Tunisia

THE ROUGH GUIDE

Written and researched by
Daniel Jacobs and Peter Morris

Additional accounts by
Linda Cooley, Lee Eltaïef and Dr Carol Higham

THE ROUGH GUIDES

MAP SYMBOLS

REGIONAL MAPS

+++	Railway
▬▬	Main Road
──	Minor Road
-----	Track or Trail
──	River
⬬	Lake
– –	Ferry route
▬ ▬	International boundary
─·─·	Chapter division boundary
⌇⌇	Mountains
⊡	Salt pan
▲	Peak
♦	Ancient site

TOWN MAPS

──	Railway
▪▪▪▪	Fortified wall
▦	Park
■	Building
⊞	Church
ᴛᵀᴛ	Muslim cemetery
⌣⌣	Jewish cemetery
₊⁺₊	Christian cemetery

GENERAL

☾	Mosque
ⓘ	Tourist Office
✕	Airport
⬚	Beach
↟	Oasis

Tunisia

THE ROUGH GUIDE

There are more than sixty Rough Guide titles covering
destinations from Amsterdam to Zimbabwe

Forthcoming titles include
Bali • Costa Rica • Mallorca • Rhodes • West Africa

Rough Guide Reference Series
Classical Music • World Music

Rough Guide Phrasebooks
Czech • French • German • Greek • Italian • Spanish

Rough Guide Credits

Text Editor:	Graham Parker
Series Editor:	Mark Ellingham
Editorial:	Martin Dunford, Jonathan Buckley, Samantha Cook, Jo Mead, Alison Cowan, Amanda Tomlin, Annie Shaw, Catherine McHale and Lemisse al-Hafidh
Production:	Susanne Hillen, Andy Hilliard, Alan Spicer, Judy Pang, Link Hall and Nicola Williamson
Cartography:	Melissa Flack
Marketing & Publicity:	Richard Trillo (UK), Jean-Marie Kelly, Jeff Kaye (US)
Finance:	John Fisher, Celia Crowley and Simon Carloss
Administration:	Tania Hummel

Continuing thanks for invaluable help on this fourth edition goes to: Joyce Brown, Catherine Cole, the Ezzine Family, Jenny Hughes, Ghislaine Morris, Jeanne Muchnick and David Leffmann, and many others in England and Tunisia. At Rough Guides, thanks go to Kate Berens for proofreading, Melissa Flack and Sam Kirby for cartography and Link Hall for typesetting. Many thanks also to Maggie Elliott, Judy Brocklehurst and the team from *Panorama Holidays*. **A number of organizations** have also given a great deal of assistance in the preparation of this edition. To all concerned, we extend our warmest thanks: ASM Bizerte, ASM Le Kef (in particular Mr Mohammed Tlili), ASM Sfax, ASM Tunis, Association pour la Sauvegarde de l'Île de Jerba, David Buckton and Elena Angelidis from the British Museum Department of Early Christian and Byzantine Antiquities, Commonwealth War Graves Commission, Maghreb Association (in particular Mr Mohammed Ben Madani), *ONTT* London, *ONTT* Bizerte, *ONTT* Gafsa and *ONTT* Tozeur.

Publishing acknowledgements

We are grateful to Oxford University Press for permission to reprint two lines of Keith Douglas's poem *Remember me when I am dead*, © Marie Douglas; and to Penguin Books for the extracts from *The Odyssey*, translation © EV Rieu, *The Aeneid*, translation © The Estate of WF Jackson Knight, and *Salammbô*, translation © AJ Krailsheimer. Also thanks for use of an extract from *Lion Mountain*, translation © Mustapha Tlili, and to the *Fondation National pour la Traduction et l'Établissement de Textes et les Études* for extracts from Abu-l-Qasim al-Shabbi's *The Will of Life*, translation © Beit al Hikma, and Ali Du'aji's *Sleepless Nights*, translation © Beit al Hikma.

This fourth edition published 1995 by Rough Guides Ltd, 1 Mercer Street, London WC2H 9QJ

Distributed by the Penguin Group:

Penguin Books Ltd, 27 Wrights Lane, London W8 5TZ
Penguin Books USA Inc., 375 Hudson Street, New York 10014, USA
Penguin Books Australia Ltd, 487 Maroondah Highway, PO Box 257, Ringwood, Victoria 3134, Australia
Penguin Books Canada Ltd, 10 Alcorn Avenue, Toronto, Ontario, Canada M4V 1E4
Penguin Books (NZ) Ltd, 182–190 Wairau Road, Auckland 10, New Zealand

Previously published in the UK by Routledge & Kegan Paul (1985), and Harrap Columbus (1988 & 1992).
Previous edition published in the United States and Canada as *The Real Guide Tunisia*

Typeset in Linotron Univers and Century Old Style to an original design by Andrew Oliver.
Printed in the United Kingdom by Cox & Wyman Ltd (Reading).

Illustrations in Part One and Part Three by Edward Briant: illustrations on p.1 and p.355 by Henry Iles.

464pp. Includes index.

Cataloguing-in-Publication Data is available from the Library of Congress.

ISBN 1-85828-1393

CONTENTS

Introduction vi

| **PART ONE** | **BASICS** | **3** |

Getting There from Britain and Ireland 3
Getting There from North America 9
Getting There from Australasia 12
Visas and Red Tape 13
Insurance 15
Disabled Travellers 17
Costs, Money and Banks 18
Health 20
Information and Maps 22
Getting Around 24
Accommodation 29

Eating and Drinking 31
Communications: Post, Phones and Media 37
Mosques, Museums and Sites 39
Hammams 40
Shopping 40
Festivals, Holidays and Entertainment 43
Travelling with Children 46
Senior Travellers 47
Sexual Issues 47
Trouble and Police 49
Directory 50

| **PART TWO** | **GUIDE** | **53** |

■ 1 **TUNIS AND AROUND 55**
■ 2 **HAMMAMET AND CAP BON 114**
■ 3 **BIZERTE AND THE NORTH 134**
■ 4 **KAIROUAN AND THE SAHEL 169**
■ 5 **THE TELL 223**
■ 6 **THE JERID 261**
■ 7 **GABES AND MATMATA 297**
■ 8 **JERBA AND THE SOUTHEAST COAST 312**
■ 9 **THE KSOUR 336**

| **PART THREE** | **CONTEXTS** | **355** |

Historical Framework 357
Architecture 379
Chronology 382
Islam: The Background 386
Traditional Society 392
Women in Tunisia 395

Wildlife 402
Legendary Tunisia 407
Tunisian Literature 412
Books 417
Language 422
Glossary 426

Index 430

INTRODUCTION

T unisia, the Arab world's most liberal nation, is recognizably Mediterranean in character and, in the north at least, predominantly European in style. Indeed, its popular image seems, at times, to verge on blandness, dominated as it is by the package-holiday clichés of reliable sunshine, beautiful beaches and just a touch of the exotic. If this seems predictable, however, be assured that it forms only one side of the picture. Beyond the white sands of Jerba and Hammamet, there is a great deal to encourage more independent-minded travel: sub-Saharan oases and fortresses, medieval Islamic cities and some of the finest of the world's surviving Roman sites.

Being such a **compact** country, especially when compared to its North African neighbours, Tunisia is also very easy to get around. Even with a fortnight's holiday, it is quite feasible to take in something of each of the county's aspects of coast, mountains and desert. The journey from Tunis, the capital on the north coast, to Tatouine, in the heart of the desert, can be made in a little over ten hours by bus or shared taxi and, while most trips are considerably shorter, the majority of journeys in Tunisia leave an impression of real travel in the transformation from one type of landscape and culture to another. This **immediacy** makes the country very satisfying to explore – an accessible introduction to the Arab world and to the African continent.

The country, sited strategically at a bottleneck in the Mediterranean, has long played an important role in the region's history. In antiquity it was the centre of Carthaginian civilization – the ruins of Carthage lie just outside modern Tunis – and, as that empire folded, it became the heartland of Roman Africa. Later, as Islam spread west, it was invaded and settled by Arabs, providing, in the cities of Kairouan, Tunis, Sousse and Sfax, vital power bases for North Africa's successive medieval dynasties. By the fifteenth century, the Europeans and Turks were also turning their attentions to Tunisia – a process that ultimately resulted in French colonization in the nineteenth century. Today, in its fourth decade of independence, Tunisia is a fully established modern nation and, by regional standards, relatively prosperous.

Where to go

If the diversity of Tunisia's past cultures and their legacy of monuments comes as a surprise to most first-time visitors, the range of **scenery** can be even more unexpected.

TUNISIA: FACTS AND FIGURES

With an **area** of 163,610 square kilometres (63,170 square miles), Tunisia is slightly larger than England and Wales, or Florida. The **population** stands at just over eight million, of whom some 650,000 live in Tunis. The official languages are **Arabic**, spoken by almost everybody, and **French**, spoken by most school-educated people. English is not widely spoken but more and more young people are studying it at school. About 99 percent of the population are Muslims, with tiny minorities of Jews and Christians. On the economic side, Tunisia's main **exports** are crude oil, textiles and phosphates and its main trading partners are France, Italy and Germany. Inflation is currently less than ten percent. The head of **state**, President Zine el Abidine Ben Ali, took office on November 7, 1987. He succeeded the founder of modern Tunisia, Habib Bourguiba, who led the country to independence (March 20, 1956) from French colonial rule. There is an elected National Assembly and a number of legal political parties – though Islamic fundamentalism is outlawed.

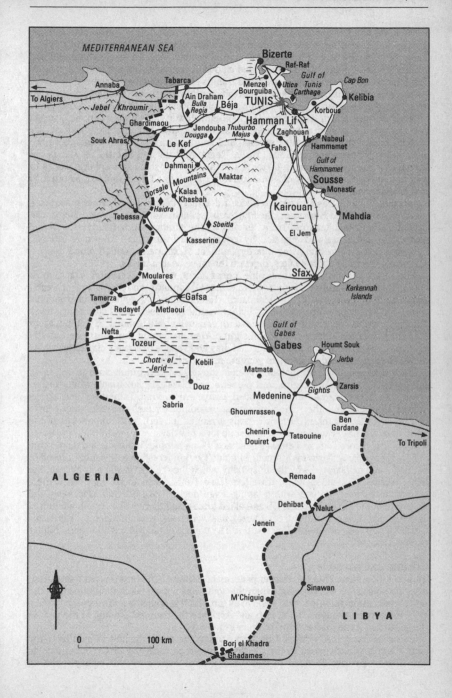

In the north you find shady oak forests reminiscent of the south of France; in southern Tunisia the beginning of the Sahara desert, with colossal dunes, oases and rippling mirages. Between the extremes are lush citrus plantations, bare steppes with tabletop mountains, and rolling hills as green and colourful (in spring) as any English county. Just offshore lie the sandy, palm-scattered islands of Jerba and Kerkennah.

In terms of **monuments**, the **Roman sites** of the north are the best-known, and, even if your interest is very casual, many are quite spectacular. At **El Jem**, in the Sahel, an amphitheatre which rivals Rome's Colosseum towers above the plain; at **Dougga** you can wander around a marvellously preserved Roman city, complete with all the accoutrements and buildings of second- and third-century prosperity; and there are sites, scarcely less grand, at **Utica**, **Bulla Regia**, **Maktar** and **Sbeitla**, as well as the legendary, extensive and much-battered **Carthage**. They're all atmospheric places to visit and at the smaller sites off the excursion routes, you'll find yourself, as often as not, enjoying them alone.

Islamic Tunisia has a varied architectural legacy, taking in early Arab mosques – most outstandingly at **Kairouan**, the first Arab capital of North Africa – and the sophisticated Turkish buildings of **Tunis**, as well as the strange Berber fortresses of the south. The latter are accompanied by equally weird structures known as *ghorfas*, honeycombed storage and living quarters, and, at **Matmata**, by underground houses. All reward the small effort it takes to get off the more beaten tracks.

For more hedonistic pleasures, the **coast** is at its most beautiful – and most commercialized – around **Hammamet**, **Sousse-Monastir** and the island of **Jerba** (connected by causeway to the mainland). Hammamet is a genuinely international resort and its satellites are spreading, but by Spanish or Greek island standards, developments remain relatively small-scale and unusually well-planned. Escaping them entirely is not hard either: even within sight of Hammamet, on **Cap Bon**, there is still wild coastline; **Bizerte**, on the north coast, has good sands and more character; whilst the **Kerkennah islands** still retain genuine fishing villages.

Your time should ideally include a spell in the **desert and mountains** as well as on the coast. The **oases** at **Nefta and Tozeur** are classically luxuriant, while further south, the *ksour* (extraordinary, fortified granaries) around **Tataouine** and dunes around **Remada** give the region an almost expeditionary feel (indeed, many people choose to go on organized "safaris", easily arranged locally). In the mountains of the northwest, **Le Kef** is an ideal place to rest up for a few days.

All of this ignores one of Tunisia's best facets – its **people**. While the hassle of some tourist areas (particularly for women) shouldn't be underestimated, visitors are often startled – and exhilarated – by the hospitality which they're shown when away from the major resorts. Few independent travellers leave Tunisia without having been invited, quite spontaneously, to stay with a family. Even during the 1991 Gulf War, when the government did not support the US and allied forces, and there was a certain amount of anti-Western rhetoric on the street, the slogans were usually transcended by Tunisians' extraordinary pleasure in meeting visitors. The politics of the wider world rarely hinder personal contact.

Climate and seasons

Tunisia follows usual Mediterranean patterns of **climate**. The best time to travel, from a scenic point of view, is **spring**, when the south has not yet reached full heat and the north looks astonishingly fertile – above all, around the orchards and vineyards of Cap Bon. Be warned, though, that March and April are the dampest months of the year in the south and it can bucket down in the north.

Summer has mixed virtues. **July and August** are much the hottest months of the year – if only slightly more so than in the southern parts of Italy or Greece – and the one time you really do need to lapse into a local way of life, for example resting through the midday hours at a café, or taking a siesta at your hotel. Obviously this goes above all for the deep south and the *ksour* (see Chapter Nine). On the more exposed beaches of the north coast, midsummer is actually a pull – some of them are only warm enough for swimming from around May until October. If you wait until **autumn**, you get the best of both worlds, with warm swimming and few crowds, even at the big resorts.

In **winter**, the north and the Tell can get distinctly cold; Aïn Draham, the highest mountain town, commonly has a metre of snow, and in 1985 it even snowed at Bizerte on the Mediterranean coast. Tunis, Cap Bon and Sousse are not so much cold in winter as dull, with sporadic rains. But this is an ideal time for covering the ancient sites at leisure and then migrating south to Jerba's beaches and the Sahara.

AVERAGE TEMPERATURES AND RAINFALL											
	Jan	Feb	Mar	Apr	May	Jun	Jul	Aug	Sep	Oct	Nov	Dec
Tunis												
Min night °C	6	7	8	11	13	17	20	21	19	15	11	7
Max day °C	14	16	18	21	24	29	32	33	31	25	20	16
Rainfall (mm)	64	51	41	36	18	8	3	8	33	51	48	61
Days with rainfall	13	12	11	9	6	5	2	3	7	9	11	14
Gabes												
Min night °C	6	7	9	12	16	19	22	22	21	17	11	7
Max day °C	16	18	21	23	26	28	32	33	31	27	22	17
Rainfall (mm)	23	18	20	10	8	0	0	3	13	31	31	15
Days with rainfall	4	3	4	3	2	0	0	1	3	4	4	4

PART ONE

THE

BASICS

GETTING THERE FROM BRITAIN AND IRELAND

Flying is the fastest and the cheapest way to get to Tunisia, with most of the best deals originating in London, no matter where you're starting from. You may well find that a package, or flight with accommodation, is hardly any more expensive than a flight alone. Using a package for a few nights' accommodation, and breaking out on your own for the rest of your holiday, usually offers good value for money. If you're determined not to travel by plane, then surface options like ferry plus train, bus or car are all feasible – if long-winded – means of getting to the country.

FLIGHTS FROM BRITAIN

A **scheduled flight** from London to Tunis is the most obvious option and, while not usually the cheapest, can give you the flexibility you may need, especially if you want to continue onwards or stay longer in Tunisia. Two airlines each operate three weekly direct scheduled flights – *GB Airways* (enquiries c/o *British Airways*) and *Tunis Air*, and the trip takes three hours.

The full scheduled economy fare is £630, but you can cut costs greatly by buying an **APEX** (Advance Purchase Excursion) ticket. These must be reserved two weeks in advance and include one Saturday night abroad; your return date has to be fixed when purchasing and no subsequent changes are allowed, otherwise hefty penalties are imposed. Current costs start at around £212 in summer, £182 in winter. However, the cheap-

est way to travel to Tunisia on a scheduled flight is usually a **SuperPEX** ticket. Unlike APEX deals, you don't have to purchase these a certain time in advance, but they are subject to availability and tend to sell out if you don't buy them well ahead, especially in summer. Your stay in Tunisia must again include one Saturday night, and flight dates both ways are fixed when purchasing, with no subsequent changes allowed. Current costs start at around £180 return in high season from London to Tunis.

Alternatively, *KLM* has some good deals on three-month return tickets via Amsterdam at £236 off-season. The other airline worth considering is *Air France* via Paris, which flies daily to Tunis and several times a week to Jerba and Sfax.

There are no direct scheduled flights from **regional British airports**, and you either need to take a charter (see below) or a connecting scheduled flight. *British Airways* fly from most places (the main exception is Birmingham) to London Heathrow, where you can connect with *GB Airways* or *Tunis Air*. A cheaper option, however, is to take a *KLM* flight from Birmingham, Bristol or Cardiff, or a combination of *Air UK* and *KLM* from Aberdeen, Edinburgh, Glasgow, Humberside, Leeds/Bradford, Manchester, Newcastle, Norwich or Teesside, changing planes at Amsterdam. The Czech airline *CSA* also flies from Manchester, changing at Prague; and *Air France* flies from Birmingham, Manchester or Edinburgh, changing at Paris. A typical fare on all these routes is around £250 return.

Charter flights are available from most British airports during the summer and from many in winter, too. In theory, charter flights are supposed to be sold in conjunction with accommodation, but it is sometimes possible just to buy the air ticket at a discount through your travel agent, or else simply not use the accommodation. Some package operators, notably *Thomson* and *Airtours*, sell deals which are basically flight-only (see below); *Transun*, which flies from airports not served by other operators, does not usually sell flights without the rest of the package, but might be worth a try just in case. Discount agents may also have charter tickets. Charter flights vary in price with the season, from about £130 in low season to about £200 at the end of July or beginning of August, and cost

AIRLINE OFFICES IN BRITAIN

Air France, 177 Piccadilly, London W1V 0LX (☎0181/742 6600).

Air UK, Stansted Airport, Essex CM24 1QT (☎0345/666777).

British Airways, 156 Regent St, London W1R 5TA (☎0181/897 4000).

CSA Czechoslovak Airlines, 72 Margaret St, London W1N 8HA (☎0171/255 1366).

GB Airways, Iain Stewart Centre, Beehive Ring Rd, Gatwick Airport, West Sussex RH6 0PB (Reservations via *BA* ☎0181/897 4000).

KLM, Plesman House, 190 Great South West Rd, Feltham, Middlesex TW14 9RL (☎0181/750 9000).

Tunis Air, 24 Sackville St, London W1X 1DE (☎0171/734 7644).

AIRLINE OFFICES IN IRELAND

Aer Lingus, 41 Upper O'Connell St, Dublin 2 (☎01/844 4777).

Air France, 29–30 Dawson St, Dublin 2 (☎01/677 8899).

Alitalia, 63 Dawson St, Dublin 2 (☎01/677 5171).

British Airways, 60 Dawson St, Dublin 2 (☎0800/626747); 9 Fountain Centre, College St, Belfast BT1 6HR (☎0345/222111).

British Midland, Nutley, Merrian Rd, Dublin 4 (☎01/283 8833); Suite 2, Sountin Centre, College St, Belfast BT1 6ET (☎01/232 241188).

KLM, Servisair Ticket Desk, Belfast International Airport, Belfast BT29 4AB (☎0181/750 9000).

DISCOUNT FLIGHT AGENTS IN BRITAIN

Campus Travel, 52 Grosvenor Gardens, London SW1W 0AG (☎0171/730 3402); 541 Bristol Rd, Selly Oak, Birmingham B29 6AU (☎0121/414 1848); 39 Queen's Rd, Clifton, Bristol BS8 1QE

(☎0117/929 2494); 5 Emmanuel St, Cambridge CB1 1NE (☎01223/324283); 53 Forrest Rd, Edinburgh EH1 2QP (☎0131/225 6111); 166 Deansgate, Manchester M3 3FE (☎0161/833

slightly more from Scotland, Wales and the north of England than from London. Bear in mind that it may be worthwhile, especially off-season or last-minute, to take a whole package for just a little more, even if you only use the accommodation for a couple of days.

The very cheapest deals of all (and some people decide to come to Tunisia simply because they happen to run across one) are **last-minute charter flights** or packages, usually for one or two weeks and often costing less than £100. These are available a week or two before the departure date and can be found in the windows of travel agents or through advertisements in the London *Evening Standard* and other local papers. Their main drawback is that availability is somewhat random, and dates cannot be changed.

For cheap deals on any of the flights mentioned above, you'll need to go to a **discount agent**. To find these in London, see ads in the *Evening Standard*, *Time Out*, the free Australasian magazine *TNT* (look for it outside

major tube stations), or magazines such as *Midweek* and *Ms London*, which are given out free to commuters. In Manchester, look in *City Life*, and elsewhere try local listings magazines or the classified section of the Sunday broadsheets. A list of the most reliable discount specialists can be found in the box above.

FLIGHTS FROM IRELAND

Ireland has no direct flights to Tunisia, so the cheapest way to get there is to pay a tag-on fare and go via Britain, Italy or France. **From Dublin**, fares start at around IR£300. A combination of *Aer Lingus* or *British Midland* with *GB Air* is usually the best deal, but *Alitalia* via Rome is sometimes cheaper.

From Belfast, your choice is with *KLM* via Amsterdam, usually the cheapest route, or a combination of *BA* and *GB Air* via London. Expect to pay around £300. Depending on the time of year, there may also be charters, which should be cheaper.

2046); 105–106 St Aldates, Oxford OX1 1DD (☎01865/242067). *Student/youth travel specialists, with branches also in YHA shops and on university campuses all over Britain.*

Council Travel, 28a Poland St, London W1V 3DB (☎0171/437 7767). *Flights and student discounts.*

Nouvelles Frontières, 11 Blenheim St, London W1Y 9LE (☎0171/629 7772). *French youth travel agency.*

South Coast Student Travel, 61 Ditchling Rd, Brighton BN1 4SD (☎01273/570226). *Student experts with plenty to offer non-students as well.*

STA Travel, 74 Old Brompton Rd, London SW7 3LH (☎0171/937 9962); 25 Queen's Rd, Bristol BS8 1QE (☎0117/929 3399); 38 Sidney St, Cambridge CB2 3HX (☎01223/66966); 75 Deansgate, Manchester M3 2BW (☎0161/834 0668); Personal

callers at 117 Euston Rd, London NW1 2SX; 28 Vicar Lane, Leeds LS1 7JH; 36 George St, Oxford OX1 2OJ; and offices at the universities of Birmingham, London, Kent and Loughborough. *Discount fares, with particularly good deals for students and young people.*

Trailfinders, 42–48 Earls Court Rd, London W8 6EJ (☎0171/938 3366); 194 Kensington High St, London W8 7RG (☎0171/938 3939); 58 Deansgate, Manchester M3 2FF (☎0161/839 6969); 254–284 Sauchiehall St, Glasgow G2 3EH (☎0141/353 2224); 22–24 The Priory, Queensway, Birmingham B4 6BS (☎0121/236 1234); 48 Corn St, Bristol BS1 1HQ (☎0117/929 9000). *One of the best informed and most efficient agents.*

Travel Bug, 597 Cheetham Hill Rd, Manchester M8 6EJ (☎0161/721 4000). *Large range of discounted tickets.*

DISCOUNT FLIGHT AGENTS IN IRELAND

Budget Travel, 134 Lower Baggot St, Dublin 2 (☎01/661 3122).

Joe Walsh Tours, 8–11 Baggot St, Dublin 2 (☎01/678 9555); 31 Castle St, Belfast (☎01232/241144).

USIT, Aston Quay, O'Connell Bridge, Dublin 2 (☎01/679 8833); 10–11 Market Pde, Cork (021/270900); Fountain Centre, College St, Belfast BT1 6ET (☎01232/324073). *All-Ireland student and youth travel specialists.*

Note that addresses and telephone numbers may not be in the same location: some airlines and agents use a single telephone-sales number for several offices.

In both the Republic and the North, the obvious people to contact first are *USIT*, who specialize in student/youth deals.

PACKAGE HOLIDAYS

Any travel agent will be able to provide details of the many operators that run **package tours** to Tunisia, which can work out a competitively priced way of travelling, often costing little more than a charter flight. Some are straightforward travel-plus-beach-hotel affairs providing a fixed base, whereas others offer archeological discovery tours, trekking or desert tours. Almost all the major British operators offer Tunisian holidays, mainly on the Nabeul–Hammamet or Sousse–Monastir coasts.

If your trip is geared around specific interests, packages can work out much cheaper than the same arrangements made on arrival. A package will include flights, accommodation and often transfers to and from your hotel, or a rental car, which can leave you more time to enjoy your holi-

day if you're on a tight schedule. Packages booked in advance can cost as little as £150 per week, and you can pick up late-availability holidays for under £100. More complete lists of package operators are available from the **Tunisian National Tourist Office**, 77a Wigmore St, London W1H 9LJ (☎0171/224 5561).

ADVENTURE TRIPS

A more adventurous package alternative, until recently, was to take one of a limited number of North African **expedition tours**. These involved overland travel for several weeks by adapted Land Rover or truck. Covering Morocco as well as Tunisia, the routes themselves were both authentic and exciting, cutting across minor *piste* roads in the Sahara and mountains. At one time there were several operators covering the "North African loop" of Morocco–Algeria–Tunisia, but Algeria is now so dangerous and unstable that no overland trips currently pass through it, nor are likely to in the near future. For up-to-date information, contact an

TUNISIAN HOLIDAY SPECIALISTS

Medward Travel, 304 Old Brompton Rd, London SW5 9JF (☎0171/373 4411). *No-frills scheduled-flight packages to a wide selection of hotels all over Tunisia, including many places served by no other operator, but rather pricey. Tailor-made itineraries possible.*

Panorama Tunisia Experience, 29 Queens Rd, Brighton, Sussex BN1 3YN (☎01273/206531); 2nd Floor, 3 College Green, Dublin 2 (☎01/6707666). *The leading specialists in Tunisian holidays, with beach hotels in Hammamet, Sousse, Port el Kantaoui, Kerkennah and Jerba, activities for kids, and golfing holidays. Charter flights from Gatwick, Heathrow, Birmingham, Glasgow, Manchester, Newcastle and Belfast.*

PACKAGE HOLIDAY COMPANIES

Airtours, Wavell House, Holcombe Rd, Helmshore, Rossendale, Lancs BB4 4NB (☎01706/260000). *Hammamet, Sousse and Monastir; charter flights to Monastir from Gatwick, Stansted, Birmingham, Cardiff, East Midlands, Manchester and Newcastle.*

Belleair Holidays, Air Malta House, 314 Upper Richmond Rd, London SW15 6TU (☎0181/785 3266); c/o *Dun Laoghaire Travel*, 12 Pembroke Rd, Dublin 4 (☎01/606035). *Hammamet, Sousse and Port el Kantaoui, plus two-centre holidays in Tunisia and Malta. Flights from Heathrow, Gatwick, Stansted, Birmingham, Bristol, East Midlands, Manchester, Newcastle and Dublin.*

Cadogan, 9–10 Portland St, Southampton, Hants SO9 1ZP (☎01703/332661). *Upmarket firm with a personal approach, using selected (mostly four- and five-star) hotels in Hammamet, Sousse, Port el Kantaoui and Monastir.*

Club Mediterranée, 106–110 Brompton Rd, London SW3 1JJ (☎0171/581 1161). *A sort of classy French Butlin's, with all the facilities you could possibly want, but rather more like being in France than in Tunisia.*

First Choice (formerly **Enterprise** and **Falcon**), First Choice House, Peel Cross Rd, Salford, Manchester M5 2AN (☎0161/745 7000). *Hammamet, Nabeul, Sousse, Port el Kantaoui and Monastir. Charter flights from Gatwick, Birmingham, Manchester and Glasgow.*

Portland Holidays, 218 Great Portland St, London W1N 5HG (☎0171/388 5111). *Hotels in Sousse, charter flights from Gatwick, Birmingham, Bristol and Manchester. The cheapest package deals, but only available direct, not through travel agents.*

Thomson (also **Horizon** and **Skytours**), Greater London House, Hampstead Rd, London NW1 7SD (☎0171/707 9000). *Hammamet, Sousse, Port el Kantaoui and Monastir. Charter flights from Gatwick, Luton, Bristol, Birmingham, Glasgow and Manchester.*

Transun, Transun House, 70 St Clements, Oxford OX14 2AH (☎01865/798888). *Holidays in Hammamet, Sousse and Port el Kantaoui. Charter flights from all regional UK airports, including ones not served by other operators.*

SPECIALIST TOUR OPERATORS

Africa Travel Centre, 4 Medway Court, Leigh St, London WC1H 9QX (☎0171/387 1211). *Specializes in overland tours. Does not currently cover Tunisia, but may do when overland tours via Algeria are on again.*

Andante Travels, Grange Cottage, Winterbourne Dauntsey, Salisbury, Wilts SP4 6ER (☎01980/610555). *Good value twice-yearly 8-day ancient history and art tours with expert guide lecturers, sometimes accompanied by a photographic advisor. Prices are around £695–750.*

Branta, 7 Wingfield St, London SE15 4LN (☎0171/635 5812). *Eight-day birdwatching tour accompanied by a Tunisian ornithologist and costing £815.*

Explore Worldwide, 1 Frederick St, Aldershot, Hants GU11 1LQ (☎01252/319448); c/o *Maxwells Travel*, D'Olier Chambers, 1 Hawkins St, Dublin (☎01/677 9479). *Fifteen-day overland adventure holiday including a 3-day camel trek from £700.*

Lotus Supertravel Golf, St Saviour's Wharf, Mill St, London SE1 2BE (☎0171/962 9494). *Seven-day golfing holidays to Port el Kantaoui, Monastir, Sousse and Hammamet from £229.*

Martin Randall Travel, 10 Barley Mow Passage, London W4 4PH (☎0181/742 3355). *Twice-yearly 8-day escorted Roman archeology tour with guest lecture, costing £885.*

Prospect Music and Art Tours, 454–458 Chiswick High Rd, London W4 5TT (☎0181/995 2151). *Twice-yearly 8-day art history and archeology tour led by an expert guide, costing £925.*

Swan Hellenic, 77 New Oxford St, London WC1A 1PP (☎0171/800 2300). *Twice-yearly 13-day art treasures tour of Roman and Islamic sites with expert guide and guest lecturer; costs £1395.*

Africa specialist agent such as *Africa Travel Centre* or *STA Travel's Africa Desk* (see p.5).

OVERLAND FROM BRITAIN

You won't save any money by **going overland** between London and Tunis but the routes are obviously worth considering if you want to take in something of France and/or Italy on the way. And if you're under 26, there are bargains to be had on rail tickets.

The route through Italy is probably the most popular. By train it takes around thirty hours from London to **Genoa** and fifty hours to **Trápani**, from where ferries leave for Tunis. An alternative route is to travel to **Marseille** (around twenty hours) for the longer ferry crossing from France. These times can be reduced by several hours if you take the *Eurostar* service via the Channel Tunnel as far as **Paris** – and depending on special offers and advance booking, it may not work out much dearer.

BY TRAIN

Standard **train** tickets for the London–Marseille run cost £84 single and £133 return, to Genoa £104/£160. You cannot buy a through ticket to Trápani in London, but London–Palermo is £132/£217 and it only costs a few pounds more to get to Trápani from there; details of routes and timetables are available from the *European Rail Centre* at Victoria Station. If you're **under 26**, there are slightly cheaper options. A *BIJ* rail ticket (available from *Eurotrain*, *Wasteels* and student/youth travel agents) costs around £84/£124 for Marseille, £84/£142 for Genoa, and £107/£174 for Palermo. These have two months' validity and allow as many stopovers as you like along the specified route. *Wasteels* sometimes have discounted tickets for not a great deal more if you are over 26.

Taking the Channel Tunnel, you'll pay £84 return from London to Paris, plus £75 return to Marseille or Genoa.

BY BUS

Buses from London to Marseille, Genoa or Rome take about the same time as trains but can cost substantially less. *Eurolines*, for example, run buses to Marseille for £56 single/£92 return. There are slight reductions for under-25s. You may find other offers in the travel pages of the magazines mentioned on p.3 under *Flights from Britain*.

BY CAR

If you're **driving** to Tunisia and want to see some of Italy, you could travel via Turin, Rome and Naples across to Sicily on the Reggio–Messina ferry, and over to Tunis by ferry from there. A more expensive but somewhat more relaxed option is to cross the Med on the ferry from Genoa or Marseille. With all these crossings, you'll need to book in advance if you're taking a car.

Crossing the **Channel** from Britain to Europe, the fastest, though not the cheapest, way is through the Channel Tunnel with *Le Shuttle*, although boarding delays can be long; it's best to book ahead if you can. The alternative cross-Channel options for most travellers are the ferry or hovercraft links from Dover to Calais or Boulogne, Ramsgate to Dunkerque, or Newhaven to Dieppe.

BY FERRY

There are **ferries** to Tunisia from Trápani and other Sicilian ports, as well as from Naples, Genoa, Marseille and Cagliari (Sardinia). In the past there have been services from Malta, but these currently only run in the opposite direction. Most services arrive in Tunisia at La Goulette, the port for Tunis (see p.102).

The **Trápani–Tunis** ferry crossing is the shortest, with one service a week run by *Tirrenia Navigazione*. The boat actually starts in Cagliari and can also be picked up there. In midsummer especially, you'll need to be prepared for a harassed and frantic time buying tickets in Trápani. Booking ahead is advisable, and

---

USEFUL ADDRESSES FOR TRAIN AND BUS TRAVEL

British Rail, European Train Centre, Victoria Station, London SW1V 1JY (☎0171/834 2345).
Eurolines, 164 Buckingham Palace Rd, London SW1W 9TP (☎0171/730 0202).
Eurotrain, 52 Grosvenor Gardens, London SW1W 0AG (☎0171/730 3402).

Eurostar, EPS House, Waterloo Station, London SE1 8SE (reservations ☎01233/617575).
Le Shuttle, PO Box 300, Cheriton Park, Folkestone, Kent CT19 4QW (☎0990/353535).
Wasteels, Victoria Station (by platform 2), London SW1V 1JY (☎0171/834 7066).

essential if taking a car across any time between mid-June and mid-September. You would also be well advised to get a full return ticket in advance, especially if you're planning to return during the last two weeks of August, when the boats are packed with returning migrant workers. For foot passengers, an alternative and quicker approach is the **hydrofoil service** from Trápani to Kelibia on Cap Bon, which runs in the summer only. There is also a weekly ferry to Tunis from **Palermo** with *Grandi Navi Veloci*, and a summer service from **Mazara del Vallo** in southern Sicily, as well as a weekly summer service from **Naples**, run by both *CTN* and *Linee Lauro*, although the latter has a reputation for foul-ups.

Ferries from Genoa and Marseille are in some respects more convenient and certainly pleasanter than those from Trápani. Car drivers, however, will need to make reservations three or four months in advance for summer crossings. Both routes are operated by *Compagnie Tunisienne de la Navigation* (*CTN* or *Cotunav*), Tunisia's national line, which runs one weekly ferry in winter rising to three in summer. From Genoa, there's also *Grandi Navi Veloci*'s weekly service via Palermo, calling at Malta on the way back.

The *ABC World Shipping Guide*, available for £42 from the *Reed Travel Group*, 6 Chesterfield Gardens, London W1Y 8DN (☎0171/355 1600), or at many public reference libraries and travel

FERRY ROUTES AND PRICES

| | | | | | cheapest single fares | | |
From	To	Operator	Frequency	Time	Passenger	Car	M/bike
Trápani	La Goulette	TN	1 weekly	10hr	£35	£60	£18
Cagliari	La Goulette	TN	1 weekly	9hr	£42	£62	£18
Trápani §	Kelibia	ULSRL	summer 3 weekly	5hr	£45	–	–
Mazara del Vallo	La Goulette	LL	summer 1 weekly	10hr	£27	£50	£12
Palermo	La Goulette	GNV	1 weekly	9hr	£57	£69	£21
Genoa	La Goulette	CTN	1–3 weekly	27hr	£85	£160	£63
Genoa	La Goulette	GNV	1 weekly	33hr	£113	£120	£34
Naples	La Goulette	CTN	summer 1 weekly	18hr	£63	£102	£45
Naples	La Goulette	LL	summer 1 weekly	19hr	£38	£73	£23
Marseille	La Goulette	CTN	1–3 weekly	24hr	£112	£244	£99

§ jetfoil

Note that fares vary with season as well as standard of accommodation; car and motorbike prices quoted are in addition to foot passenger prices.

FERRY OPERATORS

Compagnie Tunisienne de la Navigation (*CTN* or *Cotunav*): c/o *Southern Ferries*, 1⁷9 Piccadilly, London W1V 9DB (☎0171/491 4968); c/o *Tirrenia*, Ponte Colombo boat station, Genoa (☎010/258041); c/o *SNMCM*, 61 bd des Dames, Marseille (☎91.56.30.10); c/o *Tirrenia*, Molo Angioino boat station, Naples (☎081/551 2181); 122 rue de Yougoslavie, Tunis (☎01/242801), or c/o *Navitour*, 8 rue d'Alger (☎01/249500).

Grandi Navi Veloci: c/o *Viamare Travel*, Graphic House, 2 Sumatra Rd, London NW6 1PU (☎0171/431 4560); Via Fleschi 17, Genoa (☎010/550 9333); c/o *Grandi Traghetti Spa di Navigazione*, Via Marino Stabile 53, Palermo (☎0091/589629).

Linee Lauro: c/o *Viamare Travel*, Graphic House, 2 Sumatra Rd, London NW6 1PU (☎0171/431 4560); Piazza Municipio 88, Naples (☎081/551 3352); Via Amm Staiti, Trápani (☎0923/24073).

Tirrenia Navigazione: c/o *Serena Holidays*, 40/42 Kenway Rd, London SW5 0RA (☎0171/373 6548); c/o *Agenave*, 1 Via Campidano, Cagliari (☎66065/6/7/8); Corso Italia 52/56, Trápani (☎0923/27480); 2 Rione Sirignano, Naples (☎081/720 1111); 385 Via Roma, Palermo (☎091/585733); c/o *Tourafric*, 52 av Bourguiba, Tunis (☎01/341488).

Ustica Lines SRL: c/o *Tourafric*, 52 av Bourguiba, Tunis (☎01/341483).

agents, should carry current information on these ferries, as should *Thomas Cook's* European Timetables (the red volume), also available in public libraries or from any branch of *Thomas Cook*. Both are published monthly, but they aren't always up to date.

GETTING THERE FROM NORTH AMERICA

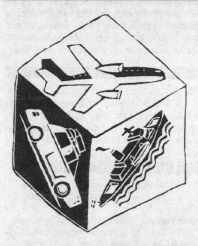

There are no direct flights from North America to Tunisia; instead you will have to rely on a flight to a European gateway city – Frankfurt and London being the main ones – and take a connecting service to Tunisia.

SHOPPING FOR TICKETS

Barring special offers, the cheapest of the airlines' published fares is usually an **APEX** ticket, although this will carry certain restrictions: you have to book – and pay – at least 21 days before departure, spend at least seven days abroad (maximum stay three months), and you tend to get penalized if you change your schedule. On transatlantic routes, there are also winter **SuperPEX** tickets, sometimes known as "Eurosavers" – slightly cheaper than an ordinary APEX, but limiting your stay to between 7 and 21 days. Some airlines also issue **Special APEX** tickets to people younger than 24, often extending the maximum stay to a year. Many airlines offer youth or student fares to **under-25s**; a passport or driving licence is sufficient proof of age, though these tickets are subject to availability and can have eccentric booking conditions. It's worth remembering that most

cheap return fares involve spending at least one Saturday night away and that many will only give a percentage refund if you need to cancel or alter your journey, so make sure you check the restrictions carefully before buying a ticket.

You can normally cut costs further by going through a **specialist flight agent** – either a **consolidator**, who buys up blocks of tickets from the airlines and sells them at a discount, or a **discount agent**, who wheels and deals in blocks of tickets offloaded by the airlines, and often offers special student and youth fares and a range of other travel-related services, such as travel insurance, rail passes, car rental, tours and the like. Bear in mind, though, that penalties for changing your plans can be stiff. Remember too that these companies make their money by dealing in bulk – don't expect them to answer lots of questions. Some agents specialize in **charter flights**, which may be cheaper than any available scheduled flight, but again departure dates are fixed and withdrawal

AIRLINES IN NORTH AMERICA

Air Canada (in Canada, call directory enquiries, ☎1-800/555-1212, for local toll-free number; US toll-free number is ☎1-800/776-3000). [Canadian toll-free numbers vary by province, and change occasionally. For the record, they are: AL ☎1-800/332-1080; BC ☎1-800/663-3721; MN ☎1-800/542-8940; NB, NS and PEI ☎1-800/565-3940; NF ☎1-800/563-5151; ON ☎1-800/268-7240; PQ ☎1-800/361-8620; SK ☎1-800/665-0520.

Air India (☎1-800/223-2420; in Canada, call directory enquiries, ☎1-800/555-1212, for local toll-free number).

British Airways (in US ☎1-800/247-9297; in Canada ☎1-800/668-1059).

Continental Airlines (☎1-800/231-0856).

Lufthansa (in US ☎1-800/645-3880; in Canada ☎1-800/563-5954).

United Airlines (☎1-800/538-2929).

penalties are high (check the refund policy). If you travel a lot, **discount travel clubs** are another option – the annual membership fee may be worth it for benefits such as cut-price air tickets and car rental.

Don't automatically assume that tickets purchased through a travel specialist will be the cheapest – once you get a quote, check with the airlines and you may turn up an even better deal. Be advised also that the pool of travel companies is swimming with sharks – exercise caution and *never* deal with a company that demands cash up front or refuses to accept payment by credit card.

A further possibility is to see if you can arrange a **courier flight**, although the hit-and-miss nature of these makes them most suitable for the single traveller who travels light and has a very flexible schedule. In return for shepherding a parcel through customs and possibly giving up your baggage allow-

ance, you can expect to get a heavily discounted ticket. Two courier outfits are listed below; for more options, consult *A Simple Guide to Courier Travel* (Pacific Data Sales Publishing).

Note that fares are heavily dependent on **season**, and are highest from around July to September 14. Shoulder season is March 20 to the end of June and September 15 to November 12; and low season, the winter months from January 5 to March 19 and November 13–23. Travellers should bear in mind that summer is also high season to Europe, which means flights book up very quickly.

FLIGHTS FROM THE USA

There are no direct flights to Tunisia from the USA, so you must fly via one of the **European gateway cities**. Transatlantic fares to Europe are very reasonable, thanks to intense competition, and currently the most convenient routing to Tunisia is

---

DISCOUNT TRAVEL COMPANIES IN NORTH AMERICA

Air Brokers International, 323 Geary St, Suite 411, San Francisco, CA 94102 (☎1-800/883-3273). *Consolidator.*

Air Courier Association, 191 University Blvd, Suite 300, Denver, CO 80206 (☎303/278-8810). *Courier flight broker.*

Council Travel, 205 E 42nd St, New York, NY 10017 (☎1-800/743-1823). *Student travel organization with branches in many US cities. A sister company,* Council Charter (☎1-800/223-7402), *specializes in charter flights to Europe.*

Discount Travel International, Ives Bldg, 114 Forrest Ave, Suite 205, Narberth, PA 19072 (☎1-800/334-9294). *Discount travel club.*

Educational Travel Center, 438 N Frances St, Madison, WI 53703 (☎1-800/747-5551). *Student/youth discount agent.*

Encore Travel Club, 4501 Forbes Blvd, Lanham, MD 20706 (☎1-800/444-9800). *Discount travel club.*

Interworld Travel, 800 Douglass Rd, Miami, FL 33134 (☎305/443-4929). *Consolidator.*

Last Minute Travel Club, 132 Brookline Ave, Boston, MA 02215 (☎1-800/LAST MIN). *Travel club specializing in standby deals.*

Moment's Notice, 425 Madison Ave, New York, NY 10017 (☎212/486-0503). *Discount travel club.*

New Frontiers/Nouvelles Frontières, 12 E 33rd St, New York, NY 10016 (☎1-800/366-6387); 1001 Sherbrook East, Suite 720, Montréal H2L

1L3 (☎514/526-8444). *French discount travel firm. Other branches in LA, San Francisco and Québec City.*

Now Voyager, 74 Varick St, Suite 307, New York, NY 10013 (☎212/431-1616). *Courier flight broker.*

STA Travel, 48 East 11th St, New York, NY 10003 (☎1-800/777-0112 nationwide). *Worldwide specialist in independent travel with branches in the Los Angeles, San Francisco and Boston areas.*

TFI Tours International, 34 W 32nd St, New York, NY 10001 (☎1-800/745-8000). *Consolidator; other offices in Las Vegas, San Francisco and Los Angeles.*

Travac, 989 6th Ave, New York NY 10018 (☎1-800/872-8800). *Consolidator and charter broker; has another branch in Orlando.*

Travel Avenue, 10 S Riverside, Suite 1404, Chicago, IL 60606 (☎1-800/333-3335). *Discount travel agent.*

Travel Cuts, 187 College St, Toronto, ON M5T 1P7 (☎416/979-2406). *Canadian student travel organization with branches all over the country.*

Travelers Advantage, 3033 S Parker Rd, Suite 900, Aurora, CO 80014 (☎1-800/548-1116). *Discount travel club.*

UniTravel, 1177 N Warson Rd, St Louis, MO 63132 (☎1-800/325-2222). *Consolidator.*

Worldtek Travel, 111 Water St, New Haven, CT 06511 (☎1-800/243-1723). *Discount travel agency.*

Worldwide Discount Travel Club, 1674 Meridian Ave, Miami Beach, FL 33139 (☎305/534-2082). *Discount travel club.*

with *Lufthansa* and either *Gibraltar Air* or *Tunis Air*, whose flight schedules mean you can be there from New York in close to eleven hours (6–7 hours' flying time on *Lufthansa* to Frankfurt and another 3–4 hours on a connecting airline to Tunis), with less than two hours' wait between flights. On other airlines, you will have a stopover or a long layover.

The low-season midweek 21-day APEX through-fare from New York to Tunis is $738, or $788 at weekends (not including $38 tax); high-season midweek fares are $1058, or $1188 at weekends. *Lufthansa* also flies out of Boston, Chicago, Washington DC and LA six times a week. Chicago low-season fare starts at $808; high-season from $1128. The fares from Los Angeles are exactly the same as those from New York.

It may also be worth simply getting a flight to **London** and taking a direct flight to Tunisia from there (see p.3), since transatlantic fares can be so cheap. There are lots of carriers flying the route: *American Airlines*, *British Airways*, *Continental Airlines*, *United Airlines* and *Air India* fly out of New York at a low-season price of $378. High-season travel will add up to $300 onto the fare, and you'll still have to add the price of a Tunis flight (see *Getting There from Britain* for prices and flight times).

FLIGHTS FROM CANADA

Canada has no direct flights to Tunisia either, and travellers need to fly to **Europe** first. *Air Canada* has a lot of Canadian gateways to Europe, and major European carriers also offer a number of options. However, *Lufthansa* again ranks as the easiest, most direct choice, with flights every day except Tuesday out of Toronto and Montréal to Tunisia via Frankfurt. Low-season fares start at Can$1340 (plus Can$19 tax and $8 German tax); Can$1628 in high season.

Again, flying via **London** is a feasible option, since competition between *Air Canada*, *Canadian Airlines*, *British Airways* and others drives off-season midweek fares as low as Can$570 for a round-trip; direct flights from Ottawa and Halifax will probably cost only slightly more. From Vancouver, Edmonton and Calgary, London flights start at Can$845 off-season. High-season travel will add a premium of $200–400 onto the fare, depending on exactly when you travel.

PACKAGE TOUR OPERATORS

For ease and convenience, **package tours** make a lot of sense, as you get to see the country without worrying too much about travel or accommodation arrangements. That said, there are very few North American companies that operate packages to Tunisia, and those there are often opt for a cultural or historical emphasis, with specific tours tailored for archeological enthusiasts or overland hiking.

NORTH AMERICAN TOUR OPERATORS

African Explorers, 197 Wall St, West Longbranch, NJ 07764 (☎1-800/474-5500). *Combines Tunisia with other African countries.*

Archeological Tours, 271 Madison Ave, New York, NY 10016 (☎212/986-3054). *Organizes tours visiting major archeological sights in Tunisia, with lectures by an archeological historian.*

Cross-Cultural Adventures, PO Box 3285, Arlington, VA 222203 (☎703/237-0100). *Emphasis on the deep south of the country, on culture and archeological sites.*

Explore Worldwide, Adventure Center, 1311 63rd St, Suite 200, Emeryville, CA 94608 (☎512/654-1879); 25 Bellair St, Toronto, Ontario M5R 3L3 (☎416/922-7584). *Fifteen-day overland adventure holiday including a 3-day camel hike in winter.*

Safaricenter, 3201 N Sepulveda Blvd, Manhattan Beach, CA 90266 (☎1-800/223-6046). *Customized jeep safaris in the desert.*

TunisUSA, 614 Lancaster Ave, Wayne, PA 19087 (☎610/995-2788 or 1-800/474-5500). *Specialists to Tunisia, with an emphasis on culture and history.*

GETTING THERE FROM AUSTRALASIA

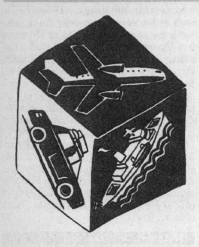

There are no direct flights from Australia or New Zealand to Tunisia, and your best bet is probably to travel via London, Athens or Cairo, or via Singapore or Bangkok.

From **Australia**, *British Airways* and *Royal Jordanian* combine to take you via Singapore or Bangkok to Amman, thence to Tunis, for A$1660–1855. You could also fly to Cairo or Athens and arrange a cheap onward flight from there: good-value fares to Cairo include *Egypt Air* (A$1620–2600), *Gulf Air* (A$1750–2000) and *Alitalia* (from A$2200), while *Olympic* have the best deal to Athens (from A$1730).

From **New Zealand**, *Singapore Airlines* can get you to Cairo and *Malaysian Airways* to Athens, both from NZ$2400. Otherwise, cheap deals to Europe include *Japanese Airlines* via Tokyo, *Garuda* via Bali and Jakarta, or *Thai* via Bangkok, from around NZ$2095–2200. **Round-the-World fares** from Australasia, which include Europe, start at about A$2000/ NZ$2500.

Reliable agents to try for flights to London (and connections on to Tunisia) are the independent travel specialists *STA Travel*, who have offices throughout Australia and New Zealand (see below).

ADVENTURE HOLIDAY COMPANIES

Explore Worldwide, *Adventure World*, 73 Walker St, North Sydney NSW 2060 (☎02/956 7766); *Adventure World*, 101 Great South Rd,

Remuera, PO Box 74008, Auckland (☎03/524 5118). *Fifteen-day overland adventure holiday including, in winter, a 3-day camel trek.*

AIRLINES

Alitalia, Orient Overseas Building, 32 Bridge St, Sydney (☎02/247 7836); Floor 6, Trust Bank Building, 229 Queen St, Auckland (☎09/379 4457).

British Airways, 64 Castlereagh St, Sydney (☎02/258 3300); Dilworth Building, cnr Queen and Customs streets, Auckland (☎09/367 7500).

Egypt Air, 630 George St, Sydney (☎02/267 6979). No NZ office.

Gulf Air, 403 George St, Sydney (☎02/321 9199). No NZ office.

Garuda, 175 Clarence St, Sydney (☎02/334 9900); 120 Albert St, Auckland (☎09/366 1855).

Japanese Airlines, 17 Bligh St, Sydney (☎02/233 4500). No NZ office.

Malaysian Airways, 388 George St, Sydney (☎02/231 5066 or ☎008/269 998); Floor 12,

Swanson Centre, 12–26 Swanson St, Auckland (☎09/373 2741).

Olympic Airways, Floor 3, 37–49 Pitt St, Sydney (☎02/251 2044). No NZ office.

Royal Jordanian Airlines, Level 20, 44 Market St, Sydney (☎02/262 6133). No NZ office.

Singapore Airlines, 17 Bridge St, Sydney (☎02/236 0111); Lower Ground Floor, West Plaza Building, cnr Customs and Albert streets, Auckland (☎09/379 3209).

Thai, 75–77 Pitt St, Sydney (☎02/844 0999 or 1-800/221 320); Kensington Swan Building, 22 Fanshawe St, Auckland (☎09/377 3886).

NOTE: ☎1-800 numbers are toll free, but only apply when dialled outside the city in the address.

VISAS AND RED TAPE

Canadian and EU citizens need no visa for a stay in Tunisia of up to three months, and US citizens for up to four.

Australians and New Zealanders need visas, which are usually issued at ports or borders, but best obtained in advance; applications take two to three weeks to process.

Visas cost around £4/$6 you'll need to provide two photos and fill in two forms.

VISA EXTENSIONS

The practice for **extending a visa** varies, but is rarely easy. If your visa is close to expiry, go to the police in good time, with some proof that you have a reason for staying in the country and evidence that you can support yourself (take along all your exchange slips). Extensions usually take between two weeks and a month to process, during which time you will be without your passport. Once granted, they usually give three months' residence. An alternative and in many ways much simpler means of getting a renewal is to take a trip over the border to Libya or even Sicily, so that you can get a new tourist stamp on re-entry.

Foreign embassies and consulates can be found in the major towns and are listed at the end of relevant town accounts under "Listings" throughout the guide.

CUSTOMS REGULATIONS

The **duty free allowances** into Tunisia are 400 cigarettes, a litre of spirits plus two litres of wine, 250ml of perfume and a litre of toilet water. Tunisian duty-free shops (often open at airports on arrival as well as departure) do not take dinars, so don't bother to save any for a bottle on your way home. They sell wine, but not the best, nor much cheaper than shops in Tunisia, but their rates for cigarettes and spirits are reasonable, and they also sell *chicha* tobacco at good prices.

Returning home, you will be subject to customs limits on what you can **bring back** before paying duty. The limit usually includes a quart or a litre of spirits (plus 2 litres of wine to the UK or Ireland, 4.5 litres to New Zealand) and 200 cigarettes (or 250g tobacco, or 50 cigars). Usual limits on the total value of goods purchased abroad are: $400 to the USA, Can$300 to Canada, £136 to the UK, IR£34 to Ireland, Aus$400 to Australia, and NZ$700 to New Zealand. Anything above these limits should be declared and duty may be charged. Any further enquiries should be directed to the following offices, which also issue explanatory pamphlets with full details.

Australia: *Collector of Customs*, GPO Box 8, Sydney NSW 2001 (☎02/226 5997).

Canada: *Canadian Customs Department*, Connaught Building, 3rd Floor, 555 Mackenzie Ave, Ottawa, ON K1A 0L5 (☎613/993-0534).

Ireland: *Office of the Revenue Commissioners*, Dublin Castle, Dublin 2 (☎01/679 2777).

New Zealand: *Collector of Customs*, PO Box 11746, Wellington (☎04/801 5007).

UK: *HM Customs and Excise*, Dorset House, Stamford St, London SE1 9PY (☎0171/202 4227).

USA: *US Customs Service*, PO Box 7407, Washington, DC 20044 (☎202/927-6724).

TUNISIAN EMBASSIES AND CONSULATES ABROAD

ALGERIA 11 rue du Bois de Boulogne, Hydra, Algiers (☎02/601388); 11 rue Nouvel Immeuble, Annaba (☎08/844567); route de Morsott, BP 280, Tébessa (☎08/974980).

AUSTRALIA 27 Victoria Rd, Belvue Hill, Sydney (☎02/363 5588).

BELGIUM 278 av Tervueren, Brussels 15 (☎02/771 7395).

CANADA 515 O'Connor St, Ottawa (☎613/237-0330); 511 Place d'Armes, Suite 501, Montréal (☎514/288-8633).

DENMARK Skinderg 23, Copenhagen (☎3315 4274).

EGYPT 26 Sharia el Jazira, Zamalek, Cairo (☎02/340 4940).

GERMANY 2 Godesbergerallee 103, 5300 Bonn (☎0228/376983).

ITALY 7 Via Asmara, Rome (☎06/839 0748); 2 Piazza I Florio, Palermo (☎091/628996).

LIBYA Sharia Bashir Ibrahimi, PO Box 613, Tripoli (☎021/31051).

MALTA Dar Carthage, Qormi Rd, Attard (☎498853).

MOROCCO 6 av de Fès, Rabat (☎07/30636).

NETHERLANDS Gentsestraat 98, The Hague (☎070/512251).

NORWAY Solliv 2A, Lysaker, Baerum (☎6753 0507).

SWEDEN Drottningatan 73, Stockholm 11136 (☎08/236470).

UK 29 Prince's Gate, London SW7 1QG (☎0171/584 8117).

USA 1515 Massachusetts Ave, Washington, DC 20005 (☎202/862-1850).

INSURANCE

Medical cover is the most important reason for taking out travel insurance. The let-out clauses regarding loss of money and possessions are getting more and more restrictive, so make sure you know exactly what the terms and conditions of your policy are. There are no reciprocal health agreements with Tunisia, so you'll have to pay for any health treatment you receive there. Remember, though, that the travel policy you buy may cover you for risks against which you're already insured (for example, theft of or damage to your property, which may be covered under an "All Risks" clause of a household policy), as well as the cost of repatriation.

Be sure to keep a note of your policy number somewhere safe and notify the insurance company immediately if you intend to make a claim. Do keep your receipts or other evidence of treatment paid for. The same goes for theft of property: you'll need to produce documentary evidence from the local police – basically a copy of their official report. Remember that claims can only be dealt with if a report is made to the local police within 24 hours and a copy of the report (*constat de vol*) sent with the claim.

Before buying an insurance policy, check to see what you are already covered for. This particularly applies to travellers from the USA and Canada. Some package tours may include insurance, but operators more commonly offer an insurance deal as an extra: it might be worth checking against alternative policies, though differences in prices

and cover are likely to be slight. Canadians are usually covered for medical expenses by their provincial health plans (but may only be reimbursed after the fact). North American holders of ISIC and other **student/teacher/youth cards** are entitled to $3000 worth of accident coverage and sixty days of in-patient benefits for the period the card is valid. University students from North America will often find that their student health coverage extends during the vacations and for one term beyond the date of last enrollment. Internationally, **credit and charge cards** (particularly *American Express*) often have certain levels of medical or other insurance included, and travel insurance may also be included if you use a major credit or charge card to pay for your trip. Finally, US and Canadian homeowners' or renters' insurance often covers theft or loss of documents, money and valuables while overseas, though conditions and maximum amounts vary from company to company.

Always check the fine print of a policy. A 24-hour medical emergency contact number is a must, and one of the rare policies that pays your medical bills directly is better than one that reimburses you on your return home. The per-article limit for loss or theft should cover your most valuable possession (a camcorder, for example) but, conversely, don't pay for cover you don't need – such as too much baggage or a huge sum for personal liability. Make sure too that you are covered for all the things you intend to do. Activities such as scuba diving are usually specifically excluded, but can be added for a supplement, usually twenty to fifty percent.

AMERICAN AND CANADIAN TRAVELLERS

For **travellers from North America**, a most important thing to keep in mind – and a source of major disappointment to would-be claimants – is that none of the currently available policies insures against **theft** of anything while overseas. North American travel policies apply only to items lost from, or damaged in, the custody of an identifiable, responsible third party (hotel porter, airline, baggage deposit, etc). Even in these cases you will still have to contact the local police to have a complete report made out so that your insurer can process the claim.

If you do want a specific travel insurance policy, there are numerous kinds to choose from: your travel agent can usually recommend one. Premiums vary, though maximum payouts tend to be meager, so shop around. The best deals are usually to be had through student/youth travel agencies – *ISIS* policies, for example, cost $48–69 for fifteen days (depending on coverage), $80–105 for a month, $149–207 for two months, up to $510–700 for a year.

BRITISH, IRISH AND AUSTRALASIAN TRAVELLERS

Travellers from the UK can obtain travel insurance from any bank or travel agent, or buy a policy issued by a specialist travel firm like *Campus Travel* or *STA*, or by the low-cost **insurers** *Endsleigh Insurance* and *Columbus Travel Insurance*. Two weeks' cover starts at around £18; a month costs from £24. For trips of up to four months, or if this is one of many short trips in one year, good-value policies for long-term travellers can be had from *Marcus Hearn & Co*: a year's cover will cost around £100, plus £26.50 to include spouse, and £16 for each child under 18.

In **Australia**, CIC Insurance, offered by *Cover-More Insurance Services*, has some of the widest cover available and can be arranged through most travel agents. It costs from A$140 for 31 days. In New Zealand, contact any branch of *STA* or one of the *Flight Centres* for similar deals.

TRAVEL INSURANCE COMPANIES AND AGENTS

AUSTRALASIA

Cover-More Insurance Services, Level 9, 32 Walker St, North Sydney (☎02/202 8000). *Branches also in Victoria and Queensland.*

Flight Centres, National Bank Towers, 205–225 Queen St, Auckland (☎09/309 6171); Shop 1M, National Mutual Arcade, 152 Hereford St, Christchurch (☎09/379 7145); 50–52 Willis St, Wellington (☎04/472 8101). *Other branches countrywide.*

STA Travel, Traveller's Centre, 10 High St, Auckland (☎09/309 0458); 233 Cuba St, Wellington (☎04/385 0561); 223 High St, Christchurch (☎03/379 9098). *Other offices in Dunedin, Palmerston North and Hamilton.*

NORTH AMERICA

Access America, PO Box 90310, Richmond, VA 23230 (☎1-800/284-8300).

Carefree Travel Insurance, PO Box 310, 120 Mineola Blvd, Mineola, NY 11501 (☎1-800/323-3149).

International Student Insurance Service (ISIS) – sold by *STA Travel*, which has several branches in the US and Canada (head office is 48 E 11th St, New York, NY 10003; ☎1-800/777-0112).

Travel Assistance International, 1133 15th St NW, Suite 400, Washington, DC 20005 (☎1-800/821-2828).

Travel Guard, 1145 Clark St, Stevens Point, WI 54481 (☎1-800/826-1300).

Travel Insurance Services, 2930 Camino Diablo, Suite 300, Walnut Creek, CA 94596 (☎1-800/937-1387).

UNITED KINGDOM

Campus Travel, head office: 52 Grosvenor Gardens, London SW1W 0AG (☎0171/730 3402).

Columbus Travel Insurance, 17 Devonshire Square, London EC2M 4SQ (☎0171/375 0011).

Endsleigh, 97–107 Southampton Row, London WC1B 4AG (☎0171/436 4451).

Marcus Hearn & Co, 65–66 Shoreditch High St, London E1 6JL (☎0171/739 3444).

STA Travel, 86 Old Brompton Rd, London SW7 3LH (☎0171/937 9921).

DISABLED TRAVELLERS

Facilities for people with disabilities are little developed in Tunisia, and disabled Tunisians are often reduced to begging, although families are usually very supportive. Blindness is more common than in the West, and sighted Tunisians are generally used to helping blind people find their way and get on and off public transport at the right stop. Wheelchairs, though often ancient, do exist, but there is little in the way of wheelchair access: some PTTs, beach hotels and the Sfax–Kerkennah ferry are exceptions.

Bus and train **travel** will be difficult because of the steps that have to be negotiated, but *louage* travel is more feasible if you can stake a claim on the front seat, assuming there is a helper to get you in and out. You should also be able to get on and off planes with a lift, but check this with the airline or tour operator.

You're likely to find travelling on a **package tour** much easier than full independence. *Thomson's* run a client welfare service on ☎0171/391 0170, which can advise people with disabilities on specific travel arrangements with them. *Panorama Tunisia Experience, Cadogan,*

CONTACTS FOR TRAVELLERS WITH DISABILITIES

AUSTRALIA
ACROD, PO Box 60, Curtain, Canberra, ACT 2605 (☎06/682 4333). *Can offer advice and keeps a list of travel specialists.*
Barrier-Free Travel, 36 Wheatley St, North Bellingen, NSW 2454 (☎066/551733). *Consultancy service for disabled travellers, with a flat A$50 fee for any number of consultations.*

CANADA
Jewish Rehabilitation Hospital, 3205 Place Alton Goldbloom, Montréal, PQ H7V 1R2 (☎514/688-9550, ext 226). *Guidebooks and travel information.*
Twin Peaks Press, Box 129, Vancouver, WA 98666; ☎206/694-2462 or 1-800/637-2256). *Publisher of the* Directory of Travel Agencies for the Disabled *($19.95), listing more than 370 agencies worldwide;* Travel for the Disabled *($14.95); the* Directory of Accessible Van Rentals *and* Wheelchair Vagabond *($9.95), loaded with personal tips.*

IRELAND
National Rehabilitation Board, 25 Clyde Rd, Ballsbridge, Dublin 4 (☎01/668 4181).

NEW ZEALAND
Disabled Persons Assembly, PO Box 10-138, The Terrace, Wellington (☎04/472 2626). *The umbrella group for all organizations dealing with disability in New Zealand.*

TUNISIA
Association Général des Insuffisants Moteurs (AGIM), Centre IMC, 1 rue Vergers,

Khaznadar, Tunis (☎01/222920). *The main Tunisian organization for people with impaired mobility.*
Fédération Tunisienne des Associations Handicapés (FTAH), 5 rue Khémaïs Ternane, 1008 Montfleury, Tunis (☎01/247190). *Umbrella organization to coordinate Tunisian disability associations.*

UNITED KINGDOM
Holiday Care Service, 2 Old Bank Chambers, Station Rd, Horley, Surrey RH6 9HW (☎01293/774535). *Information on all aspects of travel.*
RADAR, 25 Mortimer St, London W1N 8AB (☎0171/637 5400). *A good source of advice on holidays and travel abroad.*

USA
Mobility International USA, PO Box 10767, Eugene, OR 97440 (Voice and TDD: ☎503/343-1284). *Information and referral services, access guides, tours and exchange programmes. Annual membership $20 (includes quarterly newsletter).*
Society for the Advancement of Travel for the Handicapped (SATH), 347 5th Ave, New York, NY 10016 (☎212/447-7284). *Non-profit travel-industry referral service that passes queries on to its members as appropriate; allow plenty of time for a response.*
Travel Information Service, Moss Rehabilitation Hospital, 1200 West Tabor Rd, Philadelphia, PA 19141 (☎215/456-9600). *Telephone information and referral service.*

Cosmos, *Horizon*, *Intasun* and *Sunspot* also claim to cater for travellers with disabilities, but you should contact any tour operator and inform them of your exact needs before making a booking (see p.5 and 11). You should also make sure you are covered by any insurance policy you take out.

The following **hotels** claim to cater for disabled people: the *Hilton* in Tunis (☎01/782800; toll-free numbers worldwide), the *Sheraton* in Hammamet (☎02/280555; or toll-free numbers worldwide), the *Médi Sea* (☎01/293030) in Borj Cedria (Greater Tunis), *Le Prince* in Nabeul (☎02/285470), and several hotels in Sousse (see p.179). Again, you should check with them before booking. If you use a wheelchair, beach hotels are generally much more practical than cheap city centre ones, which tend to have steep staircases and narrow corridors.

COSTS, MONEY AND BANKS

The cost of travel in Tunisia compares well with southern Europe – and especially with Italy. You can get by quite easily on £100/$150 a week, with good meals, reasonable hotel rooms and a fair amount of transport, while on £150/$225 you're moving into relative luxury. At the bottom end, camping out or staying in the cheaper medina hotels, you could survive on as little as £50/$75. In general, the south of the country will be slightly cheaper than the north, and untouristed areas rather cheaper than resorts. Food, accommodation and souvenirs in Sousse, for example, can work out at almost double the price of their equivalents in Sfax.

Rooms are the most variable factor. A basic (unclassified) hotel will generally charge around £2–7/$3–10 single and £4–10/$6–15 double, while one-star places may vary from £6 to £18/$9–25 for a single, and £10 to £25/$15–40 for a double. A set **meal**, with (excellent) wine, in most local restaurants will set you back only around £8/$12 a head, or you can fill up in hole-in-the-wall

cafés for less than half that. **Transport** costs are moderate, and distances are not very great; Tunis–Sfax, perhaps the longest single journey you might think of making, costs around £5/$8 by bus or second-class train, £8/$12 by first-class train, or £6/$9 by *louage*, the shared taxis that are a standard way of getting around the country.

THE TUNISIAN DINAR

The **Tunisian dinar (TD)** is a soft currency (ie unstable in exchange value), and so illegal to export from (or import into) the country. The **exchange rate** is fixed daily on a national basis (you can find it in local newspapers under *Cours des Devises*); at present one dinar is worth about 65p sterling, US$1, or FF5, which makes prices generally cheap for overseas visitors.

An initial source of confusion is the way the dinar is written. It is divided into 1000 millimes and small, fractional prices are usually expressed in terms of **millimes** – 1,500, for example, instead of 1.5. "Whole" dinar prices, however, are usually written as "1TD", rather than "1,000mill". For the sake of clarity, prices in the guide are all expressed in dinars so that, for example, seven hundred millimes appears as "0.7TD".

Banknotes are issued in denominations of 5TD, 10TD and 20TD, with two-metal **coins** of 5TD, silver 1TD and 0.5TD coins, and brass coins of 5, 10, 20, 50 and 100 millimes – all identical in design, the last two confusingly similar in size. Small aluminium 1 millime coins are rare and useless.

BANKS AND EXCHANGE

Bank **opening hours** are irritatingly limited. In summer (July–Sept) they are Monday to Friday

8–11.30am, and the rest of the year Monday to Thursday 8–11.30am and 2–5pm, Friday 8–11.30am and 1.30am–4.30pm. In tourist areas, banks will sometimes open outside standard hours for **money exchange**, and you can often fall back on hotels; the bigger, posher ones are naturally most likely to change money for you. Always retain the receipts from your transactions for re-exchanging when you leave the country.

Away from tourist areas, exchange facilities can be few and far between and you'll sometimes find banks don't have the essential exchange rates, especially first thing in the morning. The local *STB* (Tunisia's "national" bank) is generally most reliable, and some banks will let you draw cash on *Visa* or *Access/Mastercard*. As a very last resort, if you have hard cash, you could try asking around the local *louage* (shared taxi) station, especially if it runs to any destinations beyond Tunisia's borders.

Carrying some **foreign currency** around with you in cash (French francs and US dollars rather than sterling) is a good idea; any bank will take this, as will plenty of individuals. Post offices will also often change cash. Banks and post offices will take most major currencies, including Scottish and Northern Irish sterling banknotes, but not Australian or New Zealand dollars.

Finally, it's as well to know that the **black market** offers rates only marginally better than official ones. If you're buying something expensive like a carpet, however, you may be able to get the price down by offering foreign exchange instead of dinars. *ONAT* crafts shops (see p.40), for example, often offer a discount for foreign currency.

CASH AND TRAVELLERS' CHEQUES

You are allowed to bring in unrestricted amounts of **foreign currency** and **travellers' cheques**. *Thomas Cook*, *Visa* and *American Express* are the best-known cheques and are accepted at most banks and many hotels, whether in sterling, US dollars, French francs, Deutschmarks or (usually) Canadian dollars – Australian and New Zealand dollars are not recognized. The usual commision for travellers' cheque sales is one or two percent, and it pays to get a selection of denominations. Banks in Tunisia charge a fee of 0.3TD for changing each cheque. You are supposed to keep the receipt and a record of cheque serial numbers safe and separate from the cheques themselves. However, many banks will refuse to change trav-

> ## INTERNATIONAL 24-HOUR LOST CARD OR CHEQUES FREE PHONE NUMBERS
> **American Express** ☎001-801/964 9665. *Amex* are represented by *Carthage Tours* in Tunis, Hammamet, Sousse and Jerba.
> **Thomas Cook/MasterCard** ☎0044-733/502995.
> **Visa** ☎001-415/574 7700.
> **Diner's Club**, 33 rue Lenine, 1000 Tunis; ☎01/352388.

ellers' cheques unless you show it. In the event that cheques are lost or stolen, the issuing company will expect you to report the loss forthwith to their office in Tunisia; most companies claim to replace lost or stolen cheques within 24 hours.

CREDIT AND CASH CARDS

Credit cards are of limited use outside tourist resorts, though they can sometimes be used for cash advances and are handy for items of major expense such as car rental – in fact, they're sometimes essential for car rental deposits. They are also accepted by most hotels of two or more stars, and by the more upmarket restaurants. For some reason, *Diners Club* is the best known, but *American Express*, *Visa* and *Access/Mastercard* are all usable in the right places. *Visa* and *Access/Mastercard* can also be used to draw cash from certain banks, and a growing number of ATMs, up to a limit of 50TD a day – your bank's international banking department should be able to advise on this. Make sure before you leave that you have a personal identification number (PIN) that's designed to work overseas. Remember that all cash advances are treated as loans, with interest accruing daily from the date of withdrawal; there may be a transaction fee on top of this.

WIRING MONEY

Having **money wired** from home is never convenient or cheap, and should be considered a last resort. *Thomas Cook* can telex funds to their representatives in Tunis – *ATT*, Le Colisée, 45 av Bourguiba (☎01/342710). They charge one percent of the money sent (minimum £10/$13) plus a similar telex fee, so sending £1000/$1300 will cost around £25/$34. They recommend allowing 24 to 48 hours for the transfer.

It's also possible to have money wired directly from a bank in your home country to a bank in Tunisia, although this is somewhat less reliable because it involves two separate institutions. If you go this route, the person wiring the funds to you will need to know the telex number of the bank the funds are being wired to.

LEAVING TUNISIA

There are strict regulations about the quantity of dinars that you can **change back when leaving** the country. You're allowed to reconvert up to thirty percent of the total amount you can prove you have changed since being in Tunisia – with an upper limit of 100TD. This means keeping an eye on the number of dinars you're likely to have on you when you leave, particularly if you've changed large amounts. It also means you should keep all the **exchange receipts** you're given.

Note too, that if you leave by air or sea on a ticket purchased in Tunisia with cash, you will require a **Bon de Passage**, which is a slip of paper certifying that the ticket was bought with money changed in a bank. You will first have to get a form from the ticket agent to give to the bank. But before changing your money, make sure the bank in question will issue you with the *bon*, as you cannot buy the ticket without it. The money you change when getting a *bon de passage* cannot count as part of the sum from which you're allowed to reconvert thirty percent, so it's best not to change money for other business in the same transaction.

HEALTH

Inside the country, most drugs are available but they're also expensive, so take any basics you might need, including stomach pills and suntan lotion. Travel insurance, especially to cover medical emergencies, is an essential precaution.

INOCULATIONS AND HEALTH ISSUES

Doctors differ in which **inoculations** they advise for travellers to Tunisia but many will suggest protection against typhoid, hepatitis A, cholera, polio and tetanus. The cholera jab, in particular, is now considered to be next to useless by some authorities, but many GPs like to keep their patients up to date with polio and tetanus as a matter of course. In any case, most visitors survive quite happily without having the full works, but the injections are a small price to pay for the security they provide. Tunisia is on the fringe of the **malaria** risk zone, too, and weekly pills may be worth considering if you are there in summer. More importantly, avoid mosquito bites by using a repellent on all exposed skin in the evening and at night.

Rabies exists in Tunisia, and it's wise to give dogs a wide berth and not play with animals, no matter how cute they may look. A bite, scratch or even lick from an infected animal could spread the disease; wash any wound immediately but gently with soap or detergent, and apply alcohol or iodine if possible. Find out what you can about the animal and swap addresses with the owner (if there is one), just in case. If the animal could be infected, get treatment *immediately* – rabies is invariably fatal once symptoms appear. There is a vaccine, but it is expensive, serves only to shorten the course of treatment you need and lasts no longer than three months. Dogs can be very fierce in Tunisia, especially if you're walking or cycling; as a last resort, throwing stones (or even just threatening to) should get rid of them.

MEDICAL CARE IN TUNISIA

Medical care is of a high standard in Tunisia, with most doctors trained in France or Belgium.

But state hospitals are filthy and overcrowded and basic services like food are not provided. Minor problems can be dealt with by any **infirmerie** (a surgery with a nurse), of which there's one in every town, and several in bigger ones. The larger towns all have hospitals and **cliniques** (small private hospitals that are usually more pleasant than state-run ones). **Pharmacies** administer most kinds of medicine, including some only available on prescription in Europe, and can often advise you about minor ailments too. Pharmacists usually speak French but rarely English, so you should learn a few appropriate phrases if you have special needs. In any town of reasonable size, there will be a night pharmacy, open from evening till morning when others are shut.

COMMON COMPLAINTS

Two complaints particularly liable to afflict pampered constitutions are stomach upsets and heat. Most people experience some kind of **stomach problem** during a visit, but short of starving, there's little you can do to avoid it, as there are unfamiliar micro-organisms present in everything you consume. Some people drink only bottled water or use water purifying tablets and still have trouble; others drink tap water and come through unscathed. The best policy is just to avoid obviously dirty food, wash all fresh fruit and vegetables, always wash your hands before eating and otherwise hope for the best.

If you do go down with **diarrhoea**, it's essential to replace the fluid which is lost, since dehydration can strike very quickly. In serious cases, or with children, remember that dissolving rehydration salts in water helps your body absorb it. Failing that, half a teaspoon of table salt with four of sugar in a litre of water per day should see you alright. Some say prickly pears and bananas are good if you have diarrhoea, but other fruit is best avoided, as are greasy foods, dairy products, heavy spices and caffeine. If symptoms persist for several days – especially if you get painful cramps or if blood or mucus appear in your stools – seek medical advice.

Never underestimate Tunisia's **heat**, especially in the south. A hat is an essential precaution and, especially if you have very light skin, you should also consider taking a suntan lotion with a very high screening factor, as the sun really is higher (and therefore stronger) in Tunisia than in northern latitudes. Resulting problems include **dehydration** – make sure that you're drinking enough (irregular urination such as only once a day is a danger sign) – and **heatstroke**, which is potentially fatal. Lowering body temperature, with a tepid shower or bath, for example, is the first step in treatment.

If you do decide to visit places on foot, especially in the summer, take appropriate precautions – wear a sun hat, take frequent rests in the shade and carry plenty of water.

HIV INFECTION

Although sexual encounters between Tunisians and tourists are not particularly common or likely because of traditional sexual segregation (although see p.47), it's as well to know that the incidence of **HIV infection** and full-blown **AIDS** in Tunisia is almost certainly far higher than officially known or declared. Returning emigrant workers are particularly at risk. From the point of view of travellers, a holiday affair in one of the resorts is more likely to put you at risk. Take condoms with you.

INFORMATION AND MAPS

Included in the guide are maps and plans of the main towns, cities and sites – and most other places where we think you'll need one. They can be supplemented with free handouts from the *Organisation National de Tourisme Tunisien* (*ONTT*), who print a reasonable general map of the country and a number of local town plans. Also available, though to be read with occasional irony, are a range of glossy pamphlets and reasonably full lists of hotels (usually including most of the unclassified ones).

TOURIST OFFICES

In Tunisia itself, you'll find a locally run **tourist office**, or *Syndicat d'Initiative*, in practically every town and many villages, and they tend to be friendlier and more helpful than the state-run *ONTT*; tourist office addresses and opening hours are quoted in this guide under the "Arrival" section of each town.

From these tourist offices you can get specific local information, including listings of leisure activities, bike rental, laundries and countless other things. And always ask for the free town plan. Many tourist offices also publish hotel and restaurant listings and are also often willing to give advice about the best places to go in addition to just handing out paper. They may even conduct free town tours. The *ONTT* have a main office in Tunis at 1 av Mohamed V (☎01/341077) and others throughout the country, but you can pick up most of their material in advance before you reach Tunisia from the UK, Canada and the USA.

MAPS

Free touring **maps** of Tunisia are available from tourist offices around the country, but detailed road maps are hard to come by inside Tunisia and better purchased abroad. The most reliable and best value are the 1:800,000 *Freytag & Berndt* and *World Map* Tunisia series, both with insets of Jerba, Tunis and Sousse, and the 1:1,000,000 *Michelin* (no. 958: Algérie-Tunisie), with an inset of Tunis. *Hallaweg*'s 1:1,000,000 Tunisia–Algeria map is also reasonable but less detailed, as is *Hildebrand*'s 1:900,000 Tunisia map with insets of Jerba, Tunis, Carthage,

ONTT OFFICES ABROAD

Belgium Gallerie Ravenstein 60, 1000 Bruxelles (☎02/511 1142).

Canada 1125 bd de Maisonneuve Ouest, Montréal PQ H3A 3B6 (☎514/488 0182).

France 32 av de l'Opéra, 75002 Paris (☎1/47.42.72.67); 12 rue de Sèze, 69006 Lyon (☎78.52.35.86).

Germany Kurfürstendamm 171, 10707 Berlin (☎030/885 0457); Am Hauptbahnhof 6, 6000 Frankfurt-am-Main (☎069/231891); Steinstraße 23, 4000 Düsseldorf (☎0211/84218).

Italy Via Sardegna 17, 00187 Roma (☎06/482 1934); Via Baracchini 10, 20123 Milano (☎02/871214).

Netherlands Muntplein 2111, 1012 Wr Amsterdam (☎020/224971).

Sweden Stureplan 15, 11145 Stockholm (☎08/678 0645).

Switzerland Bahnhofstraße 69, 8001 Zürich (☎01/211 4830).

UK 77a Wigmore St, London W1H 9LJ (☎0171/224 5561).

USA c/o Tunisian Embassy, 1515 Massachusetts Ave NW, Washington, DC 20005 (☎202/234 6644).

MAP OUTLETS

AUSTRALIA AND NEW ZEALAND

Adelaide: *The Map Shop*, 16a Peel St, SA 5000 (☎08/231 2033).

Brisbane: *Hema*, 239 George St, Qld 4000 (☎07/221 4330).

Melbourne: *Bowyangs*, 372 Little Bourke St, Vic 3000 (☎03/670 4383).

Perth: *Perth Map Centre*, 891 Hay St, WA 6000 (☎09/322 5733).

Sydney: *Travel Bookshop*, 20 Bridge St, NSW 2000 (☎02/241 3554).

New Zealand: *Wisers*. Branches throughout New Zealand.

NORTH AMERICA

Chicago: *Rand McNally*, 444 N Michigan Ave, IL 60611 (☎312/321-1751).

Montréal: *Ulysses Travel Bookshop*, 4176 St-Denis (☎514/289-0993).

New York: *British Travel Bookshop*, 551 5th Ave, NY 10176 (☎1-800/448-3039 or 212/490-6688); *The Complete Traveler Bookstore*, 199 Madison Ave, NY 10016 (☎212/685-9007); *Rand McNally*, 150 East 52nd St, NY 10022 (☎212/758-7488); *Traveler's Bookstore*, 22 West 52nd St, NY 10019 (☎212/664-0995).

San Francisco: *The Complete Traveler Bookstore*, 3207 Filmore St, CA 92123 (☎415/923-1511); *Rand McNally*, 595 Market St, CA 94105 (☎415/777-3131).

Santa Barbara: *Pacific Traveler Supply*, 529 State St, 93101 (☎805/963-4438; phone orders ☎805/965-4402).

Seattle: *Elliot Bay Book Company*, 101 South Main St, WA 98104 (☎206/624-6600).

Toronto: *Open Air Books and Maps*, 25 Toronto St, M5R 2C1 (☎416/363-0719).

Vancouver: *World Wide Books and Maps*, 736A Granville St, V6Z 1G3 (☎604/687-3320).

Washington DC: *Rand McNally*, 1201 Connecticut Ave NW, 20036 (☎202/223-6751).

Note that *Rand McNally* now has more than 20 stores across the US; phone ☎1-800/333-0136 (ext 2111) for the address of your nearest store, or for **direct mail** maps.

UK AND IRELAND

London: *Daunt Books*, 83 Marylebone High St, W1M 4AL (☎0171/224 2295); *National Map Centre*, 22–24 Caxton St, SW1E 6DP (☎0171/222 4945); *Stanfords*, 12–14 Long Acre, WC2 E 9LP (☎0171/836 1321), 52 Grosvenor Gardens, SW1 0AG (☎0171/730 1314), 156 Regent St, W1R 5TA; *The Travel Bookshop*, 13–15 Blenheim Crescent, W11 2EE (☎0171/229 5620); *The Travellers Bookshop*, 25 Cecil Court, WC2N 4EZ (☎0171/836 9132).

Edinburgh: *Thomas Nelson and Sons Ltd*, 51 York Place, EH1 3JD (☎0131/557 3011).

Glasgow: *John Smith and Sons*, 57–61 St Vincent St, G2 5JF (☎0141/221 7472).

Maps by **mail or phone order** are available from *Stanfords* (☎0171/836 1321).

Hammamet, Sfax, Sousse and Gabes, which are, admittedly, not as detailed as the maps in this book. Less good value are the 1:1,000,000 Tunisia maps produced by *Kimberly & Frey* and *Geographia*, although the latter has an interesting inset of Carthage with the Roman street pattern superimposed. All of these maps make some attempt to show relief, but the only maps with contour lines as such are the *Institute Géographique* 1:1,000,000 African series, rather expensive and covering the country in three separate maps. In Britain – and probably worldwide – the best map shop is *Stanfords* in London.

GETTING AROUND

Many visitors to Tunisia are discouraged from exploring the country by the high cost of car rental – around £300/$450 a week – but it's possible to reach nearly every town detailed in this guide by some form of scheduled transport or by service taxis, known as *louages*. Admittedly, the train lines are not very wide-reaching, and other forms of transport may be slow, infrequent or occasionally very crowded, but it's a reliable enough system, and distances within Tunisia are relatively short.

The one general warning to bear in mind is that transport services tend to stop at around 5pm – except in the far south, where local transport can dry up even earlier, bar buses for Tunis that leave either late at night or early in the morning. On remote routes your only choice may be the early-morning market bus.

BUSES

Buses are Tunisia's most popular form of transport and are comprehensive but complicated to master. They are run by different companies, including the **SNTRI** (*Société Nationale de Transport Rural et Interurban*) and several regional rivals known as **SRT**s (*Société Régionale des Transports*). These usually have predictable names such as *SRT Beja*, or *SRT du Gouvernorat de Medenine*, but one or two are called things like *SORETRAS* (Sfax) and *SOTREGAMES* (Gabes).

SNTRI run services in and around Tunis, linking Tunis to almost every town in the country at least once a day. Each *SRT* runs local services within its own region, and some northern ones also run services to Tunis. Only a few long-distance services don't end up in Tunis (such as Sousse–Le Kef), making it much easier to move towards or away from Tunis than across the country.

The different companies often refuse to recognize each others' existence, so it's important to ask at each individual office to be sure of finding all the buses on a given route. Some bigger towns have a central bus station, sometimes called the *gare routière*, but often the companies operate from their own separate locations, which are detailed throughout this guide. *SNTRI* generally have departure lists displayed, but with most others it's a case of persistent questioning. On some routes there are *Confort* class services, which are less crowded and faster than standard buses; the premium is slight at around twenty percent on top of the normal fare.

When travelling in the daytime, it's a good idea to consider which side of the bus the sun will be on, and choose a seat so as to avoid it. Going from east to west, the sun will be on the left all the time; from north to south, it will be on the left in the morning and the right in the afternoon.

LOUAGES

Louages – large shared taxis, usually battered Peugeot estates – are the fastest form of long-distance transport, operating non-stop along fixed routes. They leave as soon as the full complement of five passengers has appeared, or when the driver gets tired of waiting. If the car moves off without a full complement and you are the only passenger(s), make sure the driver realizes you are paying only the rate for one *place* – though you may agree with other passengers to split any empty places between you. Choice of seats is on a first-come-first-served basis; most people find the back seat uncomfortable, but you'll probably be lumbered with it if you are the fourth or fifth passenger to arrive. If you are among the first three, on the other hand, you are quite within your rights to insist on the first, second or third choice of seat. It's best to make it clear which of the remaining seats you want as soon as you find your *louage*. Allowing for five passengers, the fares are fixed at a rate a little higher than for buses. Although routes are fixed, you can, or course, rent a *louage* privately to go to a specific destination. If you think a *louage* driver is overcharging you, ask to see the official *tarif* (price list), which all *louages* must carry by law.

Louages operate from informal stations that are liable to be elusive to the uninitiated foreigner – often a particular garage or back-street yard. In larger towns, there are different terminals for different destinations. Once you've found the right place (they are detailed in the text, but they often change), ask for your destination – the signs on the cars only indicate where they are licensed, not necessarily where they are going. If you make enough noise, someone will find you a car or show you where to wait. Early morning is the best time to look for a *louage* – on many routes, they can get scarce at lunchtime and as the day goes on. If there are a lot of passengers and few *louages*, competition for seats can be fierce, and you may find yourself joining a tense group of twenty people awaiting the next arrival – the time-honoured technique is to sprint for the car when you see it in the distance, grab a door-handle, and hang on until the car stops. If you're carrying luggage, your only chance in this situation is to abandon it in the struggle for a seat then load it when the dust has settled. If this is too much for you, someone may get you a place for a little backsheesh. *Louages* will only stop for you on the road if they have a spare seat – the police are tough on drivers who carry more than the legal limit of five passengers.

In addition to inter-city *louages*, local **pick-up trucks**, known officially as *transports rurals*, run from large towns to the surrounding villages. These don't always have limit on passenger numbers and are very cheap, but rather uncomfortable.

TRAINS

Only a small and shrinking proportion of Tunisia's train lines (built by the French) have passenger services. They're run by the **SNCFT** (*Société Nationale des Chemins de Fer Tunisiens*) and cost about the same as *louages*, slightly more than buses and usually run more or less on schedule. Some routes, like the air-conditioned service down the coast, are excellent – and a real boon in summer. Prices are graded according to the type of service, and all trains have first and second class. First costs 20–50 percent more than second, and there's also a *Grand Confort* class, much the same as first but less crowded

and 10–15 percent more expensive again. A return ticket offers no savings over two singles.

Most long-distance services, especially the *climatisé* (air-conditioned), can get crowded in midsummer and should be booked in advance if possible. Even for ordinary services, turn up early to be sure of buying a ticket – if you board without, you have to pay double. Also note that, even if you already have a ticket (on the return leg of a return trip, for example), you will have to buy a 0.4TD platform access ticket in order to board your train. *Thomas Cook*'s Overseas Timetable gives a complete and up-to-date list of services. You can consult it in any public reference library. One difficulty is that most stations only have one sign, usually at one end of the platform, so you'll have to keep a sharp eye out to know where you are. Another thing to bear in mind is that trains going in different directions often pass each other at stations, there being only single track in between, and are therefore at station platforms at the same time – make sure you get the right one.

As well as *SNCFT* services, there is a local train service called the TGM from Tunis to some of its suburbs (see p.101), and a metro in the city itself.

You can buy a one-, two- or four-week train pass called the **Blue Card**, which offers unlimited train travel around Tunisia and costs per week just over twice the single fare from Tunis to Sfax, or slightly less than a return fare from Tunis to Gabes. If you plan to do a lot of travelling by train in a short time, it might be good value at 17TD for a week second-class, 24.5TD for first, and 28TD for *confort* class; for two- or four-week passes, multiply these figures by two or four. The pass can be bought at stations and travel agents and you need to bring a passport photo.

HITCHHIKING

Hitchhiking is generally good in Tunisia, for men at least. There are no problems with officialdom and, although there is remarkably little traffic, in remote areas almost anything that passes will stop. In some of these areas, hitching is a semi-institutionalized form of public transport – especially in the ubiquitous Peugeot 404 pick-up trucks – and a small contribution is expected. If there are other passengers, watch how much they pay. If you're on your own, you can either try to agree on a price in advance or risk disagreement at the end should the driver try to overcharge you; in fact this is very unlikely and waiving payment is much more common. There are no hard-and-fast rules, but the fare should be a little less than you would pay on a bus. On main routes Tunisians usually only hitch to or from places where there is no *louage* service, but traffic will probably stop for you anyway.

It can be hard to hitch out of Hammamet, and you have to walk a long way out of Tunis and Sfax, but other **routes** are fairly unproblematic. In the remote areas of the south, particularly the Ksour, local people get around by a wide and miscellaneous variety of means, details of which are given in the relevant chapters. Market days can be good for travel if you get up early enough. Transport usually heads out to a market first thing in the morning, returning late morning or afternoon. Hitching can be an excellent way of getting to meet Tunisian people. However, although **women** hitching alone or together can pick up lifts with car-renting tourists around Cap Bon or Jerba, it's not advisable elsewhere unless you join up with at least one male.

BIKES

Tunisia's terrain and climate are ideally suited most of the year to **bicycles and motorbikes**, though you may get soaked in winter and spring, and strong winds can make cycling hard work. The only drawback is the lack of maintenance facilities, as there are very few motorbikes in the country (though thousands of mopeds), and bicycles are common but basic, so you'll have to bring any specialized spare parts along. Bicycles and occasionally mopeds can be rented in big towns, but, frustratingly, only for use in the town or along the beach. If you're staying some time in Tunisia and want a motorbike for transport, it's cheaper to buy abroad and import than buy locally. **Trains** will carry a bicycle for about the same fare as a passenger; **buses** usually charge about half the passenger fare.

DRIVING AND CAR RENTAL

In such a small country **driving** ought to be the ideal way to get around. If you can afford to bring a car with you, this is true. Unfortunately **car rental charges** in Tunisia are phenomenal – among the highest in the Mediterranean. Even the smallest Renault will set you back 400TD a week and officially, at least, it's illegal to carry more than three passengers. Even at this price they'll give you a clapped-out car and if it breaks down that's your problem. Nor is

CAR RENTAL AGENCIES

AUSTRALIA
Avis ☎0800/225533.
Budget ☎0800/132848.
Hertz ☎03/698 2555.
National (Europcar/Interrent) ☎0800/655955.
Thrifty ☎0800/652008.

CANADA
Avis ☎1-800/331-1084.
Budget ☎1-800/527-0700.
Hertz ☎1-800/654-3001.
National (Europcar/Interrent) ☎1-800/CAR RENT.

IRELAND
Avis ☎021/281111.
Budget ☎0903/24759.
Europcar/Interrent (National) ☎01/668 1777.
Hertz ☎01/676 7476.

NEW ZEALAND
Avis ☎09/525 1982.
Budget ☎0800/652227.
Hertz ☎0800/655955.
National (Europcar/Interrent) ☎09/275 0066.
Thrifty ☎09/256 1405.

UNITED STATES
Avis ☎0800/331-1084.
Budget ☎0800/527-0700.
National (Europcar/Interrent) ☎1-800/CAR RENT
Hertz ☎0800/654-3001.
Holiday Autos ☎0800/422-7737.

UNITED KINGDOM
Avis ☎0181/848 8733.
Europcar/Interrent (National) ☎01345/222525.
Budget ☎0800/181181.
Hertz ☎0181/679 1799.
Holiday Autos ☎0171/491 1111.

petrol cheap, at prices very similar to those in Britain and twice the US price. If you decide to go ahead, you'll need to be over 21 and have held a licence for at least a year. You should also check the insurance and the small print very thoroughly. From this point of view, if not for price, it might be a good idea to go for one of the big agencies listed below. Hotels often have arrangements with reliable local firms. There are cheap private local companies like *Garage Lafayette*, 85 av de la Liberté, Tunis, although they tend to offer no decent bargains; if a car is cheap to rent it may not be very well maintained. One thing to always check when renting a car is the spare wheel, jack and wrench, since a flat tyre on Tunisia's ragged roads is a strong possibility. Another thing to check is the fuel tank, which should be full (you may also be expected to return it full).

Despite these hassles and expenses, driving has many advantages. You can visit the smaller and remoter villages seen only through dusty windows by those trapped in public transport, and you can make rewarding contacts with local people, especially if you pick up hitchhikers. Beware, however, on the roads into Kairouan of picking up hitchhikers whose main motive is to "thank" you by taking you to a relative's home, which turns out to be a carpet shop complete with lengthy sales pitch.

To bring **your own vehicle**, you will have to be over 21 and carry documents proving your ownership of the vehicle, a valid driving licence or an international one, and a green card covering Tunisia (if it doesn't, you can buy insurance at the frontier).

DRIVING CONDITIONS

Main **roads** are straight and surfaced and often lined with shady eucalyptus trees; A-roads are called *Grands Parcours* (GP) and B-roads *Moyennes Corniches* (MC). Driving is not as bad as people tend to make out, except, perhaps, in crowded cities — Tunis in particular is best avoided. Tunisia **drives on the right**, with priority from the right, and vehicles coming onto a roundabout or traffic circle have right of way over those already on it. **Speed limits** are (in theory, and unless otherwise indicated) 90km/hr (55mph) in open country and 50km/hr (31mph) in built-up areas, 110km/hr (68mph) on the country's only motorway from Tunis to just south of Sousse, and 70km/hr (43mph) on the island of

Jerba. However fast you're going, though, it's customary to slow down when passing **highway patrols**. It's a good idea to have your papers available because there are frequent road checks, especially in the south and around Gafsa — usually, it's your passport rather than your driving licence that they'll want to see. There are also speed traps, and seat belts are compulsory for the driver and front-seat passenger. If you get stopped for speeding you have to pay on the spot. One practice that's initially disconcerting is that the police often flag down drivers to get a lift. It's best not to argue, and if you're not going their way they won't force the matter. As far as parking goes, red and white stripes painted on the kerb tell you that it is prohibited, and in one or two places Denver boots are used to enforce this prohibition.

The biggest potential problem is the state of some of the **rougher roads**, especially in the south. Some are obviously difficult, but drifting sand on others can be insidious. Also, tarmac can be rather narrow and lorries tend to force cars off the edge of the road, accepted practice but a little worrying at first. Another hazard, especially when passing through towns, is the apparent lack of road sense among pedestrians, cyclists and moped riders, who all seem to meander quite happily down the middle of the road as if they'd never heard of the automobile; you will almost certainly end up using your horn more than you do at home, but you will also have to reduce speed and keep your eyes peeled, especially at dusk. Dipping headlights is a novel concept to most Tunisian drivers and you will be dazzled by the glare from oncoming traffic.

In the south, many of the routes are **unsurfaced roads**. Their condition varies and many are passable in any ordinary car, while others require an off-road vehicle. In any case, you will not be able to drive down them at the same sort of speed as on a tarmac road; even if it seems quite easy, remember that the road surface can change unexpectedly, and boulders can appear as if from nowhere. Car rental firms don't permit their vehicles to be driven on unsurfaced roads, and can hold you liable for "any damage caused to the vehicle through driving on dirt tracks". If you intend driving into the desert, see the box on p.352.

In case of **breakdown**, always carry a good supply of water and, if you're planning a long journey, food and blankets. There are plenty of places that will repair a puncture or more serious problem cheaply – look out for workshops with tyres outside, especially on the way into and out of towns.

FLIGHTS

Tunisia's size makes **internal flights** something of an extravagance. For the time saved, you will miss out on the satisfaction of seeing the scenery change from one region to another. However, flights are worth bearing in mind for the odd journey back to Tunis, say from the south. Tickets are relatively cheap (under £40/$60 from Jerba to Tunis) and might be worthwhile if you are pressed for time; to be sure of a flight, it's wise to book well ahead.

ORGANIZED TOURS

If time is short, you might consider an **organized tour** by Land Rover or even bus. These are offered by travel agents and hotels in most large Tunisian towns and resorts, and can generally be found in our "Listings" sections under "Excursions". The main advantage of them is that they are relatively good value (£80/$120 for three days is a typical price), and allow you to see far more in the way of sights than you could get to by public transport. Disadvantages are that they rather isolate you from the country, may move on more quickly than you would like and stop for meals at places whose prices go up when you arrive. Take note that a "safari" does not mean wildlife spotting, but is the local terminology for an organized excursion.

TRANSPORT IN TOWN

The cheapest way to get around big towns is by **bus**. These can be very crowded (you often have to fight your way on and off) and stops are not always signposted. Useful routes are indicated in the text of the guide, but it's often easier and more interesting to walk. Tunis has a so-called **metro** system that's an articulated tram rather than an underground train, and subject to most of the same provisos as buses.

Taxis are very good value for small groups. They all have meters so there's no need to fix a price before you go, though this may not apply at night – officially, they should run on the meter and charge you fifty percent extra from 9pm to 6am. You can arrange a tour (around several sites for example) by renting the taxi for the day. In this case, fix the price first. By law taxis can only take four people but if there are more of you it is possible to use a larger (and more expensive) estate car, a *louage* for example.

In towns with a large tourist presence, horse-drawn carts known as **calèches** provide a more picturesque alternative to taxis. Though slower and more expensive (and given to stopping off at souvenir stalls, where the driver gets a commission on anything you buy), *calèches* are a fun ride, especially for children. Also purely for holidaymakers are the frankly ridiculous **tourist land trains**, known as Noddy trains, which have spread like an epidemic to almost all of the country's resorts.

ACCOMMODATION

Tunisia's more expensive hotels are geared primarily to the package holiday trade. The country is adapting to the growth in independent travel – but it's a slow process. In all the main tourist centres and in most sizeable towns in the interior, you can find hotels in every price range, but in smaller places there may only be a choice between a very basic establishment with dirty sheets or a fairly expensive hotel with air conditioning and pool. In midsummer, any kind of room in the more popular towns can be hard to find on the spot – though if you get really stuck someone local will probably invite you to stay rather than see the country's reputation for hospitality diminished.

High season usually means the summer (mid-June to mid-Sept, sometimes only July & Aug); low season is over winter (Nov–March), and mid-season in between (April–June & Sept–Oct). Not all hotels have seasonal price changes (unclassified and city hotels usually do not); some charge the same prices in mid- and high-season; and one or two in the desert have high season in winter and low season in the summer. Christmas and New Year tariffs are in any case likely to be even higher than the normal high season price.

HOTELS AND PENSIONS

Classified hotels, officially approved for tourist use, are graded from one-star to five-star, with wide-ranging prices and standards within each category. The classification of a hotel depends on things like the size of rooms, windows and bathrooms, and the presence or absence of facilities (such as a swimming pool): it is not a reliable indication of the price or quality of

---

ACCOMMODATION PRICE CODES

All the hotels, youth hostels and pensions listed in this book have been price-graded according to the following scale, and although costs will rise slightly overall with the life of this edition, the relative comparisons should remain valid. Naturally, you can expect hotel prices to be higher wherever the number of tourists is greater.

The tariffs quoted are for the **cheapest available double room in high season**, although many of the cheap places will have pricier rooms with en suite facilities or sea views. Remember that prices are often seasonal and places that are expensive in the summer may have bargain-basement prices off-season when business is slack, and that prices may be negotiable, especially out of season or if you're staying for a week or more. All hotels must by law display their official maximum prices in reception, usually in the form of a price per person in a double room, with a supplement for single occupancy. Categories ③ and higher tend to include breakfast.

Classified hotels, officially considered suitable for tourists, are graded from one to four stars, with wide-ranging prices within each category.

① Up to 10TD. Very cheap. Usually a bed only in a basic, unclassified hotel or a youth hostel.

② 10.1–25TD. Budget. Bed only or bed and breakfast.

③ 25.1–40TD. Comfortable budget. Good unclassified average one-star or a cheap two-star.

④ 40.1–55TD. Mid-range. Expensive two-star, cheap three-star.

⑤ 55.1–70TD. Tourist hotel. Standard three-star.

⑥ 70.1TD upwards. Deluxe. Expensive three-star, four-star or five-star.

service. Indeed, things like room service – which you might expect in Western hotels with a rating – can be slapdash or nonexistent, and even in a three-or four-star hotel in Tunisia, rooms may have only a shower, no bath; the Western practice of adding drinks from the bar to room bills is rare.

Below the one-star category, there is a range of hotels suitable for budget travellers, even if not officially regarded as appropriate for tourists. These **unclassified hotels**, usually concentrated in a town's medina – just ask for an *auberge* (inn) or *Hôtel Tunisien* – differ widely. The best of them, often colonial relics, have high ceilings and creaking fans, and are very respectable: the equivalent of a D-class, say, in Italy or Greece, and charging 6–15TD for a double room, though in winter they may be cold and draughty with no heating. Many of the cheapest ones (3TD per person), though, can be rougher – and they're sometimes closed to, or dangerous for, unaccompanied women. In this type of place you'll often be expected to share a room, or fill it, or even pay for any beds (as many as four) which remain empty. However, there are good (and perfectly safe) places even in this range and, for men at least, they're a useful standby as you can nearly always find a bed.

Women will have to play it by ear much of the time. If Tunisian women are staying in a hotel, that should be a good sign: if all the clientele are men, think again. Male fellow travellers

may be prepared to help out by posing as "husbands" or "brothers", but this may not excise some nuisances such as the presence of Peeping Toms when you use the hotel's shared shower – and relying on male tourists can, obviously, plunge you into just the compromising situations you were trying to avoid.

Hotels are supplemented by family-run **pensions**, found mainly in the Cap Bon area and varying widely in both price and standard. At their best they really are cheap and friendly *pensions familiales*, and even at their worst they're quite adequate, and one or two are even deluxe, with prices to match.

YOUTH HOSTELS AND CAMPING

There are some thirty **youth hostels** in Tunisia, five of them run by Tunisia's *Youth Hostel Association* and the rest attached to youth centres (*Maisions des Jeunes*) run by the Ministry of Culture. Some of these, more specifically designed for accommodation, have been designated *Centre de Stages et de Vacances*. These charge 4TD a night, as much as a cheap hotel, and are usually situated on the edge of town near the municipal stadium. They tend to look like barracks and feel like changing rooms, operate curfews and turf you out early in the morning. They usually seize your passport on arrival, so you have to track it down before you

YOUTH HOSTEL ASSOCIATIONS

Australia *Australian Youth Hostel Association*, Level 3, 10 Mallett St, Camperdown, NSW 2050 (☎02/565 1699).

Canada *Hostelling International/Canadian Hostelling Association*, Room 400, 205 Catherine St, Ottawa, ON K2P 1C3 (☎613/237-7884 or 1-800/663-5777). Annual membership adults Can$25, youths (under 18) $12; children free when accompanied by parents. Adults can also take out a two-year membership for $35.

England and Wales *Youth Hostel Association* (*YHA*), Trevelyan House, 8 St Stephen's Hill, St Albans, Herts AL1 2DY (☎01727/855215). London shop and information office: 14 Southampton St, London WC2E 7HA (☎0171/836 1036); annual membership adults £9, youths (under 18) £3.

Ireland *An Oige*, 61 Mountjoy St, Dublin 7 (☎01/830 4555); annual membership adults IR£7.50, youths (under 18) IR£4.

New Zealand *Youth Hostel Association of New Zealand*, PO Box 436, Christchurch 1 (☎03/379 9970).

Northern Ireland *Youth Hostel Association of Northern Ireland*, 56 Bradbury Place, Belfast, BT7 1RU (☎01232/324733); annual membership adults £7, youths (under 18) £3.

Scotland *Scottish Youth Hostel Association*, 7 Glebe Crescent, Stirling, FK8 2JA (☎01786/451181); annual membership adults £6, youths (under 18) £2.50.

USA *Hostelling International-American Youth Hostels* (*HI-AYH*), 733 15th St NW, Suite 840, PO Box 37613, Washington, DC 20005 (☎202/783-6161). Annual membership adults $25, youths (under 18) $10, seniors (55 or over) $15, families $35.

can leave, and can't easily use it for changing money while there, but only in Tunis do they ask to see your membership card. Women's accommodation is separate – which is a boon if you're a woman travelling alone – and hostels can be excellent places for meeting young Tunisians, many of whom are dying to practise their English. *YHA* hostels charge less than *Maison des Jeunes* ones; they often have food and tend to be better run, less heavy-handed with the rules and regulations, more central and often housed in interesting old buildings. Recommended in particular are the hostels in **Tunis Medina** and **Houmt Souk** (Jerba). Those at **Remel** (Bizerte), **Kelibia**, **Remla** (Kerkennah) and **Aïn Soltane** (near Ghardimaou) are also a cut above the norm.

Although there is a mere handful of official **campsites** in the country, there are many unofficial ones, and it's almost always possible to arrange something. The official sites cost around 3TD a head; unofficial ones often a little less. Many youth hostels and hotels will also let people camp in their grounds and **camping sauvage** ("wild camping") – with a minimum of discretion – is often a positive option. While

sleeping out on the main tourist beaches like Hammamet, Nabeul, Sousse or Monastir is either expressly forbidden or likely to be cut short by the police, there should be few problems elsewhere, and it's common practice around Bizerte, Raf Raf and other places. In the interior it's a good idea to ask the permission of the land owner. If you can't find the owner, ask the local police, who are very unlikely to say no, or will suggest an alternative site. Informing the police of your presence will also help avoid misunderstandings, especially if you're in a sensitive area such as an international frontier.

MUSLIMS, ARABIC SPEAKERS AND JEWISH PILGRIMS

For **Muslims** or anyone who **speaks Arabic**, the opportunities for cheap accommodation are wider. Most likely you will move from one hospitable family to another, but if you're ever stuck, try the **local mosque or zaouia.** They often have hostel accommodation where pilgrims can stay – always an interesting place to meet people. **Jews** on pilgrimage, particularly in Jerba (see p.312), may find similar help from the local Jewish community.

EATING AND DRINKING

"Chilis were essential to the full glory of Kuss Kussu; but he did not expect mere Europeans to rise to such heights. And yet he'd known one really great Englishman, a certain Captain Gordon, who could eat more chilis than any Arab."

Reginald Rankin, Tunisia (1930).

RESTAURANT MEALS

Eating out is not really an Arab tradition but the French presence and tourism have made inroads and there are now three distinct levels of eating establishment. In big cities and tourist centres you'll come across smart and essentially French **restaurants** offering meals of several courses; these can be excellent and are usually very good value. Every town also has less elaborate restaurants serving main dishes which are virtually indistinguishable from one place to the next – simple meat, chicken, fish and vegetables kept warm throughout the day. You soon learn to recognize these places, known throughout Tunisia as **gargotes**. Last and cheapest are the **rôtisseries** which, despite their name, do more frying than roasting – if you have a low tolerance for grease, you'll probably prefer the restaurants.

Rôtisseries are usually open all day, their food laid out behind the counter so you can just point at what you want. Restaurants are open

GLOSSARY OF TUNISIAN FOOD

French, Arabic and the English translations are given where appropriate and in that order.

BASICS

L'addition	El fatura or el hisaab	Bill, check	Huile	Zit	Oil (invariably olive)
Bouteille	Darbooza	Bottle	Olives	Zitoun	Olives
Pain	Khobs	Bread	Poivre	Filfel	Pepper
Beurre	Zibda	Butter	Sel	Melha	Salt
Oeufs	Adhma	Eggs	Sucre	Sukar	Sugar
Verre	Keson	Glass	Cassecroûte	Cassecroûte	Sandwich
Couteau	Sekina	Knife	Salade	Salata	Salad
Cuillere	Mirafa	Spoon	Table	Taula	Table
Fourchette	Farchita	Fork			

FISH (poisson/samak)

(in general, the French name is used, even when speaking Arabic)

Sole	Sabidaj	Sole	Crevettes	Qambri	Prawns
Daurade	Jerrafe	Bream	Clovisses	Babush	Clams
Rouget	Trilya	Red mullet	Langouste	Fakrun b'har	Crawfish (rock lobster)
Thon	Ton	Tuna	Calmar	Subia	Squid
Mulet	Bowri	Grey mullet	Poulpe	Qarnit	Octopus
Merou	Manani	Grouper	Sépia	M'dass	Cuttlefish
Loup de Mer	Karus	Sea bass			
Roussette	Kalb el-bahr	Dogfish (rock salmon)			

MEAT AND POULTRY (viande/lahma)

Poulet	Djaj	Chicken	Biftec	Habra	Steak
Mouton or agneau	Houli	Mutton or lamb	Foie	Kibda	Liver
Boeuf	Bakri	Beef	Brochette	Safud	Small kebab

VEGETABLES (legumes/khadrawat)

Pommes frites	Batata	Chips	Pois chiche	Houmous	Chick-peas (garbanzo beans)
Pommes de terre	Batata	Potatoes			
Haricots	Loobia	Beans	Oignons	B'sal	Onions

TUNISIAN DISHES

Brik à l'oeuf One of Tunisia's great culinary curiosities – an egg fried inside a pastry envelope, the eating of which demands considerable ingenuity to avoid getting egg on your face. Sometimes made with tuna or vegetables, *briks* vary a lot in quality.

Chakchuka Vegetable stew based on onions, peppers and chick-peas, usually topped with a fried egg.

Chorba Soup. There are many varieties, but most are spicy and delicious.

Couscous (cousk-see) The classic North African dish – steamed semolina grains, served with meat or fish, and vegetables.

Deglet Fatima Fingers of filo pastry with egg or other filling.

Harissa Hot red chilli sauce added liberally to almost everything.

Kamounia Meat (lamb, beef and/or liver) stewed in a thick cumin sauce.

Kefteji A vegetable stew like a spicy ratatouille, often served with meatballs.

Koucha Lamb and potatoes in tomato sauce.

Lablabi Bread soaked in chick-pea broth, usually with a raw egg scrambled into it to cook, and spices added on top, sometimes with tuna. Very cheap – the worker's staple – and made in front of you so you can ask them to hold back on this or that.

TUNISIAN DISHES continued

Mechoui	Grilled meat.	*Schewarma*	Marinaded lamb kebab on a vertical
Merguez	Spicy sausage – eat it well cooked!		spit, carved and served in a pitta
Mermez	Mutton stew.		bread. Looks like a doner kebab but is
Ojja	Similar to a *chakchuka*, with egg		insulted by the comparison.
	scrambled into it .	*Tajine*	No relation to its Moroccan namesake,
Salade	Not a salad in the usual sense, but a		Tunisian *tajine* is a kind of baked
mechouia	mashed, spicy mix of roasted vege-		omelette or quiche.
	tables served cold.		

SWEETS (patîsseries/halawiyet)

Baklava	Honey-soaked flaky pastry	*Ftair*	A Ghoumrassen speciality –
	with a honey-soaked nut fill-		deep-fried batter pancake,
	ing – hazelnut is best.		somewhere between a
Kab el ghazal	A Tataouine speciality –		doughnut and a fritter, usually
(*corne de gazelle*)	pastry horn stuffed with		available in the morning.
	chopped almond filling.	*Halva*	Sesame-based sweet common
Draw	Lukewarm, dark grey		throughout the Middle East.
	porridge, topped by a strip of	*Loukoum*	Turkish delight.
	halva, spoonfuls of various	*Mesfuf*	Sweet couscous.
	coloured powders and a	*Millefeuille*	French cream pastry.
	hunk of cake: served by	*Makroudh*	A Kairouan speciality –
	some city cafés for breakfast		honey-soaked semolina cake
	and worth trying at least		with a date centre.
	once.	*Youyou*	Ring doughnut.

FRUIT AND NUTS (fruits/fawakia)

Dattes	*t'mar*	Dates	*Grenade*	*rouman*	Pomegranate
Orange	*burtukal*	Orange	*Melon*	*battikh*	Melon
Pomme	*tufah*	Apple	*Fraises*	*fraulu*	Strawberries
Citron	*limoun*	Lemon or lime	*Cerises*	*hbmluk*	Cherries
Raisins	*ainab*	Grapes	*Pêche*	*khoukh*	Peach
Figues	*kermus*	Figs	*Amandes*	*louze*	Almonds
Abricots	*mishmash*	Apricots	*Noix*	*zouze*	Walnuts
Figues de Barbarie	*hendi*	Prickly pears	*Pistaches*	*fozdok*	Pistachios
		(Barbary figs)	*Cacahuètes*	*kakawiya*	Peanuts

DRINKS (boissons/mashrubaat)

Bière	*birra*	Beer	*Lait*	*halib*	Milk
Thé	*té* or *shai*	Tea	*Citronade*	*asir limoun*	Real lemonade
Café	*qahwa*	Coffee	*Lait de poule*	*halib djaj*	Milkshake with egg-
Eau	*ma*	Water			white
Vin	*sharab*	Wine	*Jus*	*'asir*	Juice

mainly in the evening, and almost always display a menu – if it's in Arabic you can ask to go and look at the dishes; cheaper restaurants begin to close around 9pm, and the most popular dishes are often finished some time before then.

Women travellers may find that restaurants and cafés are some of the worst places for pestering. Your best bet, unfortunately, is to use the more cosmopolitan and expensive places in the towns and avoid those in rural areas. You will also be less conspicuous drinking coffee in a patisserie than in a café. Some restaurants have separate rooms for women diners and the waiter will automatically show you in there when you arrive. There are also one or two cafés where only women can drink, but they tend to be well hidden.

TYPICAL MEALS

If there is a **starter** at a restaurant it will probably be soup (*chorba* – oily and very spicy), Tunisian salad (basically a finely chopped green salad), or a more specifically Tunisian dish such as *brik à l'œuf* or *salade mechouia*.

There are two levels of **main course**. For around 1TD you can get a starch-based dish (couscous, spaghetti or beans) with a little meat and hot peppery sauce. Unexciting but very filling, this is what most families eat at home. Paying anything from 1.5TD upwards, you get more meat or fish, usually served with a separate plate of fried potatoes. Both grilled meat (*brochettes*) and fish can be delicious. Bread (*khobs*) is always included, along with a little plate of hot red sauce (*harissa*). There is rarely much to follow the main course except perhaps seasonal fruit.

If you are invited into a **Tunisian home**, you will probably be eating from a communal dish into which you dip bread to soak up the sauce and hold the pieces of food. Remember to **use only your right hand** – the left is used for "unclean" functions such as wiping your bottom or washing your feet – and, if there is only a little meat, not to eat more than your fair share. Men and women eat separately in a Tunisian household, but visiting Western women will probably eat with the men, especially if accompanied by one. Contrary to the popular myth, you are not expected to belch loudly to show your appreciation of the food, nor are you likely to be served sheep's eyes. Should you wish to offer your host a gift, something from home unavailable locally will go down really well, or take a box of sweets from a high-class patisserie.

VEGETARIAN AND OTHER SPECIAL DIETS

How you fare as a **vegetarian** in Tunisia depends on how strictly you avoid animal products. If you are completely vegan, you're going to have a very hard time of it. About the only things you'll be able to eat ready-cooked are chips, spaghetti in tomato sauce and *lablabi* (and even then, you'll have to watch that no eggs or tuna get into it). You can get pizzas made up without cheese or you could live on a diet of bread and olives, but you're best advised to take a spirit stove or book self-catering accommodation to take care of yourself. Staples such as rice, dried beans and pasta are available at grocers and supermarkets, fresh vegetables are easy to find in markets, and "burning alcohol" (*alcool à brûler*) is widely available at hardware shops (camping gas cannisters much less so).

If you eat **eggs and dairy products**, you're increasing your range considerably: *ojja*, *chakchuka*, *brik*, *tajine* and omelettes all become possible, and you have even more choice if you are prepared to eat fish and cheese. Even so, you will have to be watchful as the concept of vegetarianism is completely alien to most Tunisians, who may well not understand what you want.

Muslims eat meat with every meal (or aspire to) and you won't meet any Tunisian vegetarians. Nor do Tunisians exhibit much concern about animal welfare: at *Aid el Adha* most families will slaughter their own sheep and in abattoirs and markets animals are slaughtered *halal*, their throats cut without being stunned. So when you try to explain that you don't want meat with your couscous, don't be surprised if you get a blank look. And don't be surprised either if you find meat added to vegetable dishes to "improve" them. You may also ask for a dish without meat, only to find that it's a meat dish with the lumps of meat (but not the gravy) removed. The fussier you are about this sort of thing, the harder it will be for you to eat out and the more you should consider taking a stove and cooking for yourself.

Also be aware that **hospitality** is an extremely important part of Arab civilization, and if you enter a Tunisian home, you're bound to be offered something to eat. Moreover, your host may be insulted if you don't eat it. Do bear this in mind if invited into someone's house.

The Tunisian sweet tooth may be a problem for **diabetics**, especially where drinks and snacks are concerned. Artificial sweeteners are not widely used in Tunisia, diet versons of soft drinks are unavailable, and unsweetened fruit juice is expensive even if you can find it. Your only recourse is to drink water. You might consider taking some flavoured concentrate with you to mix with it, as well as some savoury crackers, since these are unavailable in Tunisia too. Sugar will usually be added unrequested to coffee unless you're quick to point out that you don't want it, and the same applies to pomegranate served broken up as a dessert in restaurants. You probably won't find sugarless tea at all.

If you only eat **kosher** meat, you'll have to stick to fish and vegetables most of the time, although two kosher restaurants exist in Tunisia

– *Robinson* in Tunis (see p.96) and a small *gargote* in Hara Kebira on Jerba (see p.328).

PATISSERIES, SNACK FOOD AND BREAKFAST

Cafés are beginning to merge with **patisseries**, French-style pastry shops which serve elaborate cakes along with almond milk and *citronade*, a refreshing drink made by putting whole lemons, skin and all, through a blender with sugar and water and straining the result. *Citronade* is a life-saver in the summer heat, but only as safe as the water that goes into it. Some patisseries also serve other fresh fruit drinks made with a blender, including *lait de poule* ("chicken's milk"), a fresh fruit milkshake with egg white. If you don't want sugar in juices or milkshakes, make it clear from the start.

The pastries served by patisseries are rapidly replacing more traditional Arab and Berber sweets, usually soaked in honey. Patisseries and cafés are also becoming institutionalized as the place to eat **breakfast** – a croissant or dry cake with coffee. In less sophisticated areas some cafés still provide the traditional *ftair* and *draw*. Those who prefer a more substantial and savoury breakfast could go for a bowl of *lablabi*, bread soaked in chick-pea broth with spices, egg and often tuna, a very cheap option that's Tunisia's answer to a fry-up.

The **perennial snack meal** is a *cassecroûte*, a thick chunk of French bread filled with vegetables, olives, oil, and either egg, tuna or sausage. It's automatically spread with *harissa* sauce, a concentration of red peppers which makes the average curry taste anaemic; if you prefer to go without, specify *sans piquant* or *bilesh harissa*. *Cassecroûtes* can be bought at most *rôtisseries* and many bakeries. Snack bars at bus and *louage* stations often sell them too.

Alternatively, grocers will often make up a **sandwich** for you when you buy the ingredients. Cheese is generally disappointing, though the soft white sheep's milk *maasoura*, similar to Italian *ricotta*, is worth a try, and sardines or tuna are other possible fillings.

The other essential for picnic meals, **fruit**, is one of Tunisia's greatest delights. Depending on the season you can gorge yourself on fresh oranges, figs, grapes, melon, dates, pomegranates, prickly pears, strawberries and cherries. Pomegranates are often served as a dessert, broken up in a dish with the bitter yellow pith removed; if you don't want sugar on top, say so when you order. The prickly pear, or "Barbary fig", was introduced into North Africa by the Spanish in the sixteenth century, after they brought it over from the Americas. In summer they are sold by the thousand from barrows. Though they are immensely refreshing and the first remedy to try for upset stomachs, you should beware of picking them or holding them unpeeled, as they are covered in very hard-to-see spines that get into your skin and are difficult to remove.

If you want to snack while you're out and about, **nuts** are available from shops everywhere – usually open quite late.

DRINKING

Wine, when available in restaurants, is good, and even the most expensive brands rarely cost more than £3/$5 a bottle. *Haut Mornag, Sidi Rais* and *Koudjat* are all excellent table wines; *Grombalia* and *Tardi* very rough standbys; while Kelibia in Cap Bon produces a distinctive and unusual **dry muscat**. Except in the tourist hotels, wine is not served in restaurants on Fridays.

Other local drinks include the rather watery *Celtia* **beer**, ubiquitous **mineral waters** (*Safia, Aïn Garci* or *Aïn Oktor*), standard fizzy drinks generically known as *gazouz*; and two **strong spirits**. Unless you have an asbestos throat it's best to drink *boukha* – a spirit derived from figs – in the standard combination with Coke; *thibarine*, a date liqueur, is more palatable. *Laghmi* (palm wine) is the sap of the date palm milked from the tree, fermented in 24 hours, and both fresh and fermented versions are available around the oases in season. If you're offered *laghmi* down south, be sure it's okay before drinking as it is sometimes mixed with dirty water or left too long. *Sirops*, distilled from fruit (pomegranate, orange, lemon, fig and even pistachio), are rather sickly in taste and garish in colour but make good mixers.

You may find alcohol at a few westernized cafés, but most Tunisian drinking is done in **bars** – exclusively male and still with an air of the bootleg about them, dense with smoke and invariably deafening. Still, they often serve excellent little snacks (melon, olives, even *brochettes*). In the European-style bars of the bigger hotels the drinks are more expensive but the atmosphere more relaxed and even Tunisian women can sometimes be seen. If you're a lone drinker you can buy alcohol in the larger supermarkets, but you mustn't carry the bottles around town in public view; take a bag which you can close. Prices displayed do not include the deposit on the bottle.

COFFEE AND TEA

Coffee-drinking in the ubiquitous card-playing cafés is a national pastime. The coffee (*qahwa* in Arabic, *café* in French) can be very good and comes in several forms. *Express* is Italian-style espresso and is almost as good as across the water. *Café au lait*, *café crème* or *qahwa bi halib* usually means filter coffee, and comes with a lot of milk. *Café filtre* is the same without milk. An espresso with milk (like a cappuccino or French *café crème*) is called a *café direct* or *crème express*. *Capucin* is not a cappuccino, but an espresso with a little milk, like a Spanish *cortado* or Italian *macchiato*. Finally, *café maure* or *café turc* is Turkish coffee – finely ground coffee brought to the boil and served with the grounds still in it, often perfumed with rose water. Two spoons of sugar are usually assumed – to avoid them, ask for *sukar kalil* (a little sugar) or *bilesh sukar* (without sugar).

Tea is either black (*té ahmar* in Arabic, *thé rouge* in French) or green with mint (*té akhdar* in Arabic, *thé vert* in French). Unfortunately, it is most commonly made by boiling the leaves in water, adding massive quantities of sugar and leaving it to stew for hours on a charcoal stove (*canoun*), which every household possesses for the purpose. The result is a powerful brew of almost pure tannin and sugar – said to result in cases of "tea poisoning" and even death – and

too pungent for most unhabituated tastes. Green tea is not usually as stewed as black and is sometimes served with pine nuts and almonds. Tea with milk is virtually unheard of, but you may get it in expensive hotels or package tour centres; anyone used to British or Irish tea, however, will not be happy with it.

Tunisian cafés still supply the traditional **hookah pipe** or *chicha*, filled with half-burned tobacco mixed with molasses. It is something of an acquired taste, but if you smoke you should certainly try it. Once strictly an old man's pastime, *chicha*-smoking has gone through something of a rennaisance of late.

RAMADAN

One thing that will probably throw your eating routine out of skew is the month of **Ramadan**, when Muslims fast from sunrise to sunset – see p.43 for specific dates. Cafés and restaurants, save those that particularly cater for tourists, are likely to close during daylight too, and bars will close altogether. Food shops are open so you can still buy things to eat but, although Tunisia is not as strict about Ramadan as some Muslim countries, you may feel that it is rude and inconsiderate to eat, drink or smoke in public when most people are committed to fasting, and that it is best to do these things in private. An alternative is to wholly or partly observe the fast too, and join local people in breaking it at sunset, hanging out late into the night enjoying the special feel that cafés have only at this time of year.

COMMUNICATIONS: POST, PHONES AND MEDIA

Post and telecommunications in Tunisia are easily up to international standards and you should have little cause to complain. Letters arrive reasonably quickly and rarely go astray, while international phone calls are a piece of cake, with direct dialling, immediate connection and reasonable charges. Indeed, Tunisia compares very favourably in this respect with much of southern Europe.

Tunisia is almost completely bilingual, so if you're competent in either French or Arabic, you can keep informed about what's happening. You should have little trouble following international news in the local newspapers or on radio or TV – though the quality of reporting and analysis is not high. Foreign newspapers, and even TV, are available in any case.

POST

Post offices (PTT) in large towns tend to follow **city opening hours** (Mon–Sat 8am–6pm, Sun 9–11am; July & Aug Mon–Sat 7.30am–1pm), while those in villages and small towns follow **country opening hours** (Mon–Thurs 8am–noon & 3–6pm, Fri & Sat 8am–12.30pm; July & Aug Mon–Thurs 7.30am–1pm, Fri & Sat 7.30am–1.30pm); these are specified as appropriate throughout the text. During **Ramadan**, post offices are open Mon–Thurs & Sat 8.15am–1.45pm, Fri 8.15am–1pm, with Sunday hours unaffected. When the PTT is closed, stamps can often be obtained from shops selling postcards.

Postal services are very reliable; **letters** to Europe and the British Isles rarely take more than a week, to North America and Australasia around two weeks. The parcel service is slower but equally reliable. Post boxes are usually light yellow in colour, are freestanding or set into walls at around shoulder height on the streets.

For **Poste Restante**, address letters clearly "Tunis R.P., rue Charles de Gaulle, Tunis" (the main post office) or to any local post office, marked "R.P." (for *Recette Postale*). To collect it, you'll need some form of identification.

PHONE CALLS

It is almost as easy to make an **international phone call** as a local one. In most towns you can dial direct on a coin phone (save up those dinar coins) at the PTT or a "Taxiphone" office. The latter is a sort of shop where you can phone Tunisian or international numbers; they're usually open later than the PTT and have plenty of change on hand. In one or two places, you make the call without coins and then pay on completion. Either way, it's rarely difficult. Three minutes to the British Isles currently costs around 3TD, to North America 6TD, and to Australasia 9TD. First dial the international code (see box), followed by the area code – leaving out any initial zeros. An occasional problem in larger towns is waiting for a booth: in summer, 2–5pm is an off-peak period.

Internal calls are not expensive: you will need hundred-millime coins, which are taken by all local pay phones. The system is fairly efficient, with area codes used in the normal way (see box).

NEWSPAPERS AND MAGAZINES

The daily **French-language newspapers** *La Presse* and *Le Temps* stay close to the Party line as, unsurprisingly, does the Party's own daily paper, *Le Renouveau*. *Le Temps* is perhaps the most substantial. They all carry listings of cultural events, exchange rates, bus, train and plane departures from Tunis, and television and Tunis cinema listings.

Periodicals, less restricted than the daily press, carry interesting items from a more radical standpoint: *Jeune Afrique*, published weekly in

DIALLING CODES

DIALLING TUNISIA FROM ABROAD

Australia ☎0011 216 + local code (without zero) + number

New Zealand ☎00 216 + local code (without zero) + number

Republic of Ireland ☎00 216 + local code (without zero) + number

United Kingdom ☎00 216 + local code (without zero) + number

USA and Canada ☎011 216 + local code (without zero) + number

DIALLING ABROAD FROM TUNISIA

Australia ☎00 61 + local code (without zero) + number

New Zealand ☎00 64 + local code (without zero) + number

Republic of Ireland ☎00 353 + local code (without zero) + number

United Kingdom ☎00 44 + local code (without zero) + number

USA and Canada ☎00 1 + local code + number

TIME

Tunisia is one hour ahead of GMT all year round, which means that the time is the same as in Britain and Ireland during the summer, an hour ahead in winter. In principle it is six hours ahead of North American Eastern Standard Time, ten hours ahead of Pacific Standard Time, seven hours behind Western Australia, nine hours behind eastern Australia and eleven hours behind New Zealand, but daylight saving time in those places will vary that difference by an hour.

USEFUL NUMBERS WITHIN TUNISIA

Emergencies ☎197
Speaking clock ☎191

Directory enquiries ☎12
International operator ☎17

TUNISIAN PHONE CODES

All Tunisian numbers are now made up of six digits. Old five-figure numbers have added an initial digit as shown in the brackets below.

☎01 – Tunis region
☎02 – Bizerte (4), Nabeul (2), Zaghouan (6)
☎03 – Mahdia (6), Monastir (4), Sousse (2)
☎04 – Sfax region (2)
☎05 – Gabes (2), Kebili (4), Medenine (6), Tataouine (8)

☎06 – Gafsa (2), Tozeur (4), Sidi Bou Zid (6)
☎07 – Kairouan (2), Kasserine (4)
☎08 – Beja (4), Jendouba (6), Le Kef (2), Siliana (8)
☎09 – all mobile phones (7)

France but with a Tunisian editor, is excellent (its credibility enhanced by occasional government bannings). The bimonthly women's journal, *Nissa,* which began publication in 1985, is in Arabic and French.

Foreign newspapers can be bought, a day late, at newsagents and big hotels in all tourist areas (*Le Monde* almost everywhere). In the resort areas, most British national dailies are available, as are the *Herald Tribune, Time* and *Newsweek.*

RADIO AND TV

There are plenty of **French-language radio stations**. *Radio Monte Carlo* is popular for music. The *BBC World Service* in **English** can be picked up from 5am to 11.15pm GMT on 15.07MHz (19.91m), but you may get better reception in the morning and evening on 12.095MHz (24.8m), or in the evening on 9.41MHz (31.88m).

There are four **local TV channels**: one in Arabic, two in French. One of the latter is a Tunisian version of the French *Antenne 2.* The news programme, *Téléjournal,* is at 8pm. The Italian station *RAI Uno* is also available, and other French and Italian channels can sometimes be picked up. Use of satellite dishes is increasing (most tourist hotels have them), giving access to many more channels in various languages, notably German, and *Eurosport* in English. TV schedules are published daily in *La Presse, l'Action* and *Le Temps.*

MOSQUES, MUSEUMS AND SITES

Tunisian history has left a substantial legacy in the form of religious and other monuments, archeological sites and museums. Increasingly aware of the need to establish Tunisia's holiday identity as more than just a cheap beach, the authorities are keen to promote their vision of Tunisia's monumental heritage, with the result that mainstream sights are well maintained and accessible. Be aware, though, that the dominance of organized tourism in Tunisia means that mainstream sights are liable to be crowded at peak hours, compared to sights lying even slightly off the beaten track that are harder to get to and often barely visited at all. When it comes to religious monuments still in use, the general rule in Tunisia – in contrast to Egypt or Turkey, say – is that non-Muslims may not enter at all, except for a few very major tourist attractions.

VISITING ISLAMIC BUILDINGS

Visiting mosques and religious buildings in Tunisia is a frustrating business. In theory, a 1972 law allows non-Muslims to visit mosque courtyards (but not prayer halls). In practice, the situation is closer to that in Morocco than Egypt or Turkey. At a few major tourist attractions, where the hours are strictly regulated, you can legitimately enter the complex but not the prayer hall. Elsewhere, to gain entry even to mosque courtyards, you'll generally need to find someone sympathetic to let you in and/or provide support in the face of the offence that you may have caused.

Whatever the building in question, respect for local custom is recommended; sadly, there are still tourists who parade around the Great Mosque at Kairouan as though it were a zoo. According to **religious regulations**, a woman entering a mosque should be covered from her neck to her ankles and wrists; she should also cover her hair and most not wear trousers. A man should be covered from his torso to below his knees (so T-shirts, but not shorts, are all right for men). Women also are not supposed to enter a mosque during menstruation.

Mosques **off the tourist trail** can be tricky, and older people will often flatly refuse you entry. Students and younger people are more helpful and often if you hang around outside someone will ask if you want to be taken in. Chances are your guide will have to argue with an older guardian – but at least while this is going on you can take a look round before gracefully retreating. Occasionally, you'll be allowed into a prayer hall, in which case you must take off your shoes. Remember, mosques are ritually clean and no Tunisian would consider entering without washing thoroughly. It is a bad idea to try to visit mosques against the will of local people, as religion is taken very seriously here.

The **zaouias**, or cult centres, are slightly different in that they are private institutions. Unless Arabic-speaking or Muslim, you're most unlikely to be allowed into a *zaouia* which is still in use, but many are now either deserted or used as domestic residences. This goes too for **medersas** – Islamic colleges. How much you impose on the occupants of secularized buildings is a personal decision; a courteous enquiry, however, can't do any harm, and many people are only too pleased to show visitors around.

ARCHEOLOGICAL SITES AND MUSEUMS

Opening hours for **archeological sites and museums** vary. In general, they open at 8–9am and close at 4–6pm, and sometimes from noon or 1pm to 2–3pm, staying open longer during the summer (July & Aug). Most are closed one day a week, usually Monday but sometimes Sunday or Friday. A student card may get you free admission, but it's unpredictable. For **photography** in museums, you are supposed to buy another ticket, and tripods (and any other professional-looking equipment, including sometimes flash) can only be used with special authorization (write to the *Institut National d'Archéologie*, Dar Husayn, Tunis). Many of the **lesser sites** out in the country have neither entry charge nor permanent guardian, and even some of the larger ones are only nominally fenced off, so outside official opening hours you can just walk in. There are reductions (in theory) for students under 32 at sites and museums.

In the large towns, something that calls itself a museum may well turn out to be a shop, and so don't be surprised if you come across a carpet "museum" with its exhibits up for sale.

HAMMAMS

It's difficult to understand the horror of the English woman in the 1850s who wrote that "a Moorish bath is one of the tortures with which the traveller in the East must make acquaintance". A hammam, or Turkish bath, is not only civilization at its most refined, it's also a bargain at around $1 or less than £1 for a steam bath, and £2–3/$3–4 with a massage. You could easily pay twenty times as much for the same treatment in the West.

Most Tunisians have at least one hammam a week, and for men Friday night at the hammam is the great social gathering; for women travellers, the hammam is the best place to make contact with Tunisian women (see p.47). Most hammams have different hours for men and women, with women usually bathing in the afternoon, and men in the morning or evening. Sometimes, especially in Tunis, hammams are exclusively for the use either of males or females, who can therefore use it all day. One or two beach hotels have mixed hammams that are rather pricey and for tourists only. To find a hammam just ask around, as plenty of them tend to be well hidden and they usually have signs only in Arabic if at all (hammam is written حَمَّام in Arabic). Some of them have a distinctive red and green front door.

Bear in mind that in Islam cleanliness is often quite literally next to godliness, and foreigners tend not to be welcome in hammams attached to mosques – which are used for ritual washing before prayer.

Hammams usually have secure lockers in which to leave any valuables. Always remember is that total nudity is not acceptable in Tunisia – you have to change discreetly, and wrap a linen towel (a *fouta*, which is provided) around your waist. Once you're suitably attired you head for the hot room to sit in or around a very hot bath. Before long, people start scratching, using the sweat that's being induced to rub off as much dead skin as possible. This process is finished by the masseur or masseuse, who first gives an expert massage, then uses abrasive gloves to remove every last particle of dead skin and dirt. After your bath, you may care to wrap yourself up in several *fouta* and relax for a while.

TRADITIONAL COSMETICS

Suek Walnut bark or root, used for cleaning teeth and reddening lips and gums, giving a slight, and not unpleasant, burning sensation.

Harqus Black skin dye used by women to decorate their hands and faces. At weddings, a spot of it is worn on the cheek.

Chab White stone used as a deodorant and to stop shaving cuts bleeding.

Henna Powdered leaves made into a paste and used for conditioning hair, and for colouring hair, hands and feet. The best henna comes from Gabes.

Tfal Fine earth used as shampoo and traditionally kept in a container called a *tafalla*.

Kohl Eyeliner made from ground antimony, sometimes with the addition of other materials.

SHOPPING

There are all sorts of souvenirs you might consider buying, depending on your taste, purchasing power and weight limit. The most popular seem to be soft toy camels – useful for young relatives perhaps but, like many items sold as souvenirs, not something a Tunisian would buy. Traditional craftwork, such as carpets and ceramics, has more lasting – and adult – appeal, but you may find that items of everyday Tunisian life make better, cheaper and more impressive souvenirs of the country.

If you're going to buy arts and crafts, it's probably worthwhile paying a visit to the local **crafts shop** run by the **ONAT** – the Tunisian crafts organization, *Organisation National de l'Artisanat Tunisien*. They have a number of workshops and a showroom and shop in most big towns – listed in the guide under "Practicalities", or in the town "Listings". Their goods are generally of a high quality, if a little overpriced, but it's worth visiting to get an idea of what sort of crafts are available and how much they should cost, and to help you weed out the imposters in the field – like the cheap Moroccan pottery sold as "Souvenir of Tunisia".

As for **opening hours**, the smarter the shop, the more likely it is to open daily 8.30am–noon and 3–6pm during the winter, and daily 8.30am–noon and 4–7pm during summer.

POTTERY AND CERAMICS

Of the two main pottery centres (whose wares you can find throughout Tunisia), **Nabeul** on Cap Bon specializes in pottery glazed in the Andalusian style, for which tourists are the main customers. Good buys include plates, vases and tiles which can be made up into a wall panel. In the other main centre, **Guellala** on the island of Jerba, ordinary Tunisians are still the main customers, and the best buys are more utilitarian. If you can cart it home, you might go for a huge "Ali Baba" jar – with room to hide at least one thief. Otherwise, you could buy a "magic camel" water jug, which is filled from the bottom, but can be poured only through the spout. An alternative souvenir from here is an octopus trap (see p.326), but if you'd prefer a used one, you should have no trouble persuading a fisherman to sell it to you. Tunisia's third ceramics centre is **Sejenane**, with its own style of "naive" ceramic sculpture not available outside the region.

CARPETS, RUGS AND BLANKETS

There are two main regions of **carpet production** in Tunisia, comprising Kairouan in the centre and Gafsa and the Jerid in the south. In **Kairouan**, where carpets are more finely knotted (quality being measured in knots per square metre – see p.196), they usually have geometric designs and deep colours. **Jerid** carpets are more psychedelic, with bright colours and stylized images. In **Tozeur** you may find carpets with the same distinctive designs used in the traditional brickwork of the houses. Other places where carpets are sold include Gabes and Jerba. *Kelims*, sold particularly in the south, are woven rather than knotted. Before buying a carpet, it's a good idea to check to see that it carries the government seal of approval, which guarantees its quality, although you

should be aware that Tunisian carpets have no special value outside the country, whatever their quality.

JEWELLERY

Tunisia's **jewellery** trade was traditionally run by Jews, most of whom have now emigrated. Nowadays, the jewellery shops of Houmt Souk on Jerba, often still in Jewish hands, are the best places to buy silver or gold pieces, or to have them made up. The Berber regions of the south also specialize in chunky silver jewellery, often set with semi-precious stones. This, however, is less openly on sale, and you may have to ask around to find something good. One typical piece is the **khlal**, a buckle consisting of a pin attached to a silver crescent that's used to fasten clothes. In Tabarca, you'll find a lot of **coral** jewellery on sale, though perhaps you should consider the plight of its source before buying (see p.166).

Common **motifs** in Tunisian jewellery include the hand of Fatima and the fish. Both are good-luck symbols used to ward off the evil eye (see p.387), though some say the fish was originally a phallic fertility symbol.

Hallmarks exist for silver and gold in Tunisia, though you don't often see them. On gold, a ram's head means 18 carat (75 percent), a goat's head is 14 carat (58.3 percent) and a scorpion is 9 carat (37.5 percent). Silver hallmarks include grapes with a figure 1 (90 percent silver), with a figure 2 (80 percent), and an African head looking to the right (80 percent or less).

WOODWORK, BASKETWORK AND METALWORK

There are masses of wood carvings around, but the nicest buys are made of **olive wood**, best bought in Sfax at the centre of the main olive-growing region. Especially attractive here are salad bowls, with the added bonus that they're not made at the expense of Southeast Asia's teak forests. **Basketwork** is common throughout the country, made from esparto grass, rushes or palm fronds, and with baskets, hats and table mats among the items produced. Another craft worth investing in is **hammered metal**. There are some excellent plates and trays available, but also a lot of shoddy rubbish. Rather than buying from tourist shops, seek out places where Tunisians might buy and check the artistry involved.

CLOTHING AND LEATHER

Traditional Tunisian **clothes** can look rather silly on foreigners, especially men, so be sure it fits your style before buying. **Chechias** (red felt hats) are one possibility, or a handsome camel hair **burnouse** (heavy men's cloak), but these are expensive. If you go for a **sifsari** (light women's shawl and head covering), get a cotton one. A cheaper way to obtain clothes is to buy the fabric and have a tailor make you something to order. Alternatively, you could try the **second-hand clothes markets** in most medinas – although much of the clothing is European, there are some outrageous garments to be found. Also available are the blue jackets (called *blusa*) that are the trademark of the Maghrebi working man.

Leather can be good but it can also be awful, so check the quality before buying, especially any stitching. Western-style gear such as jackets and handbags can be very shoddily made; more traditional items such as poufs and *babouche* slippers are usually better. **Sheepskins** are also widely available – make sure they're well cured.

ODDS AND ENDS AND ITEMS OF EVERYDAY LIFE

Often the things which will best remind you of Tunisia are everyday items sold in ordinary shops and markets. A **canoun** (charcoal stove), while not of much practical use back home, can't fail to remind you of all those cups of stewed tea you drank while waiting for *louages*. Alternatively, you could get a Tunisian **teapot** or a pot for making Turkish coffee (very finely ground coffee traditionally brought to the boil seven times), or a *chicha* (water pipe). Failing that, esparto mats, used in pressing olives, make great table mats. Olive oil and *harissa* (chilli sauce) are almost required purchases and cooks could try their hand at some real Tunisian cookery with a *couscoussier* (couscous steamer). If you own a car, buy some Hand of Fatima stickers to plaster it with.

There are all sorts of other odds and ends you might go for, from the ornate **birdcages** sold especially in Sidi Bou Said to **sea sponges**. Other possibilities include **darbouka drums**, typical of Tunisia. Try the drum souk in Tunis for these (see p.97), though if you need one good enough for a serious musician, you will probably want it made to order. **Sand roses**, the bizarrely shaped crystals of pink gypsum, dissolved out of the sand by dew over the years and found by nomads deep in the dunes, are the commonest souvenirs sold down south, and very cheap, especially around Nefta, Tozeur and Douz. They can be rather bulky but all sizes are available and you can get several very small ones for a dinar.

In the way of **antiques**, there are a lot of colonial remnants about, but nothing especially cheap. In Tunis, rue des Glacières by place de la Victoire, along with the market area around Souk des Armes and place du Marché du Blé, are likely hunting grounds for this sort of thing (see p.79). Around Roman sites, hawkers offer "Roman" and "Byzantine" coins and "old" oil lamps. Some of them are genuine (coins are sometimes found after rain and left overnight in a glass of gut-rot to clean them), though worthless; most, however, are artificially aged fakes.

BARGAINING

Whatever you buy, you will often be expected to **haggle** over the price. There are no hard-and-fast rules – it's really a question of how much something is worth to you. It is a good plan, however, to have an idea of how much you want to pay. Don't worry too much about initial prices. Some guidebooks suggest paying a third of the opening price, but it's a flexible guideline; you may end up paying only a tenth or less of the opening price, or, on the other hand, not be able to get the seller much below it. If you bid too low, you may be bustled out of the shop for offering an "insulting" price, but this is all part of the game and you will no doubt be welcomed as an old friend if you return the next day. Prices for food, cigarettes, buses and hotels are usually fixed. All hotels display government-regulated maximum tariffs, but you can try haggling anyway. You can sometimes get a better price for souvenirs by bartering – Levis and the latest trainers are always in demand.

There are certain rules of the game to remember. Never start haggling for something if in fact you do not want it, and **never** let any figure pass your lips that you are not prepared to pay. It's like bidding in an auction. Having mentioned a price, you are obliged to pay it. If the seller asks how much you would pay for something, and you don't want it, say so. And never go shopping with a **guide**, who will get a commission on anything you buy, which means a higher price for you.

DEALING WITH SALES TECHNIQUES: A TYPICAL SCENARIO

Veterans of countries like Morocco, Egypt and India will find Tunisia tame by comparison. In general, you won't be hassled endlessly by salesmen, nor will people attach themselves to you and then demand payment for having been your "guide". Similarly, shoppping in most of Tunisia is relaxed, pressure-free and often conducted over a no-strings-attached cup of tea. However, some **hard selling** is now creeping into some of the more touristed areas, notably the tourist ghettos of Cap Bon and the medinas of Kairouan and Sousse. If you're going to play the game, it pays to know the rules.

A salesman invites you into his shop, maybe **"for tea"** because it is his birthday, or "the birthday of the shop" (this is common on Jerba). You make it quite clear (and this is **fundamental**) that you don't want to buy anything, even if you half think you might. The salesman insists you should come in just to have a look. Of course, you may not want to go in. The Arabic for "no, thank you" is "*la shookran*", and if you say it with a smile then no one can take offence. A more definitive tactic is to say you already have whatever is being offered.

A **typical scenario**, if you do enter, begins as he shows you the ceiling to demonstrate what an old house he has – a "museum of carpets" (or carvings, or silver, or antiques); he will show you people at work, then sit you down and call for tea. A large number of carpets are brought and rolled out in front of you. As well as being a tradition, the tea and hospitality may make you feel obliged to him, but you should not. In a way, charming and pleasant as he may be, he has deceived you by saying that he wouldn't try to sell you a carpet, for that's exactly what he is doing. He shows you examples of the different styles, tells you how much they would be worth in your country, shows you the government seal of approval, tells you how little it will cost to send one home and demands to know why you don't want one. He brings out smaller and cheaper examples and keeps up the fluent spiel. Unless of course you do want to buy one, you will have to be insistent in decling to offer a price, and reminding the seller that it was he who insisted you "just look".

Finally, as you apologize and make to leave, he demands to know, of the carpets he has shown you, which you like. He will now probably tell you his **final price**, but any sign of interest on your part will raise it: if you're genuinely interested, you can always shop around and return any time you like. Hostility or abusiveness at this stage is still unusual, but it happens. If so, ignore it, or if you feel strongly enough, report it to the local *ONTT* and enter it in their complaints book, naming the shop concerned.

FESTIVALS, HOLIDAYS AND ENTERTAINMENT

The great national festivals of Tunisia are all related to Islam and so their dates are calculated according to the Muslim calendar. This is a lunar system so dates recede against the Western calendar by about eleven days a year.

Ramadan, the month-long fast required of all good Muslims every year (see p.387), sounds like a disastrous time to travel, and if you need food or drinks during the day it can be hard outside the resorts. But it is an exciting time, too. If those observing the fast sometimes get a little sluggish and short-tempered during the day (nothing may pass the lips between sunrise and sunset), the riotous night-time compensation more than makes up for it. Eating, drinking and smoking – with a day's consumption packed into a few hours – go on until two or three in the morning, and, for the only time in the year, café nightlife really takes off. Lights are strung up and you'll find music, occasionally belly dancing, and even puppet shows. In Tunis, the best places to look are Place Bab Souika and Bab Saadoun. If you're lucky enough to see a puppet show, it may well feature a character called Karagoz, enacting a tradition that arrived with the Turkish rulers in the sixteenth century. Ramadan ends with a flourish in a feast called the **Aid el Fitr**, or **Aid es Seghir**.

The other great national festival, the feast of Abraham known as **Aid el Adha** or **Aid el Kebir**, is more of a family affair, the equivalent of a western Christmas perhaps. Every family that can afford it celebrates the willingness of Abraham to sacrifice his son Ismail by slaughtering its own sheep and roasting the meat: you can tell the Aid is approaching by the appearance of sheep tethered by almost every house. It's a grisly business: children treat the family sheep as a pet, all the time looking forward to seeing its throat cut as if waiting for Father Christmas. There's a gradual movement away from actually slaughtering to just buying the meat, but the festival is still the time when families are reunited and transport is packed all over the country.

Other religious festivals are less widely observed, though the Prophet's birthday, **Mouled**, is a great event at Kairouan (see p.197).

It's impossible to predict **festival dates** in the lunar calendar exactly since they are set by the religious authorities in Mecca, where the new moon is sighted (see box). In addition, there are fixed **national secular holidays**, all to some extent celebrations and all meaning the closure of banks, most shops and offices (see box). Other secular holidays are **local events**, mainly recent creations designed to bolster tourism or agriculture. These are covered in the relevant chapters but, again, see the box opposite.

WEDDINGS

Weddings are extraordinarily public celebrations – almost the only chance people get to let their hair down and enjoy themselves, and they make the most of it. Cavalcades of pick-up trucks loaded with people playing pipes and drums, drive round the town (in Tunis, Mercedes hoot up and down av Bourguiba); a solemn procession carries the bride's dowry through the streets; and the celebrations, dancing and feasting can go on for several days. Sadly, you can now sign up at the big hotels for an evening at a "Tunisian wedding". Avoid these like the plague but don't decline the genuine invitations you're bound to receive if you spend any time away from the big towns.

WEEKLY MARKETS

The rest of the year, life in the country revolves around a cycle of weekly **markets**, always colourful affairs. The Sousse and Nabeul markets have been comprehensively "discovered"; but it's well worth timing a visit to other towns to coincide with the weekly event, which for many of them is the mainstay of the economy. Testour and Fahs are particularly worthwhile. Market days in each region are listed in a box at the end of each chapter.

CINEMA

Tunisians like going to the **movies**. French films and English-language films dubbed into French are especially popular in Tunis. Arabic films, mainly from Egypt, are usually a mixture of American-style soap and musical; they're more popular in rural areas and in the cities' cheaper cinemas and, even if you don't understand the plot – sometimes an advantage – can be fun. Indian movies are usually subtitled in French and Arabic, but British, American and Hong Kong films are invariably dubbed into French (still, if you've never seen Jackie Chan or Sylvester Stallone speak French . . .). Long films are not so much cut as slashed, leaving out whole reels.

Tunisia's own **film industry**, though hardly prolific, has come up with some fine movies, tending to deal with serious subjects, and more influenced by France than by Egypt, India or the United States. The first wholly Tunisian-produced feature (there had been a couple of previous Franco-Tunisian co-productions) was Omar Khliifi's *The Dawn*, a drama about the struggle for Independence. Perhaps predictably, Independence and its aftermath remained the most popular theme in Tunisian cinema for some time, but other subjects tackled have included the position of Tunisian emigrants abroad in Naceur Ktari's *The Ambassadors* (1976), social attitudes to homosexuality in Nouri Bouzid's *Man of Ashes* (1986), and rural migration to the cities in Taïeb Louhichi's *Shadow of the Land* (1982). The ill effects of tourism are well dealt with in Ridha Behi's *Sun of the Hyenas* (1977), portraying the effect of a hotel development on a small fishing village, and Nouri Bouzid's *Beznez* (1992), about

APPROXIMATE DATES FOR THE MAIN RELIGIOUS FESTIVALS

	1996	1997	1998	1999
1st of Ramadan (not a holiday)	Jan 21	Jan 9/Dec 29	Dec 18	Dec 7
Aid es Seghir (two days' holiday)	Feb 20	Feb 8	Jan 28	Jan 17
Aid el Kebir (two days' holiday)	Apr 30	Apr 19	Apr 8	Mar 28
Islamic New Year	May 19	May 8	Apr 27	Apr 16
Mouled	July 29	July 18	July 7	June 26

ANNUAL SECULAR HOLIDAYS

January 1	New Year	**May 1**	Labour Day
March 20	Independence Day	**July 25**	Republic Day
March 21	Youth Day	**August 13**	Women's Day
April 9	Martyrs' Day	**November 7**	New Era Day

LOCAL FESTIVALS AND HOLIDAYS

February Olive Festival, Kalaa Kebira (near Sousse, see p.182).

March Hammam Festival, El Hamma de l'Arad (see p.295).

April–May Orange Blossom Festival, Menzel Bou Zelfa (see p.132); Nefta Festival (see p.285).

May Matanza, Sidi Daoud (see p.130); Jewish pilgrimage, Hara Sghira (Jerba, see p.328).

May–June Drama performances in Roman theatre, Dougga (see p.233).

June Falconry Festival, El Haouria (see p.128); Malouf Music Festival, Testour (see p.230).

July Sidi Bou Makhlouf Festival, Le Kef (see p.239).

July–August Various tourist-oriented "cultural" festivals at resorts and Roman sites around the country; Carthage International Festival (see p.109).

August Festival du Borj, Gafsa (see p.266).

September Wine Festival, Grombalia (see p.132); Wheat Festival, Beja.

October Liberation Day, Bizerte (see p.136).

November Date Festival, Kebili (see p.288); Matmata Festival; Carthage Film Festival (mainly in Tunis) (see p.97).

December Tozeur Festival (see p.280); International Festival of the Sahara, Douz (see p.292).

beach gigolos. Aside from Bouzid, a Tunisian director whose films have achieved recognition outside the country is Ferid Boughedir; his best-known work, *Halfaouine* (1990), is a good-humoured boy-becomes-man tale set in the Tunis *faubourg* of the title. The social position of women is another subject popular in Tunisian cinema. Unique among Arab countries, Tunisia has a growing number of fine **women directors**, yet to achieve recognition abroad, notably Selma Baccar, who broke the male mould with *Fatma 75* in 1978.

Tunis hosts the world's most important annual Afro-Arab **film festival** every other year, with Ouagadougou in Burkina Faso hosting it the years in between (see p.97).

FOOTBALL

Tunisia is as **football**- (or soccer-) mad as every other country in the world – with the one big exception of the US. In Argentina in 1978, Tunisia's

national team was one of the early African successes at the World Cup final, and any local fan will be able to reel off the more than respectable results: 3-1 victory over Mexico, 0-0 draw with West Germany and 0-1 loss to Poland. Since then, Tunisia has failed to qualify, although its Maghreb neighbours Algeria and Morocco have been regular African representatives. Tunisian clubs have also twice won the African Cup, with CAB taking the honours in 1987, and *Club Africain* triumphing in 1980, going on to win the Afro-Asian Trophy.

While the best local players go to European leagues, Tunisia's fourteen domestic **teams** contest a league and cup each year. The teams are *Esperance Sportif de Tunis* (EST), *Club Africain* (CA), *Avenir Sportif de La Marsa* (ASM), *Club Sportif de Hammam Lif* (CSHL), *Club Athlétique Bizertin* (CAB), *Olympique de Beja* (OB), *Étoile Sportive du Sahel* (ESS), *Jeunesse Sportive Kairouannaise* (JSK), *Club Sportif Sfaxien* (CSS), *Esperance Sportive de Zarzis* (ESZ),

Olympique Club Kerkennah (OCK), *Olympique du Kef* (OK), and *Sfax Railway Sport* (SRS). They're usually referred to just by their initials.

As you might expect, the most successful teams are from Tunis and the more prosperous towns.

TRAVELLING WITH CHILDREN

Tunisians, even more than other Mediterranean people, love kids. Travelling with small children in Tunisia, you may find that people will frequently come up to admire them, to compliment you on them and to caress them, which may be uncomfortable for shyer offspring. Children are very important, and numerous, in Tunisian society, and people are not really considered complete adults until they have at least one child. In Tunisian families, children stay up late until they fall asleep and are spoiled rotten by older family members. The streets are pretty safe and even quite small children walk to school unaccompanied or play in the street unsupervised.

Hotels in Tunisia usually give a reduction of thirty to forty percent for children aged under eight or ten, though this varies with each hotel and you may have to negotiate: obviously, a child staying in your room will cost much less than a separate room. You won't find baby changing rooms in airports, hotels or restaurants, and will have to be discreet if breast-feeding – find a quiet corner and shield infant and breast from view with a light cloth over your shoulder. Beach hotels often have facilities like playgrounds and children's pools; city hotels are far less likely to cater specifically for children.

Children may well enjoy a number of things that we have not particularly recommended for adults, notably *calèche* rides, the tourist Noddy trains found in resorts, and zoos. Short camel rides should go down well too. Buckets and spades are now available at some shops in big beach resorts, but **toys** in general are poor quality, expensive, and in short supply, so bring along any you may need.

The main problem with children, especially small ones, is their **vulnerability**. More than adults, they need protecting from the sun, unsafe drinking water, heat and unfamiliar food, and are more susceptible to things like dehydration, heatstroke and stomach upsets. Diarrhoea, in particular, perhaps just a nuisance to you, could be dangerous for a child (consider carrying rehydration salts with you just in case). In fact, most hazards can be minimized or avoided simply by taking the right precautions. Take sunhats to keep the heat off young heads, and high-factor sunscreen to protect delicate skin from the sun. Make sure too that children are aware of the dangers of **rabies** – keep them away from animals and consider a rabies jab.

Of items you might consider taking, **disposable nappies** – *Peaudouce* is the commonest brand – are available at most pharmacies for prices similar to what you pay at home. You may want to take along some **dried baby food** just in case; you can mix this with hot water, which any café will supply you with. Bear in mind that Tunisian food can be very spicy, and you will probably want them to hold back on the *harissa* when serving your children.

For touring, hiking or walking, child-carrier **backpacks** such as the *Tomy Lightrider* are ideal, start at £50/$75 and can weigh less than 2kg. If the child is small enough, a fold-up buggy is also well worth packing – especially if they will sleep in it (while you have a meal or a drink).

SENIOR TRAVELLERS

Age and experience are respected in Tunisia much more than in the West. Older members of the family generally continue to live with their children (usually sons), care for their grandchildren and strongly influence family decisions. There are no state and few private pensions, so social security is a family matter.

In Tunisia, people look after their parents just as their parents looked after them, and in return they get the benefit of experienced knowledge and advice on matters ranging from business to childcare, not to mention a live-in babysitter. In this country, age commands respect, associated not so much with frailty and vulnerability as with wisdom and a lifetime of input into the family and the community. This means that even as a foreigner, you will be treated with a certain amount of deference, and shown the respect due your years.

Tunisia is a popular destination for older travellers. It's refined, quiet and safe, with all the exotics of North Africa, but none of the wildness: you will not in general be shot at by fundamentalists or offered hashish on street corners. The country is used to tourists from the West, and not particularly those of the hippy/backpacker variety, with hotels generally up to Western standards and all the amenities that you would

expect. One place in particular that appeals to older people is Port el Kantaoui, clean and pleasant, if rather sanitized, with a more sedate atmosphere than other beach resorts.

Of package tours, a number are geared especially to the needs of older travellers, and many firms run special packages for over-50s. As well as tailoring their tours and accommodation more to the needs of mature travellers, these offer the opportunity of travelling with people of your own age group. Of package firms operating out of the UK, the following have over-50s programmes: *Airtours* (Golden Years), *Cadogan* (Over 55s), *Cosmos* (Golden Times), *First Choice* (Leisurely Days), *Sunworld* (Gold Circle) and *Thomson* (Young at Heart) – see p.6 for more details. Depending on your mobility, you might want to opt for a beach hotel that is actually on the beach rather than a walk away, and to ask for a ground-floor room when booking.

If you are going for a sightseeing package tour, it is a good idea to check on the pace of the itinerary, and consider opting for a slower one with plenty of free time, rather than one which packs the maximum number of sights into the shortest possible period. Highly recommended are the usually twice-yearly art and archeology tours run by firms like *Swan Hellenic, Martin Randall, Prospect* and *Andante* (see p.6).

SEXUAL ISSUES

Because of the importance of sexual segregation in Islam, even though Tunisia is rather less strict about this than other Arab countries, male and female visitors will probably have somewhat different experiences of the country, and in general, it will be much easier for travellers of both sexes to meet Tunisian men than Tunisian women.

Sex roles and the division of labour are much more clearly defined in Tunisia than in the West, and Tunisian people may express surprise at seeing women travelling independently or men looking after children. For women, the main problem will be harassment, although men may also

experience unwanted sexual advances. These are symptoms of sexual repression in a society where, officially at least, any kind of sex outside marriage is frowned upon. Kissing, cuddling and even holding hands in public may offend people (even if they don't say so), as may going around skimpily dressed.

WESTERN WOMEN AND TUNISIAN MEN

While some women compare it favourably with southern Europe, there's no doubt that general **harassment in Tunisia** is much more commonplace than in northern Europe or the English-speaking world. It can range from comments as you pass by in the street to persistent chatting, following you or touching; on occasions, however, friendly overtures may suddenly give way to demands for sex, as if you knew what they were after all along. You'll probably face a lot of minor hassles rather than anything seriously threatening, but it can be relentless and fairly persistent. If you do feel you're in danger, don't be afraid to ask for help from passers-by or to make a scene. No Tunisian man would get away with treating a Tunisian woman in the way that some of them try to treat Western women; the Arabic word *shooma*, meaning "shame on you!" should – if shouted loudly in a public place – embarrass any man into leaving you alone.

Tactics to avoid harassment include wearing dark glasses, which prevents eye contact, including accidental eye contact on your part, hiding your hair – especially if blonde – in a scarf, and covering yourself from top to toe, which should not only cut down on harassment, but also put passers-by more definitely on your side if you do have any trouble. Mentioning a husband waiting for you nearby may also put off someone who looks likely to start.

Do be aware, however, of the Tunisian male's point of view. It genuinely is difficult for Tunisian men to know where they stand with Western women. In particular, they often seem unable to distinguish between ordinary civility and making a pass. There's a cultural difference here: Tunisian women are generally coy or aloof towards men, any other attitude being taken as a come-on (two areas where this is *not* the case are the big cities, notably Tunis and Sfax, where European sexual attitudes are emerging, and in parts of the far south, where women have always been more assertive).

The best solution is to be as stand-offish as possible, even if your attitude may be misunderstood as an insult – and even if, as occasionally happens, you're accused of racist sexual preferences (this misunderstanding is often deliberately disingenuous).

For more in-depth coverage of these issues, three **personal accounts** by Western women resident in Tunisia are included in the "Women in Tunisia" section in *Contexts* (see p.393), as is some background on issues facing Tunisian women in modern society.

WESTERN MEN AND TUNISIAN WOMEN

Generally, men experience few problems in Tunisia related to their sex. There are one or two issues to be aware of, however, which affect your relations with members of both sexes.

Men should **beware of talking to Tunisian women alone**, especially in more traditional communities. All might seem well at the time but the family may regard it as a breach of confidence and afterwards make life difficult for the woman. Male English teachers, for instance, are requested not to talk to female students alone behind a closed door.

Unless you are gay, Tunisia is not a country where **sexual relations** with local people are likely, but women – particularly those from an intellectual background – do occasionally show an interest. In such cases, however, discretion is vital. A Tunisian woman caught sharing a hotel room with a Western man, for example, faces very serious trouble indeed, as it's a criminal offence to be caught in a hotel room with a member of the opposite sex not your spouse.

Male tourists and travellers can expect the occasional **sexual proposition** by Tunisian men. A polite refusal should put an end to the matter. If you find it annoying, just remember that women tourists have to put up with far more, and that homosexuality is seen somewhat differently than at home (see below). Don't be paranoid, either; Tunisians are very tactile and touching does not usually have a sexual connotation.

GAY TUNISIA

Attitudes to **homosexuality** are very different in Tunisia to those at home, but are equally neurotic. Because of the sexual segregation endemic to Islam, homosexual activity is very widespread, but almost nobody considers themself gay, and gay people are not seen as a group in Tunisian society. Friendships are far closer than in the West and much more physical – while it is not usually acceptable for a man and a woman to kiss or hold hands in public, it is perfectly normal for two men or two women to do so. Tunisians will often say "I love him like a brother", and with such brotherly love about, it is not always easy to say where affection ends and a sexual relationship begins.

Anal intercourse between two men is illegal in Tunisia, and gay male travellers should be aware that blackmail is a possibility. To be a passive partner in such an act has connotations of femininity and weakness and is considered a disgrace, yet no such stigma attaches to the other role, and men will boast quite openly about their prowess in this position. Caution is nonetheless advised, and you should be aware that calls for money or presents in return for sexual favours are more common than sincerity. Nor should you expect a long-term relationship, since homosexual dalliances usually end with marriage, which is pretty well universal. You will, in any case, be unable to return home with your lover.

Gay women are not likely to find any hint of a community in Tunisia. **Lesbianism** is more or less invisible and its existence denied, but what we have said about friendship between men applies doubly between women. As a Western woman, however, your chances of making contact are virtually zilch.

Responses to the dangers of **HIV infection** have so far been limited but there's little doubt the problem is as grave in Tunisia as it is almost everywhere else in the world and the need for safe sex no less pressing (see "Health").

BEACH GIGOLOS

A recent but growing phenomenon in Hammamet, Sousse, Monastir and Jerba is that of the **beach gigolo** scene, known as *beznez*, from the English word "business" and the French word *baiser*, meaning to screw. Gigolos cruise the beaches looking for punters of either sex who will wine them, dine them and give them presents of money in return for sex and company. If a beach gigolo attaches himself to you and follows you into a bar or restaurant, he will expect you to pay, so make it clear if you do not intend to. If, on the other hand, you are interested in what they have to offer, be sure to use a condom as risk of HIV infection from beach gigolos is extremely high.

The phenomenon was highlighted in Nouri Bouzid's 1992 film *Beznez*, which portrayed a beach gigolo and explored the issues raised by the *beznez* business. The film caused something of a stir in France, where journalists even accused Tunisia of having a sex industry akin to that of Manila or Bangkok, something of an exaggeration to say the least. Female prostitution is a good deal more discreet, somewhat downmarket and kept well away from tourists.

TROUBLE AND THE POLICE

You are unlikely to run into any trouble in Tunisia beyond that covered in the preceding section or caused by "guides" and the hard-sell techniques covered on p.43. The police are invariably polite and helpful to tourists. Thieving, though it obviously goes on, is a lot less common than in most of Europe or North America.

THE POLICE

There are two main **types of police**: the *Sûreté* and the *Gendarmes*. The *Sûreté*, who wear grey uniforms, are the normal police force, and the people you should go to if you need to report a crime, or if you intend to camp out. They usually speak good French and should be able to give you directions if you're lost. The khaki-uniformed *Gendarmes* patrol the roads in rural areas. Drawn from conscript soldiers, they may stop you if you're driving in remote areas or near borders, ask to see your passport and question you about where you're going and why, but they won't give you any trouble.

It is just possible, though unlikely, that you will be stopped and asked for **identification** on the street (Tunisians are issued with state identity cards, which they carry at all times), but you'll be okay if you can take a police officer to your hotel and show your passport.

The **National Guard**, a branch of the military, are the people you should inform if driving across the desert.

THIEVING

Tunisians are generally honest and law-abiding and **stealing** from a visitor is considered shameful. Nonetheless, foreigners are obvious targets for theft when it does occur, the main hotspots being Sousse and Hammamet. The most common forms of theft are stealing possessions on the beach while you sleep (sometimes even from bags used as pillows); pickpocketing, especially by young kids in Hammamet, where the usual method involves an accomplice distracting your attention by asking you to change a foreign coin; bag-snatching, especially in the medina in Sousse; and leading tourists deep into the medina (Sousse and Kairouan the main ones) so that they are lost and nervous, then charging them to be led out again. Even mugging, though very rare, is not unheard of, so it is best to avoid unlit and deserted areas of towns late at night. Less nasty, and still relatively rare, is the practice of offering something as if it were a gift, and then demanding payment well over the odds for it; food or drinks offered by people you have just met may come into this category.

Many hotels operate a deposit for valuables; otherwise, wearing a body belt (cotton, with room for your passport, which you should put in a plastic bag to stop it getting saturated in sweat) might be good for your peace of mind.

If you have to **report a crime** to the police, make sure you go to the police station covering the area where the crime was committed. You'll probably have to go in office hours and put up with a certain amount of buck-passing and time-wasting; wearing your best clothes may help (and "modest" ones if you are a woman). You will need a **receipt** from the police in order to get your insurance to pay up for anything lost or stolen, and for your passport in order to get a replacement; they might ask you to call back for the receipt, but should issue one for a passport immediately – if you have to insist, do so very politely. You will not get a receipt for stolen cash.

Whatever you do, stay calm and do not get angry or shout, no matter how much they give you the runaround. For a serious charge such as assault, they may take you with them to try and locate your assailant, and will also expect you to come in and identify suspects face to face – this is not pleasant and they will not be happy if you back out of it, so make sure you are prepared to do it when you report the crime. Also be aware if you are a woman and sexual assault is involved that all police officers in Tunisia are men, and you will have to describe what happened to a roomful of them.

DRUGS

This is not Morocco or Egypt: in fact, Tunisia is more like rural France in its attitude to **hashish**. There is hardly any tradition of hashish or other drug use (though *kif* was smoked during the Ottoman period), and no sign of one emerging. Use of cannabis is frowned on, both officially and popularly, and is extremely clandestine, with very stiff penalties in force for possession of it or any other illegal drug. The situation in Algeria has in any case largely dried up imports from Morocco and, although a small amount is grown around the oases of Tozeur and Nefta, prices are high and quality low. Cigarette papers, especially gummed ones, are difficult to come by.

DIRECTORY

Abortion Women from certain European countries come to Tunisia for abortions, which are legal, comparatively inexpensive and as safe as they are in the West.

British Tunisian Society, c/o Tunisian Embassy, 29 Prince's Gate, London SW7 1QG. *Council for the Advancement of Arab-British Understanding*, 21 Collingham Rd, London SW5 0NU (☎ 0171/373 8414). *Maghreb Studies Association*, c/o *The Maghreb Bookshop*, 45 Burton St, London WC1H 9AL (☎0171/388 1840). They can supply information and books.

Cigarettes Tunisian brands are cheap but rough, with *20 Mars* strong, *Caravanes* medium and *Cristal* milder. Western brands, widely available, cost about four times as much.

Clothes Two things to bear in mind are the heat, especially in the desert, and the modesty demanded by Islam. You will certainly want a light sunhat, especially in summer, and light, loose-fitting cotton clothes. In winter, especially in the north, you will want at least one warm sweater. Be aware that many people, especially older people, can feel seriously intimidated or affronted by scantily dressed tourists wandering around town. Don't walk around the medina in a swimsuit or bare-chested, nor in shorts or short skirts.

Contraceptives Known as *Chapeaux Americains*, condoms are available from most pharmacies in large towns but ones brought from home are more reliable. Some brands of the Pill (*la pilule*) are also available, but remember that if you get diarrhoea, oral contraceptives may not stay in your system long enough to be absorbed and may thus become ineffective.

Electricity Generally 220v 50Hz, as in continental Europe, with double round-pin sockets. British, Irish and Australasian plugs will need an adaptor (double round-pin electric shavers will be all right though). American and Canadian appliances will need a transformer too, unless multi voltage. One or two old places, especially in Tunis, still have 110v voltage – check before plugging in.

Laundry There are no self-service laundries (bar one in Port el Kantaoui), but many towns have places which do washing by weight. Tourist hotels usually have an in-house service; other hotels may be able to arrange something.

Left luggage (baggage deposit) Large train stations take left luggage (ask for the *consigne*), and many hotels – especially cheap ones – have a safe room where you can leave belongings while you are away. Tourist offices may also be able to help for a short period of time, and staff at bus stations are often willing to keep an eye on your baggage for you while you wander around town between buses – often just as a favour without charge.

Photography Avoid taking photographs of government buildings, people in uniform, airports or anything even vaguely military. If in doubt, ask first or you may end up having your camera confiscated. Most of the major brands of camera film are widely available, but speeds other than 100ASA are hard to come by. Videotape for cameras is expensive if available at all.

Stoves Camping gas stoves are widely available, but the refills (*cartouches*) much less so. Ironmongers (*quincailleries*) and supermarkets

should stock them, but supplies are sporadic. Street sellers sometimes have them when the shops have run out. In Tunis, rue al Jazira is the place to look – especially pl Cheikh el Bourzouli. Much more sensible is to take a spirit stove, since burning alcohol (*alcool à brûler*) is widely available. A petrol stove is also a possibility, though somewhat messier.

Tampons Available from pharmacies in all except the remotest towns, but at around 50p/75¢ each, they are something like three times as expensive as at home. The price of sanitary towels, on the other hand, is much the same in Tunisia as in the West.

Time Tunisia is on GMT plus one now all year round, which means that the time is in principle an hour ahead of Britain and Ireland, six hours ahead of North America's east coast, ten hours ahead of the west coast, seven hours behind Western Australia, nine hours behind eastern Australia and eleven hours behind New Zealand. Daylight Saving Time in those places will, however, vary these differences by an hour. Crossing from France or Italy, there is no time difference in winter, but you will have to put your watch back an hour in summer. Flying from Britain, on the other hand, there is no time difference in summer, but you will have to put your watch forward an hour in winter.

Tipping In smarter hotels and restaurants tipping follows western practice: service is often included, and ten to fifteen percent is the standard tip for waiters. Porters and chambermaids expect something, depending on the price bracket of the hotel and the length of your stay. Taxi drivers do not necessarily get a tip, but always appreciate one. Backsheesh is also expected for small services such as loading your baggage onto buses or finding you a place in a *louage*.

Toilet paper For reasons that soon become apparent, it's a good idea to carry a stock of toilet paper around with you – it can be bought in most towns.

Work A work permit is officially required for all foreign citizens working in Tunisia: with the economy in it's present state, permits are hard to come by. English teaching is expanding rapidly, though: try writing to the *British Council*, 10 Spring Gardens, London SW1A 2BN, or direct to the *Bourguiba School of Modern Languages* in Tunis at 47 av de la Liberté (☎01/282418). Private conversation classes are sometimes possible to arrange on an informal (and illegal) basis. For almost anything else you will need at least competent French; but because the tourist industry is so highly organized there's little of the fringe market found elsewhere. The best way to see the country for free is to join one of the **international work camps** which are run most summers – contact the *International Voluntary Service*, Castlehill House, 21 Otley Rd, Leeds LS6 3AA (☎0113/230 4600); 122 Great Victoria St, Belfast BT2 7BG (☎01232/238147); 30 Mountjoy Square, Dublin 1 (☎01/855 1011); Inisfree Village, Rt 2, Box 506C, Crozet, VA 22932; c/o *Volunteers for Peace*, Box 202, Belmont, UT 05730; or 499 Elizabeth St, Surry Hills, NSW 2010 (☎02/699 1129). The North Africa coordinator is *SCI Italy*, Via dei Laterani 28, 00184 Roma, Italy (☎39-6/700 5367).

USEFUL THINGS TO TAKE

• Suntan lotion with a high screening factor.

• A wide-brimmed cotton sunhat for protection against sunstroke; in the intense heat of the desert, you can drench it in water and stick it on your head to cool you down.

• A water bottle is a must, especially if you plan to do any walking. If you plan to do any driving in the desert, it's a good idea to bring a five-litre roll-up water bag, available at camping shops.

• A pocket alarm clock – vital for catching those crack-of-dawn buses.

• A mini-padlock for your baggage.

• Insect repellent.

• Film, especially fast film (useful in the dark nooks and alleyways of city medinas) and slow film (for some serious landscape photography in the desert south).

• A sleeping bag is handy in winter if staying in budget accommodation. In any case, a sheet sleeping bag is a good safeguard against dubious sheets in cheap hotels.

• A body belt of some sort with room for your passport (which you should wrap in a plastic bag to prevent it getting soaked in sweat).

• An all-purpose knife and bottle opener – few bottles are screw-top.

• A small French dictionary or phrase book, such as the *Rough Guide* French Phrasebook.

• Condoms (more reliable than local brands).

• Tampons (more expensive than at home).

CHAPTER 1
TUNIS & AROUND

CHAPTER 3
BIZERTE &
THE NORTH

CHAPTER 2
HAMMAMET &
CAP BON

CHAPTER 5
THE TELL

CHAPTER 4
KAIROUAN &
THE SAHEL

ALGERIA

CHAPTER 7
GABES & MATMATA

CHAPTER 6
THE JERID

CHAPTER 8
JERBA

CHAPTER 9
THE KSOUR

LIBYA

CHAPTER ONE

TUNIS AND AROUND

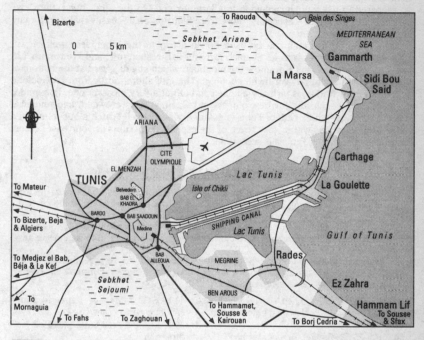

Tunis is very much a capital city: home to over a tenth of Tunisia's population, the base of government and power, and the centre of virtually all that happens in the country. It is not an attractive city – at least on first impressions. The old colonial centre is becoming increasingly submerged by anonymous housing suburbs, and the streets have a rather westernized air.

But stay a few days and you'll find that behind this unexceptional facade there is a real allure. Few package tours include Tunis, and day-trippers from the beaches tend to confine themselves to one or two standard streets and monuments in the old Arab town of the **Medina**. The rest is left to the people of Tunis and anyone else who cares to explore the narrow lanes, busy markets and unrestored monuments, including huge mosques and elaborately carved street fountains.

The Medina shelters monuments spanning six hundred years of Arab and Turkish endowment, and the French-built **New Town** is beginning to acquire a period value of its own. These distinct phases of the city's development are intricately linked in a manner which is somehow symbolic of Tunisia's ability to blend cultures. Moving from ninth-century mosque to eighteenth-century Turkish palace to nineteenth-century French boulevard seems almost a natural progression.

Away from the centre, but easily reached by public transport, are three more major attractions. The **Bardo Museum**, housed in a former regent's palace, has one of the finest collections of Roman mosaics anywhere in the world, best visited before seeing the Roman sites elsewhere in the country and then again afterwards. In the other direction, overlooking the Gulf of Carthage, are the remains of **Carthage**, ancient Great Power and the enemy of Rome, and a little further in the same direction, the picturesque resort of **Sidi Bou Said**. Carthage can be somewhat underwhelming: the Roman invaders and then time itself were such thorough conquerors that you have to go prepared to use your imagination to a large extent. On the other hand, the views over the turquoise gulf – especially those from Sidi Bou Said – easily make up for any lingering disappointment.

Any free time in Tunis can be used up on a trip to the other, less well-known, suburbs. **La Goulette**, with its Spanish fort and fish restaurants, and **Hammam Lif**, nestling below Jebel Bou Kornine – the mountain which stands guard at the bottom of the gulf – both make for worthwhile outings. The gulf shore, north from La Goulette and south from **Rades**, is virtually one beach, but not a very pleasant one. In summer even **Raouad** beach, the furthest out beyond Gammarth, is crowded, and unofficial reports claim the whole Gulf of Tunis is polluted. Alternatively, catch a bus to one of a range of destinations within easy reach of the capital. With Tunis as your base, almost anywhere in northern Tunisia is accessible.

ACCOMMODATION PRICE CODES

All the hotels, youth hostels and pensions listed in this book have been price-graded according to the following scale, and although prices will rise during the lifetime of this edition, the relative comparisons should remain valid.

The prices quoted are for the **cheapest available double room in high season**, although many of the cheap places will have pricier rooms with en suite facilities or sea views.

Classified hotels, officially considered suitable for tourists, are graded locally from one to four stars (★), with wide-ranging prices within each category. For more on accommodation prices and categories, see Basics.

① Up to 10TD. Very cheap. Usually a bed only in a basic, unclassified hotel or a youth hostel.

② 10.1–25TD. Budget. Bed only or bed and breakfast.

③ 25.1–40TD. Comfortable budget. Good unclassified average one-star or a cheap two-star.

④ 40.1–55TD. Mid-range. Expensive two-star, cheap three-star.

⑤ 55.1–70TD. Tourist hotel. Standard three-star.

⑥ 70.1TD upwards. Deluxe. Expensive three-star, four-star or five-star.

TUNIS

We arrived at Tunis, object of all our hopes, focus of the flame of every gaze, rendezvous of travellers from East and West. This is where fleets and caravans come to meet. Here you will find everything a man could desire. You want to go by land? Here are endless companions for your journey. You prefer the sea? Here are boats for every direction. Tunis is a crown whose every jewel is a district, its suburbs are like a flower-garden constantly refreshed by the breeze. If you come to her watering-places, she will quench your thirst; if you fall back on her resources, she will cure your problems; her gardens are like brides, her worth is written in many books.

El Abdari, thirteenth-century traveller

TUNIS is rooted firmly in an Arab medieval past. For a thousand years before the establishment of Islam, it was an insignificant neighbour of the port of Carthage (although in fact founded earlier) and its only historic role was as a base for invaders laying siege to the larger city. The Arabs, however, preferred Tunis's less exposed site, and as early as the ninth century the **Aghlabids** built the Great Mosque that still stands at the heart of the Medina. In the last years of their rule, from 894 to 909 AD, Tunis served as the Aghlabid imperial capital.

Largely ignored by the **Fatimids**, who ruled from Mahdia in the tenth century, the city really came into its own following the **Hilalian** invasion of the eleventh century, when Abdelhaq Ibn Khourassane established a principality here. Amid the chaos of the time, this **Khourassanid** state was such an island of stability that by the time it fell to the **Almohads**, a hundred years later, it had become the country's natural power centre. When the **Hafsids** declared complete independence in 1236, it was a capital once again.

Under the Hafsids, and especially after the fall of Baghdad to the Mongols in 1258, Tunis became the Arab world's leading metropolis – a great Mediterranean market-place at a time of expanding trade between Christian Europe and the Muslim East. Culture flourished in the cosmopolitan atmosphere, and the university in the Great Mosque – the Zitouna Mosque – was rivalled only by those of al-Azhar in Cairo and the Kairaouine at Fez. The Hafsids' own building programme included the first *medersas*, or Islamic colleges, many of the purpose-built souks, or markets, around the Great Mosque, the Kasbah with its mosque, and the city walls. It was this city that El Abdari is describing in the quotation above.

As Arab rule wavered before the **Ottoman Turks**, Tunis changed in appearance – becoming enclosed by fortifications – and in character, as a more foreign-dominated era emerged. Wealth from trade and piracy poured into the city, financing the building of more mosques, *medersas* and palaces. Christian traders were allowed to settle, and since many of the "Turkish" officials ruling the new **regency** were *mamelukes* – slaves of Greek or Eastern European origin taken as children – several of the buildings and even a few mosques have a strong European flavour.

Until the nineteenth century, Tunis still consisted essentially of the **Medina** and *faubourgs* – poor suburbs outside the walls – with a few elaborate palaces, such as the Bardo, set in gardens further away. But by the 1860s, several thousand European traders and advisers were living in Tunis and their presence was influential. The International Financial Commission set up by the colonial powers virtually ran the government, and newly found wealth gave merchants considerable power over the impoverished Beys, or Ottoman rulers. At this time a new European city – the **New Town**, or Ville Nouvelle – began to develop outside the city walls, and with the **French occupation** in 1881, the French set about draining the marshy land on the edge of the lake to extend this new colonial domain. Today its wide avenues, jammed with traffic and beginning to crumble, still feel thoroughly *belle époque*, with their pavement cafés, iron balconies and fancy stuccowork.

Orientation

Tunis lies on the shore of the large, shallow **Lac Tunis**, which stretches between the town and the Gulf of Carthage. Along the gulf shore, north and south of the narrow entrance to the lake, stretches a chain of suburbs easily reached by public transport from the city centre. An independent light train line, the **TGM** (Tunis, La Goulette, Marsa), crosses the lake on a causeway to the northern shore's suburbs, which include **Carthage** and **Sidi Bou Said**. A mainline train runs from the mainline station to the less attractive southern suburbs of **Rades** and **Hammam Lif**.

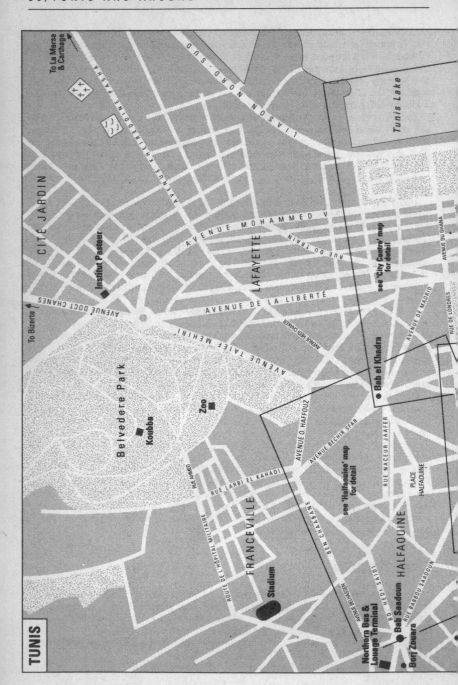

TUNIS

CITÉ JARDIN

To Bizerta

To La Marsa & Carthage

AVENUE KHEIREDDINE PASHA

LIAISON NORD-SUD

Tunis Lake

Institut Pasteur

AVENUE DOCT CHANES

AVENUE MOHAMMED V

LAFAYETTE

RUE DU TRAIN

AVENUE DE LA LIBERTÉ

AVENUE DU GHANA

see 'City Centre' map for detail

AVENUE HEDI CHAKER

AVENUE TAIEF MEHIRI

Belvedere Park

Koubba

Zoo

RUE AHMED

RUE LARBI EL KAHADI

AVENUE O. HAFFOUZ

AVENUE BECHIR SFAR

Bab el Khadra

AVENUE DE MADRID

RUE DE LONDRES

RUE NACEUR JAAFER

PLACE HALFAOUINE

see 'Halfaouine' map for detail

ROUTE DE L'HOPITAL MILITAIRE

FRANCEVILLE

BEN CHAABANE

HALFAOUINE

Stadium

AVENUE BELHASSEN

BD HEDI SAIDI

Bab Saadoun

RUE BABBOU SAADOUN

Northern Bus & Louage Terminal

Bori Zouara

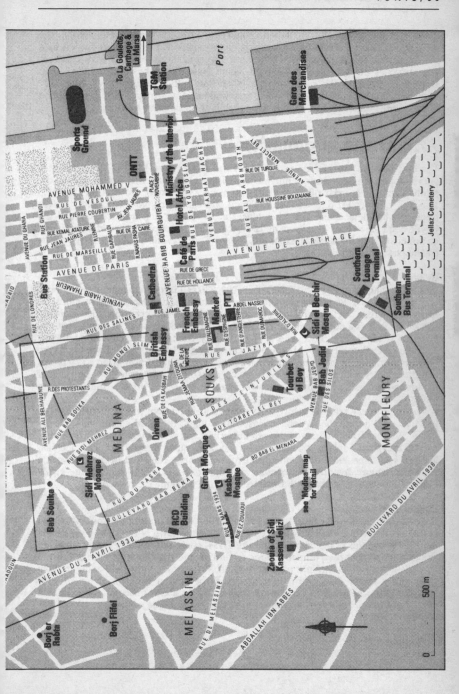

Once in the city itself, orientation couldn't be simpler. **Avenue Bourguiba**, the great central artery, flanked by ministries, smart hotels and shops, and divided by a tree-lined promenade, links the **Medina** in the west to the lake in the east. To either side stretches the grid-plan of the French-built **New Town**, bounded by the hilltop **Belvedere Park** to the north and the sprawling **Jellaz Cemetery** to the south. Everything in this central area is within easy walking distance and, with the exception of the **Bardo Museum**, there's little to be seen in the straggling suburbs.

Arrival and information

The best place to head for on arrival is **avenue Bourguiba**. Most of the reasonably priced hotels are scattered within walking distance through the streets just to the south. The main **tourist office** is nearby on place 7 Novembre (Mon–Thurs 8.30am–1pm & 3–5.45pm, Fri & Sat 8.30am–1.30pm) and can supply you with plenty of free maps and booklets. There are other offices at the airport and train station, and the **ONTT** head office is at 51 avenue de la Liberté. There is also a **Syndicat d'Initiative** on avenue Bourguiba at the junction with avenue Carthage and avenue de Paris, but its opening hours are erratic.

By air

Tunis Carthage Airport (☎01/288000, 235000, 236000) is a fifteen-minute drive northeast of the centre, 8km away on the shore of the lake, and has a tourist office, an exchange bureau and several travel agencies offering an accommodation booking service, as well as a number of **car rental** firms (☎01/288000 for all of them). If you're flying in at night, join the queue at the currency exchange immediately and leave baggage collection till later – because of currency regulations, you'll have to change some money straight away and the service is slow. You should also bring a few dinars into the country with you as they occasionally refuse to change travellers' cheques. If the bureau is closed, you may have to get a taxi to the *Hôtel Africa* or the *Majestic* to change cash.

The easiest way into the centre from the airport is by **taxi**, which should cost you less than 4TD during the day and at least 5TD at night; the TGM station misleadingly called "Aéroport" has nothing to do with the airport and is nowhere near it. Otherwise, the #35 **bus** from Tunis Marine bus station runs at frequent intervals from around 5am to 10pm and takes about thirty minutes. Drop-off points include the bottom of **avenue Habib Thameur**, **avenue Bourguiba**, near the corner of rue 18 Janvier, the **Tunis Marine** bus station, and **place Palestine**, behind République metro station.

By sea

Ferries from Sardinia, Sicily, Genoa, Marseille and Malta dock at La Goulette, a port in the city's northern suburbs. The cheapest way into town is by TGM train across the lake to avenue Bourguiba. To find the TGM, come out of the ferry terminal, go straight ahead past the *poste de douane* and follow the road round to the left. From here it's more or less straight on past the Kasbah (on your right) and another 300m or so down to the line. Turn right here and the station is 100m ahead. If your baggage is too heavy, you can always take a taxi. In a car, head for the TGM but instead of turning right for the station, cross the line and take a left across the causeway into town.

By train

Tunis's mainline **train station** is on place Barcelone (☎01/244440), right at the centre of the main hotel area, south of avenue Bourguiba (metro lines #1 and #2).

Most train services run every day but a few are non-operational on Sundays and public holidays.

By bus

Both the intercity **bus terminals** – **Bab Saadoun**, at the bottom of rue Sidi el Bechir and avenue de Carthage, for the north of the country and **Bab Alleoua**, on avenue Bougatfa, for the rest – are well connected to the centre by city bus and have metro stations of the same names nearby, although neither terminal is too far from the city centre to walk. City bus #50 runs constantly between the two terminals, though it stops by the Bab Saadoun city gate rather than outside the northern bus terminal.

By louage

Louages, or service taxis, arrive at and depart from locations right by the bus terminals (Bab Saadoun's *louage* station adjoins the bus station; Bab Alleoua's is across rue Sidi el Bechir). The exceptions are the international ones serving Libya and Algeria, which have their main stops at **Garage Ayachi** at Bab Souika (Libya) and **rue al Jazira** at place de la Victoire/Porte de France (Algeria and Morocco).

City transport

Walking isn't just the most interesting way of getting around the city centre. In summer, when the traffic seizes up in the streets and the atmosphere in the buses is as steamy as in any hammam, it's often the quickest and most comfortable way to get somewhere.

USEFUL BUS ROUTES

#1: circles the Medina
#5, #5c, #5d, #6 and **#27**: Tunis Marine–Belvedere Park
#16b and **#42a**: Belhouane–Tebourba
#20: Jardin Thameur–La Marsa
#20b: Jardin Thameur–Gammarth
#21, #26, #26a and **#26b**: Barcelone–Mornag
#23: Thameur–Borj El Amri
#27: Jardin Thameur–Raouad
#30: Tunis Marine–Bardo
#31b: Belhouane–Kalaat El Andalous
#35: Tunis Marine–Airport
#40: La Marsa–Gammarth
#44: Place Belhaouane–Kalaat El Andalous
#50: connects the two intercity bus terminals (Bab Saadoun–Bab Alleoua)
#116: Barcelone–Tebourba

USEFUL METRO STATIONS

Barcelone (lines #1 and #2): train station and interchange
République (lines #2, #3, #4 and #5): interchange
Tunis Marine (line #1): TGM station
Bab Alleoua (line #1): southern intercity bus station
Palestine (line #2): UK and Algerian consulates, US embassy
Jeunesse (line #2): football ground
Cité Sportive (line #2): Olympic swimming pool
Bab Saadoun (lines #3, #4 and #5): northern intercity bus station
20 Mars (line #4): nearest stop to the Bardo Museum until its own station opens

Bus rides in the city generally cost around 300 millimes. If you plan to do a lot of travelling by bus, buy a book of tickets from the office at the Tunis Marine bus station at the end of avenue Bourguiba, near the TGM station; otherwise, pay for your fare on board. The other main urban **bus stations** are at Jardin Thameur, place Belhouane (near Bab Souika) and place Barcelone.

More an overgrown tramway, the fairly new **metro** system runs down the middle of the street and obeys traffic lights. Outside rush hours and lunchtime, it's not as frequent as it might be nor very fast, and its lines are so arranged that almost any journey requires at least one change. At present, line #5 is not yet in operation and line #4 only runs as far as the 20 Mars station. Tickets cost about the same as buses.

The central Tunis **TGM train station** (Transport Me) is at the port end of avenue Bourguiba, next to Tunis Marine bus and metro (line #1) stations. Trains from here run every twenty minutes or so across Lake Tunis, linking the city with La Goulette, Carthage, Sidi Bou Said and La Marsa, at the end of the line and around forty minutes away. The last service is at around 1am. It's also possible to buy a sheet of TGM tickets at the TGM station. A suburban overland train line runs from place Barcelone station to Rades and Hammam Lif. The frequent service reaches Hammam Lif in about forty minutes.

Taxis in Tunis are hailed in the street in the conventional way and metered. By day you'll rarely pay more than 2TD for a ride in the city centre. They cost more at night, when meters are off and you have to negotiate the price.

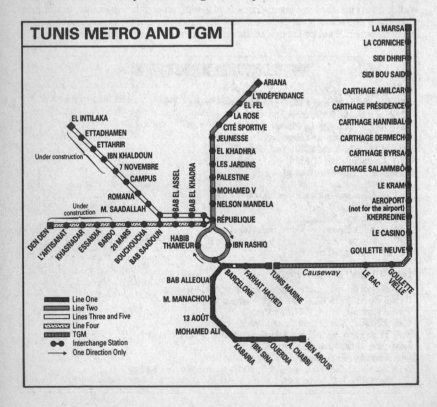

Accommodation

The *ONTT* tourist office on place 7 Novembre is of limited use in helping you find **accommodation**, and though they provide a list of hotels, they're unable to handle bookings. Many travel agencies – particularly those at the airport – offer a booking service, usually for the more expensive, classified hotels, with a few selected one-star choices at the lower end of the scale (see p.100 for airport agents). But if you haven't booked from home, the best way to find a room is to just start walking.

Central Tunis has dozens of cheap hotels, though in midsummer the more popular ones tend to fill up disconcertingly quickly and it's wise to start looking as early as possible. If everything appears to be full, it's worth knowing that at the height of the season a few hotels let people sleep on the roof. It's cheaper and makes the humidity more bearable, but is officially illegal. The only real alternative to a hotel here is the rather good **youth hostel** in the Medina – again, try to book ahead. The hotels listed below are unclassified unless stated – though classification is rarely an indication of value for money. In some you pay to use the shower and you may or may not find breakfast included, so it's important to check what the price actually covers. The **cheapest hotels** of all are in the Medina and at its edges, but can be extremely insalubrious; women travelling alone are advised to steer clear.

If you want to **camp** you have to leave the city completely to find a place to pitch a tent. The campsite at Hammam Plage/Borj Cedria, southeast of the city, closed after an attack on the nearby PLO office, but the possibility still exists of "wild" camping on Raouad beach, north of the city – though it's not exactly a peaceful getaway in midsummer when there are lots of families here.

All the hotels below are keyed on the city centre map (see p.66–67).

New Town hotels

The densest concentration of hotels – though they're also the most likely to be full – lies in the French **New Town**, between the Medina and avenue de Carthage, which cuts across avenue Bourguiba about halfway down. If you have the energy there are other cheap places to check out further south around **Bab Jazira**, especially on rue d'Alger and avenue Bab Jedid.

Rue Charles de Gaulle and around

Hôtel de l'Agriculture, 25 rue Charles de Gaulle (☎01/246394). Opposite the *Cirta* and offering good-value, basic rooms. ①.

Cirta, 42 rue Charles de Gaulle (☎01/241582). A favourite with Tunisians and tourists alike. Friendly, good value and the nearest thing in Tunis to a travellers' hotel. ①.

Commodor ★, 17 rue d'Allemagne (☎01/244941). Big, clean rooms but rather gloomy. ②.

Dar Masmoudi, 18 rue du Maroc (☎01/342248). Overpriced for the rudimentary facilities on offer. ②.

Hôtel de France, 8 rue Mustapha M'barek (☎01/245876). Nice, big, old-fashioned rooms, many with bathroom (about 1.5TD extra). Would be a great place if the management weren't so rude. ②.

Royal, 19 rue d'Espagne (☎01/242780). Cheap, but not the friendliest place in Tunis. ①.

Splendid ★, 2 rue Mustapha M'barek (☎01/242844). Rooms are quite clean if somewhat sombre, with a certain seedy charm. ②.

Zarzis, 20 rue d'Angleterre (☎01/248031). Not exactly welcoming, but dirt cheap. ①.

Around avenue de la Gare

Asma, 17 rue du Boucher (☎01/340940). Dirt-cheap but very basic accommodation. ①.

Excelsior, 7 rue du Boucher (no phone). No-frills budget option. ①.

Hôtel de la Gare, 25 av de la Gare (☎01/256754). Friendly, with clean but rather bare rooms. ①.

El Mouna, 64 rue de la Sebkha (☎01/343375). A new place that's spacious and spotless. ①.

Nouvel Hôtel, 3 pl Mongi Bali (☎01/243379). Rather Dickensian rooms and big iron beds. ①.

Savoie, 13 rue du Boucher (☎01/243779). Rock-bottom basic place. ①.

Sidi Belhassen, 23bis av de la Gare (☎01/256928). Cheery sort of place, but small rooms. ②.

Hôtel du Sud, 34 rue du Soudan (☎01/246916). Cheap and basic. ①.

East of rue Charles de Gaulle

Central, 6 rue de Suisse (☎01/240433). A bit on the seedy side but quite clean. ①.

Grand Hôtel d'Alger, 5 rue de Belgique, on pl Barcelone (☎01/246429). Cheap and grotty with peculiar management. ①.

Grand Hôtel Victoria, 79 rue Farhat Hached (☎01/342863). Not that grand, but with large rooms and right on pl Barcelone, so handy for bus, train and metro. ②.

Hôtel de Suisse ★, 5 rue de Suisse (☎01/243821). In an alley joining rue d'Hollande and rue Jamel Abdel Nasser. Pleasant rooms, a slightly grubby kitchen available and promises of a ten-percent discount for anyone brandishing a *Rough Guide*. ②.

Around rue de Grèce

Hôtel de Bretagne, 7 rue de Grèce (☎01/242146). Dirty and unfriendly with dubious security. ②.

Maison Dorée ★★, 3 rue el Koufa (☎01/240632). Spotless and rather formal place backing onto rue d'Hollande. ②.

Salammbô ★, 6 rue de Grèce (☎01/244252). Great old-fashioned rooms and a TV lounge to hang out in. ②.

Transatlantique ★, 106 rue de Yougoslavie (☎01/240680). Pleasant, colonial-style rooms and a beautifully tiled lobby. ②.

East of avenue de Carthage

Atlantic, 27 rue Daghbagi (☎01/246430). A very basic hotel in an industrial part of town, but pleasantly run. Its rooms are clean, but spartan and rather poky; no showers. ①.

Bristol, 30 rue Lt Mohamed el Aziz Taj (☎01/244836). Reasonable value. ①.

Rex, 65 rue de Yougoslavie (☎01/257397). Another colonial leftover that has seen better days but remains adequate value. ②.

St Georges ★★, 16 rue de Cologne (☎01/284525). If you can live with the location (20 minutes' walk north of av Bourguiba), this may be the best value in Tunis, with spacious, air-conditioned rooms at moderate prices. ②.

Avenue Bourguiba and north

Hôtel l'Africa Meridien ★★★★, 50 av Bourguiba (☎01/347477). A monstrous carbuncle, but the best hotel on av Bourguiba. ⑥.

Carlton ★★, 31 av Bourguiba (☎01/258167, 258168). Friendly and well situated. ③.

Capitole ★, 60 av Bourguiba (☎01/244997). Slap bang in the middle of av Bourguiba, along with the restaurant, bar and cinema of the same name. In the centre of things, but still overpriced for what it is. ③.

Continental, 5 rue de Marseille (☎01/259834). Nothing to write home about, but quite adequate. ①.

Golf Royal ★★★, 51–53 rue de Yougoslavie (☎01/344311). Business-class place with air conditioning and TV, but not many other facilities. ⑤.

Hilton Tunis ★★★★, av de la Ligue Arabe (☎01/782800). Out above the Belvedere, miles from the city centre but with a great view over it and, except in rush hours, only 10min away by taxi. ⑥.

International Maghreb Tourisme ★★★★, 49 av Bourguiba (☎01/254855). Not what you'd call a classy joint, in spite of the deluxe rating. ⑥.

Katar, imp 6, rue des Tanneurs (☎01/241222). Cheap and dingy. ①.

Hôtel du Lac ★★, rue Sinbad (☎01/258322). Discreet and tasteful it is not, but the inverted pyramid is now a landmark on the Tunis skyline and not a bad place to stay if you like a bit of luxury. ⑤.

Madrid, 24 rue Belhassen Jerad, cnr av de Madrid (☎01/353216). Has great decor, with tiles and painted ceilings, but no alcohol is allowed. ②.

Majestic ★★★, 36 av de Paris (☎01/242848). Elegant colonial architecture, especially the foyer, but the hotel in general is getting a bit shabby. ③.

El Qods, imp 6, rue des Tanneurs (☎01/340404). Next door to the *Katar* and preferable. Ask for a room with balcony. ①.

Oriental Palace ★★★★, 29 av Jean Jaurès (☎01/348846). This place has style. The decor is completely over the top and worth taking in even if you're just passing by. ⑥.

Rahma, 5 rue Qadiciyah (☎01/255566). Reasonable place with small rooms in an alley behind *La Parnasse* cinema. Avoid the neighbouring *Quercy*. ①.

Ritza ★, 35 av H. Thameur (☎01/245428). Nicely decorated but not very personable. ②.

Tej ★★, 14 rue Lt Mohamed el Aziz Taj (☎01/344899). Claims to offer a "three-star service for two-star prices". Actually the prices are three-star, but the service matches and the breakfast is excellent. ③.

Medina hotels

Hotels in the **Medina** tend to be the cheapest, but also the dirtiest and very stuffy in the summertime. Apart from the *Medina*, and the ones on boulevard Bab Menara, they are not recommended for women on their own. On the other hand, a stay in the Medina throws you headlong into a world that would completely pass you by in the safe hostelries of the New Town. If you want to experience the real Tunis, you might think about sacrificing a little comfort and security for a dose of authenticity.

Hôtel les Amis, 7 rue Monastiri (☎01/565653). Basic but clean, with kung fu videos in the TV room. ①.

Hôtel de Bonheur, 32 rue de la Kasbah (☎01/254758). Rather dubious security, but preferable to the *Soleil* next door. ①.

Hammami, 12 rue el Mechnaka (☎01/260451). Large grubby rooms in a huge and very impressive mansion near place Bab Carthajana. ①.

El Massara, 5 bd Bab Menara (☎01/263734). On the western edge of the Medina, with clean but minuscule rooms. ①.

Medina, 1 pl de la Victoire (☎01/255056). Nicest hotel in the Medina – clean, conveniently situated and naturally very popular. ①.

Riadh, 57 rue Mongi Slim (☎01/257330). On the edge of the Medina, but with rather poky and airless rooms. ①.

Sfax, 5 rue de l'Or (☎01/260275). Near pl Bab Souika. No shower but a men's hammam nearby. The beds are in a bit of a state. ①.

Hôtel de la Victoire, 7 bd Bab Menara (☎01/261224). Neighbour to the *Massara*. Cool and airy if rather noisy, but with friendly management and a painting in every room. ①.

Medina youth hostel

IYHF youth hostel "Dar Saida Ajoula" (Tunis Medina), 25 rue Saida Ajoula (☎01/567850). Clean, friendly and well run but still subject to rules and curfew (10pm winter, midnight in summer and closed 10am–4pm in July & Aug). The building is a former palace and fills up quickly in summer, so book ahead. ①.

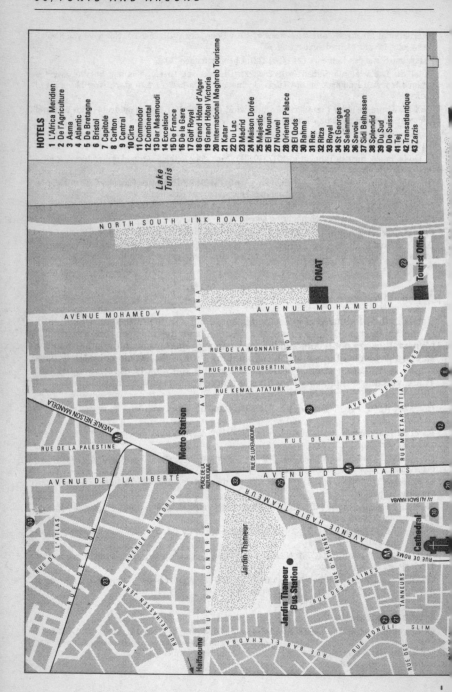

HOTELS

1 L'Africa Meridien
2 De l'Agriculture
3 Asma
4 Atlantic
5 De Bretagne
6 Bristol
7 Capitole
8 Carlton
9 Central
10 Cirta
11 Commodor
12 Continental
13 Dar Masmoudi
14 Excelsior
15 De France
16 De la Gare
17 Golf Royal
18 Grand Hôtel d'Alger
19 Grand Hôtel Victoria
20 International Maghreb Tourisme
21 Katar
22 Du Lac
23 Madrid
24 Maison Dorée
25 Majestic
26 El Mouna
27 Nouvel
28 Oriental Palace
29 El Qods
30 Rahma
31 Rex
32 Ritza
33 Royal
34 St Georges
35 Salammbô
36 Savoie
37 Sidi Belhassen
38 Splendid
39 Du Sud
40 De Suisse
41 Tej
42 Transatlantique
43 Zarzis

TUNIS CITY CENTRE

North of the Medina proper: Halfaouine

El Khir, 24 rue Souki Bel Khir (no phone). Between Bab el Khadra and pl Halfaouine. Slightly musty but not bad. ①.
20 Mars, 9 rue Sidi el Aloui (☎01/266924). Men only – and even if you are a man, hardly recommended – but at 1TD per bed in 5-berth rooms, the cheapest in town. ①.

The New Town and Belvedere Park

The area now occupied by the modern colonial **New Town** consisted mainly of waste ground until the French took control in 1881 when they immediately set about reproducing a pretentious French provincial capital. **Avenue Bourguiba** runs down the middle from the Medina to the port; to either side, the streets more or less follow a grid pattern. The city's main chunk of greenery is the massive **Belvedere Park**, which overlooks it from the north.

Although this isn't the most fascinating part of Tunis, it's where you're likely to spend a lot of your time eating or sleeping, since it contains the city's best hotels, restaurants and other facilities.

Avenue Bourguiba and around

Avenue Bourguiba is the centre of Tunis in every way. People converge here from all over the city to sit in cafés, stroll under the trees, buy a nosegay made of jasmine buds – above all, just to see and be seen. There's something very continental about it that's quite at odds with the Medina's cramped narrow streets.

The first landmark along the avenue – or to be more accurate on avenue Bourguiba's predecessor, avenue Jules Ferry – is the **Cathedral**, built in 1882 and a monstrous, bizarre mixture of Romanesque, Byzantine and Oriental styles, although the breeding colonies of common, pallid and little swifts that shelter here don't object. Just across from the cathedral, the **French Embassy** is quite modest by contrast. Built in 1862 as the advance guard of growing French influence, and as the *Résidence Générale*, the centre of the Protectorate administration from 1881, many of the important decisions of Tunisia's recent history have been made within its unassuming walls. A few blocks east, the old French **theatre**, with its bulging layers of white stucco and fantastic carved figures supporting the balcony, has just been refurbished and plays host to regular and highly recommended Arabic and classical music concerts. Here, in 1896, the Marquis de Morés made a speech condemning British imperialism in the Sudan (remarkably hypocritical, given France's colonial adventurism at the time), before making his fateful expedition to bring military aid to the Mahdi (see p.346).

South of the avenue is French Tunis's most lively area, with many of the city's restaurants, nightclubs and cinemas. There's also a huge **food market** on rue d'Allemagne, selling every conceivable kind of produce. The **Postal Museum** (office hours; free), a dark and dusty room in the main post office in rue d'Angleterre, is for ardent philatelists only, and the **Coin Museum** at 27 rue de Rome (Tues–Sun 9am–6pm; 1TD) is equally of interest only to numismatists. Beyond the train station, the grid plan begins to lose its grip near the Medina, and the same thing happens north of the avenue, where the area immediately adjoining rue Mongi Slim and rue Bab Souika – the old **Maltese and Jewish quarters** – is agreeably chaotic. The thirteenth-century **Zaraia Mosque**, on the corner of rue Zarkoun and rue Mongi Slim, is the area's main sight. The further you go along avenue Bourbuiba from the Medina, the stronger the European influence on the architecture. Both avenue de Paris and avenue de la Liberté have some wonderful examples of colonial building (see the box below), although towards the end of avenue de la Liberté things get more sombre, as you move into a zone of embassies and government buildings. Just off avenue de Paris, the **Jardin Habib Thameur** provides a small amount of greenery but is tiny and fume-laden.

Belvedere Park

Tunis is not a city greatly endowed with parks, and it is really the cemeteries – especially Jellaz (see p.89) – that provide much-needed open spaces. The exception is **Belvedere Park**, which provides an excellent reason for coming this far north. Breathing space has always been a problem in Tunis. An anonymous "English lady" of the 1850s, author of *Letters from Barbary*, reported asking to be shown a garden. Her guide led her some way through the streets, then "halted before two trees, growing against a wall, and surrounded by a plot of about four foot wide, perhaps: and this, he told us, was the biggest garden in the town." Most people today escape the summer humidity by catching the TGM to Carthage or Sidi Bou Said, but Belvedere Park, with its green lower area kept heavily watered, is a peaceful and accessible alternative. Vegetation grows much more sparsely as you climb the hill, but there's an excellent view from the top over Tunis to Bou

---

COLONIAL ARCHITECTURE

Tunis has some notable buildings, ranging from **pompous provincial style** and pseudo-Moorish kitsch to North African **Art Deco**, some in the same league as any in Algiers, Marseille, Casablanca or even Barcelona. Tunis was particularly fertile ground for Art Deco, which reached its French apotheosis in Nice and other cities on the northern shores of the Mediterranean. With its emphasis on clean geometric lines, Art Deco was felt in some quarters to be an appropriate western successor to Islam's non-representational tradition. A recent study identified over four hundred Art Deco buildings built in the Tunis area between 1925 and 1940, including the extraordinary main synagogue on avenue de la Liberté. Dominant features to look out for are semicircular balconies and elaborate ironwork.

Some of the more outstanding examples of colonial architecture around the city centre are listed below. They are disappearing quite fast, as independent Tunisia – not surprisingly – has no great interest in preserving its colonial heritage.

On and south of avenue Bourguiba

Pompous provincial: French Embassy; post office; theatre; cathedral; 48 av Bourguiba; 9 rue Charles de Gaulle; 35–37 Ahmed Tlili; 40–42 rue Oum Khalthoum; 55 av Carthage.
Art Deco: 21–25 and 61 av Ali Dargouth; 47 and 71 rue Houcine Bouzaiene; 40 rue Ibn Khaldoun; 7, 84, 96 and 114 rue de Yougoslavie; 22 rue d'Algérie; 21 rue Allal El Fassi, just south of Bab Alleoua (fine villa).

North of avenue Bourguiba

Pompous provincial: Treasury building (ex-*Société Générale* bank), pl de la Monnaie; 1 rue des Tanneurs; 11, 36 (*Hôtel Majestic*), 43 and 45 av de Paris; 30 rue Gandhi; 5 rue de Luxembourg; 6, 20, 22 and 130 av de la Liberté; 11 rue de l'Atlas (look for Hand of Fatima dated 1929 on the building opposite on rue de Zeramdine); 4, 22–28, 32 and 55–57 av de Londres.
Art Deco: 16 and 56 (*Hôtel Ritza*) av de Paris; 24 and 39 rue de Marseille; 8 pl de la Monnaie; 19, 23 and 41bis rue de Palestine; 2, 7, 41, 43 (synagogue), 45, 79, 105 and 131 (now *Club Med*) av de la Liberté; 16 rue d'Autriche (fine villa).

Kornine (see p.112). The elaborate **koubba**, or dome, standing about halfway up
was built in 1798 for a palace in the suburbs and transplanted here in 1901. Keen
ornithologists will find a range of small birds, and barn owls sometimes come to
hunt here at night.

At the bottom of the park (just above its main entrance), the old **casino** has
theoretically been converted into a **Museum of Modern Art and Cinema**, though
little progress has been made to date. Its terrace is used for theatrical performances
in summer as part of the Carthage Festival. Further round to the south is the **zoo**,
where some distressingly small cages provide an eyeball-to-eyeball perspective on
the fiercer species, as well as close contact with herds of ravening guinea-pigs. Also
here is the **Midha**, an early seventeenth-century fountain for pre-prayer ablutions,
brought here from its original site at Souk et Trouk in the Medina. The cafés in the
middle of the zoo and on the lake just outside are two of the most relaxed in the
city.

The Medina

"White, domed, studded with minarets, honeycombed with tunnel-like bazaars" – until
the nineteenth century, the **Medina** *was* Tunis: an oval-shaped walled city little
changed from its days as a great Mediterranean trading power. In the eighth century
AD, the conquering Arabs were the first to prefer Tunis's site to Carthage, exposed out
on its peninsula, and set about building the monuments that still form the heart of the
Medina, most notably the ninth-century Zitouna mosque, still surrounded by the
central souks. Along the narrow, winding streets – typical of medieval Arab – subsequent generations left behind their own distinctive legacies: mosques, tombs, palaces
and marketplaces. Most of them feature a blend of styles that mirrors the city's cosmopolitan history, although occasionally there is a more straightforward statement, such
as the Mosque of Sidi Mehrez's Ottoman domes, which would not look out of place in
Istanbul.

When the French began to build their new capital on reclaimed land east of the
Medina in the late 1800s, they made no deliberate attempt to eradicate local culture
as they had done in Algiers, but the Medina inevitably declined. After independence
in 1956, a plan was raised to drive a continuation of avenue Bourguiba through the
heart of the Medina to the government offices on the far side, which would have
destroyed the quarter for ever. Fortunately, this idea was abandoned after the
Association de Sauvegarde de la Medina (ASM) was set up to try to preserve the old
city's heritage. But the Medina remains the most tangible evidence of Tunisia's
immediate pre-colonial past and of the "decadence that made colonization possible",
to quote a senior government official in 1961. As such, it has continued to be treated
as a political football: historic buildings have been allowed to deteriorate and the
authorities have even been slow to recognize the Medina's potential touristic value.
Recently these trends seem to have been reversed, but still few of the monuments
are geared up for visitors. Many have been converted to municipal facilities of some
kind, while others remain *ukalas* – large buildings subdivided for many families or
businesses. The most distinctively Tunisian element are the magnificent doorways
which, according to El Bekri, were already famous in the thirteenth century: blue or
beige, set with black studs and a "hand of Fatima" knocker, and surrounded by intricately carved stone frames (see "Architecture", p.379).

Avoid wandering around after dark, when the Medina is deserted, ill-lit and sometimes dangerous, with incidents of pickpocketing and mugging not unknown. Although
old men are hired as watchmen (they stand on corners of the main thoroughfares with

WALKS IN THE MEDINA

There are many different ways to approach a visit to the **Medina**. Perhaps the most attractive – if not the most practical – is just to wander at random, stumbling on unexpected sights. At the other extreme, the tourist authorities have recently created and signposted an itinerary that includes many of the major monuments and provides a quick tour for excursion visitors – a leaflet showing this route is available from the tourist office on place 7 Novembre, and if your time is limited, it's a sensible option. Entrance to the monuments theoretically requires a ticket that is available only at the Zitouna Mosque (only open during the morning) and the Dar Ben Abdallah Museum, though in practice this is rarely enforced.

We have divided the Medina into five areas – the central, southern and northern Medina, Halfaouine, and the western districts; the last two are outside the walls of the medina proper and are covered under a separate heading. Each itinerary covers the main historic sights in each section and many lesser monuments. Three of the itineraries – **central, southern** and **northern** – cover the Medina itself. The other two – **Halfaouine** and the **western districts** – explore suburbs of the Medina that date back several hundred years to the Hafsid era.

Each **walk** on its own probably takes a couple of hours. They can easily be combined to create a longer outing. In terms of monuments, the centre and the souks form the densest area, followed by the south and north, and then Halfaouine and the western districts.

baseball bats, calling out the all clears at regular intervals), they hardly inspire confidence for nocturnal jaunts. Another danger in the Medina after dark is being hit by flying rubbish. It's flung from windows in the evenings for the early morning street cleaners, who supposedly arrive before the tourists, to brush it all up, as there's not much space for garbage trucks down in the narrow streets.

The central Medina

With the Great Mosque and souks set squarely in the middle, the **central Medina** was once the heart of the old city. Here, the concentration of streets, shops and people is at its greatest. At certain times of day, the main streets into the Medina from place de la Victoire are so chock-a-block you can hardly move down them. The Medina's main industry nowadays is tourism, usually of the day-trip variety, with most tour groups "doing" the same streets, the same sights and the same souvenir shops. The result is that the centre of the Medina can feel very commercial, even artificial, and the streets like a gauntlet of traders, albeit mostly amiable ones.

On **place de la Victoire**, stand for a moment and soak in the difference between western symmetry and eastern bustle. The contrast is really less fundamental than it at first seems, but it's an impression that remains striking. **Bab el Bahr**, the Sea Gate, stands alone in the middle of the square; before development of the European city began in the middle of the nineteenth century, it opened from the Medina onto more or less empty ground which led down to the naval arsenal on the shores of the lake. Once the French took over, they inevitably attached symbolic value to Bab el Bahr as the focal point of the meeting between Medina and European city. Ever the symmetrical town planners, they knocked the gate down so as to realign it with the current avenue de France, renamed it Porte de France and erected an evangelical statue behind it – now long gone – of Cardinal Lavigerie, founder of the White Fathers. Just outside the gate, until as late as the first half of the nineteenth century, the Beys used to sponsor wrestling matches between oiled Turkish wrestlers, every day during the month preceding Ramadan.

TUNIS MEDINA

Maison du Parti

RUE JEMAA EL HAOUA

PLACE DU LEADER

RUE SIDI EZ ZOUAOUI

Kasbah Walls

RUE ABDUL WAHAB

9th of April Museum

Mosque ez Zouaoui

Kasbah Mosque

PLACE DE LA KASBAH

WESTERN FAUBOURG

RUE BOUKHRIS

RUE SIDI EZ ZOUAOUI

Hôtel el Massara

BAB MENARA

Tourbet Laz

PL. DU GOUVERN-EMENT

Tomb of Anselm Tourneda

Dar el Bey

PLACE AUX CHEVAUX

Hôtel de la Victoire

Hospital

RUE EL MARR

RUE DES FEMMES

Sidi Bou Khrissane Museum

SOUK

RUE BEN MAHMOUD

Dar Haddad

Youssef Dey Mosque

BOULEVARD

SOUK SEKKA-INE

Hammouda Pasha Mosque

Souk des Armes

El Ksar Mosque

SOUK EL TROUK

RUE MOHSEN

Souk El Leffa

SOUK EL ATTARINE

Souk El Asser

RUE ABBA

Dar Husayn

SOUK DES FEMMES

Great Mosque

Bab Jedid

RUE DES FORGERONS

RUE DU RICHE

RUE DES ANDALOUS

RUE DES JUGES

SOUK EL KACHACHINE

BOULEVARD BAB MENARA

M'sid El Koubba Mosque

RUE TOURBET EL BEY

RUE DU TRESOR

SOUK EL BELAT

Former Medersa

Dar El Hedri

Zaouia Sidi Ali Azouz

Tourbet el Bey

RUE SIDI ES SOURDOU

Ichbili Mosque

RUE SIDI ALI AZOUZ

RUE SIDI KASSEM

Dyer's Mosque

Dar Bayram Turki

RUE SIDI EL BEY

Dar Ben Abdallah Museum

RUE MBAZAA

RUE SIDI EL BENNA

Dyer's Souks

RUE DES TEINTURIERS

Dar Othman

RUE EL MEKHTAR

RUE EL MEKHTAR

AVENUE BAB JEDID

RUE SIDI BOU MENOJI

RUE D'ANGLETERRE

RUE D'ESPAGNE

Sidi el Bechir Mosque

RUE EL DJAZIRA

RUE DE MAROC

PLACE BAB JAZIRA

BOULEVARD DU 9 AVRIL 1938

HALFAOUINE

BOULEVARD BAB BENAT

RUE GHARNOUTA

RUE DU PASHA

RUE BAB SOUIKA

Sadiki College

Porters' Cafe

Farhat Hached's Tomb

RUE SIDI IBRAHIM

RUE DE LA NDURIA

Bachiya Medersa

Dar Lasram

Zaouia of Sidi Ibrahim Riahi

PLACE BAB SOUIKA

Sidi Mehrez Mosque

Hôtel Sfax

RUE BIR EL HAJAR

TRIBUNAL

RUE DE LA HAFSIA

RUE EL MONASTIRI

Dziri Meusoleum

Achouria Medersa

Zaouia Sidi Mehrez

RUE ACHOUR

Dar Monastiri Hôtel les Amis

Tripoli Louage Station

R. SIDI BEN AROUS

RUE SIDI MEHREZ

AVENUE ALI BELHOUANE

Onkiya Medersa

Youth Hostel

RUE ES SAIDA-AJOULA

RUE DE L'AGHA

DU DIVAN

RUE DES JERBIENS

Zaouia Sidi Abdelkader

RUE

RUE ETTOUMI

Divan

SOUK EL OUT

KZANE

Secondhand Clothes Souk

RUE EL

R. EL

RUE DE LA KASBAH

RUE DES NEGRES

SOUK EL GRANAA

RUE BAB SOUIKA

Hôtel Hammami

THE HAFSIA

PLACE DES POTIERS

PLACE BAB CARTHAJANA

Hôtel de Bonheur

RUE DE LA VERRIERE

RUE DES PROTESTANTS

RUE SIDI EL AJAMI

Anglican Church

RUE DE LA KASBAH

RUE ZARDUN

RUE JEMAA ZITOUNA

RUE DES GLACIERES

Algeria Louage Station

British Embassy

RUE BAB EL KHADRA

Bab el Bahr

Hôtel Medina

RUE MONGI SLIM

Hôtel Riadh

CITY CENTRE

0   100 m

This area of the Medina had long been a Christian ghetto, ever since the Turks allowed the first foreign embassies inside the Medina walls to be built here in the seventeenth century (see p.57). By the mid-nineteenth century, growing European influence saw the positions reversed; the large Italianate building with shabby columns facing the gate was the office of the International Financial Commission that supervised the bankrupt Bey's administration just before the French Protectorate. These French, Italian and British commissioners forced the government to grant foreigners privileges and concessions that caused much resentment at the time, and on several occasions the building was attacked by mobs.

Rue Jemaa Zitouna leads from place de la Victoire directly to the Great Mosque, and, as the main tourist route, has turned into a cauldron of overflowing stalls and over-eager proprietors. You can buy almost everything more cheaply elsewhere, but the shops are a useful training ground for bargaining techniques, and the stall on the corner of rue Sidi Ali Azouz often has interesting old metal lamps, chandeliers and pen cases. At no. 12 is the **Church of St Croix**, the first to be built in Tunis, in 1662. In the 1860s it became a sanctuary, protected by the French, and the source of repeated confrontation between them and the Beys. Time after time the Beys had to back down and accept that the criminals and enemies who escaped here were outside their jurisdiction.

The fine door at no. 55 belongs to the **Sidi Morjani Barracks**, the third of five sets of barracks built by Hammouda Bey (1777–1813) after his Ottoman troops mutinied in 1811. Hammouda was forced to recruit tribal warriors from among the Zouaoua Berbers as auxiliaries, and built them five sets of barracks. At the end of rue Jemaa Zitouna, the **National Library** at no. 73 was originally the second barracks; entrance to the library is through the Souk el Attarine. The first of Hammouda Bey's barracks is now Aziza Othmana Hospital, near place du Gouvernement (see p.77); another is in **rue Sidi Ali Azouz**, just off rue Jemaa Zitouna (see p.80); and the fifth has since been demolished.

The Great Mosque

Bringing rue Jemaa Zitouna to an abrupt halt is the **Great Mosque** (daily except Fri 8am–noon; 3TD, ticket covers other sights on official Medina route), known as the Zitouna (olive tree) because it stands on the site of the tree under which its founder taught the Koran.

The mosque's massive size is exaggerated by the cramped alleys around it, an effect that must have been even greater when it was completed under the Aghlabids in the ninth century. While the mosque is still the heart of the Medina, for hundreds of years it was the central point of reference for the entire city: the surrounding souks were positioned deliberately around it, as well as a host of secondary buildings such as the *medersas* that housed students who had come to study at the mosque.

Successive additions over the centuries make its exterior appearance today something of a composite. In the seventeenth century Spanish architect Ibn Ghalib – who also designed the mosque complex of the second Turkish ruler, Youssef Dey – was responsible for the spacious entrance portico hanging over the Souk el Fakka (dried fruits) along the mosque's east side; the minaret at the northwest corner, which seems such a perfect fit, actually dates back only to the nineteenth century, when a new minaret was modelled directly on that of the 1235 Kasbah mosque (see p.88). In the cramped surroundings of the Medina, little else is visible of the exterior except for massive blank walls. It's worth timing a visit for the morning so that you can go inside and see the courtyard, which retains its original form – a vast empty space of polished marble. It is strongly reminiscent of the Great Mosque at Kairouan, built slightly earlier, and has the same wonderfully soothing effect after the bustle of the souks outside. As at Kairouan, the courtyard is surrounded on three sides by simple arcades, while the prayer hall occupies the fourth.

In its day, the **university** based in the mosque was one of the greatest in the world. Hundreds of years before European universities had even been thought of, students were coming to Tunis from throughout the Islamic world. Tradition records that each professor had his own column, next to which he always did his teaching. Even in the 1950s there were students here, but during the 1960s the university was brought into line with the national educational system and theological students moved elsewhere.

Coming out of the mosque, turn right along **Souk des Librairies**, one side of which is lined by a series of interconnecting *medersas* built in the early eighteenth century – the **Medersa of the Palm Tree** (no. 11), the **Bachia** (no. 27) and, on the corner, the **Slimania**, which you can visit (times uncertain). The *medersa* is a type of residential Islamic college found all over the Muslim world, and here each has the classic form of a courtyard surrounded by students' cells. These three are part of a series founded in Tunis in the eighteenth century, and the story behind two of them typifies the instability of the Husaynid dynasty. The Bachia was founded in 1752 by Ali Pasha, and only two years later he dedicated the Slimania to the memory of his son Suleiman, who had been poisoned by a younger brother. There's also a **hammam** here at no. 30.

The main souks

The close link between Islam and commerce could hardly be better represented than by the purpose-built **souks** around the Great Mosque. Even the hierarchy of trades was symbolized by their respective positions: the closer to the mosque, the more "noble" the trade, thus the Souk des Étoffes (cloth) and Souk el Attarine (perfume) were right next to it; messier businesses such as dyeing and metalwork were relegated to the suburbs.

At the Great Mosque, turn left along the **Souk de la Laine** – Wool Market – which runs up the near side. There's not much wool here any more, but a few traditional tailors and, at **no. 21**, a doorway into the mosque improvised out of Roman blocks. Opposite no. 9 is the **rue de Béjà**, where most of the wool and cotton weaving seems to have moved to. It's interesting to watch the weaving – most of the textiles are still made on hand looms. At the end of this street, a brief detour takes in some of the further souks.

Left along Souk des Femmes, you cross the Souk du Coton to a junction with **Souk el Kachachine**, with its noisy wholesale bargaining for rugs and garments. Turn right at this corner, first right onto Souk el Kouafi, then first left into **Souk des Orfèvres**. True to its name, this is still the home of gold jewellers, whose tiny shops on narrow streets reflect their need for security. Left to the junction with Souk el Leffa and then a right downhill will take you to **Souk des Étoffes**, or Cloth Market, recognizable by its red and green columns. With its deep stalls, this is the most spacious souk in the Medina; elegant and refined, it comes to an end at the far corner of the mosque. At no. 37, the **Mouradia Medersa** was built in 1673 by Mourad Bey, son of Hammouda Pasha, whose mosque is covered on p.78.

Unfortunately, the **Souk el Attarine**, which slopes down one side of the mosque, no longer specializes in perfume: in the sixteenth century it used to stay open until midnight in order to serve women, who took their hammams in the evening. On the left of this street as it descends, steps lead up to the **Midhat es Soltane**, a fifteenth-century bathing facility attached to the Great Mosque and renowned for its beauty. It's rarely accessible, so you're unlikely to see more than the facade of the

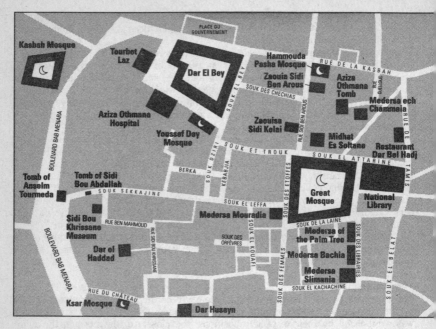

main entrance at the top of the steps, with its dramatic use of black and white marble. Reminiscent of Cairo and Syria, this technique confirms Tunis's position as a meeting place for influences from both east and west Islam. Unlike Dar Othman in the south of the Medina, though, in whose courtyard western tilework blends with eastern marble, the Midhat's interior limits itself to stark marble in an eastern style.

THE TUNIS SLAVE TRADE

Slaves were brought to Souk el Berka in Tunis – the most unfortunate from their dungeons in the Kasbah at La Goulette – where they were displayed to prospective buyers, who would first check their teeth, because unskilled slaves ended up working the corsair galleys and being fed entirely on hard biscuits. Most of the slaves were captured at sea, as far away as the English Channel – but there were also frequent raids on coastal towns in Italy, France and Spain. It was a brutal business, though western tradition has been happy to overlook the equally ferocious Christian corsairs supplying the great slave markets at Pisa, Genoa and other European trading cities. Piracy and slavery were generally accepted (even if not officially) as a lucrative adjunct of Mediterranean trade.

By the end of the eighteenth century, European fleets had forced the corsairs from the sea. Initially the Trans-Saharan trade compensated for the declining Mediterranean supply, and in the 1790s as many as six thousand African slaves were sold in Tunis every year. Over the following decades, however, taxation, along with competition from Tripoli's markets and wars in the south, ruined the trade. Then in 1846 Ahmed Bey, building his reputation as an enlightened ruler, abolished the slave trade and the markets were closed. The Africans have remained. In the past they suffered discrimination and were often reduced to the status of domestic servants, but today they are an integral part of Tunisian society.

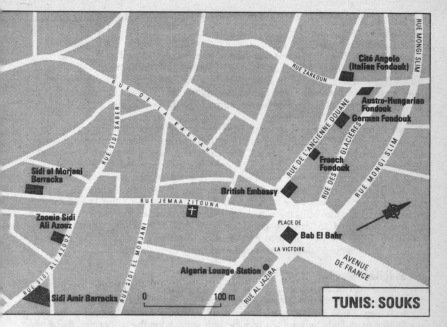

Turning back up Souk el Attarine, continue up the hill along **Souk et Trouk**, built in the seventeenth century for Turkish tailors, past the *Musée des Turcs* carpet shop, with its terrace view over the Medina. At the top, turn left into Souk Kebabjia. The open space a little way along here is the **Souk el Berka**, once the marketplace for Tunis's slave trade.

Around place du Gouvernement

Close to the Souk el Berka, the **Mosque of Youssef Bey** dates back to 1616 and was designed by the Spanish architect who added the portico to the Great Mosque. Blending local features with influences from the east, from Christian Italy and from Islamic Spain, the result is an accurate reflection of the many historical and social currents to which Tunisia's geography has always made it subject. Compared with the massive simplicity of the Great Mosque, it has a more airy, complex feel.

Most obvious here is the octagonal minaret on a square base, recalling Ottoman Turkish designs and signalling the arrival of the new Turkish rulers. The shape of the lantern, with its hanging balcony from which the muezzin would originally have issued the call to prayer, is not only the first of its kind but immediately established a standard that was to appear again and again in Tunis. Next to the minaret, the square mausoleum incorporates Spanish, eastern and Italian influences, with a green-tiled pyramidal roof recalling the Alhambra in Granada; the elaborate patterns of black and white marble, eastern in origin, had already appeared in Tunis in the Midhat es Soltane (p.75) and the palace of Othman Dey (p.80). However, the form of the prayer hall, with eight rows of six columns, is more purely North African.

Continuing up past the mosque, you emerge from the Medina into **place du Gouvernement**, an open space on what was once the western edge of the Medina proper. Formerly a royal guest house, the **Dar el Bey** is now the prime minister's office, which means that government in Tunis has returned to its original site – since the Hafsids' thirteenth-century Kasbah stood just above here. You can see the excavations over the road, and above them the gleaming PSD Party building, while to the left is the Kasbah Mosque (see p.88). The western suburb walk (p.86) begins here, running up the hill and then around to the southern end of the Medina.

Also in the place du Gouvernement is the **Tourbet Laz**, the tomb of a seventeenth-century Bey and his relations, now occupied by a family who may let you look inside. These *tourbets* (tombs) were very fashionable among rich Turkish families of the time and Tunis has several – the **Tourbet of Ahmed Kouja Dey** is just across the street from here.

Heading back past Youssef Dey's mosque, the street on your left behind the Dar el Bey is the **Souk el Bey**, suitably grand with its broad, pillared arcade. The third turning on the right here is the **Souk des Chechias**, another eye-catching market, selling the characteristic Tunisian skullcaps made from wool by a complicated process of carding, moulding and dyeing. During the eighteenth century this was one of Tunisia's most important industries, but in the mid-eighteenth century European factories flooded the market with cheap imitations and the Tunisian industry was ruined. By the 1920s the remaining manufacturers faced another recession as the wealthy turned to western dress. Now it is a disappearing industry – few Tunisians under the age of forty own or wear a *chechia* – and so the souk sits forlornly. In its centre, Tunis's oldest café sells thick Turkish coffee.

Rue Sidi Ben Arous

Right at the end of the souk at 23 rue Sidi Ben Arous is the **Zaouia of Sidi Ben Arous**, a fourteenth-century native of Cap Bon who brought back Sufi teaching from Morocco (see p.388). Built in 1437, this particular *zaouia*, the meeting place of a religious fraternity, quickly became too popular with women for the authorities' liking and was closed – only to be promptly reopened in the face of an ensuing uproar. On the opposite side of the street, at no. 18, is the late fifteenth-century Hafsid **Zaouia of Sidi Kelai**, with inscriptions and panels of leaning key-stones above its entrance. By contrast, the shocking-pink facade of the nearby **Tourbet of Hammouda Pasha** clearly belongs to a later period. With the **mosque** of the same name, it forms a complex built in 1655 and clearly modelled after the 1616 mosque of Youssef Dey, with the same octagonal minaret and detached square mausoleum, and the same use of Tunisian Cosmopolitan architectural style.

Overshadowed to the south by the Great Mosque's minaret, **rue Sidi Ben Arous** is an attractive little street with a *chechia* seller, a café and a bookshop called *Espace Diwan* (see p.98). In the other direction, its northern continuation on the other side of rue de la Kasbah is lined by the imposing doorways of what were once senior Turkish officials' houses, unfortunately mostly inaccessible.

Going down **rue de la Kasbah**, the other main street running across the Medina, the first proper street you cross is **rue Jelloud**. Impasse Echemmahia, to the right off here, surprisingly contains two important monuments. At no. 4, the **Medersa ech Chammaia**, founded by the Hafsid Sultan Abu Zakariya in 1249, was the first *medersa* built in Tunis. For all its simplicity – a one-storey courtyard surrounded by students' cells, built in plain, undecorated limestone – it is a fine example of classic Hafsid style. At the end of the same impasse (no. 9), the **Tomb of Aziza Othmana** belongs to a princess renowned for her generosity. Just before her death in 1669, she liberated her slaves and left her estate to charitable causes – funds to liberate slaves and prisoners, and a fund for poor girls who couldn't otherwise afford to marry. She's buried next to her grandfather, Othman Dey (who built the Dar Othman in the south of the Medina), and the tomb itself was built by Husayn, founder of the Husaynid dynasty and Aziza Othmana's son-in-law. The world of the Tunisian ruling classes was a small one.

The foreign fondouks

Rue de la Kasbah continues downhill and out of the Medina. Just before emerging into place de la Victoire, a tiny alley on the left – rue de l'Ancienne Douane – leads to the site of the first **French Consulate and trading post** (marked by a plaque on the wall just before the Guersin baths). Along the same street are the former Italian, Austro-Hungarian and German embassy buildings, whose first-floor balconies still bear their national insignia, the only clue to their erstwhile importance. Originally known as *fondouks* (trading posts where foreign merchants were obliged to live), they're today all *ukala*, houses divided up to accommodate several families. This is one of the most run-down areas of the Medina – at the end of the alley, rue Zarkoun is a kind of flea market and just beyond you'll find yourself in a street of brothels. The only consular building left is the **British Embassy** on the corner of place de la Victoire. When other nations were moving out to the suburbs the British obstinately stayed in the centre of town. The current embassy was built in the 1860s by Sir Richard Wood, an influential British consul in the days when Britain and France were still jockeying for position here. Wood was instrumental in obtaining for a British firm the concession for the TGM, the first rail company in Tunisia, which he then succeeded in routing through the garden of his residence in La Marsa.

It was Hammouda Pasha in 1659 who gave permission for the *fondouks* to be built. These were still dangerous times for foreigners in Tunis: in 1678 Francis Baker, the English consul, reported that one Sidi Mohammed Bey "did . . . forceably and violently seize on Charles Gratiano, Consul for the French, together with ourselves . . . swearing by the Soule of his deceased he would cutt us to pieces . . ." Fortunately Mohammed Bey fled when his brother Ali Bey returned, and the consul lived to tell the tale.

From place de la Victoire, the **rue des Glacières** leads north. Here, in the eighteenth and nineteenth centuries, huge blocks of ice, shipped from the Alps, were stored to be sold at vast profit during the summer months. Today, the street's main attractions are the shops selling second-hand furniture and bric-a-brac, most of it left by the French in the mid-1950s – Art Deco statuettes and nineteenth-century portraits of long-forgotten soldiers. If you're tempted to buy something, bear in mind that the prices asked are astronomical.

Southern Medina

Next to the central section of the Medina, the **southern area** has the greatest concentration of monumental interest, with two highlights in Dar Othman and the Dar Ben Abdallah Museum. As with all the non-central walks, though, it is the combination of continuing local life – children at school, vegetable markets – with hundreds of years of historical legacy that makes it so worthwhile getting off the main routes. This itinerary takes you from place de la Victoire down to the southern end of the Medina and then back up to finish on its western edge, not far from the beginning of the western suburb walk (see p.86).

Climbing up rue Jemaa Zitouna from place de la Victoire, you come to **rue Sidi Ali Azouz** and, turning right, at no. 7 a nineteenth-century **zaouia** of the same name. Sidi Ali Azouz was born in Fez in Morocco in the seventeenth century and settled in Zaghouan after returning from a pilgrimage to Mecca. Like Sidi Mehrez, he is one of the patron saints of the city of Tunis. Just after the *zaouia* (next left, an unnamed impasse off rue Sidi Ali Azouz) is an opportunity to see a Medina palace unaffected by the riot of decoration that covers every surface of later residences. **Dar Bayram Turki**, named after a senior official of Youssef Dey who lived here at the beginning of the seventeenth century, would originally have been approached through a typical crooked *skifa* or passage. Nowadays a simple doorway leads into a plain courtyard built of undecorated limestone, where two shallow three-arch porticoes face each other, mirrored by blind arcades on the other two sides. Compared with later courtyards, the effect is almost monastic – though far from artless: note the spaced dark stones picking out the shape of each arch, and the characteristic loop motif above. Currently the ground floor is occupied by small **workshops**, including (on either side of the entrance) a ceramics outfit which was involved in restoring Dar Othman.

A little further on, rue Sidi Ali Azouz runs past the brooding bulk of the **Sidi Amir Barracks** – one of the five built by Hammouda Bey at the beginning of the nineteenth century (see p.74). Now virtually abandoned, it feels like a massive police station – which, of course, is what it was built as. Continuing, the street merges with a dark tunnel of the **Souk el Belat**, selling mainly food. To your right, on the corner of Souk el Belat and rue du Trésor, is the tenth-century **Ichbili Mosque** with its squat fourteenth-century minaret set well back. If you're interested in another lovely palace like Dar Bayram Turki, take a brief detour behind the Ichbili Mosque to **Dar Hedri** at 12 rue du Trésor, easily identifiable by its Hafsid slanting arch-stones above the door and an open gallery running above the courtyard. Because it's now used as shared housing rather than workshops, this palace retains a more serene feeling. As in Dar Bayram Turki, the three-arched courtyard is in honey-coloured limestone, enlivened only by loop motifs (single and double). Instead of black arch-stones, a black design picks out the centre of the courtyard: a simple statement of the theme presented much more elaborately in the courtyard of the *zaouia* of Sidi Kassem Jelizi and on Dar Othman's facade.

Along rue Sidi Ali Azouz, bear right where the street forks and you're on **rue des Teinturiers** (Street of the Dyers). Ahead rises the minaret of the **Mosque des Teinturiers**, also known as the New Mosque and centre of a sizeable complex. The octagonal minaret recalls those of Youssef Dey and Hammouda Bey near the Great Mosque, though it was built a century later than Youssef Dey's, in 1716. The mosque was commissioned by Husayn Bin Ali, founder of the Husaynid dynasty, as his own memorial, and he lavished great expense on it, importing tiles for the prayer-hall from Iznik in Turkey. In the *tourbet* attached to the mosque, Husayn buried two holy men, Sidi Kassem Sababti and Sidi Kassem el Beji, reserving the space between them for his own use. Things didn't quite work out, however, and Husayn was driven from power by his nephew Ali Pasha, who buried his own father in the position of honour. A *kouttab* and a *medersa* were added to the complex later, making it an impressive, if abortive, memorial. You can see the tombs through a window, if it's open, in rue Sidi Kassem.

Dar Othman and Dar Ben Abdallah

Almost opposite the mosque, down the passage-like rue M'Bazaa, stands the superb doorway of **Dar Othman**, an attractive palace built by Othman Dey (ruled 1598–1610) to escape the intrigues and insecurities of life in the Kasbah – the gates closed off the street so that the palace could be defended if necessary. Its monumental facade consists of a welter of black and white marble patterns – an effect that was common further east in the Islamic world and may have been imported by the Turks. You may find it a little overdone here: in the *skifa* and the courtyard beyond, decoration continues unabated in the form of coloured tiles, offset by an attractive garden featuring three tall cypress trees in the corners and a lemon tree. If the garden feels out of place, that's because it's a twentieth-century addition. Dar Othman is officially covered by the Medina tour ticket (see p.71), though it is still in use as offices.

From rue des Teinturiers, turn right into rue Sidi Kassem, then left through an arch on rue Dar Ben Abdallah, where you'll find the **Dar Ben Abdallah** (daily except Mon 9.30am–4.30pm; 3TD), one of the finest old palaces in the Medina. The palace was originally called Dar Kahia after its builder, one Slimane Kahia, who achieved prominence under the reign of Hammouda Pasha (1792–1814) by marrying the daughter of the next ruler. Slimane was a senior government official and led the ruler's vital twice-yearly *mahalla* (tax-collecting expedition) to the tribes of the interior. With up to eight thousand participants, the summer *mahalla* marched to Beja and fanned out from there across the north; in winter, its base was Tozeur. When Slimane moved to live in the Bey's entourage at the Bardo, his Tunis residence was bought by the rich land-owner and silk merchant whose name it carries now.

The palace has a classic design. A *driba* (entrance hall), lined with stone benches for waiting guests, opens onto a *skifa* leading into the house proper and distancing it from the outside world. The florid decoration of the door that leads from *driba* to *skifa* is once again typical of the Italianate styles that became increasingly popular from the eighteenth century – as, too, is much of the ornamentation in the courtyard (look out for the grotesque little dolphins hanging upside down on the fountain). T-shaped reception rooms open off the courtyard; the cupboard-like rooms at the angles were some-times used as bedrooms.

The palace has been converted into the **Museum of the Traditional Heritage of Tunis**, with each T-shaped room off the main courtyard devoted to an area of tradi-tional upper-class urban life: childhood, marriage, the men's quarters. After the white stucco and light tiles of the airy courtyard, the rooms' heavily painted ceilings make for a strange contrast. Some of the rooms contain dummies dressed in traditional costumes and engaged in traditional pastimes, like drinking coffee. Notice how even the simplest of everyday items are imbued with an elaborate sense of geometric design.

The Souks of the Dyers, the Tourbet el Bey and Bab Jedid

Returning to rue des Teinturiers, there's an old **hammam** on the left, which proclaims itself the "most elegant establishment of bathing baths in marble". Opposite nos. 92 and 104 open the **Souks of the Dyers**, after whom the street is named. At one time, as part of the clothing industry, dyeing was a vital part of Tunis's economy, but now it's just one more threatened traditional craft. The first of the souks has been taken over for making drums, and piles of clay bodies line the walls waiting for skins to be tanned before being stretched over them. The other souk is still used for a limited amount of (rather gaudy) dyeing.

Continue along rue des Teinturiers, turn right on rue Sidi el Benna, then right again on rue Sidi Zahmoul, past a huge palace with lazy palm trees to the **Tourbet el Bey**. As its name suggests, this royal mausoleum, built by Ali Pasha II (1758–82), contains most of the Husaynid dynasty that followed him. Leaden, ornate and uninspired, it is one of the least successful examples of Tunisian Cosmopolitan building in the capital – perhaps because it suffers from too strong a European influence. Nearby, 44 rue Sidi Essourdou was once a **medersa** founded in the eighteenth century by Husayn Bin Ali, the first Husaynid Bey.

Turning left from the Tourbet el Bey onto the street named after it, a small detour can be made by taking a left down rue des Juges and then a right up **rue des Forgerons** (since the thirteenth century the blacksmiths' souk), bringing you out of the Medina at **Bab Jedid**, a gate built in 1276 as part of the Hafsid city wall. Up some stairs next to it is a tiny mosque, the **Khalouet Sidi Mehrez**, where the Hafsid sultans used to pay homage to the city's patron saint. You could, if you wanted, leave the Medina through Bab Jedid and join the western suburb itinerary (see p.86).

Returning to rue Tourbet el Bey and continuing along it, no. 41 is the tiny **M'sid el Koubba Mosque**, where the great historian Ibn Khaldoun used to teach. Born in 1332, at no. 33 of the same street, Ibn Khaldoun was the first to suggest that history repeats itself in cycles and in his greatest work, *A World History*, he introduced the idea of 'asabiyah (group solidarity) as the foundation of society. As 'asabiyah rises and declines, so does civilization.

A little further on rue Tourbet el Bey, just north of no. 20 and on the right as you emerge from underneath a **sabat** (a room located over the street), a decrepit stone archway leads into impasse du Jasmin. This was originally built in the seventeenth century as a weavers' workshop by the Spanish community, whose wealthy citizens lived on this street. Three and a half centuries later, a silk weaver is still making *sifsaris* in the workshop at no. 7.

Sidi Bou Khrissane and around

Backtracking slightly, go left onto **rue du Riche**, then right into **rue des Andalous**, both streets having a scattering of magnificent doorways. This is where wealthier Andalusian immigrants settled while the less well-off had to petition for land in order to found towns like Testour (see p.230). A left turn on to rue du Dey then another on rue Mohsen will bring you into a small square. On your left is the **Dar Husayn**, a palace built originally in the twelfth century and enlarged in the eighteenth. Once the town hall, then the French army headquarters during colonial rule, it's now used by the National Institute of Archeology, who will be pleased to let you have a look at the elaborate tiling and stuccowork inside – something well worth doing. Across the square is the **El Ksar Mosque**, founded around 1106 by the Emir Ahmed Ibn Khourassane. The minaret, an interesting blend of Ottoman and Andalusian styles, was added in 1647.

Ibn Khourassane's family, the Khourassanids, who ruled Tunis from 1059 to 1159, have their mausoleum just around the corner. Turn right out of the square into rue Sidi Bou Khrissane then left into rue Ben Mahmoud. On your right is the **Sidi Bou Khrissane Museum** (Mon–Sat 9am–noon, but you'll be let in at any reasonable hour if you knock; donation expected). Part of a cemetery dating back to the ninth century, it is really more a garden full of old tombstones than a museum. The Khourassanid emirs are interred under a cupola at the back.

On the way to the museum, at the end of impasse de l'Artillerie, a blind alley off rue Sidi Bou Khrissane, the sixteenth-century **mansion** of the Andalusian Haddad family will be open to the public when restoration work on it finishes.

Rue Ben Mahmoud finally runs out into Souk Sekkajine. Buried in a red and green box in the middle of the street on your left is **Sidi Bou Abdallah**, who died on this spot while defending Tunis against the invading Spanish. A Spaniard, however, is buried only a few metres further on, under an olive tree at **Bab Menara**, where Souk Sekkajine emerges from the Medina. He is Anselm Tourmeda (aka Abdallah Tourjman), a fourteenth-century Majorcan who came to Tunisia, converted to Islam and wrote religious propaganda in Arabic and Catalan.

Northern Medina

The **northern Medina** is largely free of sightseers and you'll feel less like a tourist, especially as the shops here sell goods that ordinary Tunisians buy. There are fewer sights as such, though the Mosque of Sidi Mehrez is as familiar to Tunisians as the Zitouna Mosque, but this is a much better part of the Medina if you just want to wander. This walk leads up to the northern end of the Medina, where you could detour onto the Halfaouine itinerary (see p.85); otherwise, it returns back to place de la Victoire.

Turning off rue de la Kasbah onto rue Saida Ajoula, the first left is rue Onk el Jemal, where no. 5, the **Onkiya Medersa**, was founded by a Hafsid princess in 1341. Backtracking, duck left off rue Saida Ajoula into rue du Divan. No. 3 on the right is the

Divan itself, home of the Divan council, which at first played a major role in the power structure of the sixteenth- and seventeenth-century Turkish Regency of Tunis. As authority gradually passed into the hands of individual Beys, though, the council's function became more that of a religious court. Further on at no. 16 is the **Zaouia of Sidi Abdelkader**, built in 1851 as the seat of the Kadria brotherhood, a *sufi* group.

A right at the end of rue du Divan down rue de l'Agha will bring you to an area of **second-hand clothing stalls**, where bundles of unsorted clothes arrive regularly from European and American charities to be sold off at auction. Prices are ridiculously low – you can get virtually brand-new clothes for next to nothing – but the aid organizations seem to have overlooked the impact of these cheap imports on the local clothing industry. Tunisians wear flared jeans and ludicrous second-hand suits because there's no economical alternative: traditional dress has become a luxury. Nearby, at 9 rue des Nègres, is the **Mustansiriya medersa**, founded in 1435 by the Hafsid Sultan el Mustansir and in a state of extreme disrepair. The seventeenth-century **Zaouia of Sidi Braham**, around the corner in rue el Azafine, is famous for its collection of ceramic tiles.

Back at the junction with rue du Divan, follow rue de l'Agha up to the left into little place Ramdhane Bey and have a quick look up at the elaborate set of **Ottoman windows** through the arch ahead of you in rue Bir el Hajar – a startling sight in the streets of blank exterior walls. Then head off to your right, down **rue du Pasha**, a tidy cobbled street that was the main thoroughfare of the Turkish residential quarter, with graceful doorways befitting the homes of important officials. No. 40, on the left, is the eighteenth-century **Bachiya Medersa**. Opposite no. 64 in the same street, follow a passageway into **rue de la Nouria**, which has to be the narrowest lane in the Medina. On the left as you bear left into rue du Tribunal is **Dar Lasram**, home of the Tunis *Association de Sauvegarde de la Medina* (ASM) and built for the Lasram family, an old Kairouan clan that claimed a direct line of descent back to the Arab conquest in the seventh century. This family palace dates originally from the mid-eighteenth century, a date reflected in the exuberant decoration to be seen inside. Opposite, at no. 27, is the nineteenth-century **mausoleum** of the landowning Dziri family.

Rue Sidi Mehrez and around

At the end of rue du Tribunal runs rue Sidi Ibrahim. Just to the left at no. 11 is the **Zaouia of Sidi Ibrahim Riahi**. Originally from Testour, al Riahi was a leading member of the Tijaniya *sufi* brotherhood at the beginning of the nineteenth century. Although successful as a teacher in Tunis, where religion offered greater social mobility than any other profession, he still needed a sponsor because he was not earning a decent living. Into the breach, so as to keep him in Tunisia, stepped Youssef Sahib et Tabaa, the prime minister under Hammouda Bey who later met a brutal end (see p.85).

Follow the street the other way and a dog-leg to your left at the end brings you into rue el Monastiri. Around the corner in rue Achour is the seventeenth-century **Achouria Medersa**. Rue el Monastiri runs down into **rue Sidi Mehrez**, the last incarnation of one of the main north–south arteries of the Medina. A busy shopping street, it houses the **Zaouia of Sidi Mehrez**, fronted by a long passage. At 9 rue el Monastir is the entrance to Dar Monastir, an early nineteenth-century palace currently being extensively restored.

Sidi Mehrez is still revered as a patron saint of Tunis for his efforts in the tenth century. After the city's sufferings during the revolt of Abu Yazid, it was he who oversaw its revival. The original tomb has shared many of Tunis's ups and downs, and the present building is mainly eighteenth- and nineteenth-century. Traditionally, boys come to drink from its well before their circumcision ceremony.

Opposite the *zaouia*, though not visible from the street, is the **Mosque of Sidi Mehrez**, one of Tunis's most distinctive landmarks. A little beyond the *zaouia* on the right,

THE HAFSIA AND THE JEWS

At one time the Jewish ghetto of the **Hafsia** was separated from the rest of the town by a wall and its gates were closed at night. Before the status of Jews was regularized in 1861 there were many other petty restrictions: Jews had to wear black clothes of a traditional style, as European dress was forbidden; they were not allowed to ride horses or own land outside the Hafsia. Jews had their own civil courts, but in their dealings with Muslims were subject to Islamic law, and they faced burning at the stake if found guilty of a capital offence. Although protected as a "people of the book" (those who share with Islam a reverence for the Old Testament), many Muslims regarded them as heathen and treated them as such. Occasionally riots broke out and the Hafsia was wrecked by Muslim mobs, but for most of the time the Jews lived in peace, however restricted.

It was the immigration of Maltese and Italian Jews, citizens of powerful European states, that allowed the Jews to escape these repressive laws. By the 1870s their wealth and connections with European governments had given them considerable power and new freedom. Then, under the Protectorate, they joined the middle class and many left the Medina for the suburbs. Nevertheless, when the Germans arrived in 1942 the Hafsia was still very crowded, and the Gestapo used the ghetto as an assembly point for thousands of Jews from other parts of Tunisia before sending them to their deaths. After the war most of the survivors emigrated to Israel and the Hafsia was destroyed. The remainder of the Jewish community dispersed into the suburbs.

you can climb some steps into a new arcade for the best look at its heap of white domes. Dotted with pigeons, they stand out for miles in any rooftop view of the Medina and are the city's only example of the Imperial Ottoman building style. Presumably Mohammed Bey, who founded it in 1696, wanted to stamp a truly Turkish presence on the city, but after his early death, the assassination of his brother and the rise of the Husaynids, the mosque was left unfinished. Instead of the four circular minarets that would have conferred a fully Ottoman look, it got a small square North African one; it's even named after the *zaouia* opposite rather than its own founder. The **pottery shops** at nos. 96 and 97 warrant a quick mention here: although they don't sell the fancier souvenir products, they do have a wide range of plates, cups, pots and ashtrays, all at very low prices.

Rue Sidi Mehrez emerges from the Medina into **place Bab Souika**, once a place of public execution, and nowadays the area of the liveliest cafés during Ramadan nights. Unfortunately, a controversial redevelopment plan has recently destroyed much of its character.

A right turn out of rue Sidi Mehrez along the eastern edge of the Medina and down rue Bab Souika takes you past the Anglican **Church of St George** on the corner of rue des Protestants. Among those buried in its churchyard are John Howard Payne, a nineteenth-century US consul better known as the author of the song "Home Sweet Home". The large open space opposite marks the site of the **Hafsia**, the Jewish ghetto where the Gestapo assembled thousands of Jews before sending them to their deaths. The ghetto was finally pulled down in 1953.

The Faubourgs

As well as an inner wall around the Medina, the Hafsids built an outer rampart to enclose the city's residential suburbs, or **faubourgs**, which have managed to retain a strong sense of local character and community. They are often referred to by the names of former Medina gates, thus **Halfaouine** is in the Rbat Bab Souika and **Montfleury** in the Rbat Bab Jazira.

Halfaouine

Halfaouine is one of Tunis's most fascinating areas, with a style completely its own. Originally a settlement outside the walls of the Medina proper, it was endowed with its own well and fortifications under the Hafsids. Recently, the suburb achieved a certain fame through Férid Boughedir's film of the same name, which ran away with most of the prizes at the 1990 Carthage Festival.

On the north side of place Bab Souika, a vaulted entrance leads into the **food markets** of rue Halfaouine. On the right beyond place Bab Souika is the **Abu Mohamed Mosque**, a fine example of architecture from the Hafsid era, erected by public subscription. Associated with this mosque is a tradition of religious discussion meetings during Ramadan on the subject of the *hadiths* – sayings of Mohammed.

Rue Halfaouine eventually gives onto **place Halfaouine**. Having begun life as one of the commodity markets common on the edges of the old city, this square had become the heart of an exclusive district by the eighteenth century, thanks largely to the efforts of Youssef Sahib et Tabaa, Hammouda Bey's last prime minister. Youssef rose from Hammouda's *mameluke* (slave intended for high office) at the beginning of his reign to the post of Sahib et Tabaa, the second most powerful man in the country. He owned ships in his own name and became wealthy through piracy and international trade, using some of his fortune to commission the mosque here as well as the neighbouring Souk el Jedid, site of his personal palace. Unfortunately, Youssef's forthright personality made him vulnerable after Hammouda's death, and in January 1815, only thirteen months after his master's death, Youssef was assassinated after a rival Tunisian-born official called Larbi Zarrouk convinced Hammouda's successor, Mahmoud Bey, that Youssef was a threat.

With its trees and benches, place Halfaouine retains an air of decaying quasi-European elegance, belying the fact that this quiet backwater was once notorious for nationalist demonstrations against the French. Facing the square, the **Youssef Sahib et Tabaa Mosque**, begun in 1812, is one of the most beautiful and unusual in Tunisia, closer to a Venetian palazzo than the Great Mosque of Kairouan: perhaps the finest example of Tunisian Cosmopolitan building. The blend of local and Italian elements is at its most successful here, with metal railings, Neo-classical columns and flamboyant black marble – all of them foreign – made to seem perfectly in place. The minaret was only half finished when Youssef met his premature end – which perhaps contributed to a story that the same would happen to the person who completed the minaret. It was finally completed in 1970.

Behind the mosque, at 9 rue du Salut, is the crumbling **Zaouia of Sidi Ali Chiha**, off rue Sidi el Aloui, which leads into an elongated square full of palm trees. Cross rue Bab Saadoun at the other end of the square and in front of you is the **En Nefefta Mosque** on the corner of rue des Arcs and impasse de la Mosquée. The building you see is modern, but the mosque was founded in the fifteenth century and parts of the interior structure date back to that period.

In the northwest corner of place Halfaouine is the **Souk el Jedid**, a vaulted passage leading out into rue Zaouia el Bokria. The souk, commissioned by Sahib et Tabaa, now specializes in clothes. As you emerge, keep straight ahead along **rue Sidi Abdessalem**. A small room known as a **sabat** crosses the street here at first-floor level; it houses a *kouttab* (Koranic school) attached to the *masjid* (small mosque). This complex of buildings is characteristic of old Medina quarters – the local primary school attached to the parish church, as it were. Right at the end of rue Sidi Abdessalem on a sliver of open space stands the bulbous-domed **fountain of Sahib et Tabaa**, another of his municipal works in this quarter. The fountain was originally located just inside one of the Hafsid city gates, Bab Sidi Abdessalem, so that travellers arriving from the country could refresh themselves, and nowadays it's usually surrounded by a flea market.

Boulevard Hedi Saidi to Bab el Khadra

Beyond the fountain of Sahib et Tabaa runs **boulevard Hedi Saidi**, where you can pick up a bus going west to the Bardo Museum (see p.89). A few hundred metres to the left, **Bab Saadoun**, once one of the city's outer gates but now a traffic island at a major road junction, looks rather lost. Beyond it is the bus station serving the north of the country. South of Bab Saadoun is Rabta Hill, site of two Ottoman forts, **Borj Flifel** and **Borj er Rabta**, both built in the mid-eighteenth century. Nearby, yet another fort, **Borj Zouara** (or Borj el Andalous), dates back to the seventeenth century.

Heading east from Bab Sidi Abessalem, boulevard Hedi Saidi takes you to **Bab el Assel**, yet another of the city's gates. As you approach it, you'll see the **Sidi Yahya Mosque** on your right. Built as a *masjid* in the fourteenth century by the saint whose name it bears, it was elevated to the status of *jemaa* (Friday mosque) by the Hafsids because of its strategic position. Turn left just before the mosque and have a look round behind it, and you will see the entrance to the old **Bab el Assel fort** at 25 rue du Fort, now a private house. A plaque above the doorway dates it at 1216 AH (1801 AD).

Here, too, begins a huge chunk of the **old wall**, currently undergoing restoration. It starts just past the Sidi Yahya Mosque, and then runs by the Bab el Assel sports centre, where you get a good view of it through the perimeter railings. Follow the pavement round into avenue Bechir Sfar and take the first right into rue du Miel. The entrance to the sports centre is on your right if you want a closer look; otherwise take a left down the little street full of carpenters' workshops. You'll be walking parallel with the wall, still there behind the houses on your left. The street emerges at another of the old forts, **Borj Sidi el Bsili**, again dating back to the turn of the nineteenth century. The Ministry of Culture has plans to restore it and open it to the public.

A left turn here down avenue Bechir Sfar brings you, after 100m or so, to perhaps the city's oddest gate, **Bab el Khadra**. This double-doorwayed piece of a fairytale castle is not the fourteenth-century original, but a rebuilt version dating back to 1881.

Behind the right-hand doorway is **rue de la Verdure**, a name referring, like that of the gate, to the "greenery" of the countryside which used to start outside it. Halfway along rue de la Verdure, the impasse de Sidi el Halfaoui (on the left) leads to the **Zaouia of Sidi el Halfaoui**, containing the tomb of the seventeenth-century saint after whom the Halfaouine district is named. Non-Muslims can't enter, but you can glimpse the saint's tomb through a grille by the door.

Rue de la Verdure runs onto a square from where rue Hammam Remimi will take you straight back to Bab Souika. Much better, however, is a stroll down **rue Souiki Bel Khir**, straight ahead, which runs past various interesting cul-de-sacs and under the odd *sabat* (room crossing the street at first-floor level) to end up back in place Halfaouine.

Western districts

As with Halfaouine in the north, the Medina's western and southern fringes are occupied by ancient districts dating back to Hafsid times. Directly west, the **Kasbah district** was the former seat of government, while **Montfleury**, also known as **Bab Jazira**, further south, was a residential quarter.

Place de la Kasbah, on the western edge of the Medina, is always crowded with civil servants from the various government departments located hereabouts (this makes it a good place to catch a taxi). Sweeping north around the Medina, **boulevard Bab**

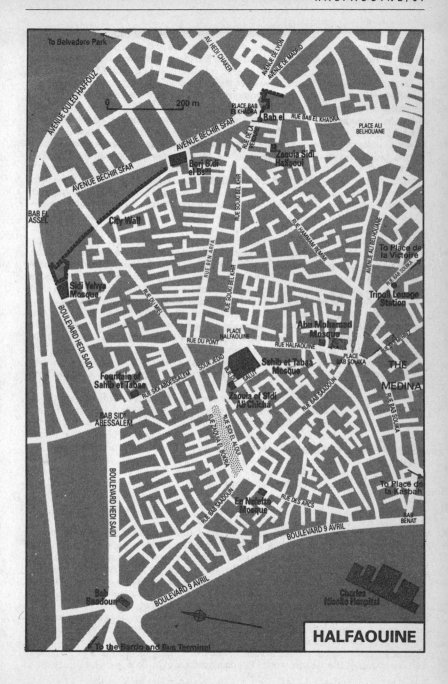

HALFAOUINE

Menara passes **Sadiki College** with its two domes, founded by Khereddin in 1875 and inevitably described as Tunisia's Eton, where Bourguiba and other future leaders were educated. Right below it, next to the street, is the **tomb of Farhat Hached**, the trade union leader murdered by reactionary French colonialists in 1952 (see p.371).

Place de la Kasbah gets its name from the fort that stood here above the Medina in Hafsid times, which has almost completely disappeared except for the **Kasbah Mosque**. Seven hundred and fifty years after it was built in 1235, though, the mosque still sets a standard for Tunisia. Arriving as part of an Almohad empire based in Marrakesh, the Hafsids wanted to make a clear statement of their origins, and this mosque's minaret – square, with decorated lozenge designs in relief – is immediately identifiable as part of the same family as the Kutubiyya in Marrakesh, the Hassan in Rabat and the Giralda in Seville. When a new Malekite minaret was needed for the Great Mosque in 1834, this was the model that the architects used. Notice that the lozenge design is more subtle than it at first looks, with a different design on the north and south faces from the one on the east and west. Perhaps because of its elevated position, the mosque signals to the rest of the city for the call to prayer: five times a day a white flag is hung out from the minaret.

The rest of the Hafsid kasbah stood on the other side of rue 2 Mars from the mosque, where a stark modern monument and plaza recently replaced the last excavations. Its last occupant was a French barracks installed in 1881 and levelled in 1957, but the Hafsid kasbah really lost its importance after the Turks moved the seat of government into Dar el Bey in the early seventeenth century. Unfortunately, the historical significance of the site has made it a favourite place for architects trying to express the more grandiose aspirations of the newly independent state, although, to be fair, the current RCD headquarters building on top of the hill was recognized as a mistake as soon as it was erected in 1974. The best thing to do is move quickly up rue 2 Mars, passing ministries on the left as well as the **9th of April Museum** (opening times uncertain; free), which is devoted to Habib Bourguiba and the struggle for independence (see p.371), complete with one of the many prison cells where the great man resided under French rule. Unless you speak Arabic and happen to be passing, it's not really worth the effort.

At the top of the hill, you pass a surviving stretch of kasbah **wall** and an old city gate, **Bab Sidi Abdallah**, before hitting boulevard 9 Avril 1938; bear left here for a couple of hundred metres until a tree-lined square opens up to your left, with the green pyramidal roof of the Zaouia of Sidi Kassem el Jelizi at the near corner (see below). Fume-ridden city artery though it may be, boulevard 9 Avril 1938 runs along the top of a ridge here and offers a fine view down over Sebkhet Sejoumi, round to the Jellaz Cemetery and beyond to Lake Tunis. From this viewpoint, it's easy to understand the city's appalling climate – as the eighteenth-century traveller James Bruce put it, "low, hot and damp".

The Zaouia of Sidi Kassem Jelizi and around

Fortunately, the **Zaouia of Sidi Kassem Jelizi** (daily 8am–4pm; free) is more than adequate compensation for coming this far: the most accessible piece of late Hafsid architecture in the city, with a strong flavour of Spain and some eastern influence as well. Abou el Fadl Kassem Ahmed as-Sadafi al-Fasi came originally from Fez, but he is thought to have learned the trade that earned him the title Jalizi ("Potter") in Spain. When his mausoleum was built, in 1490, it would have enjoyed a prominent position crowning this ridge at the edge of the Hafsid city. It begins with an entrance hall leading past a small prayer hall on the right into a courtyard. Rooms on three sides, designed originally for pilgrims and visitors but now displaying pottery exhibits, give way on the fourth to the tomb itself, whose pyramidal green-tiled roof – reminiscent of Granada and built at the time of Granada's fall to the Christians – gives the building its Spanish feel. Looking to the other end of the Islamic world, the courtyard paving's bold geometric patterns in black marble – found elsewhere in Tunis in the Midhat es Soltane and in palaces of a slightly later date – are more reminiscent of Cairo. No one is sure whether the patterns here and in the Midhat are original or whether they were added later under the Turks. Inside the tomb, however, the tone is all Spanish. In particular, don't miss the star-patterned tiles in the flat niche opposite the tomb-room entrance. Outside the mausoleum proper, a small yard shelters a large collection of headstones, the Hafsid ones having plain columns and the later Turkish examples crowned with a turban. Opposite the *zaouia*, across the place du Résidence du Leader, where Bourguiba once lived, stands the strangely squat minaret of the **Jemaa el Haoua**, founded in the thirteenth century by Queen Atif, wife of the Hafsid Sultan Abu Zakariya.

Make your way to the bottom right-hand corner of place du Résidence and out along rue Abd el Wahab. This shortly comes to a junction with rue Gorjani, across which and slightly to the right, **place aux Chevaux**, with its miniature football pitch, almost immediately becomes **place du Marché du Blé**, the start of a great junk market, where you can pick up anything from old shoe buckles to metal utensils. In the past, these two areas were the markets where city merchants would deal with farmers bringing in grain and animals from the countryside. Turn sharp left here into rue Et Tohma, following the junk, and head downhill. At the bottom of the hill, Saida Manoubia emerges under the squat minaret of the **Mosque of El Helaak**, traditionally held to have been founded in 1375 by a freed black slave who sold his gold jewellery to pay for it. Down to your right, **Souk el Asser** is a babble of eateries and food stalls. A left here will take you to **Bab Jedid**, the Medina gate visible down the hill, where you could hook up with the southern Medina tour (see p.79).

To continue, go straight ahead into the pillared tunnel of rue Hajjamine (forking right after emerging from the tunnel to stay on Hajjamine). When Hajjamine hits rue Abou Kassem el Chabbi, cross the road and continue past a green-domed tomb, down into a small open space surrounded by tombs of eighteenth- and nineteenth-century worthies. Take the lower, left-hand fork out of here and continue on Hajjamine to where rue En Naial comes in on the right – immediately opposite on the left, rue Sidi Mansour heads off downhill, passing a *masjid* with a weedy green-tiled roof at rue Er Raia, and eventually hitting **rue Bab el Fellah** – recognizable as a main drag of the old quarter.

Left on Bab el Fellah will take you back up to **Bab Jazira**, the southern gate out of the Medina, which is dominated by the minaret of the **Mosque of Sidi el Bechir**. A right on Bab el Fellah will take you further south to Bab Alleoua bus station and the **Jellaz Cemetery**, a huge and very pleasant hillside burial ground founded in the thirteenth century. According to legend, the founder was a saint whose servant bought the land from a Jew so that poor Muslims could be buried there. In 1911 it was the scene of the first mass demonstration against the French, when the municipal council threatened to requisition the land for development. A shot was fired – some said by an Italian spectator, others by a French officer – killing a young boy. In the riot that ensued, nine Frenchmen, five Italians and over thirty Tunisians died.

The cemetery is dominated by the seventeenth-century **Borj Ali Rais**, an Ottoman fortress visible from the whole city but, unfortunately, closed to the public. It's also known as Borj Sidi Bel Hassen after the nearby **Zaouia of Sibi Bel Hassen**, which was built in 1815 but dedicated to a thirteenth-century marabout said to have introduced coffee to Tunisia.

The Bardo Museum

Housed in the former Beylical Palace (the royal palace of the Bey, or Regent) west of the city centre, the **Bardo Museum** (Tues–Sun 9am–6pm; 1TD, plus 1TD to take photos) is one of those museums that is almost too well endowed. Its encyclopedic

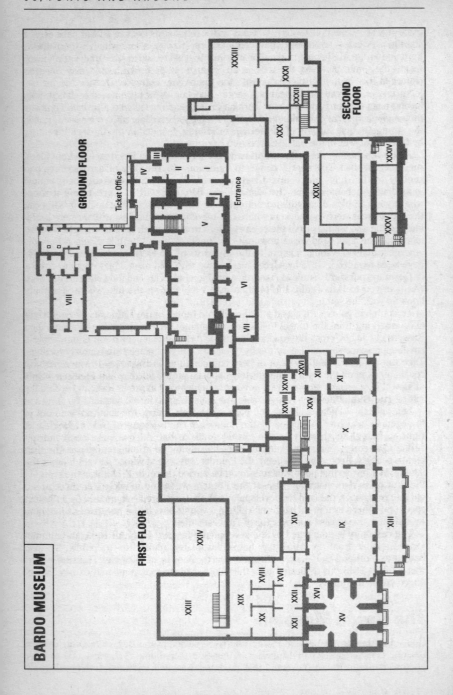

BARDO MUSEUM

GROUND FLOOR

Ticket Office

III
IV
II
I

Entrance

V

VIII

VI

VII

SECOND FLOOR

XXXIII

XXXI

XXXII

XXX

XXXIV

XXIX

XXXV

FIRST FLOOR

XXIV

XXIII

XIX

XVIII

XVII

XX

XXI

XVI

XV

XIV

IX

XIII

X

XI

XII

XXV

XXVI

XXVII

XXVIII

collection of Roman mosaics is really too much to take in on a single visit, but even a glimpse of some of the designs will flesh out the Roman sites in the country, and a second visit afterwards will complete the picture. The building itself is spectacular, built up over centuries and surrounded by gardens full of Roman and Punic stones; as you wander around the collections, note the ceilings especially.

It's a thirty-minute journey from the city centre by bus #3 from avenue Bourguiba, bus #3c, #4, #4c, #4d, #23, #23b, #23c, or #23t from Jardin Thameur, or several others from Bab Saadoun. The metro (line #4) runs to 20 Mars station, a short walk away, and should soon be extended to the museum's own station.

Confusingly, rooms in the Bardo are sometimes numbered and sometimes named after the particular sites most of the exhibits come from (and sometimes both). Another potential confusion is that the museum's collections are contained in two separate series of rooms. The larger and more impressive is the **ancient collection** (mainly Roman), which sits in rooms numbered from I to XXXV. The **Islamic collection**, called the Arab Museum, is housed in another set of rooms located within the Roman collection. In summer you might think about starting at the top of the building, so that you don't get up there just as it receives the full attention of the midday sun.

Ground floor
Punic rooms (II–IV) Clay **statues** reflect the influence of Greece on Mediterranean culture but retain an eastern flavour – those from the eighth century BC look like stiff Egyptian figures; by the third century BC you find a seated **Demeter** with drapery used in Greek style to allow the figure to break into three dimensions; but as late as the first century AD, a **Tanit** from Thinissut (just above Hammamet) still has a lion's head and the two-dimensional pose of an Egyptian or early Greek figure. Grotesquely grimacing masks from the seventh century BC are distinctively local, as are the seven men and one woman lined up on a dark **stone relief** from Chemtou (second-century BC – in the corridor outside room IV), looking like chocolates in a box.

Christian room (V) A fifth-century **mosaic** from Tabarca on the wall (A307) shows in cartoon fashion a three-aisled basilica or church similar to the many to be found in Tunisia's ancient cities. Similarly, the sixth-century four-way **baptistry** in the middle of the room (from as far away as El Kantara, in Djerba) was to reappear many times – including at George Sebastian's 1920s villa in Hammamet. A right at the top of the main staircase out of this room will take you into the **"Arab Museum"**, a series of rooms containing applied arts from Tunisia and elsewhere in the Muslim world.

Bulla Regia room (VI) The prize of this collection of monumental marble statuary is a rock star-like Apollo with his lyre, who originally stood in his own temple at Bulla Regia.

Imperial Portraits room (VII) The next room contains some fine portrait heads of Roman emperors, including one ultra-realistic one (Inv 3212) of **Gordian I**, the ill-fated elderly tax collector from El Djem who ruled the Empire for a month before committing suicide.

New Christian department (C) One of the Bardo's star exhibits is a **baptistry** (Inv 3382) from Kelibia, dedicated to Saint Cyprian, the bishop martyred in Carthage in 258, which is covered in a mosaic that is richly decorative and symbolic.

Sarcophagus and stele corridor (D) In the long corridor on the way to the Thuburbo Maius room (VIII), look for an unusual and engaging **third-century AD statue** found at Borj el Amri (Inv 3047) of a hooded man with a face like a gloomy Fred Flintstone, depicted in the realistic style common at the time; otherwise he is little more than a tailor's dummy festooned with symbols: his lionskin hood and the club he originally held in his left hand are attributes of Hercules; the drape of his tunic suggests female breasts; and in his right hand he holds a bouquet of poppies and

ROMAN AND ISLAMIC ART

Africa's **Roman mosaics**, of which the Bardo has by far the largest collection in the world, are arguably the most colourful and vivid images left behind by a Roman Empire better known for its monumental feats of engineering. Like an album of colour snapshots, they offer a direct and beautiful visual record of what was considered important by this extraordinarily successful civilization. Native Romans at home in Italy painted their walls so colourfully that they preferred their floor mosaics to be monochrome black and white. In Africa, though, wall-painting was never widespread, and mosaics developed as almost the only form of domestic decoration.

Seeing the mosaics in such exuberant quantity makes it easy to take them for granted. These were the Persian rugs of the ancient world, requiring enormous time and skill to lay out, and the fact that most were privately commissioned for homes says a good deal about the status-conscious social structure of the time.

The **subjects** were probably also chosen by the commissioner, so the emphasis on (broadly speaking) entertainment is significant. Hunting, fishing, the amphitheatre and, to a lesser extent, theatrical themes, are all indicative of the leisure activities enjoyed by the wealthy. Even the mythological and religious scenes have a strongly hedonistic slant: **Bacchus**, the god of wine and sensual pleasure in general, features heavily, often shown triumphant over the forces of evil. **Venus**, goddess of love, usually has her vampish side strongly emphasized. Most noticeable of all, though, is the feeling of abundance. The **sea** is always shown crammed with endless varieties of fish (including the lobsters which wave in the god Ocean's hair), rural **farming scenes** are a constant, and lush vines weave their way through and around almost every scene. The mosaics evoke a life of sensual gratification and plenty, neatly summed up in an inscription found at Timgad in Algeria: "To hunt, to bathe, to gamble, to laugh, that is to live."

wheat, symbols of the Greek cult of Demeter; the dog at his feet is probably the hellhound Cerberus, captured by Hercules as one of his labours.

Thuburbo Maius room (VIII) Though fragmentary, Inv 124 – a **relief** showing two Maenads (worshippers of Dionysus) twisting in the ecstasy of worship – is one of the finest pieces of sculpture in the museum. One holds above her head the knife she has used to carve up the sacrificial goat whose two halves the women hold. This first-century AD Roman copy evokes the style of high classical Greek sculpture of the fifth century BC.

First floor

Carthage room (IX) Set in the floor at the far end of this lavish central hall is the first of a series of documentary-like **mosaics** of rural life in Roman Tunisia (A105), dating from early third-century Oudna. Among the numerous pieces of statuary, keep an eye out for a stately full-length **portrait of a robed woman** leaning with one hand on an incense burner. Her pose and drapery are direct descendants from Greek originals of the fourth century BC. Five hundred years later, this fine statue was probably made in Rome to commemorate a woman who lived far away in Haidra, where it was found.

Hadrumetum (Sousse) room (X) Three semicircular scenes from the same room in fourth-century Tabarca show the components of a large agricultural estate: the owner's house (A25); the farm building (A26); and barns and store rooms (A27). From Carthage in the following century, the famous **Seigneur Julius mosaic** (Inv 1) shows Julius himself sitting at his leisure at bottom right, opposite his wife, who leans against a pillar (in a similar Greek fourth-century BC pose to that of the Haidra statue in the Carthage room). Above them in the middle panel stands their house – the domed roofs suggest a baths complex – surrounded by preparations for a hunt. Agricultural scenes

Towards the end of the Roman era, and into the Byzantine, the increasingly tense stylization of the mosaics reflects a less carefree society, permeated by a stricter spiritual discipline intended to preserve it in a hostile world. Although there's nothing here to match the early Byzantine mosaics of Ravenna, the tauter styles can come as a relief after the more florid imperial mosaics.

Because it had to be imported at great expense, **marble statuary** was less common in Africa than in other parts of the Roman world. Carthage, though, was richly stocked with figures of all types, primarily important men and women: generals, senators, sponsors, emperors and other worthies. The museum has a fine, though typically damaged selection: it's worth pointing out that the systematic **de-nosing and emasculation** of male statues was the routine work of invading Vandals, presumably mutilating and castrating their enemies in stone as well as flesh. The absence of any other kinds of representation would have endowed these statues with a significance verging on the divine that's hard to imagine in our image-glutted century.

There is also a stunning collection of bronze and marble figures and domestic furniture, recovered from the so-called **"Mahdia wreck"**. In 1907 fishermen off Mahdia found this ancient shipwreck, dating from the first century BC. Its cargo gives an impression of the style in which contemporary Romans lived.

Islamic art, which shuns the human image, is at the other extreme. The ban on the human form has not always been total, and the rooms here contain one or two rare early exceptions. But for the most part, Islamic artists have concentrated on decorative pattern and colour, a combination most brilliantly exemplified in a room of ceramic **tiles** taken from inside old mosques. The best are those brought by the Turks from Iznik, with their vegetal designs and bright colours still fresh after hundreds of years. There are other tiles from Tunisia itself, in characteristic blues, greens and yellows, and from Morocco, distinguishable by their tighter geometric patterns.

in the top panel include olives being harvested from a tree in the top left corner. Finally, an endearingly crude mosaic from **Byzantine Gafsa** (A19) suggests that the Roman's staple leisure pursuits – like chariot racing – survived the Vandal occupation and continued into the sixth century.

Dougga room (XI) The **Cyclopes Baths** in Dougga were named after A261, one of the most vivid mosaics in the museum. Three muscular cyclopes (mythical figures who usually have only one eye) wield hammers as they forge thunderbolts for Jupiter. The composition is very sophisticated, with one of the group shown from behind. Originally the floor of a *frigidarium*, perhaps this mosaic's scene was designed to warm up its chilled viewers. A382, also from Dougga, shows how bathers recovered, with two servants pouring wine from amphorae on which are inscribed the message "Drink and you will live".

El Jem room (XII) A288 shows third-century hunting scenes to delight the heart of any bloodsport enthusiast.

Althiburos room (XIII) Five named bullfighting stars carouse in Inv 3361 at a table that looks like an amphitheatre. Each of the drinkers wears a token identifying him with one of the professional gladiators' guilds. A worried-looking servant runs towards them, finger to his lips, saying "Silentium, tauri dormiant!" – "Quiet, let the bulls sleep!". Sure enough, one of the bullfighters' intended victims is struggling to its feet. After the relaxed sophistication of third-century El Jem, Inv 3618 from Beja, dated to the fifth or sixth century, looks like a child's cartoon.

Oudna room (XIV) On either side of the door, look for A150 and A152. Remains of a feast lie on a dark background: eggshells, fish heads, lemon peel, bread. Using especially fine tesserae, the second-century artist has left an astonishingly vivid still life – you can almost smell the sauce.

Virgil room (XV) This is dominated by the eponymous **Virgil mosaic**, found in Sousse and generally dated to the third century. The author of the Aeneid (see p.407) sits between Clio, Muse of History (to his right), and Melpomene, Muse of Tragedy. He holds a scroll of the Aeneid, open at line 8. Just off the Virgil room is a small but spectacular collection of **Carthaginian jewellery**.

Mahdia rooms (XVII–XXII) This spectacular collection of **Greek bronze statuary** went down in a shipwreck off Mahdia at the end of the first century AD and lay on the seabed until discovered in 1907. Greek art was highly prized in the Roman world and travelled widely around the Mediterranean – excavations in the Roman city of Volubilis in modern Morocco unearthed a good deal of it. Characteristic of a late Greek interest in the freakish are F213–215, a group of grotesque dwarves.

Mosaic rooms (XXV–XXVIII) Beyond the Mahdia rooms are a couple of rooms of **mosaics**. Inv 2884 in room XXVII shows **Ulysses** bound to the mast of his ship and heroically resisting the calls of three sirens. Nearby, Inv 2884A from Dougga has another nautical scene from myth in a more flowing style reminiscent of the Cyclopes mosaic in room XI. Some pirates in the Tyrrhenian Sea have attacked a ship only to find it's carrying the god **Dionysus**. Clad in a tunic and brandishing a lance, he has repelled the boarders, who hurl themselves overboard, pursued by Dionysus's panthers – unnecessarily, since the pirates are already metamorphosing into dolphins. The scene is completely stolen by the balding boozy Silenus, who clutches the steering oar for support.

Mausoleum Room (XXIV) Mosaic Inv 1393 once allowed wealthy citizens of Thuburbo Maius (whose floor it was), to indulge twice over in their gourmet pleasures in the *triclinium* or dining room. Munching away at their meal, they could stare at the floor and contemplate the background of a well-stocked ocean filled with various game animals and birds, bound and ready for the pot.

Second floor

Mosaic rooms (XXX–XXXII) An unlikely fourth-century scene from Le Kef in room XXX (Inv 2819) shows a herd of ostriches being prepared for the chase in an amphitheatre. Inv 3575 in the same room goes into unusually graphic detail. Beneath the placid gaze of spectators, a lion faces off against a gladiator, who jabs his spear into the lion's chest. Blood drips profusely onto the ground.

Acholla room (XXXIII) Acholla, a Roman port north of Sfax of which little remains today, produced a group of **mosaics** as spectacular as any in the country. One of these, Inv 3588, depicts the Labours of Hercules. The hero himself, equipped with lion skin, club and bow, occupies the central roundel, surrounded by others containing his opponents: triple-headed Geryon above, the River Acheloos below, and so on.

Fresco rooms (XXXIV–XXXV) One of a series of rare surviving fragments of wall painting, B84 – like so many mosaics – takes for its theme the good things of life, depicting a bottle of wine wrapped in straw, a bag full of eggs and a leg of ham.

Eating and drinking

Opportunities for **eating and drinking** in Tunis are concentrated on **avenue Bourguiba** and the streets to either side. Since the Medina closes down fairly early in the evening, there are fewer restaurants there than you might expect, though **Bab Jazira** and **Bab Souika**, at its northern and southern tips respectively, are pretty lively in the evenings, with enough tea shops and cheap restaurants to satisfy any appetite.

Restaurants

There are plenty of inexpensive **restaurants** in Tunis, most of which will fill you up for 3–4TD. Cheaper still, almost every street in the city has a rôtisserie, where you can either eat a plate of fried food standing up or take away a sandwich (*casse-croûte*). Several cluster around the junction of rue Ibn Khaldoun and rue de Yougoslavie. There are better quality places south of avenue Bourguiba and, on the northern side, the early stretches of avenue de Paris and rue de Marseille. Inside the Medina, restaurants tend to be cramped and uninspiring, but there are a few exceptions.

Fine dining is one of the legacies of French rule, and Tunis is peppered with elegant Gallic establishments. The food and ambience in these places is everything you would expect from their equivalents in France, but far cheaper: you can get a memorable meal with wine for about 15TD, or even cheaper set menus. Foreign cuisines are otherwise thin on the ground – apart from the rather awful and widely available pizzas.

We've included the phone numbers for all restaurants where you need to book.

Tunisian restaurants

Abid, 98 rue de Yougoslavie. No-nonsense nosh at no-nonsense prices.

Carcassonne, 8 av de Carthage. The four-course set menu will stuff you full and must be one of the best deals in the country.

Capitole, 60 av Bourguiba. A reasonably priced place downstairs from (but otherwise unconnected with) the hotel of the same name.

Erriadh, 9 rue Ibn Khaldoun. Another budget eatery around the corner from the *Abid* and almost identical.

Goulue, 3 rue de la Monnaie, off av Bourguiba by pl 7 Novembre. All stainless steel and glass self-service place.

Istanbul, 4 rue Pierre Courbertin. In case you wondered if there was anywhere cheaper than the *Carcassonne*, this is it. Huge servings at rock-bottom prices.

Mahdoui, rue Jemaa Zitouna. Right by the Great Mosque and something of an institution, this place is open lunchtime only but does the best couscous in town at moderate prices.

Majestic, 36 av de la Liberté (☎01/242666). Part of the hotel of the same name, the *Majestic*'s 5TD set menu remains ever-popular.

Le Malouf, 108 rue de Yougoslavie (☎01/243180). Similar fare and prices to the *M'Rabet* (see below) but less style, although there is regular live *malouf* music.

Le Marhaba, 166 rue de la Kasbah. Dirt cheap spit 'n' sawdust joint in the mid-Medina.

M'Rabet, Souk et Trouk (☎01/261729). Situated in the heart of the Medina and built over the tombs of three holy men. Probably the most stylish place in town to splurge seriously, a meal and the accompanying show (belly-dancing or similar entertainment) will cost around 20TD a head. A bit touristy.

Le Neptune, 3 rue du Caire. A less satisfying four-courser than at the *Carcassonne* but still cheap.

L'Orient, 7 rue Ali Bach Hamba (☎01/242058). A long-time budget favourite, still going strong.

French-style restaurants

Chez Nous, 5 rue de Marseille (☎01/243043). The four-course set menu is excellent value and includes a very good chocolate mousse. Muhammad Ali, Michael York and Edith Piaf are among the celebs who've patronized it and whose photos deck the walls.

Chez Slah, 16 rue Pierre Coubertin (☎01/258588). Discreetly tucked away in a small street, and possibly the best restaurant in town.

Le Cosmos, 7 rue Ibn Khaldoun (☎01/241610). Good food in a pleasant atmosphere. Recommended.

Dar el Jeld, rue Dar el Jeld, off pl Gouvernement (☎01/256326). On the western side of the Medina, this eatery is top of the range in both price and quality.

L'Étoile, 3 rue Ibn Khaldoun (☎01/240514). Good value at under 10TD a meal.

Gaston's, 73 rue de Yougoslavie. Specializes in seafood and has a cheap set menu weekday lunchtimes.

Restaurant des Margaritas, 6 bis rue d'Hollande (☎01/240632). Attached to the *Hôtel Maison Dorée*, this place is expensive à la carte, but has more a moderate tourist menu.

Le Petite Hutte, 102 rue de Yougoslavie (☎01/244959). One of Tunis's most highly regarded eateries that is as discreet and quiet as any Paris neighbourhood restaurant.

Ethnic cuisine

Hong Kong, 85 av Taieb Mehiri, up near the Belvedere (☎01/285311). A good Chinese place that's more renowned than the *Shogun*, with similarly moderate prices.

Le Robinson, 14 av de Madrid (☎01/249051). Tunisia's only kosher restaurant, doing affordable Sephardic Jewish specialities such as stuffed tongue and *boulette* (a sort of meatball), as well as kosher versions of traditional Tunisian dishes.

Shogun, 80 av Hedi Chaker. If you really can't live without a Chinese, this reasonably priced establishment is one of the nearest to the city centre.

La Mamma, 11bis rue de Marseille (☎01/241256). Your best bet for Italian food short of crossing the water, with reasonably priced pizzas, pasta and similar fare.

Vietnamien, 26 rue Amine el Abassi (☎01/282251). Better and more expensive than either of the Chinese restaurants.

Cafés, patisseries and bars

Traditional **cafés**, found all over the city and sometimes equipped with *chichas* (hubble-bubble pipes), are crowded places where men drink coffee in various forms and women may not feel very comfortable. The café's territory, however, is being gradually invaded by **patisseries** offering snacks as well as pastries, which is where Tunisian women tend to go for fast food or midday breaks – a good choice is *Ben Yedder*, 7 rue Charles de Gaulle, where you can get sandwiches and coffee, as well as the more traditional pastries, sweets and citronade. A more expensive alternative where women can feel relatively comfortable are the **café-bars** in big hotels, or the central *Café de Paris* on avenue Bourguiba, where you can happily sit and watch the crowds passing by. Try the café-bars at the *Africa*, 50 av Bourguiba; the *International*, 49 av Bourguiba; or the *Majestic*, 36 av de Paris. The best and cheapest café-bar on avenue Bourguiba, however, is the *Capitole*, open 24 hours, seven days a week, and serving up crêpes, freshly pressed fruit juice and *lait de poule*.

Tunisian **bars** – small, crowded and very male-dominated – can be found mostly around the train station, though there are others scattered through the New Town on street corners (especially along avenue de la Liberté), and most close around 8pm. The Western-style bars attached to bigger hotels or cafés tend to be much more expensive. Alternatively, you can get away with drinking in some restaurants provided you order a plate, though this can work out just as expensive as ordering your beer in a posh hotel.

Entertainment and nightlife

Tunis's **nightlife** is fairly low-key, with the exception of **Ramadan**, when the city acquires a new lease of nightlife for the month. At other times, the city closes down at about 11pm. Crowds stroll along avenue Bourguiba, and mill around the streets to either side, but facilities in the city centre are limited. You're more likely to find **live music** at Sidi Bou Said (see p.110) than in the city centre, but with money to burn there are cabaret shows at restaurants offering slick pseudo-Oriental-style evenings.

Nightclubs and live music

Discos don't offer a very exciting alternative to just sitting at a café and watching the world go by, but if you feel the urge to get hot and sweaty under the disco lights, try *Pub Sandwich* on avenue de Carthage, or *Joker*, 49 av Habib Bourguiba. There are more sophisticated places out at the suburbs of La Marsa and Gammarth.

More interesting are the displays some restaurants provide of live **traditional music** to accompany your meal: *Carstop*, 73 rue de Yougoslavie, and *Le Malouf*, 108 rue de Yougoslavie, both put on good shows. *M'Rabet*, Souk et Trouk in the Medina, is pretty touristy, and there's also a show at *Le Palais*, 8 av de Carthage.

Concerts

Watch out, too, for events such as concerts of Arabic and western classical music at the **Théâtre Municipal** on avenue Bourguiba. These can be surprisingly cheap, especially if you flash a student card and don't mind sitting in the vertiginous upper circles. Occasional one-off performances by **foreign groups** are sponsored at a government level. Many use the *Maison de la Culture Ibn Khaldoun*, 16 rue Ibn Khaldoun, which also mounts seasons of classic movies.

Films

Cinema-going is a popular pastime in Tunis, with some twenty cinemas dotted around town. Matinées start around 3pm and there are usually shows at around 6pm and 9pm. Listings are published every day in *La Presse*.

The only art-house cinema in the city is *Afrah*, 1 rue 18 Janvier, which shows French-subtitled movies. More mainstream cinemas include *ABC*, 8 rue Ibn Khaldoun, and *Hani Jawharia*, 10 rue Ibn Khaldoun. Along avenue Bourguiba, you'll find *Colisée* at no. 45 (in the arcade), *Capitole* at no. 60, *Le Palace* at no. 54, and *Parnasse* at no. 63 (in the arcade).

The **Carthage International Film Festival**, a celebration of Arab and African cinema alternating yearly between Tunis and Ouagadougou (Burkina Faso), takes over the capital's cinemas every other November (1996, 1998) – probably your best chance to see some Tunisian films. Events are listed in *La Presse* and *Le Temps*.

Ramadan

During **Ramadan** (see p.43 for dates), there's plenty of eating, drinking and making merry until the early hours of the morning during the entire month. The centre of all this activity is **place Bab Souika** at the Medina's northern end, though construction of the underpass and new shops here has, for the time being at least, dampened the excitement. Otherwise, try the lively area of **Bab Jazira**, at the other end of the Medina.

Shopping

Tunis's **souks** not only form a fascinating area of warren-like lanes and passageways to explore, but they still function as the backbone of Tunis's trading community. Souk el Kachachine (p.75) is the place to come for wholesale **rugs** and **clothes**, and Souk et Trouk (p.77), built in the seventeenth century for Turkish tailors, is where you'll find the *Musée des Turcs* **carpet** shop. Souk de la Laine (p.75) no longer trades much wool, but has a few traditional **tailors**; one typically Tunisian article, the characteristic *chechia*, or skullcap, can be bought in the **Souk des Chechias** (p.78). The Souk des Orfèvres (p.75) is still home to **gold jewellers**, but the Souks of the Dyers (p.81), once part of the clothing industry, now houses a **drum-making workshop**, along with a limited amount of **dyeing**. Souk el Belat (p.80) and Souk el Asser (p.89) have **food** stalls.

A good place to start shopping if you're interested in buying local crafts is the **ONAT** (*Organisation National de l'Artisanat de Tunisie*) showroom, located in what looks like a flimsily built warehouse on avenue Mohamed V, about 200m up from the tourist office (p.60). Prices here are high, but you can get a good sense of the range of goods available before entering the maelstrom of the Medina's central souks, which are bewildering not only for the streaming crowds but for the assortment of merchandise available.

If you prefer the idea of buying **craft goods** that ordinary Tunisians use, and at much lower prices, hold your fire until you get to the further reaches of the Medina – the stalls outside the Mosque of Sidi Mehrez, for example (see p.83). More unusual shopping ideas might include **olive wood artefacts** from a shop in rue Sidi Ben Arous (see p.78), or leftover **colonial kitsch** from the bric-a-brac and furniture shops in rue des Glacières (see p.79).

For **books**, there's a limited selection of English-language novels at 10 rue d'Angleterre; at *Librairie Ben Abdallah* on avenue de France opposite *Magasin Général*; *Claire Fontaine*, 4 rue d'Alger; or *Mille Feuilles* in La Marsa, just off the end of the TGM. For books in French about current and historic Tunisia and Maghreb, try *Claire Fontaine*, *Mille Feuilles*, *Espace Diwan* on rue Sidi Ben Arous, just up from the Great Mosque in the heart of the Medina, or *Editions Alif* at 5 rue d'Hollande. *Alif* is well worth a visit for its Medina pop-up book and jigsaw puzzle, Corsair strip cartoons and a collection of overpriced colonial postcards. For **guidebooks**, there's *Espace Diwan*, as well as stalls on avenue Bourguiba and the big hotel lobbies. Die-hard tourists will find a massive collection of **postcards** at *Tanit*, 3 rue d'el Houdaybiyah, near the cathedral, and **posters** from the *ONTT* headquarters on avenue de la Liberté (see p.60). *Alif* (see above) is also always worth a try.

Standard tourist fodder is available on **rue Djemaa Zitouna** by the Great Mosque (p.74), which has turned into a cauldron of overflowing stalls and shops that tend to be more expensive than elsewhere, but there's also the stall selling interesting old metal lamps, chandeliers and pen cases. A little beyond the *zaouia* on the right of Mosque of Sidi Mehrez are several **pottery shops** (p.84) with a good selection of low-priced plates, cups, pots and ashtrays.

Listings

Airlines *Aeroflot*, 24 av Habib Thameur (☎01/341888); *Air Algérie*, 26 av de Paris (☎01/341587); *Air France*, 1 rue d'Athènes (☎01/341568); *Alitalia*, 17 av Bourguiba (☎01/247948); *Egyptair*, 49 av Bourguiba, in the back of the *Hôtel International* (☎01/341182) (*Gulf Air* are at the same address); *GB Airways*, 17 av Bourguiba (☎01/244261); *Iberia*, 17 av Habib Thameur (☎01/340238); *KLM*, 6 rue Lucie Faure (☎01/341309); *Libyan Arab Airlines*, 49 av de Paris (☎01/341646); *Lufthansa*, *Complexe Hôtel el Mechtel*, bd Ouled Haffouz, El Omrane (☎01/352019); *Royal Air Maroc*, 45 av Bourguiba (staircases C and D, 3rd floor; (☎01/249016); *Sabena*, Centre Commercial, Hôtel Abou Nawas, av Mohamed V (☎01/259845); *Swissair*, 45 av Bourguiba (☎01/342122); *Tunis Air*, 48 av Bourguiba (☎01/785100); *Tunisavia*, c/o *Tunisian Travel Service*, 19 av Bourguiba (☎01/254239); *TWA*, c/o *Tunis Air*.

American Express c/o *Carthage Tours*, 39 and 59 av Bourguiba (☎01/254304). Mail service very efficient (Mon–Sat mornings only); exchange service less so.

Arabic courses The *Bourguiba School*, 47 av de la Liberté, runs the cheapest residential Arabic course in the Middle East, with an eight-week intensive course in July–August, with the possibility of renting accommodation in the university, and eating in the college canteen. Alternatively, the school does non-intensive courses of 4hr a week during the academic year.

Banks Banks along av Bourguiba tend to get crowded in summer. Less packed locations include the *Franco-Tunisian Bank*, 13 and 8 rue d'Alger; *Banque du Sud*, 45 av de la Liberté, next to the

Bourguiba School; *BIAT*, 21 rue d'Algérie, by Bab Jazira. The *STB* next to the *Hôtel Africa* opens late and at weekends. Outside banking hours, you can change cash at the PTT and the *Hôtel Africa*, and possibly the *Hôtel Majestic*. Travellers' cheques are trickier but you could ask around the big hotels. You are supposed to be able to change money at the airport all night, but don't count on it. As a last resort, you may find someone at one of the international *louage* stations who will change cash for you.

Car rental There are several agencies on av Bourguiba and in the big hotels. The main ones also have a desk at the airport (☎01/288000 for all of them). The smaller agencies are usually cheaper but their cars may be older. *Hertz* are said to have the newest cars. City centre offices include *Avis*, 90 av de la Liberté (☎01/780593) – also in *Hôtel Africa*; *Ben Jemaa*, 53 av de Paris (☎01/240060); *Express*, 49bis rue de la Monnaie (☎01/354099); *Garage Lafayette*, 84 av de la Liberté (☎01/280284); *Hertz*, 29 av Bourguiba (☎01/248559); and *InterRent/Europcar*, 17 av Bourguiba (☎01/340308) and 99 av de la Liberté (☎01/287235).

Car repair Any French make, and Land Rovers, can be handled at most garages. British and American dealers are in very short supply.

Churches St George's Anglican church is at pl Bab Carthajana on the edge of the Medina: very friendly weekly service. Catholics can go to Mass in the Cathedral – irregularly in English – or at Ste Jeanne d'Arc church on pl Palestine, where there's an English service at 10am every Sunday. The Greek Orthodox church is on rue de Rome (round the corner from the cathedral) and worth a visit just to see the icons.

Embassies *Australia*, c/o Canadian Embassy; *Canada*, 3 rue de Sénégal (☎01/796577); *New Zealand*, c/o UK consulate; *UK*, 141–143 av de la Liberté (☎01/792838; visas Mon–Fri 8–11.30am; consular services 8am–1pm); *USA*, 144 av de la Liberté (☎01/782566).

Emergencies Police ☎197; *Protection civil* (fire brigade) ☎198; Ambulance ☎01/341250, 341280 (for other medical numbers see "Medical Facilities", below).

Football Tunis has two main clubs, *Ésperance Sportif* and *Club Africain*, sharing the El Monza ground up in the *Cité Olympique*, where they play at home alternate weeks, usually Sunday at 2pm or 4pm, depending on the time of year. The best way to get up to El Monza is by metro to *Jeunesse* (line #2), or you could walk. To avoid the mad scramble for tickets, you're advised to arrive well before the match. Other metropolitan teams are *Avenir Sportif de la Marsa* (ASM) and *Club Sportif de Hammam Lif* (CSHL).

Hammams Ubiquitous but well hidden – ask at your hotel for the nearest. Hammams in Tunis are usually single-sex, which means that you can use them all day. One of the oldest is at 75 rue des Teinturiers (daily 4am–midnight or 24hr during Ramadan; men only), but it's rather a dump. Also for men is the *Hammam Kachachine* at 30 Souk des Librairies (daily 5am–5pm). There's a women's hammam in Souk el Belat (daily 6am–7pm) and one at 1 rue Noria (daily 6am–9pm). Further away, there's another at 45 av Lyon (daily 8am–5pm).

Laundry *Laverie*, 15 rue d'Allemagne, charges by the kilo (closed Sun).

Medical facilities Emergency **ambulance** ☎01/341250, 341280. For **minor complaints** or injuries, an *infirmerie* should be able to sort you out. A wound dressing and tetanus jab, for example, will cost around 3TD. There are **infirmeries** at 23 rue Ibn Khaldoun, 20 av de la Liberté, 32 av Bab Jedid, 59 rue al Jazira and 150 rue Bab Souika. There are two recommended **cliniques**, the *Taoufik* (☎01/288211) and the *El Manar* (☎01/891515). The best **hospital** is the *Hospital Charles Nicolle*, bd 9 Avril 1938, northwest of the Medina by Bab Benat (☎01/664215; accident ☎01/664211). For **specialized treatment**, ask your consulate for a list of doctors; in an **emergency** try the phone numbers listed in *Le Temps* or *La Presse*, which also list *pharmacies de service* – weekend and all-night pharmacies (see below).

Newspapers A wide range of foreign papers can be bought at the stands under the trees in the middle of av Bourguiba.

Passport photos A lot of places do these fast and cheaply. Try 23 rue Jemal Abdel Nasser (near the PTT), 32 rue al Jazira (on the corner of rue Ecosse), 59 rue Mongi Slim, av de France (next to the cathedral, on the corner of rue de Rome), or several places up av de la Liberté on your way to the embassy zone.

Pharmacies All-night pharmacies are located at 43 av Bourguiba, 20 av de la Liberté, 44 av Bab Jedid and 47 av Ali Belhouane.

Post and phones The main PTT, for stamps and poste restante, is on rue Charles de Gaulle. Mail is kept in poste restante for only two weeks and there is a 0.2TD charge for each item. Entrance to

MOVING ON FROM TUNIS

By air
As almost everywhere in Tunisia is within twelve hours of the capital by land, **internal air travel** is a bit of an unnecessary luxury, and internal flights are not in any case very regular: Tunis Carthage Airport, 8km northeast of the centre, has services to Jerba (9 weekly, 12 in summer), Monastir (1 weekly), Sfax (twice weekly) and Tozeur (3 weekly). For **international travel**, remember that you need a *bon de passage* (see p.20) if you buy an international air ticket with cash in Tunisia. Note also that the **duty free shop** at the airport only takes hard currency, so don't save any dinars to spend in it. For airline offices, see "Listings", p.98.

By sea
If you're leaving Tunis by **sea**, get off at the TGM's second stop, *Goulette Vieille*, and walk back alongside the track towards Tunis for 100m or so to the main road. Then turn left and continue for some 300m, past the Kasbah (on your left) until you come to a roundabout where the beach is to your left. Turn right here and continue, following the road round to the left by the *STAM/CTN* building and the *BNT* bank. The ferry terminal is right in front of you and runs services to Cagliari in Sardinia (1 weekly; 24hr); in Italy, Genoa (1–3 weekly; 24hr), Livorno (at least 1 daily; 32hr) and Naples (summer only, 1 weekly; 24hr); Marseille in southern France (1–3 weekly; 24hr); and Trápani in Sicily (2–4 weekly; 8hr). Remember you will need a *bon de passage* (see p.00) if you buy an **international ferry ticket** with cash (see p.20). **Ferry schedules** and **ticket office addresses** are given in *Basics* on p.8. In the summer, things can get hectic at the offices, so it's wise to leave plenty of time for queuing and struggling, or get your ticket in Bizerte, Sousse or Sfax instead.

By train
The Tunisian **train** service is not comprehensive and you'll find yourself relying heavily on buses – especially as trains over a longer distance are slower, less frequent and not much cheaper than buses. Tunis's mainline train station is on place Barcelone (☎01/244440), right at the centre of the main hotel area, south of avenue Bourguiba (metro lines #1 and #2). To secure a seat, it's a good idea to turn up at the station an hour or so before departure, to stake your claim as soon as the train arrives. Services down the **east coast** include El Jem (5 daily; 3hr 15min), Gabes (2 daily; 7hr), Hammamet (2 direct trains daily; 1hr 20min), Mahdia (2 daily; 4hr), Nabeul (2 direct trains daily; 1hr 40min), Sfax (5 daily; 4hr 10min) and Sousse (7 daily, or 9 in summer; 2hr 15min). The train line up to the **north coast** goes to Bizerte (4 daily; 1hr 40min) and Mateur (4 daily; 1hr); **western destinations** include Beja (6 daily; 2hr), Ghardimaou (5 daily; 3hr), Jendouba (5 daily; 2hr 30min) and Kalaa Kasbah (3 daily; 5hr 30min). There are services **south** to Fahs (4 daily; 1hr 30min), Gafsa (1 daily; 8hr 40min), Metlaoui (1 daily; 9hr 30min) and Monastir (4 daily; 3hr 10min).

There are also services out to Tunis's **southern suburbs**: Borj Cedria (half-hourly; 50min), Bou Kornine (half-hourly; 35min), Ez Zahra (half-hourly; 30min), Hammam Lif

the telephone section is off rue Jemal Abdel Nasser (open 24hr). If this is crowded, try the smaller one on rue d'Angleterre, around the corner, or *Publitel Central*, 8 rue Jemal Abdel Nasser. The **parcels** office (*Colis Postaux*) is on av de la République, just off av Bourguiba. There is a branch PTT at 1 av Habib Thameur, and a very helpful one in Bab Alleoua bus station.

Swimming Municipal pools, like the one in Belvedere Park, sporadically close. Hotels like the *International* or *Africa* may not mind or notice non-residents using the pool.

Travel agencies The many travel agencies that line av Bourguiba are all very similar, offering combinations of car rental, organized tours, flights, ferry tickets, hotel bookings and so on. *Tourafric*, 52 av Bourguiba, is as helpful and professional as any. As for student travel agents, there is *Sotutour*, 2 rue de Sparte, but its special deals are not spectacularly cheap. Many ordinary agencies will give a 25 percent discount for a student card, as will *Tunis Air* and some other airlines if you're under 31.

(half-hourly; 40min) and Rades (half-hourly; 20min). If you decide to use the **international service** to Algiers (1 daily; 20hr), consult our warning on p.376.

By bus

Buses leave Tunis regularly for all the country's main towns and there are also direct services to Libya, Algeria (see warning on p.376), Morocco and sometimes even Egypt. There are two intercity **bus terminals** – **Bab Saadoun**, at the bottom of rue Sidi el Bechir and avenue de Carthage, for the north of the country and parts of the Tell, and **Bab Alleoua**, on avenue Bougatfa, for the rest – both connected to the centre by bus and with metro stations fairly nearby, although they're close enough to the centre to walk. City bus #50 runs between the two terminals, though it stops by the Bab Saadoun city gate rather than outside the northern bus terminal. With few exceptions, the following destinations have departures during daylight hours.

Bab Saadoun mostly serves the **north** and parts of the **Tell**, with buses to Aïn Draham (4 daily; 4hr), Beja (hourly; 2hr), Bizerte (hourly; 2hr), Jendouba (5 daily; 3hr), Le Kef (hourly; 3hr), Mateur (8 daily; 1hr 30min), Medjez el Bab (half-hourly; 1hr), Tabarca (7 daily; 4hr), Teboursouk (hourly; 1hr 20min) and Testour (hourly; 1hr).

Bab Alleoua serves the rest of the country, principally the **centre** and **south**, with services to Enfida (very frequent; 1hr 30min), Gabes (10 daily; 7hr), Gafsa (8 daily; 6hr), Houmt Souk on Jerba (3 daily; 8–10hr), Kairouan (18 daily; 3hr), Kasserine (6 daily; 5hr), Maktar (2 daily; 3hr), Medenine (4 daily; 7hr), Ras Ajdir (Libyan frontier; 1 daily; 9hr 30min), Sfax (9 daily; 5hr), Sidi Bou Zid (2 daily; 5hr) and Sousse (12 daily; 2hr 30min). Bab Alleoua also serves **Cap Bon** destinations like Hammamet (hourly; 1hr 30min), Kelibia (hourly; 2hr 30min), Nabeul (half-hourly; 1hr 30min) and Zaghouan (3 daily, 1hr); and handles **international buses** to Algiers, Algeria (weekly; 18hr), Annaba, Algeria (daily; 5hr 30min), Cairo, Egypt (weekly or less; 2 days), Casablanca, Morocco (weekly or less; 2 days), Constantine, Algeria (weekly; 9hr), and Tripoli, Libya (4 weekly; 17hr). If you intend to cross the Algerian border, read our warning on p.376.

By louage

Louages, or service taxis, follow set routes and arrive at and depart from locations near the bus terminals (Bab Saadoun's *louage* station adjoins the bus station; Bab Alleoua's is across rue Sidi el Bechir). Most bus destinations are also served by *louages* – journey times are roughly three-quarters those of the bus. The exceptions are the international ones serving Libya and Algeria, which have their main stops at **Garage Ayachi** at Bab Souika for Tripoli (13hr) and **rue al Jazira** at place de la Victoire/Porte de France for Algiers (15hr) and Constantine in Algeria (7hr), and Oujda in Morocco (24hr). *Louages* depart from about 4am until about 6pm (the later departures are mostly local), and it's better to start earlier the further your destination. One or two important destinations (like Sfax) have *louages* all night, but you have to wait for them to fill up before leaving, which can take a long time in the small hours.

If you are considering crossing the Algerian border – strongly in advisable considering the current political climate – please read the warning on p.376.

GREATER TUNIS

On a hot summer evening, there's no better way of enjoying Tunis than to get out of the city centre by catching the TGM train line across the lake to one of the suburbs on the shore of the gulf, where the sea breezes clear away the city's oppressive humidity.

Carthage gave its name to a modern suburb built over and among the remains of the ancient capital of the Carthaginian Empire, later second city of the Roman world. The physical extent of the ruins can be disappointing, but not the sense of history nor the scenery. As you move up the coast from Carthage, you are also moving towards upmarket resorts that tend to cater for the more sedate variety of French tourist looking for a more refined alternative to staying in Tunis – **La Goulette**, with its Kasbah fortress and fish restaurants; **Sidi Bou Said**, a cliff-top village of considerable charm; **La Marsa**, **Gammarth** and **Raouad** for swimming and nightlife. Remember, however, that half of Tunis converges on these places in summer, especially at weekends. The TGM will get you as far as La Marsa, but past there you will have to depend on buses if you do not have your own car.

The suburbs of the southern shore are distinctly downmarket, with *bidonville* shanties spreading out beyond the boulevard du 9 Avril 1938. But **Hammam Lif**, a turn-of-the-century resort dominated by Jebel Bou Kornine, retains some character of its own.

Lake Tunis

The **causeway** on which the TGM crosses **Lake Tunis** was built in the 1870s, when the suburbs that now run from La Goulette to Sidi Bou Said barely existed. The train was originally routed directly to La Marsa (through the British Consul's garden, see p.79) along the mainland north of the lake.

Lake Tunis offers the chance to sight some of Tunisia's more exciting **birds**. Forget the northern half of the lake, whose edges are now being reclaimed for hotel and other developments, and head instead for the southern half, which attracts flamingoes, waders, gulls and terns. Numbers are particularly high in spring and autumn when they're swollen by migrants. The best vantage point is the lake's southeastern corner; take the TGM to La Bac and the ferry across to Rades port, from where you can stroll 3km down into Rades along the lakeshore.

On the **Isle of Chikli**, north of the causeway, **Fort St Jacques** sits mysteriously, built by the Spanish in the sixteenth century. Once used as a prison, it is now a stopover for migrating birds.

If you have the time or inclination to **walk**, some of the fields just north of the lake between Carthage and Sidi Bou Said have wonderful **wildflower** displays in spring; look for yellow chrysanthemums, scarlet poppies, blue borage and pink campions. Brilliant goldfinches are common in the area, while butterflies include swooping swallowtails and orange tips and, in spring, hundreds of migrating painted ladies feeding on the sea stocks at the back of the beach.

La Goulette

LA GOULETTE (the gullet, or throat) is the port of Tunis and increasingly a dormitory suburb for the capital, easily reached by the regular TGM services (every 20min; 20min). However, it still has a lively atmosphere of its own, as well as some excellent fish restaurants – the main reason for coming here, along with the ferries. The cheaper restaurants line the main avenue, with the more expensive ones down quieter side streets.

The road from the causeway and TGM towards the port (from Goulette Vieille TGM station, head back towards Tunis for 100m then turn left at the *Esso* garage) passes, on the left, a rather run-down area reminiscent of a poor district in southern Europe, complete with church. In the middle of the same road is La Goulette's **city gate**, part of the Spanish king Charles V's walls but now standing alone, shored up with concrete.

The **Kasbah**, a massive fortress built in 1535 by Charles V to defend his bridgehead in Tunisia, is a little further on the left and really the only monumental sight here. As a key strategic point in the sixteenth-century struggle for control of the western Mediterranean, it saw some torrid times, finally falling in 1574 to "four hundred and seventy-five thousand" Turks, Moors and Arabs – the figure quoted by Miguel de Cervantes, author of *Don Quixote*, who fought in its defence. Despite being captured, he and many others were glad to see the Kasbah lost – it was a "breeding-place and cloak of iniquities, a glutton, sponge and sink" of all the money spent on it in a futile policy of prestige. Over the next centuries the Kasbah was used as a dungeon for prisoners who would be taken from here to the Souk el Berka in the Medina to be sold into slavery.

An **International Museum of the Ram** (summer only, times uncertain; 1TD) has been installed in two of the rooms. Its literature proclaims it "probably unique in the world" – though mainly for an unrivalled collection of miscellaneous kitsch, including an appalling reproduction of a group of Romans using a battering ram against the besieged Jews of Masada in Palestine.

Continuing straight on from the museum takes you to the port (see p.100), but to go into La Goulette **town**, take a left up avenue Farhat Hached immediately after the Kasbah. This leads to place 7 Novembre where, if you need a.**room**, you'll find the unclassified *Hôtel Beau Rivage* (on the right, first floor, entrance round the back; ③). This is the main area of **fish restaurants** and there's a great variety, from very cheap to very upmarket. *Restaurant Venus* on place 7 Novembre is one of the smartest, charging around 13TD a head. From place 7 Novembre, avenue Bourguiba splits to the left and avenue Franklin D. Roosevelt to the right. F.D. Roosevelt is better for food, with cheap places like the *Stambli* and the *Guitoune* alongside posher establishments such as the *Monte Carlo*, the *Avenir*, the *An 2000* and the *Labidi*.

Carthage and around

> *[Walking around the city as it was being built], Aeneas looked wonderingly at the solid structures springing up where there had once been only African huts, and the gates, the turmoil, and the paved streets. The Tyrians were hurrying about busily, some tracing a line for the walls and manhandling stones up the slopes as they strained to build their citadel, others siting some building and marking its outline by ploughing a furrow . . . At one spot they were excavating the harbour, and at another a party was laying out an area for the deep foundations of a theatre; they were also hewing from quarries mighty pillars to stand tall and handsome beside the stage which was still to be built . . . Aeneas looked up at the buildings. "Ah, fortunate people," he exclaimed . . .*

Ever since Virgil wrote *The Aeneid* in the first century BC, the ancient port of **CARTHAGE** has been suffused in a legendary aura of romance, power, cruelty and decline. "Any man who could survey the ruins of Carthage with indifference," wrote one Edward Blaquière, a typical nineteenth-century traveller, "or not call to mind the scenes of its past glories and misfortunes must, indeed, be devoid of sensibility." The image is made that much more potent by the yawning gap that separates the myth from the pitiful reality. Today's remains consist of a series of widely spaced sites, with only a little standing above ground level, lurking among the plush villas of Tunis's wealthier commuters.

Still, if you approach Carthage with some imagination and a willingness to be impressed, it has a good deal to offer – not least the wide views over the Gulf and back to Tunis. It only takes a moment's thought to bring the bare bones to life, and judicious use of the TGM train line allows you to see as much or as little as you want; if you get tired, just go on to Sidi Bou Said for the evening, where the mood of dusk falling over the Gulf often revives the romance.

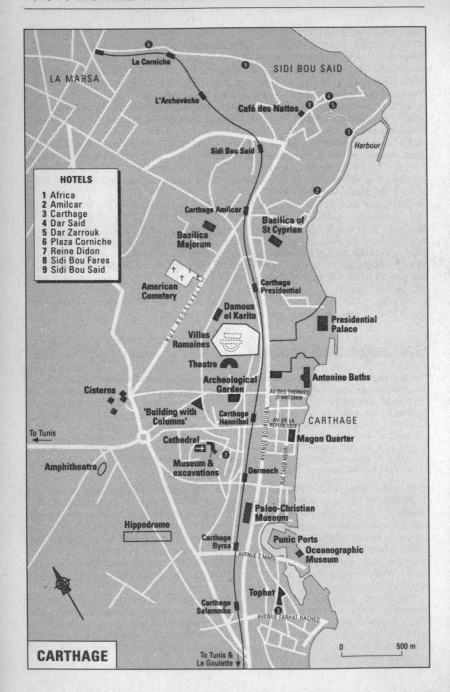

SIDI BOU SAID

La Corniche

LA MARSA

L'Archevêché

Café des Nattes

Sidi Bou Said

Harbour

HOTELS
1 Africa
2 Amilcar
3 Carthage
4 Dar Said
5 Dar Zarrouk
6 Plaza Corniche
7 Reine Didon
8 Sidi Bou Fares
9 Sidi Bou Said

Carthage Amilcar

Basilica of
St Cyprian

Basilica
Majorum

American
Cemetery

Carthage
Presidential

Damous
el Karita

Presidential
Palace

Villas
Romaines

Theatre

Antonine Baths

Cisterns

Archeological
Garden

AV DES THERMES
D'ANTONIN

To Tunis

'Building with
Columns'

Carthage
Hannibal

AV DE LA
RÉPUBLIQUE

CARTHAGE

Cathedral

Magon Quarter

Amphitheatre

Museum &
excavations

Dermech

Paleo-Christian
Museum

Hippodrome

Punic Ports

Carthage
Byrsa

Oceanographic
Museum

AVENUE 2 MARS

Tophet

Carthage
Salammbo

AVENUE FARHAT HACHED

0   500 m

CARTHAGE

To Tunis &
La Goulette

Carthage (*Qart Hadasht*, or New City) was founded, according to legend, in 814 BC by Phoenicians from the eastern Mediterranean. One of a number of such settlements on the North African coast, it gradually became the most important, especially after a 507 BC treaty with Rome banned foreign shipping from the others.

According to a myth that plays on the Phoenicians' celebrated commercial astuteness, their queen, **Dido**, landed on the North African coast and requested as much territory as could be enclosed by an ox-hide. The request willingly granted, she proceeded to cut the hide into a long strip that gave her room for a city. According to Books 1 and 4 of Virgil's epic poem *The Aeneid*, **Aeneas** – sole survivor of the Greek destruction of Troy and charged by the gods with a mission to found a new Troy in Italy – turned up while she was building the city. Taken in and sheltered by Dido, Aeneas became increasingly torn between his divine mission and his love for the Carthaginian queen. All this was probably intended as high-class propaganda to explain the rivalry between Rome and Carthage, and Rome's superiority. But Virgil found himself unable to depict Aeneas as the sort of brainless Roman hero required by the official line, and the episode became the first classic tragic love story in European literature. Historically there's no chance of it being true, as Troy was destroyed five centuries before Carthage was built.

Some history

Remarkably little is known about the appearance of **Carthage**, except that it grew up around the ports on the shore and the acropolis on the Byrsa Hill, where today's museum and cathedral now stand. The first detailed accounts come from the Romans, who gleefully describe how thoroughly they destroyed the city in 146 BC.

Having left Carthage in ruins, the Romans made Utica capital of their African province, but in 46 BC **Julius Caesar** refounded Carthage as a symbol of the planned resurrection of Africa, and it grew to a huge size – the second city of the Empire after Rome. Estimates of its population range from 200,000 to 700,000, and it was as cultured as it was cosmopolitan, with a large university. As the Empire's moral and military foundations began to tremble, Christianity became the voice of the establishment, but it was too late to halt the decline. Regarded as a typically decadent Roman city, Carthage was a natural target for Christian abuse. Saint Augustine lambasted a group of its citizens: "Up to very recently these effeminates were walking the streets and alleys of Carthage, their hair reeking with ointment, their faces powdered white, with enervated bodies moving along like women, and even soliciting the man on the street for sustenance of their dissolute lives."

Although the Vandals and Byzantines tried to keep up the imperial lifestyle, time was running out. The Arab invaders made almost as thorough a job of destroying Carthage as the Romans had done, and what was left was carted away over the next centuries for buildings in Tunis, Kairouan and elsewhere. "In the beginning of the sixteenth century," according to Edward Gibbon, "the second Capital of the West was represented by a mosque, a college without students, twenty-five or thirty shops, and the huts of five hundred peasants, who, in their abject poverty, displayed the arrogance of the Punic senators."

The sites

The two main obstacles to excavating Carthage have been that the original city was thoroughly destroyed by the Romans in 146 BC – and what was left of the Roman city after the Vandal and Arab invasions was used either for building material or, more recently, buried under suburban housing. Nonetheless, a UNESCO-inspired project involving Tunisian, French, German, British, Canadian and American archeologists has

---

CARTHAGE GLOBAL TICKET

Entry to all the major Roman sites spread for around 6km along the coast at Carthage, as well as the Carthage Museum, is by a 4TD **global ticket** (1TD extra to take photos). This is only currently available at four places: the Tophet, Carthage Museum, Antonine Baths and Villas Romaines. The sites are all open daily from 8.30am to 5.30pm.

excavated areas of the Carthaginian and Roman cities for over five kilometres along the shore on either side of the TGM train line.

Carthage's many sites lie scattered over an extensive area, so visiting them all on foot makes a good day's ramble. Though perfectly feasible, this can be quite forbidding in midsummer. An alternative would be to pick and choose, using the TGM wherever possible (trains run about every 20min), and perhaps combining Sidi Bou Said and La Marsa with a couple of sessions at Carthage. For a worthwhile abbreviated visit, you could take the TGM to Carthage Dermech for the **Carthage Museum**, which also offers a wonderful view over the gulf; wander north to the **Villas Romaines** or **Antonine Baths**; then catch the TGM again at Carthage Hannibal to move on to Sidi Bou Said or back to Tunis.

Southern sites

From Carthage Salammbo station on the TGM, head down towards the sea on avenue Farhat Hached. About 200m down, rue Hannibal leads off to the left, and 50m down that on the right are the remains of the **Tophet**, or sanctuary, of the Carthaginian divinities Tanit and Baal. A rare patch of undeveloped suburban land, dug down into deep pits and scattered with Punic stelae (headstones), this conceals a lurid past. According to legend, the Carthaginians eagerly and frequently brought their children here to be ritually slaughtered. Urns containing the ashes of children have been found on the site, but the practice was almost certainly not as common as Roman propagandists would have had people believe.

The **Punic Ports** sit just 50m away, at the end of rue Hannibal (or straight down avenue 2 Mars from Byrsa TGM station). Once the foundation of Carthaginian prosperity and power, these harbours were a source of fascination second only to Hannibal's elephants for the envious Romans. What you see today looks like two suburban ponds: the northern, circular one was the naval harbour, linked by a narrow channel (the sea opening is modern) to the rectangular merchant harbour. The best way to get a sense of what it all meant is to make your way to the small building on the edge of the naval harbour, where the British excavating team have left behind a detailed scale model (times variable; free). This shows the island as one big shipyard, surrounded by slipways. One of these, left uncovered on the far side of the island, seems surprisingly small considering the awe in which Carthage's fleet was held, suggesting that a Carthaginian naval vessel was only around 115 feet long by 16 feet wide. There's little to see at the merchant harbour, although excavations there unearthed a wealth of the kind of trade-related material that is now displayed at the Carthage museum.

Cross the bridge over the channel joining the two ports and you come to the **Oceanographic Museum** (Tues–Sat 2.30–5.30pm, Sun 10am–noon; 0.2TD), which was opened in 1924 and frankly looks its age, with such uninspiring exhibits as tanks of grumpy groupers and sad turtles and a fine collection of stuffed birds, but little else. Inland on avenue Bourguiba, between Byrsa and Dermech TGM stations, is the **Paleo-Christian museum** (daily summer 7am–7pm; winter 8am–5pm; 1TD), so called after some early Christian remains were unearthed here. It includes excavations and a building housing some fragments of mosaic and a cute statuette of Ganymede – the beautiful Trojan youth who was cupbearer to the gods – cuddling an eagle. There are explanations in English.

Byrsa Hill

Byrsa Hill, where the cathedral and museum now stand, was the heart of Carthage under Punic rule and the result of Roman fury, when they sacked the city so thoroughly in 146 BC.

Outside the museum building itself, on the southern edge of the hilltop, some meagre remains are nonetheless the most extensive remnant of pre-Roman Carthage. Ironically, it was the Romans' decision to refound the city a hundred years later that helped preserve at least this much; to provide a platform for their civic centre they levelled the top of the hill, and the Punic quarters clustered around the top of it were buried under the rubble tipped over the sides, and saved for the meticulous French **excavations** that you can see on the southeast side. The French have uncovered a domestic quarter similar to that at Kerkouane, though here the buildings were as much as five storeys high and the streets narrow, as in the Medina. Each house had its own cistern and a rudimentary drainage system. The scorched material found above these foundations has proved that vindictive Rome did indeed burn Carthage to the ground after the siege.

You can get up the hill quite easily from Dermech or Hannibal TGM stations. From Dermech, stop for a breather on the terrace of the *Reine Didon* hotel, from where you can survey the whole area. Dominating the hill is the pseudo-Oriental heap of the **Cathedral of St-Louis**, built in 1890 and dedicated to the thirteenth-century French king who died at Carthage while laying unsuccessful siege to Tunis in the hope of converting the Hafsid ruler El Mustansir. "Instead of a proselyte, he found a siege," wrote Gibbon: "The French panted and died on the burning sands; Saint Louis expired in his tent." In 1930 the French Catholic Church held a grandiose conference here to proclaim a revival of Africa's great Christian tradition, which is said to have played an important part in arousing Bourguiba's nationalist feelings.

Carthage Museum

Beyond the cathedral and housed in the former headquarters of the White Fathers missionaries of wine and "Thibarine" fame (see p.161), the **Carthage Museum** provides a substantial and informative display, with English captions, detailing life at Carthage over more than a thousand years. Beware of guides here charging outrageous rates for their services.

The museum's **ground floor** contains Carthaginian and Roman sculpture, a room devoted to Christian remains, and – unusually and interestingly – a room that illustrates the complexity of current conservation techniques. You'll find the museum's prize exhibits lying side by side at the end of the sculpture room: a life-size man and woman, carved around the fourth century BC, each lying on top of a stone sarcophagus. The man's naturalistic head would not be out of place on the statue of a fourth-century Greek philosopher, and the fall of the woman's *peplos* over her upper body is similarly Greek. But the way both lie on top of the sarcophagus suggests an Etruscan influence, while the woman's coiffure and the bird's wings protectively wrapped around her lower body are both reminiscent of old Egypt. This striking blend of different Mediterranean influences is a theme that recurs throughout Tunisian culture.

Upstairs, the **Punic room** contains many similarly pan-Mediterranean items, as well as a *tophet* in which child sacrifice was carried out, a solely Carthaginian custom. There's also a case devoted to the Punic Ports, which makes an adequate substitute for a visit to the actual site by the shore if it's too hot or you have limited time. Look out in a corner of the upstairs corridor for a pair of rare early **mosaics** which demonstrate the transition from plain pink Carthaginian floors towards the Romans' later, more elaborate work. In the fourth-century BC example, found in a house near the theatre, the band of simple square tesserae is the earliest example known of true mosaic technique in the Mediterranean. Next to it, an attractive first-century AD example incorporates a black panel decorated with sections of coloured marble. In the upper floor's final room, an excellent exhibit succeeds in bringing to life the apparently dull subject of amphorae across the centuries. A garden outside the museum is crammed with architectural bric-a-brac, including – incongruously – the tombstone of Mathieu Maximilian Prosper de Lesseps, French consul general in Tunis in the early nineteenth century and brother of the builder of the Suez Canal.

Behind the hill

The **amphitheatre** below the hill, in sketchy but recognizable condition (free entry), was the site of numerous early Christian martyrdoms. Perhaps most notorious were those of saints Perpetua and Felicitas, who were brought into the arena in 203 AD, stripped naked and placed in nets. Even Romans were horrified when they saw that "one was a delicate young girl, and the other a woman fresh from childbirth with the milk still dripping from her breasts", so they were taken out to be brought back in again, dressed in unbelted tunics; Perpetua was killed by a heifer, Felicitas by a gladiator's sword.

Just over the road is a collection of huge **cisterns**, some inhabited and others decaying, which once received part of Carthage's water supply from the Zaghouan aqueduct.

The Magon Quarter and Antonine Baths

Heading directly seawards from Hannibal TGM station or up the shore from the Punic Ports, cross avenue Bourguiba and you will find the **Magon Quarter** on your right. The German excavations here are neat, tidy and well laid-out, but not really very interesting. This residential quarter, located next to the water's edge, is named after Mago, an early king of Carthage.

A couple of blocks north, and signposted from Hannibal TGM, the **Antonine Baths** are the most extensive example of their kind in North Africa, and were once the largest in the Roman world. The entrance to the site takes you through a park full of flowers and date palms, with paths following the streets of the Roman city. You enter along Kardo 16 (a *kardo* is a north–south Roman street). Nos. 17, 15 and 14 run parallel, and all are crossed after two blocks by Decumanus (east–west street) 4. Left from the entrance is the bunker-like doorway to a little seventh-century Christian **chapel**, complete with mosaics, which has been moved here from elsewhere. The contrast between this secret cave – built about the time that the Arabs swept in from the east – and the expansive self-confidence of the Roman baths down on the beach needs no further comment. Further on, a *schola*, or young men's club, is identifiable by an unusual mosaic showing children at some sort of ritual exercise; and further still up the hill is the Byzantine **basilica of Douimes**, in which was found a poignant inscription from the Epistle to the Romans: "If the Lord is with us, who can be against us?"

The **baths** themselves are down on the beach. Once again it's a case of using your imagination, since what remains is only the basement level of a massive complex – it's almost impossible to convey the original size. The central pool alone was as big as an Olympic swimming pool, and when the curved public latrines were first discovered they were taken for a theatre. None of the original mosaics or statuary decorating the public areas have survived, but the complex remains a potent symbol of Roman imperial presence.

Next to the site is a modern **presidential palace**, whose soldiers do not like cameras to be pointed at it.

The Villas Romaines and northern sites

Heading inland from the baths, cross avenue Bourguiba, carry on under the train line and the **Villas Romaines** site is 50m up on the right. It's really little more than a series of foundations of Roman villas and an "Antiquarium" where a few stunted columns and statues have been collected to make a foreground for photographs of the gulf. The sight of modern villas below is hardly new – over 1500 years ago wealthy Tunisians and

The **Carthage International Festival** is Tunisia's biggest cultural celebration, running from June to August every year. Events of all sorts – dance, cinema, music, theatre – are staged at the restored Roman theatre (and on the terrace of the old casino in the Belvedere Park in Tunis). The events are largely in French and are well advertised on hoardings and in the press – tickets can be bought at the theatre. For details of the biennial **Carthage Film Festival**, see p.97.

expatriates were already making this idyllic stretch of coast their own. Right on top of the hill are the bare foundations of the Roman **Odeon**, a type of theatre.

A little further up the road on the same side is the Roman **theatre**, extensively restored for the modern Carthage Festival (see box) and bearing scant resemblance to the original. Carthage's theatres became infamous for the immorality they portrayed and encouraged; several hundred years later a Christian critic wrote of the last days of the African Empire: "The arms of Barbarian people were resounding against the walls of Carthage; and yet the Christian population was going wild in the theatres and enjoying itself in the circuses. Some were having their throats cut outside the walls; others were fornicating inside the walls."

Across the street, a small **archeological garden**, with a few Roman odds and ends, might be a good place for a breather. Further up, a "**building with columns**", or what's left of it, may be the Baths of Gargilius where Saint Augustine called a conference of bishops in 411 to trick the dissident Donatist church into being a party to its own prohibition.

Taking a right at the building with columns – or from the Villas Romaines site, climbing over a fence on the far side of the Odeon and cutting across the fields – brings you to the **Damous el Karita Basilica**, at 215 feet long and nine aisles wide, the largest ancient church known in North Africa. Though little more remains than a ground-plan and rows of broken grey columns, there is at least a superficial similarity between this forest of columns and the one built only a few hundred years later in the prayer hall of the Great Mosque at Kairouan – perhaps even incorporating material from here. Another example of continuity is this site's name: an Arabic transliteration of the Latin Domus Caritatis (House of Grace).

The **American cemetery** (daily 8am–5pm) beyond – cross the road and take a short cut between the fields on the other side – presents an interesting contrast in style to the British, French and German cemeteries elsewhere in the country. Most Americans killed in action in Tunisia during World War II are buried here and, in contrast to the Commonwealth cemeteries, it goes all out for size and grandeur. The caretaker is something of an authority on the war in Tunisia. Close by, to the northeast, are the scant ruins of an old Byzantine church, the **Basilica Majorum**, and east of here across the train line, another old Byzantine basilica, alleged to be the **Basilica of St Cyprian**.

Practicalities

The Roman sites lie between Carthage Salammbo and Carthage Amilcar stations on the **TGM** line that runs parallel to the coast, with regular twenty-minute services that take around thirty minutes from Tunis. There are not many places to **stay** in Carthage, and nowhere cheap at all. Most inviting is the two-star *Résidence Carthage* at 16 rue Hannibal (☎01/731072; ④), near the Tophet, which has a rather classy restaurant. The three-star *Hôtel Reine Didon* on Byrsa Hill (☎01/275344; ⑤) is a much more grandiose affair, priced accordingly, but only worth the difference for the view. Definitely not recommended is the three-star package-tourist haunt of the *Hôtel Amilcar* (☎01/740788; ④), on the beach up towards Sidi Bou Said.

Sidi Bou Said and around

Somehow, **SIDI BOU SAID**, a few kilometres north of Carthage, shrugs off its two and a half centuries as a tourist trap and remains a place of extraordinary charm. Today, it's a favourite retreat for the wealthy, but even on summer evenings, you can have Sidi Bou to yourself by wandering through the silent back streets past white, cubic houses and their blue studded doors.

You certainly won't see such a concentration of wealthy residents and visitors anywhere else in Tunisia, as Sidi Bou is as chic as they come. It seems that every artist and every writer who has visited Tunisia spent some time in this square, including Cervantes, Paul Klee, Simone de Beauvoir, André Gide and Jean Foucault. In 1939 Sacheverell Sitwell was told that Sidi Bou Said was the finest town in all Tunisia in which to see the harem ladies in their silken dresses, but gold jewellery and tanned flesh are more the style now, especially around the expensive and rather snooty *Café des Nattes*.

The first building on this strategic cliff-top was a *ribat* or monastic fortress built in the early years of Arab rule, part of the chain stretching through Sousse and Monastir to Tripoli in Libya and over whose foundations a modern lighthouse is built. The village grew up around the tomb and *zaouia* of the thirteenth-century holy man Sidi Bou Said, still celebrated in the central **mosque** and during the August festival in his honour. According to one inventive but unlikely story, the saint was none other than Saint Louis, fresh from defeat at Carthage (see p.103), who retired here incognito to marry a local girl. Around the beginning of the century the village was discovered by wealthy French and other expatriates, who bought houses and went to great lengths to "preserve" the town's character. As a result, there's very little here that is not Tunisian in origin – and nowhere else in Tunisia quite like it.

A left off place 7 Novembre up rue Dr H. Thameur takes you to the town's main square, from where rue el Hadi Zarrouk continues on to end at **Cap Carthage**; on a clear day, you can see right across the bay to Korbous. Below, the rain has exposed several fragments of **Punic flooring**, indicating the presence of villas here even in the third century BC.

Practicalities

The **TGM** from Tunis (every 20min; 35min) leaves you a five-minute walk from the town centre uphill towards the sea. Just off the square is a **bank**, the **PTT**, *Star* **car rental** agency and a *Magasin Général* **supermarket**. There's no budget accommodation in Sidi Bou Said, but you will find some excellent little retreats, in pleasant contrast to the noise and grime of Tunis. Be aware, however, that everywhere here is booked up months in advance in season, so plan ahead. The most economical option is the *Hôtel Sidi Bou Fares* (✆01/740091; ②), in the stairway of the same name off the main square. It's set around a fragrant fig tree branching all over a peaceful patio and its owner is something of a musician. Also off the main square, on rue el Hadi Zarrouk, are two very pleasant and more upmarket two-star places – the jasmine-scented former palaces of *Dar Said* (✆01/740295; ③), on the left, and the *Dar Zarrouk* (✆01/740912; ③), on the right. *Dar Zarrouk* is usually open only as a restaurant out of season. The jet-set four-star *Hôtel Sidi Bou Said* (✆01/740411; ⑥), around the cape past the lighthouse and a kilometre or so out of town, has high-class accommodation. *Résidence Africa* (✆01/740600; ⑤), down by the marina at the bottom of the cliff (access down steps beside the *Dar Zarrouk*), offers bungalows.

Eating in Sidi Bou can be tailored to your budget, and the cheapest places, like the *Bagatelle* with its local cooking, are around place 7 Novembre. Opposite, the *Restaurant Chergui* is a cheapish café; for a more elaborate meal, try *Pirates* at the bottom of the cliff by the marina, said to be one of Tunisia's best restaurants, without being extortionately expensive. For hanging out with the *beau monde*, the *Café des Nattes* in the main square may be at the heart of the scene, but the place to head for is the *Café Sidi Chabaane*, further on along rue el Hadi Zarrouk. A steep series of narrow terraces set spectacularly in the cliff overlooking the gulf, it's the perfect place in town to relax in romantic company with a glass of pine-nut tea. Doughnut fans should try a *bonbalouni* from the stall just past the *Café des Nattes*.

La Marsa

LA MARSA, next in the long chain of suburbs along the northern shore, is a place of some antiquity. In past centuries when transport was less easy, the entire court moved out here for the summer. "It is adorned with a royal palace, and pleasant places," wrote John Ogilby in 1670, "whither the rulers of Tunis in the summer go to take their pleasure, and keep their court." Behind the PTT are the remains of an early **palace**, but in the nineteenth century, when the last of Tunisia's independent Beys favoured La Marsa, many other Beylical palaces and those of their ministers were built inland – two of the best are the residences of the British and French ambassadors, both sadly inaccessible.

Today La Marsa is easy to get to on the TGM and, in summer, has become a weekend resort for all of Tunis, or so it seems. The long **beach**, with an attractive palm-lined corniche road, is what draws the crowds, and though it is slightly less crowded than those further down, you still feel like a lemming.

Practicalities

La Marsa is quite a large town compared with Sidi Bou Said. From the **TGM station** (services from Tunis every 20min; 45min), at the southern end of the corniche, follow the road up to avenue Bourguiba, heading off to the left to place 7 Novembre, where you'll find the **PTT**, **banks**, *Tunis Air*, **pharmacies** and **buses** #20, #20d and #20g to Tunis. Bus #40 for Gammarth leaves from the TGM station and can be picked up along the corniche.

Should you want to **stay** here, options are limited. *Pension Prendl*, 1 rue Mohamed Salah Malki (☎01/270529; ②), is off avenue Bourguiba about 300m from place 7 Novembre. Not the easiest place to find, it compensates with the cosiest family atmosphere of any *pension* in Tunisia. Alternatively, there's the *Hôtel Plaza Corniche* at 22 rue du Maroc (☎01/270099; ④), five minutes' walk from the station back towards Sidi Bou Said. Officially also a *pension*, it gets booked solid in season, so call ahead.

La Marsa's cheap **restaurants** are off the corniche around the avenue 20 Mars arcade. The restaurants *el Hana* and *du Peuple* are budget-priced, and the *Chez Scofe* opposite *du Peuple* has Lebanese sandwiches (including felafel) at similar prices. Midrange possibilities include two just by the bridge where the corniche crosses rue Mongi Slim and begins to skirt the beach. Above is the *Restaurant des Palmiers*, doing pizzas, crêpes, fish and similar fare for about 5TD a meal. Down below, there's nothing notably Mexican about the *Restaurant Mexicaine*, apart from the name and the cacti opposite. Upmarket places include the *Hôtel Plaza Corniche*'s restaurant. The most interesting place in town for a mint tea or Turkish coffee is the *Café Saf Saf*, opposite the mosque at the end of avenue 20 Mars, whose terraces surround a public well dating back to the Hafsid period. If you're lucky you might see a camel working the wheel, but the *Saf Saf* has clearly declined since the memorable performances of the tragic chanteuse Habiba Msika in the 1920s.

Gammarth and Raouad Beach

GAMMARTH (bus #20b from Jardin Thameur in Tunis, or #40 from La Marsa) is the next instalment of suburb along the northern coastline. It grew up around the series of beaches dubbed **Baies des Singes** (Bays of the Monkeys) by local fishermen – reputedly after the Europeans who sunbathed in the nude there in the 1950s. Up on the hill is the **cemetery** of the free French killed during World War II.

Hotels at Gammarth are aimed at the business community and priced accordingly. There's the deluxe four-star *Hôtel Abou Nawas* (☎01/741444; ⑥), the three-star *Cap Carthage* (☎01/741724; ⑤) and *Megara* (☎01/740366; ⑤), and the vacation village of *Dar Naouar* (☎01/741000; ④). The cheapest place in Gammarth is the one-star *Tour Blanche* (☎01/271697; ③).

Beyond Gammarth, civilization is almost at an end. The road runs between a salt flat and **Raouad Beach**, a broad expanse of sand where families camp en masse in summer. As there are few, if any, facilities, the water becomes almost visibly unhygienic in the peak season. You could camp out or look for a place at a holiday village such as the *Noria* (☎01/270904; ③), but frankly there are much more attractive places in Tunisia to do this.

The southern suburbs

Easily reached by train from Tunis's main station on place Barcelone, the suburbs along the **southern shore** of the gulf are for the most part shapeless areas of less affluent commuter housing, with warehouses and light industry filling the gaps between what were once smart resorts. **Hammam Lif** retains a down-at-heel allure and the **German World War II military cemetery** is a curiosity.

Rades and Ez Zahra

One of the formerly smart resorts near Tunis was **RADES**; after the Arab conquest there was even a *ribat* here, as at Sidi Bou Said. Its **beach** is the beginning of one long strand running all the way round the south bay of the Gulf of Carthage to Sidi Rais on Cap Bon; but at Rades it's crowded and dirty. With the opening of a pleasant new youth hostel in Tunis, there seems little reason to stay at the *Maison des Jeunes* **youth hostel** here (☎01/483631; ①), especially as it won't let you check in or leave your baggage before 7pm. Rades Port, 3km out of town, has a free **ferry** service to La Goulette (5min), which runs every fifteen minutes from 7am to 8.45pm.

EZ ZAHRA, the next settlement down the coast, is a little quieter than the other southern suburbs. There are two **hotels** here, the four-star *Hôtel Ez Zahra* (☎01/482550; ⑤) and the unclassified *Hôtel La Siesta* (☎01/480776; ②), and also a **youth hostel** (☎01/481547; ①) and, in summer, *La Pinède* holiday village (☎01/206036; ④).

Hammam Lif

Once the last stage on the caravan route from the south, where merchants paid tax before entering the capital, **HAMMAM LIF** was a popular spa in Carthaginian and Roman days, and emerged again as a resort under the Protectorate. Palm-lined avenues and an old seafront casino give the town a seedy sort of allure in its dramatic setting under Jebel Bou Kornine, but it rarely throws off its rather listless, Sunday-afternoon feel – except perhaps on a Sunday, market day, probably the busiest time of the week. The *Casino* (☎01/290010) is now a **bar/restaurant** – an excellent place to pop in for a beer and where women need have no worries. As for the decor, as one reader remarked, "The interior was obviously done by Elvis Presley on acid". If you want time to inspect this display, you can **stay** at the unclassified *Bon Repos*, 14 rue Ibn Rochd (☎01/291458; ②).

Jebel Bou Kornine National Park

The imposing two-pronged mountain of **Bou Kornine**, heavily forested lower down but with a more open maquis vegetation at the top, is theoretically a national park. In practice, it has become a military zone and you are liable to be arrested if you try to go further than the *Chalet Vert* restaurant, about 1km up the hill and with a fine view north over the Gulf of Tunis. A signposted road leads up to the restaurant from the main Tunis road, a few hundred metres towards Tunis from Hammam Lif.

Borj Cedria

BORJ CEDRIA, the last desultory resort before Soliman Plage, used to house the PLO headquarters, and now lacks even Hammam Lif's doubtful attractions. In 1985, to the political embarrassment of the Americans, who had been instrumental in finding a home here for the PLO after their removal from Beirut, Israeli air force jets bombed the PLO complex but failed to kill Yasser Arafat, their presumed target. Should its history fail to deter, or even intrigue you, **hotels** in Borj Cedria include the three-star *Salwa* (☎01/290830; ④) and *Médi Sea* (☎01/293030; ④; with facilities for disabled visitors), the two-star *Dar* (☎01/29018; ④), the unclassified *Younes* (☎01/293013; ②) and the *La Pinède* holiday village (☎01/206036; ④).

Just beyond the Borj Cedria turning off the main road, a discreet sign points a few hundred metres inland to the **Deutscher Soldaten Friedhof**, a German military cemetery from World War II. Built in 1975 on a slight rise near the site of the final German surrender, this grim collection of rectangular lockers represents yet another approach to the issue of the World War II dead, a stark contrast to British pastoral, American razzmatazz and French militarism.

travel details

For details of where to catch transport, timings and frequencies, see "Moving on from Tunis" (p.100).

Trains

Tunis to: Algiers, Beja, Bizerte, Borj Cedria, Bou Kornine, El Jem, Ez Zahra, Fahs, Gabes, Gafsa, Ghardimaou, Hammam Lif, Hammamet, Jendouba, Kalaa Kasbah, Mahdia, Mateur, Metlaoui, Monastir, Nabeul, Rades, Sfax and Sousse.

TGM line to: Carthage, La Goulette, La Marsa and Sidi Bou Said.

Buses

The terminals in Tunis at Bab Alleoua and Bab Saadoun have services to almost every town of any size in the country at least once a day. **Bab Saadoun** mostly serves the north and parts of the Tell; **Bab Alleoua** serves the rest of the country, principally the south, and international destinations.

Tunis Bab Saadoun to: Aïn Draham, Beja, Bizerte, Jendouba, Le Kef, Mateur Medjez el Bab, Tabarca, Teboursouk and Testour.

Tunis Bab Alleoua to: Algiers (Algeria), Annaba (Algeria), Cairo (Egypt), Casablanca (Morocco), Constantine (Algeria), Enfida, Gabes, Gafsa, Hammamet, Houmt Souk on Jerba, Kairouan, Kasserine, Kelibia, Maktar, Medenine, Nabeul, Ras Ajdir, Sfax, Sidi Bou Zid, Sousse, Tripoli (Libya) and Zaghouan.

Louages

Bus routes are also served by louages, whose journey times are roughly three-quarters the bus times.

Ferries

Tunis Goulette Vieille to: Cagliari (Sardinia), Genoa (Italy), Livorno (Italy), Marseille (France), Naples (Italy) and Trápani (Sicily).

Flights

Tunis Carthage airport to: Jerba, Monastir, Sfax and Tozeur, as well as international destinations.

CHAPTER TWO

HAMMAMET AND CAP BON

Protruding like a crooked finger into the Mediterranean, the **Cap Bon** peninsula is Tunisia's main resort area. Indeed, glancing at the brochures – with their staggering hotel capacities – it looks a little ominous, particularly along the coast from Hammamet to Nabeul. But although **Hammamet**, the best-known resort in the country, has been heavily developed, images of a Spanish-like *costa*, with tourists crowded in like cattle, don't apply. The beaches, for a start, are too big and too luxuriant, and the hotels are kept discreetly down to a few storeys, strung out along the tree-lined shore. Half an hour away, **Nabeul** has less perfect beaches and a less glamorous image, but cheaper places to stay, and good transport links for visiting other areas of the peninsula.

Among these areas, one of the most worthwhile targets is **El Haouaria**, a village at the end of the peninsula with the twin attractions of a remote white strand and a cavern full of bats. **Kerkouane**, around the coast from here, is the largest Carthaginian site yet uncovered, while **Kelibia**, a few kilometres on and dominated by a massive Spanish castle, is the quietest beach resort on the east coast. Over on the north coast of the peninsula, the ancient spa of **Korbous** is the best-known lure, but it's now heavily commercialized; if you're after seclusion and have transport, however, the coast beyond is literally one long and as yet undiscovered beach.

The peninsula is at its best in spring, when it becomes a mass of colour with its fruit orchards and vineyards. If you can make it in April, try to coincide with the Orange

---

ACCOMMODATION PRICE CODES

All the hotels, youth hostels and pensions listed in this book have been price-graded according to the following scale, and although prices will rise during the lifetime of this edition, the relative comparisons should remain valid.

The prices quoted are for the **cheapest available double room in high season**, although many of the cheap places will have pricier rooms with en suite facilities or sea views.

Classified hotels, officially considered suitable for tourists, are graded locally from one to four stars (★), with wide-ranging prices within each category. For more on accommodation prices and categories, see Basics.

① Up to 10TD. Very cheap. Usually a bed only in a basic, unclassified hotel or a youth hostel.

② 10.1–25TD. Budget. Bed only or bed and breakfast.

③ 25.1–40TD. Comfortable budget. Good unclassified average one-star or a cheap two-star.

④ 40.1–55TD. Mid-range. Expensive two-star, cheap three-star.

⑤ 55.1–70TD. Tourist hotel. Standard three-star.

⑥ 70.1TD upwards. Deluxe. Expensive three-star, four-star or five-star.

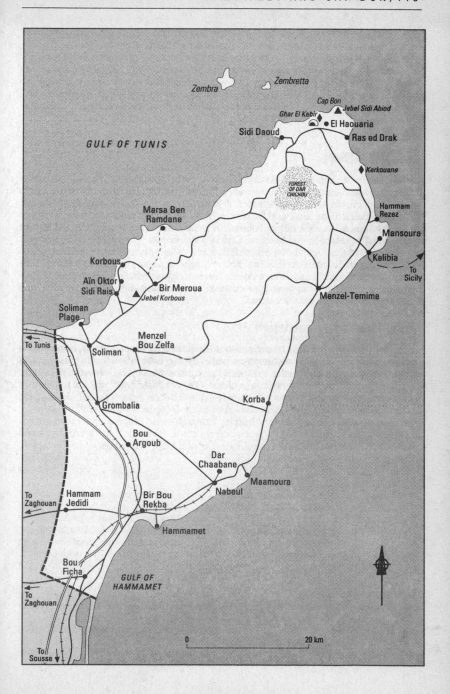

Zembra

Zembretta

Cap Bon

Jebel Sidi Abiod

Ghar El Kebir

El Haouaria

Sidi Daoud

Ras ed Drak

GULF OF TUNIS

Kerkouane

FOREST OF DAR CHICHOU

Hammam Rezez

Marsa Ben Ramdane

Mansoura

Kelibia

Korbous

To Sicily

Aïn Oktor Sidi Rais

Bir Meroua

Jebel Korbous

Menzel-Temime

Soliman Plage

To Tunis

Menzel Bou Zelfa

Soliman

Grombalia

Korba

Bou Argoub

Dar Chaabane

Maamoura

Nabeul

To Zaghouan

Hammam Jedidi

Bir Bou Rekba

Hammamet

Bou Ficha

GULF OF HAMMAMET

N

To Zaghouan

To Sousse

0   20 km

Festival at **Menzel Bou Zelfa**. By September the ground is parched – although liquid compensation is afforded by the wine festival at **Grombalia**.

Nabeul is the main centre for **transport** in Cap Bon and anyone visiting the peninsula will probably pass through here. Alternative routes are by rail via Grombalia and Bir Bou Rekba on the main train line, or by road through Menzel Bou Zelfa, or up the north coast via Soliman. With the running down of the branch line to Hammamet and Nabeul, picking up long-distance trains at Bir Bou Rekba has become a much less convenient option.

Hammamet

At the turn of the century **HAMMAMET**, some 60km southeast of Tunis, was a small fishing village making some extra money by selling lemons from its dense citrus groves to Sicily for export to America. It was only in the 1920s, with the arrival of Romanian millionaire Georges Sebastian, that the town found its true vocation. Sebastian built a fabulous villa just above the beach, described by Frank Lloyd Wright as the most beautiful house he knew. Others followed, and soon Hammamet was part of the international legend of a sensual Tunisia – somewhere between an intellectual resort and a luxurious bohemia for Europe's pre-war moneyed classes. Today, with more than sixty hotels and almost twenty thousand beds, Hammamet is considerably less exclusive, but arriving from elsewhere in Tunisia you still feel as if you've landed in St Tropez with Oriental trimmings.

Arrival and accommodation

Hammamet's two main streets begin at the Medina, with **avenue de la République** heading towards Nabeul, becoming **avenue de la Libération** further along, and **avenue Bourguiba** going inland towards the **train station**. The **bus station** is right opposite the **PTT** on avenue de la République. The *ONTT* **tourist office** is in the town hall on avenue Bourguiba, facing the beach (Mon–Thurs 8.30am–1pm & 3–5.45pm, Fri & Sat 8.30am–1.30pm; July & Aug Mon–Sat 7.30am–7.30pm; ☎02/280423).

Hammamet has almost seventy **hotels**, although most of them are spread out for miles along the beach in both directions from town. Places in town are cheaper and more convenient for transport if you want to do more than lounge on the beach. Construction recently began south of Hammamet on a new 30,000-bed *zone touristique*, known as Hammamet Sud, which will – when completed – include a yachting harbour similar to Port El Kantaoui outside Sousse.

It's about 2km west from the town centre to the most attractive swathe of curving beach, with a view of the Medina on its point. In the opposite direction, it's about 10km east to Nabeul, the route lined with hotels in the same way, although we've listed fewer as the beach here is more exposed and less attractive. Most hotels will organize excursions outside Cap Bon, ranging from a half-day to several days away; many are rather antiseptic, but still the easiest way to see the sights of the town if time is limited.

Hotels and pensions

Alya ★, 30 rue Ali Belhouane (☎02/280218). A polished place that's overpriced in summer. Ask for a room with a view of the nearby Medina. ③.

Baie du Soleil Vacation Village, av Assad Ibn el Fourat (☎02/280298). Quiet, leafy and right on the beach just east of the centre. ④.

Bellevue ★★, av Assad Ibn el Fourat (☎02/281121). Seafront location close to the Medina, with most rooms overlooking the sea. Pleasant and modern but fills up in season. ③.

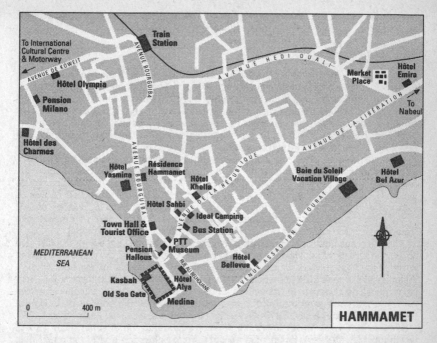

Bennila ★, av des Nations-Unies (☎02/280356). Small *pension* beyond the International Cultural Centre, west of town. ③.

Emira ★★, on the Nabeul road leaving town (☎02/281720). One of the many hotels which line the beach all the way to Nabeul. ④.

Hallous, av de la République (☎02/280525). Not the best *pension* in town but reasonable value and right by the Medina. ②.

Khella ★★, av de la République (☎02/282330). A new place similar to the *Sahbi* and just north on the same street. Fair value. ②.

Milano, rue des Fontaines (☎02/280768). A small *pension* not far from the beach west of the centre. Closed out of season. ③.

Olympia ★★, av du Kowait (☎02/280662). Rather package-oriented but perfectly adequate and quite inexpensive by Hammamet standards. The closest hotel to the train station. ③.

Résidence Hammamet, 72 av Bourguiba (☎02/280733). Only 300m from the Medina and even nearer to the beach. Four people sharing get a better deal. ④.

Sahbi ★★, av de la République (☎02/280807). Opposite the campsite and bus station. Described in their brochure as "Moorish style", rooms are big, clean and prettily furnished. Fills up with package tourists in summer. ③.

Sheraton ★★★★, av des Nations-Unies (☎02/280555). A cut above its business-class namesakes elsewhere in the world. Around 3km west of the town centre. ⑥.

Sinbad ★★★★, av des Nations-Unies (☎02/280122). Four-star deluxe comfort west of the centre, before the Cultural Centre. ⑥.

Yasmina ★★, av Bourguiba (☎02/280222). Opposite the *Résidence Hammamet* and rather more expensive. ⑤.

Campsites

Ideal Camping, av de la République (☎02/280302). A pleasant little place in the town centre with cold showers and laundry facilities. 12.5TD per person plus 1.5TD per tent.

Samaris campsite, on the Tunis road (☎02/226353). Out past the International Cultural Centre in the grounds of the one-star *Samaris Hôtel*. 1.9TD per person, 1.3TD per tent.

The Town

Hammamet's centre is a little cape sticking out into the sea with the **Medina** standing neatly on its point, the newer quarters spreading out behind, and most of the hotels spaced to either side along the beach. The tiny walled Medina is surprisingly unspoiled once you get beyond the first rash of tourist emporia, and the fifteenth-century **Great Mosque** has an attractive minaret. The over-restored **Kasbah** (daily 8.30am–6pm; May–Sept 8am–9pm; 1TD) can be safely ignored except for the view, though the **Old Sea Gate** below its walls is pretty enough.

From the Medina, avenue de la République heads towards Nabeul, passing what used to be the **municipal museum** at no. 21. Although it has long since closed down, the building is sometimes still used as a gallery: entry is free, and one or two relics remain inside. On the street corner next to it is an old olive oil press. The **town hall** on avenue Bourguiba, in the very centre facing the beach, used to be the *Hôtel de France* – packed to the rafters at one time with Europe's rich and famous. Nearby there's a **market** each Thursday near the junction of avenue Hedi Ouali and avenue de la Libération.

The main business of Hammamet, of course, is the **beach**. Even with the fast-food stalls, the forests of sunshades and the herds of bored-looking camels, the sheltered curve of the bay – backed by luxuriant greenery which conceals the low-built hotels – still manages to look even more beautiful than the brochure pictures. If you want a very slow ride along the coast to Nabeul, via all the big hotels, there's a ridiculous toytown **tourist road train** from the *Hôtel Venus*, south of town on the hotel strip, to Nabeul town centre (3 times a day; 2hr) – slower than the bus and more expensive than a taxi.

There's little more to say about the seashore than that, but at some stage it's well worth following the signs on the road west of town to **Sebastian's villa** (summer Mon, Wed & Fri 10am–noon & 3–5pm; out of season you may be able to persuade somebody to let you in; free). This has been bought by the State and turned into an International Cultural Centre to host the annual summer festival of the arts. You can look around the house and assess Frank Lloyd Wright's judgement – it really is fantasy material, with an arcaded swimming pool, a baptistry-like bath in solid marble built for four, and a black marble poolside table. During the war, the villa was used by Rommel as his Tunisian headquarters. If you can't make the visiting hours, wander into the grounds and look around the garden and the mock-Greek **theatre** built for the **cultural festival** during July and August. Although obviously directed at tourists, a lot of the events are very interesting and it's worth getting hold of a programme from the *ONTT* here or in Nabeul to check out what's on. Most events are in French or Arabic.

Lastly, 6km out of town going south along the beach, just next to the *Hôtel Samira Beach*, is the Roman site of **Pupput** (free entry). Don't expect to be impressed by the limited remains of baths and houses, although some of the Christian tomb mosaics displayed on a wall are attractive enough.

Eating, drinking and nightlife

As you'd expect, **restaurants** in Hammamet are plentiful, both in the town and in most of the hotels – and if you're on a budget it's still surprisingly easy to find a cheap Tunisian meal around the town centre. Most of the places in avenue Bourguiba between the Medina and town hall do moderately priced seafood pizzas which are usually good – try the *Grill Étage* – but they tend to be very tourist-oriented and the rest of their fare is overpriced. Two cheaper options are the *Restaurant La Brise*, 2 av de la République, which will do you a solid Tunisian meal, and the *Snack Bar Khaltoum* in rue Ali Belhouane, near the corner of avenue de la République, which has couscous.

MOVING ON FROM HAMMAMET

Buses stop on avenue de la République opposite the PTT, by *Ideal Camping*. There are departures every half-hour or so to Nabeul (15min), where you can change for other Cap Bon destinations, though there are also some direct buses to these and twelve a day for Tunis (1hr 30min). There are no *louages* in Hammamet, though in theory you could share one of the red and white taxis that do the Nabeul run if you can find one (they're supposed to leave from the bus station). Yellow taxis out to the hotels wait for business in front of the Medina.

The **train station** is on avenue Bourguiba, near the junction of avenue Hedi Ouali, but passenger services are being run down. Currently there are services to Nabeul (2 daily; 18min) and one early morning service to Bir Bou Rekba (1 daily; 7min), where you can continue to Tunis or wait for a connection going south. Other forms of transport are a better idea.

More upmarket options include the *Restaurant de la Poste "Chez le Chef"* in the main square opposite the Medina, with excellent fish and soups and an amiable polyglot staff. The nearby *Restaurant Berbère* is pricier but very good. *La Medina* and *Barberousse*, next to each other on the Medina wall, have expensive meals and good views, but the best seafood in town is to be had at the *Restaurant Chez Achour*, hidden at the end of rue Ali Belhouane. A pleasant **café** that operates only in season is the *Café de la Lune*, in a *koubba* in the grounds of the Cultural Centre.

Listings

Banks There are several banks on av de la République, and many shops and hotels (the *Alya*, for instance) will change money outside banking hours.

Car rental There's an *Avis* on av du Kowait (☎02/280164); *Mattei* on rue Assad Ibn el Fourat at the corner of rue Taïeb el Azzabi (☎02/283570); *Topcar* (☎02/281247) on av du Kowait; there are more down av des Nations-Unies on the hotel strip. *Locamop* in rue Dag Hammarskjold (☎02/280339) rents out mopeds.

Excursions If your hotel doesn't run organized excursions around Cap Bon, they are available from any number of travel agents along av de la République.

Hammams There is one in the Medina opposite the mosque, and others at 82 av Bourguiba and at av Bourguiba's junction with av Hedi Ouali. In general they're open for women from 1 to 5pm and for men in the mornings and evenings.

International phone calls The *Kaly Centre*, opposite *Ideal Camping*, has coin-operated direct-dial phones open 24 hours. Another place is below the *Berbère* restaurant opposite the Medina. You can't call abroad from the PTT.

Medical facilities All-night pharmacy at 80 av de la République. *Infirmeries* by the police station opposite 29 av Bourguiba (☎02/282333) and on av Assad Ibn el Fourat, near the *Hôtel Bellevue*.

Newspapers English-language newspapers are available in av de la République near the Medina, and at *L'Artisane* by the *Résidence Hammamet* in av Bourguiba.

PTT Av de la République near the centre. Open country hours but also Sunday mornings. No international phone calls.

Supermarket *Magasin Général* on av de la République opposite the Medina (Tues–Sat 8am–12.30pm & 3–7pm, Sun 8am–1.30pm). There's also a large grocery store at 1 av de la Libération and in rue Ali Belhouane, opposite the *Hôtel Alya*.

Nabeul and around

NABEUL, 15km east along the coast from Hammamet, is the seat of a Governorate, a market centre and the pottery and stonework capital of Tunisia, with a busy working atmosphere quite different from its near neighbour. With easier access to the fertile hinterland of Cap Bon, Nabeul has always been an industrious place. The inhabitants of Roman Neapolis supported themselves by manufacturing *garum*, a sort of fish sauce used as basic seasoning in almost every savoury dish. "Take the entrails of tunny fish", runs a second-century recipe, "and the gills, juice, and blood, and add sufficient salt. Leave it in a vessel for two months, then pierce the vessel and the *garum* will flow out." Potteries, too, are long established in this area and still the principal industry – along with tourism.

Between Hammamet and Nabeul, hotels continue right along the beach and more are being built all the time. Though the sand here is just as extensive as it is west of Hammamet, the beach lacks Hammamet's gentle curve and lush green backing. On a windy day it can feel distinctly exposed, and even on a good day it lacks the intimacy that west Hammamet has miraculously maintained.

President Ben Ali recently announced plans to build a villa on the eastern edge of Hammamet. In the hot-house world of Tunisian regional rivalry (both Bourguiba and Ben Ali are from the Sahel, and Bourguiba turned Monastir into something of a personal cult centre), this caused quite a stir.

Arrival and accommodation

Avenue Habib Thameur (av Farhat Hached) is Nabeul's main tourist strip and leads to the **louage station** and the Friday **market** site. A couple of blocks seawards is place 7 Novembre and the **train station**. The **PTT** is close by on avenue Bourguiba, north of the junction with avenue H Thameur, and you can make international phone calls there.

The *ONTT* regional **tourist office** is on avenue Taïeb Mehiri, not far from the beach (Mon–Thurs 8.30am–1pm & 3–5.45pm, Fri & Sat 8.30am–1.30pm; July & Aug Mon–Sat 7.30am–1.30pm & 3–9pm), and can supply details of the summer cultural **festival** events in the open-air theatre at the beach end of avenue Bourguiba during July and August, and the Orange Blossom Festival during April or May.

As a major tourist resort, Nabeul is not short of **hotels**. The big ones are on the beach, but the town has acquired an unusual and welcome sprinkling of *pensions familiales*, along with two youth hostels and a campsite.

Hotels and pensions

Club Aquarius ★★, Route Touristique, on the beach (☎02/285777). French *Club Med*-style establishment with full facilities, fortified against any possible intrusion by anyone or anything remotely Tunisian. Near the *Hôtel Monia Club*. Closed Nov–Feb. ⑥.

Fakir ★★, Route Touristique, next to the *Monia Club* (☎02/285477). Another small and newish place, just outside the Roman remains and within easy reach of the beach. ④.

El Habib, av Habib Thameur (☎02/287190). On the road to Hammamet by the *oued*. Clean and friendly with a small library of left-behind paperbacks. Recommended. ②.

Hafsides, rue Sidi Maaouia (☎02/285823). Behind the hospital. Another low-key pension, though its town centre location can make it noisy. Closed out of season. ②.

Les Jasmins ★, av Habib Thameur (☎02/285343). The hotel itself is not unreasonably priced, but is liable to be booked up in season. ③.

Monia Club, on the Hammamet beach road, opposite the site of Neapolis (☎02/272481). Officially a *pension*, this is really more a restaurant and bar with staying guests. You can play pool or pinball here. ③.

Mustapha, av Habib el Karma (☎02/222262). A lovely little place, clean and welcoming. Recommended. ②.

Les Oliviers, rue de Havana, off rue Abdou el Kacem Chabi (☎02/286865). Out beyond the *El Habib*, this place is closed in winter. ②.

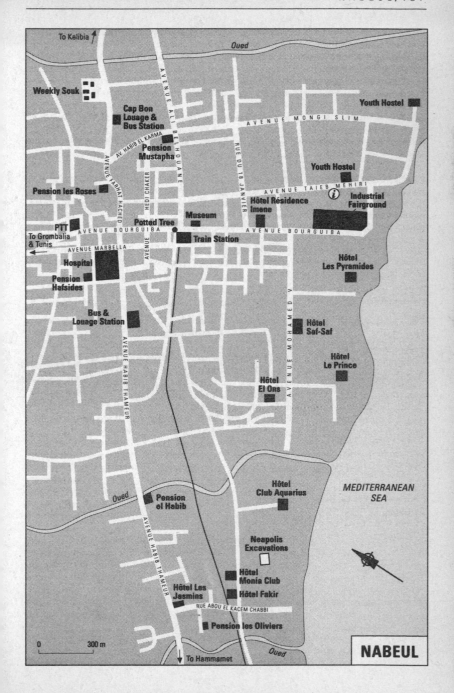

To Kelibia

Oued

Weekly Souk

Cap Bon
Louage &
Bus Station

AV HABIB EL KARMA

AVENUE ALI BELHOUANE

AVENUE MONGI SLIM

Youth Hostel

Pension
Mustapha

HEDI CHAKER

RUE DU 18 JANVIER

AVENUE FARHAT HACHED

Youth Hostel

Pension les Roses

AVENUE TAIEB MEHIRI

Industrial
Fairground

PTT

To Grombalia
& Tunis

AVENUE BOURGUIBA

Potted Tree

Museum

Hôtel Résidence
Imene

AVENUE BOURGUIBA

AVENUE

Train Station

AVENUE MARBELLA

Hospital

Hôtel
Les Pyramides

Pension
Hafsides

AVENUE HABIB THAMEUR

Bus &
Louage Station

AVENUE MOHAMED V

Hôtel
Saf-Saf

Hôtel
Le Prince

Hôtel
El Ons

MEDITERRANEAN
SEA

Hôtel
Club Aquarius

Oued

Pension
el Habib

Neapolis
Excavations

AVENUE HABIB THAMEUR

Hôtel Les
Jasmins

Hôtel
Monia Club

Hôtel Fakir

RUE ABOU EL KACEM CHABBI

Pension les Oliviers

0   300 m

To Hammamet

Oued

NABEUL

El Ons ★★, av Mohamed V (☎02/286129). A relatively new package hotel, slightly marooned behind the *Club Farah*. ③.

Le Prince ★★★, on the beachfront, off av Mohamed V (☎02/285470). Prime beachfront location, well reflected in its price. ⑥.

Les Pyramides, av Bourguiba (☎02/285444). Large, impersonal complex. ③.

Résidence Imene ★★★, av Bourguiba (☎02/222310). Very comfortable, with big rooms, but rather impersonal and fraying slightly at the edges. ④.

Les Roses, 3 rue Sidi Abd el Kader, just off av Farhat Hached (☎02/285570). The cheapest of the *pensions* and not at all bad. ②.

Saf-Saf ★★, av Mohamed V (☎02/286044). Newish place in the hotel distict that's smaller and less impersonal than many. ④.

Youth hostels and campsites

Maison des Jeunes youth hostel, av Mongi Slim (☎02/285547). The hostel's location right by the beach is great, but that's about it. It's completely full in summer and empty the rest of the year. You must pay for at least one meal during your stay. Closed Feb. ①.

Maison des Jeunes youth hostel, av Taïeb Mehiri (☎02/286689). The usual concrete splendour. Check-in after 5pm only – you can't leave your bags there in the meantime. ①.

Hôtel les Jasmins campsite, rue Abou el Kacem Chabi, near the *Pension les Oliviers* (☎02/285343). The only official site in Nabeul is attached to the hotel (see above). 1.3TD per person plus 0.9TD per tent plus 1TD for a hot shower.

The Town

The centre of town is where avenue Habib Thameur crosses the Tunis road, **avenue Bourguiba**, which runs straight through the town almost to the beach – around a fifteen-minute walk. A couple of blocks towards the sea, an unsubtle giant pot built around a pine tree in the middle of the road at **place 7 Novembre** is really the town's only landmark and proclaims Nabeul's major industry.

Nabeul's **beach** is what a lot of people come here for. Like Hammamet's shoreline, it is increasingly hotel-lined but still attractive, with nothing except tourist-oriented cafés and restaurants, and also plenty of watersport facilities – if you plan to stay a while you might want to invest in membership of the **Club des Trières**, which gives unlimited use of their equipment (subject to often heavy demand).

The town's weekly Friday **market** out on rue el Arbi Zarrouk, a continuation of avenue Farhat Hached, has become one of the country's biggest tourist attractions, with bus-loads of shoppers arriving from all over the country to pick up the local crafts (see box). There's nothing out of the ordinary about it except size and convenience – since the tourists have been coming it's sprouted an additional section specializing in holiday souvenirs. You can avoid the crowds by coming on Thursday evening for an early start next day – better still, make a point of visiting a less self-conscious market elsewhere.

No doubt the excavations of **Roman Neapolis**, down near the *Hôtel Monia Club*, will soon be developed as a paying sight. In the meantime, few of the tourists who pass through Nabeul are even aware of its existence. A Phoenician settlement was established here as early as 500 BC. If you've seen any of Tunisia's other Roman remains, you may feel Neapolis is not worth seeing, just a few fallen columns and bits of mosaic in a piece of wasteland fenced off by cacti. Officially it's closed, but you can get in from the beach by the *Hôtel Aquarius*, or climb in by the gate opposite the *Hôtel Monia Club*.

Nabeul has a **municipal museum** at 44 avenue Bourguiba, by the tree in the pot (daily except Mon 9am–4pm; 0.6TD plus 1TD for cameras). Along with some mosaics discovered locally, it also has a collection of Carthaginian pieces from Kerkouane and

NABEUL POTTERY AND OTHER CRAFTS

Many of the souvenirs on display in Nabeul, in shops with names like *Sinbad's Palace* and *Aladdin's Cave*, are standard wares available all over the country. But there's a special emphasis on **pottery** in Nabeul because, along with Jerba, this is the national centre of the craft. In fact, the potters of Nabeul originally came from Jerba, attracted perhaps by the quality of the local clay. Another important influence was the arrival in the seventeenth century of Andalusian refugees, bringing with them the artistic traditions of Muslim Spain. The same traditions were carried to Fes in Morocco, and Nabeul's ceramics often resemble those of Fes.

Pottery has a long history in Tunisia – the Roman province of Africa exported standard red tableware all over the Empire – and thanks to the tourist trade it's one traditional craft that appears to have a healthy future, even if some of the products are in highly dubious taste. Most shops will be happy to show you to the workshop of one of their suppliers (ask about an *atelier*). The industrial potters, who make bricks, are not as glamorous or well known, but are no less interesting. The small humps dotted around the eastern edge of the town, especially near the market, are the ovens in which the bricks are fired, and when they're in operation (usually in the evening) they produce a thick black pall of smoke. You'll probably be invited to clamber down into the inferno-like subterranean chamber where the oven flames are kept fired through the night.

Other crafts are worked in and around Nabeul. **Beni Khiar**, a village just along the coast road, specializes in **wool products**, and **Es Somaa**, just inland, in **straw mats**. But the big craft, after pottery, is **stone carving**. This is less amenable to souvenir production, but flourishes thanks to the policy of incorporating traditional elements in modern buildings: not just in overtly traditional ones, but in hotels and private houses too. Doorways, columns and benches in Tunisia have long been carved with intricate geometric patterns – witness the Tunis Medina – and it's fascinating to watch the process. Most of the stonework is done in **Dar Chaabane**, a small village to the east that is now virtually a suburb of Nabeul. Its main street is lined with workshops clinking to the sound of chisels, while a pile of raw stone on the pavement outside announces the trade.

In Nabeul, the **ONAT crafts shops** at 144 avenue Farhat Hached and 93 avenue H Thameur have a good selection of officially priced and officially selected items.

from Thinissut, in the hills just above Hammamet. Dating from the third century BC, the Kerkouane statuettes display the usual combination of Greek and eastern influences. Three hundred years later, in the first century AD, the terracotta figures from Thinissut – like their companion pieces now in the Bardo – show these cross-cultural influences surviving even into the Roman era: the Punic goddess Tanit's lion head, for example.

There are also two quaint but, in practical terms, useless forms of public transport in Nabeul: the **road train** to Hammamet (3 times a day; 2hr; 2.5TD) and the horse-drawn **calèches**. The *calèches* are no more traditionally Tunisian than the road train, and equally overpriced. Children adore them both.

Eating and drinking

Nabeul's two main budget **restaurants** are to be found at the bend in avenue Farhat Hached, by the *Pension des Roses*. Both the *Restaurant du Bonheur* and the *Restaurant de la Jeunesse* do cheap meals for around 3.5TD, with little to choose between them. The *Rôtisserie/Self-Service Berbère* at 34 rue Habib Karma is also cheap (1.3TD for a quarter chicken), but extremely greasy and not exactly pristine. For more refinement, the *Hôtel les Jasmins* has a restaurant with a moderately priced set menu. If you want to splash out, try *Restaurant de l'Olivier*, 6 av Hedi Chaker, on the corner of avenue Bourguiba, or *Restaurant Le Bonkif* on avenue Marbella, one of Nabeul's fanciest.

For just a coffee, the *Café le Petit Chef*, 82 av Hedi Chaker, is a popular hangout for local student types. If your French is good enough, you can peruse their little library of books and magazines to catch up on the latest news over your *thé* and *chicha*.

Listings

Banks There are lots on and around av Bourguiba, and some should be open in the morning at weekends.

Bicycle rental The youth hostel rents out bicycles at 2TD an hour.

Car rental *Express Car*, 148 av Hedi Thameur (☎02/287014); *Rent-a-Car*, 94 av Bourguiba (☎02/286679); and *TLS*, 3 rue Ibn Badis (☎02/220516)

Cinema *Palace Cinema*, 43 av Hedi Chaker.

Festivals The summer festival, a programme of cultural events for tourists, takes place over July and August in the open-air theatre at the beach end of av Bourguiba, the only time it's ever used. The Orange Blossom Festival, in April or May (whenever the orange blossom appears), is also directed at tourists.

Hammams There's one at 42 av Hedi Chaker (men mornings, women afternoons), one at 37 rue Sidi Bel Aissa, and a women-only one, *Bain Sidi Maaouria*, at 19 av Hedi Thameur.

International phone calls At the PTT, or the taxiphone office at 168 av Hedi Thameur (daily 7am–midnight).

Medical facilities The regional hospital (☎02/285633) is in the centre of town on av Hedi Thameur, 100m from av Bourguiba. The night pharmacy is opposite at 37 av H Thameur. *Infirmeries* are at 80 av Hedi Chaker and 10 rue Ibn Badis.

Newspapers English-language papers can be found at the *Librairie de l'Avenir*, 86 av Hedi Chaker, and *Imprimerie Boussan*, 131 av Farhat Hached.

ONAT crafts shops 144 av Farhat Hached and 93 av Hedi Thameur.

PTT Av Bourguiba, north of the junction with av Hedi Thameur (city hours), and you can make international phone calls there.

Supermarkets There's a large supermarket at 30 av Bourguiba and a smaller one in rue de Gafsa by the *louage* station.

North of Nabeul

North of Nabeul the coast is one endless stretch of white beach backed, as far as Menzel Temime, by unsightly salt flats, and after that by rich farmland. There are few

---

MOVING ON FROM NABEUL

Nabeul is the main transport centre of Cap Bon, and it's easy to reach most parts of the peninsula from here. The train line comes through here, but passenger services have virtually ceased, with just one early-morning service from the **train station** on place 7 Novembre through Hammamet to Bir Bou Rekba (25min), and continuing to Tunis. More convenient is the **bus station**, off avenue Habib Thameur, a five-minute walk down from avenue Bourguiba. There are lots of buses from here to Hammamet (15min), up to the Gulf of Tunis to Borj Cedria (1hr), Grombalia (45min) and to Tunis itself (1hr 30min); there are rather fewer to Fahs (3 daily; 1hr 45min) and Zaghouan (2 daily; 1hr 30min), and to southern destinations like Kairouan (1 daily; 2hr), Mahdia (1 daily; 3hr 30min), Monastir (1 daily; 2hr 30min) and Sousse (2 daily; 2hr 15min). **Louages** serve Tunis, Zaghouan, Fahs and Enfida and, if you're lucky, you may find a red and white **taxi** for Hammamet.

Buses and *louages* going up the **Cap Bon peninsula** leave from rue el Arbi Zarrouk, a continuation of avenue Farhat Hached, about 500m east of avenue Bourguiba. There are frequent bus departures for Kelibia (1hr), Korba (15min) and Menzel Temime (45min), and plenty of *louages* on the same route. Note there are no buses or *louages* through to El Haouria; you have to change at Kelibia.

towns, fewer places to stay, and little reason to stop off except for a minimal change of beach scenery.

KORBA, the next town north from Nabeul, has an exclusive *Club Méditerranée* resort as well as a Sunday souk and minor Roman remains. Birdwatchers should find it worth a stop in passing as there are lagoons and a salt marsh just to the north, which hold flamingoes, spoonbills'and avocets in the spring, a good range of migrants in spring and autumn, and ducks over the winter. Should you need them, Korba has a **PTT** (country hours) and a couple of **banks** on the main Nabeul–Kelibia road through town.

Another 25km further along the coast, **MENZEL TEMIME** has no special attractions but its **beach** (albeit rather windy and some way from town), making it a feasible alternative to the tourist ghettos of Nabeul and Hammamet. The **bus station** in town is a roundabout on the Nabeul–Kelibia road, avenue de la République. Running off it is the inevitable **avenue Bourguiba**, along which the people at nos. 29 and 31 have put a lot of work into their front doors. The **PTT** is at no. 39, and beyond that are two **banks**, with another on the main square at the end. The main square is where **louages** hang out, plying to Nabeul, Kelibia, Menzel Bou Zelfa and Tunis. Also on the square, next to a cavernous café, the two-star *Hôtel Temime* (☎02/298296; ②) offers pleasant, clean rooms (with a choice of bath or shower). If the price is too steep, there's the *Maison des Jeunes* **youth hostel** behind (☎02/298116; ①), signposted only in Arabic. There's a **cinema** next door and a couple of cheap **restaurants** on the market square beyond that. On a Tuesday, turn left at the square for the **souk**, spread out down a wide boulevard, and if you're in need of supplies at any other time, the opposite direction (the continuation of avenue Bourguiba) takes you to the *Monoprix* **supermarket**.

Kelibia and around

With all the ingredients for resort development, **KELIBIA**, 17km along the coast from Nabeul, has so far resisted touristic temptation and remains an agricultural centre with a major fishing port nestling under a huge sixteenth-century fortress. If all you want is access to a pleasant beach from a scenic town, you'll like Kelibia – although be aware that a rumoured development north of town may change the balance over the next few years.

As part of its agricultural heritage, Kelibia produces a **dry muscat wine** which is worth trying. Another Kelibia curiosity is the number of locals who bear the name *el Ingliis*, meaning "Englishman" or "Englishwoman". By one account their common ancestor was an Englishman who came to work here during the Ottoman era, converted to Islam and stayed. Another story has it that they are all descendants of shipwrecked sailors.

Practicalities

The town centre itself is focused on **place de la République**, some 2km west of the fortress and port. You'll most probably arrive in town at the **bus and louage station** on avenue Ali Belhouane. The **PTT** is on avenue Bourguiba (country hours) and there are **banks** nearby, with one on avenue Bourguiba, one on rue Ibn Khaldoun and one in place de la République. The **night pharmacy** is at the beginning of avenue des Martyrs, opposite the Maison du Peuple. There's a small food **market** where avenue Erriadh meets avenue des Martyrs, but the **Monday souk** takes place just north of avenue Ali Belhouane. Daily necessities can be bought at the **supermarket** on rue Ibn Khaldoun, or on rue Ezzouhour, off place des Martyrs. *Royal Rent a Car* (☎02/296465) is on avenue des Martyrs, just opposite the *Florida* turning. There is no tourist office in town.

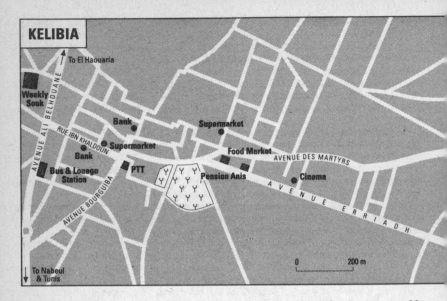

There's a reasonable selection of medium-priced **accommodation** in town, notably the old favourite *Hôtel Florida*, down the beach by the harbour (☎02/296248; ②); its rooms and bungalows cost the same but the bungalows have en suite bathrooms. The *Pension Anis*, off avenue Erriadh between the town centre and the beach (☎02/295777; ②), has spotless, airy rooms, and shared – but squeaky-clean – bathrooms; or there's the more expensive, package-type *Mamounia*, some way along the beach (☎02/296219; ②), having little in common with its Marrakesh namesake. If you're on a budget, there's also a drab, but convenient and unusually friendly *Maison des Jeunes* **youth hostel** on the Mansoura road by the port (☎02/296105; ①). You can sometimes **camp** in the grounds, and there's a small, unearthed Roman site in front of it.

The Town and around

Part of Kelibia's charm is the feeling that it's something of a backwater, but this was by no means always so. Some fine remains, which can be seen in the various patchy **excavations** around the town, bear witness to a sizeable Roman presence, and for the Byzantines, who built the first **fortress** here, *Clupea* (Kelibia) was reportedly the last place of refuge after the Arab invasion. Later, the town and fortress were sacked three times by the Spanish between 1535 and 1547.

The fortress is currently being restored and an **Islamic museum** is planned here (daily summer 8am–7pm; winter 8.30am–3.30pm; 1TD). For the moment, you'll find yourself sharing the interior of the fortifications with the *gardien*'s impressive collection of domestic fowl. At the foot of the towering fortress lies the **port**, consisting of little more than a few scattered shops and houses, as well as the State Fishing School. Kelibia is the best natural harbour before Sousse – which explains the fortress. For **watersports** in Kelibia, you could try and persuade the *Mamounia* you're a resident; the municipal club by the harbour also rents out sailboards not in use by local people.

The main **beach** lies south of the fishing port at the end of avenue Erriadh, but unfortunately it's covered in from seaweed and is not that attractive. Far more alluring is the series of beautiful coves 2km to the north at **MANSOURA**, backed by a small

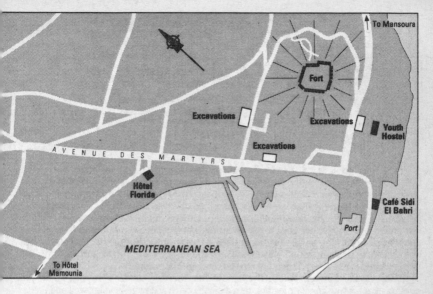

but exclusive community nicknamed "Little Paris", and with an excellent café-restaurant on its rocky promontory (hours variable). To get to Mansoura, you can catch a taxi from near the harbour in Kelibia. The *Hôtel Mansoura*, 1.5km further along the road, is closed and due for redevelopment; immediately opposite its entrance is an unlikely group of **Carthaginian rock tombs**. Take a track leading alongside a construction depot and you'll find the tombs cut in the rock to the right of the road after no more than 50m. You're almost on top of them before you see the series of rectangular openings with steps heading down, so clean cut that they look twenty years old, not twenty centuries. North of Mansoura, the shore runs in deserted and tempting swathes of white beach to the end of Cap Bon. You can combine the beaches with a visit to Kerkouane (see below) by taking some food and strolling back along the shore, though be warned that it's about four and a half hours' walk.

Eating and drinking

Not surprisingly, **eating and drinking** opportunities in Kelibia are limited. The *Florida* and the *Anis* both have pricey restaurants, where fish is the obvious thing to go for. *Restaurant de la Jeunesse* on avenue des Martyrs, opposite the *Florida* turning, is a cheap alternative that does reasonable fish dishes. *Café Sidi el Bahri*, facing out to sea just beyond the port, offers tables on the beach and mint tea with pine nuts, along the lines of Sidi Bou Said.

Kerkouane

Halfway between Kelibia and El Haouaria, a signposted side road runs about 1500m down to the Carthaginian site of **Kerkouane** (daily summer 8am–6pm; winter 9am–2pm; 1TD, plus 1TD to take photos), discovered in 1952 and the first in Tunisia to produce more than a few funerary objects – Punic jewellery and other artefacts are displayed in a small adjoining **museum** (daily except Mon, same hours), whose most notable exhibit is a wooden Punic statue found nearby.

MOVING ON FROM KELIBIA

All buses and some *louages* leave from the **bus station** on avenue Ali Belhouane. There's just one early departure to Mahdia (4hr), Monastir (3hr) and Sousse (2hr 30min), and services every hour or so through the day to El Haouaria (30min), Korba (45min), Menzel Bou Zelfa (1hr), Menzel Temime (15min), Nabeul (1hr), Soliman (1hr 15min) and Tunis (2hr 30min).

It's worth noting that a summer **jet-foil** service runs from Kelibia port to Trápani in Sicily, usually a four-hour journey but unpredictable, especially in rough weather. For more details ask around at the port, or contact *Tirrenia Navigazione* or their agents *Tourafric*, 52 av Bourguiba, Tunis (☎01/341483).

There was great initial excitement about the streets and house-plans uncovered here, but because no public buildings were initially found, the eccentric theory was posited that this was a fifth-century BC holiday resort – a sort of Carthaginian *Club Med*. It is now thought that the town's main industry was manufacturing a purple dye for which Carthaginians and Phoenicians were famous, named after a species of shell-fish called *murex*. Hundreds of these creatures were collected and left in large pits in the ground to rot; the smell must have been overpowering, but the decomposed mess was somehow made up into the dye known by the Romans as "Tyrian purple" (after the Phoenician capital, Tyre), much beloved as the imperial colour.

Almost all the **houses**, whose foundations line the easy-to-follow streets, follow the same plan: a narrow corridor leading into a small courtyard, with a water well and some-times an altar to the household gods. Kerkouane's houses are most famous, however, for their private **baths**, neatly lined with reddish cement. Virtually every house has its own, which says something about Carthaginian society – while the Romans spent vast sums on public baths, the Carthaginians kept a private, introverted profile. The town was aban-doned some time in the second century BC, after the destruction of Carthage, and never reoccupied by the Romans – which explains its remarkable state of preservation.

If Kerkouane, the largest Carthaginian site yet discovered, seems like a meagre remnant of a major civilization, it's worth remembering that outsiders were as impressed by the Carthaginians' agricultural prowess as they were by their navy and child sacrifices. This description of the interior of Cap Bon by Diodorus Siculus, a historian writing in Rome in the first century BC, but drawing on earlier accounts, would not be out of place today:

It was divided into market gardens and orchards of all sorts of fruit trees, with many streams of water flowing in channels irrigating every part. There were country houses everywhere, lavishly built and covered with stucco, which testified to the wealth of their owners . . . Part of the land was planted with vines, part with olives and other protective trees. Beyond these, cattle and sheep were pastured on the plains, and there were mead-ows filled with grazing horses.

To **get to Kerkouane**, if you don't have your own transport, you can take a bus or *louage* from Kelibia to the turn-off; take a taxi (for around 4TD – settle the price before you start); or even walk or hitch – the latter is certainly possible. Leaving the site, you'll probably have to take pot luck and hitch, or hail a passing bus or *louage*.

El Haouaria and around

Just below **Jebel Sidi Abiod**, the defiant last hump of Cap Bon, **EL HAOUARIA** is a pretty village best known as the centre of falconry in Tunisia. In an annual festival held in mid-June, young birds are caught on the mountain, trained for a month, then used for hunting game birds on the mountain and the heaths below. Two species of birds of prey are involved – sparrowhawks, which are trapped in nets on the mountain as they migrate, and peregrine falcons, which are taken as young from the nests on the rocky cliffs. The number of birds each falconer can catch is supposed to be strictly limited; they may not be sold, and the sparrowhawks are later returned to the wild, but what happens to the peregrines is uncertain. About 500m out of the village, there's an extremely helpful and informative **wildlife information centre**, with particularly good information on birds of prey, run by the *Cellule Nature et Oiseaux*. The building is called the *Aquilaria*, after the Latin for "eagle"; the name of the town is supposed to be a corruption of the same word. The village itself is a sleepy agricultural centre that turns its back on the Mediterranean to focus on Cap Bon's rich hinterland.

El Haouaria is pleasantly out of the way and all its villagers will assume you've come to see the two sets of **caves** just outside town. One of these, the **Ghar el Kebir**, is a complex of quarries right on the shore, reached by following the road straight through the village past the cemetery. Forty minutes' walk will bring you to a group of pyramid-shaped chambers poised above crashing breakers. Quarrying operations started here by the Carthaginians were continued by the Romans and Byzantines – the latter installing a military garrison – and the stone was used for buildings all around the Gulf of Carthage. Chat to the residents and you'll hear vivid stories of slaves spending their whole lives in the caverns.

The other cave complex, up on the mountain – **La Grotte des Chauves-Souris** – is full of bats. A 4km track leads from the village, but you'll need to ask around for a guide in El Haouaria itself. You'll also need a torch to make close acquaintance with the creatures. If bats don't appeal, the mountain is still a wonderful place for long windy walks, where you can reflect on the strategic position that has played such a large part in Tunisia's history; Sicily is only 150km away and the next time Africa and Europe get so close is at Gibraltar to the west and the Dardanelles to the east.

Southeast of El Haouaria, at the very beginning of Cap Bon's south coast, hides the area's most beautiful and least-known beach, **Ras ed Drak** – known as El Haouaria Plage these days. The white sands are sheltered here and given an extra dimension by the mountain's craggy shoulder. A signposted 4km road leads from El Haouaria over

---

FAUNA AROUND EL HAOUARIA AND THE CAPE

The rocky hillsides around the mountain of Jebel Sidi Abiod and the walk to Ras ed Drak beach are rich not only in flowers but also in **bird life**. The fields have abundant finches, buntings and warblers, along with stonechats – the black-headed males perching prominently on bushes and telegraph wires. Down on Ras ed Drak, the scrub behind the beach is often full of migrating birds, with the unusual blue rock thrush and Moussier's redstart both relatively common residents.

The sea is worth watching, too, and vast numbers of breeding pairs of the stiff-winged Cory's shearwater, as well as gulls and gull-billed and sandwich terns, can often be seen flying past, the last two species occurring as winter visitors and passage migrants.

The actual headland of Cap Bon is special because it is the last jumping-off point for migrating birds of prey before they cross the Mediterranean. April and May are the peak spring passage months, with lesser numbers coming back each autumn. Honey buzzards are the dominant species, although black kites, marsh harriers and common buzzards also occur in good numbers, together with a variety of migrating eagles, sparrowhawks and hobbies (the small, rather dashing falcons, midway in size between kestrel and peregrine, that prey mostly on swallows and the like – they follow the migrating swallow flocks up from Africa). The best place for viewing the migration is the top of Jebel Sidi Abiod. This requires a **permit** during the migration season: write in advance to the *Direction des Fôrets*, 30 rue Alain Savary, Tunis.

heathland to the assortment of villas and farms on the slopes behind the beach where, in season, there's a small shop on the sand. The futuristic complex on the shore to the south is a station on a gas pipeline from Algeria to Italy.

Practicalities

If you need to change any money, El Haouaria has a **bank** in the main square. There's a **louage** service from the main square to Kelibia every hour or so and less frequently to Tunis. For more local destinations like Kerkouane or the Sidi Daoud turn-off, you could hitch or share a **taxi** (0.4TD each to the Sidi Daoud turn-off). There is no tourist office here, but good budget **accommodation** in the form of the *Pension Dar Toubib* (☎02/297163; ①), tucked away down the side streets but well signposted (follow the light-blue arrows). Having tracked down the hotel, you may have to ask for the proprietor. If it seems too basic, the only alternative is the recently opened and expensive two-star *Hôtel l'Epervier* in the main street (☎02/297017; ④). **Camping** on Ras ed Drak is feasible if you're happy with water from wells and food bought from the farms. Across the street from the *Epervier* in El Haouaria, the *Restaurant de la Jeunesse* serves basic **meals**. The *Epervier*'s restaurant is priced in line with its rooms.

Sidi Daoud and around

Seven kilometres on past El Haouaria, heading west along the north coast of the peninsula, a turning on the right leads in 2km to **SIDI DAOUD**, the sleepiest of sleepy fishing villages. Almost totally dormant for ten months of the year, it bursts into life around May for the **Matanza**, a spectacular if gory tuna harvest with a technique going back to Roman times. A huge net is laid about 4km out to sea, stretching from surface to seabed to catch the fish as they migrate around the coast to reproduce. The net forms a series of chambers of decreasing size, and when the final one – the *corpo*, or death chamber – is full, it is closed. Then the boats converge around the net and raise it from all sides until the fish are virtually out of the water, at which point the fishermen jump into the net and set about the fish (some of which weigh as much as 250kg) with clubs and knives. Well and truly slaughtered, the fish are canned in the village's factory and distributed.

It used to be possible to get a **permit** from the National Fisheries Office to watch the Matanza from one of the boats but, after disagreements with the tourist authorities, this scheme has lapsed. If you're interested, it might be worth checking the permit situation with the *Commissariat Général de la Pêche* in Tunis at 30 rue Alain Savary (☎01/890761) before you come up here. Failing that, the local office is at the dockside. If you do get permission and decide to try it, be warned that the smell of fish lingers for some days afterwards.

Off the coast north of Sidi Daoud, the islands of **Zembra** and **Zembretta** are now off limits, having been declared a nature reserve under army protection. Zembra, with seabirds, beautiful scenery and excellent snorkelling, used to host a scuba diving centre run by the *Centre Nautique de Tunisie*. If you want to try for a permit to visit, you could write to the *Direction des Fôrets* at 30 rue Alain Savary in Tunis, well in advance of your trip, stating reasons; don't expect success, but if you do get permission, access to the island is by fishing boat from Sidi Daoud. There's nowhere to stay on the island so it'll have to be a day trip.

The only other diversion around Sidi Daoud is the **Forest of Dar Chichou** to the southeast. A road runs inland from Sidi Daoud, through the forest to emerge on the south coast between Kerkouane and Kelibia. On the way, you pass a fenced-off **nature reserve** devoted, strangely enough, to **gazelles**; you should be able to glimpse some from the road, especially if you stop and wait quietly for a while.

From Sidi Daoud down the Cap Bon's northern coast to Bir Meroua, the road stays several kilometres inland, skirting country that is surprisingly mountainous – even reminiscent of Scottish heathland. For most of the way, the coastline is one deserted beach, backed by farmland with any number of possible tracks down to the shore but no facilities once you are there.

There is no **public transport** from Sidi Daoud itself, but you may be able to pick up a bus or *louage* along the main road. Buses from El Haouaria to Soliman and Grombalia run along here (local people will know current times), but *louages* are likely to be full and you might have a shorter wait if you hitch.

Korbous and around

Protruding like the knuckle of Cap Bon's finger, the massif of **Jebel Korbous** looms over the ancient thermal resort named after it. Famous since Roman times and heavily developed by the French, **KORBOUS**, 30km along the coast from Sidi Daoud, has seen better days and now exudes a seedy, turn-of-the-century air reminiscent of Hammam Lif. It remains a popular weekend excursion, though, and the scenery is dramatic – especially if you have transport that will take you all the way round the mountain.

Korbous is set in a steep ravine where the Romans first came to take the waters at *Aquae Carpitanae*. At the end of the last century the modern spa was redesigned by a French civil engineer, who then retired to the precarious villa – now a presidential palace – perched on the rock overlooking the main street. There isn't a great deal to Korbous: a main street lined with souvenir stalls for the trippers on Sundays, and the fancy three-star *Hôtel les Sources* (☎02/294533; ④) for those who can afford the supervised thermal cure ("The largest dose will be taken first thing in the morning while fasting in several successive swallows", according to the *ONTT* literature). An ancient **hammam** to the left of the street (men in the morning, women in the afternoon) is reputed to go back to the Romans and, between the presidential palace and the hotel, the **Zarziha Rock** has been polished smooth by generations of women sliding down it to cure infertility. It's a pretty enough place, with waves crashing on to rocks below the Jebel Korbous's craggy green slopes. Facilities are limited, but the *Café-Restaurant Dhib*, on the main street, is pleasant and moderately priced.

Once you've seen Korbous, you'll need your own transport if you want to follow the new road around **Jebel Korbous**. A few kilometres beyond the village, a spring called **Aïn el Atrous** shoots out of the mountain through a pipe below the road. There's a narrow strip of beach beyond which people **camp** (though it looks very exposed), and at this point the recent extension of the road takes off and, before you know it, you're hundreds of metres up on the mountain's north shoulder, then dropping down onto a high plain and the village of **Douela** before meeting up again with the main road south to Soliman at the small settlement of **Bir Meroua**. If you can find some way of getting down to the long, pristine white beach of **Marsa Ben Ramdane**, it's one of the most spectacular in the country: take the track (signposted to Bekakcha) to the right about 3km outside Bir Meroua on the road to Korbous. Eleven rough kilometres further sits a magnificent white beach. Dominated by a fort that's been converted into a private house, the only permanent inhabitants down here are a few fishermen who operate from a wooden pier. In season, you might be able to rent one of the reed shacks on the beach.

Further south along the coast towards Soliman, the tiny, rickety settlement of **SIDI RAIS** was once a fashionable seaside resort, but now comprises just a row of wooden houses on stilts. One kilometre back towards Korbous, the *Hôtel Chiraz* (☎02/293329; ③) – confusingly listed under Korbous in tourist leaflets – shelters in an orchard. Shortly afterwards the road climbs onto a ledge above the shore and soon passes the spring of **AÏN OKTOR**, where the three-star *Hôtel Aïn Oktor* (☎02/284557; ④) offers thermal cures and views; outside, in a sort of concrete tent, it's possible to taste the water for free.

Soliman and around

Eighteen kilometres south of Korbous is **SOLIMAN**, a seventeenth-century Andalusian settlement whose **mosque** is almost the only remnant of that time. Today the town is a prosperous agricultural centre with an attractive tree-filled square next to the mosque, whose semicircular Spanish roof tiles can just be made out. Look out, too, for a **fountain** surrounded by colourful ceramic work.

Rue Habib Thameur runs from the town centre around the mosque to end up near the **bus station**, from where there are frequent services to Grombalia (15min) and Menzel Bou Zelfa (15min), two a day to Korbous (20min) and hourly services to Tunis (45min). There are also **louages** to Tunis and Grombalia which leave from near the bus station. There are no buses or *louages* for Soliman Plage; taxis leave from place 7 Novembre, the other side of the town centre, or you could hitch or walk. The **PTT** (country hours) is at 35 rue Habib Thameur. As for **accommodation**, there are no hotels in town itself, only at Soliman Plage.

Isolated on the edge of an empty marshy plain, **SOLIMAN PLAGE** (also known as Plage Ejjehmi) is Soliman's beach resort, 3km away. The sand is white enough and there are good views of the mountains – Jebel Bou Kornine to the west and Jebel Korbous to the east – but the desolate stretch of beach makes for one of the least attractive resorts in Tunisia. At the end of the road from Soliman is a **café** where you could stop for a cup of tea, with two **hotels** a few hundred metres up the beach to your left (to get straight to them, turn off the Soliman road 500m before hitting the beach). Between the café and the hotels, straw beach cabins are used by Tunisian holiday-makers during July and August when the beach is packed solid. The rest of the year they're abandoned and anyone could use them for a night on the beach.

Of the two **hotels**, both catering for European package tourists, the one-star *Hôtel el Andalous* (☎02/290199; ④) is the cheaper and has waterskiing and riding, but no pool. Posher and rather Teutonic is the two-star *Hôtel Solymar* (☎02/290105; ④). Beyond the *Solymar*, the beach continues round to Borj Cedria (see p.113).

Grombalia and around

Heading south from Tunis, the highway and the old GP1 cut through the fertile bottom end of Cap Bon. Originally settled by Spanish Muslim immigrants in the seventeenth century, the region was later popular with European farmers under the French regime, who left behind the many red-tiled farms and crumbling gate-posts scattered among its vast vineyards and orchards.

There's little enough reason to stop off here, unless you happen to coincide with one of the seasonal festivals. **GROMBALIA**, straddling both GP1 and the main north-south train line, is the largest market town in the area and celebrates a **wine festival** every September to coincide with the harvest – though that aside, there's little reason to come. There are frequent buses and *louages* to Menzel Bou Zelfa, Nabeul, Soliman and Tunis. Grombalia's **train station** has three services a day to Mahdia (3hr 15min), Monastir (2hr 15min) and Sousse (1hr 30min), and four a day to Bir Bou Rekba (20min, with 9 daily connections to Hammamet and Nabeul) and Tunis (45min); there are also hourly buses to Menzel Bou Zelfa (15min), Nabeul (45min), Soliman (15min) and Tunis (45min).

MENZEL BOU ZELFA, 8km east of Grombalia, has an **Orange Festival** to cele-brate the appearance of orange blossom in April or May, as well as an important seventeenth-century **zaouia**, a multi-domed structure in the centre of town. There are onward bus services to Menzel Bou Zelfa to: Grombalia (frequent; 15min), Kelibia (hourly; 1hr), Menzel Temime (hourly; 45min), Soliman (frequent; 15min) and Tunis (hourly; 1hr).

If you're mobile and fancy an excursion into the hills west of Grombalia, take the road opposite the *Société Tunisienne de Banque* on the main road, which leads 8km over the motorway up to the village of **AÏN TEBOURNOK**. Just before Ain Tebournok, look out north of the road for a grotesque **colonial mansion**, a fantasy Moorish pile, with a quasi-minaret for a central tower staring out over the plain. Aïn Tebournok itself sits in a bowl of hills, built around an ancient spring where Roman remains lie like a deserted thirty-year-old municipal facility.

Some 10km south of Grombalia on the road to Hammamet is **BOU ARGOUB**. There's little enough to this tiny village apart from a **villa** built by the Fascists of Tunisia's Italian community for Mussolini. Relations between Mussolini and the French were never good; the Italians always felt they had been cheated out of Tunisia in 1881 and had to settle for second best with Libya; Mussolini was continually preparing to invade Tunisia and, with more Italian colonists in the country than French, this appeared no empty threat. Ultimately, however, the Abyssinian campaign distracted "Il Duce" and the villa, now a girls' school, was never occupied by him.

travel details

Trains

Hammamet to: Bir Bou Rekba and Nabeul.

Nabeul to: Hammamet, Bir Bou Rekba and Tunis.

Buses

Grombalia to: Menzel Bou Zelfa, Nabeul, Soliman and Tunis.

Hammamet to: Nabeul and Tunis.

Kelibia to: El Haouaria, Korba, Mahdia, Menzel Bou Zelfa, Menzel Temime, Monastir, Sousse, Nabeul, Soliman and Tunis.

Menzel Bou Zelfa to: Grombalia, Kelibia, Menzel Temime, Soliman and Tunis.

Nabeul to: Borj Cedria, Fahs, Grombalia, Hammamet, Kairouan, Mahdia, Monastir, Sousse, Tunis, Zaghouan.

Soliman to: Grombalia, Korbous, Menzel Bou Zelfa and Tunis.

Louages

Nabeul to: Enfida, Fahs, Tunis and Zaghouan.

Soliman to: Grombalia, Menzel Bou Zelfa, Menzel Temime and Tunis.

Hydrofoil

Kelibia to: Trápani in Sicily.

MARKET DAYS

Monday – Kelibia
Tuesday – Menzel Temime
Thursday – Hammamet, Menzel Bou Zelfa

Friday – El Haouaria, Nabeul
Saturday – Soliman
Sunday – Korba

CHAPTER THREE

BIZERTE AND THE NORTH

Sparsely populated and with few roads, Tunisia's **northern coast** has played little part in the country's touristic development until recently. **Bizerte**, the one town of any size, is still more of a port than a resort, despite the excellence of the beaches in the area. Even if you get no further, Bizerte is worth a few days of your time – easily reached from Tunis, and with a monumental heritage covering centuries of strategic importance. Closer to the capital, and very much the preserve of Tunisians, are the superlative long white strands of **Raf Raf** and **Ras Sidi el Mekki**. Beaches with few equals, they are cut in two by the steep green flanks of **Cap Farina**, with its crumbling old pirate base of **Ghar el Melh**. **Utica**, a Roman city famous for its part in the civil war between Julius Caesar and Pompey, lies not far from Ghar el Melh on the road from Tunis. Inland, **Lac Ichkeul** and its national park form an ornithological highlight.

West of Bizerte along the coast, buses are infrequent and often erratic, but it's possible to reach some beautiful and remote beaches poised between deep forested headlands. **Cap Serrat** and **Sidi Mechrig** are both feasible targets; **Tabarca**, long popular as a resort for independent travellers and a recent target for major tourist development, is perhaps best of all, overlooked by a spectacular island-castle. Just inland from here, **Aïn Draham** is reckoned the coolest point in midsummer; and around, in the **Khroumirie Mountains**, there are some impressive hikes.

In contrast to the coast, the **Medjerda Valley**, formed around the country's one permanently flowing river, has always had a considerable urban population. **Beja** is the most attractive of the modern centres, though more intriguing is the Roman city of **Bulla Regia** with its underground villas, unique in the ancient world.

ACCOMMODATION PRICE CODES

All the hotels, youth hostels and pensions listed in this book have been price-graded according to the following scale, and although prices will rise during the lifetime of this edition, the relative comparisons should remain valid.

The prices quoted are for the **cheapest available double room in high season**, although many of the cheap places will have pricier rooms with en suite facilities or sea views.

Classified hotels, officially considered suitable for tourists, are graded locally from one to four stars (★), with wide-ranging prices within each category. For more on accommodation prices and categories, see Basics.

① Up to 10TD. Very cheap. Usually a bed only in a basic, unclassified hotel or a youth hostel.

② 10.1–25TD. Budget. Bed only or bed and breakfast.

③ 25.1–40TD. Comfortable budget. Good unclassified average one-star or a cheap two-star.

④ 40.1–55TD. Mid-range. Expensive two-star, cheap three-star.

⑤ 55.1–70TD. Tourist hotel. Standard three-star.

⑥ 70.1TD upwards. Deluxe. Expensive three-star, four-star or five-star.

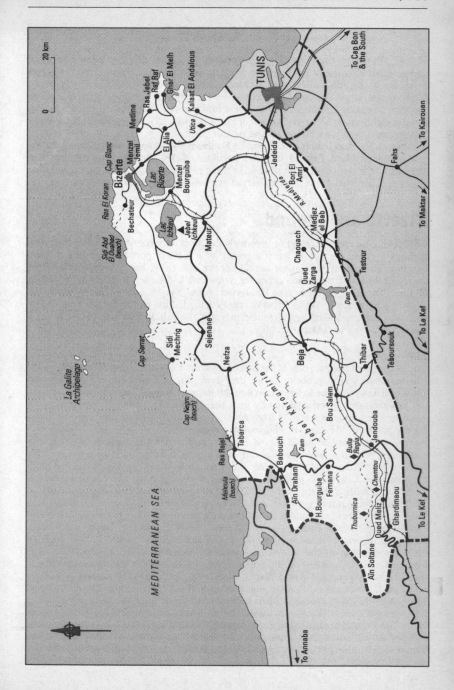

THE COAST

To visit anywhere other than the major centres along the north coast without a car means either hitching or fighting for a place in the occasional *louage*. Trains only run along the **Medjerda Valley**, with a branch line up to Bizerte; otherwise the whole north coastal region is somewhat inaccessible. The pay-off lies in the rugged, unspoiled shoreline. Soaking up the sun on the best beaches and stopping off to explore the historic sights could fill several weeks; it's best not to hurry, taking leisurely trips and avoiding confrontation with the searing summer heat.

Between **Raf Raf beach** and Tunis, the northern shoreline consists of barely inhabited alluvial farmland. Beyond, the coast becomes thickly populated and culminates in the port of **Bizerte**, where the population thins out again until **Tabarca**, recently the object of major tourist development but not yet despoiled beyond recognition.

Bizerte and around

BIZERTE, also called Benzert or Bizerta, is the most underrated of Tunisia's resorts – perhaps because it's not so much a resort as a historic port that happens to have beaches. These aren't as opulent as those of the east coast, but if you're looking for a town with both swimming and character, you won't find better. It stands at the mouth of **Lac Bizerte**, a saltwater lake connected to the sea by a canal, along which the modern port is located. An older outlet connects the fishing port to the sea. Guarded by two forts and overlooked by a dignified mosque, the fishing port is the place to get a sense of Bizerte's pre-colonial identity.

Some history

One of the great natural ports of the Mediterranean, Bizerte was exploited early by the **Phoenicians**, who improbably called their town *Hippo Diarrhytus* and dug the first channel linking the lake to the sea. When the Romans arrived they improved the existing facilities, and imperial prosperity gave the town its first taste of popularity – the Younger Pliny described it as "a town where people of all ages spend their time enjoying the pleasures of fishing, boating and swimming."

The Arabs changed the name to *Benzert*, and under the Hafsids its prosperity continued, contemporary writers mentioning a great hunting park. Bizerte inevitably found itself in the front line during the Turco-Spanish struggles of the sixteenth century, and Charles V punished the town for supporting the Christian corsair Barbarossa with a brutal raid in 1535; it went on absorbing large numbers of Andalusian immigrants, however, and was rewarded with considerable attention from the Turkish rulers, who added greatly to its amenities during the seventeenth and eighteenth centuries. **Piracy** was rife at this time but, with the demise of the slave trade and increasing European domination of the Mediterranean, Bizerte declined until the opening of the Suez Canal brought renewed strategic importance; the French set about building up the port's facilities – strictly for commercial purposes, they claimed. Even after World War II, Bizerte inspired lust in the hearts of western strategic planners, and following independence the French simply stayed on here. They still refused to evacuate when requested to do so after the bombing of Sakiet Sidi Youssef (see p.245), so, in 1961, Tunisian forces blockaded the military base. When the French tried to break the blockade, the result was the Tunisian army's first military action. More than a thousand Tunisian lives were lost before the French finally withdrew in 1963 on October 15 – no longer a national holiday, but still a day for celebrations.

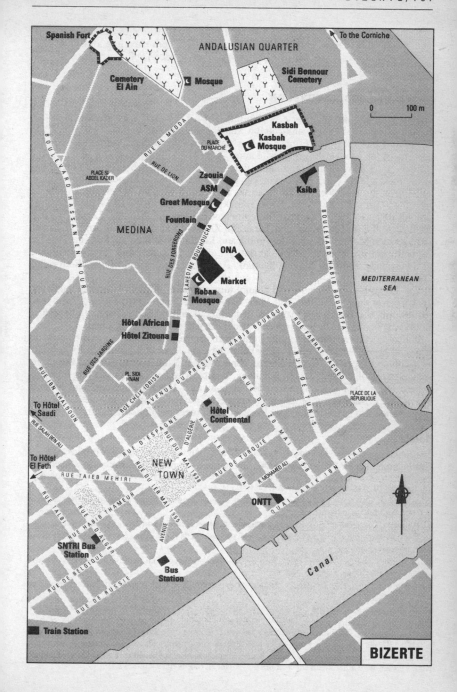

BIZERTE

Thanks to the French legacy (and departure), the main thrust of Bizerte's development has been industrial, and its naval arsenal has been converted into a vast complex including what was once North Africa's first blast-furnace. Tourism comes second place.

Arrival and accommodation

Transport in and out of Bizerte is plentiful. The *SRT Bizerte* **bus station** is at the bottom of avenue d'Algérie and rue Ibn Khaldoun, at the end of quai Tarak Ibn Ziad. Buses to Tunis (2hr) leave more or less half-hourly from here, with less frequent departures for Menzel Bourguiba (45min), Beja (2hr), Jendouba (3hr 30min), Aïn Draham via Tabarca (5hr), and one a day direct to Raf Raf (1hr), though there are plenty to Ras Jebel (1hr), where you can change for Raf Raf. Outside the bus station building is the stop for Menzel Jemil via Remel and Menzel Abderrahman. There are other buses for Kairouan, Sousse, Sfax and Jerba from *SNTRI*'s unpromising-looking depot in rue d'Alger, at the corner of rue Habib Thameur. **Louages** hang out next to the lift-bridge on quai Tarak Ibn Ziad, with loads of departures to Tunis, and plenty to Mateur, Menzel Bourguiba and Raf Raf – but none to Tabarca. Finally, the **train station** is by the docks at the end of rue de Russie and rue de Belgique, with four daily trains for Mateur (35min), Tunis (1hr 35min) and Menzel Bourguiba (30min).

You'll find the very friendly and helpful **tourist office** on rue de Constantinople, at the corner of quai Tarak Ibn Ziad (daily 8am–1pm & 3–6pm; ☎02/432703). Note that **street names** in Bizerte are mainly posted in Arabic and locals don't seem to believe in numbering houses, so locating specific places can sometimes be a problem.

In Bizerte you can choose to **stay** in the town centre, on the beaches to the north, or at Remel beach, south of town. The choice depends on what kind of hotel you want, with different types of accommodation concentrated in different areas, and the more upmarket establishments strung out along the Corniche for 5km. Take a bus from the "Cheik Driss" bus stop at the corner of boulevard Hassen en Nouri and avenue Bourguiba. **Camping** out on the main northern beaches is usually tolerated. The city centre hotels are keyed to the map; the Corniche hotels are off to the north.

Hotels

Africain, pl Slahedinne Bouchoucha (☎02/434412). Recently closed, but soon due to reopen. ①.

Continental, 29 rue 2 Mars (☎02/431436). On the corner of rue de Constantinople. Grubby but friendly with a certain run-down charm that hardened travellers enjoy. Recently closed – it's unclear if it will reopen but its worth a call just in case. ①.

Corniche ★, Corniche (☎02/431844). Fanciest of the Corniche hotels – gleaming marble and chrome, with prices to match. ⑥.

El Khayem, Corniche (☎02/432120). Cheapest of the beach hotels, and furthest from town. ②.

El Feth, av Bourguiba (☎02/430596). A recent addition that's more upmarket than the other town alternatives, but not bad value. ③.

Jalta ★★★, Corniche (☎02/434276). Run by the Austrian-based *Club Dido*, with riding, windsurfing and other facilities. Friendly, too. ④.

Nador ★★, Corniche (☎02/431848). Rather pricey, especially in high season, and mainly geared to German package tours. ④.

Petit Mousse ★★, Corniche (☎02/432185). Dating back forty years and exceptionally friendly – if you have the money and the good fortune to find an unbooked room, this is the place to stay. ③.

Remel, signposted off the Bizerte–Tunis road (☎02/440664). The *Remel*'s inconvenient location – and the difficulty in finding it – makes it a last-ditch alternative only. ④.

Saadi, rue Salah Ben Ali (☎02/437528). A nice, clean little place between av Farhat Hached and av Hedi Chaker, with a hammam three doors down. Not all rooms have windows. ①.

Zitouna, pl Slahedinne Bouchoucha (☎02/431447). A bit on the dingy side; ask for a room with a window. ③.

Youth hostels and campsites

Centre de Stages et de Vacances youth hostel, Corniche (☎02/431608). The usual charmless monolith, located behind the Spanish Fort. Check in after 6pm. ③.

Centre de Stages et de Vacances youth hostel and campsite, Remel Plage (☎02/440804). Formerly unofficial, now under IYHF auspices. Signposted from the road near the #8 bus stop (20min service from Bizerte bus station). Sylvan and peaceful place smelling of pine and eucalyptus. The sea is 300m through the trees and over a dune. 3.5TD per tent plus 0.1TD per person camping. See p.141 under "The beaches" for more on Remel Plage. ③.

The Town

Modern Bizerte begins with a shipping canal built in the 1890s. Crossed via a **lift-bridge**, the canal runs from the Mediterranean into Lac Bizerte, a large inland stretch of saltwater. The bridge looks pretty impressive when raised, its middle section towering straight up and visible right across Bizerte, which still consists of a grid-pattern **French new town** – a wholly unscenic place that has a curious gritty charm, with a green and spacious central square and grandiose buildings along the seafront. The new town sits alongside the remains of the old walled town with its harbour, the **Old Port**, built to serve as a major Mediterranean naval and military base, and guarded at the entrance by the twin forts of the **Kasbah** and the **Ksiba**. Next to the harbour are the narrow streets and monuments of the **Medina**, overlooked from the top of the hill behind town by the so-called **Spanish fort**, built by the Turks.

Until the end of the nineteenth century, Bizerte was a compact city straddling a natural channel leading from the Mediterranean into the lake, its centre standing on an island in the middle and heavy fortifications punctuating its surrounding walls. When the French colonial planners arrived they filled in most of the channel, built their new town east of avenue Bourguiba on reclaimed land and dug the modern canal to provide superior access to the lake. You can still get a sense of the historic town, though, by heading for place Lahedine Bouchoucha, on the edge of the Old Port.

The Old Port

Surrounded by cafés, narrow streets and forts (and one particularly hideous block of apartments), the **Old Port** is the heart of Bizerte. Originally it slit into two arms, one running along what is now place Lahedine Bouchoucha and one continuing around today's ONAT building. Reuniting on avenue Bourguiba, the channel left behind an island and continued on into the body of Lac Bizerte. The island in the channel – nowadays the area around the ONAT, the market and the Rbaa Mosque – lay within the city walls; in pre-colonial times, this was where the European population lived in detached splendour. Most of old Bizerte lay west of the channel, making up what is now known as the Medina. Its western wall followed the path of boulevard Hassan En Nouri up to the Spanish fort on the hill behind town, before returning back down the hill to the Kasbah.

It's a long time since any fishing boats or corsair privateers sailed all the way through town, along the channels and below the minarets, on their way to and from Lac Bizerte. But the Old Port retains a magical feeling, especially in the evening. Café tables are set out along the quay and, as darkness falls, illuminated boats chug off for the night's fishing, accompanied by the call to prayer from the minaret of the great mosque that stands just next to the harbour. In the daytime, the quaysides are a peaceful retreat where you can have a coffee, or wander up to the prosaic modern bridge between the twin fortifications of the Kasbah on the left and the Ksiba on the right.

The Kasbah and Ksiba

Standing at the mouth of the port, the **Kasbah**, with its massive walls, is hard to miss. Although its general form suggests an originally Byzantine foundation, like many of Bizerte's monuments, it dates mainly from the seventeenth century. Virtually untouched by the modern city outside, it's a wonderful place to wander around, as beyond its single, heavily defensive gate lies a miniature old town of passages, arches and walls painted in pastel shades. Through an entrance in the bastion facing the port, you can also reach a promenade running around the top of the Kasbah **walls** (daily 9am–noon & 3–7pm; 0.4TD). A café operates up here in the evening, but at any time of day it's the best place to get a view of the historic town's layout and to imagine fishing boats and privateers alike making their way through the town into Lac Bizerte.

Facing the Kasbah on the other side of the harbour channel, the Fort Sidi el Hani, or **Ksiba** (the diminutive of Kasbah, meaning "Little fort") is indeed smaller, but together the two forts must have made a formidable defensive ensemble. The effect is now somewhat muffled by the modern bridge over the channel. Parts of the Ksiba – the round tower and the wall facing the channel – date back to Byzantine times. Recently it has been turned into a small **Oceanographic Museum** (daily 3–6pm; 0.2TD).

The Medina

Overwhelmed by the colonial town and bombed during World War II, the **Medina** offers a less coherent experience than it does in some other Tunisian towns. Its most impressive monuments lie conveniently next to the old port in what was once the heart of the town. Walk up place Lahedine Bouchoucha towards the port. To your right, on what was once a prominent position overlooking the port, stands a great horseshoe in alternating black and white marble. This belonged to a **fountain** erected in the seventeenth century by Youssef Dey, second of Tunis's Turkish rulers and founder of the mosque in Tunis's Medina. Like the mosque, this fountain was designed by an architect of Spanish origin – he is identified in its inscription as El Andaloussi. The fountain's inscription advises passers-by in both Arabic and Turkish to use its water until such time as the waters of Paradise become available to them. Originally the water would have been fed by a *nouria* waterwheel powered by a camel, like the one in Kairouan, but sadly both camel and water are long gone.

Bizerte's **Great Mosque**, built in 1652, lies a little way beyond the fountain. Its minaret is visible either from the cramped rue des Forgerons or – even better – from the other side of the port, where you can watch its reflection jostling in the water with brighly coloured fishing boats, while the walls of the Spanish fort loom on the distant hillside behind. Dating, like the fountain and Youssef Dey's mosque in Tunis, from the first years of Turkish rule, the minaret belongs recognizably to the same school, its octagonal shape (signifying Hanefite sympathies) and hanging balcony reminiscent of contemporary Tunis monuments.

Just north of the Great Mosque, on a corner, the **Zaouia of Sidi Moktar** is now the headquarters of the local ASM (*Association de Sauvegarde de la Medina*), who sometimes use it to put on exhibitions about the Medina and their work in restoring and maintaining it. The ASM also has a fascinating map of Bizerte, drawn to show the city as it was in 1881, before the new town and canal were built. A little further still towards the Kasbah on rue des Forgerons is the seventeenth-century **Zaouia of Sidi Mostari**.

Just below the walls of the Kasbah, a small open square makes a pleasant place to sit at a café table. Beyond it, outside the old city wall, lies the former **Andalusian Quarter**, populated by Spanish immigrants who arrived following the Christian reconquest of Spain. There are some old streets and a whitewashed mosque, flanked by two **cemeteries** – Sidi Bennour, on empty ground outside the Kasbah walls, and El Ain, whose gravestones sprinkle the hillside below the Spanish fort.

To explore the old streets of the Medina, you can head back down rue des Forgerons, which twists the length of the old town, and take any number of side alleys. To reach the largest single remnant of historic Bizerte – the **Spanish fort** – you'll have to find your way up the hill on boulevard Hassan En Nouri. Like its contemporary at La Goulette outside Tunis, this massive fortress dates back to the sixteenth century, when Tunisia was the front line in the war between Christian Spain and Ottoman Turkey. On taking control of Tunisia in 1535, the Spanish dismantled Bizerte's existing fortifications. Later, as their struggle with the Turks continued, they realized that they would themselves need defences in this key port and began building the fort in 1570, probably not even completing it by the time the Turks ejected them in 1573. Since then it has undergone significant alterations and additions; in its original form, it was a star-shaped polygon with a central courtyard and one massive entrance gateway from the town. Although occasionally used as an open-air theatre, all it really offers now is the view from its battlements, a couple of World War II Italian guns and some rusty old cannons that were mentioned by Alexandre Dumas on his visit in 1848.

The beaches

Bizerte's main beach is the **Corniche**, a strip of sand varying in width and crowdedness as it stretches the five kilometres from Sidi Salem, by the old port bridge, north towards Cap Bizerte. Buses up the Corniche stop in town at Cheik Driss, a bus stop on boulevard Hassan en Nouri by the corner of avenue Bourguiba. Buses #1 and #2 also go up the Corniche from just north of the old port.

Three kilometres southeast of town, the beach of **Remel** (meaning "sand") is definitely lusher, if a little exposed. This is where Bizerte's other youth hostel is situated, reached by bus #8 from the Menzel Jemil stop at the bus station. The **shipwrecks** on Remel beach can be seen from the bridge over the canal, and are about a fifty-minute walk down the beach from the hostel/campsite, away from town. Both hulls, it seems, are those of Italian vessels wrecked in 1940. For beaches further afield, see p.148.

Eating and drinking

Because Bizerte is so undeveloped for tourism, its **restaurants** are rather thin on the ground, especially mid-range ones. On the other hand, there are enough cheap *gargotes* to keep you satisfied, and Bizerte is one of the best places in Tunisia for a real splurge too, with several places to treat yourself along the Corniche.

Restaurant Belle Plage, on the beach, beyond the *Petit Mousse* (☎02/431817). Mid-range prices and a reasonable menu selection.

Restaurant du Bonheur, av Thaalbi, near the corner of av Bourguiba (☎02/431047). Mid-range prices in a smart restaurant.

Restaurant la Cuisine Tunisienne, rue 2 Mars, near the corner of rue de Constantinople. Silence a grumbling stomach for around 2TD in this *gargote*.

Restaurant Eden, a few hundred metres closer to town on the Corniche (☎02/439023). A seriously classy joint specializing in seafood. Expensive, but a fraction of the price you'd pay at a similar establishment in London or New York.

Restaurant de la Jeunesse, av Bourguiba, near the corner of av Taïeb Mehiri. Another *gargote* possibility, with budget prices and good grub, but a limited choice.

Restaurant de l'Hôtel Petit Mousse, Corniche (☎02/432185). An excellent meal here will set you back around 15TD (including wine), but on Sunday lunchtimes they do a set menu. Not surprisingly, it's very popular, so get there early or dine.

Sport Nautique, bd H Bougatfa, right at the harbour mouth (☎02/431495). Another posh restaurant, with similar prices but not as much style.

Tip Top Restaurant, rue de Belgique, near the corner of rue Moncef Bey. Not as good as its name makes out, but with reasonable prices.

Listings

Airline *Tunis Air*, 76 av Bourguiba (☎02/432201).

Banks Spread around the new town, they include *UIB* on av Taïeb Mehiri at rue Moncef Bey; *L'Habitat* on av Bourguiba at av Taïeb Mehiri; *BIAT* on rue Moncef Bey at rue 2 Mars; *Du Sud* on rue H Thameur at av Taïeb Mehiri; *BNA* on rue Mongi Slim at pl 7 Novembre; *BT* on rue Ibn Khadldoun at av d'Algérie.

Bicycle rental The *Hôtel Jalta* rents out bicycles at 2TD a day.

Car rental *Avis*, 7 rue d'Alger (☎02/433076); *Budget*, 7 rue d'Alger (☎02/432174); *Hertz*, pl des Martyrs (☎02/433676); *InteRent/Europcar*, 52 av d'Algérie (☎02/439018); *Mattei*, 27 rue d'Alger.

Cinemas *Casino*, pl des Martyrs; *Colisée* on rue 1 Mai at av d'Algérie; *Majestic*, rue de Tunis; *Paris*, 43 av Taïeb Mehiri at av Bourguiba.

Excursions Some of the big hotels, notably the *Hôtel Jalta*, run trips – for example, half a day in Raf Raf and Utica, a day in Kairouan or a three-day "safari" (not a wildlife trip as such) in the south.

Festivals Liberation Day is October 15, with street celebrations and a carnival of sorts to celebrate the city's 1963 liberation from the French. Sidi Selim is a saint's day, the date of which is fixed on the Islamic calendar.

Football The local club is *CAB Bizerte*, 1987 African Cup winners. Their ground is up by Porte de Bechateur. Matches usually kick off at 2pm on Sundays.

Hammams The best one is hidden deep in the Medina. Another is in the Kasbah, and there's one in rue Salah Ben Ali, near the *Hôtel Saadi*. Hours at all of these are 6am–noon and 6–9pm for men, noon–6pm for women.

International phone calls PTT, rue 1 Mai at rue 2 Mars (daily 8am–8pm).

Medical facilities The regional hospital is up rue Ibn Khaldoun (☎02/431422), with a night-time *garde medicale* open 8pm–7am at 3 av Bourguiba near the Old Port (☎02/433673), and a night pharmacy around the corner at 28 rue Ali Belhouane.

ONAT crafts shop Behind the market, facing onto the Old Port.

PTT Av d'Algérie at rue 1 Mai (city hours); it changes cash and has phones in the side entrance.

Ferry companies *Tourafric*, 1 rue Salah Ben Ali (☎02/432315). Tickets for Tunis–Sicily.

Supermarkets *Monoprix*, rue 2 Mars, at rue Ibn Khaldoun; *Magasin Haddad*, rue 2 Mars, next to the *Hôtel Continental*.

MOVING ON FROM BIZERTE

Buses to Tunis (2hr) leave more or less half-hourly from the *SRT Bizerte* bus station, and there are daily departures for Aïn Draham (5hr), Raf Raf (1hr) and Tabarca (4hr); twice daily services to Beja (2hr), Ghar el Melh (1hr) and Jendouba (3hr 30min); there are also frequent services to Ras Jebel (1hr), where you can change for Raf Raf. Outside the bus station building is the stop for Menzel Bourguiba via Remel (8 daily; 45min). There are other buses from *SNTRI*'s unpromising-looking depot in rue d'Alger, on the corner of rue Habib Thameur, to Houmt Souk on Jerba (2 daily; 11hr), and daily departures for Kairouan (5hr), Sfax (7hr) and Sousse (4hr 30min).

Apart from buses, **louages** run from the lift-bridge on quai Tarak Ibn Ziad, with loads of departures to Tunis and plenty to Mateur, Menzel Bourguiba and Raf Raf – but none to Tabarca. There are four daily trains for Mateur (35min), Menzel Bourguiba (30min), Tinja (20min) and Tunis (1hr 35min). The **train station** is by the docks at the end of rue de Russie and rue de Belgique by the docks.

Swimming pool There's a municipal pool on the Corniche near the *Maison des Jeunes*. Otherwise, try the Corniche hotels.

Menzel Abderrahman and Menzel Jemil

South of Bizerte, the villages of **MENZEL ABDERRAHMAN** and **MENZEL JEMIL** (short journeys from Bizerte's main bus station along the Tunis road) were both founded by the Aghlabids in the ninth century and make attractive places from which to get a view of the lake. Menzel Abderrahman is right on the shore, while Menzel Jemil – now virtually a suburb of Bizerte – perches on a hillside, its a dapper old central **square** dominated by a fortress-like whitewashed **mosque**.

The Raf Raf coastline

A beach of legendary beauty, **Raf Raf**, just 30km east of Bizerte, is the best-known attraction on a stretch of coast that remains surprisingly undeveloped. Conventional tourist facilities are sparse in this area of conservative farmers, but the rewards are all the greater if you make the effort to explore, with some beautiful beaches and clifftop scenery towards **Cap Farina** and the fledgling resort at **Ras Sidi el Mekki**.

Transport to the Raf Raf area can be confusing until you master the local geography. All buses from Bizerte go through Ras Jebel before backtracking to Raf Raf Town and then down to the beach (specify "Raf Raf Plage"), and there are plenty of buses and taxis plying solely between Ras Jebel and Raf Raf. As for transport from Tunis, only one bus a day leaves for Raf Raf direct (Bab Saadoun station), but nine go to Ras Jebel, and during the summer you can usually get a *louage* direct to the beach, though you'll have to fight for a seat at weekends.

Ras Jebel

At the centre of the region is **RAS JEBEL**, a farming town which makes few concessions to visitors and is really only useful as a transport connection. The road into town divides before reaching the centre, with the main square and its towering minaret straight ahead, and the **bus stop** to the left – there are departures from here to Ghar el Melh (6 daily; 45min), Raf Raf (frequent; 30min) and Tunis (5 daily; 2hr). A street drops to the right, passing a large **café** and the **market** on the left before reaching a basic **hotel** further round to the right. The town's single other notable, and rather unlikely, feature is a Lee Cooper jeans factory.

Although Ras Jebel has its own **beach**, 2.5km down a signposted road, it's small and gets crowded in July and August, when families camp there on a long-term basis and conditions become less than hygienic. To avoid this, just walk along to the west until you find a deserted cove, though note that you'll have to bring water supplies.

Raf Raf beach

The real attraction on this part of the coast is **Raf Raf beach**, an almost endless curve of white sand backed by dunes, forest and steeply sloping fields of figs, vines and rustling cane. At its eastern edge is the long claw of **Cap Farina**, with the cliffs of its ridge hidden in shadow or gleaming in the sun; to the west a small, knobbly hill; and out in the bay the rocky islet of Pilau. If you feel an urge to do other than swim, sunbathe and eat grapes and figs (some of the best in the country), Cap Farina makes a spectacular walk. The easiest way up is from Raf Raf, along a track to the watchtower.

More daring is to climb the gash of sand visible on the mountain from the beach, from the top of which the whole coast opens out, west to Raf Raf's curve, east down to the lagoon of Ghar el Melh and Ras Sidi el Mekki beach.

The beach is popular, formidably so at weekends, but even then it's easy to escape from the crowds. If you want to **stay** here, there's the friendly *Hôtel Dalia* (☎02/447077; ②), but you may prefer to rent one of the straw shacks (in season), or you can sleep out if you're discreet.

Ghar el Melh

GHAR EL MELH, 4km along the coast from Raf Raf beach, means "Cave of Salt", perhaps a reference to the lagoon which the River Medjerda has created around the town, ruining the harbour facilities that once made Porto Farina (as it was then called) a notorious haunt of pirates. In 1654 the English Admiral Blake, in an action described by Lieutenänt Colonel Sir Lambert Playfair as "one of the most brilliant victories in the history of the British Navy", attacked and destroyed the port. By the next century, however, it had been rebuilt with three forts and an arsenal. Piracy and smuggling continued to be the town's main source of revenue well into the nineteenth century – carried out, for the most part, by British citizens, the Maltese. The government only clamped down in 1834, when a huge arsenal – kept by one of the Maltese smugglers in his basement – exploded, taking many of the surrounding houses with it. Ahmed Bey tried to turn the port to more legitimate trade, building new jetties and forts. But by this time the estuary had started to silt up, and today Ghar el Melh is a small farming town half asleep under the green flank of the mountain, where the **forts** and the crumbling walls of the **old port** are steeped in a sense of nostalgic melancholy. Buses to Ghar el Melh operate through Ras Jebel.

Ras Sidi el Mekki

Ghar el Melh should really be left to slumber gently, but its peace will be forever destroyed if longstanding plans to develop the beach at **RAS SIDI EL MEKKI**, 6km beyond at the tip of Cap Farina, are ever fulfilled. The authorities like to call this beach "Polynesian", which does at least convey the stillness of the water and the isolation. It's little known for the moment though, and its facilities consist of just a few straw cubicles and a **café-restaurant**, so camping is the ideal solution. There are rumours of a grandiose project involving ten thousand beds and a Disneyland, so try to see the beach while you can.

Just over 2km beyond Ghar el Melh, a track turns off left, while the road veers right to a new fishing **port**. The beach is another 3km from the town. If you don't have your own transport, you'll have to hitch or end up walking from Ghar el Melk, where the bus stops.

Utica and around

The ancient site of **Utica** lies in the broad alluvial plain of the **River Medjerda**, whose banks, so British traveller Sir Grenville Temple reported in the nineteenth century, "were witnesses to the well-known combat between the forces of Attilius Regulus and an enormous serpent, in 225 BC." The river – the only permanently flowing one in the country – plays a vital part in irrigating the north, but for centuries it has also been silting up this section of the coast, locking in what were once great ports. Utica lies off the main Tunis–Bizerte road, a 2km walk from the village of Zana, and just over 30km southeast from Bizerte.

Some history

Now a smallish site marooned 10km from the sea, **Utica** predated Carthage as the first Phoenician trading post on this coastline. It never really reconciled itself to Carthage's supremacy, backing the losing mercenary army in its revolt against Carthage in 240 BC and then supporting Rome in the 146 BC campaign which ended in Carthage's destruction; a century later it chose wrong again, backing Pompey against Julius Caesar in the Roman Civil War. One of Pompey's backers, Cato the Younger, was in control of the city when he heard of Caesar's decisive victory at Thapsus, near Mahdia. Having decided to kill himself rather than surrender, he fell on his sword in time-honoured fashion; and when doctors tried to repair the damage, he thrust them aside and rent his innards asunder with his bare hands. This was the sort of gesture which went down well with the Romans: they immediately erected a statue of Cato, facing heroically out to sea, and enshrined him in national myth. With the resurrection of Carthage as the new Roman capital, though, Utica began a decline that was then accelerated as silt from the river gradually put an end to the city's port and *raison d'être*.

The site

Despite the size and wealth of the Roman city, its **site** is not extensive. The central feature is the **House of the Cascade**, whose doorway still stands. The private residence of some very well-off citizen, it gives an impression of staggering affluence even without walls or decoration. The ground floor was almost entirely devoted to entertaining, with the main complex of rooms to the right of the pool in the centre of the house. In the middle of this side, the *triclinium* (dining room) is identifiable by the U-shape of its floor decoration. Couches, on which Romans lay to eat their meals (Cato was a source of amazement because, Stoic that he was, he actually ate sitting up), occupied the three sides around the walls. Of the orange and green paving in the middle of the floor, the orange "Numidian" marble came from Chemtou (see p.166), while the green was imported from Euboea, today's Evvia, in Greece. On either side of the triclinium is a garden well and another reception room: one well contains the running fountain arrangement (all in mosaics) which gives the house its name. The other rooms around the central pool are smaller reception chambers, except for a stable to the left of the entrance; note the feeding troughs. The garage for the horse-drawn carriage is on the other side of the entrance, with a wide doorway.

The residences surrounding the House of the Cascade are less affluent, but still part of an exclusive district. The **Forum** was only a block away to the north, beyond the **Punic necropolis** excavated at a lower level, and the sea was not much further. A little way west along the ancient shoreline – reminiscent of Carthage's Antonine Baths (see p.108) – stood Utica's own massive **baths complex**, whose remains are still visible. No one knows for certain where the shore was when the Medjerda started silting it up, but it must have been close to the bottom of the slope – from the House of the Cascade's roof you could have watched ships sailing in from Spain, Carthage and Alexandria.

The **museum** (daily except Mon 8am–5pm; 1TD, plus 1TD to take photos) lies just before the entrance to the site. It contains mainly domestic and funerary objects illustrating the life led by Uticans over more than a thousand years. The Punic pottery and grave reliefs (note the angular Punic script) in the early rooms date from its first six hundred years. The Phoenicians were traders and merchants, and when they weren't fighting the Greeks they were doing business with them; look out for a fine Greek *skyphos* (wine goblet) painted with a Maenad chasing a Satyr. The Roman relics, as so often, are prosaically domestic, and the quantity of marble statuary is a clear indication of the city's wealth. None of it is of a very high standard – the Reclining Ariadne and Satyr (recognizable by his tail) are poor versions of stock garden figures – and because

North Africa has no white marble of its own, all this had to be imported at great expense from elsewhere in the Mediterranean.

Kalaat el Andalous

KALAAT EL ANDALOUS, 5km from Utica, is the village just visible to the northeast of Utica, on what was once another headland in the sea. Not much is left now of the original village founded by Spanish immigrants during the seventeenth century, but it's a pleasant walk across the rich river plain and there's a magnificent view from the steep cliff on the far side, ranging from Bou Kornine and Sidi Bou Said in the south to Cap Farina in the north. Buses #44 and #44a from place Belhouane in Tunis pass through here regularly.

Lac Ichkeul National Park

The sixty-square-kilometre **Lac Ichkeul**, linked to Lac Bizerte by a narrow channel near Tinja, is too shallow to be navigable, making it an ideal habitat for fish and birdlife. In winter it's an ornithologists' delight since it's a haven for birds migrating from northern Europe – at least those that make it across the killing fields of Italy and Malta. Nontidal but slightly saline, the lake provides a unique ecosystem that the government has protected as a **nature reserve** (daily 7am–6pm; free). Unfortunately it's now under threat, due to heavy demand on its water, with two dams already constructed on its feed rivers and a further four planned before the end of the century. The combined effect of these dams and of low rainfall is that the water level in the lake is falling, causing saltwater from Lac Bizerte to flow back into it. This, together with evaporation, means that the lake is growing more saline, killing off the water plants on which its delicate ecosystem depends.

Apart from its famous ornithological attractions (see box), the lake abounds in **frogs** and **toads**, including a very handsome, vocal species with green stripes down the back; there are **terrapins** too: the Sejenane marsh on the lake's north side is a good place to look.

Getting to the park is not easy by public transport, and it's a good idea to visit the tourist office in Bizerte (see p.138) to get some advice and information. From Bizerte, the bus or *louage* to Mateur passes the southeastern corner of the lake, with the turning for the park 7km beyond Tinja. A track leads off here across a marsh to the park entrance, then back around the bottom of the mountain, past some domed bath houses, to a sign for the **ecomuseum** (daily 7am–6pm; free), which sits above the ridge. It's 9km from the Mateur road to the museum, so be prepared if you don't have your own transport. Alternatively, for viewing the northern shore of the lake, the bus from Bizerte to Sejenane skirts the water's edge, passing both the Douimis and Sejenane marshes. If you're staying at the *Ichkeul Hôtel* (formerly *Younes*) in Guengla, outside Menzel Bourguiba, take the local bus from Guengla to Tinja, and you can hitch from there either along the north or, with more promise, the south side of the lake.

Jebel Ichkeul

A superb limestone mountain, **Jebel Ichkeul** rises directly from the southern edge of the lake. It used to be a royal hunting park in the thirteenth century and **wild boar** and **jackals** still live on its flanks, as do **porcupines**, **mongooses**, **otters**, **tortoises** and a small herd of **water buffalo** – descended, it's said, from a pair given to the Bey of Tunis by the king of Sicily in 1729. During the war, American troops

BIRDWATCHING ON THE LAKE

Waterfowl are Lac Ichkeul's highspot. Ducks feed on the extensive beds of pondweed and grey lag geese on the club rush. These plants, together with the sheer size of the lake, make it North Africa's principal wildfowl wintering ground, with up to 150,000 birds at its peak.

Although huge flocks are present only between October and February, ducks remain in good numbers until the spring, with a few staying on and occasionally breeding over the summer. The birds move around the lake depending on the distribution of their food plants, but in general the best viewpoints are from the coast north of the mountain (there's a good track along it starting from the museum), or from the Douimis and Sejenane marshes on the north side. The latter marsh requires a walk along the river from the road.

As well as ducks and geese, the lake supports a variety of **wading birds** around its fringes. If the water level is high enough, both the Douimis and Sejenane marshes are good all year round for waders, with sizeable populations of avocets, black-winged stilts and Kentish plovers. These are augmented in winter by black-tailed godwits, redshanks and the smaller sandpipers. If it's wet, the edge of the Joumine marsh closest to the level crossing outside Tinja is a great spot to watch waders, but beware of the dogs around here. Herons and egrets breed among the reeds, the grey heron a resident and purple heron a summer visitor, and there's sometimes a colony of night herons in the reeds at the north edge of the mountain. The unmistakeable white storks don't breed in the park but they nest close by and often feed around the lake's edges.

The lake's **speciality birds** include the purple gallinule, a rarity rather like a huge red-billed coot, the marbled teal, a small, shy duck with a mottled brown plumage, and the white-headed duck, a universally rare bird which winters in small numbers.

With all these water birds about, as well as small mammals, reptiles and amphibians, the lake also attracts **birds of prey**. Marsh harriers are the most dominant species, identifiable by their upturned wings as they drift over the reedbeds and surrounding fields in search of small prey. Of the falcons, peregrine, lanner and kestrel all breed on the mountain, Bonelli's and short-toed eagles wheel high in the sky, and long-legged buzzards breed here too.

Don't ignore the **smaller birds**, either. Reed warblers and great reed warblers breed here in summer, nightingales are common, and bee-eaters breed in the river banks. Quail, the smallest game bird, breed in the park too; listen for their "whic whic" call from the surrounding fields in spring – they're notoriously hard to spot. Moussier's redstarts are common among the scrub on the mountain, and Sardinian warblers are everywhere. Woodchat shrikes perch on telegraph wires and lone trees in summer, and a related and very rare species, the black-headed bush shrike, breeds here in very small numbers. Boring bulbuls – like drab blackbirds but with a loud and mellifluous song – reach the most northerly part of their range in Tunisia (they're primarily Asian and African birds).

stationed nearby developed a taste for the meat and the herd was virtually wiped out.

The **flowers** up on Jebel Ichkeul are utterly dependent on the winter rains and you can walk through a carpet of colour or over barren straw, depending on the weather. As well as on the mountain, interesting flowers grow around the rivers feeding the lake – around the Douimis river on the north shore, for instance, you'll find a white Star of Bethlehem and a delightful, tiny narcissus. The **agricultural weeds** are spectacular even in a dry year, since many of the fields to the north of the lake are irrigated. Look out for fields ablaze with poppies and wild chrysanthemums, and for various colourful convolvulus species around the edges. Honeywort, with its strange pendulous yellow and brown flowers, is also common by the roadside, and there's a shocking pink soapwort in the fields.

Menzel Bourguiba and around

On the south side of Lac Bizerte, **MENZEL BOURGUIBA** (formerly the French garrison town of Ferryville) is itself uninteresting, but it's the perfect base for exploring the Lac Ichkeul nature reserve.

The centre of Menzel Bourguiba is a pleasant square with a bandstand. The only **hotel** in town is the *Moderne* (☎02/460551; ①) in rue d'Alger, which runs off the bandstand square towards the station. Cheap but very basic and somewhat grubby, it has no showers – though there are three hammams nearby. The *Moderne* is also an inexpensive eatery and the town's main bar and social focus, a pretty lively place in the evenings (except Fridays), when they serve cold beer and wine until late. During World War II, soldiers on both sides had occasion to drink here, and the venerable *patron* who served them still runs the place.

The other hotel in the area is *Hôtel Ichkeul*, some way out of Menzel Bourguiba in **GUENGLA** (☎02/461606; ②), right on Lac Bizerte. To get there, you could take a taxi or (infrequent) bus from Menzel Bourguiba town centre, or follow avenue de Palestine from the bandstand past the hospital and the craft centre opposite, turning left with the tarmac at the barracks entrance, and straight on for another 2km. The hotel is signposted on the right and you can get a pleasant room with a high-class restaurant in a tranquil setting. The proprietor also runs the *Tardi* wine company, which bottles many of the region's wines and arranges visits to the cellars at **AÏN GHELLAL**, 10km to the south. **Wildlife** enthusiasts should note that the hotel is ideally placed for exploring Oued Tinja, the river that connects Lac Ichkeul with Lac Bizerte.

The **train station**, down rue d'Alger from the bandstand, has daily services to Tinja and Bizerte, with connections for Mateur and Tunis. Turn left just before the station and continue for 100m to find the **Tunis louage station**, or cross the tracks and turn right to the site of Menzel's Wednesday and Sunday **market**, where you can pick up **louages to Mateur**. To find the **bus station**, and **louages for Bizerte**, go back up rue d'Alger, turn left at the bandstand and go straight on past a six-way roundabout and monument to the November 1987 uprising, where you'll also find the **PTT** and *Monoprix* **supermarket**. There are regular buses to Tunis and Bizerte, plus two or three daily for Tabarca, Aïn Draham and Beja.

Fifteen kilometres west on the main GP7, **MATEUR** has little of interest apart from its transport connections. *SRT Bizerte* runs the **bus station**, but other services stop here, and one way or another there are plenty of departures for Tabarca, Sejenane, Beja, Bizerte and, of course, Tunis.

West of Bizerte

West of Bizerte, the beaches run in shallow curves until the hump of **Cap Blanc**, 8km along the coast. Often said to be the northernmost point in Africa, if you're standing on top, buffeted by the winds, it's easy to persuade yourself you're at the end of a continent, although Africa's most northerly point is really a few kilometres west at **Ras Angela** (aka Ras Ben Sekka). Like all the beaches on the north coast, when the wind blows here they can feel slightly exposed, but in summer it's never unpleasant. The Roman writer Pliny the Younger tells how a boy out swimming here was befriended one day by a dolphin so tame that it carried him out to sea for rides. The dolphin soon acquired a cult following, but this was too much for the local bureaucrats of the Roman Empire, who had the dolphin killed. More conventional watersports are available today at the big hotels.

For a distant view of Cap Blanc, catch a #6 bus from boulevard Hassan en Nouri in Bizerte to the village of **BECHATEUR** – a side trip which reveals some of the unexpectedly bleak scenery behind the coast at this point. Bechateur itself is a tiny hamlet on a windswept hilltop which was once inhabited by the Romans, and blocks of their masonry can be seen in the walls of the village here and there. The bus stops at Bechateur, but a track continues for 15km to the beach of **Sidi Abdel Waheb** – worth exploring, if you have some means of getting down. The area still yields unexpected discoveries – between Cap Blanc and Ras Angela, at **AÏN DAMOUS**, a recently discovered underwater cave is said to be the entrance to Roman catacombs leading all the way to Utica.

From here, the coastline consists of a series of isolated coves, backed by increasingly heavy forests, whose inaccessibility pays dividends to those in search of wilder shores; most of the coves are uninhabited, putting them beyond the reach of all but the most dedicated, but a few are viable even if you don't have your own transport. In order to get to them, though, you'll need plenty of time, and you'll probably have to hitch, negotiate a taxi fare or charter a *louage* from **SEJENANE**, 40km west of Mateur, and the best base for any expedition to the beaches. It's a peaceful country town, living off agriculture and mining, with its own unique "primitive" style of pottery. Pots and beaches aside, there's little reason to stop here (unless it's for the Thursday market) except to enquire about transport out again – which is mainly back to Mateur.

Due north of Sejenane are the remote beaches of the promontory of **Cap Serrat**, down a well-signposted 15km track that turns off the GP51 and runs steadily down through heavily forested land. At the end of the track the mountains subside into a broad valley with a scattered settlement and a spectacular empty **beach**. If you're brave or have a four-wheel drive, or both, you might want to head west along a rougher track to the next named beach, **Sidi Mechrig**, which boasts a small settlement as well as some scanty but picturesque **Roman ruins** of a bath house. For a more staid approach to Sidi Mechrig, continue along GP7 to just before Tamra, where a signpost indicates a 17km track. Next in the line of named beaches along the coast is **Cap Negre**, reached by a track signposted about 6km after the Sidi Mechrig turning. It's barely inhabited except for a National Guard post occupying the remains of a French coral-fishing establishment, sacked in 1741 by the same expedition that ejected the Genoese from their fort at Tabarca. West of Nefza, 15km beyond the Cap Negre turning, a track leads down to yet another beach, **Zouiraa**.

Just before Ras Rajel, 10km east of Tabarca, the road passes a **Commonwealth War Grave cemetery**, whose English pastures face a filling station on the other side of the road. From the middle of Ras Rajel, a new road runs 3km north to the long-promised international **airport**, whose arrival is a sign of changing times in the Tabarca area. Currently an echoing hall that welcomes perhaps three flights a day from Tunis, Belgium and Germany, if the airport becomes successful it will be at the expense of the area's reputation as a charming backwater.

Tabarca

The setting of **TABARCA** is all that anyone could ask for – the **Khroumirie mountains** subside suddenly into a fertile plain, and in one corner is the natural harbour first used by the Carthaginians, dominated by an offshore rock that's crowned by a **Genoese castle**. Tabarca's success as a resort in recent years took what was basically a sleepy country town by surprise. Independent travellers used to arrive in July and early August, making the atmosphere like a big easy-going campsite. Towards the end of August the town would settle back to being a market centre (Friday **souk** on the Bizerte road just out of town) and small fishing port. Alas, reality has blundered into town and the tourist authorities and developers are trying to recreate in Tabarca the perceived success of a resort development like Sousse. To go with the new airport, four massive hotels and a

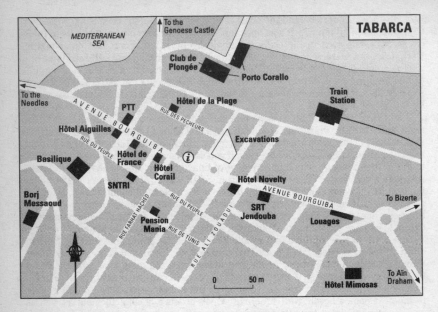

golf course have been conjured out of the previously pristine beach running east of town; downtown, the fishing port is being endowed with a luxury development called Porto Corallo, reminiscent of Port El Kantaoui. Clearly, Tabarca is undergoing significant change. Its scenic setting will remain, but you're inevitably going to find yourself sharing it with more and more fellow-visitors.

Some history

Roman Tabarca was the main port of exit for Chemtou marble from south of the mountains (see p.166), and thanks to this and grain exports it became a substantial town, wealthy enough to produce the fine early Christian mosaics on display in the Bardo Museum in Tunis. Decline set in after the fall of the Empire, but the eleventh-century geographer El Edrisi was still impressed by "ancient monuments of fine construction", and the town was – like everywhere else along the North African coast – fiercely disputed during the course of the sixteenth century. The French colonials used Tabarca as a hunting resort in a small way, but it was still considered remote enough in 1952 to be a suitable place of exile for Bourguiba. After independence, the isolation and charm remained, until recently, quite intact. **Coral** diving, and **cork** growing in the mountain forests behind the town, as well as fishing and farming, are today's important industries.

Arrival and accommodation

The town is tiny, with just a main street, avenue Bourguiba, and a few blocks on either side. Right in the middle of avenue Bourguiba is Tabarca's main square, where you'll find a covered market and the town hall. From the main square, avenue Bourguiba heads in one direction towards Aïn Draham and Bizerte, and in the other to the beach, passing the *ONTT* **tourist office** at no. 33 (daily 8am–1pm & 3–6pm; ☎08/643532).

The **train station** is by the beach, but has no passenger services at present; the **airport** is a few kilometres east in Ras Rajel (see above), though it is currently used only by infrequent charter services and twice weekly flights to Tunis. To get out there you'll need to organize a taxi or perhaps hook up with a tourist bus from one of the hotels. Meanwhile, there are two **bus stations**: *SNTRI* at 12 rue du Peuple, and *SRT Jendouba* at 72 avenue Bourguiba. *SRT Beja* buses stop in Tabarca's main square. **Louages** leave from avenue Bourguiba, by the *Hôtel Mimosas* turn-off and the *Esso* station.

The old town, on and around avenue Bourguiba, is the best place for budget *accommodation*. The *zone touristique* east of town is a source of more upscale alternatives, among them the three-star *Hôtel Morjane*, dating from 1968, a new golf course and the recent arrivals of the *Abou Nawas Montazah*, the *Mehari*, the *Royal Golf* and the *Paradis Golfe* hotels, all four-star and expensive. The inevitable tourist train links the zone with the town.

Hotels

Aiguilles ★★, av Bourguiba, across the street from the *Hôtel de France* (☎08/643653). One of the new independents, smarter but more expensive and less characterful than the *France*. ③.

Corail, corner of av Bourguiba and rue Tazerka (☎08/644455). Oldest-established budget hotel in town; adequate if unexciting. ②.

Hôtel de France ★, av Bourguiba, a block beyond the *Corail* (☎08/644577). Famous as the place where the exiled Bourguiba moved to after a disagreement with the manageress of the *Mimosas*. ②.

Pension Mamia, 3 rue de Tunis (☎08/644058). Reasonable accommodation, but not as good value as the *Aiguilles* or the *Novelty*. ③.

Mimosas ★★★, up the hill above town (☎08/644500). The elegant old-fashioned alternative to the newer hotels. Organized nightlife in town consists of discos at this hotel. ③.

Novelty ★★, av Bourguiba, just east of the central square (☎08/643008). A modern and smart new hotel. ②.

Hôtel de la Plage, 7 rue des Pêcheurs. The best-value cheapie in town: clean, bright and friendly, it gets top budget recommendation. ②.

The Town

Tabarca is built on a simple grid-plan, with the **main square** and its town hall making a focal point. Some interesting Roman remains are being unearthed on the square, watched over by a statue of Habib Bourguiba and his dog. **Avenue Bourguiba** forms the town's main artery, running from the roundabout by the *louage* station through the main square and on towards the Needles on the coast (see below).

Many of the events during the annual six-week July and August **Tabarca Festival** are put on in the garden of the so-called **Basilique**, just uphill from the *Café Andalous*. This was actually a cistern supplying the Roman town, which the White Fathers converted into a church, and is now a **museum** (daily except Mon 9am–5pm; 0.5TD),

---

CORAL

Coral, Tabarca's favourite souvenir, was one of the luxury items exported from North Africa to Europe, and avenue Bourguiba is lined with shops selling jewellery made by local artisans out of the coral brought up by divers. Prices here are considerably lower than in Tunis. The coral is Mediterranean coral, a species which has been collected for jewellery use for centuries, with the result that it is now fast declining and has been listed as an endangered species – think twice, therefore, before sanctioning this process by buying a coral souvenir in one of the many shops throughout northern Tunisia.

CORK

Cork is made from the outer bark of the cork oak, which grows all around the western Mediterranean. The first cork harvest, when the tree is about fifteen to twenty years old, is achieved by making a careful cut – so as not to damage the layer of inner bark beneath the cork – around the trunk just above the ground, and another just below where the branches begin. Four vertical cuts are then made and the oblong panels of cork carefully removed. The outer bark regrows and can be harvested every eight to ten years. Trees continue producing cork for about 150 years. Cork's springy lightness is due to millions of tiny air pockets trapped within it, which also make it waterproof and pretty well soundproof. It wasn't used to make bottle corks until the fifteenth century, and that was almost its only use until the veritable explosion – life buoys, table mats, cigarette tips and, of course, floor and wall tiles – of recent times.

featuring mosaic reproductions and old anchors. Other patches of Roman excavation are dotted around the town, including the **Borj Messaoud** halfway up the hill behind the Basilique, also originally a Roman cistern but converted into a fort by French and Italian merchants in the twelfth century.

Compared with the **Genoese Castle**, a twenty-minute walk from avenue Bourguiba along avenue Hedi Chaker, these minor monuments seem rather feeble. The castle's origins were as dramatic as its appearance is now: in 1541 the Turkish corsair Khair ed Din Barbarossa surrendered it to Charles V of Spain in return for his colleague Dragut, who had been languishing in a Christian jail, and the next year Charles sold the coral fishing rights and the island to a Genoese family called Lomellini. Having built the castle and enough of a town to support twelve hundred inhabitants, they managed to stay, despite Turkish control of the mainland, for two centuries. One of their main sources of income came from acting as agents for ransoming slaves in Tunis, a service for which they charged a three-percent commission. Then in 1741 they found themselves in need of agents when an Ottoman expedition sacked the outposts here and at Cap Negre, selling all the inhabitants into slavery.

The romance of this story was dealt a blow when the French built a causeway to the castle's island after World War II, but the silhouette on its rocky pinnacle has lost none of its allure – it's a fabulous place, especially at sunset when the sun sinks gingerly over the Needles and glints in the other direction off the cliffs of La Galite (see below). The castle itself, deemed a *zone militaire*, is now sadly closed to the public.

Just before the beginning of the causeway, a turnoff leads to the **Club de Plongée**, near the fishing port, where the local coral divers are trained. The club also offers a *"bapteme"* (first dive) to outsiders for 15TD, training to the first grade for 120TD plus 10TD membership and a medical certificate, which the Sidi Moussa Clinic in town can provide. The price includes ten dives and you must be over fifteen years old. They also rent out **boats** and **diving equipment** and do training up to the third grade.

West of town, the coast is a series of rocky coves whose beginning is marked by the grotesquely shaped **Needles**, jagged blades of rock standing in a row that juts out towards the castle.

In the other direction, the **beach** stretches 4km round the bay. A kilometre or so down towards the *Hôtel Morjane*, a few remnants of World War II wrecks just protrude from the water. You should be able to find some space on this beach, even at its most crowded. The presence of the coral makes for some of the best snorkelling in the Mediterranean. Above the beach loom the big tourist hotels, together with the golf course.

A new curiosity, perhaps created to feed the demands of the new tourist crowds, is the **Cork Museum**, a couple of kilometres outside town on the Aïn Draham road (daily 8am–noon & 2–5.30pm; free). Here you'll find the source of the extraordinary cork souvenirs that are now sold in town along with the ubiquitous stuffed camels, as well as some background to the Mediterranean cork industry. With three percent of world production, Tunisia is a small player compared with Portugal and Spain, which together account for 83 percent.

Eating and drinking

Fish is the main source of sustenance in these parts, and excellent it is too, with large, whole succulent specimens being the rule in cheap places as well as the more expensive ones. Among the bargains, the *Restaurant Trikki* in rue Farhat Hached is one of the best. For similar prices, try the *L'Athiniki* at 7 rue Ali Zouaoui, the *Restaurant des Étoiles* at 19 rue du Peuple, or two more places at nos. 31 and 35 on the same street.

With a bit more style, the *Hôtel de France* does a set menu at 4TD – and you can have a beer with it: hard drinking is done in a small garden behind the *France*, where delicious brochettes are sometimes cooked. The *Hôtel Mimosas'* menu is more expensive, but its seafood pizzas are reasonable value, and it's also good for a quiet drink or a game of pool. Also in this range is the *Café des Agriculteurs* at 43 avenue Bourguiba. If you really want to chuck your money around, the *Restaurant Khemir* at 11 avenue Bourguiba provides superior service and higher bills to match, or try the restaurants at the *Novelty* or the *Aiguilles* hotels.

For tea or coffee and a *chicha*, don't miss Tabarca's trendiest rendezvous, the *Café Andalous*, next to the *Hôtel de France*, with its bizarre, and rather atmospheric, collection of bric-a-brac.

Listings

Banks You'll find banks on the main square, at 30 av Bourguiba and at 12 av Hedi Chaker, opposite the *Hôtel de France*.

Car rental *Hertz* has an office in the Porto Corallo development (☎08/644570).

Excursions The *Mimosas* and the big hotels in the *zone touristique* all organize day excursions.

Golf The entrance to the brand-new golf course is out behind the hotels at the far end of the *zone touristique*.

Hammams There are two hammams in rue Farhat Hached (daily men 5am–noon & 5–10pm; women noon–5pm).

Medical facilities There's the Sidi Moussa Clinic at the beach end of av Bourguiba, and a night pharmacy at 5 rue Ali Zouaoui.

PTT Rue Farhat Hached (country hours).

Supermarket *Magasin Général* on the main square (Tues–Sat 8am–12.30pm & 3–7pm, Sun 8am–12.30pm).

■ MOVING ON FROM TABARCA ■

The **airport** is a few kilometres east in Ras Rajel, but flights out are still infrequent (charters to continental Europe and twice weekly to Tunis in summer). The town has two **bus** stations: *SNTRI* at 12 rue du Peuple, with five buses a day to Tunis via Sejenane and Mateur (3hr 45min), and three via Beja (more in summer); and *SRT Jendouba* at 72 avenue Bourguiba, which has five daily services to Aïn Draham (more in summer; 1hr), four to Jendouba (2hr) and one a day to both Le Kef (3hr) and Bizerte (4hr). *SRT Beja* runs two buses a day, which stop in Tabarca's main square, but if Beja is where you're headed, you may have to visit all three stops to see who has the next bus out. **Louages** – most of them for Jendouba, though you may find one for Aïn Draham if you're lucky – leave from avenue Bourguiba by the roundabout at the east of town. Otherwise, **hitching** to Aïn Draham is pretty standard practice.

FLORA AROUND TABARCA

The Tabarca region is one of the richest natural habitats in Tunisia, with the cork oak forests around Aïn Draham dropping down to the "coral coast" around Tabarca.

For a good **walk** to the west of Tabarca, go up rue Farhat Hached from avenue Habib Bourguiba, and then take a track off to the right, which scrambles up to the road by the army camp. Turn left along this road, and follow it as it winds up through shrub-covered hillside. The sandy rock doesn't support a great variety of flowers, but there are some unusual species – the Mediterranean **medlar tree** (a species of hawthorn) and heavily grazed **mastic trees** and **Kermes oaks**. Turn right off the road and head towards the coast. Look closely under the **white-flowered rockroses** on the hill and you'll find the extraordinary parasitic plant **cytinus**: with red and yellow waxy flowers and no green leaves, it gets its energy from its host plant, and is particularly common around here. In between the shrubs is **romulea**, an abundant and very beautiful tiny purple relative of the crocus. You can return along the cliffs to Tabarca, passing above the Needles. Blue rock thrushes are common on this stretch of cliffs.

La Galite

La Galite is a small volcanic archipelago 60km off the coast. The largest of the islands is only 5km long, with a tiny seasonal population that at one time included Bourguiba (on yet another of his bouts of exile). The sea here is rich in fish, with great snorkelling in summer if you get the chance, and this is the only place in the Mediterranean where it's possible to see the exceedingly rare Mediterranean monk seal – numbered in the very low hundreds at most. La Galite is now a strictly protected area and in theory closed to all except genuine scientific expeditions, although it is just possible the *Club de Plongée* in Tabarca could organize a trip if you wrote to them well in advance – contact the *Secretaire, Club de Plongée*, Port de Pêche, 8110 Tabarca (☎08/644478).

Aïn Draham and the Khroumirie mountains

In summer the mountain air is refreshing in **AÏN DRAHAM**, 20km south of Tabarca, and the town has become a resort in an unassuming kind of way, though there is little specific to do in the way of sights. The French tried to recreate here a small Alpine village in what was the equivalent of the British Simla in India, and many of the older buildings appear to have been spirited out of Switzerland and the Jura mountains in France and plumped down on this remote mountain in North Africa.

Today Aïn Draham is popular with those Tunisians who can afford to escape the heat of the capital – which means that prices have been pushed a little higher than usual (its name means, appropriately, "Springs of Money"). Most holidaymakers are here for a longish stay and rent out villas on the outskirts of the village, leaving the centre mostly unspoiled. The steep main street, **avenue Bourguiba**, lined with a few cafés and general stores – as well as the town's prettiest building, the **police station** – runs down the flank of **Jebel Bir** ("Well Mountain"), the highest point in the area at 1014m. It doesn't quite have the full Swiss Alpine atmosphere sometimes claimed, but the combination of forested slopes, fresh air and red-tiled roofs is European enough for a minaret to look incongruous.

Coming here in summer, it's almost a shock to find exercise suddenly a pleasure instead of a penance. There are two standard **walks** around town: one is to the **Col des Ruines**, the ridge opposite the village, which you can either scramble up directly, or gain access to from a side road 2km down the main Tabarca road north of Aïn Draham.

The other is the hike to the summit of **Jebel Bir**, which offers great views: east over mountains shaved with firebreaks like a reverse Mohican hairdo, north to Tabarca on its plain and west over more mountains into Algeria – you can make out El Kala as a white smudge on the horizon. A dirt road to the summit runs from the Jendouba road near the *Hôtel Rihana*: the pylon at the top is easy to spot and home in on. Both walks are about a three- or four-hour round-trip from the town and are occasionally steep but not particularly strenuous.

Practicalities

Most of the necessities of life are to be found somewhere along avenue Bourguiba, including the *Syndicat d'Initiative* **tourist office** at no. 57 (daily 8am–1pm & 3–6pm; ☎08/647115), several **banks**, and the **PTT** at no. 114 (country hours), where you can make international phone calls from an open kiosk. On avenue Habib Thameur you'll find the municipal **swimming pool**, the ONAT crafts shop and the Clinique Sidi Abdullah. There is also a regional **hospital** (☎02/647047) not far from the bus station.

The town itself has only a couple of places to **stay**. The *Hôtel Beauséjour*, near the top of avenue Bourguiba (☎08/647005; ③), is a remnant of French hunting parties, with stuffed boars' heads on the walls. Slightly further on, the *Maison des Jeunes* **youth hostel** (☎08/647087; ①) offers the usual Colditz-like accommodation, with your passport seized on arrival – you'll need to track it down before leaving. More attractive, expensive and remote are three alternatives in the surrounding forests. The *Hôtel Col des Ruines* (④) is a brand-new place, signposted off the Tabarca road, about 2km north of Aïn Draham. A kilometre beyond the *Maison des Jeunes*, on the road to Jendouba, the two-star *Hôtel Rihana* (☎08/647391; ③) is a very pleasant walk from town, and some 5km further is the two-star *Hôtel les Chênes* (☎08/647211; ③), attractively set in the forest, but a bit run-down and gloomy.

Aïn Draham is one of the few places in the country where you can eat **pork**, with wild boar available in the *Hôtel Beauséjour* and other hunting-oriented hotels during the season. The *Beauséjour* does a set menu. Other town eateries are cheaper and more *halal*. Most of them are in avenue Bourguiba, including the *Restaurant el Qods* and the *Restaurant du Grand Maghreb*, more or less opposite the *Beauséjour*, and, further down, the cheap and grotty *Restaurant de la Jeunesse* at no. 74 and the *Restaurant des Chasseurs* across the street at no. 113.

Moving on from Aïn Draham

All **buses** leave from the bus station on avenue 7 Novembre, off avenue Bourguiba at the bottom of the hill. *SNTRI* operates two services to Hammam Bourguiba (30min), three daily to Jendouba (1hr), four a day to Tabarca (1hr) and Tunis via Beja (5hr), and once-daily services to Bizerte (5hr) and Le Kef (2hr). The **louage** station is at the other end of town opposite the *Maison des Jeunes*, with most vehicles Jendouba-bound, though you might be lucky and get one to Tabarca. Otherwise, it's hitch and pay, very much the usual way of getting to Tabarca. To get to Babouch, you might have to take a taxi.

ALGERIA

A deteriorating security climate means that as of mid-1995 it was not advisable for foreigners – particularly Europeans and Americans – to visit Algeria on a casual basis. You should also be aware of heightened Tunisian sensitivities when travelling near the Algerian border – passport checks will be more frequent than normal, and you should think hard before going off the beaten track anywhere near the border. See p.376 for more details.

The Khroumirie mountains

Strictly speaking, the small eruption of forested mountains in the northwest corner of Tunisia is called the **Khroumirie**, but in practice you're more likely to hear the area called after its one sizeable village and effective capital, Aïn Draham. The region stretches from Tabarca on the coast to Fernana 50km south, and its mountains rise steeply from the sea to a height of over 1000m, covered with leafy forests of **cork oak** and ferns – and reputedly bristling with wild boar – before dipping down to the Medjerda valley at Jendouba. This sudden mountainous barrier gives rise to enormous amounts of rain which never reach other parts of the country: in winter it's not unusual to find a metre of snow at Aïn Draham.

Looking over the Khroumirie mountains, it's easy to see why the **Khroumir Berber tribespeople** who lived here were virtually independent of the country's rulers. They had a reputation for ferocity, regularly raiding the surrounding tribes and even crossing into Algeria to steal herds. But, despite their strength, they kept clear of the dynastic quarrels that embroiled – and destroyed – other tribes. When Mohammed Bey's disgruntled nephew fled here after an abortive coup in 1867, he was sent packing. Fourteen years later, however, the Bey's inability to stop cross-border raiding provided the French with the excuse they needed to invade Tunisia from Algeria in 1881.

East below the mountaintop of Jebel Bir lies the lake of the Beni M'tir dam, surrounded by forests. A detour south of Aïn Draham leads down here before rejoining the main road just before **FERNANA**, which took its name from the only tree for miles around (now vanished), which stood near this bleak settlement. The tree's singularity gave rise to a legend about its special powers. On their annual tax-collecting rounds the Bey's officials never dared penetrate further into the Khroumirie than here. The story goes that the Khroumiris would consult the tree about how little they could get away with declaring, and it would rustle its answer. According to one tale, it was the tree's error of judgement that caused the French invasion.

North from Aïn Draham, the road winds along the edge of the great natural bowl which surrounds the Tabarca plain, the only settlement it passes through being **BABOUCH**, just before the Algerian border. Like Aïn Draham, Babouch was a great hunting centre in colonial times, and the last lion and leopard were shot here eighty and sixty years ago respectively.

Babouch and Aïn Draham are surrounded by cork oak woodland, and almost any walk from either of them will take you through the forests; the valley leading from Babouch towards Hammam Bourguiba is one especially beautiful and rewarding area, although be aware that the troubles in Algeria have made the border area here particularly sensitive and you would be ill-advised to wander too far from the road. This is the only large deciduous forest in Tunisia and the wildlife is distinctive. You may notice how individual woodland birds, familiar from northern Europe, are developing differences that will, in tens of thousands of years, lead them to be classed as separate species – evolution in progress. The blue tit here has a black head; the chaffinch is pale, without a red breast; the green woodpecker is greyish and lacks the red "moustache"; and the jay is quite different, with a red, black and white head.

Louages run from Babouch to **HAMMAM BOURGUIBA**, a resort used by the ex-president, where you can take a thermal cure in the three-star *Hammam Bourguiba* (☎08/632517; ④); otherwise, try the anti-stress massage or ominous-sounding *"cure d'enveloppement"*.

THE MEDJERDA VALLEY

The **Medjerda valley** is the most fertile and best-watered region of Tunisia. In Roman times it supplied much of the grain that fed Rome, its perennial river, unique in Tunisia, allowing the fields to be irrigated and the grain transported. During the 1930s and 1950s the French improved irrigation by building numerous dams, so harnessing the winter floods for the summer. More recently, their engineering feats were surpassed by the Chinese, who built a canal that takes water to Cap Bon without a single pumping station en route. Most of the valley's towns are prosperous market centres, but the region's main attractions are its Roman ruins, most spectacularly those of **Bulla Regia**. Inevitably and enticingly, the valley forms a stark contrast to the coastal route, and it's straightforward enough to combine both in a looping, wandering journey starting and ending in Tunis.

Medjez el Bab

MEDJEZ EL BAB was a seventeenth-century Andalusian foundation on the Roman site of *Membressa*, but little remains of either except for the mosque just back from the main square and a few miscellaneous fragments in the garden of the town hall. Today it's a main crossing point over the Medjerda, one of a number of small farming centres dotted along the main roads of northern Tunisia.

Built in the seventeenth century (a plaque in the middle dates it at 1088 AH, or 1677 AD), the **bridge** is the only real reminder of that period, but only by chance did it survive the bitter battles for Medjez in the winter of 1942–43. A **Commonwealth War Cemetery**, 4km west along the Kef road, bears eloquent and emotional witness to the 2904 Commonwealth soldiers killed here, and a visit to either this or any of the other cemeteries scattered around the country is an experience you won't quickly forget. The best way of getting there is by taxi from Medjez *louage* station, or, if you're in a group, by coming to an agreement with a *louage* driver. A bus can drop you off, but then you'd have to get another one to pick you up afterwards.

WAR GRAVES

The Imperial War Grave Commission, subsequently renamed the Commonwealth Commission, was set up after World War I to arrange for the burial of Britain's **war dead** in specially designed cemeteries. Its general principle was to bury the dead near where they died, and wherever possible in the countryside. Timeless English Pastoral was the desired atmosphere, and it comes as a shock to find little pieces of England, with lawns and trees, in the middle of Tunisia. This rural ethos creates the right contrast between now and then; as you move along the seemingly endless rows of names, it's impossible and yet imperative to imagine the nightmare they represent. An unnamed grave means that the remains were not enough to identify the body, and headstones are grouped together when several remains were indistinguishable. The cemeteries are moving places, their spirit summed up best in the words of Keith Douglas, perhaps the best English poet of World War II, who fought in Tunisia in 1943 before being killed just after D-Day at the age of 24: "Remember me when I am dead / And simplify me when I'm dead."

There are Commonwealth **cemeteries** at Medjez el Bab, Messicault (1km east of Borj el Amri on the GP5 Medjez–Tunis road, some 30km from Tunis), Ras Rajel (see p.149), Oued Zarga (see below), Beja (see p.161), Thibar (see p.161), Enfida (see p.171) and Sfax. Indian servicemen are buried at Sfax, Jews at Borgel Jewish cemetery in Tunis, and victims of World War I in Bizerte International Cemetery (see p.140).

American servicemen killed in action in Tunisia (and a number of Commonwealth soldiers) are buried at Carthage American Military Cemetery (see p.109). There are also French military cemeteries at Enfida (see p.171) and Gammarth (see p.111) and a German one at Borj Cedria (see p.113).

There's no tourist office in town, but if you want to **stay**, the *Hôtel Membressa* (☎08/ 460121; ①), on the west bank of the river, overlooking the bridge, is grimy but adequate. The hotel also has a rather raucous bar and **restaurant**. Buses and *louages* stop in a square just across the bridge, where there are also two **banks**. There are frequent **buses** to Beja (1hr) and Tunis (1hr), and **louages** to Tunis, Testour and Beja. There's also a **train station**, 2km out of town on the left bank of the river, with trains to Tunis, Beja, Jendouba, Ghardimaou and Oued Zarga.

Around Medjez

After the war graves experience, it's a good idea to clear your head by taking a taxi-truck or bus up the road to Toukabeur and Chaouach, two villages high on the mountain wall to the north, for a magnificent view over the surrounding countryside and a reminder that once Medjez was a strategic point. **CHAOUACH**, at the end of the road, is built on the site of a Byzantine fort on a rocky outcrop, the fort itself assembled from the remains of Roman Sua just below. **TOUKABEUR**, 3km below Chaouach on the same road, has more scant remains – the garage on the main square is a converted Roman cistern. On April 12, 1943, a unit of the British 1st Army captured a hill just north of Chaouach. One member of the unit was Sidney Keyes, among the most promising English poets of World War II. "Algeria is a pleasant enough country," he wrote home, "but Tunisia is like what Scotland must have been in the eighteenth century, a mass of bald mountains, terribly cold at night." Two weeks later, at the age of twenty, he was killed just outside Medjez, and he lies buried in plot number 2.K.15 in the Borj el Amri Commonwealth cemetery, on the main road between Tunis and Medjez.

West from Medjez, the road hugs the north side of the Medjerda valley. When the huge **Sidi Salem dam** was completed, the river had to be diverted, and the people of **OUED ZARGA** were entirely rehoused in smart new homes. The old village was the site of a notorious massacre in September 1881, when the French stationmaster and ten other European staff were burnt alive in a sudden uprising by the local people. A conflagration more devastating is commemorated at Oued Zarga's **Commonwealth War Cemetery**, left behind in the old village. A track starting opposite the *Garde Nationale* post leads 2km downhill to the old village.

Beja and around

Twenty-five kilometres or so west of Oued Zarga, after you climb over a high ridge, **BEJA** comes into view, spread over the slopes of a mountain rather like Le Kef to the south. It's an important grain town and, although there's little of outstanding interest, it's well worth stopping off here if you're passing through, especially on a Tuesday when the weekly **souk** is held.

Some history

Since Roman times, Beja has held the biggest **grain market** in the north, and has paid the price of prosperity with a torrid history of destruction and recovery. The first of these cycles began in 109 BC, when a Roman garrison was massacred by a population keen to show its support for the Numidian **King Jugurtha**. The only survivor of the disaster, one Turpilius, turned out to have made a grave error of judgement, because when his supreme commander Metellus arrived and punished the town by razing it to the ground, he had Turpilius flogged and executed. "A man who in such a calamity could prefer dishonourable survival to an untarnished name must have been a detestable wretch," the historian Sallust explained helpfully.

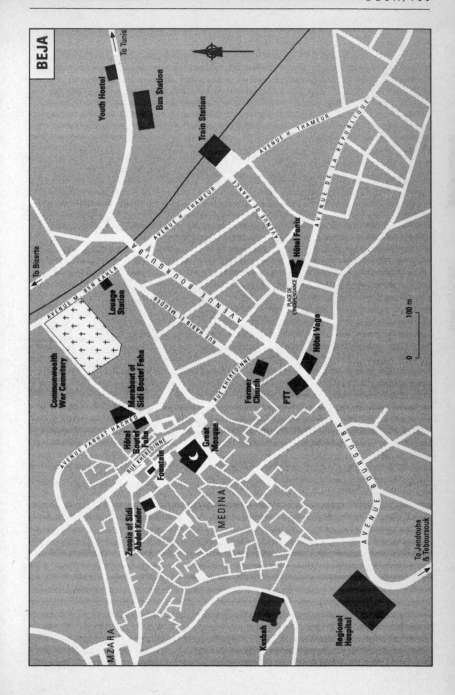

BEJA

To Tunis
Youth Hostel
Bus Station
Train Station
To Bizerte
AVENUE M. BEN KAHLA
Louage Station
Commonwealth War Cemetery
AVENUE H. THAMEUR
AVENUE DE LA REPUBLIQUE
Hôtel Fenix
AVENUE OF FRANCE
AVENUE BOURGUIBA
RUE HABIB EL MEDER
PLACE DE L'INDEPENDANCE
Hôtel Vaga
0   100 m
Marabout of Sidi Bastet Feha
RUE KHEREDINNE
Former Church
PTT
Hôtel Bourèl Feha
AVENUE FARHAT HACHED
RUE KHEREDINNE
Fountain
Great Mosque
Zaouia of Sidi Abdel Kader
MEDINA
AVENUE BOURGUIBA
To Jendouba & Teboursouk
MZARA
Kasbah
Regional Hospital

The town recovered, only to be levelled again by the Vandals in the fifth century, Abu Yazid in the tenth, and the Banu Hilal in the eleventh. By 1154, however, according to El Edrisi, it was a "beautiful city, built on a plain extremely fertile in corn and barley, so that there is not in all the Maghreb a city so important or richer in cereals." It has remained an important agricultural centre ever since, attracting large numbers of Europeans under the French, who left their mark in the form of striking buildings and a well-populated cemetery.

Arrival and accommodation

The **train station** lies on avenue Thameur, with *SRT Beja* running the city's only **bus station**, also used by *SNTRI* and a few other regional companies, on the Tunis road. **Louages** can be picked up from a station beside avenue Moncef Ben Kahla. There are **banks** along avenue Bourguiba, where you'll also find the **PTT** (city hours), just uphill from the old church, with a regional **hospital** (☎08/451431) along avenue Bourguiba, leaving town to the south, and a night **pharmacy** opposite the **cinema**, behind the church. *Magasin Général*, next to the market, and *Bonprix* in place de l'Indépendance, are the town's two **supermarkets**. There's no tourist office.

Officially, Beja only has two **hotels**. The two-star *Hôtel Vaga* on avenue Bourguiba, opposite the PTT (☎08/450818; ②), is friendly, with comfortable, pleasant rooms – if rather bizarre decor. The unclassified *Hôtel Fénix*, at 8 avenue de la République, just off place de l'Indépendance (☎08/450188; ②), is adequate, although some rooms are rather dingy with little outside light. If no one is there, try the bar round the back, at 37 avenue de France. A far better bet than either of these is the *Hôtel Boutef Faha* (①), opposite the marabout of the same name in rue Farhat Hached. Rooms are basic but clean, with a terrace, and you're right in the Medina. The *Maison des Jeunes* **youth hostel**, opposite the bus station (☎08/450621; ①), has the usual barracks-like accommodation.

The Town

Beja's backbone is **avenue Bourguiba**, which climbs from a level crossing at the bottom of the hill up to the town's main square. Bisecting the avenue, avenue de France runs east – with the **modern town** beginning in place de l'Indépendance – and rue Kheredinne runs northwest up towards the Great Mosque, with the Medina behind.

Climbing avenue Bourguiba, you'll come across the huge and extraordinary **church**, built by Beja's large colonial population in a bizarre confusion of dimly remembered European styles, with a few local additions – the tower, for example, looks like a minaret. The church is now a cultural centre. You can study more of Beja's outrageous colonial architecture further up avenue Bourguiba, at the lilac house by the *Hôtel Vaga*, and the building (now a row of shops) dated 1912 immediately behind the former church opposite the top of rue Habib el Meddeb. Reminiscent of Tunis's Christmas-cake colonial style, their early date suggests how important an agricultural centre like Beja was in the colonial scheme of things.

Beja's **Medina**, run-down though it is, has survived largely intact. It is unusually full of mosques, as well as old fountains and busy market streets, and with the cool climate which seems to prevail here, it's one of the most pleasant to wander through in Tunisia. Its main street is **rue Kheredinne**, running only a block away from the **Great Mosque**, Almohad in style, with an unusual red minaret. Rue de la Mosquée, behind it, emerges into a square as rue Blagui. Ahead, bearing right into place Bab el Aïn, you pass a **fountain** on your left dated 1219 AH (1804 AD). To the left, in another square, the 1843 **Zaouia of Sidi Abdel Kader**, with its green-tiled *koubba* dome, is now a kindergarten, but the people who work there (Mon–Sat 8am–5pm as a rule) are welcoming and will almost certainly let you in to have a look.

Taking a right off place Bab el Aïn, you're back on the main road at **place Khemais Bedda**, the centre of the Medina. A couple of hundred metres further, rue Farhat Hached on the right sweeps round to give an impressive view of the countryside to the east, passing the **Marabout of Sidi Boutef Faha** on the left, before bringing you back to the old church. Between rue Farhat Hached and rue Kheredinne is a **second-hand clothes market** where you can obtain all those ghastly 1970s fashions you missed the first time round.

Behind the Medina, the **Kasbah**, dominating the old town, was originally Byzantine, but what little remains is now occupied by the army and is out of bounds. The **Mzara** district, north of here and also above the old town, is said still to have one or two cave dwellings, but this is a very poor part of town and sightseers aren't especially welcome.

At the bottom of rue Habib el Meddeb, a left along avenue M Ben Kahla brings you to a **Commonwealth War Cemetery**, unusual for its position next to a housing estate; on its far side is a typical colonial cemetery, full of dynastic Italian family tombs now smothered in dust and cobwebs.

Eating and drinking

As far as sustenance goes, you're not exactly spoiled for choice in Beja. There are a few cheap **restaurants** in the Medina, like the *Restaurant de la Victoire* at 31 rue Kheredinne, and the restaurant of the *Hôtel Vaga*, but top recommendation, especially for its fish dishes, goes to the *Hôtel Fénix*'s restaurant (entrance in rue de France), where you'll get an excellent meal at a reasonable price. The only reservation here is that you enter through the *Fénix*'s rather raucous bar, which women may find intimidating. The bar itself is generally an all-male preserve but one of the best places in Tunisia to knock back a few beers. *Restaurant La Belle Époque*, opposite the *Fénix*, has similar prices and a quieter atmosphere.

MOVING ON FROM BEJA

From the **train station**, there are six services a day to Tunis (1hr 50min), four to Medjez el Bab (50min) and three to Oued Zarga (20min), with five a day to both Jendouba (55min) and Ghardimaou (1hr 10min) – one of which continues right through to Algiers, via Souk Ahras, Annaba and Constantine (18hr). *SRT Beja* run the city's only **bus station**, also used by *SNTRI* and a few other regional companies. There are four buses daily to Bizerte (2hr) and Aïn Draham (3hr), ten to Jendouba (1hr), six to Tabarca (1hr 30min), one to Siliana (3hr) and Sousse (4hr 30min), two to Teboursouk via Thibar (1hr), and frequent services to Tunis via Medjez el Bab (2hr). **Louages** service Tunis, Medjez, Testour, Teboursouk, Thibar, Jendouba and Nefza (for connections to Sejenane).

Thibar

Eleven kilometres south of Beja, a road turns left towards Teboursouk (see p.238), passing a farmstead that looks like a fort with an egg on top, and runs through the pleasant little village of **THIBAR**, which has a farm set up by the White Fathers, a French missionary movement, that's still in use today. Thibarine liqueur and Thibar wine are made here and, if you're lucky, you may be able to visit the **wine cellars**. Behind the farm buildings, yet another **Commonwealth War Cemetery**, a small one this time, broods among trees full of birds.

There are some scant **Roman remains** south of the village, not really worth seeing but an excuse for an hour-long stroll. Head past the site of Thibar's **Sunday souk**, taking the right-hand fork in the road, signposted "Bou Salem". At the crossroads 1.5km further on, turn right as signposted. With vineyards on your left, then a peach orchard, you're now on an avenue of eucalyptus trees. After a kilometre or so, you pass a water-pumping station on your left and, 100m beyond, a path to the left takes you around a field and across an *oued*. The remains, such as they are, lie on the other side.

Jendouba and around

JENDOUBA is just about the least interesting town in the whole country. What it does have in its favour, however, is plenty of accommodation, banking and transport facilities, making it a perfect base for visiting the impressive Roman site of **Bulla Regia** in the hills above the Medjerda valley, or the lesser remains of **Thuburnica** and **Chemtou** to the west. There are a few Roman remains in Jendouba itself, but these were lifted from Bulla Regia and now sit in a small garden, along with a monument to Jendoubans who died fighting the French for control of Bizerte in 1961 (see p.136), down rue Hedi Chaker on place des Martyrs.

Arriving in Jendouba by bus or *louage*, you're likely to find yourself at the main transport focus of place 7 Novembre, a large roundabout on the western edge of town with two and a half Roman columns poised in its middle. On one side, by a level crossing, is the **louage** station for Aïn Draham and Tabarca (you can be dropped at the Bulla Regia crossroads for the site). On the other side are the *louage* stations for Le Kef, on the left, and Ghardimaou, on the right, and beyond them the **bus** station, with ten services a day to Tunis (4hr), eight to Beja (1hr 30min), six to Le Kef (1hr 10min), four to Ghardimaou (1hr), and one daily to Bizerte (3hr 30min) and Tabarca (2hr).

To get to the town centre, take rue Hedi Chaker from place 7 Novembre, then turn left down rue Taïeb Mehiri. Here you'll find the **PTT** (city hours; international call facilities), **banks** and the easily overlooked **train station**, tucked away in a corner by the police station, with daily departures to Beja (55min), Tunis (2hr 30min), and across the border and on to Algiers. If you turn left off rue Hedi Chaker, just after place des Martyrs, rue Ali Belhouane takes you past more banks, **pharmacies** (day and night), and the *louage* station for Tunis. There's no tourist office in Jendouba.

If you're stuck out by the bus station and want to find somewhere to **stay**, the two-star *Hôtel Simitthu*, right on the roundabout (☎08/631695; ④), is the best in town. Other hotels can be found by following rue Hedi Chaker towards the centre of town. About 100m down rue Hedi Chaker, in a little street on the left – boulevard Khemaïs el Hajera – the *Pension Saha en Noum* (☎08/631595; ①) hits rock-bottom and is not recommended for women. East of the train station up rue 1 Juin, left from rue Hedi Chaker, leads to the *Hôtel Atlas* (☎08/633217; ③), slightly cheaper and correspondingly less plush than the *Simitthu*.

There are plenty of cheap **restaurants** in the town centre, and the *Simitthu* and *Atlas* hotels both do moderately priced set menus. If your stay in town becomes prolonged, there's also a **flea market** of sorts off place 7 Novembre, at the end of boulevard Khemaïs el Hajera (the street with the *pension*), and a **cinema** 100m from place 7 Novembre down the dual carriageway signposted "Le Gouvernorat".

Bulla Regia

Bulla Regia is one of the most extraordinary Roman sites to be seen anywhere in the world. The **underground villas** that form its distinctive feature were built by wealthy inhabitants and, though they have their modern parallel at Matmata (see p.305), were unique in the Roman Empire. Equally striking are the intact and beautiful **mosaics** left *in situ*, all too rare now that the museums have taken the best mosaics at other sites.

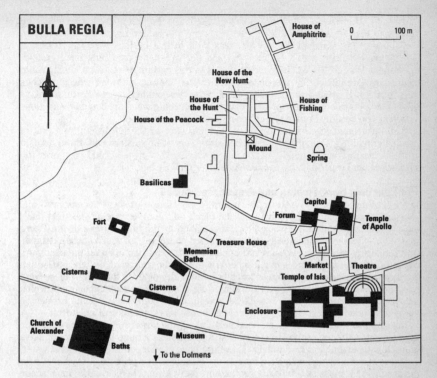

As with the troglodytes at Matmata, no one knows for certain why Bulla Regians went underground, but perhaps it was to escape the heat, as the plain surrounding Jendouba is one of the hottest areas north of Gafsa. This has always been an important region, though, and Bulla Regia played much the same market-centre role as Jendouba does today. The *Regia* in its name refers to royal connections before the arrival of the Romans, when it was associated with one of the native Numidian kingdoms. Subsequently, it became yet another prosperous Roman town and was still occupied in the Byzantine era, but abandoned after the Arab conquest in the seventh century.

The **site** itself (daily 8am–7pm; 1TD, plus 1TD to take photos) lies just north of Jendouba, 6km along the Aïn Draham road, then 2km to the right along a side road, signposted for Bou Salem. A shared taxi from Jendouba to the site shouldn't cost more than 6TD from the flea market off place 7 Novembre, or there are minibuses to the turnoff for 0.4TD from the Aïn Draham *louage* station. Make it clear that it's just the turnoff (or *croisement*) that you want; if they think you want the site itself, they'll deny all knowledge and direct you to a taxi. From the crossroads, you have to walk the last 2km – take the opposite direction from the signposted route to Chemtou. A small **museum** (same hours as the site) has some maps illustrating Bulla Regia's position in Roman Africa, some pictures of the Numidian kings to whom the town owes its suffix, and some nice neo-Punic stelae.

The Memmian Baths and Treasure House

Bullia Regia's most prominent remains – the **Memmian Baths** – stand just by the site entrance and were named after the wife of Septimius Severus, the first African emperor of Rome; the large central hall was a *frigidarium*. From here, take the track leading north to the *Quartier des Maisons*; shortly on the left is the first of the buried villas, the **Treasure House**, so called after a cache of seventh-century Byzantine coins discovered inside. The standard pattern for villas built in this curious way was to have a normal ground floor, with a dining room and perhaps bedrooms sunk underground. The relatively small Treasure House conforms to this pattern, with a large dining room downstairs (identifiable by the pattern of the floor mosaic, showing where couches were positioned around three walls), flanked by two smaller rooms. At least one of these was a bedroom, so presumably eating and sleeping were the two daily functions for which the wealthy Roman citizen most wanted to remain cool.

Back at ground level, some columns standing over to the left belong to a pair of basilica **churches**. One of them has a baptismal font at its western end. From here an artificial **mound** in the middle of the site is visible: this gives a good view over the whole area, and especially the residential quarter directly below it.

The Peacock, Hunt, Fishing and Amphitrite houses

Just left of the crossroads next to the mound is the **House of the Peacock**, with one very fine mosaic, but it's the fully excavated block on the other side of the street that's most fascinating. Almost the whole block is occupied by the huge **House of the Hunt**, whose basement even includes its own colonnaded courtyard, off which opens a magnificent dining room with its mosaics still in place. Bedrooms also open off the courtyard. Note, too, the hexagonal holes in the superstructure of the courtyard, designed to lighten the load, and clusters of what are apparently broken clay pipes in the walls – these were piled together, then plastered over, forming a light but strong construction unit which helped make these basements possible. A private baths complex and some latrines on the ground floor suggest that the owner of this house was something of a plutocrat.

Leaving the House of the Hunt, head north along the street running alongside, then take a right at the top of the **House of Fishing**. This has a huge basement built like a bunker, with a semicircular fountain that would have produced refreshing jets of water. Take the street leading north from here to the **House of Amphitrite**, justly famous for the magnificent mosaics left *in situ* on the basement level. The star of the main scene in the *triclinium* is actually Venus, not Amphitrite, but you have to admire the attendant Cupid who manages to ride a dolphin and admire his chubby features in a mirror at the same time. When Bulla Regia was first excavated, one disturbing discovery was a skeleton tied to a chair with an iron ring around its neck, inscribed: "Hold me, because I ran away from Bulla Regia." Though the victim was actually found buried in the Forum, it seems appropriate to consider her here – a sobering reminder that life in Roman Bulla Regia wasn't all mosaic floors and splashing fountains. The later building over the street was a **baths** complex.

Around the Forum

Head back down the street, then off left to the **spring** – as at Sbeitla (see p.254), the ancient source is still in use today. Beyond lies the administrative quarter of the town, the first grassy open space being the **Forum**, flanked to the west by the **Capitol**, a true-blue Roman temple on a podium, and to the north by the **Temple of Apollo**, in the African pattern of a courtyard with a small sanctuary opening off it. The best statues in Tunis's Bardo Museum were found here. A broad street leads south from the Forum, past the **market** on the right – an important facility in a town like this, its small shops around the sides could be locked up when not in use.

Continuing down the street, you pass another set of **baths** on the left, with an octagonal *frigidarium*, before reaching the back of the **theatre**. It's still possible to enter this by the original galleries, known graphically as *vomitoria*. The first three rows of seats, wider than the rest, were reserved for local dignitaries – who were separated from the proles behind by a solid railing. Bulla Regia's loose and immoral ways, focusing as ever on the theatre, were notorious. Saint Augustine preached a famous sermon here at the end of the fourth century, berating the citizens for their impropriety and imagining them welcoming strangers to the town with "What have you come for? Theatrical folk? Women of easy virtue? You can find them all in Bulla."

Immediately south of the theatre, blocked originally by the stage building, is a rectangular plaza. Making your way west from here, you pass the small podium of the **Temple of Isis**. Its remains are unremarkable, but the cult it served was a cosmopolitan one characteristic of the Roman Empire. Starting life as an Egyptian goddess, Isis was taken up as early as the first century BC by Romans searching for new deities to brighten up their spiritual lives. Isis worship became institutionalized, but always kept an air of mystery; in *The Golden Ass* it is Isis to whom Apuleius turns in his plea to be transformed back from a donkey to a man: "She is the shining deity by whose divine influence not only all beasts, wild and tame, but all inanimate things are invigorated; whose ebbs and flows control the rhythm of all bodies whatsoever, whether in the air, on earth, or below the sea."

Beyond the temple you pass a sizeable enclosure on the way back to the site entrance, with a central area, presumably once a garden, surrounded by deep water channels. A jumble of ruins south of the modern road belongs to yet another set of **baths**, next to what is now misleadingly called the **Church of Alexander**. An inscription from the Psalms was found over the door here ("May the Lord guard your coming in and your going out, now and for ever more, Amen."), and the trough-like stones (as at Kef, Haidra and Maktar) were probably connected with the distribution of food and commodities. Half a kilometre or so south of here is an area of pre-Roman **dolmens**.

Ghardimaou and around

GHARDIMAOU, 30km west of Jendouba on the GP6, is a small border town and unglamorous in the extreme. Its setting is its only virtue: a misty river plain, overshadowed on three sides by mountains that pile up steeply towards Algeria. If you intend to remain in Tunisia, however, the only real reason for coming here is to visit the minor Roman sites of Thuburnica and Chemtou, one featuring a miraculously preserved bridge and the other an ancient marble quarry once renowned throughout the Roman Empire. There's also the mountainous **Forest of Feija**, a national park 20km northwest of Ghardimaou, right on the Algerian frontier.

Ghardimaou's **train station**, crawling with customs and immigration officials, is centrally placed. There's a single **hotel** in town, should you want to stay – the *Thuburnic*, overlooking the station (☎08/645043; ①). Some social life just about succeeds in happening in its bar and restaurant but, as a depressed resident admitted, "there's no *ambience* in Ghardimaou". There's a *Centre de Stages et de Vacances* **youth hostel** (no phone; ①) in the village of **AÏN SOLTANE**, which is a good alternative to staying in Ghardimaou if you have the time. You'll have to ask around for a lift to get there, and since it's very close to the border it's advisable to inform the Ghardimaou police or border officials of your intentions. When you're ready to leave, **louages** to Jendouba depart from along the main road.

This is true border country – never more viciously or tragically so than during the Algerian War of 1954–62. In 1957, the French built the infamous **Morice Line** to prevent the Algerian ALN (*Armé de la Libération Nationale*), based in "neutral" Tunisia, from reinforcing their FLN (*Front de la Libération Nationale*) counterparts inside the country. Three hundred kilometres long, the Morice Line ran from the Mediterranean in the north to the Sahara in the south, where no one could hope to cross the border unnoticed, and it was brutally effective. An eight-foot-high electric fence, charged with 5000 volts, was flanked by minefields and defended by eighty thousand French troops using the latest in electronic surveillance technology. One three-day assault in April 1958 saw the

ALN hurl eight hundred men at the line just north of Souk Ahras. In a week-long running battle, six hundred of them were killed or captured. After the line was built, the ALN never did succeed in providing significant support across the border.

The **border crossings** here and further north at Babouch are the most heavily used in the country, and the most likely to remain open in times of tension. Be warned, though, that for 50km beyond the border, before the first Algerian town, Souk Ahras, the rugged countryside is more or less uninhabited. A deteriorating security climate means that as of mid-1995 it was not advisable for foreigners – particularly Westerners – to visit Algeria on a casual basis, and even travelling close to the Algerian border can be problematic.

Thuburnica

A visit to the Roman site of **Thuburnica** (free access) on the north side of the river plain gives ample chance to see the district's scenery. Taxi-trucks leave regularly from the turning outside Ghardimaou across the bridge towards Algeria, signposted "Turbournic 13km". The remains are an excuse for the journey, but you'll find a memorable little **bridge** carrying the track over one of the deep stream beds that hurry out of the foothills. The bridge's Roman builders are nearly two thousand years gone, but it still looks as if it might have been put up twenty years ago. The rest of the ancient town is scattered in smallish fragments over the hill to the west – a ruined Byzantine castle stands on top, and a fine two-storey **mausoleum** about halfway up.

Chemtou

The other Roman site in this area is **Chemtou** (free access), an apparently unremarkable place that was once famous throughout the Roman world as the source of "Numidian marble", a lurid red-yellow-pink variety much in vogue with imperial builders. Plainly recognizable on an isolated hill on the plain, the site lies about 2km east of Oued Meli, a town 13km east of Ghardimaou and easily reached by *louage* from either direction.

Depending on the time of year, getting to Chemtou can be tricky, because it lies on the north (far) bank of the Medjerda, unconnected by a bridge. In summer, when the river is little more than a trickle, it's easy enough to hop, hitch or drive across – look for an unsignposted track heading north from the main road, near a sign saying "Jendouba 21". This leads 3km to a ford over the river, mocked by the massive remains of a **Roman bridge**. Out of season, when the river is higher, you may have to approach along the track that runs along the north bank of the river from Tubournic to the west, or from the Bulla Regia turnoff, 16km to the east (see p.162). Completion of a sizeable new museum at the site may well bring a bridge or improved communications in some form.

Newly victorious in 146 BC, the Romans used the marble widely and closely identified it with extravagance and luxury. "No beams of Athenian stone rest in *my* house," wrote the poet Horace, "on columns quarried in furthest Africa." As a result, the industry supported a sizeable town – so far only minimally excavated by a team from Tunis and from the German Archeological School in Rome.

Saddling the middle of the hill are the marble **quarries** themselves – just gaping holes in the rock now, but their emptiness seems to preserve an indefinable memory of the skill and sheer hard work of so many men over so many years. The Romans had the industry highly organized, with every block that was cut stamped with the names of the emperor, the consul in office and the local official, along with a production number so that it wouldn't go missing or just fall off the back of a cart. The effort involved in transporting the stone from here in "furthest Africa" to its destination on the other side of the Mediterranean was enormous – it was either dragged all the way over the Khroumirie mountains to be shipped from Tabarca, or floated down the Medjerda to Utica – but of course anything which added to the cost only enhanced its value as a status symbol. The

Emperor Hadrian, a great devotee, once presented a hundred columns to Athens and twenty to Smyrna as marks of imperial favour. A number of remaining miscellaneous blocks graphically illustrate the Romans' odd sense of colour, a taste later shared in turn by the Byzantines and a nineteenth-century operation which revived the workings. If you share this taste too, small carvings in Chemtou marble are sometimes sold as souvenirs.

Other remains

On the top of the eastern summit is a partial restoration of the hilltop **altar**. You can just make out the ancient steps which were hacked into the rock leading up to it. There's something powerful about this high place of worship, which the civic dignity of official Roman religion came to lack.

Below the northern slope of the hill is a broad area of remains, originally a first-century AD military camp but taken over and adapted by some sharp Roman entrepreneur into an on-site **factory** for products of the quarries. Raw stone was delivered to the southern entrance of the camp and then passed along a primitive production line of workshops, ending up with the polishers. The finished utensils and small statues were despatched all over the Empire. Also visible north of the hill are stretches of **aqueduct** heading into the hills, from where they brought the water that fed the town.

South and west of the hill were the residential and official quarters of the town. If you can find someone to let you into the **Excavation House**, a farmhouse-like building south of the hill, it's well worth a visit for a glimpse of mosaics and other remains found on the site, among them a series of massive reliefs showing shields and other military accoutrements that decorated a Roman successor to the hilltop altar. Striking enough in isolation, these will look truly extraordinary when incorporated into the reconstruction of their original temple setting that is currently underway as part of the new museum.

Moving west from the Excavation House towards the tumbledown Roman bridge, you can make out the remains of a **basilica** and a half-buried **theatre**. The bridge, whose massive remains bear elegant testimony to the Romans' civil engineering, carried the main Sicca–Thabraca (Le Kef–Tabarca) road, along which much of the stone was hauled for export. Among the tangled ruins on the northern bank, you can see the unusual industrial feature of three parallel grooves, which forced the flowing water to drive turbines to grind grain.

travel details

Trains

Beja to: Ghardimaou, Jendouba, Medjez el Bab and Tunis.

Bizerte to: Mateur, Menzel Bourguiba, Tinja and Tunis.

Buses

Aïn Draham to: Beja, Beni M'Tir, Bizerte, Fernana, Hammam Bourguiba, Le Kef, Tabarca and Tunis.

Beja to: Aïn Draham, Bizerte, Ghardimaou, Jendouba, Medjez el Bab, Siliana, Sousse, Tabarca, Teboursouk, Thibar and Tunis.

Bizerte to: Aïn Draham, Ghar el Melkh, Houmt Souk, Jendouba, Kairouan, Le Kef, Menzel Bourguiba, Raf Raf, Ras Jebel, Tabarca and Tunis.

Jendouba to: Aïn Draham, Beja, Bizerte, Ghardimaou, Le Kef, Tabarca and Tunis.

Medjez el Bab to: Beja, Jendouba, Le Kef, Teboursouk, Testour and Tunis.

Ras Jebel to: Ghar el Melkh, Raf Raf and Tunis.

Tabarca to: Aïn Draham, Beja, Bizerte, Jendouba, Le Kef, Mateur, Sejenane, Tabarca and Tunis.

Louages

Beja to: Aïn Draham, Jendouba, Medjez el Bab, Nefza, Tabarca, Teboursouk, Testour, Thibar and Tunis.

Bizerte to: Aïn Draham, Beja, Ghardimaou, Jendouba, Mateur, Menzel Bourguiba, Raf Raf, Sejenane and Tabarca.

Jendouba to: Aïn Draham, Le Kef and Tabarca.

Tabarca to: Aïn Draham and Jendouba.

MARKET DAYS

Monday – Aïn Draham
Tuesday – Beja, Bizerte, Ghardimaou, Souk es Sebt
Wednesday – Jendouba, Menzel Bourguiba, Nefza

Thursday – Bou Salem, Sejenane
Friday – Mateur, Tabarca, Ras Jebel
Saturday – El Alia, Hammam Bourguiba
Sunday – Bezina, Fernana, Menzel Bourguiba, Thibar

CHAPTER FOUR

KAIROUAN AND THE SAHEL

K airouan – the Holy City – is only the most obvious attraction in **the Sahel***, an area that is central in every way to Tunisia. Ranging back from the east coast, these fertile plains have long been the heartland of the country's agriculture, and a focus during each shift of power. The Romans planted millions of olive trees throughout the region, and under Arab rule it was the base of the great Aghlabid dynasty, which launched a successful invasion of Sicily from the port of Sousse in the ninth century.

Monuments from this and ensuing dynasties grace most of the Sahel's larger towns. **Kairouan**, the first Arab capital in North Africa, is pre-eminent – above all for its Great Mosque, justly Tunisia's most famous building as well as its spiritual centre. But **Sousse**, **Sfax**, **Monastir** and **Mahdia** are each highly rewarding for their architecture, and **El Jem** shelters what is arguably the Roman world's finest surviving amphitheatre.

Add to this an impressive series of beaches and it's easy to understand the region's popularity – and why the **Sousse–Monastir coast** is gradually becoming the country's most highly developed for tourism. Yet there are still places – in particular, parts of the **Kerkennah Islands** – where you can find virtual isolation. Most independent travellers invariably find themselves staying longer than originally planned.

ACCOMMODATION PRICE CODES

All the hotels, youth hostels and pensions listed in this book have been price-graded according to the following scale, and although prices will rise during the lifetime of this edition, the relative comparisons should remain valid.

The prices quoted are for the **cheapest available double room in high season**, although many of the cheap places will have pricier rooms with en suite facilities or sea views.

Classified hotels, officially considered suitable for tourists, are graded locally from one to four stars (★), with wide-ranging prices within each category. For more on accommodation prices and categories, see Basics.

① Up to 10TD. Very cheap. Usually a bed only in a basic, unclassified hotel or a youth hostel.

② 10.1–25TD. Budget. Bed only or bed and breakfast.

③ 25.1–40TD. Comfortable budget. Good unclassified average one-star or a cheap two-star.

④ 40.1–55TD. Mid-range. Expensive two-star, cheap three-star.

⑤ 55.1–70TD. Tourist hotel. Standard three-star.

⑥ 70.1TD upwards. Deluxe. Expensive three-star, four-star or five-star.

---

* The Arabic name "Sahel" means coast or margin and, in the case of the sub-Saharan Sahel, the edge of the desert.

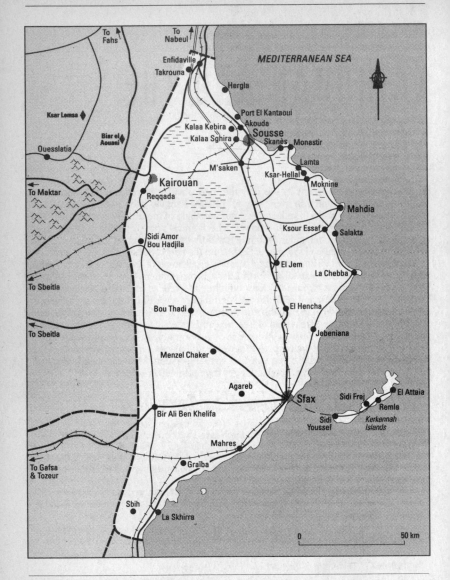

Enfida (Enfidaville) and around

ENFIDA is the administrative centre for a vast and fertile agricultural estate that was an indirect cause of French colonial intervention in 1881. The estate's original owner, the reforming Turkish official Khaireddin, put it up for sale when he was recalled to Constantinople, and the Franco-African Company immediately submitted the highest bid. The Tunisian government tried to keep the estate out of French hands, but the attempt backfired, and helped to convince the French that the time had come to take full control in the country.

The estate is still heavily cultivated, but the town has been bypassed by the coastal road to Sousse, and its dusty streets would hardly be worth a visit were it not for the breathtaking village of Takrouna nearby and the small town **museum**, in the old French church on the main street (daily 9.30am–6.30pm; May–Aug 8am–noon & 3–7pm; 1TD). The collection of mosaic epitaphs and tombstones vividly illustrates the mix of cultures and values prevalent here in ancient times – Berber, Carthaginian, Roman and Christian. Many tombstones are dedicated to priests of Saturn, a Roman transplant of the Carthaginian god Baal; hence the un-Roman symbols such as crescent moons. When Christianity came, the Berbers adapted once again, and names in the epitaphs like Filocalus, Gududa, Jades and Vernacla show that local people as well as overlords took to the new religion.

The mosaics from the nearby site of Uppena reveal persecution of Catholic Christians by the Vandals, who followed the Arian heresy. One recalls the deaths of sixteen Catholic martyrs, while two more are epitaphs to bishops summoned to a church convention in 484 AD by the Vandal king Huneric, who then kept them here until their deaths.

During World War II, heavy fighting took place around Enfida in the final weeks of the Tunisian campaign, as the retreating Germans attempted to hold a line here against the Eighth Army. A melancholy reminder of this are the two **military cemeteries** – a Commonwealth one on the western edge of town (follow signs for Zaghouan) and, 3km further on, below the looming presence of Takrouna's rocky outcrop, one for the French forces. They stand interesting comparison – the French one is positively austere and militaristic, with a helmet placed on each grave, while the Commonwealth cemetery is green and rustic, just too neat to be an English churchyard.

Practicalities

Most of Enfida is spread out along one main street. At the western end is the turnoff for Zaghouan and, less than a hundred metres east of it, the turnoff for Sousse. Beyond, on the northern side of the main street, are the **PTT** and museum, with a couple of **banks** and cheap *gargotes* opposite them. A street opposite the PTT leads to a square, off which is the main **market**. There are no hotels in town and no tourist office.

For transport, the main **bus station** is a hundred metres east of the museum, across the main road, and this is where buses and *louages* heading to or from Tunis can be picked up, with hourly bus departures for Tunis (1hr 30min) and Sousse (1hr), five a day to Nabeul (2hr) and four to Kairouan (1hr 30min), as well as two direct services to Bizerte (3hr). One or two services between Sousse and the north have to be picked up at the relevant turnoff – the people in the bus station should be able to advise you. The **louage station** for Sousse is a few metres down the Sousse road, and there is a bus stop just beyond it. For the **train station**, head east, turn right about twenty metres after the museum, and continue for a couple of hundred metres. Half a dozen trains stop here daily en route to Sousse (45min), two to Sfax (2hr 30min) and Monastir (1hr 20min), one to both Mahdia (2hr 30min) and Gabes (5hr). In the other direction, four Tunis-bound trains a day stop at Enfida (1hr 30min).

Takrouna

The victims lying in the military cemeteries died fighting for **TAKROUNA**, a Berber village 7km southwest of Enfida and perched high on a rock, whose inaccessibility had long made it a natural defensive position, though it can be reached today by local mini-bus-*louage*, picked up at the Zaghouan turnoff. The final Allied assault on it in 1943 was made by thirteen New Zealanders, most of them Maoris. The dramatic site, crowned by a green-domed marabout, and the even more mind-blowing view – from the sinister gleaming blade of Jebel Zaghouan behind to the broad sweep of the coastline – have placed Takrouna firmly on the tourist map, and busloads are rushed in and out along a specially built road. The Berbers have always cherished their independence, and this site is a typical one. Unfortunately, Takrouna's exploitation has led to the villagers exploiting tourists, and today their friendliness comes at a price. The road that goes past Takrouna continues to Zaghouan through some lovely remote heathland, passing two more Berber villages – **JERADOU** and **ZRIBA** – which are similar to Takrouna, but less visited (see p.226).

Sousse and around

SOUSSE seems to have everything going for it: a historic **Medina** containing two of Tunisia's most distinctively beautiful monuments, an excellent **museum** second only to the Bardo, and endless stretches of white **beach**. Little wonder it has become Tunisia's most popular resort. But even though there's a brash, somewhat superficial feel to the place, it has the best nightlife in the country, good swimming, cultural events and plentiful places to stay.

Some history
Thanks to its natural harbour and central position on the fertile eastern seaboard, Sousse has been important to every civilization occupying this stretch of North African coast, each remodelling it in their own image – Roman *Hadrumetum*, Vandal *Hunericopolis* and Byzantine *Justinianopolis*. Even when the all-conquering Oqba Ibn Nafi, leader of the Arab invaders (see p.362), destroyed the town in the seventh century, it wasn't long before Susa – the Arabic name still most commonly used – revived. It was the main outlet to the Mediterranean for the Aghlabids ruling in Kairouan and they launched their invasion of Sicily from here in 827. It was later occupied by the **Normans**, in the twelfth century, and **Spaniards** in the sixteenth, and was bombarded in turn by the French and Venetians in the eighteenth century. By the end of the nineteenth century the resilient town was becoming increasingly important to the French colonists. Since then Sousse's growth has been impeded only by World War II and it's now the third largest city in the country, with textiles industries balancing its unpredictable earnings from tourism.

Arrival and information

Monastir airport is 20km southeast of Sousse, connected to the town by strings of buses and the "metro" train. A number of **car rental** firms also operate from the airport, and you should be able to pick up a rental car immediately on arrival (☎03/463031), or you can catch a taxi into Sousse for around 10TD. Arriving by **bus**, you'll probably be dropped in the place du Port or by Bab Jedid, except if you arrive from Le Kef or Enfida, when you'll be dropped at the *gare routière* on avenue Leopold Senghor. The **train station** is on boulevard Hassouna Ayachi, but speedy so-called **metro** services from Monastir and Mahdia leave you on boulevard Mohamed V near Bab Jedid. The **louage station** is some 4km out of town on the Sfax road, opposite the Sunday market, and you're best off taking a taxi into town (around 2TD). If you're feeling slightly silly, you can take the **tourist land train** to Port el Kantaoui (3TD return), departing every hour from 9am to 11pm from place Boujaffar in Sousse, returning on the half-hour. Longer excursions are suggested in "Listings", p.181.

There's an extremely helpful and organized *ONTT* **tourist office** at 1 avenue Bourguiba, almost on place Farhat Hached (Mon–Thurs 8.30am–1pm & 3–5.45pm, Fri

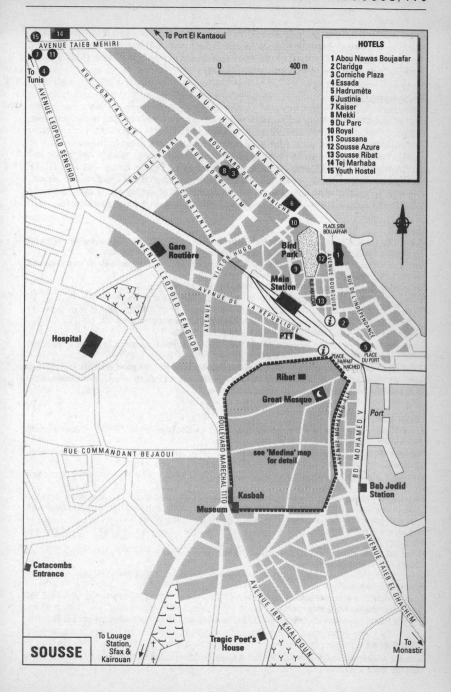

HOTELS

1 Abou Nawas Boujaafar
2 Claridge
3 Corniche Plaza
4 Essada
5 Hadrumète
6 Justinia
7 Kaiser
8 Mekki
9 Du Parc
10 Royal
11 Soussana
12 Sousse Azure
13 Sousse Ribat
14 Tej Marhaba
15 Youth Hostel

To Port El Kantaoui

0   400 m

AVENUE TAIEB MEHIRI

To Tunis

RUE CONSTANTINE

AVENUE LEOPOLD SENGHOR

RUE DE RABAT

RUE MONGI SLIM

BOULEVARD DE LA CORNICHE

AVENUE HEDI CHAKER

RUE CONSTANTINE

Gare Routière

AVENUE LEOPOLD SENGHOR

AVENUE VICTOR HUGO

AVENUE DE LA RÉPUBLIQUE

Bird Park

PLACE SIDI BOUJAFFAR

AVENUE BOURGUIBA

RUE AMILCAR

RUE DE L'INDEPENDANCE

Main Station

Hospital

PTT

PLACE FARHAT HACHED

PLACE DU PORT

Ribat

Great Mosque

see 'Medina' map for detail

RUE COMMANDANT BEJAOUI

BOULEVARD MARECHAL TITO

AVENUE MOHAMED ALI

BD. MOHAMED V

Port

Kasbah

Museum

Bab Jedid Station

Catacombs Entrance

AVENUE TAIEB EL GHACHEM

SOUSSE

To Louage Station, Sfax & Kairouan

AVENUE IBN KHALDOUN

Tragic Poet's House

To Monastir

& Sat 8.30am–1.30pm; July & Aug Mon–Sat 7.30am–6.30pm, Sun 9am–noon; ☎03/225157), with loads of useful information, including train and bus schedules and fares, as well as a *Syndicat d'Initiative* in place Farhat Hached/place Sidi Yahia (Mon 1–6pm, Tues–Sat 8am–6pm, Sun 9am–5pm; ☎03/222331).

Accommodation

Most of the cheaper **hotels** are situated within the Medina, with options in the new town tending to be classier. The gleaming white monster beach hotels begin at the end of avenue Bourguiba and go on for miles. Almost all of them offer full board and an in-house disco, so you don't actually *need* to go into town at all, and many offer bargain rates in low season and can be warmer at night than draughty Medina hotels. People **camp** out at **CHOTT MARIAM**, 18km north of Sousse, although this doesn't have official sanction and is more or less in the middle of nowhere. Camping isn't quite part of the Sousse image; it's strictly forbidden on most of the beaches – though they allow you to do it at the youth hostel.

Medina

Ahla, pl du Grande Mosquée, opposite the Great Mosque (☎03/220570). The rooms here are a bit spartan, but clean enough and excellent value, especially considering the location. ②.

Emira ★, 52 rue de France (☎03/226325). Clean and friendly, each room with its own bath and balcony, and evening barbecues on the roof terrace. ②.

Ezzouhour, 48 rue de Paris (☎03/228729). Friendly but a bit of a dive. ②.

Gabes, 12 rue de Paris (☎03/226977). Not at all bad considering the price. ①.

Medina ★, 15 rue Othman Osman, by the Great Mosque (☎03/221722). Posher than the other Medina hotels, with en suite bathrooms, but becoming a bit package oriented. ②.

Mestiri, 19 rue el Aroua (☎03/222120). Cheap and cheerful. ①.

Hôtel de Paris, 15 rue du Rempart Nord (☎03/220564). Pristine rooms, a beautiful terrace and friendly management. Recommended. ②.

Hôtel des Perles, 71 rue de Paris (☎03/224609). Rather grotty and not good value. ①.

Hôtel de Tunis, 19 rue de l'Église (☎03/224350). Cheap, but not exactly deluxe. Great views of the Ribat from the terrace, but make sure your room locks. ①.

Town centre

Abou Nawas Boujaafar ★★★★, av Bourguiba, cnr pl Boujafaar (☎03/226030). Rather a grand city hotel, but handy for the beach. ⑥.

Claridge ★, 10 av Bourguiba, off pl Farhat Hached (☎03/224759). An old favourite and city landmark, with central heating and shower or bath (but not loo) in every room. ②.

Corniche Plaza, bd de la Corniche (☎03/226763). A small place with plain but clean rooms and pleasant, efficient staff. ②.

Hadrumète, pl Assad Ibn Fourat, off pl Farhat Hached (☎03/226291). The Roman torso in the lobby is a remnant of its two-star past, and the rooms are still bright and clean here. On the fourth floor they have balconies, and many rooms have views over the port. ③.

Mekki, rue 2 Mars (☎03/227127). A clean, quiet pension in a cul-de-sac one block behind bd de la Corniche. ①.

Hôtel du Parc ★, rue de Carthage (☎03/220434). Very comfortable, with friendly young staff and a largely Libyan clientele. ②.

Royal, 4 rue Teboulba la Corniche, near the bird park (☎03/228311). A clean, friendly pension not far from the beach. ③.

Sousse Azure ★★, 5 rue Amilcar, near the bird park (☎03/227760). Spotless, with en suite bathrooms and welcoming smiles. ③.

Sousse Ribat, 8 rue Remada (☎03/226077). Rather a slapdash affair, but reasonably priced. ②.

Beach area

Essada, av Leopold Senghor (☎03/220115). A friendly place behind the *Kaiser* and *Soussana*, 700m from the beach. ③.

Hill Diar ★★★, bd 7 Novembre (☎03/241811). A pleasant and tasteful place on the beach 3km from the centre, with a mainly female staff. Minus points include piped music in the lobby and the lack of beach sports – stroll up the beach for these. ⑤.

Justinia ★★★ and **Nour Justinia** ★★★ (both ☎03/226866), both av Hedi Chaker. Sharing a pool, the nearest beach hotels to the centre are not as smart as those further up the beach, but the *Nour Justinia* is a very good deal off season, especially for full and half board, with great views from the roof. ④.

Kaiser ★★, bd Taïeb Mehiri (☎03/228111). A few doors beyond the *Soussana*, over which its main advantage is the rooftop pool and panoramic view. ③.

Soussana ★★, bd Taïeb Mehiri (☎03/228011). A reasonable place near the *Tej Marhaba*, about 400m off the beach. ③.

Marhaba Club, **Marhaba** and **Marhaba Beach** ★★★, bd 7 Novembre (☎03/242170). A group of three hotels of similar standards and identical prices that share their facilities. Good value – especially for single rooms off season – with friendly and helpful staff, and deservedly popular with British holidaymakers. ④.

Tej Marhaba ★★★★, bd Taïeb Mehiri (☎03/229800). Large and classy with lots of coming and going. Wheelchair-friendly, with a well laid-out pool, but there's 200m to walk and a main road to cross before you're at the hotel's beach. ③.

Tour Khalef ★★★, bd 7 Novembre (☎03/241844). Another well-regarded package hotel with full facilities. Wheelchair-friendly. ⑤.

Youth hostel

Maison des Jeunes youth hostel, bd Taïeb Mehiri, beyond the *Tej Marhaba* (☎03/221269). The cheapest place in Sousse if you're on your own, but there's a daily shut-out from 10am to 5pm, as well as an 11.30pm curfew (summer 12.30pm). Camping possible. ①.

The City

The hub of the city is **place Farhat Hached**, a huge "square" – if it can be called that – which becomes, on its outer fringes, variously place des Martyrs, place Sidi Yahia and place du Port. Here all traffic and activity seem to converge, and even the main train line runs straight across it. To the north is the **new town** that's been almost entirely rebuilt since the war, and to the south the **Medina**. The port is so close that it's unsettling at night to see a large ship, all lit up, apparently being towed across the square – a surreal image heightened when the train to Sfax edges its way through in front. The inevitable **avenue Bourguiba** leads from here up to place Sidi Boujaffar, where the **beach** begins, backed for a kilometre by **avenue Hedi Chaker**. Further along, **boulevard 7 Novembre** follows the coast, separated from the beach by a line of hotels all the way to Port el Kantaoui.

The Medina

The monuments in the walled **Medina** testify to the city's long-lasting importance; in particular the Ribat and the Khalef Tower indicate Sousse's strategic significance, especially to the Aghlabids. You might expect the old city in such a resort to have lost all charm and character in a deluge of tacky souvenir shops, but while there are plenty of these, with a ready spiel for eager punters – and often abuse for less eager ones – the Medina has clung to its individuality. Note that there have been one or two cases of bag-snatching in the shopping areas of the Medina, so keep your eyes open and don't dangle valuables temptingly about the place.

At the northern end of the Medina, the **Ribat** (daily summer 9am–7pm; winter 8.30am–5pm; 2TD) was begun by the Aghlabids in 821. It's a well-preserved example of a style peculiar to this period of North African history, when the Muslim inhabitants were under constant threat from marauding Christians based in Sicily. The word *ribat* is related to *marabout*, and the buildings served a religious as well as a military purpose, housing devout warrior troops broadly comparable to crusading Christian orders such as the Knights Templar. When necessary, the men would fight, at times of

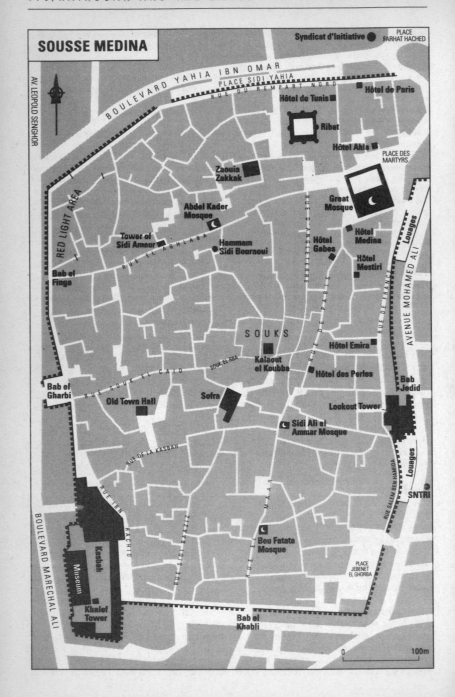

SOUSSE MEDINA

Syndicat d'Initiative ●   PLACE
                          FARHAT HACHED

AV. LEOPOLD SENGHOR

BOULEVARD YAHIA IBN OMAR

PLACE SIDI YAHIA

RUE DU REMPART NORD

Hôtel de Paris ■

Hôtel de Tunis ■

Ribat

Hôtel Ahla ■   PLACE DES
                MARTYRS

RED LIGHT AREA

Zaouia
Zakkak

Great
Mosque

Abdel Kader
Mosque

Hôtel
Medina ■

Tower of
Sidi Ameur

RUE EL AGHLABA

Hammam
Sidi Bouraoui ●

Hôtel
Gabes ■

Hôtel
Mestiri ■

AVENUE MOHAMED ALI

Louages

RUE D'ANGLETERRE

RUE DE PARIS

Bab el
Finga

RUE DE FRANCE

SOUKS

SOUK EL RBA

RUE SOUK EL CAID

Kalaout
el Koubba

Hôtel Emira ■

Bab el
Gharbi

Old Town Hall

Sofra

Hôtel des Perles ■

Bab
Jedid

RUE DE LA KASBAH

Sidi Ali el
Ammar Mosque

Lookout Tower

RUE IBN RACHID

RUE EL MAAR

RUE SALEM BEN HAMIDA

Louages

SNTRI ●

BOULEVARD MARECHAL ALI

Kasbah

Museum

Bou Fatata
Mosque

PLACE
JEBENET
EL GHORBA

Khalef
Tower

Bab el
Khabli

0   100m

peace they lived and studied in the bare cells around the Ribat's inner courtyard; the simplicity of the fort's form reflects the men's dedication to their second role. The only large communal room is the **prayer hall** over the entrance. Until superseded by the Khalef Tower at the opposite corner of the Medina, the Ribat's **tower** served as a look-out point and would pass on beacon messages – messages could be sent from Alexandria in Egypt to Ceuta in Morocco in a single night. Although the Ribat was primarily defensive, only six years after it was begun the Aghlabids were strong enough to launch a successful invasion of Sicily. The city's defences aspect remained important, however, against both Christians at sea and the Berbers inland – hence the thickness of the Medina walls on the western, inland side.

Opposite the Ribat stands the **Great Mosque**, Sousse's other great early Islamic monument (daily 8am–1pm; 1TD; dress with respect for the congregation and avoid prayer times). Although founded in the ninth century like the great mosques of Kairouan, Tunis and Sfax, this has a sparer quality, perhaps because it has received fewer later additions; the original concept of uncomplicated forms remains on view, giving added emphasis to the minimal decoration of the inscription around the wall of the courtyard. The little domed **kiosk** at one corner was added in the eleventh century to act as a minaret, its wide staircase a feature that is more commonly seen further east.

Down a side street near the Ribat you should be able to see a curious open minaret, like stone crochet-work, which belongs to the **Zaouia Zakkak** – Turkish-built, as the octagonal shape reveals. Nearby, rue el Aghlaba climbs to leave the Medina at **Bab el Finga**, passing en route the 1852 **Abdel Kader Mosque** opposite no. 29 and, a little further at no. 52, the square stone **Tower of Sidi Ameur**, like a minaret without a mosque. The area just north of Bab el Finga is a red-light district, which can only be entered here since all other exits have been walled off. Women are best off steering clear.

Back at the other end of rue el Aghlaba, rue Angleterre leads south past the tourist stalls to an area of covered souks. Turn right here onto rue Souk el Rba, and almost immediately on the right is the **Kalaout el Koubba**. No one really knows the original function of this building, though its features suggest it's eleventh-century Fatimid. It was once definitely a *foundouk*, later a café, now a council-run "cultural" exhibition gallery.

Parallel with rue d'Angleterre, running south from the Great Mosque, **rue de Paris** is the main street of tourist souvenir shops, selling the usual goods at not very bargain prices. One place worth a quick look is no. 54, an old *foundouk*. At its southern end, rue de Paris joins rue d'Angleterre. Just beyond, on the left at no. 3, you can make out the delicately carved facade of the **Sidi Ali el Ammar Mosque**, another remnant of the Fatimid period, next door to the white dome of a hammam, currently closed. A turning to the right, opposite the hammam entrance, leads to the blank and impenetrable wall which surrounds the **Sofra**, an early Islamic cistern complex. Near the end of rue el Maar you pass a small, austere mosque on the left, named after one **Bou Fatata** and built, around 840, in a style that's in marked contrast to the incipient elaboration of the Fatimid buildings. Rue el Maar comes to an end at **Bab el Khabli**, the gate of the southern wall of the Medina. From here, a left within the wall takes you to place Jebenet el Ghorba, whose small, daily market specializes in second-hand clothes, then north up rue Salem Ben Hamida and along, alongside the eastern rampart up to Bab Jedid. The woman at no. 3, a house with a lookout tower built into the wall, sometimes lets tourists climb it for a small fee. Access to the ramparts has otherwise been closed off, though if you really want to walk along them, you could try asking at the museum.

The Kasbah and museum

Leaving the Medina at Bab el Khabli and climbing the windswept promenade to your right alongside the southern wall, you come to the former **Kasbah** in the Medina's southwestern corner. The Kasbah grew up around the **Khalef Tower**, built here in 859 at the highest point in the city to improve on the view given by the Ribat tower, put up thirty years earlier. Today the Kasbah houses an excellent **museum** (daily except Tues summer 8am–noon & 3–7pm; winter 9am–noon & 2–6pm; 2TD), whose exhibits – predominantly mosaics – are of a consistently high quality, and unlike those of the Bardo don't threaten to overwhelm by sheer quantity. Many were found in the region's Christian catacombs and, distinguishable by their standard XP symbol, bear familial and domestic epitaphs. One long message reads:

> *"This was Eusebia, brothers, a rare and most chaste wife who spent with me a life of marriage, as time tells: sixty years, eight months and twenty days. God himself was pleased with her life, as I say. Truly a gentle wife of the rarest sort: I, Sextus Successus, lawyer, her husband, beg that you always remember her in your prayers, brothers."*

The earlier, more extroverted Imperial mosaics include some of the most stunning in the country. Don't on any account leave without seeing **Room 11**, across the courtyard, which contains an extraordinarily powerful group of amphitheatre scenes – almost all of them found in one villa.

Lastly, just south of the Kasbah, along rue Ibn Khaldoun and bearing right at the fork after 200m or so, is the **House of the Tragic Poet**, a tiny Roman site with mosaics of dramatic themes along the lines of its namesake in the ruins of Pompeii in Italy.

The beaches, market and catacombs

The modern town's sole pretence to culture is a small **bird park** in place Boujaffar, its entrance on boulevard de la Corniche (daily 8am–6.30pm; 0.2TD), where you can look at a motley collection of mostly tatty-looking caged birds, including a couple of ostriches, in a small and slightly unkempt park with a carousel for children next door. What brings most tourists to Sousse, however, are its **beaches**. Though inferior to Hammamet's – the shore is more exposed, urban and often windy – they have a more eminent literary history, as somewhere on the dunes beneath where the hotels now stand, the French novelist André Gide first faced up to his homosexuality.

You can take part in various **beach sports** up by the *Hôtel el Hana* and at other big hotels further along the beach and in Port el Kantaoui. Parascending (15TD a go), water-skiing (10TD) and windsurfing (7TD an hour) are all available. Beware of petty thieving by gangs of kids who will take anything left lying around while you swim or doze.

Given the large numbers of tourists who come here, it was inevitable that the **market** in Sousse would be "discovered", and images of huge camel sales are used to entice people. Market day is Sunday, and the site is a couple of kilometres out towards Sfax. Unfortunately, camels are no longer sold here, so if you were hoping to buy one you're out of luck.

Another suburban attraction is the **Catacombs**, about the same distance to the west. However, they were recently closed to the public, so check with the tourist office to see if they have reopened, and if you do manage to arrange a viewing, take along some sort of light. Access is via the Kairouan road from the Kasbah, first left onto rue 25 Juillet, then right into rue Abu Hamed el Ghazali and left after 600m. Alternatively, take rue Quatrième Tirailleur from Bab el Gharbi (the Medina's western gate), turn left after 500m, then right onto rue Abu Hamed el Ghazali and left after 100m. Several chambers, stretching for over 5km, have been discovered: the burial place of early Christians from the third and fourth centuries, they contain over fifteen thousand tombs.

Eating and drinking

Sousse has plenty of **eating places** appealing to both tourists and locals. The former provide European cooking and an ambience suited to their clientele: you'll find a number of places on the edge of place Farhat Hached between the port and avenue Bourguiba, of which the *Restaurant de Bonheur* is probably the best. The Soussi-favoured haunts have much less in the way of finesse but the food is just as palatable and the prices a lot lower. A lot of the beach hotels have buffets and set menus at moderate prices, too; the *Marhaba* in particular is good value.

Restaurants

Restaurant L'Anouina, rue de Remada. A low-priced eatery in a little street behind av Bourguiba and rue Amilcar.

La Belle Avenue, bd de la Corniche. One of the first – and best – of a host of Western-style fast-food takeaways, with cheap burgers, pizzas, chips and the like.

Restaurant le Beraka, bd de la Corniche, near the *El Hana* hotel complex (☎03/227681). A pleasant but expensive place with great fish.

Restaurant la Calèche, rue de Remada (☎03/226489). One of the better upmarket eateries in town.

Restaurant el Ferdaws, rue Braunschweig. Good food and a good-value cheapie, but tends to close early. Near the *Claridge Hôtel*.

Forum Grill, av Hedi Chaker (☎03/228399). A friendly place on the front with good food and good service; moderate to expensive.

Restaurant La Gondole, bd 7 Novembre (☎03/222778). Cosy place opposite the *Hôtel Riadh* with excellent fish soup and mixed hors d'oeuvres. Moderate to expensive.

Restaurant Le Gourmet, 3 rue Amilcar (☎03/224791). Quite a classy place with high prices in an alley off the northern end of av Bourguiba.

Hong Kong Restaurant, rue de Rabat, opposite the *El Hana Beach Hôtel* (☎03/221366). Sousse's only Chinese, with a set menu or expensive à la carte dishes, including pork and duck.

Restaurant de la Jeunesse, rue Ali Bach Hamba, just off av Bourguiba. Good food at reasonable prices.

Le Lido, av Mohammed V (☎03/225329). Tasty but expensive fresh fish.

Restaurant National, rue el Aghlaba, near the Great Mosque. Basic cheapie.

Restaurant du Peuple, rue du Rempart Nord, next to the *Hôtel de Paris*. A very pleasant, inexpensive little place.

Restaurant Populaire, 21 pl J Ben Cherifa near the Great Mosque. Tasty food at very low prices. The sign over the door is in Arabic only.

Restaurant Raphia, rue Boulogne Bilancourt, off av Bourguiba (☎03/221468). Rather pricey German and Swiss specialities, including pork dishes, for German-speaking package tourists in need of a taste of home.

Restaurant Sidi Yahia, pl des Martyrs. A decent *gargote* that's very low-priced in spite of its prime location.

Les Sportifs Restaurant, av Bourguiba (☎03/224756). Better than most, with a passable and not too pricey tourist menu.

Restaurant de Tunisie, rue Ali Belhouane (☎03/225948). Moderately priced Indian dishes when supplies are available – one of the chefs formerly worked in a UK curry house. Lots of veggie options anyhow.

Restaurant le Viking, rue de l'Algérie (☎03/228377). In a side street off av Bourguiba. Another good, central, upmarket option. Moderate to expensive.

Snack bars and patisseries

Le Cappuccino, 1 av Bourguiba, cnr of pl Farhat Hached. A bit of a tourist trap, but serves reasonable breakfasts and *schewarma* sandwiches.

Casa del Gelato, bd 7 Novembre, by the *Hôtel Hill Diar*. Delicious ice cream out in the hotel zone, in a snazzy cubic building with a pizzeria upstairs.

Patisserie Cherif, av Bourguiba, near the *Palace* cinema. Widely considered the best pastry shop in town.

Juice Bar, rue Braunschweig, by the *Claridge Hôtel*. The best place in town for real fruit juice; reasonably priced, compared to all the tourist places. Unfortunately, they only have what's in season but they also do scrumptious cakes.

Maria Luisa, 6 rue 2 Mars. Ice cream parlour and pasta takeaway run by an Italian woman, with the best ice cream in town.

Listings

Airlines *Tunis Air*, 15 av Bourguiba (☎03/227955).

Banks There are plenty of banks in av Bourguiba and always one or two open Saturday and Sunday morning. A solution to the summertime queues is to try banks further afield (such as the *BNA* on av de la République near the corner of av Victor Hugo). There are one or two places in the Medina and on av Mohammed V. After hours, try the big hotels.

Bicycle rental *El Taief* on bd 7 Novembre, opposite the *Hôtel Jawhara Club* (☎03/226519); current rates are around 1.5TD an hour, 7TD a day.

MOVING ON FROM SOUSSE

Sousse's transport system is complicated, with four different bus stations serving various parts of the country, along with two train stations, a single *louage* station and an airport.

By bus

Southbound *SNTRI* **bus services** stop by Bab Jedid, a gate in the Medina's east wall, with northbound ones running from pl du Port, an extension of pl Farhat Hached over towards the port. Most local services, including those for Hergla and the hill villages, run from pl Sidi Yahia by the Medina's north wall, but for Enfida and Le Kef you have to hike up to the *gare routière* on av Leopold Senghor (a continuation of av de la République). Bus departure times and fares are posted in the *ONTT* and *Syndicat d'Initiative*.

Bab Jedid: Douz (1 daily; 7hr 30min), Gabes (12 daily, including 7 at night; 5hr 30min), Houmt Souk on Jerba (3 daily, including 2 at night; 6hr 45min), Kairouan (11 daily; 1hr 30min), Kebili (3 daily, including 2 at night; 7hr), Matmata (1 nightly; 6hr), Medenine (6 daily, including 3 at night; 6hr), Sfax (12 daily, including 7 at night; 2hr 30min), Tataouine (2 daily, including 1 at night; 7hr), Zarzis (2 daily, including 1 at night; 7hr).

Place Sidi Yahia: Port el Kantaoui (hourly; 30min), Chott Mariam and Hergla (8 daily; 45min), Mahdia (16 daily; 1hr 30min), Monastir (12 daily; 45min).

Gare routière: Enfida (10 daily; 1hr), Le Kef (3 daily; 4hr).

Place du Port: Bizerte (2 daily; 2hr 4hr), Tunis (14 daily, including 7 at night; 2hr 30min).

By louage

All **louages** leave from a station opposite the Sunday market. There are services to La Chebba, El Jem, Enfida, Hammamet, Hergla, Kairouan, Kasserine, Ksar Hellal, Ksour Esaf, Mahdia, Moknine, Monastir, Nabeul, Port el Kantaoui, Sbeitla, Sidi Bon Zid, Siliana, Sfax and Tunis.

By train

Train services leave from the **train station** in bd Hassouna Ayachi. There are eight daily departures for Tunis (1hr 40min), four of them stopping at Enfida (45min). In the other direction, four trains a day (five in summer) serve El Jem (1hr) and Sfax (1hr 50min), two continuing to Gabes (4hr 30min) and one to Gafsa (6hr 30min) and Metlaoui (7hr 15min).

A fairly quick service known as the **metro** runs to Monastir (hourly; 1hr 30min) via the **airport**, from 6am until 7pm (the last train doesn't run on Saturdays) from Bab Jedid station, 200m south of pl Farhat Hached on bd Mohammed V. About half of the metro trains continue to Mahdia.

By air

Monastir airport (☎03/461314) is 20km southeast of Sousse, with scheduled flights to Brussels, Frankfurt, Geneva, Jerba, Luxembourg, Lyon, Malta, Nice, Paris, Rome, Palermo and Tunis. The airport is connected to town by strings of buses and the metro train. Taxis cost around 7TD, depending on your bargaining skills. Otherwise, try some of the package tour hotels to see if there are groups taking the same flight as you whose bus would give you a lift.

Books The second-hand bookstalls by Sidi Yahia bus station have the odd English title.

Car and motorbike rental *ATL*, bd 7 Novembre, up in the hotel zone (☎03/241828); *Avis*, bd de la Corniche (☎03/225901); *Budget*, 63 av Bourguiba (☎03/227614); *Express*, av Hedi Chaker (☎03/229731); *Hertz*, av Bourguiba (☎03/225428); *Interrent/Europcar*, 49 bd de la Corniche (☎03/226252); *Topcar*, bd de la Corniche (☎03/226070). Motorbikes, scooters and mopeds can be rented from *El Taïef* on bd 7 Novembre, opposite the *Hôtel Jawhara Club* (☎03/226519).

Cinemas The *Théâtre Municipal* on av Bourguiba, a block north of the *Hôtel Claridge*, hosts arty films (as well as plays and classical concerts). Otherwise, there's the *Palace* a few doors up, the *ABC* on av H Thameur or the *Nejma* on bd de la Corniche.

Excursions Try the big hotels, or agencies like *Cartours* on bd de la Corniche (☎03/224092), who do trips such as a three-day "safari" (not a wildlife expedition) around the south for about 125TD, or a day in Gabes and Matmata for around 45TD. You should book a couple of days in advance.

Ferry companies *CTN*, rue Abdallah Ibn Zoubeir, off pl du Port (☎03/229436). The Italian companies are represented by *Tourafric*, 14 rue Khaled Ibn el Walid, off rue Ali Belhouane by *Magasin Général* (☎03/224509).

Festivals Both Sousse and Port el Kantaoui have high-season programmes of cultural events for tourists known respectively as the International Festival of Sousse and the El Kantaoui Festival. There's also an Olive Festival in Kalaa Kebira at the end of November.

Football The main local team is *Étoile Sportive du Sahel* (ESS), whose ground is west of the Medina (out of Bab Gharbi and straight ahead up rue Commandant Bejaoui for 2km), and matches are usually played on Sunday afternoons.

Hammams *Hammam Sidi Bouraoui* in rue Sidi Bouraoui (off rue Aghlaba by no. 23) is one of the oldest in the Medina (daily except Tues men 4am–3pm, women 3pm–midnight).

International phone calls Most taxiphone offices stay open from 7 or 8am to 10pm. Try off rue du Caire, behind the *Hôtel Claridge*; pl Farhat Hached; next to the *Hôtel Hadrumète Palace*; off av Ayachi, 60m north of the station (open till midnight); av Hedi Chaker, under the *Hôtel Nour Justina*; on bd de la Corniche, by *Ciné Nejma*.

Medical facilities Farhat Hached University Hospital (☎03/221411) is on av Ibn el Jazzar, off av Leopold Senghor, behind the Medina. The *Clinique des Oliviers* on bd 7 Novembre (☎03/242711), opposite the *Hôtel Scheherezade*, and generally preferable. There is a night pharmacy at 38 av de la République, quite a way up, and a night doctor service just past it (☎03/224444).

Newspapers English-language papers can be found at the stall in the main train station, and at *Cité du Livre* in av Bourguiba at the corner of rue Ali Bach Hamba.

PTT At the corner of av de la République and bd M Naarouf (city hours), with a bureau de change for cash.

Supermarkets There's a *Monoprix* at the beginning of av Bouguiba by pl Farhat Hached, and two branches of *Magasin Général*, one on rte de la Corniche and one behind pl Farhat Hached on rue de l'Indépendance.

Swimming pools Hotel pools in Sousse are not usually open to non-residents, but there's always the sea.

Around Sousse

Sousse is surrounded by the very old and the very new – the latter in the form of a massive tourist development at **Port el Kantaoui**, and the former covering the cliff-top village of **Hergla** and a group of timeless hamlets in the hills a few kilometres inland. For amateur naturalists, too, the area is interesting, with marshland, mud flats and salt-pans all the way down the Sahel coast and around the bay of Gabes, attracting large numbers of wading birds and associated species. The best areas around Sousse to see these are the **Oued Sed** and **Sebkha Kelbia**.

Port el Kantaoui

Nine kilometres north of Sousse, **PORT EL KANTAOUI** offers package tourism 1990s-style. With the help of Kuwaiti investment, a vast pleasure complex has been conjured out of a stretch of empty coast, including a "genuine" Tunisian yacht harbour in "authentic" Andalusian style. This is Tunisia without tears, built for the delectation of the international tourist. Call it artificial, soulless, even anemic, it has nonetheless become one of Tunisia's most popular resorts and, if you don't mind being in a tourist ghetto cut off from the rest of Tunisia, it does have a lot going for it. Prices are, needless to say, much higher here than elsewhere in the country, and this is certainly not the best place to sample Tunisian culture, but if sun, sea and sand are what you're after, you'll certainly find them aplenty here. Tunisian people, incidentally, find the place fascinating and come down by the busload in season to see how the other half lives and to join foreigners in dancing the night away.

The **marina** is a popular winter refuge among Mediterranean yachting folk, who come here for its mild climate and very reasonable mooring fees – you'd have to go through the Suez Canal into the Red Sea to beat either – while package tourists flock to the marina for its tasteful layout, well-designed hotels and wide range of facilities. Most of the hotels here have everything you could possibly want for a fortnight in the sun, and around the marina you'll find shops, a nightclub, car and boat rental offices, banks, a post office, a doctor and an *ONTT* **tourist office** (Mon–Thurs 8.30am–1pm & 5.45pm, Fri & Sat 8.30am–1.30pm; July & Aug Mon–Sat 7.30am–1.30pm & 3.30–6.30pm, Sun 9am–noon; ☎03/241799). Representatives of the main tour operators are based at the *Hammamet Travel Service* office, not far away. Port el Kantaoui is also home to Tunisia's favourite **golf course**, currently 18-hole, but soon to be expanded to 27 holes, while **riding stables** nearby rent out horses, camels and *calèches*.

The first-built **hotels** in the centre of the resort are generally the best, while the newer ones to the north and south tend to be more slapdash affairs, built to cash in on the resort's name. Right on the Mediterranean, north of the golf course, are the three-star *Hôtel Mouradi* (☎03/246355; ⑤), with its own hammam, pinball machine and video games, the three-star *Hôtel Abou Soufiane* (☎03/242844; ⑤), on a smaller scale, with fewer facilities and a touch less class, and the very stylish five-star *Hôtel Diar Andalous* (☎03/246200; ⑤), with comfy rooms, bars and restaurants in massive grounds with twenty free tennis courts. Closest to the marina are the five-star *Hôtel Hannibal Palace* (☎03/241577; ⑤), whose rooms mostly have sea views, the quiet and restful four-star *Hôtel Hadstrubal* (☎03/241944; ⑤), with its large pool, the four-star *Hôtel Kanta* (☎03/240466; ⑤), not as classy as some, and its self-catering annexe, the four-star *Hôtel Résidence Kanta* (☎03/240466; ⑤). There's also the four-star *Hôtel Marhaba Palace* (☎03/243633; ⑤), with a palatial lobby, pleasant rooms and cheerful service. Slightly west of the marina, the four-star *Hôtel Golf Résidence* (☎03/242713; ⑥) caters especially for golfers, and has a calm and friendly atmosphere.

Transport in the form of **buses** to Sousse or Hergla, and *louages* to the same destinations, can be picked up on the main road, although most tourists seem to prefer the rather silly **Noddy train** which leaves for Sousse from the main entry to the marina area on the hour, every hour (3TD return). Two daily buses to Tunis will pick up passengers at the turnoff for the motorway. For **car rental**, try *Kantaoui Rent* (☎03/241318).

Hill villages

More typically Tunisian, if a little nondescript nowadays, are three hill villages just a few kilometres inland from Sousse – **KALAA SGHIRRA**, **KALAA KEBIRA** and **AKOUDA** – all of which date back to Aghlabid times. To get to them, take the bus from place Sidi Yahia in Sousse.

Seen from a distance, the villages are highly picturesque, each on its green hill topped by a mosque but, once inside, their attraction is more a sort of bustling venerability; the ancient winding streets and doorways are a bit decrepit but full of the sense of a life that stretches far back into the past. In 1864 their tranquillity was shattered when the villagers

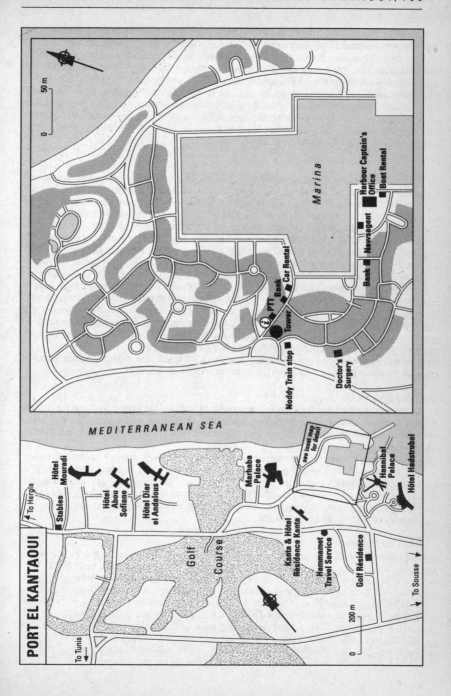

PORT EL KANTAOUI

To Tunis

To Hergla

MEDITERRANEAN SEA

Stables

Hôtel Mouradi

Hôtel Abou Sofiane

Hôtel Diar el Andalous

Golf Course

Marhaba Palace

Kanta & Hôtel Résidence Kanta

Hammamet Travel Service

Golf Résidence

To Sousse

see inset map for detail

Hannibal Palace

Hôtel Hadstrabal

200 m

Marina

Harbour Captain's Office

Boat Rental

Newsagent

Bank

Bank

Car Rental

PTT

Tower

Doctor's Surgery

Noddy Train stop

50 m

joined forces with the tribes from the interior in a revolt against the Bey's demands for increased taxation. They came near to overthrowing the government but soon fell out with each other, giving General Zarrouk a chance to gather his troops and defeat them piecemeal. The retribution he exacted was terrible, with heavy fines imposed on the villagers, while those who could not pay were seized, tortured and executed. Landowners with no cash were forced to sell their acres to merchants from Sfax, who had wisely remained loyal to the Bey, and thus the villagers became labourers rather than landowners. Many were totally impoverished. Even today, Zarrouk's name is considered synonymous with cruelty, and historians identify the year 1864 as the turning point in the region's economy. Thereafter a steady decline set in.

Hergla

HERGLA, a pretty village perched on a cliff about 30km north of Sousse (buses and *louages* from place Sidi Yahia), has a long history, including a time when it marked the boundary between two Roman provincial subdivisions. This romantic setting should have belonged to a pirate's lair, but the inhabitants have always made their living from weaving **esparto grass** – brought from as far inland as Kasserine – into filters used in pressing olives for oil. A fishing harbour has now been built, a spectacular place with whitewashed houses and topped, as in the hill villages, by a mosque. Built in the eighteenth century and named after a local man called Sidi Bou Mendel (who, it's locally agreed, flew back from Mecca in the tenth century on his handkerchief), the mosque overlooks a cemetery and a drop to the deep blue sea. The paltry remains of Roman **Horrea Coelia** (a few mosaics) are half a kilometre down the cliff road to the south: turn left at the junction 100m beyond the end of the tarmac, and it's on your right (winter Tues–Sat 9.30am–4.30pm, Sun 9.30am–1pm; summer Tues–Sat 8am–noon & 2–6pm, Sun 8am–noon; 1TD). To the north of the village is a **beach**, narrow and flotsam-strewn but deserted. There are also snorkelling possibilities.

There is nowhere to stay in Hergla, but there's a **bank** and a couple of **restaurants** – the medium-priced *Le Paix* and the more expensive *Boumendil*.

Oued Sed

An interesting wetland area some 20km north of Sousse, the **Oued Sed** is a freshwater and reedbed area, whose river flows under the main road and eventually ends up in **Sebkhet Halk el Menzel**, a salt lake close to the sea. Any bus heading north from Sousse can drop you off here.

As always, freshwater is a magnet for **birds** and, if there's enough water in the river and the lake, it's well worth a trip, with all the usual wading and waterside birds plus occasional sightings of purple gallinule and marbled teal. Peregrine falcons and marsh harriers hunt over the area – the latter feeding on the abundant frog population. **Flamingos** are present whenever there's enough water, and you can sometimes see large flocks of migrating cranes, too.

Sebkha Kelbia

Sebkha Kelbia is a huge salt lake inland 30km west of Sousse. In the past it was a major site for wintering wildfowl and waders, but dams have been built on its feed rivers, and it has been completely dry since 1982. After a very wet winter, though, it would certainly be an outstanding site. The lake can be best explored from the village of **DAR EL OUESSEF** at the northern tip where the Oued Sed flows out, or (with a bit of a walk) from the village of **BIR JEDID** at the southwestern corner.

The fields around Kelbia are rich in **gypsum**, and, in spring, hold a very colourful and characteristic **flora**. Vast areas of the lake itself, in common with all *sebkhas* or salty mud-flats, are dominated by shrubby species of salt-resistant glasswort. Tamarisk bushes form a shrubby fringe, and are worth scouring for small warblers.

Monastir and around

Coming to this area from almost any other part of the country, it's a shock to discover just how densely populated the small triangle south of Sousse is, with a thriving town every few kilometres. Even in Roman times this was the case, and the coastline is still littered with vestigial remains of their many settlements. But it was under the Aghlabids, when the capital was Kairouan, that this area moved ahead of the rest of the country.

Most of the towns are virtually indistinguishable with crowded streets and a purposeful atmosphere that's very different from the rest of the country. **MONASTIR**, however, has a special appeal. A former fishing port on the Sahel coast just 15km southeast of Sousse, it has never been allowed to forget that **Habib Bourguiba** (born here on August 3, 1903) emerged from its industrious middle class, which later provided his power base. With a festival every year on the ex-president's birthday, along with the Bourguiba family mausoleum, the Bourguiba Mosque, and a presidential palace much used by Bourguiba, Monastir has uneasily adjusted to a role in the national limelight. As well as this attention, the town has also had to cope with the international film industry and a level of tourist development which has all but swamped it. Needless to say, all this detracts somewhat from its older heritage.

Arrival and accommodation

Monastir airport is right in the middle of the country's tourist haven and connected to Monastir and Sousse by buses and a so-called metro train, whose platform is 100m from the air terminal. A number of **car rental** firms also operate from the airport, and you should be able to pick up a rental car immediately on arrival (☎03/463031). You can catch a **taxi** into Monastir for around 7TD. The **train and bus stations** are both

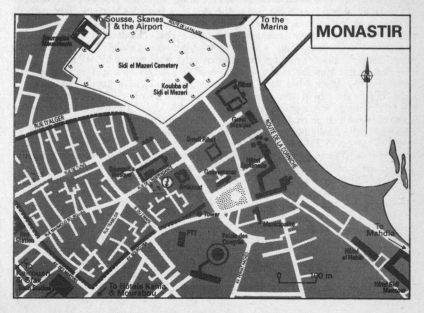

on avenue des Martyrs. The rather useless *ONTT* **tourist office** is on rue de l'Indépendance, in a square opposite the Bourguiba Mosque (Mon–Thurs 8.30am–1pm & 3–5.45pm, Fri & Sat 8.30am–1.30pm; ☎03/461960), and there's another just up the coast in Skanes, near *Les Hôtels* metro station (same times; ☎03/461205).

Hotels in Monastir are almost all reserved for package tours, with only one central budget place apart from the youth hostel.

Hotels

Esplanade ★★★, rte de la Corniche (☎03/460148). Most central of the hotels, almost within spitting distance of the Ribat. ⑤.

El Habib ★★★★, rte de la Corniche (☎03/462944). Part of a comfortable complex which includes the 3-star *Résidence el Habib*, where you can rent apartments from 36.5TD in season. ⑥.

Kahla, av 7 Novembre (☎03/464570). On a roundabout about 800m up the Ksar Hellal road from the junction of av Bourguiba and av des Martyrs. Self-catering apartments as well as rooms. ②.

Mourabou, rte de Khniss (☎03/461585). A stone's throw from the *Hôtel Kahla*. Central heating and a free bus to the beach once a day. ②.

Yasmin, rte de la Falaise (☎03/462511). Clean and does a good breakfast, but 2km out of town. ③.

Regency ★★★★, Port de Plaisance (☎03/460033). Monastir's poshest gaff, right by the marina – park your yacht while you pop in for dinner. ⑥.

Sidi Mansour ★★★★, rte de la Corniche (☎03/461311). Beach holiday hotel with the usual facilities, near the fishing port. ⑤.

Youth hostel

Maison des Jeunes youth hostel, rue de Libye, near the bus station (☎03/461216). Rather basic, but central and the cheapest place in town. ①.

The Town

The heart of the town is the **Medina**, skirted to the north and east by rue d'Alger, to the south by avenue Bourguiba, and to the west by avenue des Martyrs. Some parts of its story-book walls are eighteenth-century, others more recent, and there are gratuitous additions in the 1980s Andalusian style used at Port el Kantaoui. This is acceptable at Kantaoui, where everything is avowedly fake, but when genuine and counterfeit are mixed indiscriminately you begin to wonder if the whole ensemble is just a film set. The **Bourguiba Mosque** in rue de l'Indépendance follows classic Hafsid design, but the rest of the Medina has been so blatantly gentrified that it hardly even merits a stroll. In fact, the real Medina was originally the area around the Ribat; what is called the Medina today was a walled suburb, like the *faubourgs* of Tunis. One little curiosity is the **tower**, which protrudes, for no apparent reason, from the wall opposite the PTT. Close by is the small, dusty **Museum of Traditional Costume**, in rue de l'Indépendance by the *ONTT* (Mon–Sat 9am–noon & 2–5.30pm; 0.8TD), with its fairly diverting display of local clothes, and the equally unnoteworthy **Museum of the National Movement** in rue Trabelsia (Mon–Sat 10am–1pm & 2–5pm; 0.8TD).

To go with its new national prominence, the town centre east of the Medina has been emptied of habitation and replaced by a bleak esplanade designed to show off Monastir's monuments to the best advantage. The **Bourguiba Mausoleum** is undoubtedly the most eye-catching of these, just to the north, unmistakeable with its gilt cupola and twin minarets. It stands in a cemetery named after the **Koubba of Sidi el Mezeri**, the tomb of a twelfth-century saint. The inscription on the gateway, apparently written by the saint himself, mentions one Princess Mona, and many believe that the town takes its name from her.

Compared to Bourguiba's monuments, the old **Ribat of Harthema**, overlooking the sea, is rather more restrained (daily 8.30am–5pm; 1TD, plus 2TD to take photos).

Begun in 796, it has undergone so many reworkings that even experts have difficulty in assigning its parts to the correct period. The core structure follows the same plan as at Sousse, however, with a courtyard surrounded by cells for the fighters, and on one side a prayer hall now used as a **museum** to display ancient Islamic writings, fabrics and pottery – look out here for eleventh-century Coptic fabric from Egypt and an ornate 1774 Turkish marriage certificate. A map of the original Medina shows how comprehensively the old town was levelled in the pursuit of modernity, creating the sterile esplanade outside the Ribat. One fortunate side effect of the museum's existence might be to make it less easy for the Ribat to resume its erstwhile role as a favourite cinematic ancient world; biblical epics are filmed here by the dozen – this is where Jesus trod the battlements in Zeffirelli's *Life of Christ*, as did Brian in Monty Python's alternative scenario. The ninth-century **Great Mosque** stands next door, and the smaller **Ribat of Sidi Dhouwayeb** between the mosque and the Medina.

The **old fishing port** stands a few hundred metres to the east in a rocky inlet. It must have been a pretty place once, but the corniche is now so loaded with hotels that it looks distinctly out of place. In the other direction, the road leads west along the coast past more resort development and Bourguiba's favourite **palace**. The **house** where Bourguiba was born is in place 3 Août, way down the promenade past the *Hôtel Sidi Mansour* towards the fishing port. Further on is the rather mixed collection of amateur sculpture at the **El Helm Museum** (Mon–Sat 10am–1pm & 2–5pm; 1TD).

Eating, drinking and nightlife

Good, cheap **eating** is hard to come by in Monastir. If you're staying here, you're best advised, if possible, to opt for full or half board in your hotel, although there are a couple of fast-food places opposite the *ONAT* by the cinema, and one or two restaurants in the Medina – the *Bonheur*, in rue 2 Mars, isn't too bad. If you feel like a splurge, the *Hôtel Regency* does set menus which are good value by Monastir standards. Otherwise, the Marina is full of fancy establishments, or in town there is the *Rempart* on avenue Bourguiba (☎03/460752).

If you're here in June, July or August, you can seek **evening entertainment** from the summer programme of events every Thursday and Saturday at various hotels. These, laid on by the *ONTT* and hotels, include donkey racing, mock weddings, orchestras both traditional and less so, and an item billed mysteriously as "majorettes". For the rest of the year nightlife is typically low-key.

Listings

Airlines *Tunis Air*, in the *Hôtel el Habib* complex (☎03/464210).

Banks Near the PTT on av Bourguiba, and more on pl de l'Indépendance in the very centre of the Medina.

Car rental *Mattei*, rue de Jammel (☎03/461243).

Cinema Rue d'Alger, opposite the *ONAT* crafts shop.

Excursions It's possible to visit the Kuriat Islands, a deserted archipelago 15km off the coast, from Monastir's diving centre, *Monastir Plongée et Loisirs*, down at the marina (☎03/462509). The minimum charge for a day trip is 200TD and forming a group makes it cheaper.

Golf There's a golf course next to the Ouardanine road, which leads from the town centre towards Kairouan, and another way out along the hotel strip near the *Sunrise Hotel*.

Hammam Rue de Tunis, in the Medina (daily men 6am–1pm, women 1–5.30 pm).

International phone calls International calls can be made from the taxiphone office diagonally opposite the *Central Bank of Tunisia*, next to the train station.

Medical facilities The regional hospital is on av Farhat Hached, out past the Sousse *louage* station (☎03/461144), and there's a night pharmacy in rue Chedli Kallala, off av Bourguiba near the PTT.

MOVING ON FROM MONASTIR

Monastir's **train station** is southwest of the Medina on av des Martyrs, near Bab el Gharbi, with two daily departures to Enfida (1hr 20min), Bir Bou Rekba (2hr) and Tunis (3hr 10min), and hourly services to Sousse (1hr 30min), and eight a day to Mahdia via Ksar Hellal and Moknine (1hr 10min), with four on Sundays. The **bus station** is a short walk up the street, by the city wall, with one daily departure to Sfax (2hr), Nabeul (2hr 30min) and Tunis (3hr), frequent services to Sousse (45min), and **louages** to Tunis. The rest of Monastir's *louages* leave from south of the Medina (follow av des Martyrs past the station towards the hospital) but only go as far as Ksar Hellal, Moknine and Sousse.

To get to the **airport** (☎03/461314), the metro is the obvious means, although there are buses too. When none of those are running, you'll have to take a taxi (around 7TD), or try to get a lift with a tour group on the same flight as you.

ONAT crafts shop Rue de l'Indépendance, on the corner of rue d'Alger.
PTT Av Bourguiba opposite the Medina wall (city hours).
Supermarkets There's a *Magasin Général* on rue de l'Indépendance, and *Monoprix* on av Bourguiba, with longer opening hours (Mon–Sat 8am–7pm & Sun 8am–1pm).

South of Monastir

Direct public **transport** between Monastir and Mahdia being nonexistent, any journey by road involves a change of vehicle at either Ksar Hellal or Moknine (see below), though there are now daily trains calling at Lamta, Ksar Hellal, Bekalta and Moknine. The settlements in this area are constantly expanding and merging with each other, and travelling through them – to the buzz of a thousand *mobylettes* (mopeds) – you get a vivid sense of why this region is such an economic powerhouse.

Two thousand years ago, the area was already industrious and heavily settled. **LAMTA**, 15km southeast of Monastir, was once *Leptis Minor*, cousin of the much larger *Leptis Magna*, whose ruins on the modern Libyan coast are among the most spectacular Roman sites in the world. The brand-new **museum** (daily except Mon 9am–1pm & 2–6pm; 1TD) on the northern edge of town, next to the Monastir road and quite a walk from the train station, is worth a visit if you are passing or interested in industrial-type archeology, which seems to be a speciality of this region. Like the British team at Salakta, an American-funded excavation team here focused on pottery, as Leptis exported so-called red slipware all over the Mediterranean for five hundred years. The museum explains techniques and processes – thankfully with English captions – and also has one unique piece of fine art in a carved Christian sarcophagus found in 1975 and probably imported from France or Rome.

A few kilometres south of Lamta, bustling **KSAR HELLAL** is an old textile centre where silk is still made. The thread is dyed in large vats, and handlooms are still used to weave the cloth. Sadly, the resulting article is disappointing – usually plain, with none of the geometric designs that you find on coarser textiles, and very expensive. The town's other claim to fame is as the venue for the Neo-Destour Party Congress where Bourguiba emerged as leader. From here disciples went throughout the country encouraging strikes and civil disobedience that came close to overthrowing the Protectorate. Ksar Hellal fades into **MOKNINE**, another sprawling town, which has a small regional **museum** (times uncertain; 1TD), 100m to the left on the main road entering town, and housed in a disused **mosque**, exhibiting principally money, manuscripts, pottery and weapons from all periods. If the exhibits themselves fail to entertain, the labelling certainly will.

On the coast 6km east of Bekalta, Roman **Tapsus** was the site of a battle in 46 BC that ended the Roman civil war between Julius Caesar and Pompey.

Kairouan

"What a Hell of a place to put a Holy City", wrote *The Times'* military correspondent of **KAIROUAN** in 1939; in midsummer, when the town bakes like a brick on its barren plain, it's hard to disagree. But Tunisia's oldest Arab city and Islam's fourth most holy centre – after Mecca, Medina and Jerusalem – is an exceptionally rewarding place. Its architectural interest is unrivalled, and the strong Eastern flavour it has retained is a particular shock after Sousse. All of this can best be appreciated by staying a while in its venerable Medina.

Some history

Not surprisingly, perhaps, it was divine inspiration that led to the choice of this infernal site. In 670 **Oqba Ibn Nafi**, advancing west, called a routine halt here with his army. A golden cup was found on the ground, which he recognized as one he had lost at Mecca, then a spring was discovered, and declared to be connected to the holy well of Zem Zem at Mecca. Having first banished for eternity the "noxious beasts and reptiles" which had been present in some abundance, Oqba founded his capital on the spot. There was sound strategic sense behind the inspiration, as the new city was a reasonably secure and central base for the new rulers, halfway between the seaborne threats of the Mediterranean and the mountainous homes of the rebellious Berbers. Despite this security, extremist **Kharijite** Berbers took the city in 757, and their behaviour (such as massacring their opponents and stabling horses in the Great Mosque) shocked more moderate Kharijites, who drove them out and installed one Abderrahman Ibn Rustam as their ruler. In 761, Egyptian forces loyal to the Caliph retook the city, and Ibn Rustam set up shop in Tahirt (Algeria), from where his family (the Rustamids) ruled the south of Tunisia.

As the **Aghlabid** capital, Kairouan quickly developed into one of the world's great cities, its monuments surpassed only by the level of its scholarship and its influence, which reached far across the Islamic world. The Kairaouine Mosque in Fez – still the centre of Morocco's religious life – takes its name from the origins of the Kairouan native who founded it in 857. There was a decline under the Fatimids, who moved the capital to Mahdia, and a low point was reached in 1057 when the town was sacked by the Banu Hilal. But although the Hafsids made Tunis their political capital, Kairouan has never lost its ancient, holy status, with seven visits to Kairouan supposedly equivalent to one pilgrimage to Mecca. The town was jealously guarded from infidels and, before the arrival of the French, Christians needed a Beylical permit to enter the walls; no Jew dared even approach them. In 1835, Sir Grenville Temple had a permit, and may have exaggerated in reporting that "if we were known to be Christians, whilst walking about, we might be torn to pieces by the infuriated populace". Members of the 1881 **French invasion force** were, indeed, distinctly apprehensive as the tribes assembled in a wide arc around the town. But when it came to the final battle their defence crumbled and, much to the surprise of the French column, the town surrendered without a shot being fired.

Modern Kairouan is a successful market centre for agricultural goods, especially apricots and almonds, and a major producer of carpets and *Caravanes* cigarettes. But it remains intensely religious – a living centre of Islamic doctrine. Through the post-Independence years, its religious authorities periodically created friction over Bourguiba's attempts at secular reform. In 1960, when he urged national abandonment of the Ramadan fast (see p.387), Kairouan pointedly observed it a day later than the rest of the country and simultaneously with Egypt, in a gesture of Arab–Islamic solidarity. The town's avenue Bourguiba was only named after the president made a visit of conciliation in 1969 and it has now been renamed again. Kairouan also has a special place in international Islamic consciousness, and representatives from all over the world converge on the city for the *Mouled* celebration of the Prophet's birthday.

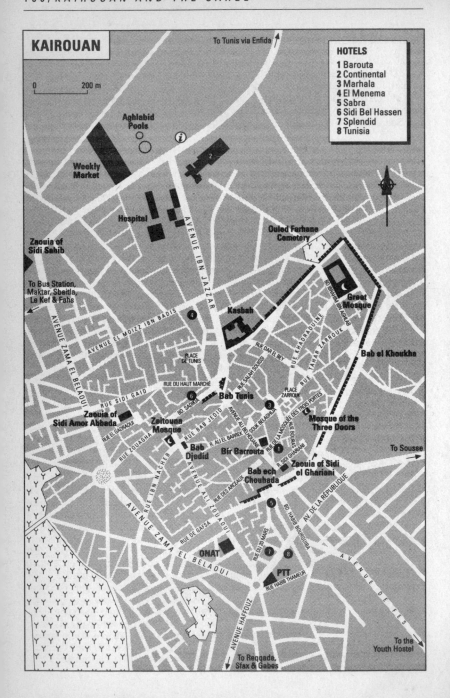

KAIROUAN

To Tunis via Enfida →

HOTELS
1 Barouta
2 Continental
3 Marhala
4 El Menema
5 Sabra
6 Sidi Bel Hassen
7 Splendid
8 Tunisia

0   200 m

Aghlabid Pools

Weekly Market

Hospital

Ouled Farhane Cemetery

Zaouia of Sidi Sahib

To Bus Station,
Maktar, Sbeitla,
Le Kef & Fahs →

AVENUE IBN JAZZAR

BD BRAHIM IBN AGHLAB

Great Mosque

Kasbah

AVENUE EL MOIZZ IBN BADIS

RUE DAR EL BEY

RUE KHADRAOUINE

RUE TAHAR ZARROUK

Bab el Khoukha

PLACE DE TUNIS

RUE DU HAUT MARCHÉ

RUE SALAH SOUSSI

AVENUE ZAMA EL BELAOUI

RUE SIDI GAID

BD SADNA

RUE DE LA MOSQUEE DES TROIS PORTES

PLACE ZARROUK

Bab Tunis

RUE DES PORTES

RUE BAB JEDID

AVENUE ALI BELHOUANE

Mosque of the Three Doors

Zaouia of Sidi Amor Abbada

RUE EL GAORAOUI

Zeitouna Mosque

RUE ZOUAGHA

R ALI EL BARREK

Bir Barrouta

R SIDI GHARIANI

Zaouia of Sidi el Ghariani

To Sousse →

Bab Djedid

AVENUE ALI ZOUAOUI

RUE IBN NACHEB

Bab ech Chouhada

RUE DES ARCEAUX

BD HABIB BOURGUIBA

AV. DE LA RÉPUBLIQUE

RUE DE GAFSA

AVENUE ZAMA EL BELAOUI

RUE DU 20 MARS

ONAT

PTT

RUE HABIB THAMEUR

AVENUE HAFFOUZ

AVENUE DE FÈS

To Reqqada,
Sfax & Gabes ↓

To the
Youth Hostel →

Arrival and accommodation

The **bus station** is inconveniently located northwest of the Medina, beyond the Zaouia of Sidi Sahab, while **louages** from Tunis, Sfax and Sousse arrive at place Bab Tunis, just outside the Medina walls at the northern end of avenue Ali Belhouane. Maktar and Sbeitla *louages* leave from a T-junction 400m down the Gafsa road.

The new **French quarter** to the south of the Medina contains the banks and administration, but most of the life of the town remains centred on the main street through the Medina, avenue Ali Belhouane (formerly avenue Bourguiba), at one end of which is Bab Tunis, from where avenue Ibn el Jazzar leads north to the new *ONTT* **tourist office** by the Aghlabid Pools (daily 8am–6pm; ☎07/220452).

Hotels in Kairouan run the gamut from cheap and basic to four-star luxury. There are good hotels in all categories and you should have no trouble finding one to suit.

Hotels

Barouta, off av Ali Belhouane, opposite Bir Barouta. A real dive with uncertain security; dodgy in the extreme. ①.

Continental ★★★★, av El Moizz Ibn Badis (☎07/221135). Out by the Aghlabid Pools, this is the swankiest hotel in town. ⑤.

Marhala, 35 Souk Belaghjia (☎07/220736). Well hidden inside the souk, this converted Koranic students' hostel has rooms with showers, and a shared but spotless loo (with paper). Ask for a room right at the top. Recommended. ②.

El Menema, rue Moizz Ibn Badis (☎07/220182). Clean and pleasant. ②.

Sabra, pl des Martyrs (☎07/220260). Excellent value, clean and spacious, with hot showers and a roof terrace, but no reduction for sleeping there. Recommended. ②.

Sidi Bel Hassen, bd Sadikia (☎07/220351). Turn left just out of Bab Tunis for this, the cheapest place in town. Basic but clean. ①.

Splendid ★★★, rue 9 Avril, off av de la République (☎07/220041). Big rooms, and rather classy if you ignore the linoleum floor. ③.

Tunisia ★★, av Farhat Hached (☎07/221855). Big, clean rooms with a choice of bath or shower. ③.

Youth hostel

Maison des Jeunes youth hostel, av de Fes (☎07/220309). Out near the now closed *Hôtel des Aghlabites*, with a midnight curfew, but it is open all day. ①.

The City

Kairouan's **Medina** stretches east to west, the **Great Mosque** at its far corner, and its main street, **avenue Ali Belhouane**, seeing most of the city's life. The city's ancient suburbs lie to the north and west, with the new **French quarter** to the south. When planning your route, especially on a hot day, bear in mind that two of the city's main attractions lie some way out of the Medina – the Aghlabid Pools, right next to

---

STREET NAMES IN KAIROUAN

Streets in Kairouan seem to change their names even more indiscriminately than elsewhere in Tunisia, and many streets have two or more names. Thus, for example, rue Farhat Hached was formerly called av de la République; av de la République used to be av Zama el Balaoui; av Ali Belhouane was av Bourguiba; and bd Hedi Chaker (alongside the city wall between pl des Martyrs and rue de Gafsa) was av Ali Belhouane. Av Ali Zouaoui is also called bd Driss I. To add to the confusion, most maps of Kairouan are extremely inaccurate and name streets wrongly in any case. Great pains have been taken with our city map, but we would appreciate notification of any errors which may have crept in.

THE GREAT MOSQUE

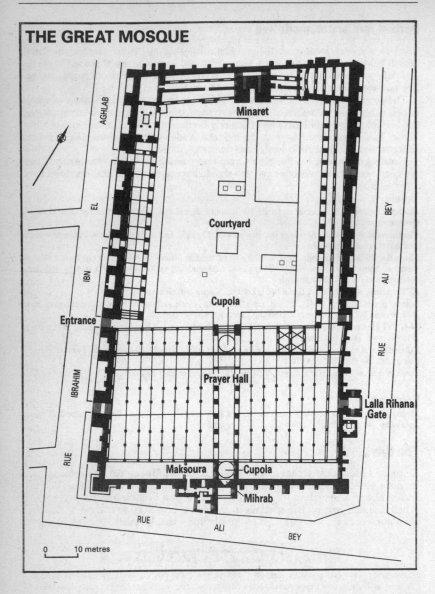

the tourist office, and the Mosque of Sidi Sahab to the northwest, not far from the bus station.

The Medina

Although the **Medina** can't compare in size with that of Tunis, it has a mystique which has always affected Western travellers. At the beginning of this century the artist Paul

Klee remarked that the Medina was "the essence of A Thousand and One Nights, with a 99 percent reality content". Lurking just east of avenue Bourguiba, the tunnel-like **souks** are surprisingly easy to miss, as is the **Bir Barouta**, which looks more like a mosque than a well. Up some steps is an unlikely camel, clad in a natty set of green fluffy blinkers, tramping endless circles to draw water that you can drink. Some say that this is the well connected to Mecca which Oqba found in 670, but its name refers to a holy man of the thirteenth century whose prayers for water were answered when his dog, Routa, scrabbled in the ground until water gushed forth. A taste of the water, it's said, will bring you back one day to Kairouan.

The Medina **walls** were originally built by the Zirids on foundations dating from 761, but it was only a few years before they were wrecked by the Hilali invasion, and they have undergone repeated destructions and restorations ever since. The most recent depredation was during World War II, when the Germans needed to build an airfield in a hurry.

At the Medina's eastern end, the **Great Mosque**, or mosque of Oqba (closes daily at 2.30pm, Fri at noon), in all its relentless simplicity, is one of the oldest, largest and most important mosques in the country. Compared with the delicate elaboration of later periods, its massive buttressed walls feel more like a fortress; yet it's hard not to be moved by its enormously powerful and beautiful expression of faith. At least, that is, when it's not packed with tour parties; the best times to visit are early or late morning.

Only one of the several monumental entrances is now used, but the **Lalla Rihana Gate** on the east side, dating from 1294, deserves a quick detour. Typically Hafsid, with the characteristic arches and cupola, the gate was built more than four hundred years later than most of the present mosque, which was erected by the Aghlabid Ziyadatallah in 836 and greatly influenced mosques built at the same time in Sfax, Sousse and Tunis.

Framed by Hafsid and Turkish colonnades, the vast **courtyard** was never just an aesthetic addition. In a town so short of natural water sources, the courtyard was turned to use as a catchment area, with rainwater made to flow down to the curiously shaped drain in the centre and into huge cisterns below. The **drain**'s odd form is a gift for mischievous guides, who for years told credulous tourists that the curious notches were for animals coming to drink. They were actually designed to decant dust from the water before it went down into the cistern. The **well-heads** used to draw from the cisterns are made out of antique column bases, and the grooves in the rims come from centuries of rope friction. The oversized **sundial** in the courtyard is one of two; the second, a smaller one for afternoon use, is on the superstructure of the eastern colonnade. Although the age of the **minaret** is disputed, its lowest storey is thought to date from 730, a century before most of the present mosque. This might explain why it stands off centre, and it certainly makes it the oldest surviving minaret in the world. The minaret's blunt form is more imaginative than it first appears – notice how the size of the windows increases as the ascending storeys grow smaller. Two blocks bearing Roman inscriptions are built into the minaret, one of them upside down.

GLOBAL TICKET

Entrance to the most important of Kairouan's **monuments** is by a 2TD ticket which can only be bought from the tourist office out by the Aghlabid Pools (daily 8am–6pm for tickets). The ticket is valid, in theory, only on the day of issue, but you can usually get away with using it for a day longer. The seven places it covers are the **Great Mosque**, or Mosque of Oqba, the **Zaouia of Sidi Sahab**, or Mosque of the Barber (aka the Mausoleum of Abu Zomaa el Balaoui), the **Aghlabid Pools**, the **Zaouia of Sidi el Ghariani**, **the Museum of Islamic Art** at Reqqada, the **Zaouia of Sidi Amor Abbada** (currently closed) and **Bir Barouta**. All of these sites are open from 7am to 6pm, except on Friday, when they close at noon.

Neither the minaret nor the courtyard is symmetrical, which emphasizes by contrast the layout of the **prayer hall**, which has six aisles to either side in the colonnade and eight in the hall itself, with the entrance set off by the cupola above. The elaborate wooden doors into the prayer hall date from the nineteenth century. With its roof supported by columns (mainly from Roman sites), the hall has been likened by centuries of pilgrims and travellers to a forest. The central aisle, higher than those on either side, is further marked out by stone reliefs below the ceiling. A transverse aisle, connecting the Gate of Lalla Rihana to another on the far side, is also distinguishable. Wooden pillows separate the capitals from the higher elements of the columns, designed to soak up any shifts caused by earth tremors. There are endless stories about these columns. According to one, anyone who counts them all will become blind; in another, the pairs operate as a sort of proverbial Muslim eye of the needle – those who cannot squeeze between them, it is said, will never reach Paradise. Dimly visible at the far end of the central aisle are 130 faïence tiles around the *mihrab*, imported from Baghdad in the ninth century. The wooden *minbar* just next to the *mihrab* is another important example of early Islamic decorative art, also carved in the ninth century by order of Ibn Aghlab himself. The wooden enclosure, or *maqsoura*, to the side of the *minbar*, was installed by a Zirid ruler in 1022 so that he did not have to pray among the hoi polloi.

Just outside the wall by the Great Mosque, the little **Ouled Farhane Cemetery** with its whitewashed gravestones makes a pretty backdrop for souvenir snapshots, while at the other end of boulevard Ibrahim Ibn Aghlib, **Bab el Khoukha** is the oldest of the Medina's remaining gates, originally called the "Sousse Gate" when built in 1705.

THE MOSQUE OF THE THREE DOORS

If you turn left up rue Bouras and then right down rue de la Mosquée des Trois Portes, you come to the **Mosque of the Three Doors**. Closed to non-Muslims, it is a rare example of a small ninth-century mosque. Notice the inscriptions above the three doors: the top two bands date from the mosque's foundation, the lower band and minaret from later additions. Between the top two bands of inscriptions is a row of stones with floral decorations, of which no two are decorated the same.

A few minutes' walk away is the **Bab es Chouhada**, the gate at the southern end of avenue Ali Belhouane, and the **Zaouia of Sidi el Ghariani**, with its formidable entrance. Although the building dates from the beginning of the fourteenth century, it is now named after a native of Gharian in Libya, who died a hundred years later. In 1891, according to Sir Lambert Playfair, the hereditary governor of Kairouan was still one of Abd el Ghariani's descendants; since then the *zaouia* has seen hard times, but it has been restored and is now the home of the ASM (*Association de Sauvegarde de la Medina*). Notice especially the green and black columns of the *mihrab*, and the typically dark wooden ceiling of the tomb. The *zaouia* is not where it's marked on most maps; that spot, about 100m further along the street, is an old Beylical palace, now a carpet shop. The salesman will entice you in by asking for your ticket and claiming the shop is a museum. Go in if you like, but be prepared for the hard sell.

The Aghlabid Pools and the Mosque of Sidi Sahab

Around a kilometre from the Medina at the other end of avenue Ibn el Jazzar, the **Aghlabid Pools** were wrongly ascribed to Roman engineers by many chauvinistic nineteenth-century French historians, on the grounds that Arabs could not have completed such a technically complex project. After extensive restoration, the pools have the bland feel of a municipal waterworks – not surprisingly, since that's what they were. Just remind yourself, though, that the newly arrived Arab builders were conjuring a city out of the desert over a thousand years ago. The larger one is said to be more than a kilometre across and the buttresses around the sides have something of the

Great Mosque's monumental purity. Water was brought here by aqueduct from Jebel Cherichera, 36km to the west, to be decanted and stored in the basins. Such utilities were an essential feature of urban life in this area, and there were once as many as fourteen of them. As well as holding the water, it was hoped that the pools would produce humidity over the town to relieve the summer heat – instead, they were a terrific mosquito breeding ground and consequent source of malaria. The small stand in the middle of the larger pool held a pavilion in which the Aghlabid rulers could recline.

Following the main avenue de la République to the west, you arrive at the **Mosque of Sidi Sahab**, or more correctly the Mausoleum of Abu Zama el Belaoui or Mosque of the Barber. Its occupant was a companion, or *sahab*, of the Prophet, and his distinguishing characteristic was that he always kept with him three hairs of the Prophet's beard – one under his tongue, one on his right arm and one next to his heart, hence the tendency to call him the Prophet's barber. The mosque and its surrounding complex are still a much venerated place of pilgrimage, where families – both Berber villagers and prosperous town-dwellers – still come to pay their respects. Most of the existing buildings date from the seventeenth and nineteenth centuries, and their elaborateness contrasts with the less fanciful form of the Great Mosque. The entrance to the main complex ducks under an Andalusian-style minaret, where an ornate passage of marble columns and Italianate windows leads to an equally rich courtyard, its walls and ceilings lined with green-blue tilework and white plaster stucco. In a small room to the left of the courtyard is the **tomb of Sidi Shrif Bin Hindu**, the architect of the Great Mosque. Sidi Sahab himself lies buried in the room on the far side (closed to non-Muslims). This central court is a wonderfully peaceful place to sit on a hot afternoon, with the trees outside waving overhead. The mosque is also a popular place to have boys circumcised, and the climax of the ceremony happens in this courtyard. Over the preceding weeks the boy's family will have filled a large jar with sweets and nuts before sealing it. At the moment of the big snip, the jar is smashed in the centre of the courtyard, and the watching children scramble for its contents.

The Zaouia of Sidi Amor Abbada

Outside the mosque of Sidi Sahab to the west, before you reach a group of satellite marabouts, there used to lie a pile of four huge **anchors** that belonged to the **Zaouia of Sidi Amor Abbada** – Sidi Amor Abbada was a nineteenth-century blacksmith who must have operated very successfully to build this seven-domed tomb, now a museum of some of his artefacts. This *zaouia* itself (currently closed) can be found by continuing south along avenue de la République for 500m or so and then taking a left down rue Sidi Gaid. As for the anchors by the Mosque of Sidi Sahab, he claimed that they had come from Noah's ark on Mount Ararat, and that they would anchor Kairouan to Tunisia forever. More prosaic rival theories suggest that they came from the silted-up port of Porto Farina, now known as Ghar el Melkh (see p.144).

The quarter you pass through to reach Bab Jedid (the way back to the Medina from here) one of the town's ancient suburbs, and particularly well endowed with **doorways** painted in disturbing colour combinations, featuring the brown and blue that seem to be a Kairouan speciality.

The Carpet Museum

The former *ONAT* crafts shop on avenue Ali Zouaoui, just up from the PTT, no longer sells carpets but functions as an informal **carpet museum** (daily 9am–noon & 3–6pm; free), with examples of the many types hung on its walls. It is heavily involved in quality control, and every carpet for sale is inspected and awarded a rating – *Deuxième Choix*, *Première Choix* and *Qualité Supérieure* – which is then stamped on it. Any carpet without this rating has not been passed. The shops on parallel avenue Bourguiba offer tempting credit facilities as part of their hard sell – sceptical caution is advisable.

Eating, drinking and nightlife

Buses between Tunis and the south often have to wait, even in the middle of the night, while all the passengers get off at Kairouan to buy the **sweets** for which it is famous – the best known of which is *makroudh*, a honey-soaked cake with a date filling. The city's foremost patisseries are in the Medina along avenue Ali Belhouane.

For something more substantial, the budget-priced *Restaurant Fairouz*, just off avenue Ali Belhouane behind Bir Barouta, will feed you for next to nothing; their couscous in particular is recommended. Otherwise, there's a number of cheap *rôtisseries* around the PTT where, for a dinar or two, you can fill up with a *schewarma* sandwich or a kebab. As a conservative town, Kairouan has little indigenous nightlife, but three more upmarket establishments in the hotel district south of the Medina are the *El Karawan*, rue Souhaire Bint el Houssein (☎07/222556); the *Sabra*, right next to the *Hôtel Tunisia* (☎07/225095); and the *Roi du Couscous*, rue 20 Mars, near the roundabout (☎07/221237), where the drinking can get raucous.

CARPETS

Carpet making in Kairouan belongs to a tradition going back many hundreds of years. The authorities will tell you that every Kairouan woman – doctor, lawyer or shop assistant – knows how to make them, and that 5000 families in the town are engaged in the industry.

Knotted carpets

All the carpets are handmade, but there are two basic types. The more expensive ones, recognizable by the pile, are **knotted** to either 40,000, 90,000 or 160,000 knots per square metre. These carpets are luxury items produced by a sophisticated urban culture and their designs are based on a central diamond-shaped lozenge derived originally from the lamp in the Great Mosque, but infinite variation is possible. Traditionally, each design is passed on and evolved from generation to generation within the family. An important subdivision is between *Alloucha* and *Zarbia*. *Alloucha* carpets use a range of colours which can be naturally derived from the wool – beiges, browns, whites and blacks – a recent innovation, perhaps in deference to Western "ethnic" tastes; the traditional *Zarbia* carpets use rich polychrome shades of deep blue and red.

Woven carpets

Woven carpets, or *Mergoum*, come from a very different culture, the nomadic Berbers. Instead of being urban luxuries, they were literally the roof over a family's flocks. *Mergoum* use brighter colours, the sort of intense reds and purples which Berber women still wear, and more strictly linear geometric patterns. Because *Mergoum* are cheaper, they're more open to abuse, and the designs of roofline mosque silhouettes have very little to do with traditional forms. For a look at some traditional designs, call in at the carpet museum, which has a small collection of old *Mergoum*.

The carpet market

If you're really committed to bargaining, it's possible to buy the carpets direct from the women who make them at the Saturday **carpet market** in Souk Belaghjia, near the *Hôtel Marhala*. Be aware, however, that the retailers don't like foreigners cutting into their business, and if you don't speak Arabic you'll need a translator. The scene is fairly frenetic, with a row of women sitting on one side of the alley displaying their carpets and a row of merchants standing on the other; in between them runs an independent auctioneer who takes bids for the carpet on offer. The whole thing is done at feverish pitch and the atmosphere is electric. It's well worth a look, even if you don't intend to buy. If you do, then prices can be less than half those in the shops; though watch out – the nicest old lady can be a shark and you could easily pay good money for junk. Around 1–2pm on Saturday is the best time to go.

> **MOVING ON FROM KAIROUAN**
>
> The **bus station** is northwest of the Medina, beyond the Mosque of Sidi Sahab, and as the town is pretty central, there are buses to most parts of the country run by all the main bus companies – including eighteen daily services to Tunis (2hr 15min), thirteen to Sousse (1hr), three to both Gafsa (4hr) and Sfax (2hr), two to Houmt Souk, Jerba (7hr) and Le Kef (3hr 30min), and only one to Gabes (4hr), but with several more at night. **Louages** for Tunis, Sfax and Sousse leave from place Bab Tunis, just outside the Medina walls at the northern end of av Ali Belhouane. For Maktar and Sbeitla, they go from a T-junction 400m down the Gafsa road. There are no *louages* for El Jem: you have to go via Sousse.

Listings

Airline *Tunis Air*, rue Khawarezmi (☎07/220422).

Banks There are several in the centre around Bab es Chouhada and rue Farhat Hached. One of them should be open weekend mornings.

Car rental *Hertz*, av Ibn el Jazzar (☎07/224529).

Cinema *Casino Municipal*, on the same roundabout as the PTT.

Festival The *Mouled* festival, to celebrate the Prophet's birthday, is a big event in Kairouan. A seasonal pudding called *assida* is a speciality of the celebration, whose date varies according to the Islamic calendar (see p.45).

Hammams Men can use the hammam attached to the *Hôtel Sabra* (daily 5am–4pm). Women can only use it by arrangement after 4pm, if there's a group of you. Failing that, you will have to find the women's hammam alleged to be close by, but very well hidden. There is another hammam in the Medina near Bir Barouta.

International phone calls Taxiphone office in av Haffouz, opposite the PTT across the roundabout (daily 8am–1am). Also in av Zama el Balaoui near Sidi Sahab Mosque (daily 7am–9pm).

Medical facilities The Ibn el Jazzar University Hospital is on av Ibn el Jazzar (☎07/220036), near the *Hôtel Continental* and the Aghlabid Pools. There's a night pharmacy on av Ali Zouaoui, less than 100m north of the junction with bd Hedi Chaker, on the right.

PTT On a large roundabout where av de la République meets av H Thameur (city hours; bureau de change).

Supermarket *Magasin Général* on bd Bourguiba, behind the tourist office.

Swimming pool 2TD to use the pool in the *Continental*.

Around Kairouan

On the flat plain surrounding Kairouan are the remains of some palace complexes built by the ninth-century Aghlabid rulers, testimony to their feelings of insecurity even in such a prosperous period. The minimal remains are hardly worth a visit for their own sake, but those at **Reqqada** could be combined with a visit to the National Museum of Islamic Art.

Reqqada

The main reason for visiting **REQQADA**, 10km south of Kairouan, is the **National Museum of Islamic Art** (daily except Mon 9am–4pm; included on Kairouan global ticket), which recently opened to great fanfare in a former presidential palace. Actually, it's a bit of a letdown, with somewhat dry exhibits like ancient Koranic manuscripts, old gold and silver coins from the earliest period of Arab rule, ceramics, glassware and stonework. Explanations are in Arabic only, and without at least some comprehension, little in the museum makes much sense.

To get there, take the bus for students, which leaves every hour between 8.15am and 11.15am from Kairouan's avenue Haffouz by a hexagonal kiosk, about 200m down on the right from the PTT. Otherwise, there are buses and *louages* 200m further on. When you arrive at the stop, the museum is a kilometre further and signposted to the right.

As you walk towards the museum from the bus stop, you'll find the minimal remains of the **palace**, built in 876 by the Aghlabid sovereign Ibrahim II, in a field on the right. The Aghlabids' reasons for wanting a palace out of town included avoiding troop rebellions and being able to have a reasonably pleasurable lifestyle beyond the withering gaze of Kairouan's religious lobby. Another reason for choosing Reqqada was its agreeable climate, believed to have dynamic powers: "Every time the doctor Zian Ibn Khalfoun left Kairouan for Reqqada," wrote El Bekri, the early traveller, "he took off his turban in order to receive directly on his head the beneficial effects of this atmosphere."

Raqqada's predecessor was **El Abbasiya**, built 5km southeast of Kairouan after a troop rebellion of 809, in which the Kairouanis had joined. Even less remains of this than of the palace in Reqqada, but it has given rise to an intriguing theory. El Bekri's description of a minaret which once stood there fits that of the Leaning Tower of Pisa, itself built in 1174. The theory leads to the question of whether this is more than a coincidence, given that Pisan ships took part in the Norman campaign in Tunisia from 1141 to 1160.

Scanty remains of another old palace, **Sabra**, are to the left off the Reqqada road a couple of kilometres out of Kairouan, and not easy to find. The palace was built for the Fatimid ruler El Mansour on the site of his final victory over the Kharijite rebel Abu Yazid (see p.363) in 947. Abu Yazid is said to have died of his wounds exactly a year later.

Biar el Aouani

Route 3, the direct road north to Fahs and on to Tunis, skirts the southern edge of the Zaghouan massif, last remnant of the Dorsale range, before reaching an easy run

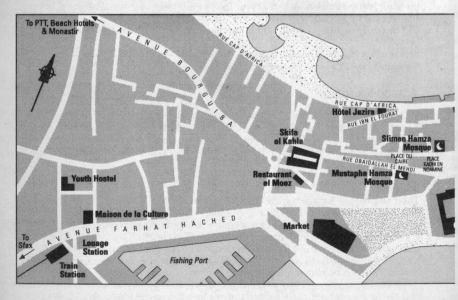

across flat empty country all the way to Kairouan. The only diversion on this route, 20km north of Kairouan, is **BIAR EL AOUANI**, with its perfect turreted Byzantine **fort** on the bare hillside, and a little local museum (variable hours) whose curator rushes up to greet any car that stops. The isolation makes the site all the more attractive.

Mahdia

Georges Sebastian, whose fabulous villa helped launch Hammamet as an internationally famous resort, thought **MAHDIA**, 50km south along the coast from Sousse, was the only place in Tunisia which could compare. Until recently, he was right. It was one of the most beguilingly unspoiled towns in the country and had made only a half-hearted gesture towards mass tourism. Unfortunately, in the last few years the tourist authorities and big money developers have decided to take Sebastian at his word and endow Mahdia with a massive *zone touristique*. However, while this will gradually erode some of Mahdia's former charm, the historic old town ought to remain comparatively immune.

Some history
Set on a narrow peninsula in the belly-like bulge of the Sahel coast, Mahdia's geographical position has defined its history. After defeating the last of the Aghlabids in 909, the new Fatimid ruler of Tunisia, the self-styled **Mahdi** (see p.427), needed a capital to provide security from the hostility of the Sunni majority. The heretical Fatimids overthrew the complacent Aghlabids with the aid of Berber dissidents, but were neither popular nor concerned to be so. They just wanted Tunisia as a base to conquer Egypt and Iraq, the heart of the Arab world. It was with this in mind that the historian Ibn Khaldoun later called Mahdia a "dagger held in the fist".

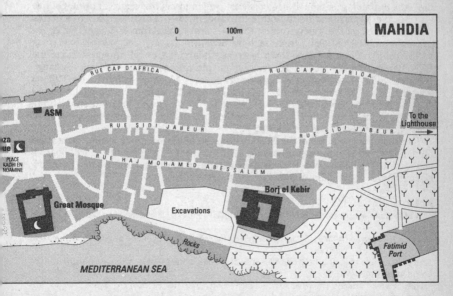

Mahdia made the ideal capital, its narrow entrance easily closed off by the massive wall begun in 916. Behind the wall the Mahdi built a Great Mosque, a harbour, a palace and other installations, with everything else relegated to a suburb outside the wall. A few merchants were allowed to trade inside, but they had to live outside, and the Mahdi claimed•that his aim was to separate them from their wives during the day and from their goods at night.

For the next six hundred years, Mahdia was to be one of the most formidable fortresses in the Mediterranean. Its first test came with a siege in 944–45 by **Abu Yazid**, "the man on a donkey" (see p.363), and his Kharijite revolt from Tozeur, but this was soon beaten off. After the Fatimids left for Cairo in 970, Mahdia shared the chequered fortunes of other coastal towns. In 1057 the **Zirids**, supposedly the country's rulers, were forced to take refuge here by the invading Banu Hilal, and thirty years later a joint Genoese–Pisan force seized the city, and the Zirids had to buy it back. Taken again by the Norman king Roger II of Sicily in 1148, the return to Islamic control in 1160 brought prosperity through trade and piracy and, in 1390, another unsuccessful siege by French, English and Genoese. The wars of the sixteenth century, however, brought Mahdia's period of greatness to an end. In 1547 the corsair **Dragut** made the town his centre of operations, causing the Spanish to storm it in 1550. Rather than have to return, when they left in 1554 they brought the walls down. Since then – apart from routine pillagings by the Spanish in 1597 and the Knights of Malta in the seventeenth century – Mahdia has been a peaceful fishing port.

Arrival and accommodation

The bus and *louage* stations are both by the fishing port to the west of the Medina, with **buses** on the side by the market, and **louages** on the other side. The **train station** is past the *louage* stand, opposite the *Maison de la Culture*, now the local **cinema**.

Next to the port is a main square, with the town hall, police station and entrance to the Skifa el Kahla gate-tunnel (see opposite), which forms the centre of town. On one side lies the Medina and on the other the modern town. There are plenty of **banks** nearby, as well as the **tourist office** (Mon–Thurs 8.30am–1pm & 3–6pm, Fri & Sat 8.30am–1pm; ☎03/681098), just through the Skifa.

Stretching off into the **new town** is avenue Bourguiba, on which you will find the **PTT** after about 500m on your left (city hours; international phone and cash exchange facilities) and a *Magasin Général* **supermarket** at no. 63, about halfway to the PTT on your left (Mon–Sat 8am–noon & 2.45–7pm, Sun 8am–12.45pm). The regional **hospital** is in rue Mendes France (☎03/681005). When the PTT is closed, **international phone calls** can be made from the *Hôtel Mehdi* or the *Shell* station in the main square, or from a taxiphone office opposite the market.

There is only one **hotel** in the Medina, with the others out along avenue Bourguiba on the beach west of the centre, costing a lot more but all offering full or half board if you want it. If you like a beach location without the luxury prices, there's also an unofficial **campsite** between the *Sables d'Or* and the *Mehdi* hotels.

Hotels

Cap Mahdia ★★★, Corniche (☎03/681725). Relatively long-established member of the *zone touristique*. ⑤.

Corniche, Corniche (☎03/694201). A friendly new independent right on the beach, about 1km west of the Skifa. ②.

Jazira, 36 rue Ibn el Fourat (☎03/681629). The only hotel in the Medina, with lovely bedrooms but horrid bathrooms. ②.

Mehdi ★★★, Corniche (☎03/681300). Rather snooty, but cheaper than the *Sables d'Or* for full board. Way overpriced in season. ⑥.

Pension Rand, 20 av Taïeb Mehiri (☎03/680525). Just 300m from the beach, though a bit isolated in the new town. ②.

Sable d'Or ★, Corniche (☎03/681137). Rooms or roomy bungalows. A little bit run-down, but the friendliest of the beach hotels. ③.

Youth hostel

Maison des Jeunes youth hostel, rue Ibn Rached (☎03/681559). Follow signs off av Farhat Hached opposite the *louage* station. ①.

The Town

Mahdia's **Medina**, on a peninsula poking out to sea, is only a tiny quarter now of what's otherwise a typical, thriving Sahel town, but its maritime atmosphere sets it apart from Tunisia's other old cities. The sea provides the dominant smell here, and even the stones of the houses look more seaworn than weatherbeaten. The dominant sound, on the other hand, is not the breaking of waves, but the working of looms, since weaving is the main cottage industry here.

Forming the dividing line between the old and new towns is the **Skifa el Kahla** gate, a sixteenth-century reconstruction of what the departing Spaniards blew up in 1554, which dominates the main square. The gate – once the only entrance to the city – stood in the middle of a wall as much as ten metres thick, stretching right across the neck of the peninsula. It's a staggering thought that the defences destroyed by the Spaniards, four hundred years ago, were already six hundred years old. The Skifa in particular had quickly become legendary: each section of its vaulted passage could be closed off by lowering an iron grill weighing as much as eight tons; but it was the narrow passage itself, immortalized in the name *Skifa el Kahla*, "The Dark Passage", which became most notorious: "So dark," according to John Ogilby, translating Olfert Dapper's book of 1670, "that it is terrible to strangers, seeming rather a murdering den than an entrance into a city." Nowadays the murdering den is an informal souk, with stuffed camels making an unwelcome recent appearance.

The street on the far side of the Skifa leads past a renovated souk, on the left, to **place du Caire**, one of the most perfect little squares in all Tunisia. Sitting at the café here under the small minaret, the only reminder of time passing is the tortoise-like movement of old men who shift their seats slowly round the square in pursuit of shade.

Also worth a visit if you want to know more about the Medina is the local **Association de Sauvegarde de la Medina** (variable hours), which has set up shop in an old palatial residence on rue Cap Africa east of the *Hôtel Jazira*. If you're interested in **weaving**, the Medina is full of workshops whose loom workers are friendly and usually willing to chat about their job to passing tourists.

Straight on from place du Caire, beyond another Turkish mosque on the left, the **Great Mosque** dominates an open plaza. By the 1960s the whole building was so decrepit that it was entirely reconstructed – what you see now is a twenty-year-old version of the thousand-year-old original built by the Mahdi in the tenth century, incorporating some characteristic Fatimid elements. Most obvious of these is the monumental entrance, a Fatimid innovation which owes its form to Roman triumphal arches and its function to the elitism of Fatimid doctrine. Only the Mahdi and his entourage were allowed to use the main entrance, and the same distinction carried over to the prayer hall, where the central aisle was reserved for those in the ruler's favour. Deep niches, used in the entrance gate and in the prayer hall facade, represent another Fatimid innovation, and the two bastions at either corner of the north wall were cisterns for collecting water from the roof. The courtyard was used as a cemetery by the Spaniards in 1551, but when they left in 1554 they exhumed the bodies and took them to Palermo. Non-Muslims are unlikely to be allowed even into the courtyard.

Most of the peninsula itself is rocky, but some steps going down from the *Café Sidi Salem* on the southern Corniche road, below the Great Mosque, provide good **swimming** off the rocks below the excavation site.

The hilltop fort in the middle of the peninsula, the **Borj el Kebir** (Mon–Sat 8am–noon & 2–6pm; 1TD), dates from only 1595. When it was first built it was just a simple rectangle, the corner bastions being added in the eighteenth century. As forts go, this one is bleak and uninteresting, but it does offer a great view over the town (mornings are best for photography). The *gardien* will probably tell you that a subterranean tunnel off the narrow entrance passage leads to El Jem, and the story is that elephants carried the building blocks for an amphitheatre from the port at Mahdia to the middle of the Sahel. But it is unlikely that there was any Roman settlement here, as the crumbling **port** below the fortress was built by the Fatimids: it once had a tower on either side of the entrance with a chain suspended between (which Christian attackers broke through in 1088). Long obsolete, the old harbour and the few confused remains of the Mahdi's **palace** almost breathe melancholy, an impression not helped by the fact that the end of the peninsula is a large cemetery. The **harbour** that once held a Mediterranean strike-force now shelters a few painted fishing boats, themselves left behind by the modern vessels in the new port in town.

The daily fish **market** by the modern fishing port – the country's fourth biggest – and the weekly Friday market are both lively affairs; look out especially for octopuses, which are sold by the bunch, rather like grapes. They're caught by boys who can be seen any morning picking their way round the shallow rocky pools on the peninsula's shore, armed with spiked canes. Stretching off into the **new town** to the west of the Medina is avenue Bourguiba, running parallel to the **beach** as it curves away to the north. Thankfully, the *zone touristique*, with its nine massive new hotels, doesn't start until some way along.

Eating and drinking

You don't have to stray far from the main square by the port to get some great **food**, at prices you won't believe if you've just come down the coast from Sousse or Monastir. In the *Restaurant el Moez*, in a passage parallel to the Skifa, you can fill up on excellent and very moderately priced fish soup and a deliciously spicy *kamounia*. For not much more, the *Restaurant de la Medina*, in the same building as the market, does some seriously succulent fish served by a handlebar-moustached waiter in a bright yellow three-piece suit. There are more upmarket restaurants along the quay, best of which are the *Lido* and the *Quai*, but the difference in price and attitude isn't matched by any notable difference in the food. Another pricey alternative on the north shore is the *Neptune*, just along from the *Hôtel Corniche*.

South of Mahdia

About 10km south of Mahdia, **KSOUR ESSAF** was the birthplace of Bourguiba's Neo-Destour Party in 1934; there's little to distinguish it from any other textile town in the Sahel, but it's the jumping-off point for **SALAKTA**, a few kilometres south, a small

---

MOVING ON FROM MAHDIA

There are regular **buses** to Ksar Hellal (30min) and Sousse (1hr 30min), one bus daily to Nabeul (3hr 30min) and Tunis (4hr), and two a day to Sfax (2hr 30min). **Louages** run to Sousse, Sfax, Ksour Essaf, La Chebba and El Jem, but if you're going to Monastir you have to take one to Moknine or Ksar Hellal and change. The **train station** is a little further past the *louage* stand, opposite the *Maison de la Culture*, and has two daily trains to Tunis (4hr), eight to Ksar Hellal (four on Sunday; 1hr 10min) and four direct to Sousse (1hr 40min).

village on the site of Roman *Sullecthum*. The **ruins** are really only for the enthusiast, though it's a pleasant enough place with a new fishing harbour. Shared taxis ferry to and fro between Ksour Essaf and the shore. Right on the beach is a Roman **cemetery**, next to a new **museum** (daily except Mon 9am–1pm & 2–6pm; winter 9.30am–4.30pm; 1TD) that contains the mosaic of a lion 4.5m long from nose to tail, and the funerary breastplate of a general from Hannibal's army. Also in the museum is an enlarged photograph of a mosaic found in Ostia, Rome's port town, showing ships in front of the office of a group of traders who specialize in trade with *Sullecthum* – a vivid reminder of how close trade links across the Mediterranean were. If you're interested in archeology of a more industrial bent, much of the museum here is devoted to the work of a British-funded team on Roman pottery from the region, with the added bonus of English captions.

South along the shore are other vestigial **remains** of baths, houses and walls, some of them actually in the sea. A little further on are the **Catacombs of Arch Zara**. If you want to look for them, follow the coast road south from the museum for just over a kilometre until you come to a junction. Turn right inland, and continue for about 300m until the tarmac turns right again, but instead of following it, turn left with the main power lines. After nearly 1.5km of piste, a track to your left heads towards a building with a blue-tiled onion dome on the roof. The path takes you after 100m to three pits, one of which has steps leading down into the catacombs, or *Ghar Dhaba*, quite an extensive series of niche-lined tunnels, which you'll need a light of some kind to explore. Just before the path, also on your left, an old Roman **cistern** is used by a local family to keep their rabbits in. The piste continues 500m to emerge on the Ksour Essaf–Sfax road by the "Sfax 87/Mahdia 18" marker.

Between here and Sfax the coast is largely bare, but the town of **LA CHEBBA**, 20km south, has beaches of a sort, and a couple of places to stay. In town, the *Hôtel Lahmar* (☎03/683077; ①) is reasonable enough, and there's the *Centre des Jeunes* **youth hostel** (☎03/683815; ①) 1.5km off the main road, 5km north of town; a couple of hundred metres away is a sand and rock beach, full of black seaweed and washed-up garbage, but free of people. You can **camp** at the hostel but meals are only available in the summer.

The peninsula protruding into the sea for 4km east of town ends in the most easterly point in the belly of the Sahel, **Ras Kaboudia**, a corruption of *Caput Vada*, its ancient name. A **lighthouse** standing here incorporates the remains of a Byzantine fort.

Another Roman site, **Acholla**, lies on the coast between here and Sfax. Originally founded by Maltese Phoenicians, its mosaics have been plundered and hauled off to the Bardo in Tunis, but ruins of a **bath house** and two **villas** – one the home of a second-century AD Roman senator – remain.

El Jem

The extraordinary **amphitheatre** at **EL JEM**, 40km southwest of Mahdia, is the single most impressive Roman monument in Africa, its effect magnified by the sheer incongruity of its sudden appearance, surrounded by a huddle of small houses in the middle of the flat Sahel plain, halfway between Sousse and Sfax. There's a reasonable hotel here, but transport is good and there's no reason to stay longer than it takes to see the amphitheatre and the museum. If you do stay, however, you can get up early and visit the amphitheatre before the tour groups arrive from 8am onwards.

Some history

Ancient El Jem was probably larger than the modern town, full of the luxurious villas of men who had grown rich on the proceeds of selling olive oil to Rome. As the Romans expanded from grain into oil, so the Sahel began to grow rich, and it was during the second century AD that **Thysdrus**, set here at a crossroads of the area, first started to expand so spectacularly. Prosperity brought luxury villas, mosaics and the amphitheatre – but eventually also the town's downfall. Some time in the 230s the citizens rose in revolt against the level of Roman taxation, killing the collector of taxes and proclaiming as Emperor of Rome an eighty-year-old Imperial official called **Gordian**. This action introduced an unsettled period of fifty years for the Empire as a whole and did Thysdrus little good. The one memorial to Gordian's short rule (soon defeated, he committed suicide) is the amphitheatre, begun in his time and left unfinished at his death. According to an unlikely legend, the amphitheatre saw the last heroic stand of **Kahina**, Jewish prophetess and leader of **Berber resistance** to the Arab invasion in the seventh century. Certainly it would be even better preserved today if in 1695 Mohammed Bey had not blown up most of one side in order to evict the followers of Ali Bey.

The Town

What is left of the **amphitheatre** (daily 7am–6.30pm; winter closes 6pm; summer closes 7pm; 4TD, plus 1TD to take photos) still amounts to its being one of the best preserved of its kind – finer than the Colosseum in Rome, and not a great deal smaller. It actually stands sixth largest in the world league table of amphitheatres. Estimates of its original capacity run to around thirty thousand, more than the total population of Thysdrus itself. People must have come from all around to watch the games here, a boost for the town's civic prestige.

Chambers underneath the middle of the arena held gladiators, animals and theatrical scenery, and an elaborate system of lifts allowed them to be delivered direct to the arena. Animals would be hoisted up in their cages, which could then be opened in safety from below using pulleys. Following extensive restorations, you can wander around this subterranean backstage complex, and it's well worth going down there. Think of any amphitheatre mosaics you've seen, add the atmosphere of a bullfight or any other contemporary sporting stadium; then imagine the roars and stench of animals and the fear of those about to face them in this claustrophobic space lined with marble so neither combatant nor animal could escape.

The **museum** (same times and ticket as amphitheatre), south of the amphitheatre next to the Sfax road, is worth the effort even on a hot summer day, as its small collection of mosaics includes several that are as fresh and vigorous as any in the country. In the courtyard, two peacocks – almost Art Nouveau in their stylization – look ready to leap off the wall. A metal frying pan in the room to the right is an unusual domestic touch, displayed alongside amphitheatre scenes. But the large room at the far side of the courtyard contains the masterpieces, with mosaics featuring an almost abstract peacock-tail design, a balding, drunken Silenus being bound by three boys for a nymph, and a child riding a tiger. There's one small field of **excavations** next to the museum, with typical peristyle house plans and some mosaics in place.

Over the road from the museum and across the rail line are the remains of a **smaller amphitheatre**, hardly in the same state as the big one but open all the time, with no gates, no fences, no tour groups and no charges. This small version was built first.

Another patch of **Roman excavations** can be found just outside town; take avenue Hedi Chaker – the Sousse road – west for about a kilometre until you come to the last house on the right. Then turn sharp left up a track that heads straight back towards the big amphitheatre. The excavations begin immediately on the left, with another group 100m straight in front. A left turn there will take you to a third group, and beyond that a fourth. Frankly though, unless you want a walk in the sun, none of these scattered bits of stone is really worth the effort.

ROMAN ENTERTAINMENT

Circus shows were the opiate of the Roman masses, used unashamedly by rulers to keep their huge urban proletariats happy, and the whole ritual played an important part in cementing the paternalistic relationship between rulers and ruled. A royal box was situated at each end of the arena (so that seasonal comfort could be assured) from where the charitable sponsor of the show would watch the proceedings and intervene when necessary. The defeated gladiator in a duel had the option of throwing himself on the mercy of the ruling official in his box, which he signalled by lying on his back and raising his left arm. If the crowd thought his courage had earned him his life, they would signal it by giving the thumbs-up sign – but the final decision was the official's alone: if *his* thumb was pointed down, the victim was killed on the spot. Doubtless prudent officials tended not to offend the crowd too often.

The only disadvantage of the shows as far as the rulers were concerned was their in-built inflationary spiral. The more spectacular the show, the higher the expectations next time. All they could do was to go on increasing the brutality quotient. **Wild animals** played a large part in the proceedings and, since Africa was Rome's principal supplier, they must have been plentiful here. They would be pitted against each other or against gladiators, or else unarmed victims would be thrown into their midst; on the day that Rome's Colosseum opened, five thousand animals are said to have been slaughtered. But the public's appetite grew stronger and stronger for human blood. **Christians** were all too literally easy meat (see p.105 for martyrdoms at Carthage), but human life was sufficiently cheap for **armed gladiators** to be in plentiful supply. Most of them were prisoners or criminals, or even bankrupts on a contract which would pay off their debts – if they survived. Gladiators were surrounded by a macabre sort of glamour: they had their own fan clubs, and sometimes open banquets were put on at which the public could meet the next day's victims.

The most disquieting aspect of all this is that it would not have happened unless people enjoyed it – this really was **mass popular entertainment**, not in any way the freakish interest of a perverted minority. Ordinary concerns and interests circulated all around the slaughter, and the poet Ovid even describes how to pick up girls at the circus. And when a gladiator was on the point of dispatching his victim, the crowd would scream "Bene lava!" ("Wash yourself well [in blood]"), a homely little tag usually found in its literal meaning on the doorsteps of houses and public baths.

Practicalities

The **train station** lies on the central square, with four or five daily departures for Sfax (50min), Sousse (1hr) and Tunis (3hr), and one daily service to Gafsa (5hr 10min) and Metlaoui (6hr), and two to Gabes (3hr). **Louages** cluster directly opposite, most of them headed for Mahdia, but some for Sousse and the occasional one to Tunis or Sfax. *SNTRI* **buses** runs four daily services to Sfax (1hr 15min) and Tunis (3hr 45min) that stop across the square, and *SRT* buses go from down the road in front of the archeological institute by the museum, with four daily runs to Sousse and Mahdia, and two to Sfax. Note that there's no direct public transport to Kairouan.

There are a couple of **banks** in town, a **PTT** (country hours) and a **taxiphone office** (daily 8am–9pm) on the way to the museum, and a *Magasin Général* **supermarket** in the main square. **Market day** is Monday and there is a programme of cultural events posing as a **festival** in July and August. If you want to **stay** in town, the one-star *Hôtel Julius*, right next to the station (☎03/690044; ②), is very respectable for its rates, and you can even get a room with a view of the amphitheatre. **Food** is available at the hotel, at the *Restaurant du Colisée* next door or the *Restaurant du Bonheur* opposite that. For something cheaper, there are a couple of *gargotes* around the marketplace by the main square. The hotel is the only place in town where alcohol is served.

Sfax

The writer Ronald Firbank once took it into his head to call **SFAX** "the most beautiful city in the world", for which he has been ridiculed ever since by travel writers, their readers and at least one mayor of the town. Granted some exaggeration, Sfax *is* a much more attractive place than is usually supposed. Somehow everything seems a little easier here, from bureaucratic operations to a certain no-nonsense attitude that other Tunisians often dislike. Indeed, with its two excellent museums and consistently under-rated Medina, Sfax can claim to be the most sophisticated town in the country. Ferries also run regularly to the **Kerkennah Islands**, another good reason for passing through.

Some history

Sfax's lack of interest in tourism is significant: as the wealthiest, most successful city in the country, it has no need to rely on tourists either for revenues or for self-esteem. Founded in 849 near the site of a small Roman town, *Taparura*, Sfax took its name from a species of cucumber (*faqous* in Arabic) and made its money from a trading fleet and the products of the Sahel's olive trees. By the tenth century it was already wealthy.

During the **Hilalian invasion**, a member of the Zirid family, one Ibn Melil, set up a principality in Sfax, with hopes of reuniting Tunisia around it, but the Normans already had their eyes on it, and it fell to them in 1148. The Sfaxians plotted their resistance and began manufacturing arms in secret. Posing as beggars, they went from door to door recruiting fighters. As a signal they would be given beans of a number corresponding to the number of combat-worthy men in the house. Then, on New Year's Eve 1156, cele-brated by the Christians with fireworks and a procession of bejewelled cows, they mingled with the Normans and surprised them mid-carnival, retaking the town. With money from the cows' gold, they built the "Cisternes des Vaches" a few hundred metres northwest of the Medina – the site is now a school, but the district still bears the name – and even today, New Year's Eve is celebrated in Sfax with beans and fireworks.

In 1546, under the crumbling rule of the Hafsids, Sfax again became a principality under the cruel adventurer **El Mokkani**. It was rescued fifteen years later by the pirate **Dragut**, who reunited it with the rest of Tunisia. Then began the period of Sfax's great-est prosperity, at its height in the eighteenth century. When the French came in 1881 they met fiercer resistance here than anywhere else, and the city was bombarded by nine warships and four gunboats. Having taken Sfax, the French proceeded to sack the city, profane its mosques and kill hundreds of its inhabitants. Later it was here that **Farhat Hached**, the UGTT leader, found fertile ground for Trade Unionist resistance to French rule.

Today, Sfax occupies a unique position in Tunisia. Politically, the Sfaxian lobby is a very powerful one, its clout coming from its commercial pre-eminence, which by now is Tunisian lore. Sfaxians are known as "the Jews of Tunisia" (an indication of residual anti-Semitism), and the stories and proverbs about their competitive nature are endless; according to one of them, if a Jerban grocer (Jerbans are the other notoriously sharp operators) sets up in Sfax, two locals will immediately move in on either side to squeeze him out. Feelings about Sfax in the rest of the country consist of a mixture of admiration, envy and resentment, while the Sfaxians just go about their business, because they know – as everyone else knows – that the town is successful.

Arrival and accommodation

Sfax's **airport** (☎04/240879) is 7km west of town on the route de l'Aéroport, a 3TD taxi ride away. The **train station** sits right at the eastern end of avenue Bourguiba, close to the southeastern corner of the Medina, while **buses** have depots all over town – on rue

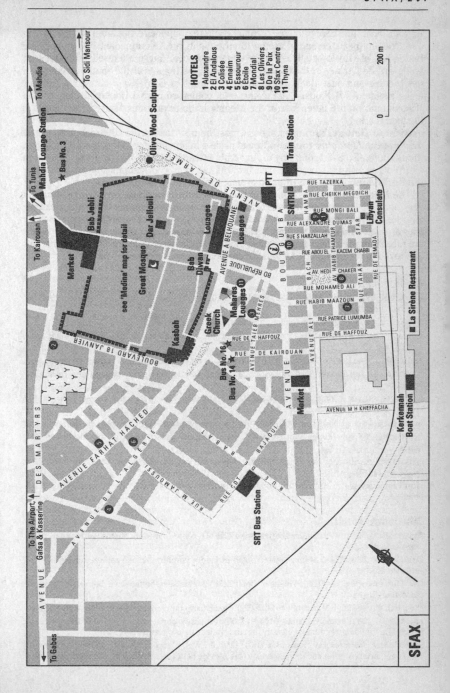

HOTELS
1 Alexandre
2 El Andalous
3 Colisée
4 Ennaim
5 Essourour
6 Etoile
7 Mondial
8 Les Oliviers
9 De la Paix
10 Sfax Centre
11 Thyna

SFAX

Haffouz near the corner of rue Leopold Senghor, opposite the train station in rue Tazerka, and near the end of avenue Bourguiba in rue Commondant Bjaoui, opposite the end of rue du Rabat. The **louage** situation is even more confused, with stops on boulevard de l'Armée at the corner of avenue Ali Belhouane at the southeast corner of the Medina and, just 100m away, another in front of Bab Diwan, as well as further down avenue Ali Belhouane, at the corner of boulevard Farhat Hached in front of Bab Kasbah, and on the other side of the Medina in boulevard des Martyrs, just north of the food market.

   Avenue Bourguiba runs straight across the new town from the train station, past the *Syndicat d'Initiative* **tourist office** in place d'Indépendance (Mon–Sat 8.30am–1pm, Mon–Thurs also 3–5.45pm; July & Aug daily 7.30am–3.30pm; ☎04/224606), housed in a turn-of-the-century bandstand, and towards the main bus stations and the turnoff for the **Kerkennah boat station** down avenue Mohamed Hedi Khefacha.

   The Medina has a variety of cheap and basic **hotels** for those on a budget – mostly very basic and unsuitable for women travelling alone (exceptions being the *Ennasser* and the *Medina*) – and there are a couple of classy joints in the town centre for those who are not. Mid-range, you get a slightly wider choice, and if the town centre hotels are full, there are others further afield, notably to the west of town. The Medina hotels are keyed to the map on p.211, and the city centre hotels to the map on p.207.

Medina hotels

El Andalous, 64 rue Mongi Slim (☎04/220903). Grotty but friendly. No showers but two hammams nearby. ①.

Besbes, 23 rue Borj el Nar (no phone). Far from luxury, but OK for the price. ①.

Ennacer, 100 rue des Notaires (☎04/299919). Bright, clean and welcoming, with hot water and a roof terrace. ②.

El Habib, 25 rue Borj el Nar (☎04/221373). Similar to the *Besbes*, but with a warmer welcome. ①.

El Jerid, 61 rue Mongi Slim (☎04/298929). Small rooms, but clean enough and reasonable value. ①.

El Jemia, 89 rue Mongi Slim (☎04/221342). Marginally less grotty and correspondingly less friendly than the *Andalous*. ①.

El Magreb, 18 rue Borj el Nar (☎04/220057). Best and friendliest of the rue Borj el Nar hotels. ①.

El Medina, 53 rue Mongi Slim (☎04/220354). Cheapest and cleanest of the rue Mongi Slim hotels. ①.

Moktar, 19 rue Borj el Nar (☎04/220892). Only worth considering if the other rue Borj el Nar hotels are full. ①.

Hôtel du Sud, 42 rue Dar Essebai (no phone). Tunisian workers' hotel with extremely basic conditions. ①.

City centre hotels

Alexandre ★, 21 rue Alexandre Dumas (☎04/221911). Next door to the central *la Paix* and rather more sedate. ②.

Colisée ★★, 32 av Taïeb Mehiri (☎04/227800). Friendly, comfortable and central. Air conditioning available. ③.

Les Oliviers ★★★, av Habib Thameur (☎04/225188). Has seen better days, but retains a certain old-fashioned charm. ③.

Mondial, 46 rue Habib Maazoun (☎04/226620). Dodgy city centre place with an attitude problem. ②.

La Paix, 17 rue Alexandre Dumas (☎04/221436). An old favourite, and cheapest of the city centre bunch. The building is getting a bit tatty, but the smiles are as warm as ever. ①.

Sfax Centre ★★★★★, av Bourguiba (☎04/225700). Well-placed hotel with all mod cons including a pool, but rather business-oriented and the service is not as attentive as you might wish. ⑥.

Thyna ★★, 35 rue Habib Maazoun (☎04/225266). Pleasant enough rooms, tatty corridors, and a rather dubious upstairs bar. ②.

Hotels out of the centre

Amin ★, rue Mejida Boulila (☎04/245600). On a busy road north of town near the hospital, this place is clean enough, but not particularly welcoming. ②.

El Andalous ★★★, av des Martyrs (☎04/299100). New and brash and not to be confused with the hotel of the same name in the Medina. ④.

Ennaim, 46 rue Mauritanie (☎04/227564). Off av de l'Algérie beyond the *Étoile* and the *Essourour*. Pleasant rooms with a café downstairs. ①.

Donia ★★, rte de l'Aéroport (☎04/247714). Used as an overnight stop by Land Rover tour groups or by visiting sports teams. Rather pricey but handy for the sports stadium. ④.

Essourour, 142 av Farhat Hached (☎04/223172). Basic and a bit grubby. Not recommended for lone women. ①.

Étoile, 9 rue Mohamed Janoussi (☎04/296091). Off av Farhat Hached west of town, the *Étoile* is quiet, amiable and good value. ②.

Hannibaal, rue Mohamed Rachid Ridha, off rte de Mahdia (☎04/234329). 2km from the centre, Sfax's only pension is quiet and respectable, if a bit worn at the edges. Spacious rooms, massive bathrooms and the possibility of full board. ②.

Syphax ★★★★, rte de Soukra (☎04/243333). Way out of town and hardly worth the effort considering the price, though the pool and gardens are very pleasant. ⑤.

Youth hostel

Maison des Jeunes youth hostel, rte de l'Aéroport (☎04/243207). At the beginning of the airport road. Open all day with clean dorms but dirty loos, although it's currently being renovated. Students half-price and camping possible. ①.

The New Town

At first the city seems to vindicate all criticism with its sprawling suburbs of housing and industry, but Sfax's centre is as compact as that of Sousse. The Medina is separated from the port by a French grid-plan **new town** that is pretty light on things to see but contains almost everything you need in the way of facilities. **Boulevard de l'Indépendance** connects the Medina's main entrance at **Bab Diwan** (by the main *louage* station) to the thoroughfare that runs through the new town, **avenue Bourguiba**.

The new town was largely rebuilt after heavy bombardment during World War II, and today it's less crowded and more open than the Medina, with paved esplanades, genuinely green spaces and tree-lined streets. Being right on the sea, the climate is also less oppressive, and there's a large port with a busy daily **fish market**.

Very stylish, if a touch incongruous, is the French-looking clock tower on the **town hall** in place Hedi Chaker, which houses the excellent **Archeological Museum** (Mon–Sat 8.30am–1pm & 3–6pm; 1TD). There are only six rooms of exhibits, but for variety and quality they're hard to beat. Room 1 (the entrance hall) holds Islamic antiquities; Room 2 has early Christian relics from La Skhirra and Thyna, including a magnificent stylized Daniel in the lions' den; Room 3 contains Roman relics, including – unusually – wall paintings and delicate glass; Rooms 4, 5 and 6 are also Roman; and Room 7 (under the stairs) contains prehistoric stone tools from near Gafsa, evidence of the Capsian culture.

Admirers of Art Nouveau architecture will want to snatch a glance at **nos. 39–41 avenue Bourguiba**, a stucco confection on the corner of rue Patrice Lumumba, and at **no. 10 rue d'Athènes**, a cherub-encrusted concoction behind the Greek Orthodox church.

The Medina

Sfax's **Medina** differs from many in Tunisia in that it is still a thriving community. This is no tourist spectacle, but a real city where people live and work, and you won't find souvenir stalls or tour groups trailing after a guide. Not that you'll be made to feel in any way unwelcome; on the contrary, the pleasant reaction you get in ordinary shops where Sfaxians make routine purchases comes as a refreshing contrast to the tedious "Kommen Sie hier, mein Freund" of Tunis and Kairouan's souvenir emporiums.

Another difference are the Medina's near-complete **walls**, which make for a dramatic first impression. In view of the many bombardments the city has endured, the walls are in remarkable shape, with some parts dating back to the ninth century. If you want to walk around the walls on the inside, you can follow them almost all of the way in the Medina's western corner from Bab Jedid to Bab Gharbi. One curious feature of the Medina is the multitude of first-floor **workshops**: narrow staircases lead up to these cramped rooms, where small businesses – tailors, shoemakers, engravers – beaver away in an almost antiquated atmosphere. Few of them mind being interrupted, and their terraces offer wonderful rooftop views.

The **Kasbah** in the Medina's southern corner was originally constructed in 1849 as a *ribat*, and was later the governor's residence and the headquarters of the town's militia. It has now been restored and turned into a **Museum of Architecture** (daily except Mon 9.30am–4.30pm; 1TD), featuring exhibits on private, public and religious buildings, but the best thing about it is that you can climb up the bastions and walk along the battlements. On leaving, check out the tiled doorway of the school across the square. Just north is the whitewashed **Sidi Karray Mosque**, dating back to 1654 and surrounded by some classic Sfaxian doorways decorated in pink Gabes stone, notably that of 31 rue Ben Kaddour. The mosque is the focus of Sfax's *Mouled* festivities to celebrate the Prophet's birthday.

Rue de la Kasbah runs alongside the southern wall from the Kasbah, past *Café Diwan* and into place de la Journée de Tunis. On the corner as you come into the square is the **Zaouia of Sidi Bahri**; note the double inscription above the door, again in pink Gabes stone. If you cross the square from here, the multiple arches of **Bab Diwan**, the Medina's main entrance, are to your right. As at Tunis, Bizerte and Sousse, this main gate into the Medina was once much closer to the sea. Only its westernmost, horseshoe entrance is ancient, going back to the fourteenth century. Along with Bab Jebli, it was one of just two original city gates, both still retaining their iron-clad doors, which were once closed nightly.

The Dar Jellouli Museum and around

To your left, opposite the inward side of Bab Diwan, is the **Ajouzin Mosque**, restored in the last century. Rue de la Grande Mosquée runs next to it, up towards the Great Mosque. Straight on down rue Borj el Nar, the **Amar Kamoun Mosque** – right, after about 150m – is between nos. 50 and 52. Look out for its small stone minaret. The mosque was rebuilt, like so many of Sfax's monuments, in the eighteenth century when the city became a major commercial centre. But the style of the minaret gives away its earlier origins.

Another 200m along the same street to the end, then a right, and a right at the end again, brings you to the entrance of the **Borj Ennar**, a fortress built to guard the Medina's eastern corner, now accessible to the public and the headquarters of the ASM.

Continue past the Borj's entrance down some cobbled steps into a small square. On the left is a gateway out of the Medina; on the right a small archway brings you back into rue Borj el Nar, emerging between nos. 76 and 78. Cross rue Borj el Nar and take rue Dar Essebai, straight ahead of you. At the end, turn left into rue de la Driba, past **Hammam Sultan** on your left, Sfax's oldest bath house, restored in the eighteenth

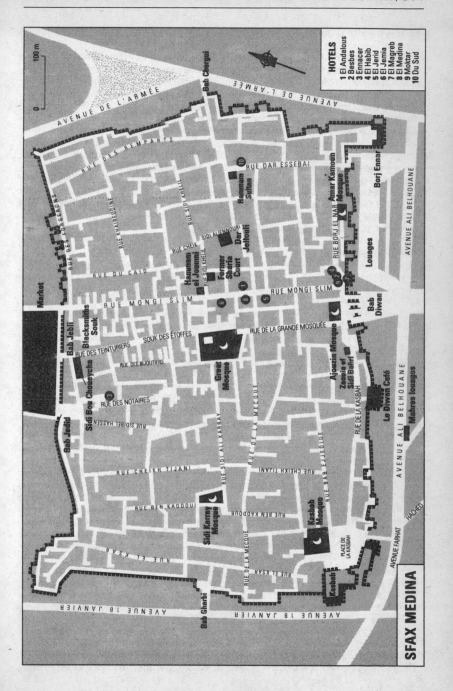

SFAX MEDINA

HOTELS
1 El Andalous
2 Besbes
3 Ennacer
4 El Habib
5 El Jerid
6 El Jemia
7 El Magreb
8 El Medina
9 Moktar
10 Du Sud

century but dating back to Hafsid times; after the hammam you will see the Dar Jellouli Museum just to the right ahead of you, in rue Cheikh Sidi Ali Ennouri.

The **Dar Jellouli Regional Museum of Popular Arts and Traditions** is not to be missed, housed in a seventeenth-century residence as interesting as the exhibits themselves (daily except Mon 9.30am–4.30pm; 1TD, plus 1TD to take photos). As in the Dar Ben Abdallah museum in Tunis, these illustrate local life, with costumes, utensils and manuscripts. One exhibit demonstrates how rose water is made, another shows how Tunisian women traditionally prepare their *kohl* eyeliner. There's even an old *kif* pipe similar to the ones still used in Morocco (though not Tunisia) today.

Leaving the museum, turn left and continue up rue Cheikh Sidi Ali Ennouri, which brings you to a small square. Rue Sidi Khelil, left off the square under a small archway, takes you past the former courthouse on the left (nos. 36–40) and the **Hammam el Joumni** at no. 25 opposite. Just beyond the hammam, you cross **rue Mongi Slim**, one of the Medina's main thoroughfares and perpetually bustling. Rather than get caught up in the flow, however, carry straight on past **place Souk el Jemaa**, the site of a hectic Friday market, and you come out into rue de la Grande Mosquée, facing the northeastern wall of the Great Mosque.

The Great Mosque

Sfax's **Great Mosque**, though at first sight lower and less imposing than its contemporaries at Kairouan and Sousse, repays closer inspection. Unfortunately, it is not possible to enter unless you are a Muslim, but you can see in through the windows, which are normally open.

Begun in 849 by the Aghlabids, it was extensively rebuilt in the tenth century under heavy Fatimid influence and remains one of the most distinctive buildings left from that era – more so even than Mahdia's own Great Mosque. The most characteristic feature is the series of niches on the east facade, crowned by tooth-like rims – a form of articulation quite foreign to both the simple Aghlabid style and the later, more sophisticated calm of the Hafsid styles.

This love of movement in external decoration is even more apparent in the **minaret**, whose wedding-cake layers of decoration are highly unusual for this region; the geometric bands, round windows and religious inscription seem almost frenzied compared to the Kairouan minaret. You can see the minaret from the northern corner of place Souk el Djemaa, or climb up a terrace for a clearer view – the best is to be had from a staircase in the entrance to the teahouse at 5 rue des Aghlabites, which also does an excellent cup of green tea.

A curiosity worth looking out for is the stone embedded above the fourth window from the left in the northeastern facade. Originally Byzantine, it depicted two peacocks (the ancient Greek symbol of eternity or immortality) surrounded by grapevines and small birds, with a Greek inscription above and probably a cup or fountain between them. Such obvious pictures of animals and plants are very rare in Islamic architecture, but the spirit of the inscription ("Good deeds and happiness along with them enrich Your holy abode") was considered sufficiently Muslim for its inclusion in the mosque.

The souks

Heading north from the Great Mosque, you pass under an arch into rue des Aghlabites, on the other side of which is the area of the main souks. More or less straight ahead is the **Souk des Étoffes**, specializing in fabrics, with rich garments all around, gradually giving way to carpets as you move up the souk. Parallel, one street to the left, is rue des Bijoutiers, the **jewellers' souk**. Cross rue Okba at the end of souk des Étoffes, and follow rue des Teinturiers (once the dyers' souk) until you come to **Bab Jebli**.

Just to the right is the **Sidi Bou Choueycha Mosque**, currently under restoration. The older of its two prayer halls is Zirid or Hafsid, but the later one, added in 1683, marked a new phase in Sfaxian architecture, establishing a style which was to dominate eighteenth-century construction in the city. In the other direction, opposite no. 19 in rue des Forgerons, an archway leads through to the **blacksmiths' souk**, where the smiths are hard at work amid the noise and grime. However, a glance at the upper storey, reached via a staircase to your left as you go through the archway, reveals that this was once a *foundouk* and dates back to the tenth century. It was associated with Bab Jebli, outside which there was a marshalling point for trans-Saharan caravans, whose passengers would stay overnight at the *foundouk*.

Coming out of the blacksmiths' souk, a right turn brings you to the end of rue Mongi Slim, which leads straight back to Bab Diwan. Opposite the end of rue Mongi Slim, crowds squeeze through a narrow Medina entrance in a crush worthy of Cairo. On the other side of it is a large food **market** complex, one of the most successful modern uses of the old vaulted forms to be seen in Tunisia, and, unlike so many other new market buildings, a delight to wander through.

Eating and drinking

As with accommodation, the Medina is the obvious place to go if budget **eating** takes precedence. On the other hand, if you feel like treating yourself, you'll find the expense well worth it, as Sfax has some first-class restaurants at prices that are ridiculously cheap by Western standards, and very reasonable by Tunisian ones, too.

Restaurants

Hôtel Alexandre, 21 rue Alexandre Dumas (☎04/221911). Discreet high-class eating that's pricier than the town's other upmarket options, but still very good value for money.

As You Like It, 19 rue Tahar Sfar, cnr rue Abou el Kacem Chabbi. Offers budget-priced "hot fast food" with ketchup on everything.

Restaurant Au Bec Fin, pl 2 Mars, opposite the PTT. Pleasantly situated and with decent if not very exciting moderately priced fare.

Restaurant Baghdad, 63 av Farhat Hached (☎04/223856). Excellent if pricey Tunisian cooking; there is a set menu, but à la carte may work out cheaper, depending on what you order.

Restaurant Bahloul, 25 rue Hannon. Hidden away inside the Medina, this clean and good-value budget eatery unfortunately closes around 4pm.

Restaurant Besbes, 79 av Bourguiba. On the corner of av M.H. Khefacha, with inexpensive couscous, meat or fish dishes. Great value and open all hours.

Restaurant Carthage, 63 av Ali Belhouane. Handily located, more or less opposite Bab Diwan. Moderately priced seafood treats include octopus in sauce and clams marinières.

Restaurant Colombia, 2 rue Tazerca, opposite the train station. A convenient place to grab a reasonably priced bite before travelling.

Le Corail, 33 rue Habib Maazoun (☎04/227301). Fairly chic, but angling for the moneyed tourist market.

Chez Nous, 26 rue Patrice Lumumba (☎04/227128). Good food and meticulous service, but it's the latter you pay for.

Le Printemps, 55 av Bourguiba (☎04/226973). Very smart, with excellent and pricey French cooking. Set menu available.

Restaurant Saada, 22 rue Mongi Slim. Best of a number of cheap places just inside Bab Diwan.

Le Sirène, by the port (☎04/224691). Across the train line from the bottom of rue Haffouz, or across the bridge from the Kerkennah ferry port. Excellent, expensive fish restaurant – choose your fish and have it barbecued while you wait, but beware of ordering the octopus salad entrée or you may be too full for your main course.

Drinks and snacks

For a cup of tea or coffee after your meal (or any other time), head for the *Café Diwan*, off rue de la Kasbah by no. 27 – an amazing place, actually inside the city wall. Go upstairs for a better view. With pine-nut tea, rose-water Turkish coffee, a relaxed atmosphere and, arguably, the smoothest *chicha* in the country, it's recommended for women as well as men. Other coffee bars – and alcohol bars – are located around boulevard de la République and in the grid zone south of avenue Bourguiba. These tend to be rather raucous and very male-dominated. A quieter beer can be had at the bar of the *Hôtel Colisée*. When these places are shut, you'll get your last beer of the evening in the *Hôtel les Oliviers*, where you pay a bit more for it.

Listings

Airlines *Air France*, 15 rue Taïeb Mehiri (☎04/224847); *Tunis Air*, 4 av de l'Armée (☎04/228028).

Banks Banks are mainly concentrated on av Bourguiba and bd de la République; *STB* in bd de la République is probably the best, but even they may refuse to change money until the daily rates come in around 9am. One bank should be open at weekends. When the banks are shut, you can usually change cash for similar rates and buy or sell Libyan dinars at Bab Diwan *louage* station.

Car and moped rental *Avis*, rue Tahar Sfar, at rue H Maazoun (☎04/224605); *Budget*, rue P Lumumba (☎04/222253); *Hertz*, 47 av Bourguiba (☎04/228626); *Interrent/Europcar*, 40 rue Tahar Sfar (☎04/228540); *Mattei*, rue P Lumumba (☎04/296404); *Solvas*, rue H Maazoun, at rue Tahar Sfar (☎04/229882). Mopeds can be rented in the middle of rue Ali Belhouane, opposite the Borj Ennar, at the southeast corner of the Medina.

Cinemas *Baghdad*, 14 av Farhat Hached, at rue H Maazoun; *Le Colisée*, 27 rue Tahar Sfar, av Hedi Chaker; *Atlas*, rue Hedi Chaker; *Etoile* and *Theatre*, opposite each other in bd de la République.

Consulates *Libya*, 35 rue A Dumas (☎04/23332). The Libyan embassy in Sfax is more likely to issue visas than its counterparts in Tunis, but at last check is issuing them only to those with an invitation from someone in the country. *UK*, Moncef Sellami, 1st Floor, 55 rue Habib Maazoun (☎04/223971): the prospective honorary consul.

Ferry companies *CTN*, 73 rue H Maazoun (☎04/298322); *Tourafric* (*Alimar's* agent), 35 av Hedi Chaker (☎04/229089).

Football Sfax's main club, the *Club Sportif de Sfax* (CSS), has its ground behind the youth hostel near the beginning of the airport road.

Hammams *Hammam Sultan*, 78 rue de la Driba, near the Dar Jellouli museum (daily men 6am-noon & 4-11.30pm, women 1-4pm). The nearly *Hammam el Joumni*, 25 rue Sidi Khelil, off rue Mongi Slim, is open similar hours.

International phone calls In the PTT, at a booth near the *Syndicat d'Initiative*, and another booth on bd de la République (all daily 8am-10pm). Another at the train station should stay open until 12.30am.

Medical facilities The main hospital is on route de l'Aïn, west of the town centre (☎04/244511), with the *Polyclinique Ettawfik* at bd des Martyrs near Bab Jebli (☎04/229306). There's also a night pharmacy at 24 rue Leopold Senghor.

Newspapers British papers are available at a kiosk on the corner of av Bourguiba and bd de la République, in a little square diagonally opposite the town hall; also at pl Marburg at the junction of rue Habib Maazoun and rue Leopold Senghor, in front of the *Hôtel Thyna*.

ONAT crafts shop 10 rue Lt Hamadi Taj (Mon-Sat 9am-noon & 3-7pm).

PTT Av Bourguiba, by the train station (city hours).

Supermarkets *Monoprix* has a branch at 12 rue Abou el Kacem Chabbi, and another in bd des Martyrs near the Mahdia *louage* station (daily 8.30am-12.30pm & 3-7pm).

Swimming pool There's a municipal pool on rte de l'Aérodrome, near the youth hostel (Mon-Fri noon-3pm, Sat noon-4pm, Sun 9am-1pm; 1TD per hour, students 0.5TD).

South of Sfax

The outstanding **saltpans of Sfax** stretch almost continuously from Sfax to Thyna, and produce some 300,000 tonnes of top-grade sea salt a year. More significantly, they're the Mediterranean's single most important site for **wintering wading birds**, making them a focus of international scientific interest. The combination of a shallow coast and a tidal range of between one and two metres – a highly unusual

MOVING ON FROM SFAX

Public transport from Sfax – buses and *louages* especially – is complicated by the multiplicity of parking areas and *louage* stands. The **train station**, at least, is easy to find, right at the eastern end of av Bourguiba, with four daily services (five in summer) to El Jem (50min), Sousse (1hr 50min) and Tunis (4hr), two the other way to Gabes (2hr 30min), and a night train to Gafsa (4hr) and Metlaoui (5hr).

As for **buses**, city bus #16 to the war cemetery and out towards the Thyna turnoff can be picked up in rue Haffouz near the corner of rue Leopold Senghor, and #3 to Sidi Mansour from just off bd des Martyrs opposite the Mahdia *louage* station. Both run every twenty minutes during the day. Otherwise, **SNTRI buses** stop opposite the train station in rue Tazerka, with five daily and six nightly departures to Sousse (2hr 30min) and Tunis (5hr) – four via El Jem (1hr) and eight via Mahdia (2hr 30min) – with one continuing to Bizerte (6hr 30min), and a total of thirteen (six at night) to Gabes (2hr), six to Medenine (3hr 30min), five to Jerba (4hr 30min), three to Kebili (4hr 30min), two to Tataouine (4hr 30min), Zarzis (5hr) and Ben Gardane (5hr 30min), and one to Douz (5hr). The **SRT bus station** is down near the other end of av Bourguiba in rue Commandant Bjaoui, opposite the end of rue de Rabat. From here, there are seven daily buses to Gabes (2hr 30min), five to Gafsa (3hr 30min), three to Mahdia (2hr 30min), and one each to Kairouan (1hr 30min), Kasserine (3hr), Le Kef (4hr 30min) and Jerba (4hr 30min). There are also around a dozen a day to Mahres (40min) and La Chebba (1hr 30min), two to Sidi Bou Zid (2hr) and seven to Agareb (30min).

The **louage** situation is even more confused, with *louages* for Tunis, Sousse, Gabes, Medenine, Tataouine and Kebili leaving from bd de l'Armée, at the southeast corner of the Medina; just 100m away, in front of Bab Diwan, is the *louage* station for Gafsa, Sidi Bou Zid and Tripoli. The Mahres and Skhirra *louage* park is further down av Ali Belhouane, at the corner of bd Farhat Hached in front of Bab Kasbah, and *louages* for Mahdia, La Chebba and Ksour Essaf have their own station on the other side of the Medina in bd des Martyrs, in front of a building with a "Sfax 2000" sign on it.

Ferries for the hour-long journey to the Kerkennah Islands are operated by *Sonotrak*, Porte de Kerkennah, rue M Hedi Khefacha (☎04/222216), and leave four times a day for most of the year, with up to eight departures a day at the height of summer; prices are 0.5TD for foot passengers, 3.5TD for a car and 1.5TD for a motorbike. Unusually, there is easy access for wheelchairs.

Sfax's **airport** (☎04/240879) is not very well connected, but it offers flights with *Tunis Air* and *Air France* to Paris (2 weekly), and with *Tuninter* to Tunis (9 weekly) and Jerba (5 weekly). Otherwise there are charters – including an occasional one to London. The airport is 7km west of town on rte de l'Aéroport, but it is a military airport, so procedures are strict, and they won't take kindly to you getting your camera out. Bus #14 from rue de Kairouan, just north of av Taïeb Mehiri, drops you 1km or so short, but your best bet is to take a cab, which shouldn't cost more than 3TD or so.

feature in the largely tideless Mediterranean – exposes huge areas of mudflats at low tide that are rich in the small creatures which form the bulk of a wading bird's winter diet.

You can access the saltpans by venturing south down Sfax's avenue Bourguiba and, after less than 2km on the Gabes road, left at a road signposted to the fishing port. Walk up that, and the mudflats start on your right just before the port. The entrance to the saltpans has a gate and a high wire fence and is marked *Cotusal*, but while the mudflats are public land, they're unsafe to walk across, as well as being foully polluted with Sfax's effluent; the best way to see the birds is to wander along the banks on the seaward side of the saltpans – private land, for which you'll need to ask permission to enter at the gate. The birds are found on the mudflats at low tide, and on just a few of the saltpans, depending on their salinity. There are fifteen square kilometres of saltpans, so it may take some time to find the birds' location.

Ten kilometres south of Sfax, **Thyna** (free access) is the site of Roman *Thaenae*, and the source of some of the mosaics in the Sfax museum. The turnoff from the Gabes road is signposted, but not too conspicuously, so keep your eyes peeled. Any bus bound for Gabes or Mahres should drop you there (ask for the Thyna *croisement*), and city bus #16 leaves you 300m short. From the turnoff, follow the Thyna road left towards the sea until you see a lighthouse; go straight on towards it, but take a track off to the right, following the arrow, just before you reach it. This track runs alongside the ramparts of the Roman town. On the other side of it are the main buildings so far excavated, including a **temple**, whose mosaics have been carted off to the museum, then a **Roman street** with remains of houses. Seaward of this, the main relic is the **Baths of the Months**, whose mosaics are still in place but covered with sand. The desultory remains to the south are a smaller **bath house**. Chances are, the *gardien* of the site will find you and give you a guided tour. There are plans afoot to develop Thyna as a tourist site, but, in the meantime, the area on the other side of the light-house is a military zone, so be careful not to trespass and avoid taking photographs.

WILDLIFE OF THE SALTPANS OF SFAX

The saltpans south of Sfax support high winter populations of **flamingos**, rare **spoon-bills**, and a variety of **herons**, **egrets**, **gulls** and **terns**. The whole area offers exceptional birdwatching, partly because of the sheer numbers and range of species, but mostly because the birds have become used to saltpan workers and shell fishers, making them very approachable. If you're remotely interested in wildlife, it's not a site to pass up.

The little inlet closest to Sfax is magical in the early morning sunlight, with hundreds of wading birds among the shell fishers. Although the biggest numbers of birds are recorded from November to the end of February, many are still present through to April, and some species (such as avocet, blackwinged stilt and redshank) stay on to breed in the coastal salt marshes surrounding the mudflats.

The feeding grounds in the mudflats beyond the saltpans are the actual reason why the birds congregate at Sfax, and a few hours watching the area gives a fascinating insight into their **feeding habits**. You'll see everything from flamingos doing their inverted side-to-side sieving of the shallow water with their huge bills, to spoonbills with their own usefully shaped mouthparts; from herons and egrets standing poised, ready to pounce, to the true waders (stints and dunlins, curlews and godwits) probing the mud, each species to a different depth and for different prey.

As well as the waders, Sfax is a good place to watch for **seabirds**, including the region's largest tern, the Caspian, with its long red beak. In winter, you can also see hundreds of **black-necked grebes**, bobbing on the water like miniature round ducks.

Mahres and La Skhirra

Continuing south for 30km or so, you pass through **MAHRES**, an unexciting beach resort with a Monday market and three hotels. The **beach** is not really suitable for swimming, being covered with slimy green seaweed, but there's a very pleasant sandy one at **Chafaar**, 5km north along the shore or 8km up the main road; turn seaward just after a level crossing and continue down a track for 4km. You should be able to **camp** in the open air here.

If you want to **stay** in the centre of Mahres, you'll find the clean and bright *Hôtel Younga* (☎04/290334; ②), with the hotel entrance at the back and a very reasonable low-priced eatery at the front. Just north of town is the two-star *Marzouk* (☎04/290261; ③), with clean rooms and a small pool; next door is the new and very friendly *Hôtel Tamaris* (☎04/290950; ④), with a rather posh restaurant. Mahres' three **banks**, **taxi-phone office** and, bizarrely, the skeleton of a whale, are to be found along the main street. **Buses** and **louages** for Sfax can be picked up by the *Hôtel Younga*, and there's

OLIVE TREES

Whether you find the roads out of Sfax scenically appealing depends on your reaction to row upon row of **olive trees** – the age-old industry of the Sahel ever since the Romans introduced them to replace grain. It was in the early nineteenth century, however, that the olive plantations really came into their own. Most of the olive oil was shipped to Europe where, too coarse and strong-tasting for dainty European palates, it was made into soap. The markets seemed bottomless and the price high, encouraging many Sfaxians to occupy lands belonging to the surrounding Methelith tribes in order to plant trees. By the 1830s, the German traveller Prince Puckler-Muskau claimed that the trees already stretched further than the eye could see.

Most of the trees are planted a standard twenty metres apart, the optimum distance, and the harvest begins in November. As it has to be done by hand, the process is highly labour-intensive, with teams of seven combing the branches, protecting their fingers with hollowed-out goat horns (more recently with plastic substitutes). An average tree around Sfax produces 50kg of olives a year, almost all of them sent to factories on the outskirts of the city, where they are converted into 15kg of oil.

Unfortunately, recent increases in productivity and production – not only in Tunisia but throughout the Mediterranean – have led to overproduction. In the last decade prices have tumbled, and after a good harvest Tunisia can't sell the bulk of its oil, whatever the price. Now the government encourages farmers to uproot the older plantations and plant cereals, and so history has turned full circle.

a bus station 100m south on the other side of the road and a **train station** inland, with two daily services to Gabes, Sfax, Sousse and Tunis, and one to Gafsa and Metlaoui.

If you're a sucker for ruined castles, you might make the effort to get to **Borj Younga**, a Byzantine fortress rebuilt by the Aghlabids, 11km south of Mahres. The turnoff is marked only by a stop sign, just before a couple of lone shops in the middle of nowhere. From there, it's a 3km walk down a track to the fort, the shell of which remains, adorned by graffiti, next to a marabout, a couple of houses and a well. It looks rather more impressive from a distance than it does when you actually reach it. As the turnoff is not served by public transport, bar the odd Gabes-bound bus, your best bet for getting there is probably to hitch.

Forty-five kilometres further south, **LA SKHIRRA** is a big oil terminal for pipelines coming from Algeria and Tunisia. Just over a hundred years ago it was simply a summer camp for the Mehadhaba tribes, then, in 1871, the Perry Bury Company of Lancashire began exporting esparto grass for paper manufacture from here. It quickly became one of the region's most important commodities and the town grew up on this British link. There is an archeological **site**, many of whose finds are now in the museum in Sfax, but the site is within the bounds of the oil terminal and off-limits to the public.

If you're lucky, you might be able to get someone down at the port to take you over to **Kneiss Island**, a few hundred metres offshore, for some isolated birdwatching, but check with the port police first.

The Kerkennah Islands

Throughout history the **Kerkennah Islands**, 20km off the coast of Sfax, have been a place of exile – the Carthaginian general Hannibal, Roman outcasts, adulterous Muslim wives and Habib Bourguiba have all been sent here at one time or another. Now this isolation is an attraction for tourists. Conventionally promoted as the poor folk's Jerba, the islands are distinctively quieter and make an ideal spot for doing nothing for a few days or weeks – even energetic swimming is out of the question as the sea is so shallow.

Some history

The islands' name came from the nymph **Circe** who, according to legend, imprisoned Odysseus here because she could not bear to let such a handsome man leave. Since then, the only historical events interrupting the islands' calm were their 1286 seizure by **Roger de Lluria**, the Catalan ruler of nearby Sicily, their 1335 repossession by the **Hafsids**, and an attempt to occupy them in 1510 by the Spanish. At the time, the Spaniards held Tripoli and felt they needed a back-up base. They tried to take Jerba without success, and left four hundred men on Kerkennah to occupy it. All were massacred by the Kerkennians within the next year, and they didn't hold Tripoli for long either.

Today, many of the islands' people understandably find the desert island atmosphere less appealing than do the tourists, and depopulation has been a problem for some years. In the early 1960s a company called *Somvik* was set up to exploit the tourist potential and revive the islands' fortunes, but this has done little more than bring a small strip of low-key hotels, so isolated that unless you're staying in one it would be easy not to notice them at all. Happily, there are signs that the economy is picking up, and the island people remain some of the most hospitable in the country.

The Islands

Strictly speaking there are two inhabited islands – **Chergui** ("Eastern") and **Gharbi** ("Western"), also called **Melita** after the village at its centre – but the channel between them was bridged by a causeway in Roman times, so for all practical purposes there's only one. It's now a hypnotic expanse of wind-blown date palms on sandy ground that never rises more than three metres above sea level. The trees are rather tatty and their dates generally inedible (although figs grow well here), but many people think this the most beautiful spot they know and return year after year. Apart from the dominant palms, there are some interesting **flowers** – in particular a small type of asphodel, and a low plant with sprawling thin leaves and a beautiful flat purple flower that goes by the inelegant name of *fagonia*. Other common seaside plants include dandelions and cotton-weed, covered with fine silvery hairs and with yellow "everlasting" flowerheads. Both of these species combine with pale blue sea lavender to form a fine carpet of colour at the edges of the beaches and rocks. **Birdwatching** in Kerkennah is also generally good, with a number of waders easily spotted in the shallow waters around the islands. Bounouma, El Attaya, Gremdi and the causeway are among favoured locations.

There are six daily **ferries** to and from Sfax (1hr) from mid-June to mid-September, with eight at the height of summer and only four the rest of the year. Island **buses** connect with the boats and run to Remla, Sidi Frej and El Attaia. The other way, they leave Remla an hour before the boat's scheduled departure time (although the journey only takes twenty minutes); all bar the first bus of the day call at Sidi Frej. There's also a more expensive minibus service from the *Grand* and *Farhat* hotels in Sidi Frej, once a day to Remla and three times a day to meet ferries.

On Kerkennah the ferry docks at **SIDI YOUSSEF**, the westernmost tip of the first island, not far from a crumbling **Turkish tower** 3km along the north shore. The island's sole bus line rumbles north along its single road and over the causeway to Chergui. A turning to the left serves the hotel strip known as **Sidi Frej**. If you're heading this way, make sure you take the right bus when you get off the ferry, otherwise you could get dropped off at Ouled Yaneg, just over the causeway, and be left with a 2km walk.

Sidi Frej and around

Kerkennah's main resort is **SIDI FREJ** on the island's west coast, a very pleasant and low-key place compared to the costas of Hammamet, Sousse and Jerba, although it is rather isolated, with just one overpriced souvenir shop, a few hotels and nothing else.

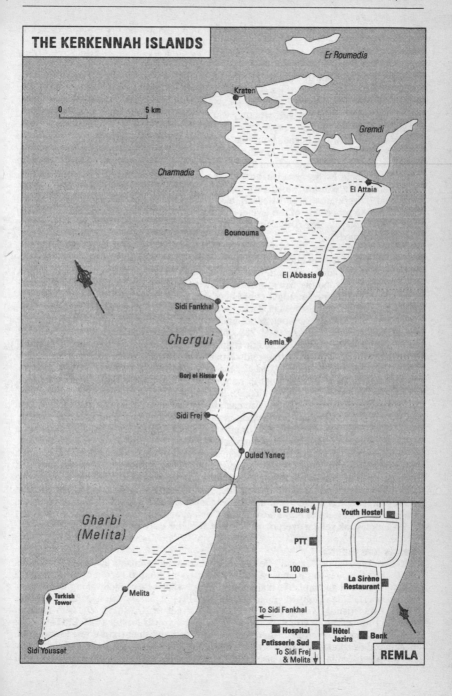

THE KERKENNAH ISLANDS

0   5 km

Er Roumedia

Kraten

Gremdi

Charmadia

El Attaia

Bounouma

El Abbasia

Sidi Fankhal

Chergui

Remla

Borj el Hissar

Sidi Frej

Ouled Yaneg

Gharbi
(Melita)

Turkish
Tower

Melita

Sidi Youssef

To El Attaia

Youth Hostel

PTT

0   100 m

La Sirène
Restaurant

To Sidi Fankhal

Hospital   Hôtel   Bank
Patisserie Sud   Jazira
To Sidi Frej
& Melita

REMLA

Consequently, much revolves around the swimming pools and organized activities in the hotels.

The **beach** at Sidi Frej is certainly not the best on Kerkennah, and the *Grand Hotel* really has the only bit of it worthy of the name, though both it and the *Farhat* have swimming pools (small charge for non-residents; the *Aziz's* is not open to non-residents, but you can use it if you're eating there). The *Grand* also has the best facilities, including **windsurfing** (free for residents, 5TD an hour for outsiders, compared to 4TD an hour at the *Cercina*, whether you're staying or not), and a **kids' club** organized by the *Panorama* tour rep.

To see more of the islands, you could rent **bicycles** from the *Cercina* (the *Grand* charges half as much again). One short trip is to **Borj el Hissar**, a ruined fort 2km or so up the coast along a track from the hotel zone, put up by the Aghlabids on a Roman site, later rebuilt by the Spanish, and destined to become a museum. In front of it on the shore, some **Roman mosaics** have been excavated. Five kilometres further, **Sidi Fankhal** is Kerkennah's finest beach, also accessible by piste across a salt flat from Remla on the other side of the island. Alternatively, *Salem's Horse and Camel Hire* in Sidi Frej (enquire at the *Grand* for details) offers rides to Borj el Hissar on the eponymous quadrupeds.

Most places to **stay** are by the beach. The first is the *Hôtel Cercina* (☎04/281228; ②–③), with a choice of cheap, rather poky "bungalows" set among sweet-smelling fig trees and closed in winter, and small but passable rooms with their own bathrooms, open all year. Beyond the *Cercina*, the *Kastil* (☎04/281212; ②) has the cheapest accommodation in Sidi Frej, in small cubic huts posing as bungalows that are closed off-season or whenever business is slack. Further up, the *Résidence Club Vacation Village* is closed, but hopes to reopen soon, and past that, on the right and away from the beach, the *Appart-Hôtel Aziz* (☎04/259405; ③) offers large, cool rooms or family suites, with a self-catering option, although supplies are only available from the "drugstore" within the hotel. Finally, at the end of the road are two hotels catering for mainly British package tourists: the *Hôtel Farhat* (☎04/281236; ④) is the quieter of the two, though its rooms are decked out in rather loud colours, while the longer-established *Grand Hotel* next door (☎04/281266; ④) is more soberly decorated, but rather noisier, with good facilities for children. You can **change money** six mornings and five evenings a week at the *Grand*, three evenings at the *Farhat*, and sometimes at the *Cercina*. The *Farhat* has a **nightclub** open to all in July and August, the *Grand's* **bar** being a favoured evening gathering place the rest of the year.

You can **eat** at all four Sidi Frej hotels and, if you're lucky, try local Kerkennah specialities such as *tchich* (octopus soup) and *melthouth* (something between pasta and couscous). The *Farhat* and the *Grand* do moderately priced set menus; otherwise you'll be paying slightly more at the *Cercina*, more still at the *Aziz*, and slightly less at the *Kastil*, although the *Cercina* has the best food. A good suggestion, if your budget is up to it, is to stay at the *Farhat*, eat at the *Cercina*, and use the *Grand's* facilities. Apart from a mini-souk selling overpriced bottled water, there are no shops in Sidi Frej.

Remla and around

REMLA, the islands' "capital", lies on the east coast and contains about three-quarters of all the shops on the islands. As a beach, it has nothing to recommend it, but as a village it is quiet and amiable, making no attempt whatsoever to jolly along the islands' sleepy way of life. Eight kilometres from Sidi Frej, it boasts the islands' only other **hotel** – the friendly *Jazira*, right on the main street (☎04/281058; ②), with clean, if spartan rooms. The *Centre de Stages et de Vacances* **youth hostel** (☎04/281148; ①), a couple of hundred metres further up the main road and then right down towards the beach, is clean and welcoming, with a mix of Tunisian and foreign youth and the option of **camping**. Remla also has a **bank** (down from the *Jazira* towards the sea), a **hospital**

in the opposite direction, a petrol station, two taxiphone offices and a PTT (country hours). The *Patisserie Saïd* opposite the *Jazira* sells excellent cheap sandwiches, and you can also eat at the *Jazira*, whose set menu is cheap to moderate, depending on the current price of fish, or at the more expensive *Sirène Restaurant* by the beach.

From Remla, the road keeps straight on for 12km to end at the fishing village of **EL ATTAIA**, reached by four daily buses from Remla (the last returning at 3pm). A turning to the left on reaching El Attaia leads through some small settlements before reaching an unlikely **museum** (variable hours) devoted to Bourguiba's dramatic escape from French custody in 1945, when he passed through the village. The boat he used, the house he sheltered in and some of the letters he wrote from various international places of exile have all been faithfully preserved. Across a narrow stretch of water lies the uninhabited island of **Gremdi**, to which local fishermen will row you for a small consideration and come and collect you by arrangement. Together with the beach at **BOUNOUMA**, 6km west of El Attaia, Gremdi is a favourite spot for a bit of **camping sauvage**. Finally, en route to El Attaia, you might try to find the meagre **Roman remains** near the village of **EL ABBASIA**, 4km north of Remla; the same village, was also the birthplace of Farhat Hached, the UGTT leader gunned down by diehard French settlers in 1952.

Fishing excursions

Doing anything energetic on Kerkennah really defeats the object of coming here, but a popular **excursion** is to go out with one of the fishermen who take people aboard for a small fee, usually cooking a meal of fresh fish into the bargain. The islanders use a curious fishing technique involving screens made of palm fronds set in V shapes in the waters all around the shore (see p.325). A trip in one of their small sailing boats, as the sun falls behind the palms and floods the sea a deep blood red, is one of Tunisia's most idyllic experiences. The going rate is about 10TD per person for half a day; contacts are easily made at the *Jazira* in Remla and the *Cercina* in Sidi Frej, or by just asking around the fishing boats.

travel details

Trains

Enfida to: Grombalia, Mahdia, Monastir, Sfax, Sousse and Tunis.

El Jem to: Gabes, Gafsa, Metlaoui, Sfax and Tunis.

Mahdia to: Ksar Hellal, Monastir, Moknine, Sousse and Tunis.

Monastir to: Enfida, Ksar Hellal, Mahdia, Moknine, Sousse and Tunis.

Sfax to: Gabes, Gafsa, El Jem, Mahres, Metlaoui, Sousse and Tunis.

Sousse to: Enfida, Gabes, Gafsa, El Jem, Mahdia, Metlaoui, Monastir, Sfax and Tunis.

Buses

Enfida to: Beja, Hammamet, Kairouan, Le Kef, Nabeul, Sousse, Tunis and Zaghouan.

El Jem to: Kairouan, Sfax, Sousse and Tunis.

Kairouan to: Gabes, Gafsa, Houmt Souk, Le Kef, Sfax, Sousse and Tunis.

Mahdia to: Ksar Hellal, Moknine, Nabeul, Sfax, Sousse and Tunis.

Monastir to: Ksar Hellal, Moknine, Nabeul, Sfax, Sousse and Tunis.

Sfax to: Douz, Gabes, Gafsa, El Jem, Houmt Souk, Kairouan, Kasserine, Kebili, Le Kef, Sbeitla, Mahdia, Medenine, Nefta, Sousse, Tozeur, Tripoli and Tunis.

Sousse to: Beja, Ben Gardane, Bizerte, Douz, Gafsa, Hammamet, Houmt Souk, El Jem, Kairouan, Le Kef, Gabes, Mahdia, Medenine, Monastir, Nabeul, Sfax, Tataouine, Tunis and Zarzis.

Louages

Enfida to: Sousse

Sousse to: La Chebba, Enfida, Hammamet, Hergla, El Jem, Kairouan, Kasserine, Ksar Hellal, Ksour Essaf, Mahdia, Monastir, Moknine, Nabeul, Port el Kantaoui, Sbeitla, Sfax, Sidi Bou Zid, Siliana and Tunis.

El Jem to: Mahdia and Sousse.

Sfax to: La Chebba, Gabes, Gafsa, Kebili, Ksour Essaf, Mahdia, Mahres, Medenine, Sidi Bou Zid, La Skhirra, Sousse, Tataouine, Tripoli and Tunis.

Ferries

Sfax to: Kerkennah Islands.

Flights

Monastir to: Amsterdam, Brussels, Casablanca, Düsseldorf, Frankfurt, Geneva, Istanbul, Jerba, Luxembourg, Lyon, Malta, Marseille, Munich, Palermo, Paris, Rome and Vienna. Most of Monastir's air traffic is seasonal charters from Europe and the UK.

MARKET DAYS

Monday – La Chebba, El Alia, El Jem, Kairouan, Ksour Essaf, Mahres, Msaken

Tuesday – Bir Ali Ben Khelifa, Ksar Hellal, Remla (Kerkennah)

Wednesday – Agareb, Menzel Chaker, Moknine

Thursday – Bou Thadi, Ksiba el Mediouni, Sbih, Sidi el Hani

Friday – Ej Jemaa, Jebiniana, Jemmel, Mahdia, Ouesslatia, Sfax, La Skhirra

Saturday – El Hencha, Hammam Sousse, Monastir

Sunday – Enfida, Graïba, Ksar Hellal, Sousse

CHAPTER FIVE

THE TELL

T he **Tell** begins with fertile plains – good, well-watered farming land – but rises quickly into the **Dorsale mountains**, the highest in the country, forming a barrier across the country from Zaghouan to Kasserine. Beyond lie empty and infertile steppes which fade towards the coast into the Sahel. The plains have been heavily populated since Roman times, though the southern parts, over the centuries, were steadily taken over by esparto grass and left to sheep and camel herds. The tribes that lived here in the nineteenth century were notorious for their banditry; the **Hammama**, centred on the tomb of Sidi Bou Zid, used to raid as far as the very gates of Sfax. During the Protectorate large areas of public grazing land were taken over by colonists and the tribes were left to fight over the scraps. Most of the population lived by working on colonial estates and gathering esparto grass. The economy has been severely depressed ever since and, even in larger towns like Le Kef and Kasserine, most people now leave to look for work in Tunis or the Sahel – often without success. The feelings of frustration which haunt the region found expression in January 1984, when the **bread riots** started in Kasserine, leading to the deaths of eighty people (see p.374).

Lack of attention from tourism contributes to this sense of neglect. Tour groups make their way from the coast to the main Roman sites of **Thurburbo Majus, Maktar, Sbeitla** and above all **Dougga**, but they largely neglect the region's less obvious attractions. **Zaghouan**, an unspoiled market town just an hour from Tunis, sits below the country's most spectacular mountain, **Jebel Zaghouan**, whose foothills harbour a group of isolated Berber villages. **Testour** was built up by Andalusian settlers and retains a very Spanish flavour, with a glorious seventeenth-century minaret more like a Toledo church tower. Over by the Algerian border is **Le Kef**, a historic mountainside

---

ACCOMMODATION PRICE CODES

All the hotels, youth hostels and pensions listed in this book have been price-graded according to the following scale, and although prices will rise during the lifetime of this edition, the relative comparisons should remain valid.

The prices quoted are for the **cheapest available double room in high season**, although many of the cheap places will have pricier rooms with en suite facilities or sea views.

Classified hotels, officially considered suitable for tourists, are graded locally from one to four stars (★), with wide-ranging prices within each category. For more on accommodation prices and categories, see Basics.

① Up to 10TD. Very cheap. Usually a bed only in a basic, unclassified hotel or a youth hostel.

② 10.1–25TD. Budget. Bed only or bed and breakfast.

③ 25.1–40TD. Comfortable budget. Good unclassified average one-star or a cheap two-star.

④ 40.1–55TD. Mid-range. Expensive two-star, cheap three-star.

⑤ 55.1–70TD. Tourist hotel. Standard three-star.

⑥ 70.1TD upwards. Deluxe. Expensive three-star, four-star or five-star.

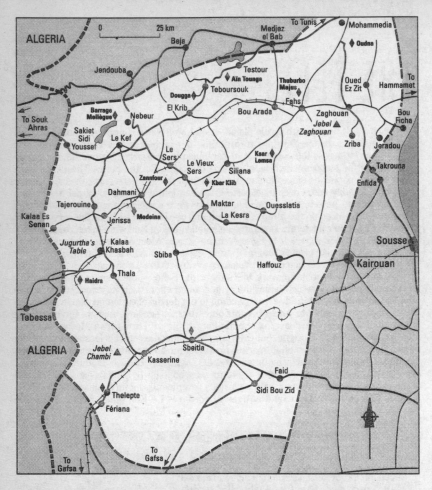

town that looks out over landscapes reminiscent of the American West. Hidden here, and virtually unvisited, are **Haidra**, one of the most majestic Roman sites in the country, and **Jugurtha's Table**, a flat-topped mountain that served as a bandit's lair for many centuries.

The Tell does not have a very integrated system of **transport**. Le Kef and Kasserine are the main transport centres, reasonably well connected to other parts of the Tell and beyond, and places on the edge of the region often have better connections to other parts of the country. Sbeitla and Kasserine have train lines but no passenger services.

Zaghouan and around

Almost alpine in feel, with its green slopes and the grey crags above, **ZAGHOUAN**, 50km south of Tunis, is perhaps the most refreshing town in Tunisia. The old town's steep, narrow streets crisscross a low ridge of **Jebel Zaghouan** – not quite the highest mountain in the country, but easily the most spectacular. Cold water gushing from the mountain springs used to supply Carthage via a 70km Roman aqueduct and now splashes from taps at every street corner.

One end of the ridge is punctuated by the old church spire and the new mosque's minaret; nearer the middle are the nineteenth-century **Great Mosque** and the **Marabout of Sidi Ali Azouz**, named after the patron saint of Tunis, where he is commemorated with his own *zaouia* (p.79).

The place to head for is a café below the Roman remains, which lie about 3km above the town centre (follow signs for the *Nymphes* hotel). Here you can sit and enjoy the **view**, extending over the bare plain below and up into a gash of the mountain behind. The Roman **"temple"** here is little more than a backdrop – not a temple at all, in fact, but a grand fountain of the type found in all Roman towns. The twelve niches above the basin once held a statue for each month of the year.

If you feel inspired to climb the craggy, limestone ridge of **Jebel Zaghouan**, either take the 16km track leading to the relay station on the summit (from where there are superb views over the countryside), or scramble up directly from the temple in a couple of hours. It's very hard-going, rough on exposed legs and a good place to twist an ankle, and the mountain is not a place to get caught out after dark.

Jebel Zaghouan, rising 1300m above the surrounding plains, is the most typical of the ranges that form Tunisia's backbone. From a naturalist's point of view, its highlight is an abundance of **birds of prey**, of which up to a dozen species can be sighted in a few hours, including eagles, vultures, kites and falcons, wheeling around their nest sites, or soaring hundreds of metres before gliding out over the plains in search of food. They're active most of the day, but early morning and evening are the best times to watch.

Public transport around Zaghouan is not that extensive, but interesting excursions are available west to Fahs and Thuburbo Majus, or southeast to the Berber villages of Zriba and Jeradou.

Practicalities

Although a fair number of tourists stop by to see the Roman ruins, few stay long, leaving the town surprisingly unspoiled. If you have the choice, come on a Friday, **market day**. The cheapest **accommodation** is the *Maison des Jeunes* **youth hostel** (☎02/675265; ①), a barrack-like affair on top of the next ridge over from the town centre. The only hotel, the expensive *Nymphes* (☎02/675094; ④), along the shady lane leading behind the town towards the ruins and high up among the trees, is sometimes open to bargaining. This same road continues to a café-restaurant just below the remains where they may allow **camping**.

Transport in Zaghouan operates from the bottom of the old town near the Roman arch, with three daily **buses** to Enfida (45min), eight to Nabeul and Hammamet (1hr) and to Fahs (30min), two to Sousse (2hr) and hourly departures to Tunis (1hr). There are **louages** to Tunis and occasionally to Nabeul, Fahs and Enfida.

South to the Sahel: Berber villages

Southeast towards Enfida and the Sahel, the roads lead past a couple of dramatic **Berber villages** perched in the dying fall of the Dorsale mountains and similar to Takrouna outside Enfida (see p.171).

The most remote is **ZRIBA**, 12km southeast of Zaghouan and confusingly located amidst Hammam Zriba and Zriba Village. You'll need to find your way first to Hammam Zriba – turn right 8km out of Zaghouan towards Enfida on the MC133 road

– and continue through the modern settlement to the shops around the hammam, which occupies the opening of a narrow gorge leading into the hills. You should be able to find a bus or a lift from Zaghouan as far as this – especially at weekends, when the hammam is a popular excursion. If you're interested in a scramble, this gorge is apparently where Flaubert came to get in the mood for *Salammbo*'s chapter about the massacre of the mercenaries. To continue to Zriba, you'll need to find a rough 5km track that heads southeast past the entrance to an ugly open-cast mine. As you walk or bump over the hills, you'll catch glimpses of the village in the distance, clinging to the edges of an outlying jag of the mountain behind. The village itself is less striking than its setting, with narrow lanes crawling up and down the steep ridge.

Similar to Zriba, **JERADOU** is more accessible if you have transport – less so if you don't. A track leads east to it from the Zaghouan–Enfida road. Or there's a more straightforward surfaced approach from the Zaghouan–Bou Ficha road. Like Zriba, Jeradou occupies an outlying pinnacle of a mountain and consists of narrow streets leading up to a saint's shrine on top of the ridge. Look out for Roman remains in the field of olives below the village.

From Jeradou, a minor road leads south through **SIDI KHALIFA**, a small settlement with a multi-domed shrine. A track leads a short way south from here towards a low forested hill, at whose foot lie the unexpected remains of Roman **Pheradi Maius** – baths, a triumphal arch and, on the hilltop above to the east, a temple to Baal. The road through Sidi Khalifa goes on to join the coast road halfway between Bou Ficha and Enfida.

Sidi Jedidi and Oued ez Zit

The direct road from Zaghouan to Hammamet (MC28) leads north off the Bou Ficha road through empty countryside. Five kilometres before Hammam Jedidi, a young forest plantation lies a little way north of the road, beyond an old colonial farmhouse. A reader reports having found some rusting tanks, remnants of a World War II battle, here. Beyond Hammam Jedidi, the Tuesday market at the village of **SIDI JEDIDI** has become the target of tourist excursions from Hammamet. From the top of the ridge here you can look down towards the coast, where your first sight of the resort complex is of parasails floating above the beach.

The main road back to Tunis from Zaghouan runs northwest to join the GP3, the road to Fahs. If you have transport or happen to find a lift, you might want to think about taking the back road to Tunis, which runs northeast across the fertile plain below Zaghouan to **OUED EZ ZIT** ("River of Oil"), a small village with some Roman remains. Here the route enters a lonely pass between Jebel Zit and Jebel Marchana, either of which would make attractive walking country. Towards the end of the pass, the road offers a dramatic view of the back of Jebel Ressas, the lonely trapezoid mountain more usually seen lurking behind Jebel Bou Kornine from Sidi Bou Said. Beyond the mountain, the road runs through vineyards towards the straggling southern end of Tunis.

Fahs and around

FAHS is a sizeable but nondescript market town, and the only reason to come here is to see the Roman site of Thuburbo Majus, 3km north. The town has few attractions of its own, with the exception of the **Saturday market**, one of the largest in the area and totally devoid of tourist buses. The marketplace is next to the train line and **buses** stop on the main road, with two services a day to Le Kef (3hr) and Sousse (2hr), three to Nabeul (2hr) and Zaghouan (30min), and six daily services to Kasserine (4hr), Maktar

(2hr) and Tunis (1hr 30min); **louages** also stop nearby on the main road and serve Maktar, Siliana and Tunis. East and west of Fahs, good minor roads lead through empty country (with limited public transport) to Zaghouan and Mejez el Bab. More heavily travelled are the main roads south to Kairouan and southwest to Siliana and Maktar. There's no tourist office nor any hotels in town.

La Mohammedia and around

Sixteen kilometres from Tunis on the road to Fahs, Ahmed Bey (1837–56) built a summer palace called **La Mohammedia** that he hoped would surpass even Versailles in its grandeur. Senior state officials had long kept country residences here, including two of the ill-fated *Sahib at Tabaa's* – Youssef, who built the mosque in Tunis (see p.77), and Shakir, both of whom met early deaths. Ahmed Bey began to build a palace complex here in the 1840s, and following his state visit to France in 1846, he aimed to incorporate some of what he had seen in Europe. This included a French optical telegraph system – then the latest in telecommunications technology – which the French, rulers of Algeria since 1830 and already jockeying for position in Tunisia, were only too glad to provide. Lines were set up linking Mohammedia to the Bardo Palace and to La Goulette, but for some reason the system was barely used before being abandoned.

Little but a shell now remains of Ahmed's palace complex. All the roofs have collapsed and most of the tiles have been pillaged, but the site still has the bare outlines of the palace buildings and associated barracks. Tunisia has a large number of redundant and ruined Beylical palaces, perhaps because of the superstition that it was unpropitious for a Bey to rule from the palace of his predecessor.

A few kilometres beyond La Mohammedia, the road runs parallel to the Roman **aqueduct** which carried water from Zaghouan to Carthage. First built in the second century AD, it was reconstructed by the Byzantines after the Vandal invasion, and later by the Fatimids and Hafsids. Where the road meets the aqueduct, an 8km track leads directly to the minimal remains of Roman **Oudna** – some excellent mosaics have gone to the Bardo, leaving (most recognizably) a Byzantine fortress.

Thuburbo Majus

The ruins of **Thuburbo Majus** (daily 8am–5pm; 1TD, plus 1TD for photos) lie behind a low rise 3km north of Fahs on the Tunis road, beyond a bridge over the Oued Miliane. Under French rule, Fahs was known as Pont du Fahs, and as you cross the river you can see the remains of a bridge left behind by Roman colonists in the riverbed to the east. If you're on foot, ignore the signpost for the site – which seems to take you halfway around northern Tunisia – and walk instead straight up to the dip between two small hills, the eastern edge of the Roman city.

Thurburbo Majus was a Berber-Carthaginian settlement long before the Romans arrived. The name was actually based on a common root in the indigenous local language, used in place names like Thuburbo Minus (modern Tebourba), Thuburnica near Ghardimao (see p.166), and Teboursouk near Dougga (see p.238). For the Romans (and later the French) it was an important market centre and grew rich on the proceeds. Like so many other provincial towns, it acquired the trappings of Rome – a Forum, a Capitol, and the semblance of an orderly grid plan at the heart of an older, meandering town. The site was abandoned after the seventh-century Arab invasion and was only rediscovered in 1875. As Roman sites in Tunisia go, it lags slightly behind the likes of Maktar and Sbeitla but is easier to reach from Tunis and the coastal resorts.

The Forum

The town's public buildings, the expression of its citizens' collective pride, date mainly from the great imperial era of the second to third century AD. The **Forum** – the paved

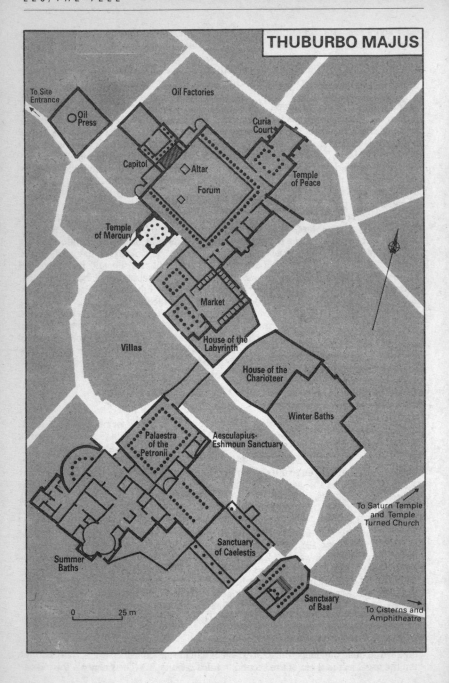

THUBURBO MAJUS

To Site Entrance

Oil Press

Oil Factories

Capitol

Altar

Forum

Curia Court

Temple of Peace

Temple of Mercury

Market

House of the Labyrinth

Villas

House of the Charioteer

Winter Baths

Palaestra of the Petronii

Aesculapius-Eshmoun Sanctuary

Summer Baths

Sanctuary of Caelestis

To Saturn Temple and Temple Turned Church

Sanctuary of Baal

To Cisterns and Amphitheatre

0   25 m

open space at the centre of the site, laid out between the years 161 and 192 AD – was its most characteristically Roman feature, something that any self-respecting imperial town had to have. A colonnade ran around three sides, the fourth left open for the **Capitol temple**, which catered for the imperial cult of Jupiter, Juno and Minerva. The podium and the vertical emphasis of the columns are very much the norm, and if you walk round behind it's easy to see just how much effort had to go into giving the temple a massive base so that it would dominate the Forum in the prescribed manner. In fact, the whole of one side of the Forum had to be raised on an artificial platform to create the required level space – a graphic illustration of the influence of the Roman role model over status-conscious provincial citizens. The area of housing behind the Capitol was later converted into **oil factories**. You can see clearly where one massive circular press was installed so that the oil would drip into a pool originally designed for human bathing – a grim illustration of the change in Thuburbo's circumstances, with industry supplanting leisure. To the north, one of three surviving **triumphal arches** marks the outskirts of town.

The Temple of Mercury and market

Behind the colonnade on the other three sides of the Forum stood temples and municipal buildings. On the right-hand side as you look from the Capitol is a curious **Temple of Mercury**, built in 211 AD according to the local and not the Roman pattern, and featuring an outer courtyard – circular, with niches making corners – leading into the sanctuary. Mercury was the god of trade (as well as of thieving), and the three split-level courtyards below the temple formed the town's **market**, where stalls can still be made out. The Mercury temple looks out over an area of jumbled streets and houses, predating the Forum, in a layout that was anathema to the Romans. Several hundred metres beyond, towards another triumphal arch in the distance, is a second residential quarter with regular streets, a Roman addition as the town expanded. In many ways, the contrast between the two areas is similar to the difference in modern Tunisia between traditional medinas and French grid plans – like the Romans before them, the nineteenth-century colonial powers imported their own ideas when it came to town planning.

However rambling the streets in the quarter below the Forum, though, the houses in this central district were as Roman as their wealthy inhabitants could make them. Some fine colourful mosaics are visible in a house where columns have been re-erected around the central courtyard.

The Palaestra of the Petronii and around

Just east of here stands a well-preserved row of blue-grey columns which still support an entablature. These made up one side of the 225 AD **Palaestra of the Petronii**, where young men took part in boxing, wrestling or running before going on to the **Summer Baths** behind. Carved in the paving of the Palaestra's southern corner, you'll find some letters that make up a Roman game used to learn the alphabet. The most striking part of the baths beyond, confused in plan after being remodelled in 361 AD, is an impressive semicircular portico which housed not statuary but latrines – whose users sat over a still-visible channel of running water.

Nothing could be more Roman than the Palaestra, but three hybrid centres of worship are reminders of the cultural blend in Roman North Africa. In the far corner of the Palaestra is a small **shrine** to the healing god Aesculapius, here worshipped under the joint name of Aesculapius-Eshmoun. An inscription reveals that those wishing to enter the sanctuary had to observe a three-day ritual when they were forbidden beans and pork, bathing, shaving and sexual relations. A street leads off to the right here towards a small temple podium. This **Sanctuary of Baal**, the top deity in the Phoenician pantheon, was erected in the second century under Roman rule. The courtyard just over the street (with its entrance re-erected) was a **Sanctuary of Caelestis**, the Roman version of Carthaginian Tanit. Later it was used as a church.

Ruins discernible on the hillside south of the Baal temple comprise perhaps the most monumental **cistern** to be seen in Tunisia, even boasting an inner gallery around the top of the deep storage tank. An **amphitheatre** above is just recognizable – there's a fine view from here of Jebel Zaghouan dominating the whole region, and across to the eastern **gate** of the town on the next hill. Above this gate are the remains of a **Temple of Saturn**, the Roman equivalent of Baal whose temples tend to stand near the city boundaries, as at Dougga.

The route from the centre of town to the eastern gate leads past the **Winter Baths** – mediocre except for their impressive facade – and a late **church**, fashioned out of another large temple. Standing among the columns of its nave and two aisles, you can easily make out how a rectangular church plan was imposed on the existing square courtyard. An apse is recognizable at one end, a baptistry at the other.

Southwest to Maktar

Heading southwest, the MC4 road makes up one side of the Fahs–Maktar–Kairouan triangle which contains some of the most remote country in the Tell. It's scenically rewarding, but difficult to reach without your own transport. The most obvious single sight is the massive Byzantine **fortress** of **KSAR LEMSA**, 20km down a left turn off the Fahs–Siliana road towards Ouesslatia. Sitting below the massive presence of Jebel Bargou, it guarded one of the routes north into the more fertile but vulnerable areas of the Tell. Continuing south along the Ksar Lemsa road will bring you to a fork where you can go east to Kairouan or west to Ouesslatia.

Back on the Siliana road heading southwest, a left turn 20km east of Siliana at **BARGOU** (also known as Robaa) offers a scenic one-way route into the heart of the **Jebel Bargou** massif. Twenty kilometres further on, **SILIANA** itself is, like Ouesslatia, a lowland equivalent of Maktar, a dull modern farming centre where you wouldn't want to stay for its own sake. It is, however, the site of one of the few **hotels** in this area – the *Zama* (✆02/870751; ②) – and has reasonable transport connections, which makes it one of the few feasible bases for exploring the Fahs–Maktar–Kairouan triangle.

Roman remains within reach of Siliana, just accessible down a 9km track and recommended for enthusiasts only, are the vestigial ruins at **JAMA** of what is thought to be *Zama Minor*, site in 202 BC of the climactic battle of the Second Punic War, in which Scipio (soon to become Scipio Africanus) defeated Hannibal.

It's uphill most of the way from Siliana to Maktar (see p.250). About 10km outside Siliana, a minor road turns west to cut across for 20km to the Maktar–Kef road. About halfway down this lonely road, which bumps up and down over steeply rolling country, you pass two solitary Roman-era monuments, both easy to miss. The first, known as **Ksour Toual Zouamel**, is a two-storey square mausoleum which sits below and to the north of the road, halfway up a hill. About 1km further, the second, known as **Kbor Klib**, is a couple of hundred metres south of the road on the ridge of the same massif. A huge block of masonry, originally 45m long by 15m wide and 6m high, it remains uncertainly identified, and is said to be either a Numidian sanctuary, similar to the one which stood on top of the hill at Chemtou, or a victory altar erected by Julius Caesar to celebrate his Civil War triumph.

Testour and around

Approaching the Tell from Tunis, the main westward route splits at Medjez el Bab, where the northern fork climbs over the Teboursouk range (see Chapter Three). The southern branch follows the Medjerda River before reaching **TESTOUR**, 75km west of the capital and the most undiluted remaining evidence in the country of the Spanish immigration of the early seventeenth century.

A cluster of tiled roofs on a mound above the River Medjerda, Testour looks so Spanish that it's no surprise to find that it was built by Andalusian refugees in the 1600s. Its appearance and the local people's way of life have changed very little since, and this, along with the almost pristine rural feel of the place, gives it a particular fascination, the more so if you can coincide with the Friday regional **market**. At all events, it's worth a stop en route from Tunis to Dougga and Le Kef, an easy enough road to travel by bus or *louage*.

Some history

Some of the **Andalusian Muslims**, evicted from Spain in the wake of the Christian reconquest, were wealthy enough to settle in Tunis itself, where the rue des Andalous is a reminder of their presence. Others had to petition the authorities for land, and in 1609 were granted the old Roman site of *Tichilla*, today's Testour.

The new Andalusian communities were renowned throughout North Africa for their commercial abilities and hard work, but were conscious of their outsider status. Both feelings are neatly expressed in a myth about Testour's foundation. According to this story, the first group of settlers originally stopped about 12km north of the current town, where some of them planted vineyards. The Turkish authorities were so impressed when they saw the result that they slapped on taxes at a punitive level – whereupon the disgusted settlers uprooted their vines and themselves and moved on to Testour's current site.

From its foundation, Testour's economy centred on the agricultural activities of the region – for which it still provides an important market – but there were also skilled artisans among the immigrants. The town was long famed for its **chechias**, skullcaps made from the wool of local flocks. These have almost disappeared, but the other main trade – traditional **tile production** – has survived. A factory can be seen down by the river below the Great Mosque, one of only two left in all Tunisia (the other is at Tozeur), where some two thousand tiles are produced every week.

The Town

In Testour, the bourgeois pride and culture of the Andalusian settlers found permanent expression in mosques and public buildings that are redolent of rural Spain. The **Great Mosque**, unmissable with its distinctive tiled octagonal minaret, is the largest and most beautiful of an extraordinary number of mosques built in the town in the early seventeenth century. It stands at the end of the main street, its walls the texture of crumbled biscuit, surmounted by a ribbed tile roof. Inside, the delicate arcades of the two courtyards – one hung with white jasmine – are in marked contrast to the generally heavier local styles. Yet even here you can see that Roman bits and pieces – doorframes, capitals, columns and oil presses – have been reused in the paving. One corner column in the main courtyard sports a milestone proclaiming "Carthage 66 miles", which, as it happens, is just about right.

But it is the **minaret** that dominates the mosque, just as it dominates the town and the surrounding river valley, with its nostalgia for Spain. Most obviously Spanish is the superimposition of an octagonal crowning section, lavishly decorated with tiles, on a square base, which recalls church bell towers in Aragon and Castile. In the base, the builders used a Toledan technique in which rectangular patches of rubble somehow become decorative when surrounded by brick. Least obvious, but perhaps the biggest giveaway, is the sundial clock on the south face; this is standard for a church bell tower but doesn't appear on a minaret anywhere else in the world.

Testour's Spanish immigrant citizens could hardly have provided a clearer demonstration of their identity or proof of their success than this mosque and its minaret. This is actually the second great mosque that they built. The remains of the first one – a floorplan, a bricked-in *mihrab* and the bottom half of a smaller minaret – lie not far to the northeast of the existing one.

Local tradition has it that there were once fourteen mosques here, built on virtually every side street off the main avenue and serving the specific needs of local communities, playing host to business and municipal meetings as well as everyday prayer. Only a handful remain today, but almost without exception they consist of a bell tower-like round crown on a square base. The **Abdellatif Mosque**'s minaret, just north of the main street on rue Kortouba, has some rows of faïence tiles. "Kortouba" refers to Cordoba in Spain; just before it, on the same side of the main street, notice also rue Ichbilia ("Seville").

South off the main street, at the end of rue 26 Fevrier 1953, stands another graceful reminder of Andalusian culture – the **Zaouia of Sidi Naseur el Baraouachi**, built around his tomb in 1733. It begins in a lengthy passage and passes through a green door whose studded nails have been painted a hallucinatory red. Inside, however, all is calm, with a tiny paved courtyard surrounded by small chambers under a tiled arcade and almost swamped by an orange tree. The tomb itself, under its green-tiled dome and decorated with stucco and faïence tiles, is still an object of veneration; the stains on its far wall were made by hands coated in henna to ward off the evil eye.

Most of the Andalusian immigrant communities established in Tunisia included Jews as well as Muslims, though many have left for Israel over the last decades. Testour was formerly the site of a Jewish pilgrimage from all over Tunisia to the tomb of one Rabbi Fraji Chawat, said to be a native of Fez who died here. More recently, the town became tangled in the torrid story of a Jewish woman called Habiba Msika, born in 1895, who became one of the country's best-known singers and actresses during the musical revival of the early part of the century. She is remembered today for the manner of her early death in 1930, when her jealous lover Elyaou Mimouni – a wealthy native of Testour – doused her in petrol while she slept and burned her alive. Look out for the film about Msika that is rumoured to be in the making.

Mimouni's house now serves as Testour's **Maison de Culture** on rue Kortouba, beyond the Abdellatif minaret, with an Arabic plaque on the wall in which the fateful year of 1930 is recognizable. If you can find someone to show you round this incongruously lavish 1920s mansion, you can see Mimouni's massive safe, some splendidly vampish photos and even an auditorium that was purpose-built for Msika. The *Maison de Culture* is also the place to ask about Testour's annual **Festival of Malouf Music**, which takes place in June and July in the large and hideous new café opposite the great mosque.

Practicalities

There have been few incursions into the fabric of the old town – most of the straggle of **new development** flanks the main road heading west to Le Kef. One of the last of these buildings, the *Hôtel Ibn Zeitun*, looks well and truly abandoned, and there are no other hotels in town, no PTT and no tourist office. **Buses** stop at the *Restaurant el Qods*, on the main road west of town, and run hourly to Teboursouk (30min) and Le Kef (2hr), as well as to Medjez el Bab (30min) and Tunis (1hr 30min).

Aïn Tounga

At **AÏN TOUNGA**, 9km west of Testour on the Le Kef road, there is an ancient site which includes one of the most impressive **Byzantine fortresses** to be seen in Tunisia. Remains of its walls and towers, some half-buried but still enormous, loom over the modern road. Above an entrance to the southwest tower is a Latin inscription – which doesn't seem strange until you reflect that the Byzantines spoke Greek. The local people must still have spoken Latin after a century of Vandal rule, an interesting testament that the language was not just living but also tenacious.

Above the fortress are the remains of Roman **Thignica**: a residential quarter crowned by a temple, with the outline of a theatre, baths and an arch hidden away in a garden below to the right.

Dougga and around

"Dougga very big city, monsieur" is what the hopeful guides hanging around the entrance will tell you, and they're right. The Roman site of **Dougga** (daily 8am–5pm; 1TD, plus 1TD to take photos) is both the largest and most dramatic in Tunisia, and it contains what some consider the most beautiful single Roman monument in North Africa. If you see only one Roman site in the country, it should undoubtedly be "these magnificent remains of taste and greatness, so easily reached in perfect safety by a ride along the Medjerda, as pleasant and as safe as along the Thames between London and Oxford", as James Bruce noted in 1765.

Dougga's name suggests non-Roman origins, as does its site high on the side of the valley, as the Romans preferred flatter sites more suited to their standardized urban forms. Here they seem to have adapted well to a town that had already been described in the fourth century BC as being "of an impressive size". By the second century BC it had become the seat of Numidian king **Massinissa**, whose support for Rome in the last war against Carthage gained much credit for the town. From the second century AD, under Roman administration, it began to enjoy a period of great prosperity. At its peak the Roman town had a population of ten thousand and although the surrounding countryside now looks empty, aerial photography has revealed no fewer than ten other settlements within a ring of just six square kilometres.

The Byzantines built huge fortifications and, after their departure, the local inhabitants remained among the ruins until excavating archeologists at the end of the last century forced them to move down the hill into the purpose-built village of **NOUVELLE DOUGGA,** a drab modern place on the Tunis–Kef road.

Dougga is quite remote, and **getting there** can involve some effort if you don't have your own transport. The site lies on a hillside about 6km west of the modern town of Teboursouk and 3km north of Nouvelle Dougga. Approaching from the east, it's best to head for Teboursouk, from where a side road follows the wall of the valley up and around to Dougga. There's no public transport from Nouvelle Dougga, and you'll need to walk, hitch or organize a taxi – a return trip should cost around 8TD. Approaching from the west, you could consider an alternative approach through Nouvelle Dougga, from where it's a shorter 3km walk up the valley side along a new road that leads to the site.

The theatre and temples

The road to Dougga from Teboursouk winds into the site past a heavily restored **theatre,** almost at the top of the steep slope over which the grey remains are spread. Originally built in 168 AD, the theatre was one of a string of monumental projects of the second and third centuries financed with the money Dougga's leading families made out of the agricultural land it surveys. In this case, an inscription let everyone know that one Publius Marcius Quadratus had erected the theatre, the halls flanking the stage, the porticos, the statue platform and the scene building. Today the theatre is used for occasional summer performances of the French classics in May and June.

Up on the hilltop behind the theatre are some early and peripheral odds and ends, beginning with the **Temple of Saturn** whose skyline columns overlook the road.

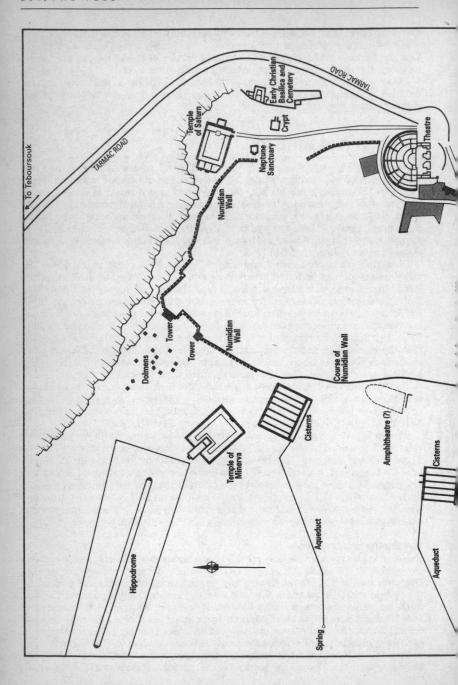

To Teboursouk

TARMAC ROAD

TARMAC ROAD

Early Christian Basilica and Cemetery

Temple of Saturn

Crypt

Theatre

Neptune Sanctuary

Numidian Wall

Tower

Tower

Numidian Wall

Dolmens

Course of Numidian Wall

Amphitheatre (?)

Cisterns

Temple of Minerva

Cisterns

Aqueduct

Aqueduct

Hippodrome

Spring

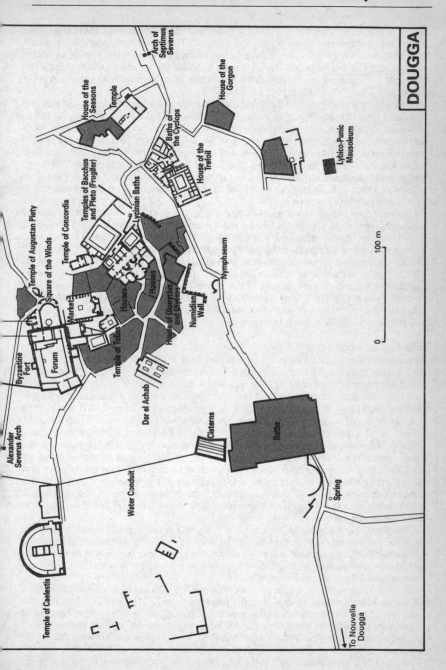

DOUGGA

Arch of Septimius Severus

House of the Seasons

Temple

House of the Gorgon

Baths of the Cyclops

House of the Trefoil

Temples of Bacchus and Pluto (Frugifer)

Lycinian Baths

Lybico-Punic Mausoleum

Temple of Augustan Piety

Temple of Concordia

Square of the Winds

Nymphaeum

Temple of the Winds

Market

Houses

Houses

House of Dionysius and Ulysses

Numidian Wall

Byzantine Fort

Forum

Temple of Tellus

Dar el Achab

Alexander Severus Arch

Cisterns

Baths

Water Conduit

Spring

Temple of Caelestis

To Nouvelle Dougga

100 m

0

These columns formed the facade of a courtyard which in turn led into three inner chambers, the typical African pattern for a temple. This is not surprising, since underneath the second-century Roman remains were found traces of a pre-Roman sanctuary of Baal, the Carthaginian god. In the paving opposite the central sanctuary chamber, look out for a pair of mysterious footprints in the floor, remnants of some unknown ritual.

From the top of the cliff by the Temple of Saturn, you could cut across west to some occupied houses that still huddle under the remains of the pre-Roman Numidian defensive wall. Otherwise, return to the theatre and make your way along the main track leading towards the Capitol at the centre of the Roman town. This in turn becomes a paved Roman street that seems narrow and twisting compared to the norm – another sign that the Romans here inherited a well-established earlier settlement. The small semicircular **temple**, on the left as you approach the town centre, was dedicated to Augustan Piety, and beyond it is what used to be a **mosque**, built on the foundations of a Roman Temple of Fortune.

Because this temple stood at an oblique angle, the open space below was rounded off with a semicircle – most unusual for conservative Roman planners – that introduces an unexpected note of intimacy. The plaza is called the **Square of the Winds**, after a compass-based inscription in the paving below the Capitol temple which names all twelve winds. As with mosaics illustrating the four seasons, or the months of the year, this is typical of the important role the natural world played in the imagery of Roman Africans. It's likely that the Square of the Winds was commissioned at the end of the second century by the Pacuvii family, who were also sponsors of the **Temple of Mercury** on the north side and of the **market** to the south, surrounded by individual stalls whose foundations have been restored.

The Capitol and Forum

You're now face to face with the huge temple of the **Capitol** – or you would be, if the Byzantines hadn't built some highly disorienting fortifications around it, which, ironically, are the reason for the Capitol's excellent state of preservation. The Capitol really is a magnificent sight as it looks out over the town and the valley below, and is so well proportioned that you have to get close to appreciate just how huge it is. It was a gift to the city in 166 AD – just two years before the theatre was built – from the parents of the proud theatre donor, and an inscription records its dedication to "Jupiter, Juno and Minerva for the safety of Marcus Aurelius and Lucius Verus", joint emperors at the time. Some fragments of the massive cult statue of Jupiter that originally stood six metres high in the *cella* (inner sanctum) – a potent symbol of Roman power – are now in the Bardo Museum in Tunis. The relief sculpture in the temple pediment shows a human figure being molested by a large bird – the previous emperor, Antoninus Pius, undergoing his apotheosis at the hands (or claws) of an eagle, and a singularly uncomfortable reward it looks, too.

The open space west of the temple is the **Forum**, lavishly decorated with columns of polychrome marble, but modest in size because of the lie of the land. Although the Byzantine fortifications now make this difficult to appreciate, the Square of the Winds may have been built so as to increase the sense of open space around the Capitol and thus enhance the sense of Romanness.

A track leads west among the olive trees behind the Capitol to the **Triumphal Arch of Alexander Severus**, named after the emperor from 222 to 235 AD, when the arch was built. Further along, set in the gentle lap of the valley side, is the **Temple of Caelestis**, possibly the most likeable of Dougga's monuments. Built at the same time as the nearby triumphal arch, it's dedicated to Juno Caelestis (Heavenly Juno), the Romanized version of the Carthaginian god Tanit, and thus makes a pair with the Temple of Saturn on the far side of the city; but it's the truly Roman cult which is given central position in the Capitol. The temple itself, featuring podium and columns with attractive Corinthian capitals, is nothing out of the ordinary, but the semicircular colonnaded portico behind it is, like the Square of the Winds, unusual in the conservative architectural atmosphere of Roman Africa. Far away at the other end of the Roman Empire (Turkey and Palestine, for instance), this sort of touch was commonplace, but in Tunisia innovation seems to have gone against the grain of the Roman designers. The portico was inscribed with the names of distant provinces of the empire – Dalmatia, Judaea, Mesopotamia, Syria and Laodicea – as well as Carthage and Thugga. They may all have been centres of the Caelestis cult.

An ancient residential quarter

Head back towards the city centre along the track which turns into a Roman street just below the Forum and runs past an imposing doorway to the right. This is now known by the Arab name of Dar el Acheb, and the original function of its courtyard is not known. Beyond Dar el Acheb, the main street cuts through the centre of the town's most exclusive residential quarter. Large houses are crammed into all available spaces on the narrow side streets, and it's hard to imagine how it once looked when the walls stood to their full height. As the street follows the contour of the hill around, one sharp left and a left again leads between houses to the **Temple of Tellus** (Earth), dated to 261 AD and identifiable by a small peristyle (columned courtyard) leading to a sanctuary room with niches in the far wall, a recognizably African temple pattern. Further round the hill, the **House of Dionysus and Ulysses** is named after the famous mosaic of Ulysses tied to the mast of his ship while the Sirens sing; it's now in the Bardo (see p.93).

By now you are below the fortress-like remains of the **Licinian Baths**. Look for a barrel-vaulted passage – originally a tradesmen's entrance – which takes you into the baths from here. The official entrance was down some steep steps into a room on the northwest side of the complex, where mosaics and columns still stand. A headless statue here provides an eerie reminder of the forgotten bourgeoisie who placed such store by this sort of facility, and quite probably it represented one of the Licinii family who donated the baths to the city in the third century AD. The large central room was the *frigidarium*, which opened through a smaller *tepidarium* to the southwest on to the *caldarium*, situated above the tradesmen's entrance and facing south to catch the sun. In the other direction, the large peristyle room in the northeast corner was the *palaestra*, a sort of training room for athletes.

Continuing along the main street, then right at its end, the large **House of the Trefoil** has had its history censored – a stone with a relief of a phallus used to stand outside the door, identifying the town brothel, until it was removed some 1800 years later by authorities concerned for tourist sensibilities. A staircase leads down between two standing columns to a wide courtyard surrounded by rooms, one (its roof heavily restored) in the clover-leaf shape that provides the building's name – a name that carefully avoids any suggestion of the house's original function.

Beside the brothel stood a small private **baths complex**, now named after the magnificent mosaic in the Bardo of three bodybuilder Cyclopes swinging their hammers to forge Jupiter's thunderbolts. The baths were presumably connected with the brothel and still contain a well-preserved row of **toilet seats**.

The Arch of Septimius Severus and the Libyco-Punic Mausoleum

Heading down the hill past the baths leads eventually to the **Triumphal Arch of Septimius Severus**, built in 205 AD, a few years before the one near the Caelestis Temple. A track originally left the city through this arch to join the main road below from Carthage. Septimius Severus, who came from Libya, was the founder of the dynasty of Roman emperors which ended with Alexander Severus (dedicatee of the

Triumphal Arch near the Caelestis temple). It was Septimius's wife whose accent was notorious at Rome; but not that of the emperor himself, according to one tactful poet: "Your speech is not Carthaginian, nor your dress, nor is your spirit foreign: you are Italian, Italian . . .".

A track to the right, just before the arch, winds down to the **Libyco-Punic Mausoleum**, built in the second century BC for "Ateban, son of Ieptamath, son of Palu", which is important as one of the few surviving examples of pre-Roman monumental building in Tunisia. Although the mausoleum managed to survive the Roman Empire more or less intact, in 1842 it fell victim to the British Empire when the British consul, Sir Thomas Reade, dismantled it so as to get at the bilingual inscription which provides the names above. The inscription remains in the British Museum in London, where it permitted the deciphering of Libyco-Phoenician for the first time. Ironically, it was with the help of a sketch by James Bruce that the French authorities reconstructed the mausoleum at the turn of the century.

Like other remnants of immediately pre-Roman North Africa – the sarcophagi in the Carthage Museum (see p.107), for example, and the temple at Chemtou (see p.166) which is currently being reconstructed – the mausoleum is a melange of different influences. Greek culture contributed the Ionic order in the second storey, but most of the elements are recognizably more Eastern, influenced by Carthage's Phoenician links; the overall form is similar to Anatolian and Syrian monuments, and the lotus-flower pilaster capitals on the corners of the first and third storeys speak with an Egyptian accent.

The Temple of Minerva and around

On the summit of the hill behind the Capitol are a few traces of the pre-Roman town, as well as some peripheral Roman structures. A track which veers right, uphill, from the Roman road between the theatre and Capitol leads past a group of seven massive **cisterns** on the right, each 35m long and 5m wide, with newly restored pink roofs. An aqueduct fed water into these from the spring located a little way west. Above the cisterns, a **Temple of Minerva**, built in the second century AD, follows the African pattern, with a colonnaded courtyard leading into a sanctuary room. Beyond the temple, the track runs along what looks like a long, flat field that was once the municipal **Hippodrome**. Two small heaps of rubble facing each other 190m apart were the ends of the *spina*, the central barrier around which the chariot races were run. If this seems like a bleak kind of place to watch a chariot race, sitting on the bare rocks opposite, the man who donated the land to the city in 214 AD knew better – he provided it "ad voluptates populi" (for the pleasure of the people), and numerous mosaics in museums around the country support his judgement.

Back to the east, beyond the end of the *spina*, is an area of **dolmen tombs** dating from the third century BC to the first century AD, sited just below the walls of the Numidian city, of which some remains and even a tower can be seen behind.

Teboursouk

For most tourists, **TEBOURSOUK**, 30km south of Beja, is simply a point of transit on the way to Dougga. While it's probably not worth visiting for its own sake, there is enough to repay a brief wander – it is a venerable and attractive market town in its own right, with a Thursday **souk** just off the main road to Le Kef, and a Byzantine **fortress** dominated by a **marabout** clinging to the hill above. Like Dougga, just along the valley side, it affords balcony views south over the broad agricultural lands of the Tell.

The only place to **stay** in town is the *Maison des Jeunes* **youth hostel** (☎08/465095; ①), otherwise there's the two-star *Hôtel Thugga* below the town on the main road

(☎08/465713; ③), with various Roman artefacts tastefully arranged outside. **Buses** stop by a roundabout in the centre of town, with hourly services to Testour (20min), Le Kef (40min), Medjez el Bab (1hr) and Tunis (2hr 20min), and two a day to Thibar (30min) and Beja (1hr). **Louages** stop opposite and serve Beja, Gaafour, Medjez el Bab, Nouvelle Dougga, Thibar and Tunis.

Mustis

Twenty kilometres after Teboursouk, the road to Le Kef runs past a well-preserved triumphal arch standing casually by the side of the road. This was the outskirts of Roman **Mustis** (free access), today a site of middling-to-limited interest whose central ruins sit right by the edge of the road near an attractive **zaouia** a little further along.

Mustis was originally an unremarkable farming town much like modern Le Krib, a kilometre further down the road. On the left of the entrance sit remains of the **temples** of Ceres and Apollo. Then a paved Roman street leads uphill through an arch, with two massive pieces from an olive press leaning against a wall at the top of the street; the remains of the structure they came from are recognizable over to the left, beyond the **Temple of Pluto**. Just north of here are traces of a three-aisled Christian **church** ending in an apse.

From here you can already see the walls of the Byzantine **fort** that dominate the site – a sign that Mustis, like so many other similar towns, ended its life as a frontier outpost. From inside, the fort offers a vivid sense of the precariousness of life at the turn of an era. Perhaps this is because it is smaller than the likes of Aïn Tounga or Haidra, and there is barely room for it to contain everything the inhabitants would have needed, like cisterns, living quarters and defensive walls.

Le Kef (El Kef)

The first sign of **LE KEF**, just 45km east of the Algerian border, is a gleaming ribbon of rock that twists round Jebel Dyr just below the mountain's summit. Clinging just below the southern end of the table top is the old town, while the newer quarters spill ever wider down the hillside below. It's a breathtaking setting – the more so in its isolation close to the Algerian border – and the kind of place where you feel involved just wandering round, contemplating the vistas below. But there's more than just views here: the town's long history has left a legacy of monuments, and it has also recently acquired an interesting regional culture museum.

Some history

Although still regarded as the unofficial capital of western Tunisia, Le Kef's historic predecessors enjoyed more prominence. The area was inhabited very early: Neolithic hunters left their tools nearby and the Numidians built megalithic tombs here before the urban centre entered history as Carthaginan **Sicca** after the Second Punic War. Unable to pay its defeated mercenary army, Carthage packed them off here, a gesture which rebounded when the mercenaries rose in revolt to wage a four-year struggle in which they were only suppressed with the aid of yet more mercenaries. The war – of a legendary brutality – inspired Flaubert's blood and guts novel *Salammbô*, which includes a chapter entitled "Sicca". The town was annexed in 46 BC by the Romans, who added the title "Veneria", giving it a rather dubious name. The Arabs, who took it in 688, called it *Chakbanaria*, but renamed it El Kef ("The Rock") in the seventeenth century.

Since the Islamic conquest, Le Kef's strategic position between the Tunisian hinterland and the Algerian interior has put it at the centre of so many inter-factional strug-

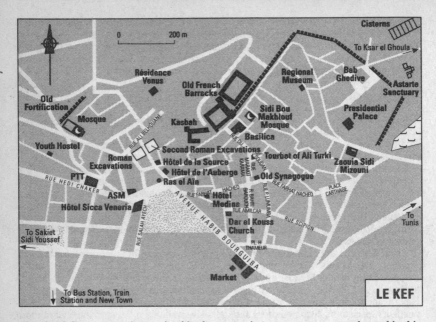

gles that it has never quite regained its former eminence – a process accelerated in this century when the train line to Algeria was built through Jendouba and Ghardimaou to the north. Algerians have, however, had occasion to be thankful for Le Kef, which was the main base and command centre of the FLN (Algerian armed resistance) until 1962.

In the years since Independence the town has felt itself a victim of the national bias towards the Sahel region – feelings which erupted particularly strongly in the 1984 troubles. For a town of its size it is desperately short of work and recreational outlets, and even though the townspeople are proud to have one of the largest schools in Africa, the pupils it educates find little employment here.

Arrival and accommodation

The **train station** is right at the bottom of the hill, but the **bus** and **louage** stations stand about halfway up, from where it's a short walk past the modern administrative buildings to the town centre. The road at the top of the hill heads left towards Sakiet Sidi Youssef, or right to **place de l'Indépendance** at the centre of town. Rue Hedi Chaker heads east from here, and continues down past the **PTT** (city hours) to meet the Sakiet Sidi Youssef road. There is no tourist office in town, just the friendly and enthusiastic Romdhane Ayachi in the **ASM office** on place de l'Indépendance in the upper town (hours variable; weekday mornings best), which promotes interest in Le Kef's history and functions as a tourist office; it also serves as an unofficial social club.

Le Kef has several **hotels**, including one of Tunisia's most memorable, the *Hôtel de la Source*, and a decent youth hostel.

Hotels

Hôtel de l'Auberge, rue de la Source (✆08/220036). A couple of doors from the *Source*, the *Auberge* is reasonably clean but a bit gloomy. ①.

Medina, 18 rue Farhat Hached (☎08/220214). Newer than the *Hôtel de l'Auberge*, with clean, pleasant rooms, but no hot water – there's a hammam up the street at no. 33. ①.

Nouvelle Ere, 59 rue Habib Karma (no phone). At the very bottom of the scale and extremely basic. ①.

Sicca Veneria ★, av Bourguiba (☎08/221561). Formerly Le Kef's most comfortable abode, with all mod cons and a choice of bath or shower, but now beginning to show its age. ③.

Hôtel de la Source, rue de la Source, near the beginning of av Bourguiba (☎08/221397). Rather wonderful if a bit seedy, with a lovely air of fading decadence. It has a legendary room, the four-bed *chambre de famille*, where a huge double bed reposes under an ornate vaulted stucco ceiling; this may be the nearest you'll come to sleeping like an eighteenth-century Tunisian bey, give or take the odd grubby sheet (check them first). ①.

Résidence Venus, off rue Ali Belhouane (☎08/224695). A friendly, laid-back pension recently opened by the owners of the restaurant of the same name, who can also give you complicated directions to find it. It's five minutes' walk west of pl de l'Indépendance, and if your budget's up to it, this is the best bet in town. ③.

Walid, on the Dahami road, 1.5km south of the town centre (no phone). A new unclassified hotel behind the Ministry of Transport building with nothing going for it unless everywhere else is full. ①.

Youth hostel

Maison des Jeunes youth hostel, 8 rue Mohamed Gammoudi (☎08/220424). Very friendly and right in town near the PTT. ①.

The Town

Le Kef – or plain Kef as it's usually known – is a great place just to wander at random, catching glimpses, between houses or over the trees in the park, of the plains below. The old quarters huddle below the southern end of the mountain plateau, with the new districts spreading out down the slope below. From the central **place de l'Indépendance**, **avenue Bourguiba** follows the curve of the hill round to the right, a tremendous belvedere for the chequered plains below.

On the uphill side of avenue Bourguiba is the **Medina**, with narrow cobbled streets winding up to the Kasbah at the cliff's edge. The Medina's main street is **rue Farhat Hached**, which begins at avenue Bourguiba near place de l'Indépendance; a third of the way along it is the old synagogue. Here rue Marakit Karama ascends to the Basilica in **place Bou Makhlouf** and to the **Kasbah** beyond that, while rue Bahri Barbouch drops to place Habib Thameur, just off avenue Bourguiba above the market.

Place de l'Indépendance and around

Place de l'Indépendance forms the heart of the town, but is little more than a crowded traffic junction bordered on the south side by a park. Just north of here, the **spring** of *Ras el Aïn* rises in the open space just below the *Hôtel de la Source* on the square; it has always supplied the cities on this site, receiving cult reverence through the centuries. Roman blocks which channelled the water can be made out. Just next to the locked door of the spring proper is a small niche, a **shrine** to a supposed Islamic saint called Lalla Mna; in fact she was originally a Roman nymph, now renamed and Islamicized. Hers is still a living cult, and there are often recent offerings in the niche.

Back along rue de la Source, past the **Mosque of Sidi Ahmed Gharib**, is a confused area of **Roman remains** which are permanently but slowly in the process of being excavated and restored. Above the street is the entrance to a huge Roman **cistern** which stored the water that fed the more interesting complex across the street. Here at the far end is a **nympheum**, or fountain, which would have been lined with statues, and a **baths complex**, which contained the impressibly solid hexagonal room.

The baths were subsequently converted into a church whose geometric mosaics are visible. A wall is lined with the tombstones of Roman worthies. Before emerging onto rue Ali Belhouane, rue de la Source runs through an attractive old **vaulted passage** containing food shops.

The Medina

Le Kef's main attraction is its **Medina**, which has managed to retain not just monuments from successive periods in its history, but also a neighbourhood feeling, away from the bustle of the new town. Closest of the monuments is the well-preserved **Dar el Kouss Church** – take the first right off rue Farhat Hached immediately after it leaves avenue Bourguiba, and the church is on the first corner. Dating from the fourth century, it has been restored for use as an open-air theatre, but is currently closed to the public. A small room in its far right-hand corner has a curiously carved lintel stone combining a Greek cross and a palm frond.

Rejoin rue Farhat Hached and turn right to meet rue Marakit Karama going up the hill and rue Bahri Barbouch coming down it. With rue **Bahri Barbouch** you take a leap forward to Turkish times, when the street was reserved for the town's Jewish community. The building on the northeast corner of this junction is the former **synagogue**, recently – and remarkably, here in the distant interior of an Arab country – restored. The synagogue's walls are now lined with items evoking the not-so-distant world of Tunisia's Jewish community, such as Hebrew tablets, photos of local life in the 1950s and a wedding invitation from 1960. You should be able to find a *gardien* to let you in.

Le Kef was one of three *ghribas* in the eastern Maghreb – the other two being in Annaba, Algeria (presumably disappeared) and Jerba (see p.328). The town had a sizeable Jewish community, though virtually all left for Tunis, France or Israel in the years following World War II and especially during Independence. Their traditional specialization in jewellery lives on in the shops which line rue Bahri Barbouch, where you will also find spectacular wedding costumes and one small jewellery shop with a fine old painted wooden shade.

Racial segregation was once common in North African towns, and the next street along – formerly **rue des Nègres** – used to be the centre of the black community. Following the abolition of slavery in 1846, black people became a free community, and today there's little difference in culture or lifestyle between black and white Tunisians.

It was during Turkish times, with the rise and internecine struggles of the Husaynid dynasty, that Le Kef was most directly involved in recent Tunisian history. The father of Husayn Bin Ali, the dynasty's founder, is entombed just up the hill. You pass his somewhat derelict **Tourbet of Ali Turki** at the top of rue Bahri Barbouch and rue du Soudan. Ali Turki was born in Crete but came to Tunisia and enrolled in the army during the reign of Murad Bey. While serving in Le Kef he married two local Tunisian women, each of whom gave birth to a son: one of them was Husayn Bin Ali, founder of the Husaynid dynasty (ruled 1705–35, see p.367), the other was the father of Ali Pasha, Husayn's successor (ruled 1735–56).

Carry on up along rue du Soudan and you'll come up to **place Bou Makhlouf**, an open space below the Kasbah that lay at the heart of the souks of the old town. Here was the town's Great Mosque, the monumental building now known as the **Basilica**, which was used for hundreds of years for Muslim worship. For much of that time it had a minaret, which was only dismantled to be reused elsewhere in the town after Independence, when the building was secularized and returned to its current state. The building now serves as a **museum** of local antiquities (daily 8–11am & 3–6pm; free), although it is more interesting for its own sake – even though very little is known for certain about its origins. Built either in late Roman or Byzantine times, it takes the form of a spacious courtyard (look for columns of unusual green stone) which leads into a cruciform room ending in an apse. Both the apse and the arms of the cross are lined with niches (23 in all), with a carved lintel running above them.

The diminutive **Mosque of Sidi Bou Makhlouf** at the end of place Bou Makhlouf, along with the complex of streets around it, is one of the most captivating spots in Tunisia. The mosque – named after the patron saint of Le Kef, who originally came from Fez – is a small masterpiece, the bare whitewashed courtyard leading into a domed prayer hall resting on antique columns and lined with white stuccowork. On the outside, its dome has an unusual ribbed appearance. At the beginning of the nineteenth century this complex became home to Le Kef's branch of the Aissaouia *sufi* brotherhood, renowned for some of the more outlandish *sufi* rituals. On one side of the cobbled street leading up to the mosque is a blue door into a former *foundouk* which has a Roman tombstone for a tap in its central water trough. Opposite it is the *Café of the Souks*, sadly now open only during the month of Ramadan, but the perfect place to sit and watch the changing patterns of light over the plains – magical under a full moon.

The Kasbah

Another place to admire the view is the **Kasbah** above, recently abandoned by the army. The smaller and lower of the **forts** here is a legacy of the border struggles under the Beys: Hammouda Bey added it in 1813 to house a guard of ultra-faithful troops, stationed here to guard against Algerian designs on the town. Excavations here during the current refurbishment uncovered the remains of innumerable Turkish clay pipes made in Smyrna (now Izmir) on Turkey's Aegean coast. The older, larger fort dates back to 1601 and was converted into a prison for Tunisian nationalists, with its Beau Geste cells, a French sentry box and Turkish gateway.

The Kasbah is now being renovated to house a **cultural centre** in the large fort, with a cinema, open-air theatre and cultural archives, and a hotel and bar-restaurant in the small fort; the dungeons will become a small museum. All this will no doubt be very twee – and is already viewed unenthusiastically in some quarters – but at the very least will increase Le Kef's recreational facilities. The project is not yet complete, and meanwhile the Kasbah is open to the public and entry is free.

Follow rue el Kasbah round above the Basilica and rue Sidi Bou Makhlouf to place Ben Aissa, where you'll find the worthy **regional museum** (daily except Mon 9am–3.30pm; 0.8TD), housed in a restored *zaouia*. Exhibits concentrate on and beautifully evoke the way of life of the nomads whose tents are still to be seen on the surrounding plain. Put up in 1784, the building that houses the museum was originally the headquarters of a *sufi* religious brotherhood called the **Rahmania**.

The old town walls run almost continuously from the Kasbah around to the east, finally encircling a **presidential palace**. This is something of a sore point in the town, as it occupies a prime site but is hardly ever used; a swimming pool beckons invitingly in its grounds, while the municipal pool in the park has never been opened. Just below the palace walls is the nineteenth-century **Zaouia of Sidi Mizouni**, or Zaouia of the Qadriya.

Bab Ghedive and beyond

Just above the palace, **Bab Ghedive** ("Gate of Treachery") gives entrance to the town and earned its name in 1881 when the governor and town notables, having received no orders to fight, opened the gate to the French army on its "temporary mission" – even though the townspeople were prepared for a long siege. They surrendered the most important frontier defences without a shot being fired.

Once through the gate, the transition from town to country is startlingly abrupt. Just ahead, an iron ladder leads down into a vast **Roman cistern** that's twelve gloomy chambers in length and one of the coolest places in Kef – but an alcoholics' den at night.

Over to the right from here, across the road, are more fragmentary remains, the first set of which may be the ancient **Sanctuary of Astarte**, so notorious for its erotic mysteries. Roman moralists professed shock that young Carthaginian girls of noble birth were forced to sacrifice their virginity here to the goddess, ensuring the fertility of the land on which Sicca depended, but it was the Romans who gave the town the suffix "Veneria". Sex still enjoyed a high profile here in Christian times; the second area of remains, below the disused **Christian cemetery**, may have been the **Ksar el Ghoula Basilica**, which reputedly possessed a magic mirror; men who suspected their wives of infidelity could look at the glass and find the face of their rival. Beyond it, a **Jewish cemetery** stretches all the way back to the wall, the part nearest to it being much older than the rest of the Jewish and Christian cemeteries.

Eating and drinking

For **food**, *Restaurant el Andalous*, in rue Hedi Chaker opposite the PTT, is cheap and highly recommended. They do salad with homemade mayonnaise and great couscous. The *Restaurant de l'Afrique* two doors down, *Des Amis* on the steps by the *Hôtel de l'Auberge*, and *El Hana*, in avenue Bourguiba above the market, are all similarly priced.

For a smarter meal, try the *Hôtel Sicca*'s restaurant. Alternatively, if you've never had supper at a filling station, the *Esso Restaurant*, above the pumps in rue Hedi Chaker, 50m past the PTT, serves a surprisingly good meal. A final more upmarket alternative is the *Restaurant Venus*.

If you want to **drink** in the evening, try the *Hôtel de l'Auberge*'s bar (which does food too) – but don't expect instant service. There's also a cheap, unnamed bar-restaurant up behind the PTT at 4 rue Salya. The *Sicca*'s bar is only slightly more refined than these two.

Listings

Banks There are several banks around town, especially at the top of rue Salah Ayech and rue Ali Belhouane; others in av Bourguiba above the market, and opposite the bus station on the hill down into the new town. They run a weekend rota, so there should be at least one open Sat & Sun am.

Cinemas *Ciné Pathe*, av Bourguiba (not signposted and, in fact, not easily identified).

Consulates The Algerian consulate is right down the bottom of rue Hedi Chaker at no. 3. You could try them for a visa, but they will probably tell you to go to Tunis and apply there.

Hammam Pl Habib Thameur, at the bottom of rue Habib Karmna, and one at 33 rue Farhat Hached.

MOVING ON FROM LE KEF

The bus and louage station is on the hill between the old and new towns, about halfway down on the left. There are **buses running** hourly to Medjez el Bab (1hr 30min), Teboursouk (40min), Testour (1hr) and Tunis (3hr), six a day to Jendouba (1hr 10min), Kalaa Khasbah (1hr 30min) and Thala (1hr 45min), five to Tajerouine (30min) and Kasserine (4hr), three to Beja (2hr), two daily departures to Fahs (2hr), Kairouan (3hr 30min), Sakiet Sidi Youssef (1hr), Sfax (4hr 30min), Sidi Bou Zid (3hr) and Sousse (3hr 45min), and one daily departure for Bizerte (4hr), Gafsa (4hr 45min), Maktar (2hr), Nabeul (4hr) and Ras Ajdir on the Libyan border (8hr).

Louages serve El Ksour, Jendouba, Kalaa Khasbah, Kalaat es Senam, Tajerouine and Tunis. The **train station** is right down the bottom of the hill, rather pretty and well-kept, but with only one very early departure to Sers (30min), Le Krib (1hr), Gaafour (1hr 30min), Fahs (4hr) and Tunis (5hr 30min).

Medical facilities There is a hospital on the Sakiet Sidi Youssef road (☎08/420900), and a night pharmacy in rue Souk Ahras – turn right just before the PTT in rue Hedi Chaker and it's 100m up on your left.

PTT Rue Hedi Chaker (city hours); international phones.

Supermarket *Monoprix* is 100m off to the left of the hill down into the new town, about halfway down, just above the bus station.

Around Le Kef

If the view across the plains around Le Kef tempts you, there are several good hiking possibilities and particularly rewarding excursions. One of the best short walks is to **SIDI MANSOUR**, a small village around 4km north of town. Leave Kef by Bab Ghedive and scramble up the rocks below the TV mast. A rough path leads north through a small eucalyptus plantation and onto the top of the plateau, opening out on an immense view over the broken forests along the Algerian border and the glint of the lake behind the Mellegue Dam. The village, a small farming community, is soon reached; its spring water is locally reputed, but for what it's difficult to establish. Just to the west, beyond a deep river canyon, are wide caves gouged in the rock – a popular picnic spot inhabited in prehistoric times. North of the village, it isn't far to the other end of the plateau; or you can climb up to the east, then bend down and around and come back into Kef by the palace.

The artificial **Lake Mellegue** that's visible from Sidi Mansour, gleaming in the distance, was created by damming the River Mellegue. Buses head out in this direction from Kef to the attractive village of **NEBEUR**, 17km northeast below the northern tip of the mountain of Jebel Dyr, and then 5km on to **BARRAGE MELLEGUE**, a small cluster of houses on the dam itself. The water crashing out at the bottom is the colour and consistency of liquid chocolate. The reason for coming to the dam, though, is to walk back to Kef through open country – a five-hour hike, but a rewarding one. There's no danger of getting lost since Jebel Dyr is always in sight and, once you get to the mountain, Kef is only 5km further on.

If you aim for the top of **Jebel Dyr**, then head round its western face below the cliff edge, you should hit a winding tractor track which runs all the way to Sidi Mansour. At first it climbs through clumps of pines, foothills of the mountain proper, then emerges on to broader slopes which sweep up like waves against the rock. The scenery is tremendous, but it's only part of the value of the hike. Just as impressive is the insight you gain into the pace of life in the countryside of Tunisia, and above all the dominating need for water. When you set out on the walk, take as much as you can carry, but even so you'll probably need refills. For these you're dependent on the infrequent springs that isolated local farmhouses rely on for all their daily needs. When you finally reach a small pipe, you're usually surrounded by a group of children who have walked several kilometres with donkeys and cans to fetch the day's supply.

At the other end of Lake Mellegue, the restored Roman spa of **Hammam Mellegue** is at the end of a 12km piste off the road to Sakiet, 10km west of Le Kef. Hot spring water provides a communal bath (women in the morning, men in the afternoon), which is very popular with people from the surrounding villages. Walking is the only sure way of getting to it, though you might try sticking your thumb out just in case. Alternatively, ask around for a lift at the market in Le Kef.

Thirty-five kilometres west of Le Kef, **SAKIET SIDI YOUSSEF** is the last village before the Algerian frontier. The border post here is sometimes open, and accessible from Le Kef by *louage*, but you should check on this before setting out – the main crossing is 30km north at Ghardimaou (see p.165). The Algerian consulate in Le Kef might know the latest situation; on the other hand, they might just feed you an unhelpful story with no bearing on reality when you actually get there.

There's little other reason for visiting Sakiet, although it does have a historical notoriety. It was here, in the midst of the Algerian War in 1958, that the French bombed the civilian population. The incident was denounced as a "new Guernica" and caused a rapid decline in relations between France and newly independent Tunisia. One outcome was the Tunisian attempt to eject the French navy from their base at Bizerte.

South of Le Kef

The area **south of Le Kef** – before the fertile plains climb up onto bleaker steppes around Kasserine – is right off the tourist routes. Yet, using Le Kef as a base, it's a quietly rewarding region to explore. The scenery, always impressive, becomes eerily compelling around the craggy mountain of **Jugurtha's Table**, and there are two unexcavated but well-preserved Roman sites at **Medeina** and **Haidra**. Each of these – particularly Haidra – has an aloof grandeur in its remoteness, inspiring an excitement quite absent from the more domesticated major sites.

Tajerouine and Jugurtha's Table

TAJEROUINE is the first town of any size on the main road, 25km south of Le Kef, and is quite a transport centre. The **bus** station is in the middle of town on the main road, with plenty of buses to Le Kef and Sakiet Sidi Youssef. **Louages** stop nearby, down a road next to the mosque. Tajerouine has a **Monday souk**, and there are **banks** and a *Magasin Général* **supermarket** opposite the bus station, but no hotel and little character: it's hardly more than a roadside sprawl.

But beyond the town, you emerge on to the plains – vast open spaces with jutting isolated **mountains** that bob like ships on a calm sea. There is a good deal of mining on the plain, with major producers of iron and phosphates dotted about here.

The place to head for, however, to reap the best rewards of the scenery around here, is **KALAAT ES SENAM**. Just 6km from the Algerian border, this small village sits at the foot of the mountain known as **Jugurtha's Table**, a flat-topped peak like Jebel Dyr to the north but more sharply defined, with its tilting plateau standing out for miles around. *Louages* go to Kalaat es Senam either direct from Le Kef or with a change at Tajerouine. Stock up with water while you can, because it's a good two hours' walk from the village to the steps in the middle of the mountain's north side, though the steps themselves make for an easy ascent.

The name Jugurtha's Table refers to the tradition that it was the stronghold of the Numidian king **Jugurtha** in his second-century BC struggles against the Romans; a role echoed in more recent times by the name of Kalaat es Senam – "Seat of Senam" – after a local bandit who made similar use of the mountain against the armies of the Beys. With the surrounding scenery so reminiscent of the American southwest, comparisons with Butch Cassidy and the Hole-in-the-Wall gang are irresistible. This dramatic past seems very close as you climb the steps to the summit, which are hacked into the rock and lead to a Byzantine gateway. The lunar-like surface is littered with remains which include troglodyte **caves** and a spooky **marabout**. Romance apart, the mountain also provides a magnificent view, and if you have the equipment, it's an extraordinary place to spend the night. At the last visit, the only visible inhabitants were six overheated cows – how they got up there is a mystery.

Kalaa Khasbah and Haidra Town

KALAA KHASBAH (also known as Kalaa Jerda) is an old Italian mining town still redolent of the colonial presence, with its tiled houses, profuse greenery and aban-

TRAVELLING TO ALGERIA

A deteriorating security climate means that as of mid-1995 it was not advisable for foreigners – particularly Westerners – to visit Algeria on a casual basis. You should also be aware of heightened Tunisian sensitivities when travelling near the Algerian border – passport checks will be more frequent than normal, and you should think hard before going off the beaten track anywhere near the border. See p.376 for more details.

doned mining machinery, including an enormous chimney stack. But the real reason for coming here is to find transport to the Roman site of Haidra, just down the road.

This is the terminal for passenger **train** services, and it gets three trains a day to Tunis (5hr 30min) via Sers (1hr 40min), Gaafour (2hr 45min) and Fahs (4hr); even though Haidra is on the train line, there are no passenger trains further than Kalaa Khasbah. There are five onward **buses** daily to Thala (2hr) and Kasserine (2hr 30min), and six to Le Kef (1hr 30min), with **louages** to Thala and Kasserine. **Hitching** to Haidra from Kalaa Khasbah is quite easy – there's only one road, so virtually everything that passes will stop. On your way back down this road, look out to the north for glimpses of Jugurtha's Table, ducking above and below the skyline – more than ever reminiscent of the prow of a ship. The modern settlement of **HAIDRA TOWN** has even more of a dead-end border feel than Ghardimaou, enlivened only by a grotesque **train station**. With its extraordinary combination of Classical order and 1930s Deco, this would look weird anywhere, let alone miles from anywhere on a North African frontier. The **border post** here is usually open, but little used.

Haidra

The Roman site of **Haidra** (free entry), 18km southwest of Kalaa Khasbah, is remotely positioned by the Algerian frontier and only minimally excavated, meaning that the surviving monuments are exceptionally well preserved. Coming upon them, you feel something of the awe early travellers must have experienced when confronted with remains of a mysterious and magnificent past.

Ancient Haidra, Roman *Ammaedara*, was in its way a border post like the modern village of the same name, founded as a base for the Third Augustan Legion, whose job was to protect Rome's new province from hostile incursions. When the Legion was moved further west, the camp became an important town – but after the Islamic conquest reverted to its border role.

The ruins sprawl beside the road just to the east of the modern settlement. If you've got a ride in from Kalaa Khasbah, you might want to get yourself dropped off outside the Byzantine fort at the centre of the ancient remains, opposite a French customs post dated 1886, whose military occupants are sensitive about cameras.

The site

East of the customs post, identifiable by a hemispherical arch, are the remains of Haidra's "building with troughs" (see also p.253). A **Vandal Chapel** behind it is so called because of the crude inscriptions in its paving stones dating it to the reigns of the kings Thrasamund (510 AD) and Ildirix (526 AD), who sound as though they come from an Asterix and Obelix storyline.

On the west side of the customs post, a **market** can just about be made out as a square depression, followed by the **Capitol** temple with only its podium recognizable, and then the more interesting **Basilica of Melleus**, featuring two rows of columns, some in Chemtou marble, clearly defining the nave. Entrance to the church was through three doors at the eastern end, which connected with a courtyard. An apsidal

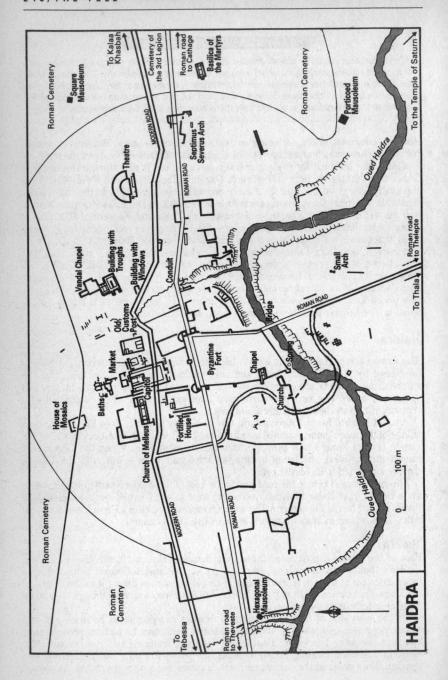

HAIDRA

Roman Cemetery

Square Mausoleum

To Kalaa Khasbah

Cemetery of the 3rd Legion

Roman road to Carthage

Basilica of the Martyrs

Roman Cemetery

To the Temple of Saturn

Porticoed Mausoleum

Theatre

MODERN ROAD

Septimus Severus Arch

ROMAN ROAD

Oued Haidra

Vandal Chapel

Building with Troughs

Building with Windows

Conduit

Small Arch

Roman road to Thelepte

ROMAN ROAD

To Thala

Bridge

Old Customs Post

Market

Baths

Capitol

Byzantine Fort

Chapel

Spring

Church of Melleus

Fortified House

Church

House of Mosaics

Roman Cemetery

0   100 m

Roman Cemetery

MODERN ROAD

ROMAN ROAD

Hexagonal Mausoleum

Oued Haidra

To Tebessa

Roman road to Theveste

MAN BITES LION

The area around Haidra was notorious among early European travellers for the lawlessness of its inhabitants. Although James Bruce, passing this way in 1765, managed to avoid mortal danger, he did have a curious gastronomic experience. A recent predecessor, one Dr Shaw, had claimed that the inhabitants of Haidra ate lions, but was promptly accused of "traveller's licence" by the learned doctors of Oxford University, who "took it as a subversion of the natural order of things, that a man should eat a lion, when it has long passed as almost the peculiar province of the lion to eat man". Ever the vigorous empiricist, Bruce was not much impressed by expert opinion, and was glad to be able to report that he had "eaten the flesh of three lions – that is part of three lions – in the tents of the Welled Sidi Boogannim". He found the texture like old horse flesh, palatable except for a strong smell of musk. As for the locals, he sniffed, "a brutish and ignorant folk, they will, I fear, notwithstanding the disbelief of the University of Oxford, continue to eat lions as long as they exist."

---

structure at the western end was the *presbyterium*, reserved for clergy. Spidery inscriptions from the sixth and seventh centuries, still visible in the paving stones, suggest something of Haidra's turbulent history. They include the gravestones of two bishops buried here – Victorinus, a Vandal Aryan Christian, and Melleus, a Byzantine Catholic.

Across the road from the Basilica lies a fortifed house, and over to the east the five empty windows of a **"building with windows"**, whose function is not known. Behind looms the northern wall of the mother of all Byzantine **fortresses** in Tunisia. Built to guard an important frontier crossroads when the Byzantines retook Tunisia from the Vandals in 533 AD, its north wall was rebuilt much later under the Turks. Two hundred metres long by a hundred metres wide, with stretches of wall and towers still standing ten metres high, the fortress stretches down to the river valley at the bottom of the hill. Roads from Carthage and Tebessa entered through fortified towers at the top of the fortress, while the road from Thelepte crossed a Roman **bridge**, whose remains can still be seen in the river bed, and then entered through the southeastern tower. The interior presents a jumble of unexcavated remains except for the evocative **chapel**, built against the southwest wall, with its apse and green columns. Sit alone for a while, with the wind from Algeria and the sound of cocks crowing in the village, and watch the donkey traffic coming to the spring in the river bank below the fortress's southwest corner. If smaller Byzantine fortresses such as Mustis reek of panic on the frontier, this one conveys instead the determination, however doomed, of a Byzantine empire based thousands of kilometres away to defend what it saw as its rightful inheritance.

The site's eastern outskirts contain two well-preserved square **mausoleums**, the golden-coloured southern one with its four-columned second storey standing in splendid isolation above the river. Between them, next to the modern road, stands the **triumphal arch** of Septimius Severus (195 AD). Like the arch at Maktar and the Capitol at Dougga, this owes its crisp preservation to fortifications that the Byzantines built around it; here, the Byzantine work has been only partially dismantled, and the arch emerging from its casing looks for all the world like a piece of sculpture coming out of a plaster cast. West of the site, again just above the river, stands another well-preserved **mausoleum** – this time hexagonal.

Thala

Continuing from Kalaa Khasbah to Kasserine, the only village of any size is **THALA**, 10km south of Kalaa, on the steep slope dividing the plains of Kef from the more forbidding steppes around Kasserine. At an altitude of 1017m, it is a refreshing place in summer but a cold one in midwinter. The village's only claim to fame is a notorious incident in 1906, when a marabout, **Amor Ben Othman**, inspired the local Fraichich tribes to take up arms against the colonists who had stolen their lands. In the ensuing riot sixteen men, women and children died, causing an outcry across North Africa. Amor Ben Othman was brought to trial and the press clamoured for his execution. Only Myriam Harry, a reporter on *Le Temps*, cared to look behind the scenes and describe the poverty and deprivation suffered by the Fraichich tribe as a consequence of colonization. "Oh little Joan of Arc of this desert," she wrote, "what pity you inspire in me." Unfortunately her sympathy was inadequate protection for the marabout and his accomplices. All were hanged with great ceremony as a warning to others.

There are a few minor **excavations** on the main street in Thala, and a **marble factory** in the lower outskirts of the village, but, unless you arrive on a Friday, market day, they make little enough reason to linger. Should you want to **stay**, the *Hôtel Bouthelja* (no phone; ②), just off the main street, is reasonable enough. There are also a couple of cheap **restaurants** and a **bank**. Up the hill, there's an *STK* **bus station**, with five daily services to Kasserine (45min), and six to both Tajerouine (30min) and Le Kef (1hr 45min); opposite is a **louage stop** for Kasserine and Haidra. The *SNTRI* stop for the four daily buses to Tunis (5hr) is down the hill.

Medeina

Medeina, Roman *Althiburos*, isn't the easiest site in Tunisia to reach. You have to get the bus from Le Kef to Dahmani (also known as Ebba Ksour), a small tree-shaded farming town, and then walk or hitch 7km down the Jerissa road; the turning to Medeina is on the left,·and the site about a four-kilometre walk away.

Despite its present remoteness, Medeina once stood on the main Roman road from Carthage to Tebessa. Today its ruins are attractive enough, rambling above a green river bed, though hardly extensive. The first glimpse is of a third-century AD **Triumphal Arch**, almost hidden in a field to the left. Beyond, towards the centre of the site, the most distinctive building is the **Capitol**, just above the river bed, to one side of the paved **Forum**, opposite the remains of a **temple**. A street runs southeast through the Forum, and following it you find a well-preserved **fountain** on a street corner. Further in this direction are the remains of a **theatre**.

Back in the Forum, alongside the temple opposite the Capitol is the **House of Sixteen Bases**, whose name refers to the unusual reliefs on the bases of its inner portico. Some way north of here, across a stream bed, is the **Building of Aesclepia**. No-one knows its precise function, but having begun life as a private house it seems to have become the home of some sort of cult connected with the healing god Aesclepius. This explains the extraordinary number of baths found here, and the quality of the mosaics – most of them third- or fourth-century AD, and now removed to the Bardo Museum in Tunis.

Maktar and around

It's well worth going through the town of **MAKTAR** for the scenery alone. The road from Le Kef winds 60km through some preliminary foothills to Le Sers, a French railway town sitting in the middle of a vast natural bowl that contains some of the most fertile land in the country. Passing through Le Vieux Sers, a few kilometres further south, are a couple of rough tracks leading to the unexcavated but quite substantial remains of Roman *Assuras* at **ZANNFOUR** (6km), and of **ELLES** (9km), with megalithic tombs and a meagre Roman settlement that produced the Bardo's bizarre fourth-century mosaic of a stressed Venus being crowned by two female centaurs (see p.89).

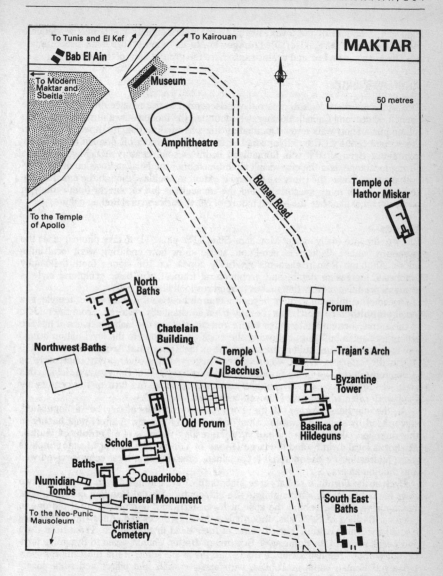

The main road goes on to climb up the side of the bowl, and on neighbouring hilltops beyond the rim are the ancient and modern towns of Maktar, separated by a modern road junction at a Roman triumphal arch.

Modern Maktar, across a ravine from the ancient town, is quite a tempting place to stay. At nearly 1000m altitude, the air is fresh, the scenery tremendous, and there's a relaxed feel to the town that can come as a welcome relief. **Market day** is Monday. **Buses** to and from Le Kef, Fahs, Kairouan and Kasserine leave from a balustraded road at the bottom of the town; nearby is the unpretentious but perfectly adequate *Hôtel Mactaris* (☎08/876014; ②). **Louages** are to be found on the main street higher up. The town's main **bar** and **restaurant** share the ground floor of the hotel.

Ancient Maktar

The site of **ancient Maktar** was only rediscovered in the nineteenth century by the French officer, one Captain Bordier, who founded the modern town on a neighbouring hilltop just a short walk away. Dominating the surrounding country, it was founded in the second century BC by a Numidian king trying to protect his domain from Berber incursions. Even after it was Romanized in the second century AD, Maktar kept a strong local tone, and the city wasn't abandoned until the Hilalian invasion of the eleventh century. Today the ruins are of similar extent to Sbeitla's, though the mountaintop setting is much more spectacular and the museum is full of objects (tombstones in particular) that illustrate the hybrid nature of North Africa's rural Roman culture.

The site

Entry to the **site** (daily except Mon 8am–5pm; 1TD, plus 1TD to take photos) is via the **museum**, whose displays of neo-Punic stelae show how enduring were local influences. Although Roman elements gradually appear on the stones (note the family emphasis, increasing depth, and architectural frames), the basic sculptural style is always a primitive naivety that makes the figures look like rag dolls.

Outside the museum garden, beyond a church built on top of an earlier temple, is a small **amphitheatre** which has recently been substantially restored. From the middle of the arena, surrounded by gates where you can still see the slots for doors, it has the feel of a Spanish bull ring. Following the track up the slope to the level hilltop brings you to a scant **Forum**, built at the same time as the **Triumphal Arch**, dedicated in 116 AD to the Emperor Trajan, whose career history still sounds pretty impressive as "Conqueror of the Germans, Armenians and Parthians". As at Dougga and Haidra, this arch was fortified by the Byzantines and used again at the turn of the century by Captain Bordier, who installed himself in the Southeast Baths.

At the northeast corner of the Forum, a **marketplace** can be distinguished, surrounded by stalls and with an altar dedicated to Mercury. A short walk further in this direction takes you to the not very interesting remains of a **Temple of Hathor Miskar**, a local divinity, and the large **House of Venus**. The Hathor Miskar temple is more interesting for the material it contained, revealing that local cults survived well into the Roman era.

Back at the Forum, a solitary tree just south of the triumphal arch stands over two rows of double columns belonging to the fifth-century Vandal **Basilica of Hildeguns**. Its baptistry, hidden behind the apse at its eastern end, is reminiscent of the one in Sbeitla's Basilica of St Vitalis, though less lavishly decorated. After the Byzantines ejected the Vandals, they buried some of their dead in the church. From here it's a short walk south to the unmissable **Southeast Baths**. Thanks again to Byzantine fortifications whose remnants can be made out, these are some of the most impressively preserved Roman baths in Tunisia, with massive walls and pillars and some lovely geometric mosaic floors still in place.

Back at the triumphal arch, a smooth paved road leads west past a **Temple of Bacchus** on the right (look for the cave uncovered in its cellar) and an irregular paved open space on the left. This is another **Forum**, an older African one that predates the rigid Roman lines of the model next to the triumphal arch. The original wasn't any less functional than the new Forum; it's just that form demanded one in the Roman style.

The **Châtelain Building** at the road junction is named after its excavator but is little understood, while the **North Baths** date from Byzantine times. The **Northwest Baths** date from the second century AD, but were converted into a church in the fifth or sixth century. Roman blocks were cut down (look for an interrupted inscription) to obtain the square posts that define the nave and two aisles.

A path leads southeast from here to the prettily ruined **Schola**, its columns and trees reminiscent of Olympia in Greece. This was basically a clubhouse for a young men's association, where well-born youths of the town would meet both socially and as a sort of police force. Their complex here consisted of the main building, later confused by being turned into a well-defined church with apse and columns, and just to the south the so-called *quadrilobe*, whose windows with troughs make it one of the mysterious **"Buildings with Troughs"** (see p.247). Here the troughs were perhaps used for the collection of contributions by the association's members.

It was this sort of voluntary association, with its implicit faith in the Roman order, that formed the backbone of the Empire. If it had been able to offer more to the rural Berbers as well as to the urban bourgeoisie, it might have lasted longer. A remarkable gravestone found at Maktar, belonging to the so-called "Maktar Reaper", records a rare case of upward mobility. The inscription, thought to date from the second half of the third century AD, tells the "local boy made good" story with relish – how the dead man worked his way up the social scale by the sweat of his honest brow. You too, it concludes encouragingly, can be a success: "Learn, mortals, to lead a blameless life. Those who have lived honourable lives have earned an honourable death."

Behind the Schola, some jumbled remains belong to a **cemetery** that was in use for six hundred years; its earliest tombs were megalithic chambers, in widespread use before the arrival of the Romans and still being used in the first century AD. Five hundred metres west of here, outside the site wall, beyond a **Muslim cemetery** that surrounds a white-domed **koubba**, stands an oriental-looking neo-Punic **mausoleum** similar to the one at Dougga. Getting over the site wall is a bit of a scramble – you may prefer to go back to the site entrance and walk up the road. The mausoleum's pyramidal roof and angular design are distinctly un-Roman, though the monument may in fact have been built during the imperial epoch. Another 500m northwest of here is an African-style **Temple of Apollo**. If you come up here by the road, or return down it, don't miss the **herm** (entry stone with phallus) which stands outside the excavation headquarters. A second triumphal arch below the museum is difficult to miss; the square **Mausoleum of the Julii**, across the road from the museum, is easier to miss. And easiest of all to miss is the tumbledown **dolmen tomb** in the middle of town, on the right of the road on to Kairouan.

The route to Kairouan

The most exciting way out of Maktar is the **road to Kairouan**, which runs through some of the most rugged scenery in the country. After about 10km you enter the vast **Forest of Kesra**, a blanket of bright green Aleppo pine named after **LA KESRA**, a Berber village clinging almost invisibly to a mountain face at an altitude of 1078m.

Side roads connect the village to the main route from both east and west, the western one slightly shorter at about 3km – the western junction, with stores and a school, is also where you're more likely to find a lift. If it ever opens (currently only the bar is functioning), the *Hôtel des Chasseurs*, 1km west of the junction on the main road, will offer spectacular views up to the village and down onto the plain. Although steep, the climb up to La Kesra offers a foretaste of the *ksour* in the south, as well as a reminder of similar villages further north, such as Chaouach (p.158) and Jeradou (p.226). The houses merge with the slope, leaving no doubts about the defensive attitudes which saw settlements like these built, faced with the dangers of the open plains to the south – Maktar shared the same vulnerability. Nowadays the only defence is a pair of **cemeteries** at either end of the village, each surrounding a white-domed tomb of a saint.

Back below, at a village called El Garia, the main road soon punches through the last ridge of hills, a final reminder of the Tell before you descend onto the plain of the Sahel. If you're going through to Kairouan, you face another 90km of barren emptiness, broken by only the barest of diversions. Just east of the roadside town of **HAFFOUZ**, 35km east of Kesra, is an old and neglected French **war cemetery** for Muslim soldiers "morts pour la France". Twenty kilometres further, as the road crosses Oued Chnihira, look out to the north of the road for remains of the **aqueduct** which carried water from the mountains to Kairouan's Aghlabid pools (see p.194).

Alternatively, about 15km beyond the tunnel at El Garia, a turning goes left to **OUESSLATIA**, another 10km away. This road offers an alternative route into the exciting Fahs–Maktar–Kairouan triangle. Another drab modern farming settlement of little interest for its own sake, Ouesslatia is the principal settlement inside the triangle, lying in the broad valley between Jebel Ousselat to the southeast and Jebel Seri to the northwest. In the eighteenth century, and for hundreds of years before, these mountains were the home of the eponymous Ousselatia, a tribe that, like the Khroumirs, remained outside the control of central government in Tunis. In the dynastic quarrel of the 1730s they made the mistake of backing Husayn Pacha, and on his death in 1740 the mountain was taken by his rival, Ali. The chronicler Mohammed Seghir Ben Youssef cut down all the olive trees and exiled the survivors to the corners of the Regency, from where they were never allowed to return.

Despite its fertility, the mountain is still deserted, its empty villages having remained untouched for two hundred years. Like much of the terrain around here, it's good walking country with limited public transport.

This same road, if followed north all the way, leads past the Byzantine fort at Ksar Lemsa to Fahs. The other road out of Ouesslatia heads northwest to Siliana, round the flank of **Jebel Serj**, which at 1360m is only slightly lower than Jebel Chambi, outside Kasserine, the highest mountain in the country. Ten kilometres along this road, as it climbs up to enter the mountain massif, the remains of Roman **Aggar** tumble down the slopes to the north of the road. A little further, the massive pillars of a Roman **bridge** march across a river bed next to a rickety-looking modern equivalent.

Sbeitla and around

The dusty modern market town of **SBEITLA**, 30km east of Kasserine, is unexciting in the extreme, enlivened only on Wednesdays by the weekly **souk**. What makes a detour here advisable is its proximity to the site of Roman **Sufetula**.

There is very little recorded about the Roman town, apart from its one moment of abortive glory in 646 AD, when the Byzantine Prefect Gregory declared the African province independent here in anticipation of the coming Arab invasion. Much good it did him or the province; the Arabs won a famous victory here in 647, making Sbeitla the shortest-lived of all Tunisia's capitals. What remains of Roman *Sufetula* sits on a level plain with little scenic interest, but it does boast the best-preserved complex of Forum temples in the country. These have long been famous, inspiring one of Sir Grenville Temple's (see p.418) prints in 1835 (an enlargement of this is on display in the new museum). It also has some fine Christian remains and the most unadulterated Roman city plan in Tunisia.

The site

The **site** (daily 8am–5pm; 1TD, plus 1TD to take photos) lies along the Kasserine road, northwest of the new town. To get there, walk straight ahead out of the bus station about half a kilometre up rue Taieb Mehiri, past a **triumphal arch** on the right of the

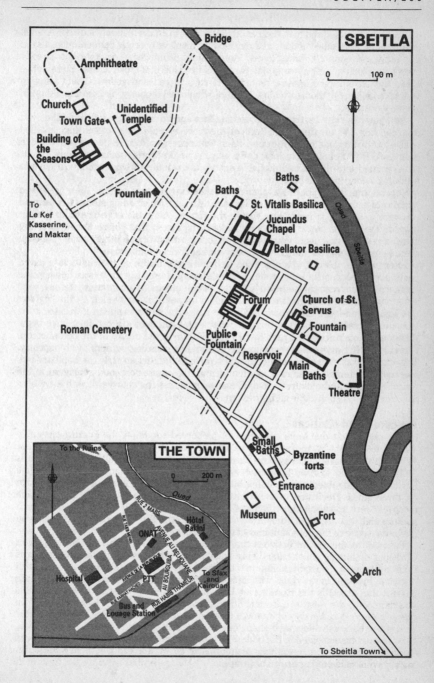

SBEITLA

Bridge

Amphitheatre

Church

Town Gate

Unidentified
Temple

Building of
the
Seasons

Fountain

0   100 m

Baths

Baths

St. Vitalis Basilica

Jucundus
Chapel

Bellator Basilica

To
Le Kef
Kasserine,
and Maktar

Forum

Church of St.
Servus

Fountain

Roman Cemetery

Public
Fountain

Reservoir

Main
Baths

Theatre

Small
Baths

Byzantine
forts

Entrance

Museum

Fort

Arch

THE TOWN

To the Ruins

0   200 m

Oued

RUE 2 MARS

RUE TAIEB M'HIRI

Hôtel
Bakini

ONAT

AVENUE ALI BELHOUANE

Hospital

AVENUE 6 LA SEPTEMBRE

PTT

AV. BOURGUIBA

RUE HABIB THAMEUR

RUE FARHAT HACHED

To Sfax
and
Kairouan

Bus and
Louage Station

To Sbeitla Town

road which straddled the main Roman highway east to *Hadrumetum* (Sousse). A small **museum** of archeological finds and explanatory displays recently opened opposite the site entrance (same hours; closed Mon). Apart from the Temple print already mentioned, look out for a round fifth-century altar table that looks at first like an olive press and an attractive mosaic featuring a cross in red and yellow. Touts hanging around outside sell "Roman" coins, some of which may actually be genuine although almost worthless.

You enter the site past a small Byzantine **fort** and an immediate left turn takes you past another one on the right. Both of these were really little more than fortified houses, with no door on the ground floor (entrance would have been via a wooden staircase). If you climb up to look down into the second fort, you can see how rooms are crammed into the limited available space: you would not have wanted to have to withstand a long siege in here.

Beyond the fort, opposite a plan of the site on the left, are the best-preserved remains of an **olive press** in Roman Tunisia, with massive standing stones that remind you what a serious industry this was in the region. After the olive press, turn right towards the centre of the site. It's immediately apparent that you're already walking along a regular grid-plan, suggesting that, unlike most of the other major Tunisian sites, Roman Sbeitla did not grow out of an earlier African foundation.

After two long blocks, you reach the well-preserved **baths** on the right, with paved pools and hypocaust heating systems visible everywhere. Entrance was down some steps from the street on the north side; the double pillars of a *palaestra* exercise yard are straight ahead through two rooms, flanked immediately to the left by the *frigidarium* and, beyond, the *caldarium*. Below the baths the sad remains of a **theatre** overlook the river. It's not hard to imagine what a pleasant spot it must once have been. Back on the main road that runs towards the Forum at the centre of the complex, the **Church of St Serverus** is recognizable by the four standing corners of its baptistry. This church was carved out of an existing temple in the African style. Its baptistry was originally the temple sanctuary, reached through a square-porticoed courtyard to the south; the body of the church was laid east–west across the courtyard, with a *presbyterium* apse just recognizable at the west end.

The Forum and basilicas

Highly photogenic due to its uniquely well-preserved condition, the **Forum** ensemble – dated to 139 AD by an inscription on the entrance archway – is Sbeitla's big draw. Although the Byzantines may have made use of the enclosure wall as a defence, it is probably too thin to have been built as a fortification and, in any case, the original Forum was undoubtedly surrounded by a wall, as well as a colonnaded portico inside on three sides. Dedicated to the trinity of Juno, Jupiter and Minerva, the two side **temples** were approached by flights of steps, while Jupiter's in the middle stood on a podium and was accessible only from the side. For the first time here in Tunisia, you get a real sense of the dominant impact of a Roman civic centre.

Pass out of the Forum between the temples and turn right towards a complex of Christian buildings, which after being installed on top of existing Roman structures then underwent constant shifts in configuration to reflect changes in Christian doctrine. Furthest to the right, with an apse at each end (and tombs visible in the apse nearest the street) is the **Basilica of Bellator**. In its first Christian incarnation, this was flanked to the west by a freestanding baptistry, later converted into a chapel. You can see where a reliquary column was inserted in the middle of a baptistry basin that was in the curiously elongated shape characteristic of Sbeitla. The relics in question, which would have resided in the hollow on top of the column, are thought to have been those of one Jucundus, a Catholic bishop martyred by the Vandals, hence the building's current name of **Jucundus's Chapel**.

Beyond Jucundus's Chapel lies the largest building in the complex, the **Basilica of St Vitalis**, with five aisles divided by rows of double columns. Dating from the end of the fifth century, it would have had only fifty years of use before Gregory's defeat by the Arabs in 647. Even so, like Bellator's Basilica, it went through adjustments which produced an apse at both ends of the central nave. In its original form it would have had only the one nearest the street, behind which is hidden a magnificently decorated baptistry basin. The inscription in its mosaic says that the basin was built at the instigation of Vitalis and Cardela. Beyond the northwest corner of the cathedral is a baths complex.

The northern end of the site

In the distance, looking north, you should be able to see a **bridge** over the *oued*. Built by the Romans, the bridge is still in use (though admittedly heavily restored), providing access to a spring on the far bank whose water is pumped directly to Sfax. Just about level with the bridge, a solitary square ruin known as the **"unidentified temple"** stands over the northwest limit of the town. Both feature in the foreground of Temple's sketch of the ruins in 1835, as the frame for some picturesque imaginary Arab hunters standing over an equally imaginary dead lion. Look out here for the foundations of a **Triumphal Arch** over the street, and the attractive **Building of the Seasons** on the far side, its colonnade carved with a vine in typical local style. Beyond, a low mound outside the town is all that remains of the **amphitheatre**.

Practicalities

The modern town of Sbeitla has one **bank** and a **PTT** (country hours) in avenue Farhat Hached, between the bus station and the town centre, but no tourist office. If you want to **stay**, there are two two-star hotels – the clean and comfortable *Bakini*, near the mosque on rue 2 Mars (☎07/465244; ③), and the pricier *Sufetula* on the Kasserine road beyond the site (☎07/465074; ④), which caters mainly for organized tour parties, but is more spacious and has a view over the ruins plus a swimming pool – non-residents can use this for a small charge.

For **food and drink**, the *Bakini* has a sedate bar and restaurant. Rather raucous by comparison, the *Hôtel Ezzohour* opposite the bus station, at the start of avenue Bourguiba, is no longer a hotel, but still dispenses beer. Basic food can be found in the *Restaurant des Ruines* at the other end of avenue Bourguiba, near the roundabout in the centre of town.

The train station has no passenger services, but the **bus station**, in rue Habib Thameur at the southern end of town, has six services daily to Kasserine (30min), four a day Sidi Bou Zid (1hr) and Tunis (3hr), two to Gafsa (2hr) and one to Sfax (3hr), and there are also **louages** to Sidi Bou Zid and Kasserine. **Hitching** to the site on the main road is generally easy.

Sidi Bou Zid

Moving on, the road east to Kairouan skirts the eastern edge of the Dorsale range, though there's nothing to entice a stop along the way. Similarly, the route to Sfax fails to provide even this limited interest. If you can get a lift to the first big crossroads, it's a good place to hitch to Gafsa. Some 17km east of this junction, then 8km south of the Sfax road, is **SIDI BOU ZID**, a notoriously drab town, most of whose population works in Sfax. About the only thing of interest in town is the **Zaouia of Sidi Bou Zid** and the nearby *zaouia* of his son. Unexciting from the outside (and entry is reserved for Muslims), this marabout is a centre of pilgrimage and the historical base of the Hammama tribal confederation.

The **bus station** is one block from avenue Bourguiba, behind the square – which, with its trees and pavement cafés, can be taken as the town centre. There are services five times a day to Kairouan (1hr 30min), four a day to Gafsa (2hr), Sbeitla (1hr), Sfax (2hr) and Tunis (4hr), twice daily to Gabes (4hr 30min), Kasserine (1hr 30min) and Le Kef (3hr), and only one to Tozeur (4hr 30min); there are also *louages* to Ben Aoun, Gafsa, Haffouz, Meknassy, Sfax, Sbeitla and Tunis, but none direct to Kasserine. There's a clutch of **banks** and a couple of cheap **restaurants** by the bus station, and a **market** too, although the weekly **souk**, on a Saturday, is held a few blocks behind, near the *zaouias*.

There are two one-star **hotels** in Sidi Bou Zid, both in the direction of Sfax from the bus station and main square. The *Hôtel Chems* on avenue Bourguiba (☎06/430515; ②) is comfortable and welcoming, and its budget-priced restaurant does an excellent steak *au poivre*. *Hôtel Horchati*, on rue de Meknassy, 400m off avenue Bourguiba down rue de Palestine (☎06/430217; ②), is also clean and friendly. The *Maison des Jeunes* **youth hostel** is on avenue Bourguiba (☎06/430088; ①), 200m in the Gafsa direction on the right. Before you reach it, you'll pass the **PTT** on your right, with a **taxiphone** office opposite and a *Magasin Général* **supermarket** on the left.

Kasserine and around

From the edge of the high steppes at Thala, the Gafsa road passes through empty and unrelenting country populated mainly by lonely shepherds and their flocks. Fifty kilometres south of Thala – and just 30km west of Sbeitla – **KASSERINE** proves a sprawling and unattractive town under the equally uninspiring **Jebel Chambi**, Tunisia's highest mountain at 1554m. The town centre is focused on a huge barracks and a conspicuously ugly American-aided cellulose factory; a depressed as well as a depressing place, it's no surprise that the bread riots of January 1984 began here. Although it is the site of the remains of Roman *Cillium* and a large mausoleum, both are some way from the town centre and barely worth the effort except for enthusiasts.

The main square that marks the town centre boasts trees and flowers, three **banks**, a couple of cheap **restaurants** and the *SNTRI* station, with six daily buses for Fahs (4hr), Gabes (4hr), Gafsa (1hr 30min), Maktar (2hr), Sbeitla (30min) and Tunis (5hr), five services to Le Kef (4hr) and Kalaa Khasbah (2hr 30min), two to Sfax (4hr 30min), and one to both Le Kef (2hr) and Tunis (5hr). The *SRT Kasserine* and **louage station** is also on one side of the main square, in front of the train station (no passenger services). *Louages* serve Tunis, Sbeitla, Feriana and Thala, but not Le Kef or Gafsa. There's a **hospital** (☎07/470022) out towards the ruins, with buses running from the bus station every fifteen minutes. There's no tourist office in Kasserine.

There are quite a few **hotels** in town, with budget places like the *Hôtel du Golf* on the main square (☎07/471044; ①) – not recommended for women, the *Hôtel Ben Abdallah*, 40 rue Habib Thameur (☎07/470568; ①), down beside the *Magasin Général*, and the usual Colditz-style barracks of the *Maison des Jeunes* **youth hostel** (☎07/470053; ①), 1km from the town centre on avenue Bourguiba, on the left going towards *Cillium*. More comfortable are the *Hôtel de la Paix* on avenue Bourguiba, 50m from the main square towards Sbeitla (☎07/471465; ②), the *Hôtel d'Algérie*, avenue 7 Novembre (☎07/471876; ②), three blocks behind the main square, and the rather officious one-star *Hôtel Pinus*, 350m from the main square towards Sbeitla (☎07/470164; ②). Top of the list is the friendliest hotel in town, the three-star *Hôtel Cillium*, near the junction with the Thala road (☎07/470682; ④), by the ruins of the same name, with huge rooms, nice views of the ruins and a swimming pool (open to non-residents). **Food** is available on the main square, and behind it in avenue Taïeb Mehiri, where there are several patisseries, rôtisseries and cafés. There are a number of **bars** on avenue Bourguiba near the main square, the *Hôtel de la Paix* has one, and there's another next door.

Cillium and the Mausoleum of the Flavii

The remains of Roman **Cillium** are well out of town past the *Hôtel Cillium*. If you don't fancy walking all the way or taking a taxi, get a bus to the hospital and walk from there, taking a left 100m beyond the hotel. The ruins begin a short way up this path, and are spread out over quite an area. The most impressive feature of a not very outstanding site is the third-century **arch**. Nearby is a group of rather pretty whitewashed **marabouts**.

On the way to *Cillium*, and more engaging than its rather limited remains, is the **Mausoleum of the Flavii**, the best-preserved example of its kind in the country, which stands three storeys high next to the main road, decorated with a 110-line falteringly poetic inscription to the dead Flavius. Four lines sum up the Roman dedication to conspicuous consumption:

> *"Who could fail to be mind-blown as he stands here, who would not marvel at this construction and be staggered at the wealth which has caused this monument to rise to the heavenly skies . . . ?"*

Onward to Gafsa and Tébessa

There's nothing to stop off for on the road between Kasserine and Gafsa, one of the bleakest in the country. The only town of any size is **FERIANA**, 5km after the minimal remains of Roman **Thelepte**, which look more than usual as if someone has just scattered a handful of hefty blocks across the road: the basilicas, baths and a theatre in the home town of Saint Fulgentius (467–532) are barely visible. If through some mishap you do get stuck in Feriana, it offers the *Hôtel Mabrouk* (✆07/485202; ②) on the main road, along with a couple of **banks**. A road to Tébessa in Algeria splits off at Thelepte, but the current political situation in Algeria makes crossing the border inadvisable.

travel details

Trains
Kalaa Khasbah to: Fahs, Gaafour, Sers and Tunis.
Le Kef to: Fahs, Gaafour, Le Krib, Sers and Tunis.

Buses
Kalaa Khasbah to: Kasserine, Le Kef and Thala.
Kasserine to: Gabes, Gafsa, Kairouan, Kalaa Kasbah, Le Kef, Sbeitla, Sfax, Tozeur and Tunis.
Le Kef to: Beja, Bizerte, Fahs, Gafsa, Jendouba, Kalaa Khasbah, Kasserine, Maktar, Medjez el Bab, Nabeul, Ras Ajdir, Sakiet Sidi Youssef, Sfax, Sidi Bou Zid, Sousse, Teboursouk, Testour, Thala and Tunis.
Sbeitla to: Gafsa, Kasserine, Sfax, Sidi Bou Zid and Tunis.
Sidi Bou Zid to: Gabes, Gafsa, Kairouan, Kasserine, Le Kef, Sbeitla, Sfax, Tozeur and Tunis.

Teboursouk to: Beja, Le Kef, Medjez el Bab, Testour, Thibar and Tunis.
Thala to: Le Kef, Kasserine, Tajerouine and Tunis.

Louages
Kalaa Khasbah to: Kasserine and Thala.
Kasserine to: Feriana, Sbeitla, Thala and Tunis.
Le Kef to: El Ksour, Jendouba, Kalaa Khasbah, Kalaat es Senam, Tajerouine and Tunis.
Sbeitla to: Kasserine and Sidi Bou Zid.
Sidi Bou Zid to: Ben Aoun, Gafsa, Haffouz, Meknassy, Sbeitla, Sfax and Tunis.
Thala to: Haidra and Kasserine.
Teboursouk to: Beja, Gaafour, Medjez el Bab, Nouvelle Dougga and Tunis.

MARKET DAYS

Monday – Maktar, Tajerouine
Tuesday – Dahmani, Haffouz, Hajeb el
  Ayoun, Kasserine, Le Krib
Wednesday – Menzel Chaker, Sbeita,
  Sers

Thursday – El Aroussa, Le Kef, Siliana,
  Teboursouk
Friday – El Houareb, Testour, Thala
Saturday – Sidi Bou Zid
Sunday – Rohia

CHAPTER SIX

THE JERID

Rich in the phosphates which play a major role in Tunisia's economy, **the Jerid** – the parched terrain spreading west from Gabes all the way to the Algerian frontier – is an arid land of bare pink hills punctuated only by mining towns and sporadic oasis-villages built around springs and deep gorges. These take time to explore, but are memorable places to experience the precariousness of oasis life. In contrast, the oases at **Tozeur** and **Nefta** – both reached quite easily – are vast folds of luxuriance, set right at the edge of the **Chott**, a bizarre salt lake of shifting colours and mirages. Nefta has long been a centre of Sufism whose monuments add an

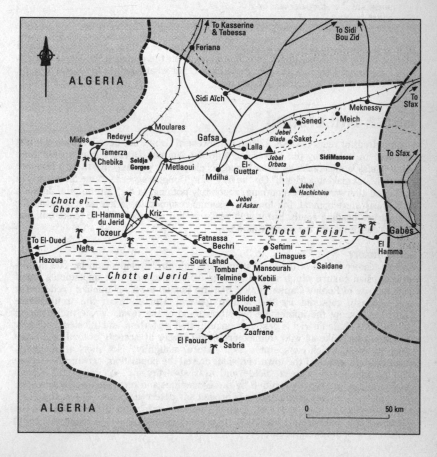

ACCOMMODATION PRICE CODES

All the hotels, youth hostels and pensions listed in this book have been price-graded according to the following scale, and although prices will rise during the lifetime of this edition, the relative comparisons should remain valid.

The prices quoted are for the **cheapest available double room in high season**, although many of the cheap places will have pricier rooms with en suite facilities or sea views.

Classified hotels, officially considered suitable for tourists, are graded locally from one to four stars (★), with wide-ranging prices within each category. For more on accommodation prices and categories, see Basics.

① Up to 10TD. Very cheap. Usually a bed only in a basic, unclassified hotel or a youth hostel.

② 10.1–25TD. Budget. Bed only or bed and breakfast.

③ 25.1–40TD. Comfortable budget. Good unclassified average one-star or a cheap two-star.

④ 40.1–55TD. Mid-range. Expensive two-star, cheap three-star.

⑤ 55.1–70TD. Tourist hotel. Standard three-star.

⑥ 70.1TD upwards. Deluxe. Expensive three-star, four-star or five-star.

---

intriguing dimension to its character. Across the Chott lie further oases – the scattered centres of the Nefzaoua, under constant threat from the dunes of the Great Eastern Erg. **Kebili** and **Douz** are the two main towns, but what supplies the interest is the access they offer to smaller villages around.

Gafsa and around

For hundreds of years **GAFSA**, 130km northwest of Gabes, has been inspiring the sort of comment quoted by the Edwardian traveller Norman Douglas from an old Arab song: "Gafsa is miserable; its water blood; its air poison; you may live there a hundred years without making a friend." On the face of it, Douglas agreed – "One dines early in Gafsa and afterwards there's nothing, absolutely nothing, to do." After a brief flirtation with tourist development, the town now seems resigned to its fate as a stopover for tour parties heading south. But it isn't really as bad as people like to make out, and worth a day or two for the scenery alone.

Some history

Gafsa's history is one of the longest in the Maghreb, let alone Tunisia. The prehistoric Capsian culture which spread all over Africa is named after implements found near the site of Roman **Capsa**. In 107 BC, the Roman town's Numidian predecessor was famously captured by the Roman general **Marius** from the troublesome Jugurtha. "Except the immediate neighbourhood of the town," wrote the historian Sallust, "the whole district is desolate, uncultivated, waterless, and infested by deadly serpents, which like all wild animals are made fiercer by scarcity of food, and especially by thirst, which exasperates their natural malignity." Not short on malignity himself, Marius sacked the town and slaughtered the population – giving the excuse that the inhabitants were a "fickle and untrustworthy lot". An important Roman colony, Capsa was heavily fortified by the Byzantines and renamed **Justiniana** after the emperor – neither of which moves proved any deterrent to Arab **Oqba Ibn Nafi**, who captured the city and took eighty thousand prisoners in 668. Despite the conquest, and large-scale conversion to Islam, El Edrisi reported Latin still being spoken here in the twelfth century.

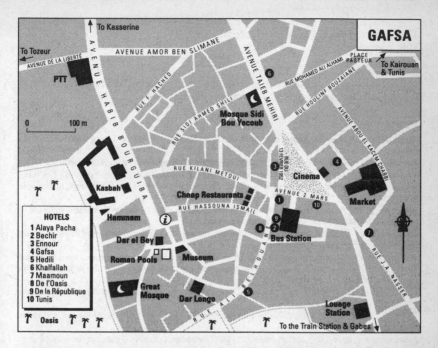

Gafsa's most recent world headlines were in January 1980. On January 27 a mysterious group of unidentified soldiers took over the town in a night-time operation. It took several days for the army to evict them, after 48 deaths; of the 60 captured, 13 were hanged on April 17. To this day the incident remains shrouded in mystery. Rumour has it that the leader was a native of Gafsa who had fled to Libya in the wake of the Ahmed Ben Salah purges of 1969, and the one consistent element in suggested explanations seems to be that the men came from Libya. As to their purpose, however, nothing is clear; if the Tunisian south was expected to rise spontaneously and declare allegiance with Libya, its mood had been severely misjudged. But it is significant that Gafsa was chosen as the target. As the economic and administrative capital of the Jerid, whose phosphates play such a large part in the national economy, there is some resentment among the citizens that they don't benefit more from the industry. True or not, the common view in the town, that the profits all go to rich businessmen in Sfax, suggests considerable disenchantment.

Arrival and accommodation

The centre of town is marked by the nondescript triangular garden of **place 7 Novembre**, tucked in between avenue Taïeb Mehiri, avenue 2 Mars and avenue 13 Février. The Medina lies to the west of here, across avenue 13 Février, which continues round the edge of the old town as **rue Ali Belhouane**, where most of the budget hotels are located. Across place 7 Novembre, **avenue Taïeb Mehiri** is Gafsa's main thoroughfare, and where you'll find the central **market**. On the other side of the Medina is **avenue Bourguiba**, running from the Roman Pools up to the PTT. Off to the left there, avenue de la Liberté is the Tozeur road. The *ONTT* **tourist office** is next to the museum (Mon–Thurs 8.30am–1pm & 3–5.45pm, Fri & Sat 8.30am–1.30pm; ☎06/221664), by the Roman Pools.

Arriving by **train**, you are left way out in the suburb of Gafsa Gare on the Gabes road, 3km to the southeast. Your best bet is to take a taxi into town (3TD or so), or walk (bear right opposite the station and straight on) up to the main road, where there are more taxis – and some buses, but not early enough for the arrival of the morning train.

Most of Gafsa's budget **hotels** are on rue Ali Belhouane, and upmarket hotels – such as there are – can be found close to the centre of town. Mid-range accommodation is a little thin on the ground, but not impossible to find.

Hotels

Alaya Pacha, 4 rue Ali Belhouane (☎06/222232). Rooms are clean, bright and inviting, the management less so. ①.

Bechir, 40 rue Ali Belhouane (☎06/223239). Friendly and clean but the rooms are small. ②.

Ennour, 41 rue Mohamed Khaddouma (☎06/220620). On a little road parallel with rue 13 Février and easier to spot from the back than the front. The best of the cheapies: nice rooms, nice people, nice breakfast. ①.

Gafsa ★, 10 rue Ahmed Snoussi (☎06/224000). Discreetly classy place with a warm welcome, in spite of all the tour groups. The best upmarket option. ③.

Hedili, 108 rue Ali Belhouane (☎06/221887). A warm welcome and good views of the Medina and the oasis, especially from the top floor. ①.

Jugurtha ★★★★★, Sidi Ahmed Zarroug (☎06/221315). Four kilometres west of town in a small oasis (see p.267). Currently closed for renovation and upgrading. Owned by the same firm as the *Maamoun*, where you can check to see whether it's reopened. ⑥.

Khalfallah, av Taïeb Mehiri (☎06/221468). A touch classier than the other budget hotels, but also pricier. ②.

Lune ★, rue JA Nasser (☎06/222212). Two hundred metres down from the *Maamoun* and rather better value for money. ③.

Maamoun ★★★, av Taïeb Mehiri (☎06/222433). The poshest place in Gafsa, but the only thing it's got on the *Gafsa* and the *Lune* is its swimming pool. ④.

Moussa, av de la Liberté (☎06/223333). Out on the Tozeur road, about 300m past the PTT. Clean, neat and good value. ②.

Hôtel de l'Oasis, 7 rue Ali Belhouane (☎06/222338). The people who run it are pleasant, but the rooms are dark and gloomy. ①.

Hôtel de la République, 28 rue Ali Belhouane (☎06/221807). The management are friendly but the rooms dirty, with cockroaches galore. ①.

Tunis, 62 av 2 Mars (☎06/221660). The rooms are reasonably clean, the beds rickety and crammed in. ①.

Youth hostel and campsite

Maison des Jeunes youth hostel, rue Mongi Bali (☎06/220268). Three- to four-person dorms and a 10pm curfew. To get there, take the Tozeur road past the *Hôtel Moussa*, then the next right and the first left; the reception is on the corner, and the hostel itself 100m down on the left. Camping possible. ①.

The Town

Gafsa's centre must have changed very little since Norman Douglas's day. It's still not a town for great sightseeing, and anything of interest is concentrated around the Roman Pools in the corner of the Medina at the bottom end of avenue Bourguiba. The skyline is dominated by the majestic minaret of the spacious **Great Mosque**, overlooking the town from nearby, with the oasis and distant desert beyond it.

Gafsa's focal monument is the **Piscines Romaines** (Roman Pools), which every small boy will automatically assume you've come to see. A left turn at the end of rue Hassouna Ismail (off rue Ali Belhouane by the *Hôtel de l'Oasis*) will bring you to two

PUTTING THE DEVIL BACK IN HELL

Gafsa has a literary claim to fame in Boccaccio's 1353 classic, the *Decameron*, being the home of Alibech, the innocent virginal heroine of the book's thirtieth and most infamous tale. Setting off into the desert to learn how to serve God, Alibech encounters the pious young hermit Rustico, who agrees to teach her. Rustico, however, soon gets other ideas and persuades her to join him in a rather unorthodox enactment of putting the devil into hell, thus coining a sexual euphemism current in the Italian of the time. In the story, when the women of Gafsa found out how Alibech and Rustico had been serving God out in the desert, "they burst into such laughter that they are laughing still". English translators, though, found it no laughing matter and, even into this century, they refused to put the crucial parts into English, printing them untranslated. Their readers were left to fathom the finer points of Rustico's method from the original Italian text.

open, rectangular pools in familiar Roman masonry. Apart from the fish, look out for the inscriptions on the side of the larger, upper pool, and the hot spring which you can see coming up through the bottom of the smaller, lower one into which, if there are enough tourists about, young boys will daringly leap from the overhanging palm trees in return for some backsheesh. The arcaded building over the lower pool is called the **Dar el Bey** after the ruler who built this house, and on the far side steps lead down to a hammam using the pools' overflow; unfortunately, as well as being open only to men, this is more a toilet than a bathhouse – one whiff at the doorway should be enough to convince women that they're not missing out.

On the square by the pools, a small **museum** (daily except Mon 7am–4pm; 1TD) exhibits Capsian artefacts, and some mosaics from Roman Zammour, the latter an example of the Tunisian jigsaw approach to archeology, but worth a look.

The path behind the large pool and the *Café des Piscines Romains* leads back to rue Ali Belhouane. As it widens to accommodate cars, check out the large whitewashed mansion on your right, known as **Dar Longo**. Currently under restoration, it is worth a look around if you can get somebody to let you in, and the roof offers excellent views over the town – although the best vistas over both the town and oasis are to be had from **Jebel el Meda**, the rocky hillock opposite the *Hôtel Moussa* on the Tozeur road.

A little way up avenue Bourguiba from the Roman Pools stand the pinkly picturesque crenellated walls of the **Kasbah**. It has had a chequered career since it was built by the Hafsids on a Byzantine foundation – it resisted a Turkish corsair's siege in 1551, only to surrender to the same opponent five years later; its worst moment came in 1943, when an Allied ammunition dump blew out most of one wall. This was subsequently replaced, to universal dismay, with new law courts, and the Kasbah remains a rather soulless place until sunset, when the walls glow in harlequin shades of limpid colour. The best view of it is from the back, where the walls remain intact.

On the southern side of the Kasbah, a small egg-domed **marabout** hides beneath it another **hammam** using water from the Roman Pools. This one is actually Roman in origin and, if open, admits women one side and men on the other. Next to the men's hammam, right up by the walls of the Kasbah, is an ancient **Jewish ritual bath**.

The road south from here skirts the oasis and passes the Great Mosque before meeting up with rue Ali Belhouane. At the corner where they meet, if you're here at the right time of year, you can see some vintage technology in action in the form of an electric-powered **olive oil press**, used during the November to January harvest.

Gafsa is situated at a transitional point between the last remnants of the central steppes and mountains to the north and the incipient desert to the south, a position which has always made it an important place. The scenery is still the most striking feature, one long tongue of bleak hills passing behind the town to the west, another parallel in the southern distance. On the edge of this pocket is the **Gafsa oasis**, west of the Kasbah, large but more diffuse than those of Tozeur or Nefta. If those oases are islands in the desert, then Gafsa is the big port on the shore.

Eating and drinking

Most of the **restaurants** around the bus station and cheap hotel area are pretty bad value and are little more than overpriced greasy spoons. Decent low-priced eats can be found by taking rue Hassouna Ismail off rue Ali Belhouane by the *Hôtel de l'Oasis,* and then the second right, where there are three restaurants doing basic cheap meals. The one on the corner of rue Kilanai Metour is the best of the three, but sometimes gets quite packed out.

More sophisticated eating places include the rather sedate *Restaurant Semiramis* on rue Ahmed Snoussi, the *Gafsa* next door, and the rather pricier *Hôtel Maamoun* down the street. If you're looking for somewhere priced in between the two ends of the market, *Le Grill* on rue Abou el Kacem Chatti does, as its name suggests, mixed grills (pronounced "mix-ed").

Listings

Banks There are several in av Taïeb Mehiri, and a couple by the cinema. There is a weekend rota, so one bank should be open Saturday and Sunday mornings.

Cinema In av Taïeb Mehiri, opposite the *Tunis Hôtel,* next to the central market, and the *Maison de Culture* behind the Kasbah, which is also a theatre.

Consulates The Algerian consulate is behind 37 rue Houcine Bouzaiane (entrance in rue Abou el Kacem Chabbi; ☎06/221366). If it becomes possible (and safe) to visit Algeria again, you may be able to get a visa here.

Festival The Festival du Borj is a series of theatrical and musical presentations in the Kasbah throughout August.

Hammams The newest and cleanest is *Hammam Karaouli* at 15 rue Sidi Ben Yagou, up rue Honcine Bouzaiane to pl Pasteur, then left (daily men 6–11am; women 11.30am–5pm). More central is the one at 101 rue Kilani Metoui, with two doors – the right-hand one for men, the left-hand one for women (men daily except Mon 4–11am & 4–8pm; women Mon 4–11am, Tues–Sun 11.30am–8pm). There's also one by the Kasbah, which may be open (see p.265).

International phone calls 17 rue Houcine Bouzaiane at pl 13 Février (daily 7am–9pm). Also in the bus station in av Taïeb Mehiri, opposite *Hôtel Khalfallah,* and in the *Hôtel Moussa,* which claims to be open 24 hours.

MOVING ON FROM GAFSA

The **bus station** is off avenue 2 Mars, right in the centre of town behind several cheap hotels, and has eight daily departures for Tunis (four of them overnight; 7hr), seven to Kairouan (4hr), six to Sidi Bou Zid (2hr), five to Kasserine (2hr), Sfax (3hr 30min) and Redeyef (1hr 30min), four to Gabes (2hr 30min) and one each to Kebili (2hr), Douz (2hr 30min), Sousse (5hr 30min), Le Kef (4hr 45min) and Ras Ajdir (5hr). There is also a total of seventeen buses a day to Metlaoui (30min), twelve to Tozeur (1hr), ten to Nefta (1hr 30min), fourteen to El Guettar (30min) and three to Sidi Aich (1hr).

Louages for El Guettar hang out by the cinema on avenue Taïeb Mehiri, but a yard off the Gabes road, opposite the *Agil* station, is the stop for services to El Guettar, Gabes, Meknassy, Metlaoui, Redeyef, Sfax, Sidi Bou Zid, Tozeur and Tunis. There is also a **train station**, rather inconveniently located 3km down the Gabes road in the suburb of Gafsa Gare, reached by shared taxi (0.3TD) from in front of the *Hôtel Maamoun.* There's a single overnight train to Tunis (9hr) via Sfax (4hr) and Sousse (7hr), and a less useful one to Metlaoui (35min), very early in the morning.

Medical facilities The regional hospital is in rue Ibn Sina (☎06/220177), up rue Houcine Bouzaiane to pl Pasteur, then right. There's a night pharmacy at 16 av Amor Ben Slimane.

ONAT crafts shop Off av de la Liberté (Tozeur road), the first left coming from the PTT. Closed for renovation on last check, but due to reopen. The Jerid has its own style of carpet with designs quite unlike those found elsewhere and the *ONAT* shop is good for checking out styles and prices.

PTT On the corner of av Bourguiba and av de la Liberté, the Tozeur road (city hours).

Around Gafsa

Gafsa's significance as a desert "port" can be best appreciated by visiting two of its small satellite oases. Local buses leave regularly from the *Hôtel Tunis* for the **Lalla oasis**, 7km east of town. Stay on the bus until it turns around at the end of its route, then walk on a bit further to a small café and two prolific springs. The stark contrast here between shady green and glaring pink hills really brings home the fragility of oasis existence. **Sidi Ahmed Zarroug**, the other oasis, lies 4km west of town and is now occupied by the luxurious *Hôtel Jugurtha* (see p.264). If you're here in the winter – the only time of year suitable for energetic scrambling – the view out over the desert from the bald ridge which towers over the hotel is little short of magnificent.

There is an **animal park** at **ORBATA** (daily 7am–7pm; 0.1TD per person, car or bus 0.5TD), a few kilometres out on the Tunis road, where gazelles and ostriches roam about freely, although there are one or two cages too. On Wednesdays there's a live-stock **market** next door. Orbata can also be reached by local bus from the *Hôtel Tunis*.

Some 20km east of Gafsa on the Gabes road is another oasis, **EL GUETTAR**, reached by bus or *louage* from Gafsa. It's nothing much in itself, a ribbon of modern concrete houses along the road, but the huge palmery is rarely visited and farmers still use old techniques such as the *noria*, a device to draw water from wells by animal power. The oasis is known for its pistachio nuts. At the end of the village, a road to the left leads to the remote Berber mountain villages of **SAKKET** (14km), **SENED** (27km) and **MEICH** (42km) – highly worthwhile targets if you're prepared for a moderate adventure and to be a genuine visitor and not just another tourist (see box below).

Getting to these villages is difficult. It's possible to catch a bus to El Guettar but from there you'll have to walk, or, if you're lucky, get a lift. Another possible approach, to Sened at least, is from Sened Gare, on the Gafsa–Sfax road. East of El Guettar, the main GP15 highway continues across the steppe to **SIDI MANSOUR**, a small village with an important marabout, and thence on to Gabes (150km from Gafsa). Buses run regularly both ways.

TRADITIONS IN THE BERBER VILLAGES

Outsiders aren't that welcome in Sakket, Sened or Meich – as you arrive, the women hide in their houses and the men gather into groups to discuss the *hawaja*, or foreigner. Little has changed here in the past two centuries. As in Berber villages in the far south of the country, the villagers retain their distinct ethnic identity (though none have spoken Berber since the last century), and traditional dress and customs persist. Women wear the *bakhnug*, a shawl embroidered with geometrical patterns to shelter them from the eyes of strangers. Many of the men wear the knee-length trousers that used to be common before the last war. At the centre of each of the villages are marabouts' tombs, with rags and flags hanging from poles: the last place in Tunisia where you can see votive offerings to these village saints. The village oil presses are still animal-powered and women grind their own flour by hand. In winter many people migrate into the pastures with their herds, and the villages are virtually deserted. Today, however, a different type of migration is slowly eroding the community, as many families abandon their villages for an easier life in the city.

There are two Roman **mausoleums** at the village of **SIDI AÏCH**, 48km north of Gafsa on a turning off the Sidi Bou Zid road. They stand in splendid isolation just outside the village at the beginning of a *piste* to Feriana with a lovely backdrop of jagged mountains striped with layers of rock. The original Roman inscriptions are joined by more recent carvings, some as modern as the last century. Regular pick-ups, and three buses a day, reach Sidi Aïch from Gafsa.

Meknassy and Bou Hedma National Park

The road from Gafsa to Sfax takes you across the barren steppes between the Dorsale mountains to the north and the Chotts to the south. The only town of any size on this route is **MEKNASSY**, just under 80km east of Gafsa, where you might conceivably need to change *louages* (they go from here to Sfax, Gafsa, Sidi Bou Zid and direct to Tunis).

With your own vehicle, you could visit **Bou Hedma National Park** (see below), just south of Meknassy, where an ambitious programme is in progress to reintroduce gazelle, oryx and addax, as well as ostriches, which only disappeared from the south of the country this century. To visit the park, you'll first need permission from the *Direction Général des Forêts*, 30 rue Alain Savary, Tunis (☎01/891497). You may be able to phone them and arrange to pick up your permit at the forestry office (*Direction de Forêts/Triq el Ghaba*) opposite the train station in **MAZZOUNA**, 25km east of Maknassy. From there, you take the Skhirra road, turning right (no signposting) after 7km and arriving at the park after 10km of tarmac and, currently, 10km of *piste* due to be surfaced. Even then, much of the park is inaccessible without a four-wheel drive.

JERID WILDLIFE

The steppes cover a vast area of the centre of the country – from the southern foothills of the Dorsale ridge down to the Chott el Jerid. Most are degraded forests; it's a sobering thought that Hannibal probably got his **elephants** from this region a few thousand years ago. Over the centuries, the wood has been felled and the land grazed by sheep, goats and camels, resulting in a landscape only barely productive for agriculture.

The steppes, and particularly the low hills and wadis rising up from them, are rich in unusual **small birds**. Worth special mention are crested larks, hoopoe larks (so called because of their long decurved bill and black and white wings), and the even more peculiar Temminck's horned lark, a striking bird with a black and white head pattern and, in breeding plumage, two distinct black "horns". In the rockier parts, look out for the trumpeter finch, a thick-billed pink bird with a weird nasal call. **House buntings** are common in villages and, as they're treated with some reverence by local people, are extremely tame.

Out in the wilder areas, you may see – with some patience and luck – some of the true **desert mammals**. Jerboas and gerbils are reasonably common, as are susliks, a sort of short-tailed ground squirrel with an upright "begging" posture. Most of the larger desert **antelopes** have been reduced to extinction by excessive hunting, but an ambitious reintroduction programme is underway at the Bou Hedma National Park (see above).

Metlaoui and around

In 1896 a French army vet and amateur geologist, Philippe Thomas, found phosphate deposits around **METLAOUI**. Previously known only for his work on goat diseases, the discovery made Thomas a national hero and turned an insignificant village into an important mining centre.

The transformation took little over a decade. Thousands of miners were recruited from Algeria and Libya, for local people were at first reluctant to work in the mining towns and were later excluded because the mine owners feared they would campaign for better conditions. Conditions were certainly bad; companies provided no accommodation and huge *bidonvilles* grew up without any planning or services. At work there were few safety measures, and one third of employees had to retire – without compensation – because of injury. Unions were discouraged by the companies' policies of maintaining a high turnover of personnel and by pitting one ethnic group against another, paying Algerians more than Libyans, and Libyans more than Sudanese. So tense were relations that fights used to break out between the groups, and on one occasion the Algerians burnt down a Libyan shantytown, killing over a hundred people. It was only in the 1930s that the unions managed to unite the workforce and direct their anger against their bosses rather than each other – and conditions then improved radically.

By 1899, phosphate from Metlaoui was being exported to France via the new railway to Sfax and other mines were being dug in the surrounding hills. The *Compagnie des Phosphates de Gafsa* was established after independence, and Tunisia is now the fourth largest phosphate producer in the world, although mining is problematic as the value of phosphate is unstable and the rock here is of poor quality. In 1977 the workers went on strike because of low wages and their action led to the national crisis the following year that for a while threatened to overthrow the government.

Metlaoui itself is an odd jumble of French houses dwarfed by overhead phosphate conveyors and heavy mining equipment. English writer Norman Douglas came here in 1930 and found "trim bungalows", an "air of neatness and well-being" and workers who "would slit your throat for a sou". The workers in question no doubt saw things somewhat differently.

Philippe Thomas's legacy lives on in Metlaoui, not only in the form of the phosphate works, but also through a **museum** built to house his natural history collection and due to open in revamped form about 800m up the Tamerza road, just before the *louage* station.

The Gafsa road runs through the centre of town until it meets the Tamerza–Tozeur T-junction by a filling station, bank and cinema. Metlaoui's only **hotel**, the *Ennacim* (☎06/240271; ②), is 300m towards Tozeur on the left. The rooms, each with bath or shower, are presentable, if a bit institutional. You can also get a medium-priced set menu in the restaurant, and the hotel bar is one of only two places in town with beer. If you'd prefer a cheaper eating house, there are several along the Gafsa road. The **PTT** is off the Gafsa road (country hours), about 200m from the main junction, and there's also a *Magasin Général* **supermarket** about 700m up the Tamerza road, just before the museum.

The **bus station**, about 800m up the Gafsa road from the main junction, just past the level crossing, is served by both *SNTRI* and *SRT Gafsa*, with seventeen daily departures to Gafsa (30min), sixteen to Tozeur (45min) and Nefta (1hr 15min), and nine to Redeyef (1hr). Five buses a day serve Kairouan (4hr 30min) and Tunis (6hr 30min), with one direct to Sfax (4hr), Kasserine (2hr 30min) and Sidi Bou Zid (2hr 30min). **Louages** operate from a station about a kilometre up the Tamerza road and run to Gafsa, Redeyef, Tamerza, Tozeur and Tunis, but they can be a bit sparse, depending on the time of day. If they don't find enough passengers, they may cruise around town looking for them.

The **train station** is 1.5km from the main junction on the Gafsa road, but services are sparse, with one overnight train a day to Tunis (9hr 40min) via Gafsa (45min), Sfax (4hr 40min) and Sousse (7hr 40min); you could also get to Gabes (8hr 40min) if you're prepared to wait two hours at Sfax or Mahres (4hr) for your connection; there's an afternoon service the other way to Redeyef (1hr 30min).

Until recently, there was also a special **tourist train**, the *Lézard Rouge*, running four times weekly (Tuesday, Wednesday, Friday and Sunday) to Seldja and back for a return fare of 10TD. Originally used by the Bey, the train consisted of original nineteenth-century carriages, restored in red velvet. Lately, however, the train has been under repair and out of commission. Further information is available from the *Transtours/Lézard Rouge* office in Metlaoui (☎06/240634), through whom, if the train is running, reservations can be made. The office is about 100m into town from the train station, although you should be able to turn up at the station just before the train's 11am departure and buy a ticket there and then.

Seldja and around

SELDJA, 16km west of Metlaoui, comprises only a neat white signal box stuck in the middle of nowhere, built by the French along with a remarkable series of bridges and tunnels. Previously, the Romans had diverted the water from these ravines, building an aqueduct to supply nearby agricultural land. Coming from Sbeitla, their caravans took a short-cut through here en route to Ghadames in present-day Libya. From the signal box you can walk back down the tracks to some of the more impressive parts of the gorge, its sheer sides worn completely smooth by the river. Norman Douglas nearly met his end in one of the tunnels, and phosphate trains do still pass at regular intervals, so watch your step. As well as the *Lézard Rouge* (see above), you can get to Seldja from Metlaoui on the afternoon Redeyef train, returning on the same train an hour and a half later. An alternative route to the gorge is by road from Metlaoui, where a track leads out over the flat plain for 5km – too hot to walk – to a rock passage known as the **Coup de Sabre**, or sword thrust. Legend says that the warrior Al Mansour cut into the rock with one stroke to prepare a bed for Leila, a princess escaping from her husband. There's a 4km path along the foot of the gorge to the signal box – if you walk it, you'll see the wheeling silhouettes of birds of prey overhead.

Redeyef

REDEYEF, the last of the mining towns, is 17km further on and, like Metlaoui, has grown up around an old French community, with its bungalows and church. There's nothing much to see here, but you may find yourself passing through on your way to or from Tamerza, and it's a pleasant enough little town. The Gafsa road meets the Tamerza road in front of the **PTT** (country hours), and another road off the main junction leads to the square, with a **mosque** and, in front of it, rather resembling a toy train, a mining locomotive and bogeys built by Schötter GmbH of Bremen, Germany. Beyond the main square is the **market**, at its busiest on Sunday, and also the **bank**. Should you need to **stay**, the *Maison des Jeunes* **youth hostel** is a hundred metres up the Gafsa road from the PTT (☎06/245388; ①), with a **campsite**, meals and even a swimming pool.

From the bus station at the beginning of the Gafsa road there are four local services a day to Tamerza (1hr), plus eight to Moulares (20min) and Metlaoui (1hr), four continuing to Gafsa (1hr 30min), the other four to Tozeur (1hr 45min) and Nefta (2hr 15min). *SNTRI*'s overnight bus to Tunis (8hr) via Kasserine (3hr 30min) and Siliana (5hr 30min) leaves from the main square, while pick-ups for Tamerza leave from the other end of the market. The train station, with its single late-afternoon departure for Metlaoui (1hr 25min), is a hundred metres up the Tamerza road and off on the left.

Tamerza and the Chott el Gharsa

West, beyond Redeyef, the towns lose their industrial ugliness and become a series of lovely oases that some consider the most beautiful in the country. Certainly, their remoteness and inaccessibility leaves them unspoiled compared to places like Tozeur and Nefta; but it also means that facilities are few and public transport, beyond Tamerza, nonexistent. South of Tamerza, the recently ruined road to Tozeur crosses the Chott el Gharsa, a smaller salt-plain giving a taste of the Chott el Jerid itself.

TAMERZA, 85km west of Gafsa, with its high cascade and dense cultivation, is one of the least spoiled of all the Jerid oases. The oldest mud-and-stone houses (to the south of the road from Redeyef) were abandoned after torrential floods in 1969, and the new village, a kilometre further on, is built in traditional Arab style with high blank brick walls facing the main street. Three **marabouts** are still maintained in the old village, the most striking that of Sidi Dar Ben Dhahara with its pointed green dome. The four-star *Hôtel Tamerza Palace* (☎06/453844; ⑥), perched on the other side of the *oued*, has excellent views over the oasis and old village from its poolside terrace and each of its cool rooms. Tamerza's only other accommodation is in the rather grotty and overpriced palm-frond bungalows of the *Hôtel des Cascades* (☎06/453732; ②), down a street to the left as you go through the new town, and, as its name suggests, just above one of Tamerza's two **water-falls** – the other is beyond the edge of town, a couple of kilometres towards Chebika. There are panoramic views over the second one from the Chebika road.

The mountain oasis of **MIDES**, a few kilometres west, is reached by a new surfaced road from a junction 4km west of Tamerza towards Redeyef (a *piste* from the same junction passes a customs post before crossing the border into Algeria). The alternative route is on foot or by donkey along the valley floor from Tamerza – the *Hôtel des Cascades* can arrange the latter. If you do this trip, take some water with you, and in summer take precautions against heatstroke – it can get roasting hot. The walk takes a couple of hours.

The new Mides settlement and the older **Berber village** stand at opposite ends of the oasis, where the palms provide shade for pomegranates, which in turn shelter lemon and orange trees. Only from the top of the hill, above the ruins and the network of narrow paved streets, can you make out the spectacular position of the old houses, clinging to the sheer rock face of a deep gorge. This stretches for 3km around the village, providing a natural defensive position. The only place to **stay** in town is the rather basic *Camping de l'Oasis*, a very friendly, cheap site that doesn't always have running water, along the gorge from the old village. They can also arrange donkey rides to Tamerza for somewhat lower prices than coming the other way, sell drinks and a variety of fossils, including sharks' teeth, and can prepare meals. Otherwise, there's nowhere to get provisions in Mides, so it's a good idea to bring your own.

From Tamerza to Tozeur

The road south beyond Tamerza leads across the Chott el Gharsa to El Hamma du Jerid and Tozeur. There are no buses or taxis, and if you try hitching, be prepared to wait. Flooding can sometimes render this road impassable to all but four-wheel drive vehicles for months at a time, so check before setting out. The alternative is to go the long way around via Metlaoui, which you can do by a combination of pick-ups and *louages*, or by direct bus four times a day.

TRAVELLING TO ALGERIA

A deteriorating security climate means that as of mid-1995 it was inadvisable for foreigners – particularly westerners – to visit Algeria on a casual basis. You should also be aware of heightened Tunisian sensitivities when travelling near the Algerian border – passport checks will be more frequent than usual, and you should think hard before going off the beaten track anywhere near the border. See p.376 for more details.

The first section of road is surfaced but rough, characterized by sharp bends, sheer drops and breathtaking scenery before it comes down onto the plain for the last 5km before the small oasis of **CHEBIKA**. Behind the new settlement by the road, the old village perches on a rock platform, bordered by palms and, on the far side, a steep gorge. As at Tamerza, a cascade falls from high up the cliff, feeding the streams and the agricultural land below. This was the site of the Roman outpost of **Ad Speculum**, from where signals were sent by mirror (*speculum*) tracking the caravans en route to Tozeur. Because of its exposed position, the village was later named Qasr el Shems (Castle of the Sun). The springs are said to have risen up at a point where a wandering camel carrying the body of a holy man, Sidi Sultan, finally came to a halt; the **marabout**, attributed with the usual powers, is buried in the tomb near the ravine.

Chebika is the village described by Jean Duvignaud in his book *Change at Shebika* (see p.420), where he tells of the open rivalry between Chebika and Redeyef since mining began. Wealthy miners bought land here in the oasis, when an annual cathartic ritual stood in for open warfare right up until Independence. The people of Redeyef used to go to a selected spot between the villages, lay out some bread and then hide behind a rock. The people of Chebika soon arrived on the scene and pretended to steal the bread, whereupon the owners would run out and start a mock fight before both sides settled down to eat together. Throughout his book, Duvignaud describes how similar traditions led to the destruction of the very community they were supposed to sustain. The men from here, for example, often married women from El Hamma, and ceded land from the oasis to the bride's father, depriving the village of its property and increasing the power of the absentee landlord. Agricultural production seldom increased, since the new owners (like the miners) were unskilled, and local families had to borrow to survive.

The Chott el Gharsa and El Hamma du Jerid

Beyond Chebika, the road cuts across the corner of the **Chott el Gharsa**, a salt lake lying in a depression below sea level. Like the Chott el Jerid, it's not really a lake – though mirages suggest it must be – and the surface is inundated only in the wet season. The road itself is surfaced for all but 13km, which should be no problem in even an ordinary car. On the other side of the Chott, **EL HAMMA DU JERID**, with its six springs and 110,000 palms, signals the beginning of the large oases around Tozeur. The waters of the Hamma, rising to a temperature of 38°C, were much favoured by the Romans; one later traveller compared the bath to a mustard plaster, and emerged feeling like a boiled lobster. If you would like to try them, the baths are at the northern end of town, just off the road from Chebika, with separate pools for men and women, and are allegedly open around the clock.

Tozeur

TOZEUR has always been the commercial and political centre of the Jerid, and for many years had greater regional power than the central government. This it owed to the date harvest, which made the town an important market and attracted caravans and merchants from the far south. Parts of the old fourteenth-century quarter still survive, but the oasis is the main feature.

In recent years, like so many other parts of the country, Tozeur has been gearing itself up as a major tourist centre. First came the jeep-loads of day-trippers on "safari" from the coast, then the airport with a few charter flights, and finally the "Route Touristique", lined with package hotels to make this a fully-fledged desert resort.

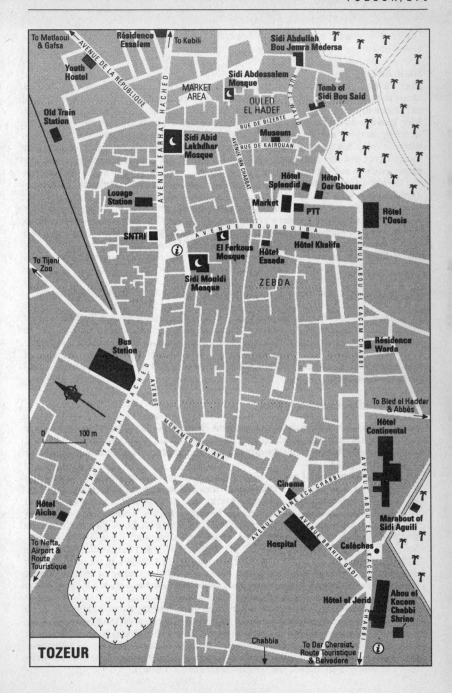

To Metlaoui & Gafsa
AVENUE DE LA RÉPUBLIQUE
Résidence Essalem
To Kebili
Youth Hostel
Old Train Station
RUE EL MAOUJ
Sidi Abdullah Bou Jemra Medersa
Sidi Abdessalem Mosque
MARKET AREA
OULED EL HADEF
Tomb of Sidi Bou Said
RUE DE BIZERTE
AVENUE FARHAT HACHED
Sidi Abid Lakhdhar Mosque
Museum
RUE DE KAIROUAN
AVENUE IBN CHABBAT
Louage Station
Hôtel Splendid
Hôtel Dar Ghouar
Hôtel l'Oasis
SNTRI
Market
PTT
AVENUE BOURGUIBA
To Tijani Zoo
El Ferkous Mosque
Hôtel Essada
Hôtel Khalifa
AVENUE ABOU EL KACEM CHABBI
Sidi Mouldi Mosque
ZEBDA
Bus Station
Résidence Warda
To Bled el Haddar & Abbès
AVENUE FARHAT HACHED
AVENUE MOHAMED BEN AYA
Hôtel Continental
0   100 m
Cinema
AVENUE LAMINE ECH CHABBI
AVENUE BRAHIM GADI
AVENUE ABOU EL KACEM CHABBI
Hôtel Aicha
To Nefta, Airport & Route Touristique
Marabout of Sidi Aguili
Hospital
Calêches
Hôtel el Jerid
Abou el Kacem Chabbi Shrine
Chabbia
To Dar Cheraiat, Route Touristique & Belvedere

TOZEUR

Tozeur still retains much charm, but you do feel a bit like just another punter here nowadays.

Some history

After the first **Arab invasions**, the Berbers of Tozeur joined the Arab army, which swept west through the Maghreb. By 900, however, Tozeur's radical **Kharijite sect** had begun to resist the rule of the Shiite Fatimids, and in 944 the legendary figure of **Abu Yazid** (or Abu Himara, "the man on the donkey") moved north from Tozeur to lay siege to the Fatimid capital at Mahdia. The rebellion failed and Abu Yazid was killed in 947, but the legend of the unruly southerner became part of Tunisian mythology. Over the next centuries, Tozeur continued to be a centre of revolt; the **Almoravids** found strong support here when they tried to overthrow the **Almohads**, and the town's rebelliousness was only finally suppressed by the **Hafsids** in the fourteenth century.

Thereafter Tozeur lost its military might but developed as the major trading post for southern Tunisia. When Dr Shaw arrived in 1757 (see p.418), he noticed the "great traffick" in slaves, brought from as far away as the River Niger; the exchange rate was one black slave for two or three quintals of dates. James Bruce, heading for the Nile in 1765, reported that Tozeur was used by merchants from Timbuktu and other Saharan oases, dealing in sufficient wool and dates to load twenty thousand camels each year. But by the middle of the nineteenth century, the Saharan trade had dwindled to one or two small caravans each year, and the oasis was thrown back on its own, still plentiful resources.

Until the French occupation the town had a strangely ambivalent relationship with the Beys. Although there was a governor, or *caid*, who usually lived in Tunis, the town was actually administered by its own council of elders. Every winter the Bey had to send a *mahalla*, a military expedition to force the town and surrounding tribes to pay their taxes and allow the *caid* to carry out his administrative duties. After a couple of weeks the *mahalla* would leave and the town once again became autonomous – until the following winter.

Arrival and accommodation

Tozeur's backbone is its main street, **avenue Bourguiba**. Lined with tourist souvenir shops, it can feel like a gauntlet of eager merchants trying to sell you carpets and sand roses. About two-thirds of the way down is the central **place Ibn Chabbat**, flanked by the **market** and **PTT**.

At the northern end of avenue Bourguiba, **avenue Farhat Hached** is the main Nefta–Kebili road, and where you'll find the **bus** and **louage stations**. If you arrive by **air**, there's no public transport into town except taxis (around 3TD), although the local *Interrent/Europcar* rep claims to meet all incoming flights. Tozeur has two **tourist offices**: the friendly and knowledgeable *ONTT* on avenue Abou el Kacem Chabbi by the *Hôtel el Jerid*, which employs some English-speaking staff (Mon–Thurs 8.30am–1pm & 3–5.45pm, Fri & Sat 8.30am–1.30pm; ☎06/454503), and the *Syndicat d'Initiative* (Mon–Sat 8am–1pm & 3–6pm, sometimes Sun; ☎06/450034), more conveniently located at the northern end of avenue Bourguiba by the corner of avenue Farhat Hached. They can both arrange camel and *calèche* tours of the oasis at 5TD per person on a camel or 15TD for up to five people in a *calèche*.

Tozeur is blessed with quite a selection of pleasant **hotels**, and you should have no trouble finding a place you like, whatever your budget. Women on their own need have no worries, except possibly in the very cheapest places. The Route Touristique has an ever-increasing number of hastily built three- and four-star tourist hotels, all with swimming pools, nightclubs and money-changing facilities ready for package tourists arriving at the local airport. In fact, the only thing missing is a beach.

Town centre hotels

Aicha ★, av Farhat Hached (☎06/452788). On the Nefta road, towards the airport turnoff. Neat and spotless, with welcoming smiles, showers in most rooms, and a choice of room decor. ②.

Continental ★★★, av Abou el Kacem Chabbi (☎06/450411). Similar to the *Jerid*, in spite of the extra stars, and rather shabby beyond the facade. ③.

Dar Ghouar ★★, rue de Kairouan (☎06/452870). Tozeur's only two-star hotel. New and rather bare, it lacks a lived-in feeling. ③.

Essada, off av Bourguiba, opposite the market (☎06/450097). The cheapest place in town, but not for the fussy; the beds are on the soft side, and lone women should think twice about staying here. ①.

Résidence Essalem, av Farhat Hached (☎06/452981). A quiet, family-run place on the Kebili-Degache road, east of town. ②.

El Jerid ★, av Abou el Kacem Chabbi (☎06/454488). This is where they stick tour groups whisked in from Hammamet and Monastir on quick jeep "safaris" of the south. ③.

Khalifa, av Bourguiba (☎06/450858). More than adequate, but check your room has an outside window. In summer you can sleep on the roof. ②.

Hôtel de l'Oasis ★★★, pl des Martyrs (☎06/452699). Rather a classy joint, but friendly with it. ⑤.

Splendid, rue de Kairouan (☎06/450053). Behind the PTT on the edge of the Ouled el Hadef district. A very decent mid-range hotel, but more splendid than the rooms is the collection of banknotes in reception. Ask for a room with a shower and outside window. ②.

Résidence Warda, 31 av Abou el Kacem Chabbi (☎06/452597). Very clean and pleasant. Recommended. ②.

Route Touristique hotels

Abou Nawas Tozeur ★★★★, Route Touristique (☎06/453500). Tozeur's poshest hotel, pleasantly peaceful with tastefully decorated rooms. You may even rub shoulders with the odd VIP. ⑥.

Basma ★★★, Route Touristique (☎06/452488). Friendlier and more relaxed than the neighbouring *Ras el Ain*, with a younger French clientele. ⑤.

Dar Cheriaiat, Route Touristique (☎06/452100). If the *Abou Nawas* isn't pricey enough, you could go right to the top of the market by renting a luxury suite in the museum complex. ⑥.

Hafsi ★★★, Route Touristique (☎06/452558). First of the bunch along the route but it still looks newly built. Rooms are airy and light, if a bit hard and bare. ④.

Palmyre ★★★, Route Touristique (☎06/452016). Classy if a bit staid, but nicely done out in traditional brickwork with Roman artefacts strewn about, satellite TV in every room and lots of palms, but no palmyras. ⑥.

Phedra ★★★, Route Touristique (☎06/452185). A friendly place with views of the sunset over the Belvedere from everywhere – even inside the pool. Ask for a room with a view. ⑤.

Ras el Ain ★★★, Route Touristique (☎06/452698). Run by *Club Med* and all a bit Frenchly formal. Showers but no baths in rooms. Library of French and a few English books. ⑥.

Youth hostel and campsites

Maison des Jeunes youth hostel, av de la République (☎06/452335). A couple of hundred metres up the Gafsa road from its junction with av Farhat Hached. Up and out by 8.30am; and curfew at 10pm. Camping possible. ①.

Campement les Beaux Rêves, av Abou el Kacem Chabbi (☎06/451242). five hundred metres beyond the *ONTT*. Sleep in your own tent, in a Bedouin version, in a palm-frond hut or on a hammock hung between two date palms. It's very pleasant with trees, a stream to bathe in, running water, showers, toilets and café.

Camping du Belvédère, up by the Belvedere (no phone). Friendly but very primitive with no running water but hot and cold springs nearby, places to bathe and toilets of a sort. Shelters for those without tents.

The Town

Between avenue Farhat Hached and avenue Bourguiba is the ancient **Ouled el Hadef** quarter, the most interesting part of Tozeur, where the architecture, like the lives of its people, is largely traditional. **Avenue Abou el Kacem Chabbi** runs west, parallel to avenue Farhat Hached, alongside the quarters of **Zebda** and **Chabbia**, which have been less zealous about preserving their traditions than Ouled el Hadef. Various turnings from the main road lead into the **oasis**. At the end of avenue Abou el Kacem Chabbi, the tarmac turns a corner by the Dar Cheraiat Museum to become the **Route Touristique**, meeting up with avenue Farhat Hached at the airport turnoff. Straight ahead, off the tarmac, is the road out to the **Belvedere**.

Ouled el Hadef

The oldest part of town, fourteenth-century **Ouled el Hadef**, backs onto the *Hôtel Splendid*, its entrances marked by plans of the quarter. As at Tamerza, its high walls are faced with small rectangular bricks, presenting a blank exterior to the narrow streets. The windowless walls ensure the privacy that is prescribed in the Koran – in fact, the Arabic word for a house, *maskin,* is related to *sakina,* which means "peaceful and holy". A fifteenth-century legal ruling of one Sidi Khalil, brief and to the point, states that "anyone may climb up his date palm but only if he previously informs the neighbour into whose house he might obtain a view". Only traditionally made bricks are used and the brickwork in the quarter is almost unique in Tunisia (see below); the only other place it can be found is in neighbouring Nefta. The bricks themselves are made near the Belvedere.

This is an excellent place to wander around and get lost, despite groups of young boys who seem to delight in baiting tourists. Things to look out for, apart from the brickwork, are the palm-trunk ceilings overhead as you pass under archways, and the large doors equipped with three knockers that are still fitted on some houses. Men, women and children each have a different one with its own tone, so that any visitor can be greeted by the appropriate member of the household.

The main street of the quarter, **rue de Kairouan**, leading from the *Hôtel Splendid* and the *Hôtel de l'Oasis*, runs from one side of it to the other. On the right is the **tomb of Sidi Bou Aissa**, now converted into a **Museum of Popular Art** (Mon–Sat 8am– 6pm, Sun 8am–2.30pm; 1TD). Among the exhibits are objects from the traditional marriage ceremony – the wooden chests for the bride's clothes, an Egyptian silk dress, and ornamental green and yellow pottery. There is also a collection of manuscripts, including a timetable for the distribution of water through the oasis; this was devised by Ibn Chabbat in the thirteenth century as a way of ensuring equal supplies for every landowner and only set out in print by the French. In the courtyard, among miscellaneous statuary, is a pair of traditional three-knocker doors, in case you missed them on your wanderings around the old quarter.

BRICKWORK IN TOZEUR AND NEFTA

The **building style** of the houses in the old quarters of Nefta and Tozeur is unique in Tunisia. Constructed of yellowish handmade bricks, they are picked out in relief with ornate geometrical designs. The unique ornamental shapes and motifs made with the bricks are repeated on local carpets and shawls. This decorative technique was first used in Syria and Iraq during the eighth century and carried west by the Arab invaders in the tenth. The only other place where it can can be seen today is in Iran.

Although the archways and covered passages have been extensively restored, the materials are usually traditional; local clay and sand are mixed, soaked in water and left to mulch for a day. Then the mixture is shaped in a wooden frame and left to dry in the sun. Finally, the bricks are baked in a kiln for three days at temperatures of up to 1000°C. The industry is on something of an upturn at the moment as people are returning to locally made bricks – which provide better insulation against extremes of temperature than breeze blocks.

DATES AND DATE FARMERS

Deglat en nour dates

Of all the 120 varieties of **date palm**, the finest is the *deglat en nour*, or "finger of light", so called because of the translucent quality of the ripened fruit. Tozeur and Nefta produce 1000 tonnes of these dates every year, and most are exported to Europe for Christmas. According to legend, a poor village woman died before she could make the pilgrimage to Mecca and was buried with her humble string of beads, made from date stones. The tears the Prophet shed in sympathy germinated the stones and created not only an oasis but also the new variety of date. The palms are artificially pollinated in April and June each year, and the fruit harvested by hand at the beginning of winter. Each tree is expected to yield some fifteen or twenty clusters of dates, each weighing about ten kilos.

Palm wine, the notorious *laghmi*, is simply the sap of the palm, collected from the top of the trunk or through incisions in the bark. It only takes 24 hours to ferment, and is available in sweet (fresh) and fermented versions. The latter needs to be treated with caution as it's unpredictably potent and occasionally adulterated. *Laghmi* is generally available between April and October – ask around in the oasis. As for buying the dates themselves, in season the market in Tozeur is as good a place as any.

The sharecroppers' tale

Most of the palms are owned by wealthy, and often absentee, landlords who employ labourers as **sharecroppers**. Instead of a salary, they each receive a share of the harvest. Out on the plains where the main crop is barley, this share is about one-fifth – a share that gives them their name, the *khammes*. In the oases, however, the figure falls to one-tenth, sometimes even less, because the date harvest is so valuable.

Without capital of their own, and since they are paid only at the end of the agricultural year, the *khammes* have to borrow from their employers to tide them over. Paying high rates of interest on these loans forces them into heavy debt, which, after a poor harvest, they are often unable to repay. And so they fall into a sort of debt bondage, bound to the employer in perpetuity because they cannot pay off the ever-increasing loans. Since Independence the government has tried to improve their status by introducing a union to combat the employers. Strangely enough the *khammes* have remained apathetic. They see the weather, the cause of poor harvests, as the source of their condition and not the employers' ruthless exploitation of their poverty.

At the far end of rue de Kairouan, two right turns will take you down rue de Bizerte. The rue el Walid, left at the end, leads to the **Medersa of Sidi Abdullah Bou Jemra**. Nearby, the finely carved **tomb of Sidi Bou Said** bridges the narrow street. The mosque whose minaret dominates the quarter is that of **Sidi Abdessalem**, by the side of the market.

The mosques on avenue Bourguiba are of limited interest. The **El Farkous Mosque**, with its tall, slender minaret, is attractive and distinctive, but not very ancient. The **Mosque of Sidi Mouldi**, down the road by the *Syndicat d'Initiative*, has a minaret in a similar style, restored in 1944, but you probably won't be allowed up it to admire the view.

South of town

Avenue Abou el Kacem Chabbi is named after the great Tozeuri poet (see p.412) whose shrine is tucked away by the *ONTT* tourist office. With the northern edge of the oasis on one side, it also skirts the quarters of Zebda and Chebbia. **Zebda** borders avenue Bourguiba, across which it glared angrily at Ouled el Hadef, the two in a state of mortal feud until the last century. **Chabbia**, a little further west along the road, was one of the last places in Tunisia where the bride still rode in a camel-borne litter at her marriage ceremony. The camel still joins the procession, but nowadays the bride walks alongside it. If you want to see the real thing, you'll have to go to Jerba.

Behind the *Hôtel Continental*, near where the camels and *calèches* hang out, is the little **marabout of Sidi Aguili**; there's nothing very special about it really, except that it's remarkably photogenic and appears anonymously on numerous postcard depictions of "the South". See how many you spot around the country.

At the end of avenue Abou el Kacem Chabbi is the **Dar Cheraiat complex** featuring a museum, an Arabian Nights theme park, a restaurant, café and deluxe apartments, with all sorts of additions and extensions in the pipeline. The **museum** (daily 8am–midnight; 2.5TD) gives an upmarket, sanitized view of Tunisian life, but it's well laid out, with treasures formerly belonging to the Bey, among other fascinating antiques, all with English explanations. If you so desire, attendants dressed up like the Bey's servants will escort you round. The **theme park** (same hours as museum; 5TD), with sundry waxwork scenes from the Arabian Nights tales – which are mainly set in Egypt and Iraq and don't actually mention Tunisia at all – is expensive by Tunisian standards, but a snip compared to Madame Tussaud's in London. The café is a handy place to stop for a drink, so long as you don't mind paying well over the odds.

The road and sand track to the left of Dar Charaiat follow the main water course out to the signposted **Belvedere** – a grandiose name for several large boulders which are, nonetheless, big enough to give a beautiful view over the oasis if you climb up them. You can make out the precise boundaries of the cultivated land hemmed in by sand. During the Ottoman period the protecting bamboo fences were removed and the oasis went to ruin, battered by the south winds.

A hundred metres or so past the Belvedere, shards on the ground like broken glass glinting in the sun are in fact **rock crystals**. A little further is the traditional **brick factory** (open office hours), where the workers will be happy to show you how they make the bricks used in Tozeur's distinctive architecture. The scrub area beyond the Belvedere is also an excellent and easily accessible place for spotting desert birdlife.

The Oasis

The main attraction of Tozeur, its vast **oasis**, covers around ten square kilometres planted with some 200,000 palms and fed by 200 springs, its water channelled along dykes, or *seguias*, and controlled by a series of sluices. At the time of Ibn Chabbat, these streams were blocked with sections of palm trunks, which were opened and closed by orders of the warden.

The main road into the oasis starts in avenue Abou el Kacem Chabbi by the *Hôtel Continental*. Just over 500m along it is the village of **BLED EL HADDAR**, site of Roman **Tusuros**, where a heavily restored brickwork **minaret** stands on a course of Roman stonework in a square to the right of the main road. Also in the square is the **Great Mosque**, built around 1190 by the Almoravid Ibn Ghaniya who, like so many others, came to Tozeur to start a rebellion. Its beautiful stone **mihrab**, all the more striking in this plain interior, was the work of craftsmen from the Balearic islands. Like many Islamic buildings, the mosque exploits sunlight, which, during the afternoon, streams through the narrow windows down the central nave to the *mihrab*. The classic minaret above begins as a circle, develops into an octagon and ends up square; the bird's nest is a later addition. On the other side of the tower, a path leads to the reconstructed **tomb of Ibn Chabbat** (first built in 1282), who devised the complex irrigation and cultivation system used in the oasis.

The road continues through some of the oasis's best cultivated land, reaching, after a couple more kilometres, the little village of **ABBÈS**. Just beyond it is the **marabout of Sidi Bou Lifa**, overshadowed by a huge **jujube tree** planted by the saint himself; both are reputed to be over seven hundred years old. Jujube trees, which originated in

China, bear fruit which can be eaten fresh or dried, tasting a little like dates and traditionally used in the United States to make large sucking sweets. From here the road meanders lazily a few pleasant kilometres through the oasis, before bringing you back to Tozeur near the top of avenue Bourguiba.

A few hundred metres past the tree and marabout is a garden and zoo, unassumingly called **Paradis** – a somewhat untended version, sadly (daily 8am–nightfall; 1TD). The menagerie has gazelles, several tormented baboons, snakes, and a family of lions, all kept in overcrowded captivity. If you arrive at the same time as a tour group, you can also see performing scorpions and such spectacles as a Coke-drinking camel. Children should appreciate it. More interesting for adults, though overpriced, are the pistachio, rose, violet and pomegranate syrups made from plants in the garden and sold at the entrance.

Back in town, animal lovers will also want to avoid the **Tijani Zoo** – left from avenue Bourguiba into avenue Farhat Hached, then signposted (right) after some 150m and off to the right a few hundred metres up (daily 8am–6pm; 1TD). This was once a snake farm, but the reptiles are nowadays a very minor attraction, neither labelled nor easy to see beneath their wire gauze. Otherwise it's the typically depressing spectacle of bears, jackals and other miserable beasts pacing back and forth frustratedly in their undersized cages. Domestic animals lighten the atmosphere, but even they are only enjoyable if you tag on behind a tourist party and watch them watching the inmates.

Eating, drinking and nightlife

There are a number of budget-oriented **restaurants** along avenue Bourguiba, avenue Abou el Kacem Chabbi and avenue Farhat Hached. Just off the southern end of avenue Bourguiba, opposite the newspaper kiosk, the *Restaurant de la Medina* does standard fodder at low prices. A hundred metres down towards avenue Farhat Hached, and left through the arches, the *Restaurant de la République* is pretty similar, while the *Restaurant du Paradis*, just by the *Hôtel Essada*, is even better value, with large helpings of good food. On avenue Farhat Hached, the *Restaurant el Amal* provides cheap fare just behind the *Syndicat d'Initiative*, or there's the *Restaurant du Sud* a couple of hundred metres east, opposite the *Agil* station. Slightly more refined options are available on avenue Abou el Kacem Chabbi, in the form of the *Restaurant du Soleil* at no. 48, opposite the *Résidence Warda*, and better, the *Restaurant Diamanta* at no. 74, opposite the road to Bled el Haddar. Neither of these should burn a hole in your pocket.

For something a little classier, your best bet is in the restaurants of the various starred hotels, most of which do set menus and/or buffet lunch and supper. The cheapest is the *Aicha* (closed Fri), but the *Continental*, *L'Oasis* and *Dar Ghaouir* all have buffets or set menus. The *Restaurant le Petit Prince*, off avenue Abou el Kacem Chabbi near the top of avenue Bourguiba, is a bit of a tourist trap and rather expensive for what you get, but the price includes a floor show. Finally, if money is no object, why not lunch or dine at the *Dar Charaiat*, whose prices are extravagant by Tunisian standards.

If breakfast is not available at your hotel, the pizzeria/sandwich bar halfway down avenue Bourguiba should sort you out, or, for a dinar or so, you can breakfast at the *Hôtel Khalifa*. A couple of patisseries on avenue Abou el Kacem Chabbi, notably the *Diamanta* near the corner of avenue Bourguiba and another at no. 29 next to the *Warda*, do freshly squeezed orange juice in season (or you can pay more for it on avenue Bourguiba). For a quiet beer, your best bet is the **bar** of the *Hôtel Splendid*.

Listings

Airlines *Tunis Air*, on the Nefta road, opposite *Hertz* (☎06/450038).

Banks Two on av Bourguiba, and two more just round the corner in av Farhat Hached.

MOVING ON FROM TOZEUR

Tozeur's **bus station** is off avenue Farhat Hached. There are no fewer than sixteen daily departures to Metlaoui (45min), of which four continue to Redeyef (1hr 45min) and Tamerza (2hr 45min), the rest to Gafsa (1hr). Five of these (run by *SNTRI*) go on to Kairouan (5hr) and Tunis (7hr), one to Sfax (5hr 30min). Three buses a day run to Kebili (1hr 30min), one continuing to Gabes (3hr 30min), the others to Douz (2hr 15min): you may have to change buses – you'll know if everyone gets off the bus and you find your baggage taken out of the trunk and dumped on the tarmac. In the other direction, there are regular departures to Nefta (30min), the last around 8pm; in the morning, one of these continues to the Algerian border at Hazoua (1hr 30min).

Louages leave from a yard off avenue Farhat Hached, about 100m east of avenue Bourguiba. You should have no trouble getting a vehicle from here to Tunis, Nefta, Metlaoui, Gafsa, Kebili, Degache or El Hamma du Jerid. There is no public transport along the direct road north to Tamerza, 13km of which is unsurfaced though usually passable in a two-wheel drive car.

Tozeur's **airport** (☎06/450388), 3km out of town, has services once a week to Jerba (50min), Lyon (2hr 15min) and Paris (2hr 45min), with between three and seven a week to Tunis (1hr 10min). There are no longer any passenger train services to or from Tozeur.

Car rental *Eurorent, ATL, Hertz* and *Interrent/Europcar* all have offices on the road to Nefta and the airport. *Avis* (☎06/453547) is on av Farhat Hached, a few metres west of the junction with av Bourguiba. *Hertz* (☎06/450214), *Express* (☎06/451520) and *ATL* (☎06/452404) are all by the *Magasin Général* supermarket, a few hundred metres west towards the airport turnoff, while *Interrent/Europcar* (☎06/450119) is 200m further still.

Cinema Av Lamine ech Chabbi (off av Abou el Kacem Chabbi opposite the *Hôtel Continental*) – about 100m down on the right, at the corner of av Brahim Gadi.

Festival Every year around December, a series of camel races and Bedouin spectacles takes place on a site 500m off av Abou el Kacem Chabbi.

Hammams There is a hammam three doors away from the *Hôtel Essada* (daily men 5–10am & 3.30–7pm; women 10am–3pm); you may have to go in the back way, which can be tricky to find. Another lies behind the *Syndicat d'Initiative* (daily men 4–10am & 4–9pm; women 10am–3.30pm).

International phone calls In the PTT's back entrance (Mon–Sat 8.30am–1pm & 2.30–5.30pm, Fri & Sat 8.30am–1pm), or at the taxiphone office opposite (daily 7.30am–2pm & 4–10pm). Other taxiphone offices are located behind the *Syndicat d'Initiative* and off av Abou el Kacem Chabbi more or less opposite *Résidence Warda*. You can also use the phones at the *Hôtel Splendid*, at "reasonable" times, or any time if you're staying there.

Medical facilities The regional hospital is on av Brahim Gadi (☎06/450476), off av Abou el Kacem Chabbi, opposite the *Hôtel el Jerid*.

Newspapers *Time, Newsweek* and some English-language papers are available at a kiosk at the southern end of av Bourguiba, between the *Hôtel Khalifa* and av Abou el Kacem Chabbi.

PTT In pl Ibn Chabbat, just off av Bourguiba (city hours); changes cash, phones at the back.

Supermarket *Magasin Général*, av Farhat Hached, out towards the airport turnoff (Tues–Sat 8am–12.30pm & 3–7.15pm, Sun 8am–12.15pm).

Swimming pool If you don't fancy the oasis pools, the hotels *Jerid, Continental* and *Oasis* have pools you can use for few dinars (the *Continental* is currently cheapest), as do the hotels on the Route Touristique (the *Phedra*'s with a view).

Nefta

After travelling the 25km from Tozeur through almost totally barren and dusty land, the oasis at **NEFTA** is quite a shock. You don't notice it immediately – the drab buildings on the edge of the town shield its beginnings – but suddenly its extent becomes clear, as does that of the **Corbeille**, a crater-like depression densely planted with palm trees. The

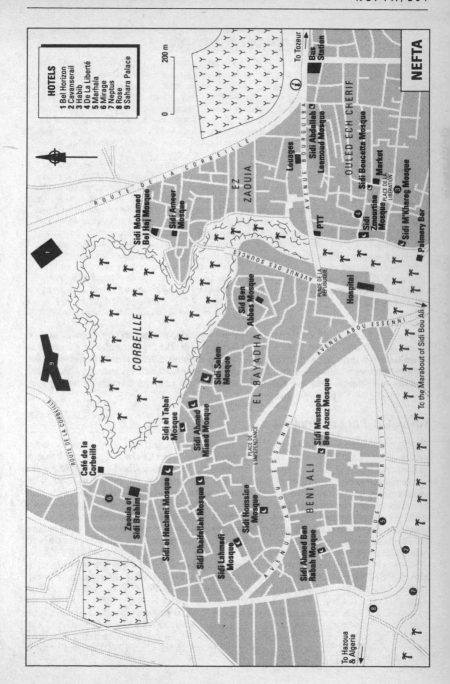

NEFTA

HOTELS
1 Bel Horizon
2 Cavanserail
3 Habib
4 De La Liberté
5 Marhala
6 Mirage
7 Neptus
8 Rose
9 Sahara Palace

200 m

To Tozeur

Bus Station

OULED ECH CHERIF

Sidi Abdallah

Laamoud Mosque

Sidi Boucetta Mosque

Market

PLACE DE LA LIBERATION

Sidi Zmourine Mosque

Sidi M'Khareg Mosque

Palmery Bar

PTT

AVENUE BOURGUIBA

Louages

EZ ZAOUIA

Sidi Mohamed Bel Haj Mosque

Sidi Ameur Mosque

ROUTE DE LA CORBEILLE

CORBEILLE

Café de la Corbeille

ROUTE DE LA CORBEILLE

Zaouia of Sidi Brahim

Sidi el Hachani Mosque

Sidi Dhaiatlah Mosque

Sidi Lahmadi Mosque

Sidi el Tabaï Mosque

Sidi Ahmed Miaad Mosque

Sidi Houssine Mosque

Sidi Ahmed Ben Rabah Mosque

PLACE DE L'INDEPENDANCE

Sidi Mustapha Ben Azouz Mosque

BENI ALI

AVENUE ABOU ESSENNI

AVENUE DES SOURCES

Sidi Ben Abbas Mosque

Sidi Salem Mosque

EL BAYADHA

AVENUE ABOU ESSENNI

PLACE DE LA REPUBLIQUE

Hospital

AVENUE ABOU ESSENNI

To the Marabout of Sidi Bou Ali

AVENUE BOURGUIBA

To Hazoua & Algeria

Sufism, *Tasawwuf* in Arabic, is the Divine Wisdom contained within the *Tariquah*, the spiritual way or path laid down in the Koran. Participants are called *faqirs* or dervishes, meaning "poor", and strictly speaking the Sufi is one who has reached the end of the path, which is a direct personal experience of the Unity of God. A Sufi teacher, variously called a *faqir, sheikh* or *murshid*, prescribes the chants, recitations and body exercises which have made this sect so famous. Besides the Koran and the *Hadith* (sayings of the Prophet), the Sufi looks to the *Hadith qudsi*, in which God speaks in the first person through the Prophet. "My slave," reads one typical verse, "comes ever nearer to me through devotion of his free will, until I love him, and when I love him, I am the hearing with which he sees and the hand with which he fights and the foot with which he walks."

Sufism has often had an awkward relationship with orthodox **Sunni Islam**, threatening to usurp religious law and to substitute mysticism for the knowledge of the truth contained in the Koran, a problem partially resolved as early as the eleventh century by saying that Sufism was a way of "apprehending reality", not of finding out new facts about God. In Tunisia Sufis have long held considerable power; with the breakdown in the control of central government (from the Almohads in the thirteenth century onwards), the *sheikhs* had great influence in rural areas, setting up *zaouias* which provided shelter, teaching and administered justice. In the twentieth century, Tunisian liberals as well as the French attacked their autonomy and what they considered an obsolete code of conduct. Many devout Muslims, however, continued to practise the **hypnosis**, trancelike **meditation** and **saint worship**, or *maraboutism*, with which Sufism had always been linked.

site of Roman *Nepte*, Nefta, according to the legends, was settled by Kostel, "son of Shem, son of Noah", at the place where water boiled for the first time after the flood. It is now one of the most important religious centres in Tunisia, traditionally linked with the mystical brotherhoods of **Sufism**; the ridge above the Corbeille is cluttered with simple whitewashed domes and the old quarters somehow manage to pack in twenty-four mosques and over a hundred shrines.

Arrival and accommodation

Avenue Bourguiba, the main road from Tozeur to the Algerian border, splits the town neatly in two. Coming in from Tozeur, it descends into the **Corbeille**, which it bridges at the narrowest point – the area south of here is **Ouled ech Chrif**, one of Nefta's old quarters, and over the bridge is **place de la République**, the centre of town. The main road swings south from here, skirting the quarter of **Beni Ali** on one side, and the main hotel zone on the other, before continuing on its way towards Algeria. South of the hotels is the **oasis**, and beyond that the silvery gleam of the Chott, which really does look like a sea from here. Should you wish to literally drive around the town, the whole ensemble is now neatly encircled by a belt of tarmac, the northern part of which goes right round the top of the Corbeille.

Nefta's **bus station** is on avenue Bourguiba next to the *Mobil* petrol station, opposite the *Syndicat d'Initiative*, and **louages** leave from avenue Bourguiba, halfway between the bridge and the *Syndicat d'Initiative* **tourist office** (daily 8am–6pm; ☎06/430236), 300m out towards Tozeur on the left. The office is very helpful and rents out camels (3.5TD per person per hour), donkeys (1.3TD) and *calèches* (1.5TD), all with a compulsory guide (5TD per 1–2hr excursion). Alternatively, you can just rent the guide, who may be able able to smooth your way into some of the monuments. They also offer two- and three- person car trips around Nefta (2hr; 10TD) or to Chebika, Tamerza and Mides (day trip 35TD).

Nefta doesn't have the widest choice of **accommodation** in Tunisia, but you can find hotels in all categories, and their number is increasing as Nefta limbers up to become an overnight stop for tour groups "on safari" from the beach resorts.

Hotels

Bel Horizon ★★★, rte de la Corbeille (☎06/430328). Up beyond El Zaouia. Not such a nice view over the Corbeille as the *Sahara Palace*, but the nearest thing till that reopens. ⑤.

Caravanserail ★★★/★★★★, Route Touristique (☎06/430355). Opposite the *Marhala*, and with a choice of old three-star or new and more expensive four-star wings. ⑤–⑥.

Habib, pl de la Libération (☎06/430497). Nicely located and handy for the morning *SNTRI* bus to Tunis, especially as the driver spends the night here. ②.

Hôtel de la Liberté, off av Bourguiba (☎06/430643). Take the path off av Bourguiba by the PTT, first left up the steps by Sidi Zmourtine mosque and look for the sign on your left. Rather basic old-school travellers' hotel, which should appeal to anyone vaguely till hippyish. Run by a genial local character called Mahmoud and set around a patio complete with grapevine. ①.

Marhala, Route Touristique (☎06/457027). Less slick but a better deal than its three-star neighbours. You can also camp here and use the hotel's facilities. Choice of an older, cheaper wing or the new wing, which has air conditioning and offers greater comfort. ②–③.

Mirage, rte de la Corbeille (☎06/457064). Near the *Sahara Palace* and somewhat cheaper. Closed for rebuilding at last check. ③.

Neptus ★★★, Route Touristique (☎06/457378). Nice airy rooms – ask for one with a view of the oasis. ⑤.

Le Nomade, av Bourguiba (☎06/430052). On the Tozeur road close to the edge of town. Clean rooms with showers, and a pool, but rather inconveniently located. ②.

Rose ★★★, Route Touristique (☎06/430696). A mainly German clientele frequents this comfortable tourist hotel. ⑥.

Sahara Palace ★★★★★, rte de la Corbeille (☎06/457046). Nefta's most chic hostelry, patronized by the likes of Brigitte Bardot. Closed for renovation at our last check, but should reopen soon. ⑥

The Town

The most rewarding pastime in Nefta is wandering round the **old quarters** – Ouled ech Cherif, El Bayadha, Ez Zaouia and Beni Ali – where you can admire the distinctive local architecture and, through the ancient doorways, see the looms and rugs which provide a living for most of the people.

Sadly, torrential rain and flooding in January 1990 caused considerable damage to Nefta's ancient buildings – especially in El Bayadha, when a chunk of the old quarter fell into the Corbeille. Although a lot of the mosques have already been rebuilt, traditional methods of rebuilding and restoration make this a very drawn-out process. Meanwhile, Ouled ech Cherif remains the quarter least affected if you fancy a walkabout to check out the traditional brickwork (see p.276). Otherwise, take a look around the other quarters and survey the damage.

Coming into town from Tozeur along avenue Bourguiba, **Ouled ech Cherif** lies to your left. At its heart is place de la Libération, the main square of the quarter. The streets north of place de la Libération are a maze of brick alleyways and tunnels roofed with palm beams, while the quarter's most outstanding mosque, that of **Sidi M'Khareg**, stands on the edge of the oasis, its four-domed minaret recently restored after damage in the floods.

Continuing down avenue Bourguiba, you come to place de la République, where a left turn takes you into the heart of the oasis, while a right turn up **avenue des Sources** takes you along the edge of the Corbeille and then crosses it into the **Ez Zaouia** quarter. The edge of the Corbeille here offers good views but in general Ez Zaouia is less interesting than the other old quarters and still sustains considerable flood damage. Of its two mosques, **Sidi Mohamed Bel Haj** got away reasonably unscathed, but **Sidi Ameur** remains virtually a ruin.

Some of the most important monuments in Nefta are near the *Café de la Corbeille* in the **El Bayadha** area, at the Corbeille's northwestern tip although much of El Bayadha remains a wasteland, with repairs to flood damage in progress here and there. Unfortunately, many residents cannot afford to do repairs in the traditional way, and the quarter will never again look as it once did, although the mosques have been well restored. Just down the road from the café is the **Zaouia of Sidi Brahim**, a complex of tombs, courtyards and teaching rooms belonging to the Qadria, the most important of the Sufi orders represented here. Members of the order are often buried here near the saint, who also belonged to it. Beside the *zaouia*, a track leads round a ridge over the Corbeille, past five **mosques**, all small, simple in design and packed closely together. The first you come to is the **Sidi el Hachani Mosque**, then the **mosques of Sidi et Tabaï** and **Sidi Ahmed Miaad**. The oldest is the **Mosque of Sidi Salem**, sometimes called the Great Mosque, approached through an unobtrusive doorway off the narrow street; apart from one strip of carving around the walls, its fifteenth-century courtyard is completely unornamented. Finally comes the **Mosque of Sidi Ben Abbes**, the smallest. The road continues from here across an open space that was until recently the town brickworks. The brickworks have moved 5km out of town along the Hazoua road and the site now hosts Nefta's Thursday **market**. Beyond it, the road leads out onto avenue des Sources near place de la République.

Don't take it personally if the guardians of the *zaouia* and mosques turn you away. Nefta is considered a religious city, and local people generally don't like tourists wandering around their monuments. If you can't get in by yourself, you may be luckier with a *Syndicat d'Initiative* guide.

The Corbeille

The **Corbeille** is a vast sunken extension of the oasis, like a massive crater full of palm trees gouged out of the middle of Nefta, with steep sides to protect it from the harsh desert wind. North of the bridge, it bends around to the west, spreading into a wedge that takes out a large chunk of town. At its northern extremity, the Corbeille measures almost a kilometre across, and here beneath the defile well up the springs which irrigate it. Presiding over them, the chic *Hôtel Sahara Palace* is the pride and joy of the local tourist board, now newly refurbished. Beneath the *Café de la Corbeille*, hidden by the palms, is an open-air **bath**. Women generally use it in the mornings, men in the afternoons, and it's not a good idea to intrude on the opposite sex. Beware of going there at night, as there's no lighting and there have been one or two cases of muggings. The best way through the Corbeille is to walk by the hot stream, which saves trampling on the cultivated land and leads from the west to the east end of the valley. Look out for the local eccentric Mohammed, who lives in his garden by the hot stream, growing henna, tobacco and bananas, and selling tobacco pipes.

Norman Douglas liked the Corbeille so much that he wanted to make another at Tozeur – "all the elements are present", he explained, "it only requires a few thousand years of labour, and what are they in a land like this?"

The Nefta Oasis

The **oasis** proper, on the other side of the main road, extends for some ten square kilometres. In addition to over a hundred natural springs, new wells were drilled here in the 1960s, which seem to have reduced the flow from the springs in both the oasis and the Corbeille. Numerous tracks lead through the palm groves, all best explored on foot. Set right in the heart of the oasis is the **Marabout of Sidi Bou Ali** – take the road south from place de la République past the hospital and continue for 500m. This is a major place of pilgrimage, particularly on the third day after the Aid el Kebir. For this reason the marabout is closed to non-Muslims, but it's worth the short walk just to get among the surrounding gardens and to see the other, smaller marabouts along the way. Sidi Bou Ali was born in Morocco and came to Tunisia in the thirteenth century, hoping to resolve the religious disagreement which had divided the area. The legend that he planted the first palm trees in the Jerid (bringing the plants from Touggourt in Algeria) doesn't seem very likely, since Ibn Chabbat had already reorganized the oasis at Tozeur.

Many of the **pools** are used for bathing by women in the early morning and men in the afternoon. As ever, avoid intruding on the opposite sex, but otherwise the bathers are very welcoming. Running around barefoot, as local kids do when swimming, is inadvisable, too, as the oasis is infested with scorpions. If you do get stung you might do worse than follow the advice of Shaw in 1757, who recommended either burying the patient up to the neck, to make them "perspire" or, in "less serious" cases, applying hot ashes or powder of henna, with two or three slices of lemon. In practice a sting hurts like hell, but is rarely fatal.

Eating and drinking

There's a dearth of **restaurants** outside the hotels, but the best of the cheapies is probably *Restaurant des Palmiers du Sud* in place de la République, which does a pretty mean couscous. Others worth trying include *Restaurant Jamel* in avenue Bourguiba by the tourist office, and *Restaurant les Amis* in place de la Libération. The *Bar de la Palmerie*, just inside the oasis south of the Sidi M'Khareg mosque, is good as well, and in the party atmosphere everybody makes a great fuss of unexpected guests. Women may, however, find the atmosphere a little bit intimidating.

Of the **hotel restaurants**, the *Marhala* has the cheapest. The *Nomade*'s restaurant is also quite reasonable, but tends to be monopolized by groups in season. If you feel like splashing out, there's always the *Sahara Palace*. Otherwise, the *Bel Horizon* has a buffet, while the *Caravanserail* and the *Neptus* both have set menus.

The best place in Nefta to have a cup of tea is probably the *Café de la Corbeille* at the northwestern corner of the Corbeille, where you get the best view of the town. It is, however, rather touristy. For a rowdier drink, try the *Bar de la Palmerie* mentioned above.

Listings

Banks Two on av Bourguiba, one opposite the bus station, the other between that and the PTT. When they're closed, you might be able to persuade the big hotels to change some money for you.

Festivals The *Festival Populaire de Nefta*, held over three days in April in pl de la République, features a range of performing arts as well as Sufi chanting and dancing. The *Dakhla* pilgrimage centred around the Marabout of Sidi Bou Ali on the third day after Aid el Kebir (see p.45) also features Sufi chanting and dancing, but is a much more religious affair.

Hammams If the baths in the Corbeille and the oasis are not what you seek, there's the *Hammam el Baraka* in pl de la République (daily men 5am–noon, Tues–Thurs, Sat & Sun also 5pm–midnight; women 1–5pm, Mon & Fri also 5pm–midnight)

Medical facilities The regional hospital (☎06/457193) is on av E Riadh, south of pl de la République and the Sidi Ben Abbes mosque. There's a pharmacy on av Bourguiba between the PTT and *Syndicat d'Initiative*.

PTT On av Bourguiba just by the bridge on the southern side (country hours). International phone calls and cash exchange facilities available.

Swimming pool The *Neptus* has the lowest fee for use of its pool by non-residents. Diners at most hotels can use their pools without charge.

MOVING ON FROM NEFTA

Nefta's **bus station** is on avenue Bourguiba next to the *Mobil* petrol station, opposite the *Syndicat d'Initiative*. Buses coming from Tozeur (30min) generally continue past place de la République and do a loop just before place de l'Indépendance before heading back. The exceptions are the two *SNTRI* buses to Tunis (8hr 30min) via Metlaoui (1hr), Gafsa (1hr 30min) and Kairouan (5hr 30min), which park up in place de la Libération. All *SRT* services east of Tozeur, except the ones to Douz, in fact start at Nefta going to Gabes (1 daily; 5hr), Gafsa (7 daily; 1hr 30min), Kebili (1 daily; 2hr), Metlaoui (11 daily; 1hr), Redeyef (4 daily; 1hr 45min) and Sfax (1 daily; 6hr). The only other services from here are three a day to the Algerian frontier at Hazoua (1hr). **Louages** leave from avenue Bourguiba about halfway between the bridge and the *Syndicat d'Initiative*, serving Tozeur and Hazoua.

At present, **Algeria** is in a state of turmoil with all foreigners declared targets (see p.376). Under the circumstances, travel in the country would be foolhardy. Should this situation change, you will find occasional Algerian *louages* plying the four or five kilometres between the two border posts, but you may have to walk. On the other side, there are frequent buses to El Oued. You can buy Algerian dinars at the border post, but only for cash.

The Chott and Kebili

The **Chott el Jerid** was once called the "Lake of Marks" – after the palm trunks planted across its normally parched surface to guide trading caravans. Here in 1885, Sir Lambert Playfair was shown a circular platform in the middle of it, called the "Middle Stone", where camels could pass the night. Although the Chott can be crossed on foot at virtually any point for ten months of the year, tradition has it that leaving the recommended path can be fatal. Tijini, the fourteenth-century Arab historian, recounts the apocryphal story of the death of a thousand camels and their attendants in black mud beneath the thin salt crust. Now the army has built a causeway and road right across, and daily buses from Tozeur to Douz via Kebili have been introduced, making this once lengthy journey quick and easy.

DEGACHE sits 10km northeast of Tozeur and claims to have the very best dates in the region. If you find yourself **staying**, the excellent *Bedouina Camping* (☎06/420209) has the usual campsite facilities among date and olive trees, with rooms (②) and Bedouin-style tents for those who don't have their own. The town has basic facilities such as **banks**, a **PTT** (country hours) and a municipal **swimming pool** (mid-June to mid-Sept only). Apart from a couple of rather unappetizing places in the centre, the campsite is the only place to **eat**, even though it's a little bit pricey, but there's cold beer, a floorshow with dinner, reduced rates if you're staying and a cheap and very good breakfast.

A couple of kilometres beyond, at **ZAOUIET EL ARAB**, a newly rebuilt but originally ninth-century brick **mosque** stands in the oasis by the remains of the old town – take a track off the main road to the right (south), just after the date packing plant. A glance at the base of the minaret reveals that, like the one at Bled el Haddar, it rests on Roman foundations. The minaret with four cupolas is typical of the region, unlike that of the Salaam Mosque on the main road, which bears a striking resemblance to a church tower. Just north of the main road at the eastern end of town, past the police station, the pretty white **marabout of Sidi Mohammed Krisanni** sits behind a more recent, and less picturesque, wall of grey breeze blocks.

KRIZ, a couple of kilometres further, has hot spring **baths**, up the hill on the Gafsa road at the edge of town (daily men 6am–8pm front entrance; women 7am–6pm side entrance). After Kriz, the road turns southwest and begins to drop down towards sea level as you cross the Chott, giving a perfect view of the pale expanse of salt and sand, marked only by a single black tarmac strip. To the east, the mountains gradually march into the distance and the crystal surface is concealed by shimmering mirages on every side. In the heat, water always seems to begin a few hundred yards ahead of you and the shore constantly recedes. This is a surreal land, the optical effects dreamlike and reminiscent of a Tanguy painting. After rain, it really is covered in water, but even that is illusory, being only a few inches deep.

Nefzaoua

The southern side of the Chott, the region called **Nefzaoua**, is an area full of oases, smaller but more frequent than those further north, with lonely clumps of palms standing among the dunes or on the salt flats.

Most of the **oasis villages** are stretched out along the road from Tozeur. They are largely pretty ugly, with little to recommend them, but if you want to see traditional oasis agriculture it's interesting to roam around the palmeries, where villagers will proudly show you their plots and present you with fruit straight from the trees. Just get off the bus or ask the *louage* to stop at any point; the road is busy, so you should be able to get a lift on to Kebili later.

SOUK LAHAD, as its name suggests, hosts a lively Sunday market, as well as a couple of cafés and a bank. Seven kilometres to its north, there's also a three-star hotel, the *Les Dunes* (☎05/499195; ④), complete with swimming pool, restaurant and the usual amenities. It might not be a bad place to stop for lunch if you're passing (the set menu's not too pricey, but a buffet costs twice as much), since the tour groups who are its main customers tend to arrive in the evening and depart the next morning, leaving it pretty quiet around midday. The hotel's outstanding feature is a tower which you can climb to survey the surrounding landscape.

Six kilometres south of Souk Lahad, a road off to the east, just after the village of Tombar (signposted "Rabta"), leads in 4km to **MANSOURAH**, where you can bathe in

---

ROUDAIRE AND PLOUGHSHARE: PLANS FOR THE CHOTT

In 1876, one **Captain Roudaire**, working for the French Ministry of War, put forward a plan to dig a canal from the coast at Gabes to the Chott el Fejaj, a finger-like extension of the main Chott pointing eastwards towards the coast. The sea water, he supposed, would flood the entire area of the salt lakes, creating a huge inland sea. In part this scheme was prompted by legends from the past: Roudaire thought the Chott was the site of the ancient **Bay of Triton**, birthplace of Poseidon, crossed by Jason with the Argonauts, and a Roman galley had been found on the northern shores. The Bey would not agree to "so dangerous an experiment", but once the French had occupied Tunisia, engineers no longer had to worry about his opinion. The project looked set to go ahead and Ferdinand de Lesseps, architect of the Suez Canal, became involved. At that point, to general embarrassment, preliminary surveys revealed that the Chott was, in fact, above sea level.

If Roudaire's project sounds daft, then still worse was to follow. In 1962 the American Atomic Energy Commission set up the benignly named **Ploughshare Program** to enquire into "the peaceful use of nuclear explosions". In an associated paper, a leading scientist explained how the radiation would be just an "operational nuisance, quickly localized and easily controlled". For some reason, he couldn't put his finger on anywhere in the USA worthy of detonation, but the Bay of Triton seemed like an ideal place. With the mighty atom, the whole of the south and parts of the Sahara could be turned into a lake, open to mineral exploration and tourism. Like the programme itself, the idea was quietly cast aside.

pools originally built by the Romans (daily men 5–9am & 5–9pm; women 9am–5pm). The village itself is famous for its melons. About a kilometre further on, you reach **TELMINE**, now a compact place whose **oasis** was reputedly planted by conquering Egyptians. It was one of a series of outposts used by the Romans to guard against insurrection, and later became a thriving city – which the Almohads destroyed in 1205. The houses, crowded around narrow streets, still give it a medieval look, and a couple of Roman **reservoir pools** still survive.

On the peninsula of higher land that juts out into the Chott, the water comes from tunnels, called *foggara*, dug up the slope to reach high aquifers. Teams of workers dig holes along the course of the *foggara* and excavate the earth and rock. As you drive along the road these circular pits, some of them 30 to 40m deep, are all you can see and, close up, the amount of work that has gone into the miles of tunnels below becomes evident. But these are considered small; in Iran, where the idea came from originally, some of these *qanat*, as they term the *foggara*, extend for hundreds of kilometres.

Kebili

KEBILI, an important market town for slaves until the last century, is now the administrative centre of the Nefzaoua, 85km southeast of Tozeur. There is not a great deal here of interest, but it is an important interchange, especially if you're going to or from Douz.

Just before you get to the pools, a road on your right, signposted "Ancienne Kebili", leads down a hill and then 4km through the oasis to Kebili's **original site**, complete with a couple of marabouts and a mosque, deserted since 1980 – but still blaring out the "Allah-o-akbar"'s five times daily – although the November festival is still held here. Should you be thirsty after your walk, follow the power lines past the mosque to a generating station, next to which a **spring** in the form of a large pipe emerges from the ground, with a tap for drinking purposes. Just before reaching the old village, a left turn leads, after 500m, to the ruins of **Dar el Kehia** (the chief's house), named after Ahmed Ben Hamadi, Kebili's first local administrator appointed by the French. A cruel opportunist, Ahmed raced across the Chott to surrender to the French while the elected village *sheikh* vacillated. His reward was command over his fellow villagers whom he ruled tyrannically for three terrible years. His palace, as he liked to call it, was built from the stones of his neighbours' homes, which he had destroyed.

Practicalities

The road from Tozeur brings you to a roundabout by a *Total* filling station at the bottom of a hill. At the top of the hill the *SORTREGAMES* (Gabes *SRT*) **bus station** is just to your right, almost opposite a *Magasin Général* **supermarket**, with an hourly shuttle service to Douz (30min), three daily buses to Blidet (30min), one to Nouail (45min) and a couple each to Tozeur (1hr 30min) and Gabes (1hr 30min). *SNTRI*, just behind *Magasin Général*, runs four daily buses to Tunis (8hr 15min), one via Tozeur (1hr 30min), Gafsa (2hr) and Kairouan (5hr 30min), the others via Gabes (1hr 30min), Sfax (3hr 30min) and Sousse (6hr). Also behind the supermarket is a **bank** as well as the **louage station**, which serves Douz, Tozeur, Gabes, Gafsa and sometimes Tunis and Sfax. **Pick-ups** to Blidet can be found down the hill on the Blidet road.

The town's main square, **place de l'Indépendance**, is about 200m down avenue Bourguiba from the *louage* station in the Douz direction. There you'll find two more **banks** and the **PTT** (city hours), with change facilities and an international coin phone. There's also a **taxiphone office** in avenue Bourguiba near the *louage* station, and the **regional hospital** is on the edge of town out on the Gabes road (☎05/490401). In a more upbeat vein, Kebili's regular **market day** is Tuesday and there's a **date harvest festival** held in Old Kebili at the end of November. Hot springs, on the left of the Douz road, about 1km out of the town centre, provide natural **baths** in the open air – the men's pool (Roman in origin) is by the road, the women's behind it. If you prefer to bathe in an indoor **hammam**, you'll find the same baths covered 50m further along the road, on the left (both sexes daily 4am–10pm; separate entrances).

You may want to get straight on to the Saharan outpost of Douz, but if you do decide to **stay** in Kebili, there's the *Hôtel Ben Saïd* on avenue Bourguiba (☎05/491573; ①), a cheap, clean and pleasant place in the centre, and the two-star *Hôtel Fort des Autruches* (☎05/491117; ④), signposted left off avenue Bourguiba, just out of the town centre towards Douz. Otherwise, there's the friendly and plush three-star *Hôtel Oasis* (☎05/491436; ⑤) opposite the *Fort des Autruches*, not a massive jump from its neighbour in spite of the extra star, and the two-star *Hôtel Kitam* on avenue 7 Novembre (☎05/491338; ③), on the Gabes road at the edge of town, which is comfy enough, with a pool under construction. At the other end of the scale, the *Maison des Jeunes* **youth hostel** is behind the *Total* station where the Tozeur road begins (☎05/490635; ①). There's an 8am kick-out time and a 10pm curfew (midnight in summer).

Very simple **restaurants** and a **café** are located around place de l'Indépendance and opposite the *louage* station. For something with a bit more class, try the *Fort des Autruches* restaurant.

Douz and around

The road south from Kebili takes you along the edge of the **Grand Erg Oriental**, the Great Eastern Sandy Desert, where the dunes reach hundreds of metres in height. Here at its northerly extent, they are a touch less impressive, but you can at least get the feel of the desert. And to add a little local colour, scattered around are date palms fed by small springs and several nondescript hamlets.

Twenty-five kilometres south of Kebili, **DOUZ** calls itself "the gateway to the Sahara" and with some justification. Even though it has become the tourist centre of the region, it's remarkably unspoiled by crass tourism: the people are an amiable lot and their town is a pleasure to stay in. It is also a good base from which to explore the isolated oases to the south.

A lot of people here are descended from slaves of west and central African origin who were once bought and sold in neighbouring Kebili. Both black and white people will tell you, however, that racial discrimination is a thing of the past, while intermarriage, frowned on in both communities until only twenty years ago, is now quite normal.

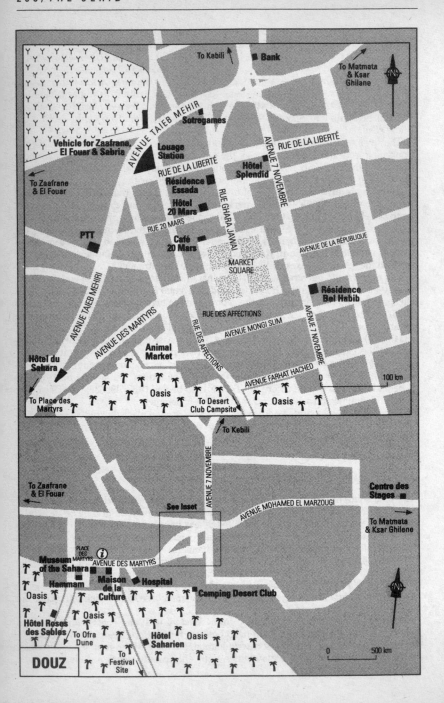

To Kabili

Bank

To Matmata & Ksar Ghilane

Vehicle for Zaafrane, El Fouar & Sabria

AVENUE TAIEB MEHIR

Sotregames

Louage Station

RUE DE LA LIBERTÉ

AVENUE 7 NOVEMBRE

RUE DE LA LIBERTÉ

Hôtel Splendid

To Zaafrane & El Fouar

Résidence Essada

Hôtel 20 Mars

RUE GHARA JAWAI

RUE 20 MARS

PTT

Café 20 Mars

MARKET SQUARE

AVENUE DE LA RÉPUBLIQUE

AVENUE TAIEB MEHIRI

Résidence Bel Habib

RUE DES AFFECTIONS

AVENUE DES MARTYRS

AVENUE MONGI SLIM

AVENUE 7 NOVEMBRE

RUE DES AFFECTIONS

Hôtel du Sahara

Animal Market

AVENUE FARHAT HACHED

0   100 km

To Place des Martyrs

Oasis

To Desert Club Campsite

Oasis

To Kebili

To Zaafrane & El Fouar

AVENUE 7 NOVEMBRE

Centre des Stages

See inset

AVENUE MOHAMED EL MARZOUGI

To Matmata & Ksar Ghilane

PLACE DES MARTYRS

Museum of the Sahara

AVENUE DES MARTYRS

Hammam

Maison de la Culture

Hospital

Camping Desert Club

Oasis

Oasis

Hôtel Roses des Sables

To Ofra Dune

Hôtel Saharien

Oasis

0   500 km

DOUZ

To Festival Site

THE MRAZIG

Douz is the centre for the **Mrazig**, one of the nomadic peoples who still live in the Nefzaoua and now number about 15,000. With the promise of schools, medical facilities and housing, many of the nomads have abandoned the life which led them to three different areas every year. Some of the people still move south in spring, though, when the rains have provided pasture for the sheep and goats; during April the sheep are sheared and the women work on the rugs later sold in the large towns; by the summer the community has largely returned to the comparatively cool oasis, and while the men look after the land and dates, the women again prepare food for the winter. Two months later, the animals are taken north to fresh lands near Gabes or Gafsa, and the people set up their tents nearby. At the beginning of winter they return to pick dates or press olives, and spend the cooler months around their home base.

Arrival and accommodation

The *Syndicat d'Initiative* **tourist office** in place des Martyrs (daily 8am–noon & 3–7.30pm; ☎05/495351) is very helpful and provides services such as camel rental at 3.5TD per person per hour and *calèches* at 1.8TD; the *ONTT* (daily 8.30am–1pm & 3–6pm; ☎05/470351) in the same building is extremely officious and doesn't seem to approve of tourists staying in the cheap city-centre hotels. Arriving by road, the **bus and louage stations** are both nearby on avenue Taïeb Mehiri.

Most of the budget **hotels** are near the market square, with more upmarket places out in the oasis. If none of these appeal, however, or if you yearn for the vastness of the open desert, you could opt instead to stay at the hotels in the nearby oases of Zaafrane or El Faouar (see p.294).

Hotels

20 Mars, rue 20 Mars (☎05/495495). In the street behind the café of the same name on the market square. Not luxury by any means, but one of the nicest hotels in the whole country. Great people run it, they play music and dance every night – with guests joining in – and the multi-bed rooms are clean and pleasant. ②.

Résidence Bel Habib, av 7 Novembre (☎05/495115). Another travellers' favourite that's clean, friendly and well run. ②.

Caravanserail ★★★, by the Great Dune (☎05/495123). Standard three-star stuff, ready to process the punters. Some rooms have showers rather than baths. ⑤.

Résidence Essada, rue Ghara Jawai (☎05/495465). Cheap and very adequate. ①.

Hôtel du Sahara, av des Martyrs (no phone). Very cheap but rather grotty. ②.

Splendid, av 7 Novembre (no phone). Nice rooms but dubious and not recommended. ①.

Roses des Sables, off av des Martyrs in the oasis (☎05/495484). Turn left at the very end of av des Martyrs and it's 300m down on the right. Pleasant, with private bathrooms, heating in winter and air conditioning in summer. Pool under construction. ②.

Saharien ★★, in the oasis (☎05/495337). Left off av des Martyrs before the tourist office and it's 500m down on the left. It's not too formal, with mostly bungalows, a pool and all mod cons. ③.

Touareg ★★★, by the Great Dune (☎05/470057). Much the same as the *Caravanserail*. Again, specify if you want a bath rather than a shower. ②.

Méhari ★★★, by the Great Dune (☎05/495088). The first of the Great Dune hotels but, if anything, even more impersonal than the others, although it does have a hot spring pool. ⑤.

Sahara Douz, ★★★, by the Great Dune (☎05/470865). There's an indoor hot spring pool, all rooms have baths and the staff even smile. ⑤.

THE FESTIVAL OF THE SAHARA

At the end of December the **Festival of the Sahara** celebrates everything from popular pottery and a traditional marriage to camel fighting (camel versus camel that is), sand hockey and even greyhound racing. It all takes place at a special festival site out beyond the *Hôtel Saharien*. Associated cultural activities such as music, singing and poetry contests take place in the *Maison de la Culture* in place des Martyrs. Note that hotels tend to fill up quickly at this time of year, so arrive early or book ahead.

Youth hostel and campsite

Camping Desert Club, rue des Affections (☎05/470575). European-style campsite with a pitch for every tent or vehicle, complete with electric socket. Passports must be surrendered on arrival. Fees are cheap, breakfast expensive by local standards.

Centre des Stages et des Vacances campsite, rte de Ksar Ghilaine (no phone). Three kilometres out on the edge of town and rather more rustic than the *Desert Club*. Run by the Tunisia YHA, with kitchen, hot water and bedding, and shelter provided if necessary. ①.

The Town

On Thursdays Douz is transformed by the weekly **market**. Townspeople, nomads, people from nearby villages and tourists pour in to participate in one of Tunisia's most engaging souks, and it says something for Douz that the presence of tourists seems to add to rather than detract from the whole affair. The centre of activity is, of course, the market square itself. Here you can find many of the traditional goods (jackets, leather shoes and slippers) which end up in the cities. You can also buy souvenirs like petrified wood or the inevitable sand roses, or get desert shoes made to measure overnight (in the square's southeastern corner). In season, you'll find the region's famous *deglat en nour* dates for sale behind the southern side of the square.

Most of the tourists, however, are here to see the **camels**. These are not the most important livestock commodity, but you will find them on sale with the other animals – mainly sheep and goats – if you take the western exit (av des Martyrs) out of the square, then the second left, and follow the throng.

Another popular attraction for tour groups on one-day visits is the **Great Dune**, out of town past the *Hôtel Roses des Sables*. It's a chance to play in the sand for those without the time to get further into the desert – or go to the beach. You should, of course, ignore the rumour that the dune was built with the aid of bulldozers.

The **Museum of the Sahara**, near place des Martyrs (Mon–Sat 8.30am–1pm & 3–6pm; 1TD), is barely worth looking into: its exhibits are mostly about local fabric making and explained only in Arabic. Roads into the oasis from here take you to the bigger hotels.

Eating and drinking

Most of Douz's cheap hotels double up as **eateries** and offer the likes of couscous, stew and chicken for a couple of dinars. The *Bel Habib* and *20 Mars* are safe enough bets. Otherwise, there's the *Restaurant des Caravanes* by the bus stop in avenue Taïeb Mehiri, the *Restaurant la Rosa* in avenue 7 Novembre, and the restaurant between the ONTT and the *Syndicat d'Initiative* in place des Martyrs. A cut above these is the *Restaurant el Kods* up at the end of avenue des Martyrs, on the left just before place des Martyrs. You'll be hard-pushed to find any upmarket eating in town, but the hotels by the Great dune are the most promising. However, Douz's greatest culinary experience has got to be the *Restaurant Ali Baba* on the Kebili road opposite the bank, with its legendary couscous, fine Mrazig welcome and relaxed atmosphere. You can eat in a Bedouin tent out the back, or go out there for a tea and a chat after your meal, and the prices are as sweet as the staff.

Listings

Banks *Banque du Sud* is on av 7 Novembre, just north of the junction with av Taïeb Mehiri.

Cinema At the *Maison de la Culture* in pl des Martyrs (Wed & Fri).

Excursions The only licensed operators are *Douz Voyages* on av Taïeb Meluri, opposite the Kebili turnoff (☎05/470178) and, slightly cheaper but less renowned, *Abdelmonla Voyages* on av des Martyrs, just before the tourist office. A two-day jeep trip to Ksar Ghilane is currently about 300TD for up to six people, camels around 40TD per person per day. All the cheap hotels in town can organize lower-priced camel trips, but you risk falling in with dubious operators – make certain you are insured. You can also get good deals for camel trips in Zaafrane. Be aware that the desert can get extremely cold at night, so come prepared.

Hammams *Hammam el Hana*, north of the *louage* station past the cemetery, is open mornings and evenings for men, afternoons for women, but far better are the natural hot-spring baths found by taking the first left off av des Martyrs past pl des Martyrs (signposted to the *Hôtel Roses des Sables*). Just round the bend on the right, these are open 7am–noon & 2.30–8pm for both sexes (separate entrances) and offer the choice of bath or pool.

International phone calls There's a taxiphone office on av des Martyrs between av Taïeb Meluri and the market square; otherwise, try the *Hôtel Saharien*.

Medical facilities The hospital (☎05/470323) is just off av des Martyrs, 100m east of the tourist office.

Newspapers *Librairie el Manar*, opposite the taxiphone office, sometimes has English-language papers.

PTT Av Taïeb Mehiri, opposite the end of rue 20 Mars (country hours). Changes cash and has a coin phone.

Supermarkets *Magasin B Abdennour* on av Taïeb Mehiri, opposite the *Hôtel du Sahara* (daily 7.30am–8pm), is very friendly. Otherwise, there's one just called *Magasin*, 100m down the Zaafrane road opposite the cemetery, which is open slightly later.

Swimming pool The municipal pool behind the water tower off pl des Martyrs is open in July and August (daily 9am–6pm; 0.2TD). Otherwise, you can use the *Hôtel Saharien*'s pool for a few dinars.

West of Douz

The road out of Douz to the oases of Zaafrane, El Faouar and Sabria is now tarmac all the way. As well as the five daily buses from Douz, pick-ups do the run cheaply

---

MOVING ON FROM DOUZ

Buses leave from opposite the *SOTREGAMES* (Gabes *SRT*) office on the corner of rue Ghara Jawai and avenue Taïeb Mehiri. As well as departures to Kebili (30min), of which there are plenty (the last at around 4.30pm), two daily buses run direct to Tunis (9hr 45min) – one via Gafsa (2hr 30min), the other through Gabes (2hr), Sfax (4hr) and Sousse (6hr 30min) – with two more to Gabes (3hr), one to Tozeur (2hr 15min), and five to Zaafrane (15min), Sabria (40min) and El Faouar (1hr).

The **louage** station is just a block away, at the end of rue de la Liberté and rue el Hanine, opposite the Zaafrane turning. Basically, all the vehicles are for Kebili, but you may be lucky, especially on market day, and find one going on to Gabes or Tozeur. Various **pick-ups** for Zaafrane, El Faouar and Sabria leave from the turning by the cemetery in avenue Taïeb Mehiri, opposite the *louage* station.

Lastly, if you're tempted to try the road across the desert to Ksar Ghilane, you'll need four-wheel drive or a dromedary. Both can be arranged (see "Excursions" above). The road to Matmata should be negotiable, with care, in a two-wheel drive rented car.

enough, but remember that transport back to Douz dries up around 4pm, so head back by 3.30pm or so if that's where you plan to spend the night. If driving in this region, take the usual precautions for desert driving (see p.352).

ZAAFRANE is the real gateway to the Grand Erg Oriental. The village lies close to the main through track and is surrounded on one side by endless dunes, on the other by a cool **oasis**. Life centres around the café, a grocery store and the main well, while a small brickworks provides employment. Most of the houses are off to the left and many have been built for the nomadic **Adhara**, who still migrate to Ksar Ghilane during the spring. Their large black tents, often pitched nearby, are made from long strips of wool and goat hair, supported by two wooden poles. Paths lead from the main road to the sand dunes at the far edge of the village. From here the desert stretches into the distance, beyond the remains of old stone houses, washed over by the sand. If you would like to follow the Adhara's migration route, either check out the camel operators in the large open space to your left as you enter the village, or the *Syndicat d'Initiative* **tourist office** at the other end of town (variable hours; ☎05/ 490750), where the dunes start in earnest. Prices tend to be slightly lower here than in Douz and you should be able to negotiate a one-week trip to Ksar Ghilane by camel for around 200–250TD all inclusive.

There is a **hotel** here, the *Zaafrane* (☎05/495074; ②), which is not a bad old place, mostly bungalows with bathroom and heating or air conditioning, and also Bedouin tents between March and October. They usually allow **camping** in the grounds, have a bar if you're in need of a cold beer, a low-priced set menu, and you can use their pool for a couple of dinars, or for free if you're eating there.

Whether or not you take the bus to Zaafrane, you'll probably end up hitching back to Douz or on to El Faouar; most passing vehicles will pick up hitchhikers.

Sabria and El Faouar

Beyond Zaafrane there are still pick-ups going to Sabria and El Faouar and it's no problem getting a lift. The main attraction is simply the drive through the desert. **SABRIA**, 25km west of Douz and 3km off the El Faouar–Zaafrane road, is the centre for the people of the same name, Arabized Berbers who are part of the larger Ghrib confederation. Spectacular views over the desert greet you when you climb up some of the high dunes around Sabria, with a vast expanse of sand stretching in every direction, dotted with little green oases.

Sabria is one of the few places where the "Danse de la Chevalure" is still authentically performed. On the first night of the marriage ceremony, the women remove all their jewellery and woollen head coverings and parade before the assembled men and musicians. To the beat of the tambour, and encouragement of the crowd, each dancer whirls her long hair round her head faster and faster. Over several hours the women gradually drop out, and the dance ends when just one is left on the floor.

The road divides after 25km and most traffic goes straight to **EL FAOUAR** (also called Sabria el Faouar), which has a Friday souk. This is the home of the **Ghrib** who, until recently, were a wholly nomadic community, breeding cattle and sheep. A small group of stone houses stands below the *Garde Nationale*, and around the edge of the **oasis** are the huts, made from mud and palm fronds, used in preference to tents during the summer.

The one **hotel** – the three-star *El Faouar* (☎05/491576; ③–④) – is a pretty reasonable place, especially when not too swamped. Off on the left as you come into the village from Zaafrane, it has a bar and restaurant (low-priced set menu) and a free pool; it also lends out sand skis gratis. As well as the rooms, each decorated with its own mural, there is the option of sleeping in cheaper Bedouin-style tents. Behind the hotel, the dunes begin. While not as huge as the dunes deeper into the erg, the sand mountains round here still stretch immensely to the horizon and satisfy most visitors' desires to be, at last, really in the desert.

There are other, smaller oases, unmarked on any of the available maps, between El Faouar and Zaafrane. If you're hitching, you might be dropped off on the way, but there will always be shade and an occasional car later in the afternoon.

North of El Faouar

Paved roads branching off on your right (if coming from Douz) 5km before Zaafrane and 10km after El Fouar (signposted "Dergine") lead back to Kebili via **NOUAIL**, where a *campement* offers **accommodation** in rather grubby "bungalows" and may allow you to pitch a tent (☎05/495584; ②).

Between Nouail and Kebili is the picturesque village of **BLIDET**, with a ruined **medina** on a hill topped by a **marabout** and flanked by minor **oases**. Aside from a very early bus from El Faouar, the only way to get from there or from Zaafrane to Blidet without your own transport is to hitch, but you can reach Blidet from Kebili by means of regular pick-ups and three daily buses.

Towards the coast

For Shaw in the 1750s, the area east of Kebili to the coast was a "lonesome and uncomfortable desert, the resort of cut-throats and robbers." He recalled, "We saw the recent blood of a Turkish gentleman, who, with three of his servants, had been murdered two days before by these assassins." Nowadays there's no blood and little of interest until El Hamma. At **SAIDANE**, 30km east of Kebili, the old French fort, once a hotel, is now a *Garde Nationale* post, so resist the temptation to photograph it as you pass. What may pass the time is looking out for the desert birds and mammals that can be spotted along the road.

EL HAMMA DE L'ARAD is 50km east of Saidane. Its **hot baths**, which have long attracted visitors from far and wide, gave it the Roman name *Aquae Tacapitanae*, and there is still a **hammam festival** in March. Leo Africanus was not keen, noting somewhat irrelevantly, "the hot water tastes like brimstone so that it will in no way quench a man's thirst". The open-air **baths** (daily 7am–8pm; 0.6TD) are in a modern building, based on Roman foundations, opposite the marketplace; the entrance on the left is for women, men go round the corner to the right. The spring water rises at 47°C and heats up still further in the sunlight, and you sit on submerged stone seats in a shallow pool. If you don't have your own towel, you pay slightly extra for the wrap-round towels worn in the water.

In the sixteenth century, unlikely as it may seem, El Hamma was a substantial town and a major **staging post** on the trans-Saharan routes. Then, in the 1630s, the **Matmata** who lived here refused to pay their taxes to the Bey, and the town was razed to the ground and its citizens expelled. A **fort**, the remains of which can be seen beyond the spring, was built to ensure Turkish sovereignty and the Beni Zid nomads were allowed to settle in place of the recalcitrant Berbers. Today there is nothing of the old town left and the modern buildings that have been built on the site are uninspiring to say the least. The **tomb of Rabbi Sidi Youssef** is the scene of an annual Jewish pilgrimage around December, but you would need a certain dedication to coincide and participate in any way.

El Hamma also has two **banks** and a *Magasin Général* **supermarket** and, on Mondays, an additional attraction is the **market**. There are regular buses to Gabes (20min), five a day to Kebili (1hr 30min) and one *SNTRI* departure to Tunis (8hr 10min) via Sfax (3hr) and Sousse (5hr 30min).

travel details

Trains
Metlaoui to: Gafsa, Mahres, Redeyef, Seldja, Sfax, Sousse and Tunis. There are no services to Moulares or Tozeur.

Buses
Douz to: El Faouar, Gafsa, Kairouan, Kebili, Sfax, Sousse, Tozeur and Tunis.

Gafsa to: Douz, El Guettar, Feriana, Gabes, Kairouan, Kasserine, Kebili, Le Kef, Metlaoui, Nefta, Ras Ajdir, Redeyef, Sfax, Sidi Aich, Sidi Bou Zid, Sousse, Tamerza, Tozeur and Tunis.

Kebili to: Blidet, Douz, Gabes, Gafsa, Sfax, Tozeur and Tunis.

Metlaoui to: Gabes, Redeyef, Nefta, Sousse, Tozeur and Tunis.

Nefta to: Gabes, Gafsa, Hazoua/Algerian border, Kebili, Metlaoui, Sfax, Tozeur and Tunis.

Tozeur to: Gabes, Gafsa, Hazoua/Algerian border, Kairouan, Kebili, Metlaoui, Sfax, Tamerza and Tunis.

Louages
Douz to: Kebili. Pick-ups to El Faouar, Sabria and Zaafrane.

Gafsa to: El Guettar, Gabes, Meknassy, Metlaoui, Redeyef, Sfax, Sidi Bou Zid, Tozeur and Tunis.

Kebili to: Douz, Gabes, Gafsa, Sfax and Tozeur.

Metlaoui to: Gabes, Redeyef, Tamerza, Tozeur and Tunis.

Nefta to: Hazoua/Algerian border and Tozeur.

Tozeur to: Degache, El Hamma du Jerid, Gafsa, Kebili, Metlaoui, Nefta, Sfax and Tunis.

Flights
Tozeur to: Jerba, Lyon, Paris and Tunis.

MARKET DAYS

Monday – El Hamma de l'Arad
Tuesday – Kebili, El Guettar
Wednesday – Gafsa
Thursday – Douz, Nefta

Friday – El Faouar
Sunday – Metlaoui, Moulares, Redeyef, Souk Lahad, Tozeur

CHAPTER SEVEN

GABES AND MATMATA

he towns of Gabes and Matmata lie in a tract of land that swoops below the belly of the Sahel, the fertile terrain stretching south of Sousse. For the most part nondescript, it is punctuated by fecund emerald oases and hemmed by mile upon mile of coast along the gulf. Almost every traveller heading south passes through **Gabes**, but few take the time to explore its historic quarters and adjacent oasis – both remnants of a turbulent era in Tunisia's past, when the extensive oases were important staging posts for caravans from the other side of the Sahara.

Better known – and decidedly more spectacular – are the weird lunar landscapes and troglodyte villages around **Matmata**, a town blown to fame by the filming there of

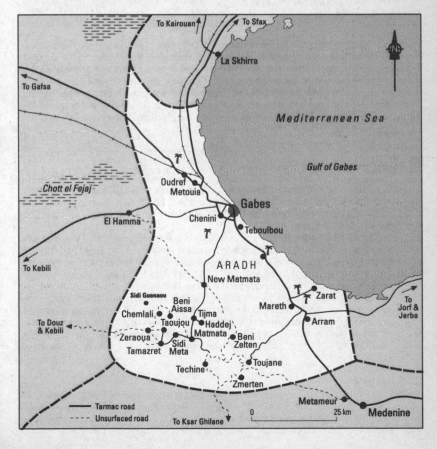

To Kairouan

To Sfax

La Skhirra

Mediterranean Sea

To Gafsa

Chott el Fejaj

Gulf of Gabes

Oudref
Metouia

Gabes

El Hamma

Chenini

Teboulbou

To Kebili

A R A D H

New Matmata

Sidi Guenaou

Beni
Aissa

Zarat

Chemlali

Tijma

Mareth

To
Jorf &
Jerba

Taoujou

Haddej

To Douz
& Kebili

Zeraoua

Matmata

Arram

Sidi
Meta

Beni
Zelten

Tamazret

Toujane

Techine

Zmerten

Metameur

— Tarmac road

0   25 km

Medenine

‑‑‑ Unsurfaced road

To Ksar Ghilane

ACCOMMODATION PRICE CODES

All the hotels, youth hostels and pensions listed in this book have been price-graded according to the following scale, and although prices will rise during the lifetime of this edition, the relative comparisons should remain valid.

The prices quoted are for the **cheapest available double room in high season**, although many of the cheap places will have pricier rooms with en suite facilities or sea views.

Classified hotels, officially considered suitable for tourists, are graded locally from one to four stars (★), with wide-ranging prices within each category. For more on accommodation prices and categories, see Basics.

① Up to 10TD. Very cheap. Usually a bed only in a basic, unclassified hotel or a youth hostel.

② 10.1–25TD. Budget. Bed only or bed and breakfast.

③ 25.1–40TD. Comfortable budget. Good unclassified average one-star or a cheap two-star.

④ 40.1–55TD. Mid-range. Expensive two-star, cheap three-star.

⑤ 55.1–70TD. Tourist hotel. Standard three-star.

⑥ 70.1TD upwards. Deluxe. Expensive three-star, four-star or five-star.

---

scenes in the *Star Wars* movie. Sometimes the demands of tourism seem disturbingly overbearing in this region, geared to – indeed springing from – the film's success. Outside the tour groups, however, it's none too easy to make your way around without a car. If you've got one or are willing to hitch, the most genuine experiences are to be found some way off the beaten track – in Berber villages around Matmata like **Haddej**, where the underground way of life continues unaffected, or others further afield like **Tamezret** and **Taoujou**, which are isolated and barely visited, deeply traditional and extremely scenic.

Gabes

In 1886, a French administrator arrived to take up a post at **GABES**, the coastal town billed as the port of the Sahara. "Imagine my surprise", he wrote to his superior, "when I had to disembark onto the beach and walk up the dusty path that is the main street to reach the only building, my office."

Today Gabes has grown in size but is still rather a disappointment. The busy new town, rebuilt after World War II, stretches for miles away from the coast and, though the palm groves reach to the sea, they're largely inaccessible at this point, surrounded by the port and industrial complex. On the other hand, Gabes's pivotal position between the sea and the *chotts*, or salt flats, ensures that virtually all traffic between the south and centre of the country passes through here – and there are things worth stopping for. Tucked among the alleys of the old quarters are several fascinating **mosques**; the well-preserved **markets** are as alive with daily commerce as they ever were; and the long, sandy **beach** has the benefit of being almost undeveloped. Most alluringly, away from the main streets, parts of the vast **oasis** really are a haven of peace and shade.

Some history

First occupied by the Phoenicians, Gabes was later a major port of **Roman Africa**, its name, *Tacape*, meaning "a wet and irrigated place". In medieval times it was the terminus for many of the Trans-Saharan **caravans**, while the main *haj* caravan, carrying pilgrims on their obligatory trip to Mecca, passed through on its way to Tripoli and Cairo before reach-

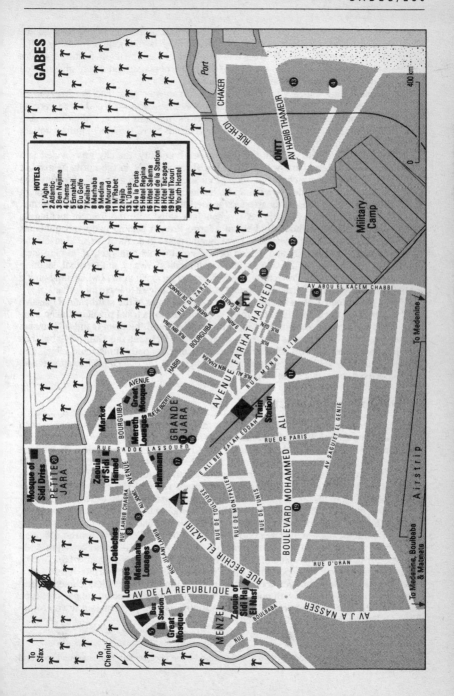

GABES

HOTELS
1 L'Agha
2 Atlantic
3 Ben Nejima
4 Chems
5 Ennakhil
6 Du Golfe
7 Kailani
8 Marhaba
9 Medina
10 Mourad
11 M'Rabet
12 Najib
13 L'Oasis
14 De la Poste
15 Hôtel Regina
16 Hôtel Salama
17 Hôtel de la Station
18 Hôtel Tacapes
19 Hôtel Tkouri
20 Youth Hostel

Port

CHAKER

Military
Camp

Airstrip

To Sfax
To Chenini
To Medenine
To Medenine, Boulbaba & Matmata

AV J A NASSER

BOULEVARD MOHAMMED ALI

RUE D'ORAN

RUE DE PARIS

AV SAGUIET EL GENIE

RUE DE TUNIS

RUE DE MONTPELIER

RUE DE TOULOUSE

RUE BECHIR EL JAZIRI

MENZEL

AV DE LA REPUBLIQUE

Bus Station

Great Mosque

Zaouia of Sidi Haj El Nasr

BOULBABA

RUE JILANI

Louages Matmata Louages

Caleches

Louages

Zaouia of Sidi Hamed

Mosque of Sidi Driss

PETITE JARA

RUE LAHBIB CHAGRA

AV ALBANE

RUE SADOK LASSOUED

Market

Meireth Louages Mosque

Great Mosque

GRANDE JARA

AVENUE BOURGUIBA

AVENUE BOURGUIBA HABIB

Hammam

PTT

E ALI BEN SALAH EDDAH

RUE ALI BEN KHALIFA

RUE 6 AZESTE

RUE BEN SINA

RUE DE FRANCE

AVENUE DE FRANCE

9 AVRIL

RUE DE GAULLE

RUE GEN

RUE MONGI SLIM

AVENUE FARHAT HACHED

Train Station

AV ABOU EL KACEM CHABBI

PTT

RUE HEDI

AV HABIB THAMEUR

ONTT

400 km

0

ing the holy city itself, bringing along with it thousands of merchants and their goods. Gabes was also famed for its **silk**, made from silk worms raised on mulberry bushes in the oasis. But even in those times the oasis had its seamier side. The tenth- century traveller Ali Mahalli complained that the oases were "the home of plague and death" and advised others to avoid the place or stay as short a time as possible.

Like Jerba, Gabes fell easy prey to seafaring European states, with the **Aragonese** first to invade in 1279. However, when central government was weak and there were no Europeans about, the town was quick to reassert its **independence**. It did this during the Hilalian invasions and, later, whenever the Hafsids were too busy fighting among themselves to do much about it.

By the time of the Ottomans in the late sixteenth century, the city was divided into three separate quarters: **Jara**, with a large Jewish community, in the north, **Menzel** in the west and **Boulbaba** a couple of kilometres south. According to Leo Africanus, the entire region was surrounded by a dyke which could be flooded in times of war – though for much of the time the city quarters expended their energies fighting one another. Their quarrels came to a head in 1881, when Jara sided with the French, inciting its neighbours to attack. Without the help of a large French landing party and gunboats offshore, the Jews would inevitably have been massacred. As it was, Menzel and Boulbaba were fined heavily and denied permission to hold a market, so forcing local trade into the hands of the **Jews**. The communities' rivalry and mutual loathing simmered throughout the Protectorate period, exploding again in 1942 when anti-Semitic riots, encouraged by the Germans, persuaded most of the Jews to leave for Jerba.

Under the French, Gabes became the key garrison point of the south, and a massive **fort** was built on the outskirts of the town in readiness for a tribal revolt or Italian invasion. Today the region remains strategically sensitive, and the town is full of Tunisian conscripts. Their presence is also explained by the fact that the Gulf of Gabes has considerable reserves of **oil**, which have been claimed by both Tunisia and Libya. The dispute was finally settled in 1981 and relations between the two countries, often tense, have improved somewhat since then.

Arrival and accommodation

Arriving by **train**, you find yourself bang in the middle of town on rue Mongi Slim and not a long walk from the beach. The **bus and louage stations** are opposite the *calèche* stand at the far western end of town, where avenue Farhat Hached meets avenue de la République and the road to Sfax. From here, two main roads head east through the city centre, with most of the services and shops concentrated along them. Rue Lahbib Chagra branches northeast to become **avenue Bourguiba**, which curves past the main **market** (daily except Mon) before turning a sharp bend to continue seawards past the main **PTT** (city hours) and several of the town's best hotels and restaurants. Gabes's other main artery, **avenue Farhat Hached**, follows a more or less straight line towards the sea, meeting avenue Bourguiba again at the other end of town. Just beyond here is the **tourist office** on the corner of avenues Habib Thameur and Hedi Chaker (Mon–Thurs 8am–1pm & 3–5.45pm, Fri & Sat 8.30am–1.30pm; July & Aug Mon–Sat 7.30am–1.30pm; ☎05/270254), with a list of hotels and tariffs posted up outside, along with a timetable of bus departures.

Gabes has plenty of budget **accommodation**, although there is less choice among the more expensive hotels, with nothing over two stars except a couple of package-type places by the beach. Apart from these, most hotels are in the centre of town around avenues Bourguiba and Farhat Hached.

Hotels

L'Agha, 101 rue Sadok Lassoued (☎05/276569). Good-value cheapie with rooms around a central patio. ①.

Atlantic ★, 4 av Bourguiba (☎05/220034). At the junction of av Farhat Hached, this enormous white French colonial building creaks with character. Ask for a large room. ②.

Ben Nejima, 68 rue Ali Jemel (☎05/271591). On the corner of av Farhat Hached. Clean rooms and friendly management, but a bit noisy. ②.

Chems ★★★, on the beach (☎05/270547). Massive bungalow complex next door to *L'Oasis*. Slightly pricier but all on one level and can cater for wheelchairs. Non-residents can use the swimming pool for a few dinars. ⑤.

Chella Club, near Chenini (☎05/227442). A slightly tacky "vacation village" out in the oasis (see p.303). ③.

Ennakhil, behind the bus station (☎05/273598). Shared rooms and hardly luxury, but handy for that early bus. One room is reserved for women or married couples. ①.

Hôtel du Golfe, av Abou el Kacem Chabbi (☎05/271807). Low-priced, rather bleak rooms alongside the military camp. ①.

Keilani, 134 av Bourguiba (☎05/270320). Clean and friendly. The same price, in theory, for a double room as a single. ②.

Marhaba, av Farhat Hached. Opposite the Matmata *louage* station, with dusty rooms and rickety beds. ①.

Medina, rue Haj Jelani Lahbib (☎05/274271). A pleasant enough place in the Menzel quarter, between av Farhat Hached and av de la République. ①.

Mourad, 300 av Bourguiba (☎05/270513). Above the *UIB* bank. Clean, quiet and good value. Most of the upstairs rooms have bathrooms. ①–②.

M'Rabet, rue Ali Zouaoui (☎05/270602). Off bd Mohammed Ali, near the station. Most of the nice, clean rooms have showers, some a loo and/or balcony. ②.

Nejib ★★, av Farhat Hached (☎05/271686). At the junction of bd Mohammed Ali. It may not have the most stars, but this is the classiest hotel in town. ③.

L'Oasis ★★★, on the beach (☎05/270381). A reasonably posh tourist hotel with the usual facilities. ④.

Hôtel de la Poste, 116 av Bourguiba. Favoured haunt of backpackers, but rather grubby and not actually very good value unless you are prepared to haggle the price down. Outside windows are in short supply. ①.

Regina, 138 av Bourguiba (☎05/272095). Slightly upmarket budget option. The main minus point is that the windows all open onto the noisy interior patio. ②.

Salama, 262 av Farhat Hached (☎05/272233). At the corner of rue Sadok Lassoued. Cheap and friendly but rather grimy. ①.

Hôtel de la Station, 330 av Farhat Hached. Extremely basic, predominantly male and none too clean. ①.

Tacapes ★★, 55 av Bourguiba (☎05/270700). Comfy enough, but getting a bit shabby. ②.

Tkouri, 399 bd Mohammed Ali (☎05/277706). Quiet and clean but not very central. ②.

Youth hostel

Centre de Stages et de Vacances youth hostel, rue de l'Oasis, Petite Jara (☎05/270271). Not tremendously friendly, but camping is possible and you can come and go as you please. ①.

The Town

Gabes is not primarily a seaside resort. The swimming and the long sandy **beach** are reasonable, but no match for Kerkennah and still less for Jerba. Indeed, while the fishing **port** to the north can get quite lively, it almost seems that the beach has been stuck on the eastern end of town as an afterthought. The town itself has all the facilities you would expect from such a pivotal communications centre, but its places of real interest are concentrated in the **old quarters** of Jara, Menzel and Boulbaba. The **oasis** stretches north and west of the town.

Jara and Menzel

Jara is divided into two parts. The larger chunk of **Grande Jara** extends outwards from the western end of avenue Bourguiba. Its main attraction is the market, open every day except Monday. To the north of the main street, lined with cheap cafés and *gargotes*, a covered passage leads through to the **marketplace** once crowded with caravans from Ghadames and Algeria. Around its entrance stand bulging panniers, filled with the henna for which Gabes is renowned. This area, being near Jara's Great Mosque, is reserved for "clean" goods – mainly clothes, rugs and spices. Among the adjoining shops are the gold- and silversmiths, while the cobbled street leading down to the river is the territory of the so-called "dirty" crafts pursued by blacksmiths, knife-sharpeners and metal-workers. By the river itself is the unhygienic cattle market, well away from the mosque.

The **Great Mosque** on avenue Bourguiba is recent, as are most of the mosques in Grande Jara, but the **Zaouia of Sidi Hamed**, around the corner at 44 rue Sadok Lassoued, is worth a look for its *koubba* dome and doorway carved in local pink stone.

The other part of the quarter, **Petite Jara**, is across the rue de l'Oasis bridge. The **Sidi Driss Mosque** (rarely open) was built here in the eleventh century by an Arab prince of the Banu Jami, descendants of the Banu Hilal invaders. The prayer hall, like much of Jara, has been built using stone from old Roman columns. Many of Jara's other historic mosques, however, have disappeared since World War II, along with its old synagogues and most of its Jewish heritage.

The monuments of **Menzel** – the area around avenue de la République – seem to have survived rather better than Jara's, such as they are. Menzel's **Great Mosque**, in a square just west of avenue de la République, and the **Zaouia of Sidi Bnei Isa**, down a side street on the other side of the avenue, are both old and attractive buildings, and a stroll down rue Bechir el Jaziri will take you past the **Zaouia of Sidi Haj el Nasf**. Even without tracking all these down, however, Menzel is the only quarter of Gabes that really retains its ancient feel, and is definitely the best part of town for an aimless wander. It also has its own **market**, on rue Omar el Mokhtar.

Boulbaba

The third of Gabes's historical quarters, **Boulbaba**, is somewhat removed from the town centre, down at the end of avenue de la République and along avenue J A Nasser, then along rue 6 Octobre, some twenty minutes' walk away – look out for the tall mina- ret. Bus #3 or #3b will also get you to Boulbaba from the centre; ask the driver for Sidi Boulbaba. It is worth making the effort to get out here to see Gabes's most important and oldest religious monument.

The **Mosque of Sidi Boulbaba**, on the opposite side of the square from the mosque with the tall minaret, contains the seventh-century tomb of the saint who was Mohammed's barber. Its courtyard is particularly beautiful, surrounded by colonnades and decorated with tiles. Boulbaba arrived here in the seventh century and, like many holy men and marabouts in the south, united warring factions to bring prosperity to the town – of which he is now the patron saint. The surrounding village, which took his name, stood on the site of Roman *Tacape* and was closed to local Jews and Christians. Non-Muslims may now enter the courtyard of the mosque, but not the prayer hall.

Next to the mosque is an imposing old *medersa*, built in 1692 and now a **Museum of Popular Arts and Traditions** (daily except Mon winter 9.30am–6pm; summer 8am– 1pm & 4–7pm; 1TD). The people who run it are welcoming and happy to show you around. The pink stone building is really more interesting than the exhibits, although these include everyday objects, textiles, a Punic ossuary and a little garden planted with henna, pomegranates, bananas and grapes. Some locally excavated Roman artefacts decorate the grounds.

The Gabes Oasis

Part of the **Gabes oasis** starts just behind Petite Jara, leading along to the Sfax road and, in the other direction, to the sea. There are 300,000 palms here, but many are in poor health, spoiled by the damp sea air. The land has changed little since the days of Roman writer Pliny, who wrote: "Here in the midst of the sand, the soil is well cultivated and fruitful. Here grows a high palm and beneath that palm are olives and under that a fig tree. Under the fig tree grows a pomegranate and beneath that again a vine. Moreover, beneath these there are sown corn, then vegetables or grass." This tiered intercropping continues today, allowing farmers to cultivate an astonishing range of crops, some 400 varieties in total, including henna and spices as well as food produce.

The main oasis villages are on the other side of the Gabes–Sfax road. Most worthwhile – although also most touristed – is **CHENINI**. Bus #7 from Gabes leaves every hour from opposite the school near the *Hôtel Medina* on rue Haj Jelani Lahbib, or you can go by taxi. Alternatively, you could walk from Gabes – past the *calèche* stand, taking a right turn over the river, just after the bus station – but it's a long, hot trudge. What most people do is take a *calèche* tour of the oasis. These all follow much the same route, with obligatory stops to buy souvenirs, but the tours are not too expensive (10TD for up to four people).

The small direct road winds around the irrigation ditches in a swirl of right-angle bends and ends up at **EL AOUADID**, some 3km away. If you turn left here, the road continues past the *Café des Cascades* in the palm trees to a **Roman dam**, made up of several layers of stone holding back a small reservoir. Next door is a **crocodile farm** (Tues–Sat 7.30am–6pm; 0.5TD) containing a rather unimpressive **zoo**. A path behind the dam goes on to the *Chella Club* (see p.301) and finally to some impressive **gorges** at the southwest tip of the oasis. This is where the springs rise, but the club has concreted parts of the rock to build a swimming pool. The road along the top leads past the **Marabout of Sidi Ali Bahoul** and on to Chenini itself.

Eating and drinking

Food certainly isn't one of Gabes's high points, but reasonable meals can be found in every price range if you know where to look. If your budget is really tight, there are some *gargotes* in avenue de la République and around the market, with a couple opposite the Matmata *louage* station in avenue Farhat Hached.

Amori, 84 av Bourguiba. Watch French TV while you eat the cheap, copious meals served up here.

Restaurant el Andalous, av Abou el Kacem Chabbi, just off av Farhat Hached. Low-priced couscous and similar fare.

Pâtisserie Ben Amor, 65 av Bourguiba. Cakes and seasonal fruit juice.

Hôtel Ben Nejima, 68 rue Ali Jemel. A similarly priced alternative to the *Boukachouka* opposite. The bar is the best bet in town for a quiet beer.

Boukachouka, 60 rue Ali Jemel. Tasty food and low prices. A good place for breakfast.

Café la Chicha, rue Ibn Jazar. A refined if slightly pricey place for a coffee, unsweetened fruit juice and *chicha*, at the junction of av Bourguiba and av Farhat Hached.

Restaurant el Mazar, 39 av Farhat Hached (☎05/272065). Highly regarded, very refined and rather expensive.

Hôtel Nejib, av Farhat Hached (☎05/271636). A slightly posher set menu than the *Tacapes*, at the junction of bd Mohammed Ali.

Restaurant de l'Oasis, 17 av Farhat Hached (☎05/270098). Gabes's top restaurant. Old, established and with excellent food.

Restaurant la Pacha, 34 av Farhat Hached (☎05/272418). Rather more finesse than most of Gabes's restaurants and consequently expensive.

Pizza Pino, 144 av Bourguiba. A pleasant and inexpensive little place, doing very passable pizzas, a few doors from the *Hôtel Regina*.

Restaurant Pizzaria el Khalij, 142 av Farhat Hached. An alternative address for pizzas or pasta, a little pricier than the *Pino*. On the corner of rue 9 Avril.

Hôtel Tacapes, 55 av Bourguiba (see above). Not a bad place to eat, although the *Amori* across the street is better value.

Listings

Banks Several on av Bourguiba, including four near the Gabes Centre and one at no. 300 under the *Hôtel Mourad*. There are three more on av Farhat Hached, near the corner of rue 9 Avril.

Bicycle rental Bicycles and mopeds can be rented at 142 av Bourguiba, two doors up from the *Hôtel Regina*, but give your chosen mount the once-over first.

Car rental *Avis*, 4 rue 9 Avril (☎05/270210); *Express*, 145 av Farhat Hached (☎05/274222); *Hertz*, 30 rue Ibn el Jazzar, near the corner of av Farhat Hached (☎05/270525); *Interrent/Europcar*, 6 av Farhat Hached (☎05/274720).

Cinemas *El Khadra*, rue Abou el Kacem Chabbi, near the corner of av Farhat Hached; *El Jaouhara*, 288 bd Mohammed Ali.

Excursions To cover some of the more inaccessible parts of the south with ease, mostly by Land Rover, you might consider a **tour** run by operators like *Voyages Najjar Chaabane* at 159 av Farhat Hached (☎05/271983), or *Sahara Tours* at 11 av Farhat Hached (☎05/270930).

Hammams The most central is in rue de Palestine, just off rue Sadok Lassoued – look for the blue and white door (daily men 5am–noon & 6–9pm; women 1–5pm). There is also the *Hammam el Hana*, rue Général de Gaulle, just off av Bourguiba (daily men 6am–1pm & 6–10pm; women 1–6pm).

International phone calls Try the PTT, or one of the number of taxiphone offices around town. Most close by 9pm, but there are a couple on av Farhat Hached which should be open till 10pm: one on the north side just east of Sadok Lassoued, and one on the other side at the junction of rue Ali Ben Salah Eddahri.

MOVING ON FROM GABES

Gabes is the main transport link between the south and the centre of Tunisia, and almost everything passes through here, so it's a very good place to pick up connections to anywhere in the country. Although the town has an airport, there are no passenger flights, and the **train station** off rue Mongi Slim has just two daily departures (one of which is overnight) to Tunis (7hr) via Mahres (2hr), Sfax (2hr 40min), El Jem (4hr) and Sousse (5hr). If you take the night train, you can change at Mahres or Sfax for Gafsa (6hr 15min) and Metlaoui (7hr), but it's a long journey.

The **bus station** operates *SNTRI*, Gabes's own *SRT* (called *SOTREGAMES*), and three other *SRT* services, running twelve buses a day to Sousse (4hr 30min) and El Hamma (45min); two daily buses to Bizerte (8hr), Kasserine (3hr 30min) and Tataouine (2hr 15min), and one service a day to Nefta (5hr), Sidi Bou Zid (3hr), Toujane (1hr) and Tozeur (4hr 30min). There are also buses to Ben Gardane (7 daily; 2hr 45min), Douz (3 daily; 3hr), Gafsa (4 daily; 2hr 30min), Houmt Souk on Jerba (10 daily; 2hr 30min), Kairouan (5 daily, 4 of them at night; 5hr 30min), Kebili (5 daily; 2hr 30min), Mareth (frequent; 30min), Medenine (14 daily; 1hr 15min), Sfax (20 daily; 2hr 15min), Tunis (16 daily, including 9 overnight; 6hr 30min), Zarzis (8 daily; 2hr) and Zarat (6 daily; 30min). Closer by, nine daily buses serve Matmata (1hr). Many of the Tunis or southern buses leave around midnight, arriving in the early morning. All except one of the buses serving Kairouan also run at night, dropping you in the holy city at a most inconvenient hour.

The main **louage** station is right in front of the bus terminus, with regular departures for Tunis, Sfax, Sousse, Kebili (and sometimes Douz), Medenine, Tataouine, El Hamma, Ben Gardane and Tripoli. *Louages* for Mareth leave from av Bourguiba by the Great Mosque, while those for Matmata leave from av Farhat Hached, just west of the junction with rue Haj Jelani Lahbib and rue Ali Jemel. Buses for Matmata stop here too, but most of the *louages* only go to Nouvelle Matmata, where there are onward connections for Matmata by pick-up.

Medical facilities The regional hospital is in rue Romdhane Ali Dhari (☎05/272700). More central is the *Clinique Bon Secours* at the eastern end of rue Mongi Slim (☎05/271400), which has an emergency department. There's an all-night pharmacy at 234 rue Mongi Slim, at the corner of rue Ali Ben Khalifa.

Newspapers *Librairie Nefoussi* at 16 rue 9 Avril carries the *Herald Tribune*, UK papers and *Time* and *Newsweek*. A place at 240 av Bourguiba, near the bend, also occasionally has British papers.

ONAT crafts shop Av Farhat Hached, opposite the PTT (Mon–Sat 9am–12.30pm & 3–6pm).

Supermarkets *Magasin Général* have two branches, one in Menzel at the corner of rue Omar el Mokhtar and rue Bechir el Jaziri; the other at the junction of bd Mohammed Ali and rue Mongi Slim. Both are open Sunday mornings, but closed Monday.

Swimming pool The *Hôtel Chems* will let you use their for a few dinars.

Matmata and around

Like the Romans of Bulla Regia once did, the Berbers of **MATMATA**, some 40km due south of Gabes, live underground in caves and courtyards dug into the soft, crumbly sandstone. In Iraq and Iran people escaped from the intense heat by building wind towers, a primitive kind of air conditioning which forced any breeze down into the living rooms; at Matmata, as at Bulla Regia and Gharian in Libya, the natural insulation of the earth was even more effective in providing cool temperatures during the summer and warmth in the winter.

Sadly, the travelling bus tours and the three large underground hotels have completely changed the local way of life. The attempt to exploit custom and tradition now threatens their very existence, and the use of Matmata as a location for the *Star Wars* movie proved another nail in the town's coffin. You'll get repeated invitations into people's houses and you should be prepared to buy the local handicrafts in exchange for a quick peep. This is tourism at its most voyeuristic, and barbed wire and dogs around many of the pits demonstrate that not everyone in town is happy about it. Stardom and hustle aside, however, Matmata remains interesting in its own right and useful as a base from which to explore the other villages of this remarkable region.

Arrival and accommodation

Matmata is spread out around three main roads – to Gabes, Toujane and Tamezret respectively. Where the three meet – the centre of town – you'll find a *Syndicat d'Initiative* **tourist office** (daily 8am–1pm & 3–6pm; ☎05/230114), whose staff are very amenable, though you may have to track them down in the *Ouled Azaiz* café opposite. They can organize camels, donkeys and other such rustic means of transport. There are **no banks** in Matmata (the nearest are in Gabes and Mareth) so bring enough dinars to see you through.

Three of Matmata's **hotels** are converted pit-dwellings, so staying in one is a good way to become familiar with the design of a traditional Matmata home.

Hotels

Les Berbères, off the Tamezret road, near the centre of town (☎05/230024). A friendly hotel in a converted pit-dwelling and often booked up by tour groups, so phone ahead. ②.

Sidi Driss, off the Toujane road nearer the centre of town (☎05/230005). Slightly more basic than the other two pit-dwellings, with each room crammed chock-full of beds. ②.

Marhala, off the Toujane road (☎05/230015). The most popular place in town was the location of the famous *Star Wars* disco scene. Tourists troop along to this pit-dwelling to eat, but many return to Gabes in the evening. ②.

Matmata ★★, off the Toujane road, just before the *Marhala* (☎05/230066). Spacious, spotless rooms and a pool, non-residents can use for a small fee, but not a traditional pit-house. ③.

Les Troglodytes ★★★, 1km up the Tamezret road (☎05/230088). This is where the upmarket tour groups stay, with its bar, restaurant and "Moorish" café. Very quiet during the day as they're all out touring. Non-residents can use the pool for a few dinars. ④.

The Town

Driving from Nouvelle Matmata, you climb to the top of the Demer mountains and descend to Matmata in the valley on the other side. With the virtual absence of any buildings, the place looks deserted; in fact, five thousand people still live in the "craters" which come into view as you head further down the road. Nonetheless, spread out as it is across the saddle of the mountain, Matmata seems almost too diffuse to be a village; the structures which have sprung up above the ground now give the lie to its much heralded "lunar" landscape, while the busloads of snap-happy day-trippers and camel-riding tourists manage at times to completely swamp the place.

Before the bulk of the Matmata tribe moved here in the sixteenth or seventeenth century, a very much smaller community lived in ancient Matmata, around the *kala'a*, or **fortress**, just discernible on the heights above today's town. Their homes, built into the mountainside, have been abandoned in favour of pit dwellings, and trying to climb up there is most inadvisable since the *kala'a* overlooks the army camp on the road to Toujane, and your appearance on its ramparts is likely to lead to trouble.

Many of the **pit dwellings** in Matmata follow a regular design some four hundred years old. Each is based around a circular pit with vertical walls, some seven metres deep by ten in diameter. A small, covered passageway, lined with recesses for animals and their fodder, leads from ground level down to the sunken courtyard, which is surrounded by small rooms and cisterns dug into the sandstone. Holes in the ceiling allow grain to be poured from ground level straight down to the lower store rooms. The largest houses consist of two or three pits linked together.

If no one approaches you with an invitation to visit their home, try walking out along the Gabes or Tamezret roads, where some of the pits have signs outside inviting tour-

---

THE MATMATA BERBERS

The **Berber tribe of the Matmata** once lived near the hot springs of El Hamma (see p.272), but were pushed back into the mountains by the nomadic northern Arab tribe of Beni Zid in the sixteenth or seventeenth century. While some Berbers did join the Hilalian armies that swept west into Morocco, the tribe preserved its autonomy until the end of the seventeenth century. The Ottomans always had trouble collecting taxes in this area, and Mohammed Bey was forced to build forts at El Hamma to the north and Bir Soltane in the desert to the west in order to keep the Matmata under control. By the eighteenth century, however, these forts had been abandoned and military expeditions remained the only means of asserting government authority, sometimes with success, sometimes ending in humiliating failure. In 1869, for instance, General Osman led his army into the foothills only to be surprised at night and forced to flee, leaving behind his artillery and richly adorned tent.

Under the French, the Berbers maintained their own tribal court, called the **miad**, which settled questions according to Berber law. In common with all the villages in the south, Matmata was still ruled by a *sheikh*, or administrator of the community, answerable to a *khalifa* (deputy governor) and the *caïd* (governor) at Gabes. The system continued until Independence, and the French officers of the *Service des Affaires Indigènes*, who supervised tax collection and public works, usually kept out of village affairs. Yet, although they enjoyed some autonomy, the government presence was still strong, as the fort on the outskirts of town – now an army base – testifies.

ists to view – in return for some backsheesh, of course. Alternatively, there is a **museum** off the Gabes road, near the centre of town (daily, no set hours; donation expected), consisting of a pit dwelling with three rooms and an assortment of everyday items, as well as clothes modelled on cute painted wooden figures. Unfortunately, all the explanations are in Arabic only, and the staff are totally unforthcoming, so don't expect any help from them.

Eating and drinking

Your best bet for **food** in Matmata is to try one of the hotels in town. The *Marhala*, *Berbères* and *Sidi Driss* all do very reasonable set menus, and although the *Matmata's* is pricier, you get your own table. Otherwise, you can try the *Ouled Azaiz Café Restaurant* in the very centre of town, or the cheaper nameless restaurant next door. For smarter eating, your only option is the restaurant in the *Hôtel les Troglodytes*.

As for **drinking**, the obvious place to take your custom is the *Hôtel Marhala* – though the company down in the bar isn't as lively as you may recall from *Star Wars*.

MOVING ON FROM MATMATA

Nine daily **buses** do the run to Gabes (1hr), with an evening *SNTRI* departure to Tunis (7hr 30min) via Sousse (5hr 30min) and Sfax (3hr), and a lunchtime bus to Tamezret (20min), returning three hours later (there's an evening one too, but you wouldn't be able to get back). There are also two daily to Techine (30min). Few **louages** serve Matmata, but you should be able to hitch or get on a pick-up to Nouvelle Matmata (about 1TD), from where there are *louages* to Gabes. Depending on prevailing conditions, the road to Ksar Ghilane (see p.350) may be just about passable in a two-wheel drive rented car, but you should take pains to check this out locally before setting off, and always inform the National Guard of your plans and heed the advice on desert driving on p.352.

Haddej and Tijma

To get some idea of what Matmata must once have been like, it's worth backtracking to **HADDEJ**, 3km northeast, which was formerly the region's most important village and home of the *khalifa*. A primary school among the palm trees marks the centre of town, and the **pit dwellings** lie up ahead. As soon as you arrive, the village children will appear, asking for pens and offering to show you around (for a little backsheesh, of course). It's a good idea to take up their offer as the buildings are even better concealed than those at Matmata, and the kids will probably follow you in any case. Many of the pits were abandoned after the floods of 1969, when the water covered the courtyards for a week, but an underground **grain store** at the top of the slope is in remarkably good condition. Two tiers of interlocking, arched storerooms have been built into a rock, like the *ghorfas* which dominate the landscape further south.

On the left-hand side of the path leading to the pit dwellings is the village **olive press**, also dug into the ground. At the centre of a small domed chamber is a circular stone, connected by a wooden shaft to the ceiling; a stone roller fixed to an axle is pulled around this shaft, crushing the olives spread out on the slab. The skins are taken from the stone and pressed again by a heavy palm trunk fastened at one end to the wall. Oil runs through a series of esparto grass mats into a jar, and the underground location provides the warmth in winter that's needed to separate the waste, which is fed to camels. In a final room, the olives are fermented to give the oil the rancid taste the people of the south appreciate.

Nearby is an underground **marabout** occupied only by its custodian. Another pit house, to the left of the olive press, was used for the village's **marriage ceremonies**. Seven days before the wedding, the bride's family went into the large underground room to prepare the feast. On the wedding day the bride was brought here on a camel and taken into a small room, reached by the steps leading up from the basement (take some matches if you visit). The husband, who was staying in a cell further inside the rock, went through to see the bride and to sign the marriage contract. Taking a back staircase up to ground level, he was led round to the front door to be formally received. When the feast was over, bride and groom would be taken into an airless cave, at the far end of the house, to remain in conjugal seclusion for several days. Meanwhile, the celebrations went on outside with a company of African comics, jesters and dancers.

The tourist office in Matmata (see above) may be able to sort out **transport** to Haddej if there are five or six of you; failing that, it's a question of walking or hitching 4km along the main road to Tijma, where you turn right for Haddej (signposted), about 3km up into the hills. There's a direct footpath between Matmata and Haddej but it isn't easy to find.

Tijma

The **House of Fatima** in the tiny settlement of **TIJMA**, about 4km north of Matmata, has long been owned by a woman of that name, and offers itself as a typical pit dwelling. Due not least to its unusually sanitized condition, this house is now on the tourist route and the current Fatima, plus daughter, receives the hordes with much aplomb. A bedroom, with its *dukkana* (a sort of bench used as a bed), and a kitchen, with pots and postcards for sale, are both open to view.

Walking through the valleys from Tijma towards Haddej, the luxuriance of the olive, almond and fig trees contrasts with the barrenness of the slopes. The trees flourish on hidden reservoirs of water stored in the thick soil of terraces, or **jessour** – winter downpours are channelled off the valley sides by shallow ditches and walls and contained for the long dry summer, helping olive and fig trees thrive in this inhospitable environment. The work involved in building these *jessour* was formidable, with huge quantities of earth piled up behind barriers built across the valley floors to make the terraces – a garden of one quarter-hectare (30m by 80m) behind a barrier 30m long would take about six months' work for one person, so it's hardly surprising that they're no longer built or even repaired. Most of the local men work in the cities and agriculture has been neglected, with the result that the region's terraces, its agricultural capital, are literally being washed away.

Beni Aissa

Neither easy to find nor to get to (there's just one daily minibus from Nouvelle Matmata), **BENI AISSA** is a lovely little village where the people live in the same sort of homes as in Matmata. About one and a half kilometres west of Matmata, an unpaved road leads off to the right. Some 4.5km along here is another turn-off (left), and a couple of kilometres along that, brings you into the village. A rented car will cover the route with no difficulty.

Look out for the group of **marabouts** 100m or so beyond the school, bus stop, shop and post box that mark Beni Aissa's centre. Courtesy and consideration for local people make a big difference to how you'll feel about the village, and how the villagers view you – the importance of privacy in Islamic society is hard to overstress, and Beni Aissa is a far cry from tourist-driven Matmata.

West of Matmata

The main road west from Gabes to Tamezret skirts the edge of a valley cultivated using the *jessour* system (see above). About halfway between Matmata and Tamezret, set a kilometre back from the road to the right, is the village of **SIDI META**. The first you see of it is a white *koubba* high up on the hillside, all that remains of the old village. At some time in the last two centuries the villagers moved down into the valley below, where, as at Matmata, they dug houses into the soft soil. Like Beni Aissa, Sidi Meta is rarely visited by tourists, and the people, as a result, are very accommodating. There's an **oil press** and an **underground mosque** that are worth seeing and the village also has a shop where you can buy bottled drinks.

TAMEZRET, built above ground, is packed around several steep slopes, topped by a **mosque**. One path between the tumbledown houses will take you to the **café** at the summit, the village's main tourist trap, where you can get a so-called traditional cup of almond tea and climb onto the roof to see the village of Zeraoua in the distance. Tamezret – and the villages around – is known for its **woollen shawls**, the ceremonial *bakhnoughs*, with striking geometric designs identical to the facial tattoos sometimes seen on older women. Be sensitive to the locals, especially if you have a camera, as tourism is creeping in, but so far it is not too obtrusive. Getting to Tamezret may be a problem, however, as there is only one practicable bus that runs the 10km from Matmata and cars are few and far between.

The tarmac road continues as far as **TAOUJOU**, beyond which is the village of **ZERAOUA**. Both are walkable from Tamezret – 4km and 7km respectively – but, like Tamezret, neither has accommodation (although someone may take pity on you and put you up). The views across the plateau and into the desert are stupendous, as are the villages – tightly knit communities living in compacted houses that look like a continuous wall from a distance. If you have reliable four-wheel drive transport and are rash – or confident – enough to want to cross the desert, a track leaves Tamezret for Kebili. It also goes direct to Douz (take a left after 26km).

Southeast of Matmata

An alternative route from Matmata, starting out from by the *Hôtel Marhala*, leads to Metameur (55km) and Medenine (both in the *Ksour* chapter) by way of Toujane. There are no buses at all in this direction and the bad surface, especially after Toujane, makes it hard-going in a car without four-wheel drive and not a very good prospect for hitching – if you want to try, walk out beyond the military zone. Most traffic prefers the easier approach to Toujane from Mareth on the Gabes–Medenine road (see p.310).

About 3km from Matmata, the road begins to flatten out, revealing the **Marabout of Sidi Moussa** on a peak to the left. In the early summer this is the scene of an ancient *ziarad*, a tribal pilgrimage atttended by thousands of villagers from Matmata, and on the rocks around the tomb you can see the blood stains from animal sacrifices. Some 8km further along, just off the road, is the village of **TECHNINE**, known for its furniture, made from branches covered with clay, plaster and whitewash. It also has a traditional olive press, worked by a donkey.

A further 4km on – 15km from Matmata – a turn off on the other side of the road winds for 8km down an incredibly steep gorge and out onto the plains to reach **BENI ZELTEN**, perched – like Tamezret – on the top of a small hill. Here though, the hill-top village has been deserted in favour of troglodyte dwellings and houses on the valley floor. Nevertheless, it remains a remarkable site, and one that's unknown to most visitors. The road beyond the village continues to Nouvelle Matmata.

Ignoring these detours and continuing along the steadily deteriorating Medenine road, you cross a series of deep gorges and then pass along the escarpment with spectacular views of the plains below. Suddenly the road drops again, this time giving a bird's-eye view of **TOUJANE**, 23km from Gabes. The old town – not to be confused with Nouvelle Toujane (or Dkhila) down below – is one of the most dramatic of the Matmata villages, spreading across two sides of a deep gorge and built around the foot of a mountain, from whose heights rear two brooding *kala'a* (fortresses). Once isolated and untouched, Toujane is now sufficiently on the beaten track for a **"café-musée"** to have sprung up. The cursory collection of artefacts is a rather feeble excuse to relieve passing tourists of a little cash, but lovers of instant coffee will be pleased to know that's all they have in the café.

Mareth and around

Midway between Gabes and Medenine, **MARETH** has long suffered from its important strategic position, commanding the narrow coastal plain between the Gulf of Gabes and the mountains. In 1936, the French army built a **defensive line** here to withstand a possible attack by the Italians in Libya. The line was first taken by Rommel and, in 1943, it blocked the Allied advance from the east; in the ensuing battle and Allied capture, the line and Mareth itself were virtually destroyed.

Apart from the busy Wednesday **market**, the new town is not wildly interesting, but if you're **staying** the options are the *Hôtel el Iman* (☎05/236035; ①), on the main road, left just past the *louage* station as you go south, or, slightly cheaper, the *Hôtel du Golfe*, 100m further on the right (☎05/236135; ①), a friendly place that only lacks hot water. You could stop at either hotel for a drink and a bite to eat.

Three kilometres south of Mareth, just before the Jorf turn off, the main road crosses **Oued Zigazou** on a zig zag bend. It's a seasonal river, dry most of the year, with the main emplacements of the Mareth Line spread out along it. On the *oued*'s north bank is the **Military Museum of the Mareth Line**, run by the Ministry of Defence (daily except Mon 9am–5pm; 1TD). Exhibits include maps and reconstructions illustrating Tunisia's role in World War II and the Battle of Mareth, as well as various small arms, and a French gun emplacement that looks remarkably like a dalek; the ticket includes a guided tour in English. Outside the museum are **concrete bunkers** that were actually part of the Mareth Line. These have been dug out – they were previously half-buried – and you can go inside them.

Should you wish to see **Rommel's command post**, as illustrated in the museum, it has also been tidied up by the army and is open to the public (variable hours, check with museum). To get there, take the unsignposted Toujane road from Mareth – west off the main road, by the taxiphone sign between the two hotels – for 5km to the village of **AZAIZA**, just beyond which there's a track to the right – look for an upright rectangle on top of a hill, which is in fact a seismograph. Follow the track for 2km, round the back of the hill with the seismograph, and you will see the command post. The left-hand of the two entrances leads into the sleeping quarters, but you'll need a light of some kind in order to see anything.

At the top of the hill by the seismograph are the remains of **trenches**, and a stunning view over the whole plain, which illustrates very clearly indeed how strategic the position was. Rommel set up his HQ here following orders from the Axis high command to strengthen the Mareth Line after their October 1942 defeat at the battle of El Alamein. Fortifications were built up along Oued Zigazou, and the post was chosen for its commanding view over the plain and the whole of the Mareth Line.

A kilometre north of Mareth, a road branches off east to the town of **ZARAT**. It's a bit of a wind blown, dead-end place, but 2km beyond it is a **beach**, marked by a line of roofless white beach huts. Though not the nicest in Tunisia – the sand is hard and the shoreline covered in black seaweed – you won't see another tourist here. Zarat town is connected to Mareth by six daily buses (all continuing to Gabes) and regular pick-ups.

Leaving the area, there are **buses** out of Mareth north to Gabes and south to Medenine or Houmt Souk. Further afield, there are buses to Tunis, Sfax, Sousse and Kairouan. Other services reach Tataouine, Zarzis, Ben Gardane and Ras Ajdir. More locally, there is a bus to Toujane. **Louages** go to Gabes and Medenine, but not Houmt Souk. However, it is not difficult to hitch to Jorf, from where you can pick up the ferry to Jerba (see p.312). **Pick-ups** serving local villages leave from behind the *louage* station. Destinations include Toujane, Zarat and Azaiza.

The **road to Toujane** is not signposted, but turns west off the main road in the centre of Mareth by the taxiphone sign between the two hotels, bearing right after 500km. It was this route, then a path, that allowed the eighth army to outflank the German lines by advancing during a single night.

travel details

Trains
Gabes to: El Jem, Gafsa, Mahres, Metlaoui, Sfax, Sousse and Tunis.

Buses
Gabes to: Ben Gardane, Bizerte, Douz, El Hamma, Gafsa, Houmt Souk, Kairouan, Kasserine, Kebili, Mareth, Matmata, Medenine, Nefta, Ras Ajdir, Sfax, Sidi Bou Zid, Sousse, Tataouine, Toujane, Tozeur, Tunis, Zarat and Zarzis.

Mareth to: Ben Gardane, Gabes, Houmt Souk, Kairouan, Medenine, Ras Ajdir, Sfax, Sousse, Tataouine, Toujane, Tunis, Zarat and Zarzis.

Matmata to: Gabes, Sfax, Sousse, Tamezret, Techine and Tunis.

Louages
Gabes to: Ben Gardane, El Hamma, Houmt Souk, Kebili, Mareth, Medenine, Nefta, Sfax, Sousse, Tataouine, Tripoli, Tunis and Zarzis, with the odd one direct to Douz and Nouvelle Matmata.

Mareth to: Gabes and Medenine, but not Houmt Souk.

Matmata to: Gabes.

Pick-ups
Mareth to: Toujane, Zarat and Azaiza.

Matmata to: Nouvelle Matmata.

Nouvelle Matmata to: Matmata.

MARKET DAYS

Monday – Matmata and Mareth

Daily except Monday – Gabes

CHAPTER EIGHT

JERBA AND THE SOUTHEAST COAST

T he island of **Jerba**, joined to the mainland by a causeway since before Roman times, perches at the southern end of the Gulf of Gabes, enclosing the smaller **Gulf of Bou Grara** between island and mainland. Eastwards, the coast dips past the modern town of **Zarzis** and the Bahiret el Biban lagoon before disappearing over the border into Libya.

This sun-soaked corner of Tunisia boasts some of the finest **beaches** in the Mediterranean, arguably the finest. Unfortunately, the best of these, in the island's northeastern corner – from **Sidi Mahares** round to **Aghir** – have largely been swamped in recent years by large-scale package tourist developments, and beach hotels are beginning to spread, too, along the mainland parts of the coast around Zarzis. In midsummer it's probably a good idea to seek nirvana elsewhere.

However, there are deserted beaches if you have the means to get to them. On the **west coast** of Jerba and **southeast of Zarzis** are strands where you won't see another tourist, and not many Tunisians either, though these tend not to be the best ones, and you should, in any case, check with the local police or National Guard before heading to potentially sensitive areas close to the Libyan border.

JERBA

On the tenth [day] we made the country of the Lotus-Eaters, a race that live on vegetable foods . . . I sent some of my followers inland to find out what sort of human beings might be there, detailing two men for the duty with a third as messenger. Off they went, and it was not long before they were in touch with the Lotus-Eaters. Now it never entered the heads of these natives to kill my friends: what they did was to give them some lotus to taste, and as soon as each had eaten the honeyed fruit of the plant, all thoughts of reporting to us or escaping were banished from his mind. All they now wished for was to stay where they were with the Lotus-Eaters, to browse on the lotus and to forget that they had a home to return to. I had to use force to bring them back to the ships, and they wept on the way, but once on board I dragged them under the benches and left them in irons. I then commanded the rest of my loyal band to embark with all speed on their fast ships, for fear that others of them might eat the lotus and think no more of home. They came on board at once, went to the benches, sat down in their proper places, and struck the white surf with their oars.
So we left that country and sailed on sick at heart.

Homer, *The Odyssey (Book IX)*

Jerba, along with Gozo and Menorca, claims to be the legendary land of the **Lotus-Eaters** and – low-lying, semi-desert island that it is – it makes good territory for such

ACCOMMODATION PRICE CODES

All the hotels, youth hostels and pensions listed in this book have been price-graded according to the following scale, and although prices will rise during the lifetime of this edition, the relative comparisons should remain valid.

The prices quoted are for the **cheapest available double room in high season**, although many of the cheap places will have pricier rooms with en suite facilities or sea views.

Classified hotels, officially considered suitable for tourists, are graded locally from one to four stars (★), with wide-ranging prices within each category. For more on accommodation prices and categories, see Basics.

① Up to 10TD. Very cheap. Usually a bed only in a basic, unclassified hotel or a youth hostel.

② 10.1–25TD. Budget. Bed only or bed and breakfast.

③ 25.1–40TD. Comfortable budget. Good unclassified average one-star or a cheap two-star.

④ 40.1–55TD. Mid-range. Expensive two-star, cheap three-star.

⑤ 55.1–70TD. Tourist hotel. Standard three-star.

⑥ 70.1TD upwards. Deluxe. Expensive three-star, four-star or five-star.

myth and fantasy. The coast consists largely of beautiful sandy beaches while, inland, unique mosques and houses are scattered among palm groves. Its history and culture are to some extent different from those of the mainland; its architecture is quite distinctive, its ethnic background more diverse. Unfortunately, its seductive packageable charms and easy access through an international airport have brought **tourism** on a big scale. Dozens of hotels line the northern coast, which the government has declared a *zone touristique*, and many of the people who come to stay here see the island as nothing more than a beach in the sun. And indeed Jerba is an excellent **beach resort**: the palm-rustled strands themselves are wonderful, the sea warm and limpid, the mood relaxed and the general scene idyllic. Moreover, the hotels here are some of the country's best and more than adequate by any standard. If all you want is sun and sand, it's just the place to come; on the other hand, if that is all you want, you're missing out.

The island's intimate, farm-divided **interior** exudes a certain magic you won't find anywhere else, a district of country lanes through date and olive groves, with the sea never far away. The beautiful whitewashed, fortified mosques are unique in Tunisia and the island also boasts three historic forts and scattered Roman remains, so far unexcavated. It's a big enough area (around 25km wide by 22km long) to explore in a genuine sense but small enough to do so by bicycle.

By road, Jerba can be reached easily enough from the south or north. From the south, most **buses** take you straight through to Houmt Souk, via Zarzis and the causeway. Coming from Gabes and the north, it's faster to use the Jorf–Ajim **ferry**, although many buses still go the long way round via Medenine and Zarzis.

For **travelling around** the island, **taxis** are probably your best bet. These are more expensive than buses, but metered and still very reasonable. You may also be able to share with someone and cut costs. Failing that, remember that **hitching** is very easy in Jerba (you may have to resort to it to get back to Houmt Souk anyway), and, depending on the heat, even **walking** is not out of the question for getting around parts of the northwest of the island. If you are **driving**, note that Jerba has a 70km per hour maximum speed limit, rarely obeyed but sometimes enforced. Jerbans seem to know where the police are waiting to pounce, and tourists are better off keeping within the limit.

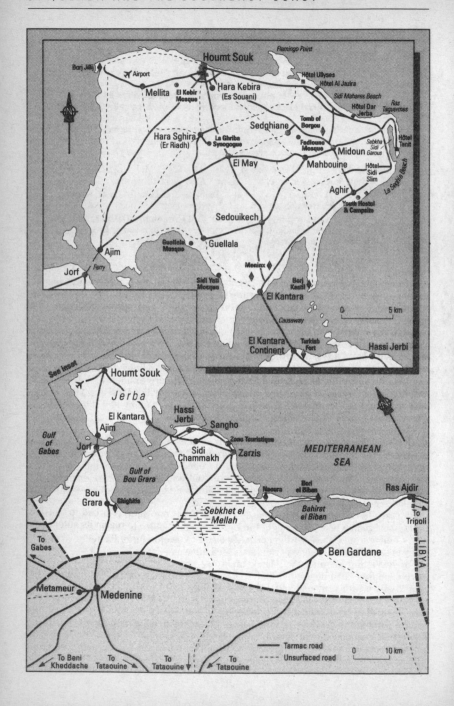

Jerba's **airport** is at Mellita (☎05/650233), 6km from Houmt Souk and 12km from the heart of the hotel strip at Sidi Mahares. There are three daily buses into Houmt Souk, with buses from there to Sidi Mahares and Aghir. If you don't have transport laid on by a hotel, and if the buses fail to connect with your arrival, you will have to take a metered taxi, costing around 3TD (5TD at night) to Houmt Souk, and around 10–15TD to the hotel zone, depending on the time of day and where exactly your hotel is. *Avis, Hertz, Europcar, Express* and *Mattei* all have **car rental** desks at the airport (☎05/650233). There are also three buses a day out to the airport.

Jerba has some reasonably inexpensive **flights** back to Tunis (8 daily; 1hr), as well as various flights to Monastir (2 weekly; 30min), Sfax (5 weekly; 30min) and Tozeur (1 weekly; 50min), along with international flights to Brussels (2 daily; 3hr 15min), Frankfurt (1 daily; 4hr 30min), Geneva (1 daily; 2hr 15min), Lyon (1 daily; 2hr 15min), Marseille (1 daily; 2hr), Paris (3 daily; 2hr 45min), Rome (1 daily; 1hr 30min), Zürich (1 daily; 2hr 30min) and Vienna (1 daily; 2hr 45min).

Some history

The **Carthaginians** who first settled on Jerba called it *Meninx* – "land of the receding waters", a reference to the highest tides anywhere in the Mediterranean. With its virtually landlocked gulf, it was an ideal haven for any sheltering fleet, and quickly gained a reputation for trade and commerce. The **Romans** built an extensive city on the southern shores, exporting cloth (dyed imperial purple with the murex shellfish) throughout the Empire.

Under the **Arabs**, Jerba was a centre of almost permanent revolt as it constantly struggled to assert its independence from its overlords. The island strongly supported the **Kharijite rebellion** in 740 and, when the Aghlabids retook the north of Tunisia, Jerba became part of the Rustamids' Kharijite state (it is still one of Kharijism's last strongholds). Later, Jerba supported **Abu Yazid**'s 944 Kharijite rebellion against the **Fatimids**, and also rose unsuccessfully against their successors, the **Zirids**. Throughout the centuries leading towards French domination, it remained a hotbed of defiance, never at peace for long.

From the twelfth century, Jerba came under serious threat from the Christian kingdoms, especially whichever one had control of Sicily, just across the water. Like Sicily, Jerba's strategic position made it an object of Muslim–Christian rivalry. In 1135, Sicily's Norman king **Roger II** invaded Jerba, massacring or enslaving much of the population. The island resisted with little success and, a century later, suffered much the same fate under **Roger de Lluria** of Aragon. When Jerba again rose up in 1310, Aragonese troops under **Ramon de Muntaner** murdered or enslaved three-quarters of the island's population and strangled its economy with punitive taxes. Even when returned to Muslim rule by the **Almohads** in 1159, Jerba made repeated attempts to regain its autonomy. The Christians tried to retake it several times, but local resistance rebutted them. For much of the fifteenth century, at least, Jerba under the **El Samumni** family was virtually independent.

Piratical **merchant-sailors** wrought havoc in Jerba in the sixteenth century. The corsair Aruj **Barbarossa** made his base here in 1510, as did his protégé **Dragut** in 1535. Dragut, trapped with his fleet by the flotilla of Charles V of Spain in 1551, made a famous and daring **naval getaway** (see p.366) from the island. Later putting himself at the disposal of the Turks, Dragut returned with an **Ottoman** fleet to set up shop in 1560, and completely trounced the coalition of European forces under Philip II of Spain that attempted to drive him out.

Under the **Ottomans**, Jerba became a centre of silk and wool production and its economy thrived. It was also a major terminal for trans-Saharan goods until its main commodity, African slaves, was banned in 1846. European merchants preferred to trade here rather than with the unpredictable mainland – if there was an uprising on the mainland, business could go on as usual on the island. This is just what happened in 1881; the islanders, fearing that Jerba would be occupied and sacked by the rebellious tribes on the mainland, welcomed the **French** invaders, gaining for themselves the lasting gratitude of the conquerors.

Houmt Souk

Although **HOUMT SOUK** is becoming increasingly commercialized, the *Association pour la Sauvegarde de l'Île de Jerba* has made great efforts to preserve its distinctive architecture over the last decade. The island's capital and its one real town, Houmt Souk (the town's name means "marketplace", and it was originally just the site of the island's market, with everything built outwards from the souk) remains a lively and interesting place and, at only 1500m from end to end, a very easy one to find your way around.

Arrival and accommodation

If you're not arriving by plane (see p.315), Houmt Souk's **bus station**, run by *SRTG Medenine*, is in avenue Bourguiba just south of the town centre, with the **louage station** opposite; local buses serve the hotel zone of Sidi Mahares and Midoun. For transport between Houmt Souk and the hotel zone with the maximum possible delay, there's a **tourist train** twice a day at 3TD for the return trip (children 2TD) from outside the *Syndicat d'Initiative*. The main *ONTT* **tourist office** is on rue Ulysse, the coast road to Sidi Mahares (Mon–Thurs 8.30am–1pm & 3–5.45pm, Fri & Sat 8.30am–1.30pm; ☎05/650016), and there's a *Syndicat d'Initiative* on avenue Bourguiba, opposite place Mongi Bali (same hours; ☎05/650915). Most services and shops are on the two main north–south roads, **avenue Bourguiba** to the west and **avenue Abdel Hamid el Kadhi** to the east, with **banks** around place Farhat Hached and avenue Bourguiba (the best being *CFCT* on the corner of avenue Bourguiba and avenue Mohamed Badra). If you want to rent a **car** immediately on arrival, *Avis*, *Hertz*, *Europcar*, *Express* and *Mattei* all have desks at the airport (☎05/650233).

Unless you want to stay by the beach at Sidi Mahares or Aghir, you'll probably end up in one of Houmt Souk's **hotels**. Five of these (including the town's excellent youth hostel) are old converted **foundouks** or *caravanserais*, once offering food and shelter to itinerant merchants and pilgrims. They share a common plan, with a large open courtyard surrounded by arches or colonnades. At the centre camel trains would be tethered by the well, their goods securely stored on the ground floor. If you're **camping**, Jerba's only two campsites are at Aghir, or you can camp wild at Flamingo Point, Ras Taguermes or on the west coast. In Houmt Souk itself, a park on rue Ulysse by the Borj el Keir is sometimes used as a campsite by the scouts and it's just possible that you could pitch a tent and use such facilities as there are, but you'd have to find someone to ask, and that's easier said than done.

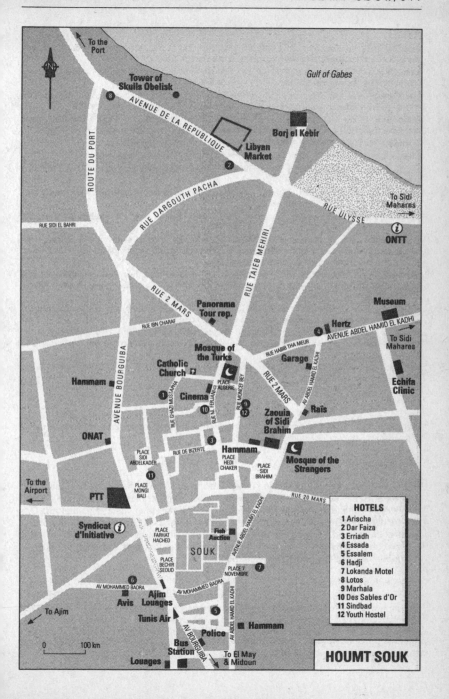

To the Port

Gulf of Gabes

Tower of Skulls Obelisk

8

AVENUE DE LA REPUBLIQUE

Borj el Kebir

ROUTE DU PORT

RUE DARGOUTH PACHA

Libyan Market

2

RUE TAIEB MEHIRI

RUE SIDI EL BAHRI

RUE ULYSSE

To Sidi Mahares

ONTT

RUE 2 MARS

Panorama Tour rep.

RUE IBN CHARAF

Museum

Hertz

4

AVENUE ABDEL HAMID EL KADHI

To Sidi Mahares

RUE HABIB THA MEUR

Mosque of the Turks

Garage

RUE 2 MARS

AV ABDEL HAMID EL KADHI

Catholic Church

PLACE D'ALGERIE

Echifa Clinic

Hammam

RUE GHAZI MUSTAPHA

Cinema

RUE EL FERJANI

PLACE MONCEF BEY

1

10

9

12

Zaouia of Sidi Brahim

Rais

ONAT

PLACE SIDI ABDELKADER

RUE DE BIZERTE

3

Hammam

PLACE HEDI CHAKER

PLACE SIDI BRAHIM

Mosque of the Strangers

AVENUE BOURGUIBA

11

PLACE MONGI BALI

PTT

RUE 20 MARS

To the Airport

Syndicat d'Initiative

PLACE FARHAT HACHED

Fish Auction

AVENUE ABDEL HAMID EL KADHI

PLACE BECHIR SEOUD

SOUK

PLACE 7 NOVEMBRE

7

6

AV MOHAMMED BADRA

Avis

Ajim Louages

AV MOHAMMED BADRA

Tunis Air

Bus Station

5

Police

AV BOURGUIBA

AV ABDEL HAMID EL KADHI

Hammam

To Ajim

Louages

To El May & Midoun

0   100 km

HOTELS
1 Arischa
2 Dar Faiza
3 Erriadh
4 Essada
5 Essalem
6 Hadji
7 Lokanda Motel
8 Lotos
9 Marhala
10 Des Sables d'Or
11 Sindbad
12 Youth Hostel

HOUMT SOUK

Hotels

Arischa ★, 36 rue Ghazi Mustapha (☎05/650384). Near the church. Most attractive of the old *foundouks*, its court festooned with vines and enclosing a shallow pool. ②.

Ben Abbes, 158 av Bourguiba (☎05/650128). Out towards the hospital, each of these self-catering apartments has its own kitchen. ③.

Dar Faiza ★, rue de la République (☎05/650083). Up near the Borj. A charming and well-run place with a small pool, family atmosphere and customers who come back year after year. ③.

Erriadh ★, 10 rue Mohamed Ferjani, off pl Hedi Chaker (☎05/650756). Rooms have bathrooms but windows open only onto the central patio. The most expensive of the *fondouks*. ③.

Essada, 6 rue Habib Thameur (☎05/651422). Nice rooms, shame about the attitude. ②.

Essalem, rue de Remeda, off pl 7 Novembre (☎05/651029). Big comfy rooms. ②.

Hadji ★, 44 av Mohamed Badra (☎05/650630). Rather formal with large rooms and all the mod cons. ②.

Laroussa, av Bourguiba (☎05/650788). The clientele in this clean and quiet place are mostly holidaymakers from other Arab countries. ②.

Lokanda Motel, passage de la Municipalité (☎05/651513). Not the best hotel in town, but the rooms are clean enough. ①.

Lotos, 18 rue de la République (☎05/650026). Opposite the tower of skulls obelisk. Large, clean rooms with bathroom. Run by the same people as the nearby and slightly dearer *Hôtel Dar Faiza*, whose pool and tennis courts are open to *Lotos* guests. ③.

Marhala, 13 rue Moncef Bey (☎05/650416). An old *foundouk* next door to the youth hostel, and run, like its namesakes in Nefta and Matmata, by the Touring Club of Tunisia. Pleasant though rather basic rooms, and the best bar in town. ②.

Nozha ★, 150 av Bourguiba (☎05/650381). Friendly, if a little shabby, and out by the hospital. Rooms have balcony and bathroom, and some have air conditioning. ③.

Hôtel des Sables d'Or, 30 rue Mohamed Ferjani (☎05/650423). Not a *foundouk* but an old palatial house built around a central patio. The rooms are clean, with private showers but shared loos. ②.

Sindbad, pl Mongi Bsali (☎05/650047). No singles so a bit pricey if you're on your own. Not as nice as the other *foundouks*. ②.

Youth hostel

Maison des Jeunes youth hostel, 11 rue Moncef Bey, off pl Hedi Chaker (☎05/650619). The best youth hostel in the country: very friendly and well-run converted *foundouk*, with double rooms and a distinct lack of rules and regulations. ①.

The Town

With a history as stormy and an identity as strong as Jerba's, it is hardly surprising that its capital is full of interest. Houmt Souk's nooks and crannies are gradually being pedestrianized, and its cottage industries are giving way to shops and restaurants that are hardly there for the benefit of Jerbans. But in spite of this onslaught, it still has loads of charm and remains one of the country's most pleasant towns. While you can't, unfortunately, enter any of the mosques or *zaouias*, the **fort and museum** are open to the public, and both are worth investigation.

The Souk and around

At the very centre of the town is its **souk**, with two *qaysarriya*, arched and covered passageways where traditionally the most expensive goods were sold, such as prized Egyptian cloth and filigree silver. Coral and jewellery are now the market's pricey mainstays; the leather goods are often pretty shoddy. Be ruthless when you barter – it's often not unreasonable to make an initial offer of a tenth of the quoted price. In the less tourist-oriented part of the souk, the daily **fish auction** is interesting to visit.

Mondays and Thursdays are the souk's busiest days, with traders coming in from around the island. The market is then full of people selling straw baskets and mats, along with musicians from Midoun (see p.326) playing and selling their instruments.

Next to the souk, the **Zaouia of Sidi Brahim**, with its heavily buttressed walls, is typical of the ascetic Ibadite style of architecture (see box on p.329) and looks much more military than religious. Building was begun in 1674 but only completed thirty years later by the Bey, Mourad Ben Ali, and it was then used for worship, teaching and as a rest house for travellers. Today it contains the tomb of the saint and his followers but, although a small door into the courtyard is usually open, non-Muslims are not allowed to enter. Across the road is the extravagant **Mosque of the Strangers**, whose contrast with the *zaouia* could hardly be greater – this mosque is covered with domes and topped by an extravagantly carved minaret. Again, sadly, it is closed to non-Muslim visitors.

Avenue Moncef Bey, just opposite, leads to the smaller **Mosque of the Turks**, the most interesting of all Houmt Souk's mosques. The distinctive minaret was built by followers of Ibn Abdul Wahab, an eighteenth-century Islamic reformer from Arabia who introduced a fundamentalist and staunchly nationalistic brand of Islam. The unusually shaped minaret was first dubbed "phallic" by the Victorian polymath Sir Harry Johnston – a contentious epithet that has rather stuck. Johnston was convinced of "an unrecognized system of phallic worship throughout the south, and on Jerba all but the most recently built mosques have a phallic emblem on the summit of the minaret".

Just around the corner in a quiet cul de sac, the **Catholic church** offers no such mysterious symbols for interpretation: this strange baroque building was once the centre of a thriving Christian community on Jerba. From the 1840s Greeks, Italians and Maltese came to the island for the sponge-fishing. Some stayed on and, by the 1890s, several thousand Europeans were living here. With Independence, however, most left and the church fell into disrepair, eventually to be turned over to more secular uses. Today it's a gymnasium.

Opposite the *Hôtel Marhala* is another reminder of the island's European links, the **Maltese foundouk**, where merchants and sponge-collectors once stored their goods.

The Borj el Kebir and Libyan market

From the Mosque of the Turks, rue Taïeb Mehiri leads to the fort, variously called the **Borj Ghazi Mustapha** or **Borj el Kebir** (daily except Fri summer 9am–7pm; winter 9.30am–4.30pm; 1TD). The site was originally occupied by the Romans, but a fort was first built here by the Aragonese King of Sicily, Roger de Lluria, in 1289. Its most famous moment came in 1560 when, after Philip II of Spain's armada was wiped out by Dragut's Ottoman fleet, his men retreated inside the fort, only to be massacred by the Turks. The skulls of the Spaniards (by various accounts numbering 500 or 5000) were piled up in a great tower – which stood until European powers prevailed on the Bey, despite strong local opposition, to bury them in 1848. All that remains now of this tower of skulls is a discreet **obelisk** marking the site, 100m over towards the port.

The fort has been excavated but the site is hard to interpret for the untrained eye; for clues, look towards the new bridge over the ditch on the south side, which leads first into a hall (*skifa*) and then into a courtyard between two perimeter walls. On the far side, the tomb of Ghazi Mustapha (who rebuilt the fort under the Turks) stands on the site of a thirteenth-century mosque. The west wall, with its four massive towers, is original.

In a walled enclosure next to the Borj el Kebir, a **"Libyan market"** takes place on Monday and Thursday mornings, with bargains and goods brought in from across the border. At one time, most of the traders were Libyan and all sorts of rarities unavailable elsewhere in Tunisia could be found here. Nowadays, the market has become much like any other in Tunisia, though still worth a browse, but if you want the real thing, you have to go to Ben Gardane (see p.333).

The Museum of Arts and Popular Traditions

For more concrete historical evidence than that offered by the obscure remnants of the fort, take a look at the concise **Museum of Arts and Popular Traditions**, at the eastern edge of town on avenue Abdel Hamid el Kadhi (daily except Fri summer 9am–7pm; winter 9.30am–4.30pm; 2TD).

The museum's first room, once the *zaouia* of Sidi Ameur, contains **costumes** worn on special occasions and in different parts of the island. Search out in particular the old *fut'a*, a wrap-around garment worn by Berber women, and the traditional shawl or *bakhnug*. The long ornamental brooches in the cabinets are worn to indicate tribal allegiance: a Malekite would wear such a brooch on the left, a Berber in the middle and a Bedouin on the right. As in all the regions of the south (much more so than the north), Jerba has its own **marriage rituals**, now threatened by increasing costs and the demand for high dowries from the bride's father. Exhibits illustrate the ceremonies that begin six weeks before the wedding day, when red or yellow eggs are sent as invitations to the guests. During the week before the wedding the bride will receive presents from her husband and his family, including jewellery and ceremonial dress of the kind on display in the museum. She must also apply henna (on two different occasions) to the whole of her palms, fingers and feet; a Berber, though not a Malekite, might use a black paint called *ouchi*. At some stage, both the man and woman will be led in procession around a fertile olive tree, striking their companions with a branch to hasten other marriages in the village. On the Friday before the wedding the bride is formally presented and unveiled to her family, who traditionally throw money at her feet. Finally she is carried to the groom in the privacy of a *palanquin*, a screened canopy placed on the back of a camel.

The museum's second room, the former **shrine of Sidi Zitouni**, has an original pottery roof (although the stuccowork on its walls has been restored). Display cases contain ornamental **jewellery** made by the island's Jewish community. Downstairs is a reconstruction of an old pottery workshop of the sort still used at Guellala (see p.328). A room across the next courtyard was once used as a **kitchen** by pilgrims staying at the sanctuary. The large "Ali-Baba" **jars** are used as marriage chests, since there's little wood on the island. As you leave the museum, have a look at the **weaver's hut**, the *harout*, with its triangular front and sunken external buttressing; like the *houch* (see p.326), these are unique to Jerba.

Eating and drinking

Houmt Souk has a reasonable range of **restaurants**, with plenty of tourist ones around place Hedi Chaker and place Sidi Brahim, and cheaper places tucked away around town. Patisseries and cafés are cheap and plentiful, and a couple of hotel bars provide a pleasant enough backdrop for an evening drink.

Restaurants

Aladin, 40 av Mohamed Badra. Next door to the *Hôtel Hadji*. The latest-closing moderately priced eatery in town. Till 11pm nightly.

Berbère, 9 pl Farhat Hached. Quite refined but still inexpensive and very central.

Central, 128 av Bourguiba. Near the bus station. A calm atmosphere with pretty good and reasonably priced couscous.

Hôtel Dar Faiza, rue de la République (☎05/650083). The best of the hotel restaurants, with good fish and a medium-priced set menu, but it does tend to cater for guests who don't like spicy food.

Essada, 12 pl Bechir Seoud. Not as sophisticated as the nearby *Berbère*, but cheaper.

Essalem, 21 av Mohamed Badra. Basic and cheap fried fare.

El Hana, pl 7 Novembre (☎05/650568). Tucked away by the souk entrance. You can get a meal for around 12TD or order more expensive specialities like Sole Lord Nelson or a "Captain Hornblower Feast".

Restaurant de l'Île, pl Hedi Chaker (☎05/650575). A reasonable alternative to the *du Sud*, just opposite, with high prices.

Les Palmiers, pl d'Algérie, at the end of rue Mohamed Ferjani, near the church. Solid and inexpensive Tunisian food.

Patisserie Pizzeria Dar, 161 av Abdel Hamid el Kadhi. Very passable and reasonably priced wood-oven pizzas to eat in or take away.

Populaire, 29 av Mohamed Badra. Very cheap, but rather a greasy spoon.

La Princesse d'Haroun, at the harbour (☎05/650488). A rather posh and pricey fish restaurant down at the harbour.

Sportif, 147 av Bourguiba. Good-value, good-quality food. The liver in particular is worth a try.

Restaurant du Sud, pl Sidi Brahim (☎05/650479). Better than most of the tourist traps although still expensive; à la carte may be cheaper than the set menu, depending on what you order.

Tunisien, in the central souk. Bargain place for a good feed. Fish is especially recommended. Open lunchtimes, only.

Cafés and bars

Cafés and **patisseries** are popular places to start the day, with croissants, pastries and sandwiches on sale from early morning onwards. The café on place Bechir Seoud is a cut above the rest, with fresh croissants and loads of pastries, and there's another on place Hedi Chaker with a garden. Two patisseries worthy of mention are the ones at 145 avenue Bourguiba and 35 rue Mohamed Ferjani, which both do good sandwiches.

As for **drinking**, most places, as usual, are closed by 8pm. The *Hôtel Marhala* has Houmt Souk's liveliest bar, with its courtyard serving as its saloon bar and staying open later, but it's sometimes restricted to hotel guests. The *Arischa* is also quieter and sometimes stays open late in summer. After closing time, your best bet is to find a restaurant where you can get away with ordering only beer, and perhaps a snack to go with it. Otherwise, you'll have to get a taxi out of town to a hotel such as the *Strand*, where you can drink till late. Make sure you can arrange transport back if you do this.

Listings

Airlines *Air France*, 131 av Abdel Hamid el Kadhi, pl 7 Novembre (☎05/650239); *Tunis Air*, av Bourguiba (☎05/650159).

Car and bike rental For cars, try *Avis*, 51 av Mohamed Badra (☎05/650151); *Ben Jemaa*, 1st floor, 4 av Mohamed Badra (☎05/650340); *Budget*, rue 20 Mars (☎05/650185); *Express*, av Abdel Hamid el Kadhi (☎05/650438); *Hertz*, 10 rue Habib Thameur (☎05/650196); *Intercar*, 173 av Abdel Hamid el Kadhi (☎05/651155); *Interrent/Europcar*, 161 av Abdel Hamid el Kadhi (☎05/650357); *Mattei*, av Abdel Hamid el Kadhi, at rue H Thameur (☎056/651367); and *Topcar*, 19 rue 20 Mars (☎05/650536). *Avis, Hertz, Europcar, Express* and *Mattei* all have desks at the airport (☎05/650233). Land Rovers cannot be rented without a driver. The place to rent **motorbikes** is *Holiday Bikes* out in the hotel zone (☎05/657169), 100m before the Midoun turnoff from the main road; they also do scooters. In town, **scooters** and **mopeds** can be rented from *Raïs*, 155 av Abdel Hamid el Kadhi (☎05/650303). The hotels *Arischa* and *Sindbad* rent out **bicycles**, but they are cheaper from *Raïs* or from a nameless place at 15 rue 20 Mars, by pl Sidi Brahim.

Cinema Pl d'Algérie, opposite the Mosque of the Turks.

Excursions Land Rover trips of the south are more worthwhile than bus tours, which stick to main roads and isolate you somewhat from the country. *Evatour*, on the airport road, 200m west of the PTT (☎05/653172), is the best and friendliest, offering week-long tours of the south for 380TD or two-day trips to Ksar Ghilane in the south for 100TD.

Festivals There's a summer Ulysses festival, and a yacht regatta all around the island at the beginning of September.

Hammams The oldest, friendliest and most central hammam is by the *zaouia* at 17 pl Sidi Brahim (daily men 5am–noon; women 1–6pm). The *Hammam Ziadi* at 93 av Bourguiba is cleaner but dearer and less friendly (daily men 6am–noon; women 1–6pm). There is another one with similar hours at 117 av Abdel Hamid el Kadhi.

MOVING ON FROM HOUMT SOUK

Houmt Souk's **bus station**, run by *SRTG Medenine*, is in avenue Bourguiba, just south of the town centre. **Local buses** serve the hotel zone of Sidi Mahares (#11), Midoun and Aghir (#10), with services to Hara Sghira (#14), El May (#10 and #16), Guellala (#14), Ajim, Sedouikech (#16) and the airport (#15). For leisurely transport between Houmt Souk and the hotel zone, there's a **tourist mini road train** every two hours (2TD).

Intercity buses serve Ben Gardane (3 daily; 2hr), Gabes (10 daily; 2hr 30min), Medenine (9 daily; 2hr), Tataouine (2 daily; 3hr) and Zarzis (11 daily; 1hr). For destinations north of Gabes – especially Tunis (4 daily; 8hr 30min) – buses are often full and need booking in advance. **Louages** to Tunis, Gabes, Zarzis, Ben Gardane, Medenine, Sfax and Tripoli leave from next to the bus station, and those to Ajim, their only destination within Jerba, leave from the traffic island in the middle of avenue Bourguiba, opposite the corner of avenue Mohamed Badra.

International phone calls As well as the PTT, there are various taxiphone offices around town, including one in pl Sidi Brahin and another in the back of a newsstand opposite the PTT. An office just up the street at 73 av Bourguiba is open until midnight, as is the one at 18 rue Sakiet Sidi Youssef, off av Bourguiba.

Medical facilities The regional hospital is at the southern end of av Bourguiba (☎05/650018). There's also a private clinic, the *Echifa*, near the museum (☎05/652215). One GP used to treating foreigners is Dr Ben Sabah at 164 av Bourguiba (☎05/650238), and there's a late-night pharmacy at 166 av Bourguiba.

Newspapers British papers are available at 127 av Bourguiba, near the PTT, along with *Time*, *Newsweek* and the *Herald Tribune*.

ONAT crafts shop Av Bourguiba, 100m north of the PTT.

PTT Av Bourguiba, opposite pl Mongi Bali (country hours). Pay phone section open until 7.30pm weekdays.

Supermarket *Grand Magasin* at the corner of rue Tahar Battikh and av Abdel Hamid el Kadhi; *Société Commerciale de Distribution* is in the souk near the fish auction.

Sidi Mahares beach and around

East of Houmt Souk, before the package tourists' haven of Sidi Mahares, the low sandy peninsula of Ras Rmel – known as **Flamingo Point** – stretches lazily out into the sea. Between November and March, you'll see a lot of the pink waders here, and often **dolphins** too, just a few yards offshore. A lot of Tunisians and Libyans **camp** out here in summer, as they do at the other end of the hotel zone, and there is no reason why you shouldn't join them.

Bus #11 from Houmt Souk will take you past Flamingo Point and out along **Sidi Mahares beach**, past the tourist complex and the string of hotels along 8km of beach and surf until you reach the lighthouse at Ras Taguermes. The bus stops at most of the hotels en route, and you specify which one you want as you buy the ticket; the first on the beach is the *Hôtel Ulysse Palace*. Prices for staying at these hotels – unless you're pre-booked on a package – are very inflated, especially in summer, though most are good and easily bear comparison with their equivalents in, say, Greece or Spain. Only a few operators – among them *Panorama* and *Medward* (p.6) – offer package holidays here from the UK.

As far as facilities go, **beach sports** are available at most of the hotels and include parascending, waterskiing, wetbiking and windsurfing. Most of the hotels also run stables for horseriding, and rent out bicycles, and a new 27-hole golf course has opened up to the east of the *Dar Jerba*. Unfortunately, pollution is a problem on the beach, and most of the hotels provide diesel to wash tar off feet.

Practicalities

On Sidi Mahares's main road, which runs about 200m inland from the beach road, you can rent a **scooter** or **motorbike** from *Holiday Bikes* (☎05/657169), 100m west of the Midoun road that starts just by the *Hôtel Djerba Beach*; *Daly Cyclos* (☎05/657840), 50m east of the turnoff for the *Hôtel al Jazira*, rents out **mopeds** or **bicycles**. A **supermarket** next to the *Hôtel al Jazira* sells a modest selection of European goods such as ham, salami, Camembert cheese, Italian biscuits and German sweets, all at rather inflated prices, and English-language **newspapers** are available at hotels used by UK tour operators, currently the *Djerba Palace* and the *Djerba Beach*.

Ordinary Tunisian **eating** at ordinary Tunisian prices is available at the *Restaurant des Palmiers* just by *Daly Cyclos* and, 50m up the Midoun road from its junction with the main road near *Holiday Bikes*, the very aptly named *Restaurant de l'Oasis* offers good honest grub in a desert of tourist traps.

Hotels

Al Jazira ★★★, at the western end of the beach (☎05/657300). The grand-daddy of all Jerba's beach hotels, put up in 1962 and now showing its age. ⑤.

Le Beau Rivage, at the western end of the beach (☎05/658730). A friendly, intimate little pension between the *Ulysse Palace* and the *Al Jazira*, 100m from the beach. ④.

Beau Séjour, at the western end of the beach (☎05/657109). Another pension, opposite the *Ulysse Palace*, pricier than the *Beau Rivage* and without any appreciable advantages. ⑤.

Dar Jerba, at the eastern end of the beach (☎05/657191). An enormous complex containing four hotels: the four-star *Dahlia* (⑥), the three/four-star *Narjess* (⑥), the two/three-star *Yasmine* (⑤/⑥), and the two-star *Zahra* (⑤), with all the facilities anyone could want. You could spend your whole holiday inside this place. The two-star rooms, incidentally, are very reasonably priced out of season.

Djerba Beach ★★★, at the eastern end of the beach (☎05/657200). Smaller, quieter and friendlier than the *Djerba Palace*, and right on a very nice bit of beach. ⑥.

Djerba Palace ★★★★, at the eastern end of the beach (☎05/658600). Cosy rooms and the full range of facilities. ⑥.

Hadstrubal ★★★★★, at the eastern end of the beach (☎05/657650). Formerly the poshest hotel, now rather upstaged by the *Royal Garden*. ⑥.

Iberotel Royal Garden ★★★★★, at the eastern end of the beach (☎05/658777, reservations 658765). If only the best will do, this is the newest, smartest, most expensive and most luxurious hotel on the island. ⑥.

Résidence Dar Ali, at the western end of the beach (☎05/657671). Next door to the *Beau Séjour* and very similar. Like the two other pensions, its clientele is mainly German tour groups. ⑤.

Strand ★, at the western end of the beach (☎05/657430) 300m east of the *Al Jazira*. Cheaper but rougher and readier than the other beach hotels, without any of their facilities. Its main interest lies in the fact that its bar is reasonably priced and open till midnight. ④.

Ulysse Palace ★★★★, at the western end of the beach (☎05/657422). Westernmost of the beach hotels and at one time the best. Nowadays just one of many, but still among the most expensive. ⑥.

Ras Taguermes

The cape at the end of Sidi Mahares beach, called **Ras Taguermes**, is marked by a red and white striped **lighthouse**, and the main local attraction here is the **go-kart track** (daily 9am–6pm; 6TD for ten laps).

Across from the lighthouse begins a **sand spit** enclosing the **Sebkha Sidi Garous** lagoon. In summer, *camping sauvage* is the order of the day here, as Tunisian and Libyan families pitch tents or sleep out on the beach. Some 5km down the spit, the two-star *Hôtel Tanit* (☎05/657132; ⑤) offers an alternative for those who don't want to camp out. The spit continues for another 2km beyond the hotel. In winter, look out for **flamingos** and other birds in the lagoon behind.

La Seguia and Aghir

Around the point of Ras Taguermes, on **La Seguia beach**, is a carefully restricted *Club Med* with three branches – *Jerba la Fidèle, Jerba la Douce* and *Calypso. Jerba la Fidèle* actually has the nicest beach on the island fenced off and monopolized, so you won't be able to use it unless you either stay there or make like a *Club Med* Euro-yuppie and sneak in on the sly.

A couple of kilometres beyond here, the beach at **AGHIR**, while not quite up to Sidi Mahares's standards, is a lot less crowded. After storms, however, the water tends to be infested with jellyfish. At its northern end, the two-star *Hôtel Sidi Slim* (☎05/657021 ⑤) has a **campsite**, though the facilities leave much to be desired; the *Centre des Stages et Vacances* down the road is somewhat preferable (see below). The hotel **restaurant** does a moderately priced set menu.

A little further, the pricey but rather jolly and well-managed three-star *Club Palma Djerba* (☎05/657380; ⑥) has the best bit of Aghir's beach. Next door, near the Midoun–El Kantara junction, the *Centre des Stages et Vacances* **youth hostel** and **campsite** (☎05/657366; ①) offers the choice of four-bed dorms, cheaper huts or your own tent. Friendly, if a bit run-down, it hopes to be able to rent out bicycles and wind-surfing boards, but only does food if there's a group staying. Otherwise, you have the choice of eating at neighbouring hotels, going into Midoun or getting in supplies at the

---

JERBAN SOCIETY

Jerban society is quite distinct in many ways from that of mainland Tunisia. Its population forms a patchwork of different **ethnic and linguistic groups** – Arabs, Berbers and Black Africans, Muslims (both Ibadite and Sunni) and Jews – who vary markedly in their traditions, style of dress, the names they bear and the way they speak. However, all these people share a common Jerban identity: their traditions differ from those of the mainland as much as from each other, and each has a place in Jerban society.

Today, however, with the present **tourist influx**, it seems no exaggeration to talk of a **crisis** in Jerba's identity. Nowhere in Tunisia is there such an obvious and direct clash between a still very traditional society and the demands of foreign culture. Services have become strained, prices inflated, and local culture and agriculture increasingly ignored. If you consider that the average package tourist gets through more meat and dairy products in a week than the majority of Tunisians consume in an entire year, it's easy to see just how drastic recent changes have been.

Even more serious a threat to the Jerban way of life is **emigration**, with traditional communities disrupted by the departure of Jews to Israel and of young men off to seek their fortunes elsewhere, usually by opening corner shops (known in Tunisia simply as *Jerbans*). Through the centuries the business acumen of its people – especially the Ibadites and Jews – has been of lasting importance to Jerba. People from the island now work as grocers all over Tunisia, and there are Jerban communities throughout Europe and as far away as Brazil. Following independence, the government attempted to introduce national cooperatives in order to modernize the shops and to stop tax evasion and profit hoarding, but the islanders would have none of it and the scheme eventually had to be abandoned.

grocery store a couple of kilometres up the road by the junction between Aghir and La Seguia. In the way of **transport**, there are ten daily **buses** from Aghir to Houmt Souk via Sidi Mahares or Midoun.

El Kantara and around

A single 12km road leads south from Aghir to **EL KANTARA**, passing some deserted beaches on the way. Halfway along on the left, a track heads 8km over the sand and out along a strip of land to the fort of **Borj Kastil**, built by Alfonso V of Aragon during his brief mid-fifteenth-century tenure of the island. The surrounding rocks are said to be good for underwater fishing.

It was the Carthaginians who created the **causeway** which stretches 7km from El Kantara to the opposite shore. In 1551, Dragut the pirate, trapped with his fleet by the flotilla of Charles V of Spain between the causeway and the fort, made his famously daring naval getaway. To gain time, he barricaded himself in the fort and held off the Spaniards while his men, under cover of darkness, dug through the causeway, enabling his fleet to escape into the Gulf of Bou Grara. Although it could still be forded at low tide in the intervening period, the causeway was not repaired for over four hundred years, finally reopening in 1953.

The site of ancient **Meninx** is spread around the road junction by El Kantara. Very little now remains of the city established by the Phoenicians and rebuilt by the Romans, but if you want to explore, there are two patches of **unexcavated remains** (freely accessible). One area is spread up the Aghir road for 2km or so on both sides, the main area of blocks and fallen columns being about 1km from the causeway on the seaward side of the road. The other patch of remains is about 100m north of the *piste* to Guellala, less than a kilometre from the causeway (just before the date palms begin). Roman debris then lines the *piste* for another 200m beyond that. There is nothing spectacular to be seen, but the site is good for a stroll, and a number of nooks and crannies repay closer inspection.

The west coast

Long and wild, virtually uninhabited and empty of tourists, the **west coast of Jerba** is not as postcard-pretty as the other coasts, nor as good for swimming, with a rocky shore and shallow water for quite a way out. It is, however, *the* place to really get away from it all – if you can get there, that is. At its northern end is the island's airport; to the south, Ajim, Jerba's main port; and in between no transport at all. If you stay anywhere along this 20km shore, you're down to looking after yourself, camping or just sleeping out – no hardship so long as you have adequate supplies of food and water.

Two roads run out to Jerba's west coast from Houmt Souk. The first leads past the radio tower to the **airport** (for details of departures, see p.315). **MELLITA**, the nearest village, has some of the oldest *menzels*, or divisions of land, on the island. The road continues to the eighteenth-century fort of **Borj Jillij**, now a lighthouse. From Borj Jillij you can drive or cycle back along a track by the sea to Houmt Souk, a distance of about 11km. The west coast is the best part of the island for **fishing**, and a series of *zribas*, traps made from palm fronds, stretch in a line away from the shore. The fish are caught by the current in a triangular enclosure and then swim into a smaller trap called an *achoucha*. A hole, which looks like an escape route, leads into a net, or *drina*, which can be lifted from the water.

The main Houmt Souk–Gabes road leads through dull countryside to the fairly dreary port of **AJIM**, the most important centre for sponges, which are still taken from the sea floor by divers – now mainly Tunisians but originally Greeks and Maltese. Ajim is also a centre for the local date harvest, though compared with the *deglat* variety of Tozeur the crop here is poor – three varieties of palm provide nothing edible at all, and are kept only for *laghmi*, or palm wine (see p.35). Some say it was this natural brew that knocked out Ulysses's companions. Be careful, too, if you go swimming here, as the channel swarms with large jellyfish, constantly chewed up in ferry propellors. The channel is also full of octopuses and all along the quay are stacked piles of **octopus traps** in the form of ceramic pots, which are laid on the sea bed in the evening. The creatures, looking for hiding places at the end of a night's foraging, crawl into them only to be hauled out in the morning.

The Ajim–Jorf **ferry** runs every half-hour between 4am and 10pm, and every hour or two through the night. Foot passengers go free, cars pay 0.6TD. In a vehicle, try to avoid using the ferry in the evening at weekends, when there can be long queues (at Jorf on Saturdays and at Ajim on Sundays). Between Ajim and Houmt Souk, there are frequent *louages*. If you need to change money, Ajim has a **bank** – but there are no hotels.

Inland Jerba

Even today, Jerba is not really an island of towns and villages, but of individual homes. The only villages as such are the two Jewish "ghettos" of Hara Sghira and Hara Kebira. Houmt Souk, once just a marketplace (which is what its name means), only became a town this century. Other places marked on maps – Midoun, Mahboubine, El May, Guellala – really are little more than markets. People shop and work in them, but few people live there.

Midoun and around

MIDOUN, the island's second town, is really little more than a bunch of souvenir shops, a pair of banks and a few restaurants, but it's quite a lively place during the Friday souk, when there's also a livestock **market** just out to the southeast. The other event of the week is a mock **Berber wedding** put on for tourists every Tuesday afternoon in the central square.

Midoun's underground **oil-press** (*massera*) is worth a look (Nov–Jan variable hours). It is located between the mosque on avenue Farhat Hached (the Sidi Mahares road) and the taxiphone office on avenue Salah Ben Youssef – look for the ground-level

---

JERBAN HOMES

Jerban homes, spread around the countryside, take the form of a *houch* (traditional house) inside a *menzel* (piece of land), each one belonging to a different family. From the outside, a *houch* looks like a small square fortress, with blank white walls and a small tower at each corner. Like the mosques, these houses were designed in response to numerous invasions from the eleventh century onwards, and it's been suggested that the basic plan was taken from the Roman forts, or *limes*, on the mainland. Three large rooms surround the central courtyard, each used by one section of an extended family. The parents in each section sleep in the tower, called a *ghorfa* or *kouchk*, often crowned with a dome. This is the only part of the house with external windows, traditionally placed higher than a man on horseback, but the breeze is fed down below through holes in the floor. Near the house is a simple guest room (usually facing east) and a threshing floor. The distinctive Jerban well is flanked by two upright supports for a system of pulleys operated by camel or mule; a system you can see all over the island.

dome. As at Haddej and Matmata, underground air ensures humidity throughout the winter, necessary to separate the oil. A mule or camel used to turn the stone roller around its base, crushing the olives, but the press is now motor-driven. After pressing, the skins are transferred to a sieve (*chamia*) which is squashed by the weight of a palm trunk, hinged at the wall; the oil and vegetable water drip through into a jar and separate. Around the main room are storage chambers, used by each family for their olives.

Otherwise, in practical terms, there's a **hammam** (Thurs–Sat men 6am–12.30pm & 6–10pm; women 12.30–5.30pm), at least one all-night **pharmacy**, a **hospital** (☎05/657280) and a very reputable **doctor**, Dr Massabi, the mayor's wife, at 20 avenue Bourguiba, by the town hall. If you should want to **stay**, the *Hôtel Jawhara* (☎05/657363; ②) is clean and pleasant, but ask for a room with a window. The *Restaurant de l'Orient* on the main roundabout does cheap and filling Tunisian **food**, and there's a similarly priced place at 11 avenue Mohamed Badra, advertising "Eine heimische Küche". For more refined eating, there's the *Restaurant le Pêcheur* on boulevard 7 Novembre (the Houmt Souk road), while the *Restaurant el Guestile*, just off the market square, is more tourist oriented and does good seafood.

Frequent **buses** run to Houmt Souk via Mahbouine and El May, and there are also plenty of buses to Aghir and the hotel zone. **Taxis** wait for custom by the main roundabout. On Fridays, the **Noddy train** also does a run to Midoun from the beach hotels.

If you take the direct road from Midoun to Houmt Souk, there are a couple of things en route worth breaking the journey for. Two kilometres out of Midoun, a pyramid-shaped pile of weather-worn sandstone blocks north of the road marks the Punic **Tomb of Borgou** (freely accessible). The sarcophagus was in an underground chamber which is normally accessible, since its entrance has usually been broken open by the drunks who use this as a nocturnal meeting place. The **Fadloune Mosque**, 1km further on the south side of the road, appears anonymously on numerous postcards of the island. It is no longer used for prayers so you should be able to go in and look around. Another couple of distinctive Jerban **mosques** appear after another 8km or so to the north: the **Ben Yakhlef** with its stumpy minaret is just by the road, with the **Mouzline**, like a sleeker version of the Fadloune, a little way beyond.

A more picturesque route from Midoun to Jerba is by way of Mahboubine and El May, through the vineyards and fruit and olive groves. All along this road, behind the high banks (or *tabia*), are the traditional Jerban houses (*houch*), each commanding the *menzel*, or estate, of a different family. All the sand tracks to the north of the road here lead past one *menzel* after another – a district best explored by bicycle from Houmt Souk.

MAHBOUBINE, a couple of kilometres northwest, itself has little more than a central square, a couple of cafés and a nineteenth-century mosque inspired by the Blue Mosque in Istanbul. Rather more distinctive is **EL MAY**, 8km further on, with its typical Jerban **Mosque Umm et Turkia**. Like the Zaouia of Sidi Brahim in Houmt Souk, the low walls of this fortified building are supported by thick buttresses, the minaret a squat, rounded stump. Around its walls a Sunday **market** takes place; other signs of business include two **banks** and a **PTT**. **Buses** pass through here regularly between Houmt Souk and Midoun or Sedouikech.

Hara Sghira (Er Riadh)

Two kilometres from El May, in the direction of Houmt Souk, the road turns off left for Guellala. On the way is a Jewish settlement called **HARA SGHIRA** ("Small Ghetto"), now officially Er Riadh. Buses pass through seven times a day each way between Houmt Souk and Guellala.

Hara Sghira **synagogue of El Ghriba** ("the miracle") is 1500km out of the village down a well-signposted road. It is a place of pilgrimage for Jews from all over North

Africa on *Lag be Omer*, the 33rd day after Passover, and a large new hostel for pilgrims reflects the importance of the site. The present building, dating only from 1920, is covered inside with rather garish tiles. The original synagogue was apparently constructed at the place where a holy stone fell from heaven: an unknown woman arrived, miraculously, at the same time, to direct operations. If the Jews ever leave Jerba, it is said that the synagogue's silver key will be thrown back to heaven. An inner sanctuary contains several manuscripts, including one of the oldest Torahs in the world. One plaque on the wall offers a benediction for the Supreme Combatant, Bourguiba, and another asks for donations (these are not optional – less than 0.5TD and you will be promptly shown the door).

THE JEWS OF JERBA

Opinion about when **Jews** first came to Jerba is divided between 566 BC, following the fall of Jerusalem to Nebuchadnezzar, and 71 AD, when the city was taken by Titus. The island community today numbers about 1500, some of whom have evidently returned here after emigrating to Israel. Historically, Jewish **artisans** worked here as jewellers, playing a considerable part in developing the island's commercial reputation.

Jerban **Jewish colonies** sprang up over much of the south, often made up of shopkeepers or itinerant blacksmiths. But while they established small communities in remote villages, they kept their bonds with Jerba, returning to the island during the summer and for important religious festivals.

To begin with Jews were tolerated, but only while they kept to their own community and traditional occupations. **Under the French** their position improved, but they remained second-class citizens relative to the Europeans and European Jews. Their own attitude helped maintain this position, for while other communities took advantage of the educational and financial resources of world Jewish organizations, the Jews of Jerba rejected aid, preferring to keep their strict and distinctive form of Judaism untainted. Consequently they won a reputation as intransigent **traditionalists**, gained far less from the Protectorate than other communities, and became the target of French and Arab anti-Semitism.

The new state of Israel offered an opportunity to make a new life in the Promised Land, and by the early 1950s many Jews were leaving. After Tunisian Independence the trickle of emigrants became a flood and the community shrank. Perhaps as a result of Bourguiba's attempts to encourage integration, overt anti-Semitism is rare, and Jerban Jews generally have good relations with their Muslim neighbours. However, anti-Zionism ("We have nothing against Tunisian Jews, it is only the State of Israel we object to") still provokes – or provides a rationale for – occasional outbursts of hatred. As recently as 1985, a policeman, apparently incited by radio broadcasts from Libya, burst into the Ghriba in Hara Sghira and killed three worshippers before he could be restrained.

Hara Kebira (Es Souani)

The other Jewish village, **HARA KEBIRA** (now officially Es Souani), near Houmt Souk, is rather more workaday than Hara Sghira. It boasts no fewer than eleven synagogues, but none as interesting as El Ghriba, and a small *gargote* which is one of only two kosher restaurants in the country. One thing to look out for as you wander around the village are the symbols painted in blue on house doorways to ward off the evil eye. As well as the usual fish and hands, these include a five-armed version of the normally seven- or nine-armed *menorah* (Jewish candelabra).

Guellala

GUELLALA, on the island's south coast, rivals Nabeul in Cap Bon as a centre for handmade, mass-produced **pottery**. The clay is dug out of the hillside on the road to

---

IBADITES AND BERBERS

From the earliest Arab invasions, Jerba became a centre for the **Kharijites**, an ascetic Islamic sect hostile to the Caliphs who ruled the Arab empire, and whose origins go back to the very beginning of the schism between Sunni and Shiite Muslims. The Sunnis supported the Ummayad Caliphs and their Abbasid successors, while Shiites believed that only the prophet's son-in-law Ali and his descendants had the right to the Caliphate. But in the early days of the dispute, when Ali agreed to arbitration over the question, a group of his followers withdrew their support, declaring that God was the only arbitrator. Taking their name from the Arabic for "to leave" (*kharaja*), they became an ascetic and highly puritan sect, hostile to Sunnis and Shiites alike (it was a Kharijite who eventually assassinated Ali), but they had a considerable following among the Berbers. With the fall of their North African states based at Sijilmasa in Morocco and Tahirt in Algeria to the Fatimids in 909, Jerba, along with the Mzab in Algeria, the Jebel Nafusa in Libya, and the island of Zanzibar in Tanzania, became one of their last refuges.

Ibadites, as they are known today, form nearly half of Jerba's Muslim community and are concentrated in the south and west of the island. They are extremely strict in their religious practice, and follow the dictates of the Koran even more scrupulously than other Muslims. They also differ from Sunni (orthodox) Muslims in certain details of their religious rituals. The austerity of their religion is best expressed in their architecture: they built the most simple and severe of all the 300 mosques and marabouts around the island. In times of war these semi-fortified buildings would serve as a place of refuge for those outside the *houch* or *menzel*, the country houses in the interior (see p.326).

Most of Jerba's dwindling minority of **Berber-speakers** are Ibadites. They live in the south of the island, especially around Ajim, Guellala and Sedouikech. Because they speak a different language, they tend to be at a social disadvantage (getting a job is always a problem, for example), and the low social status of Berber is the main factor behind the decline of the language.

Sedouikech (the one prominence on the island), then bleached and cleaned in the sea. All the products were once exported from a port down the road, and people used to travel around the markets near Tataouine selling their goods. The staple of the industry, the large terracotta vessels used for storing and cooling water and oil, went to markets as far afield as Benghazi and Constantine. Workshops line the main street, though of the ones operating, only one is still in the original style, partly underground and insulated with stone and soil to protect the drying clay from the heat and wind. The three hundred kilns in the village are constructed with special bricks, made from earth which has been washed with alluvial deposits. Most of the glazed ware is garish and geared to the market in cheap souvenirs, though the Berber bowls, baked at the lowest temperatures, are more authentic and interesting. A Guellala speciality nowadays is the "magic camel", a water jug in the shape of a camel with a hole in the base through which it's filled. When placed the right way up, the water miraculously fails to escape from this hole and pours only from the mouth. (Guellala has a **bank**, should you need to change any money to invest in a bit of pottery.)

The town has an underground oil press (through the shop with the ceramic map on the door), but the **oil press** in use today, out on the edge of town by the El Kantara road, is actually much more interesting – a wonderful piece of vintage science museum technology – specially so if you manage to call in when it's being used.

Out of town, along the shore, are a couple of interesting mosques and a few bits of Roman masonry. The **Guellala Mosque**, by the beach, dates back to the fifteenth century. Half a kilometre west up the beach, you'll find the odd piece of Roman wall; there's more underwater just offshore, and local farmers often turn up pieces of marble and mosaic in their fields. In the other direction, 1500m east along the coast, the tenth-century **Mosque of Sidi Yati** stands disused and crumbling by the shore.

There are seven **buses** a day to Houmt Souk, while a **taxi** costs about 3.5TD, and it's not hard to **hitch** via either Sedouikech or Hara Sghira.

THE SOUTHEAST COAST

The **mainland behind Jerba** basically consists of the small towns of Jorf and Bou Gara and, on the country's remote southeast coast, the nascent resort of Zarzis and the route into Libya via Ben Gardane. With most people heading for Jerba's lotus-eating shores, this corner is still a rarely visited part of Tunisia – but it's a region that's likely to become increasingly the subject of tourist development over the next few years, so long as Tunisia's giant neighbour continues to assent.

Jorf and Gightis

JORF, the mainland ferry terminal, is not the most inspiring town in Tunisia. However, the ferry services ensure that you won't be stranded for long, with half-hourly services between 4am and 10pm, running roughly hourly throughout the night for the fifteen-minute crossing over to Jerba; try to avoid crossing on weekend evenings when there can be long queues. There are *louages* to Medenine, but not to Gabes (either change at Medenine, or walk up to the turnoff and hitch). Between Jorf and Gabes the only town is Mareth (see p.310), from where adventurous travellers can strike off to Toujane. En route to Medenine you could stop off to visit the Roman port of Gightis – though as passing *louages* tend to be full, it can prove difficult to continue on afterwards.

Gightis

GIGHTIS was established by the Phoenicians and became a trading post under the Carthaginians. The Gulf of Bou Grara could provide shelter for a large fleet and, recognizing its strategic importance, the Romans attacked the city during the first two Punic wars. After the campaign of Julius Caesar from 46 to 40 BC, the Romans assumed control and for the next two hundred years Gightis flourished as a major port of Africa Proconsularis and Byzacenia. The Roman trade route went from Carthage via Hammamet, El Jem and Gabes to Gightis and then on to Oea, Leptis Magna and Ghadames in Tripolitania. The city was later sacked by the Vandals, but the Byzantines thought it worthy of restoration. With the Arab invasion of the seventh century, however, the port was destroyed and the site covered over until excavations in 1906.

The **site** of Gightis (daily except Fri 8am–5pm; 1TD) lies next to the main road, 1km south of the village of Bon Grara. In fact, it is not fenced off and you can go in any time, although the *gardien* may come and ask you to pay the entrance fee. The larger central square, the **Forum**, dates from the reign of Emperor Hadrian (117–138 AD) and is overlooked by a **temple** dedicated to Serapis and Isis. A long flight of steps leads up to the top of the red sandstone podium, but little remains of the columns or interior walls. The stone-flagged road down to the port begins by the arch at the other end of the forum and passes, on the left, the **Temple of Bacchus**. Behind the portico, where only the fragments of columns remain, is an underground passage and several small rooms, their purpose unknown. The **port** has long since silted up but a partly submerged row of stones marks the site of a **jetty**, once 140m long. Stone foundations by the road also give an idea of the town's extent – stretching to the Capitol Temple, at the top of a slight hill, towering above the shops and houses. On the right-hand side of the forum (as you face the sea) are the **baths** and several scraps of mosaic. Walking through the baths, away from the square, the **market** is ahead and just to the right; built in the third century, it consists of a central courtyard surrounded by a walkway, fitted out with shops. Nearby are the remains of villas and a temple of Mercury.

Bou Grara

The new village of **BOU GRARA** is a kilometre up a side road, past the ruins. From the rock, on the right of the site, there's a sweeping view of the inland sea, mud flats and the older fishing port down below. Although French naval architects believed they could build a second Bizerte in this natural harbour, the modern port never quite lived up to the promise of its ancient predecessor: the water was far too shallow to accommodate heavy military vessels and the plans were scrapped.

Jerba to Zarzis and the Libyan frontier

Across the causeway from its namesake in Jerba, **EL KANTARA CONTINENT** has nothing special to commend it except a ruined **Turkish fort** gazing languidly at Borj Kastil across the water. From here, there are two roads to Zarzis, a coastal road via Hassi Jerbi, passing the tourist hotels and beach zone, and a less scenic but more direct route via Sidi Chammakh.

Some 12km down the coastal road, 9km north of Zarzis at **SANGHO**, two "hotel clubs" aim to provide everything you need – fortunately, as they're in the middle of nowhere. The three-star *Hôtel Club Oamarit* (☎05/680770; ⑥) boasts a "semi-Olympic swimming pool with its basin for children" and "various restorative services" intriguingly available from reception. It also has several bars and restaurants, including a pizzeria and a nightclub. The three-star *Sangho Club* next door (☎05/680124; ⑥) is more *Club Med* in style and altogether more exclusive than the *Oamarit*, although only slightly more expensive. You can rent bicycles from both clubs, and both have **car rental** offices – *Hertz* at the *Sangho*, *Eurorent* at the *Oamarit* – or you can rent a car from *Mattei* outside (☎05/682600). Sports such as waterskiing, wetbiking and windsurfing are available on the beach, and horseriding is also possible.

Rather more refined than either of these, though in the same price bracket, is the *Sultana Residence*, less than a kilometre south along the coast (☎05/682206; ⑥). A tranquil, relaxing little place, it's like a classier version of a *pension de famille*, with a pool and a jacuzzi, nine rooms, each one different, and a pier for sea swimming. A little luxury they also provide – the only place in Tunisia to do so – is mosquito nets.

Zarzis

Halfway down the coast that nearly encloses the Gulf of Bou Grara, **ZARZIS** has a good, long beach with new hotels, though it pales in comparison with Houmt Souk and much of Jerba. Even so, French officers considered it the cushiest posting in the south, a paradise after the parched heat of the interior. It was also the only place south of Gabes that suffered settlement by French colonists. Unfortunately, they didn't get on too well with the military, who feared that if too many colonists arrived they would lose their holiday resort to the civil administration, and did everything they could to make their lives difficult. The colonists, in turn, sent frequent complaints to the government, claiming that the army ruled with "the sword and the bull whip rather than any legal code". In the end, independence arrived before the military could be persuaded to abandon the town.

There isn't much to see around Zarzis. Like Sfax, the town is surrounded by olive plantations, most of which were planted this century. Until recently, few travellers ever bothered to go further east, but since Libya has tentatively (though sporadically) started allowing entry to tourists, Ben Gardane and Ras Ajdir are slightly more on the beaten track. The **beach** at Zarzis's *zone touristique* has the best swimming in the

Zarzis area, and the *Zarzis* and *Zita* hotels have new pools, reputed to be the best in Tunisia. Barriers at the hotels' entrances prohibit roaming Tunisians, but tourists should be able to get in.

Market days in the souk are Monday and Friday, and on other days there is little of interest in Zarzis, although there is a small **museum** of traditional clothes and artefacts in avenue Habib Thameur (daily 8.30am–1pm & 3–5.45pm; 1TD). Zarzis celebrates a **sponge festival** in the last week of July every year.

Avenue Mohamed V is the main road in from Jerba. At **place de la Jeunesse**, the town's central roundabout, there are a few **banks**. The third exit from place de la Jeunesse is rue Hedi Chaker, leading to **place 7 Novembre**, where there are more banks, while the **PTT** (country hours) is just off the square, with the **cinema** opposite. There's a **taxiphone office** (daily 8am–10pm) next door at 3 avenue Farhat Hached, a *Magasin Général* **supermarket** at the next roundabout; the **hospital** (☎05/680302) is just around the corner from here in avenue 20 Mars, and there's a **night pharmacy** down the road. From place 7 Novembre, avenue Habib Thameur leads off towards the **port** and avenue Bourguiba towards Ben Gardane. The "Plan de Zarzis", issued by the tourist board, looks promising enough, with a seaside restaurant and a fishing port marked, but the coastal road leads through a large unmarked military camp – hardly designed for an evening stroll – while the restaurant is closed.

Zarzis has a brand-new **bus station** down towards the port, beyond the end of avenue Habib Thameur. From here, eleven buses a day head off for Houmt Souk (1hr), six for Ben Gardane (1hr), three for Tunis (9hr), two of which continue to Bizerte (10hr 30min), and nine for Medenine (1hr), one continuing to Tataouine (2hr). A total of eight buses serve Gabes (2hr), three go to Sfax (5hr), and two each to Sousse (7hr) and Kairouan (7hr 30min). The tourist zone can be reached from the bus station by local bus #1. **Louages** leave from outside the bus station, serving Medenine, Houmt Souk, Ben Gardane and Tunis.

On the main road outside the hotels in the *zone touristique* are the **car rental** offices of *Avis* (☎05/681706), by the entrance to the *Zephir*, and *Hertz* (☎05/680284) and *Express* (☎05/683105), nearer the *Zarzis*, with a motorbike and moped rental shop between the two hotels (☎05/681016). There are also **buses** and **taxis** into town, an *ONTT* **tourist office** (variable hours; ☎05/680445), and a taxiphone office for **international calls**.

Zarzis has a number of budget **hotels**, most of them not too great and many often closed for no accountable reason. More upmarket beach hotels can be found in the *zone touristique*, 4km north of town along the coast.

Hotels in town

Afif, av Mohamed V (☎05/681639). A very reasonable second best to the *Corniche*: cheap and clean. ①.

Corniche, av Tahar Sfar (☎05/682833). Off pl 7 Novembre towards the sea. The best-value cheapie in Zarzis: friendly, bright, clean and low-priced. ①.

El Hana, av Farhat Hached (☎05/680408). Opposite the *Olivier*. Rock-bottom prices, rock-bottom conditions. Pretty much men only. ①.

Haroun Errachid, rte de Ben Gardane (☎05/681332). At the beginning of the Ben Gardane road. Reasonable if slightly dingy rooms, some with shower (but no loo), some with windows. No apparent reception, and the staff are sometimes hard to locate. ①.

Medina, off av Farhat Hached, near pl de la Jeunesse (☎05/681388). The best hotel in town. Large, airy rooms, mostly with their own bathrooms. ②.

L'Olivier, av Farhat Hached (☎05/681340). 100m up the road from the *Du Sud*. Adequate, but with rather a couldn't-care-less sort of attitude. ①.

Hôtel de la Station, av Farhat Hached (☎05/680661). By the *SNTRI* station. Very adequate rooms, many with bathrooms. Probably the best hotel in town. ①.

Hôtel du Sud, 18 av Farhat Hached (☎05/681340). Across the street from the *Medina*. Reasonably clean and pleasant, but ask for a room with an outside window. ①.

Hotels in the tourist zone

Amira, on the beach, 100m south of the *Zephir* (☎05/680188). Cheap and friendly, with a beach bar. ②.

Errachid. A small place on the main road between the *Zephir* and the *Zarzis*, with a mainly Libyan clientele. ②.

Nozha (☎05/681593). Homely and comfortable, with its own bit of rather exposed rocky beach, halfway between the town and the tourist zone. ③.

L'Oasis (☎05/681465). A quiet little hotel on the main road by the *Zephir*. No single rooms. ②.

Zarzis ★★★, about 200m north of the *Zephir* (☎05/680160). Slightly classier than the *Zephir*, with a clientele made up mainly of German sun-seekers. ⑤.

Zephir ★★★ (☎05/681026). The first of three package hotels known as *"les trois zeds"*, catering for a mainly German clientele. ④.

Ziha (☎05/681304). A fourth "zed" set to reopen soon just south of the *Zephir* and off the beach. The pool and rooms are smaller than in the other "zeds", but so are the prices. ③.

Zita ★★, north of the *Zaris* (☎05/680246). A lower-key place that closes out of season. ④.

Youth hostel

Maison des Jeunes youth hostel, rue d'Algérie (☎05/681599). Near the PTT. Don't excactly welcome you with open arms. Curfew 9pm. ①.

Eating in Zarzis

The best place to eat in town is probably the *Restaurant de Caravans*, 11 rue 9 Avril, just off place de la Jeunesse. Another place worth trying is the *Restaurant Tunisien*, just up avenue Farhat Hached. Both of these are somewhat preferable to the overpriced *Palmier* by the *Shell* station. Cheaper eats can be found further up avenue Farhat Hached at the *Restaurant Zarzis*, by the *Hôtel L'Olivier*, and the *Restaurant de la Station* near the hotel of the same name.

More upmarket eating can be found in the *zone touristique*. *Le Pirate*, opposite the *Hôtel Zephir*'s entrance, will set you back about 7.5TD a go, *La Pacha*, a little way up towards the *Zarzis*, costs slightly more. Across the road is a cheap *rôtisserie*.

East of Zarzis

The road south towards Ben Gardane (there are buses and regular *louages*) skirts the **Sebkhet el Mellah**, a large salt flat which used to be the site of a mustard gas factory during World War I and today contains a massive salt mine. Seventeen kilometres south of Zarzis, a road leads to the village of **Biban**, at the end of a long spit. Beyond it (and inaccessible without permission), an old Turkish fort, **Borj el Biban**, sits on a little island of its own. There are a few sandy beaches, mainly on the southern side of the spit – not up to Jerba's standards, but totally deserted if you can get to them. From the east, another spit stretches out towards Borj el Biban, the channel between them once marking the border with Libya. The lagoon enclosed by the two spits, **Bahiret el Biban**, is full of fish and rich in birdlife, notably flamingos, spoonbills and other waders. Easily accessible sites for spotting them can be found back on the main road, a few kilometres south of the Biban turnoff, where it crosses the eastern corner of the lagoon.

Ben Gardane

Off the beaten track for many years, **BEN GARDANE** is the last main town before the Libyan frontier, and now a staging post on the route to Libya. It is also host to no fewer than three markets. The weekly Saturday **souk**, in the centre of town, is very lively and far more agricultural than others in the south, but there is also a **Libyan market** similar to the one in Houmt Souk, but bigger and less tourist-conscious, in a walled enclosure about a kilometre up the Zarzis road. This operates every day and is especially good on Sundays, with various goods and brands not normally seen in Tunisia brought in from across the border, much of it sold from the back of pick-up trucks in the style of a giant car boot sale. Finally, on the road to Mouamarat, 3km south of town (take the road south of the hospital, bear right at the fork after 500m and continue for a couple of kilometres), there is a Thursday morning **livestock market**.

In addition to these, Ben Gardane has the usual **banks** (though money changers at the *louage* station and on the Ras Ajdir road buy or sell Libyan dinars and will also sell Tunisian dinars for hard currency), a **PTT** (country hours), **taxiphone offices** opposite the *Hôtel Pavilion Vert* and opposite the *SRTGM* bus station, and a *Grand Magasin* **supermarket**, about 50m towards Ras Ajdir from the PTT.

There are around a dozen **hotels** in Ben Gardane. The biggest and poshest is the *Pavilion Vert* on the Ras Ajdir road (☎05/655355; ①–②), though in fact, if you take a double room without bathroom, it won't cost you much more to stay here than in most smaller, grottier places. Other reasonable hotels include the *El Ouns* (☎05/665920; ①), a decent enough, dusty city hotel, and the cheap and cheerful *Hôtel de la Confiance* (☎05/665173; ①), its name posted in Arabic only. Snacking options in Ben Gardane, consist of a number of cheap *gargotes* on the main road through town. For something a little more refined, your only option is the 6TD set menu at the *Pavilion Vert*.

The *SRTGM* **bus station** is on the roundabout where the roads to Zarzis and Ras Ajdir meet. Buses tend to peter out around midday, but there are services to Ras Ajdir (regular shuttle; 40min), Houmt Souk (2 daily; 2hr), Medenine (3 daily; 1hr) and Zarzis (4 daily; 1hr). From the *SNTRI* office, 50m up the Zarzis road, there are two daily departures to Tunis (9hr 30min), via Sfax and Sousse or Kairouan, all passing through Medenine and Gabes. If you don't coincide with a bus, you'll find **louages** just around the corner on the Medenine road, with regular services to Medenine, Zarzis, Ras Ajdir, Gabes and Tunis. For Tripoli, you'll have to change at Ras Ajdir.

Onward to Libya

If you're striking out for **Libya***, the Tunisian frontier post is at **RAS AJDIR**, 33km east of Ben Gardane, but you'll encounter several police checks on the way. At Ras Ajdir, the prevailing atmosphere is one of complete chaos as you get out of your vehicle to go through the various **formalities**, which include filling out a departure card and getting your passport stamped. There are 24-hour **exchange facilities**, but you should avoid using them unless desperate (apart from the queues, the rates are bad and they may decide on a whim not to change travellers' cheques).

Buying Libyan dinars is quite easy on the road to the frontier. Money changers line the road all the way from Medenine, waving their wads of bills at passing cars. Ascertain the going rate before you start haggling (it's usually about three times the official rate). Remember that it is officially illegal to import or export Tunisian currency in or out of Tunisia, or to take Libyan currency into Libya.

There are always plenty of vehicles at the border, and you should have no difficulty finding **transport** to Tripoli, 196km away (4hr). Note that *louages* in Libya are called *taxi binasser*, or service taxis. Once over the border, the first thing you notice will probably be the improved state of the roads. At present there is no customs or immigration on the Libyan side and the police check your passport further along the road. If the cross-border tourist traffic grows, this is likely to change.

---

* For further information about Libya, see p.376.

travel details

Buses

Ben Gardane to: Houmt Souk, Medenine, Ras Ajdir, Tataouine, Tunis and Zarzis.

Houmt Souk to: Ben Gardane, Bizerte, Gabes, Kairouan, Medenine, Sfax, Sousse, Tataouine, Tunis and Zarzis.

Ras Ajdir to: Tripoli and Tunis.

Zarzis to: Ben Gardane, Bizerte, Gabes, Houmt Souk, Kairouan, Medenine, Sfax, Sousse, Tataouine and Tunis.

Louages

Ben Gardane to: Gabes, Houmt Souk, Ras Ajdir, Tunis and Zarzis.

Houmt Souk to: Ajim, Ben Gardane, Gabes, Medenine, Ras Ajdir, Tunis and Zarzis.

Zarzis to: Ben Gardane, Houmt Souk, Medenine and Tunis.

Ferries

Jorf to: Ajim.

Flights

Jerba to: Brussels, Frankfurt, Geneva, Lyon, Marseille, Monastir, Paris, Rome, Sfax, Tozeur, Tunis, Vienna and Zürich.

MARKET DAYS

Monday – Houmt Souk, Zarzis
Tuesday – Sedghiane, Sedouikech
Wednesday – Ajim, Guellala, Mouansa
Thursday – Houmt Souk

Friday – Midoun, Zarzis
Saturday – Ben Gardane, El May
Sunday – Ajim, Guellala

CHAPTER NINE

THE KSOUR

O f all Tunisia, the **south**, the region that dips down towards the border with Libya and Algeria, is the most exciting and remote, and has long been this way. In the Middle Ages, Arab travellers avoided the area because the tribes were notorious for their lawlessness and banditry. It was a reputation that

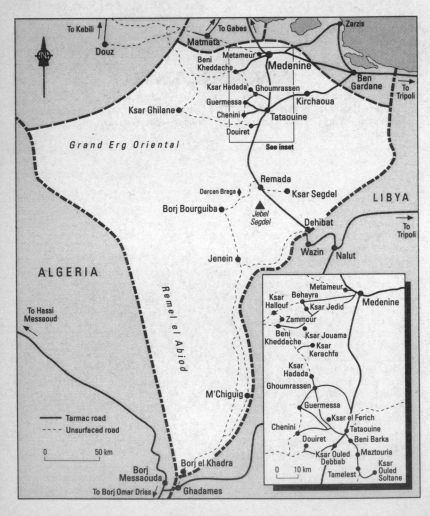

Tarmac road
Unsurfaced road

0   50 km

See inset

was passed on to later generations, for during the eighteenth and nineteenth centuries few European travellers entered the region, and only three are known to have visited **Medenine**, still the largest and most important town in the area. Even the intrepid James Bruce, who went on to discover the source of the Nile, preferred to take the boat from Gabes rather than risk his neck with these tribes. When the French army invaded in 1881 they, too, gave the region a wide berth; it was many years before it was fully integrated, and it remained under military administration until 1956.

With their steep escarpments, the south's arid mountains are impressive in themselves, but even more striking are the **ksour** (*ksar* in the singular), fortified communal granaries, and the mountain villages of **Douiret**, **Chenini** and **Guermessa** that they hide. Strange and extraordinary as monuments, they are even more remarkable as living settlements in so barren a land.

The people themselves are another reason to visit; there's little of the hassle that you tend to expect in the north, and people here are cool and reserved – in part, perhaps, due to the comparative absence of tourists. There are few hotels and few facilities to attract visitors, and those who do come tend to be on whistle-stop Land Rover tours. If you want to explore in more depth, you'll have to put up with "roughing it in a very moderate way", as Sir Harry Johnston put it in 1892.

Transport is the greatest problem you'll face in travelling independently. The road network is sparse, and joins modern French towns like **Zarzis** (covered in the previous chapter), **Medenine** and **Tataouine**, rather than the more interesting villages. Buses are few and the *louage* service is less dependable than in the north, so you may have to resort to hitching, arranging a lift or hiring a taxi. There is always more transport in the morning and it often dries up completely by the afternoon, so the earlier you set out the better. But there's always some way of getting where you want, and the effort is generously rewarded.

Medenine and around

Before the French occupation, **MEDENINE** was the focus of everything that mattered in the south, with a huge weekly market attracting merchants from as far afield as

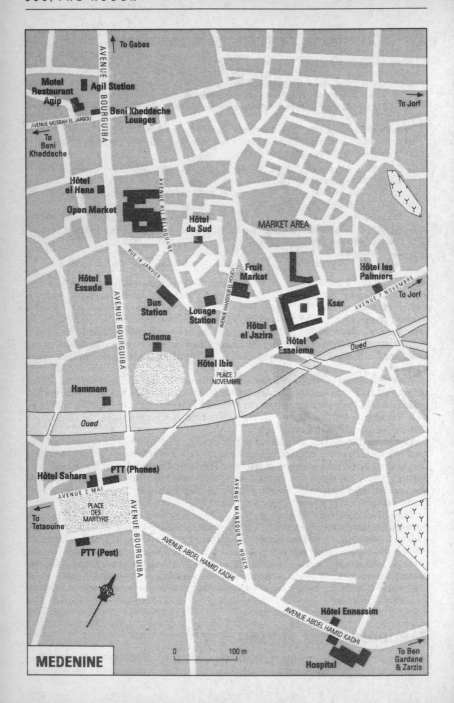

To Gabes

AVENUE BOURGUIBA

Motel
Restaurant
Agip

Agil Station

Beni Kheddache
Louages

AVENUE MOSBAH EL JARBOU

To
Beni
Kheddache

Hôtel
el Hana

Open Market

AVENUE ALI BELHOUANE

Hôtel
du Sud

MARKET AREA

To Jorf

RUE 18 JANVIER

Hôtel
Essada

AVENUE BOURGUIBA

Bus
Station

Cinema

Louage
Station

AVENUE MANSOUR EL HOUCH

Fruit
Market

Ksar

Hôtel les
Palmiers

AVENUE 7 NOVEMBRE

To Jorf

Hôtel
el Jazira

Hôtel
Essaiema

Oued

Hôtel Ibis

PLACE 7
NOVEMBRE

Hammam

Oued

Hôtel Sahara

PTT (Phones)

AVENUE 2 MAI

PLACE
DES
MARTYRS

AVENUE BOURGUIBA

AVENUE MANSOUR EL HOUCH

To Tataouine

PTT (Post)

AVENUE ABDEL HAMID KADHI

AVENUE ABDEL HAMID KADHI

Hôtel Ennassim

MEDENINE

0   100 m

Hospital

To Ben
Gardane
& Zarzis

Tunis, Tripoli, Tebessa in Algeria, and even Bornu in present-day northern Nigeria. It was also the central granary of the **Touazine** and **Khezour**, tribes belonging to the powerful **Ouerghamma confederation** of Berber-speaking tribes (see p.428), who had moved from Ghoumrassen on the advice of their marabout, Sidi el Assaibi. As a base for the confederation, Medenine grew rapidly from about 1800, and, at its height, the town's *ksar* had some eight thousand *ghorfas*, or cells to store grain (see box on p.341). The French established their southern headquarters here and its flimsy appearance hasn't improved much since. Nevertheless the town is the regional centre and you'll have to pass through it at some point, probably even stay the night.

Sadly, Medenine's **ksar** has gradually been demolished since the beginning of the century, when the tribes began to store their grain in silos near the fields rather than carry it all the way into town. One large courtyard remains, right in town on avenue 7 Novembre. With its *ghorfas* converted into curio shops, busloads of holidaymakers are driven in to look at it (nearby cafés double their prices for anyone looking remotely like a tourist). There are some more **ghorfas** behind it, mainly abandoned, but up to three storeys high and giving a much better idea of the original construction. On the whole, the *ksar* is a disappointment, but it forms an introduction to those to the west and further south, which, although originally far smaller, are much better preserved.

Practicalities

The town centre is concentrated down by the Oued Medenine el Gueblaoui at **place des Martyrs**, where you'll find the **PTT**, with its postal section (city hours; coin phone) across the square from the **phones** section (open country hours). **Avenue Bourguiba** leads north across the river from here, past the open-air **souk**. Market day is Sunday but there are stalls out every day of the week.

Taxiphone offices (daily until about 8pm) are located on the north bank of the *oued*, further up avenue Bourguiba opposite the junction of rue 18 Janvier, while **banks** are mostly by the main roundabout, place 7 Novembre, or on avenue Bourguiba up above its junction with rue 18 Janvier, with one open on Saturday and Sunday mornings. There's a **cinema** at the top of a pedestrian area between avenue Bourguiba and place 7 Novembre, and a **hammam** the other side of avenue Bourguiba just by the *oued* (daily men 5am–noon & 6pm–midnight; women 1–6pm). If you want a **newspaper** in English, try the newsagent up avenue Bourguiba near the corner of rue Mosbaa el Jarbou, who sometimes has the odd English-language title. Lastly, for essential supplies, there's a *Grand Magasin* **supermarket** at 18 avenue Bourguiba, and a **night pharmacy** further up at no. 46. The **hospital** (☎05/640830) is on the Ben Gardane road, about 400m up from place des Martyrs.

Medenine's **hotels** are generally lousy, with budget places dingier than usual and only one option at the top of the range and one in the middle. If you don't like the look of any of the following, the closest alternative is Metameur (see p.340).

Hotels

Essada, 87 av Bourguiba (☎05/640300). Rather spartan, but reasonably clean and with windows opening onto a central terrace. ①.

Essalema, 85 av 7 Novembre (☎05/640509). Infested mattresses, squalid bathrooms and toilets, but a young and friendly management and nice views over the *ksar* opposite. ①.

El Hana, av Bourguiba (☎05/640690). Up past the *Essada*. Some of the rooms are a bit claustrophobic, but okay for one night. ①.

Ibis, pl 7 Novembre (☎05/643878). Medenine's newest, brightest and most deluxe hotel – an oasis in the desert for those who can afford it. ④.

El Vazira, off av 7 Novembre, by the *Ksar* (no phone). Clean rooms and low prices – the best of the cheapies. ①.

Sahara, rue 2 Mai, next to the PTT phone office (☎05/640007). Once quite posh, the *Sahara* is now pretty shabby, but acceptable for a night or two. ②.

Hôtel du Sud, rue Abderrahim Ibn Khaldoun, off av Ali Belhouane (☎05/640354). Basic and not recommended for women. ①.

Youth hostel

Maison des Jeunes youth hostel, rue des Palmiers (☎05/640338). Unsignposted in a group of white buildings about 500m past the *ksar* on the left. Curfew at 10pm, up and out at 8.30am; a bit of a disinfectant-and-wire-brush school barracks. ①.

Eating and drinking

Medenine is not the place for gourmets, and even cheap **restaurants** are thin on the ground. The best of them is the nameless eatery off rue 18 Janvier by the side of the *Hôtel Ibis*, with good food at low prices. Alternatives in the same price range include the *Restaurant Chrigui*, on avenue Bourguiba by the *Hôtel el Hana*, and the *Restaurant Carthage*, opposite the bus station in rue 18 Janvier. Pizzas can be had at the *Pizzeria Plaza* in avenue Bourguiba, a block beyond the *Hôtel el Hana*. For more refined meals, try the moderately priced restaurant of the *Hôtel Sahara*, or the more expensive *Hôtel Ibis*, either of whose bars is a reasonable place for a quiet beer.

MOVING ON FROM MEDENINE

The **bus and louage stations** face each other about halfway up rue 18 Janvier. There are nine daily **buses** to Tunis (7hr 30min), six of them overnight, with two of the day services and three of the night services going via Sfax (3hr 30min) and Sousse (6hr), the others via Kairouan (6hr); one of each continues to Bizerte (9hr). A total of fourteen daily buses serve Gabes (1hr 15min), six go to Tataouine (1hr), nine to Zarzis (1hr), seven to Ben Gardane (1hr 30min), with one continuing to Ras Ajdir – en route, at the Zarzis turnoff, look out for the signpost to "Cairo 2,591km". There are also nine buses to Jerba (2hr), five to Ghoumrassen (1hr if direct) and two to Beni Kheddache (45min). **Louages** serve Ben Gardane, Beni Kheddache, Gabes, Ghoumrassen, Houmt Souk (Jerba), Sfax, Tataouine, Tunis and Zarzis. For Ben Kheddache, they leave from the beginning of rue Mosbah el Jarbou, next to the *Agil* station. For a day trip round some of the *ksour*, a group of four or five may find it economical to negotiate a rate with a *louage* or taxi driver.

Metameur

The 600-year-old **ksar** of **METAMEUR** has a dramatic silhouette, standing isolated in the plain. Though quite small, with three courtyards and *ghorfas* that reach only three storeys, it's remarkably well preserved and hasn't been converted wholesale to tourist use. It's a short bus ride 6km along the Medenine–Gabes road, or an easy enough hitch from the top of avenue Bourguiba in Medenine to the turnoff, from where it's a 1km walk to the village.

The village was founded around the thirteenth century by a local marabout, Sidi Ahmed Ben Adjel, who set up shop in a cave, and the local nomads who followed him. Today the village is still occupied by Sidi Ahmed's descendants, the **Temara**, and the descendants of his followers, the Berber **Harraza**. At one time each Harraza family would pay its Arab Temara masters in wheat, barley, oil and the much-prized local wood. In autumn and winter the *ksar* is barely used by the Temara and Harraza tribespeople as they're out in the plains with their herds; it is at its busiest in summer. On Fridays the **Mosque of Sidi Ahmed Ben Adjel**, housing the saint's tomb, also draws a congregation mainly comprised of nomads from the surrounding pastures.

GHORFAS, KALA'A AND KSOUR

Throughout the south, people stored their grain in **ghorfas**, small stone cells (the Arabic word means room – you can ask for a *ghorfa* in a hotel) a couple of metres high and five to ten metres long. The cells were generally constructed on top of one another and side by side, at times reaching eight storeys. Individual units were always built in the same way, with grain sacks full of earth placed between the two side walls to act as a support during the construction of the roof. A layer of matting was placed over the top of these sacks, in the form of an arch, and then covered with clay, mortar and gypsum. When it had dried, the clay was chipped away, the sacks and net removed, and a palm wood door fitted at the front. The rough inner walls were covered with plaster, usually with stucco figures such as handprints or fish to ward off the evil eye, sometimes with inscriptions or geometric patterns.

In the first years of the Arab invasion, the Berbers retreated inland to the high mountain tops, building **forts** (or *kala'a*) near their cave dwellings. Once the Arabs had occupied the fertile land the Berbers were forced into peace treaties and the *kala'a* were replaced by the **ksour** (*ksar* in the singular), fortified granaries belonging to each tribe. The outer defensive wall consisted of the back of these *ghorfas*, presenting a blank facade to the would-be assailant. The shape of the perimeter was dictated by the site, whether along a hilltop, as at Ksar Jouama, on a hillside as at Ksar Ouled Soltane, or down in the more spacious river valley, like Medenine.

The best preserved of the *ksar*'s courtyards is now the excellent *Hôtel les Ghorfas* (☎05/640128; ②), where you can stay in a *ghorfa* and still enjoy such modern luxuries as tea and hot running water. Most overnighters take half-board as there is nowhere else to eat in Metameur. Its gregarious proprietor, Hachim Drifi, is very knowledgeable about local culture, and happy to converse on the subject for as long as you let him. He is also planning an art centre in part of the *ksour*, and brushes and paper are now freely available to anyone who cares to use them. In winter it's a good idea to arrive early or phone ahead as he sometimes gives up and goes home around nightfall if there are no customers.

When you're ready to move on, there's a **bus** back to Medenine, as well as a *piste* from Metameur to Toujane and Matmata, 56km west, which you could try hitching down – but you'll need luck on your side. You can cover the *piste* in a rented car without four-wheel drive, but progress is slow, and it's faster (and safer) to go the long way round via Gabes.

The Jebel Haouia

Although there's a main road south from Medenine straight to Tataouine, it goes through the plain, a route that's uniformly dull. A spectacular alternative is to make a detour to the west via **Ksar Jouama** and **Beni Kheddache**, straight through the rugged mountains of **Jebel Haouia**, where the most impressive of the *ksour* sit perched on mountain spurs.

If you plan on doing this, take note that it's not easy. **Public transport** and surfaced roads run southwest from Medenine as far as Beni Kheddache, and strike north from Tataouine up to Ksar Hadada, but making the connection between the two roads if you don't have your own car involves hitching the 22km of dirt track that link Beni Kheddache with Ksar Hadada. This road is due to be surfaced in the near future, though there's no promise of public transport along it. In the meantime, therefore, the easiest way to get to Ksar Hadada is from Tataouine in the south (see p.344).

Ksour west of Medenine

Two minibuses a day run west along the road from Medenine to Ksar Jouama and Beni Kheddache, and there are also two *louages* from the beginning of avenue Masbah Jarbou (left off avenue Bourguiba, at the top of the hill by the *Agil* station). Failing that, you could try hitching from further along the same road.

The minibus from Medenine stops briefly after 20km at **KSAR JEDID** ("New Ksar"), built in the 1890s when the security imposed by the French army allowed the mountain tribes to store their grain safely in the plains. This was the first stage in the process of abandonment: within thirty years, the tribes had stopped using *ksour* altogether, keeping their grain in unprotected silos near the fields.

From Ksar Jedid the road climbs the escarpment for 8km – check out the amazing view from the top – to **KSAR JOUAMA** and the modern village of the same name. The *ksar* is just visible on the crest of a steep hill to the right, and there's a path from the road, a little walk back from the bus stop and village shop, which leads past a deserted **mosque** to the bottleneck of the *ksar* and its entrance **gate**. An inscription gives its Islamic date as 1174 AH (1764 AD), but the *ksar* was almost certainly here before then. Decades of disuse have taken their toll – the outer **wall** is now crumbling and some of the **ghorfas** have collapsed – but it still makes a strong impression. If you've taken an early bus, it's possible to stop off at Ksar Jouama and catch the next one – if you can attract the driver's attention. Or try hitching, as it's a busy road.

BENI KHEDDACHE is 8km further on, a large village that used to be another mountain *ksar*. Reginald Rankin, who came here in the 1890s, described it as "a sort of Saharan Windsor", with walls twenty metres high and a ninety metres long and a courtyard covering eighteen thousand square metres. Unfortunately it was demolished by the French just before the last war to make way for a market. However, a few **ghorfas** survive behind the **mosque**, whilst the *ksar* has become a settlement – a village and market centre for the surrounding tribes. Souk day is Thursday.

There are no hotels in Beni Kheddache, though in cases of severe hunger there is a place off the market square on the Ksar Ghilane road that serves sandwiches and chips. You'll no doubt want to leave before long – the last bus back to Medenine goes at about 6pm. There are also *louages* and pick-ups to Medenine and Ksar Hallouf, but none south to Ksar Hadada. You could try **hitching** down there, but start early as the road is very quiet. The road way out west to Ksar Ghilane (see p.350) is pretty well impossible to use unless you have your own four-wheel drive.

Just 2km north of Beni Kheddache is **ZAMMOUR**, where a track to the right leads up to a **ksar**. Small and largely ruined, it compensates with great views. There is a **"station touristique"** here (☎05/647196; ②), where you can have dinner and sleep in a cave, but it's all rather rudimentary. Beyond Zammour, 12km of *piste* brings you to **KSAR HALLOUF**, a small thirteenth-century *ksar* overlooking a fertile valley, itself overlooked by a ruined **kala'a**. It's worth climbing up for the views of the plain, with Jerba visible in the hazy distance. In the *ksar*, as well as a traditional camel-worked olive press, there's a *Relai* **hotel** (☎05/647037; ②), where you can spend the night in a *ghorfa*. Sleeping conditions are a bit basic, but if you don't want to stay there, you could just stop off for a reasonably priced couscous dinner.

Pick-ups run a shuttle service to Beni Kheddache, while the *piste* from Zammour to Hallouf is passable in a regular two-wheel drive car, continuing for another 8km to Behayra, where it meets the paved road to Ksar Jedid and Medenine.

Beni Kheddache to Ksar Hadada

The road south over the plateau from just outside Beni Kheddache heads towards Tataouine via Ksar Hadada and Ghoumrassen. Unsurfaced beyond the first kilometre (though passable, with care, in any car), it winds across the hillocky plateau of the Jebel Haouia, through dense plantations of olive and figs that use the same *jessour* technology as in the Matmata (see p.308). General Jamais, commanding a punitive expedition into the region in 1883, called it "a true paradise in the desolation of the south", and the contrast with the desert plains is, indeed, staggering.

The plateau is the home of the **Haouia**, intractable enemies of the French. Part of the Ouerghamma confederation, they are one of the few communities who still practise transhumance, the seasonal movement from pastures in the desert to the coastal plain. In the winter months they camp in the plain or in the **Dahar** – the arid plateau to the west of the mountains – returning to their fields in summer for the fig and olive harvests. Since the beginning of the century, however, the Haouia have abandoned their *ksour* and now live in scattered houses and cave dwellings among their fields.

One of the most impressive of the old *ksour*, **KERACHFA**, can be reached along a turning to the east 10km down the road from Beni Kheddache. The 5km winding approach road is surfaced, a fact that will seem less strange soon, when the main road is paved. The **ksar** itself is a ruin of startlingly Gothic appearance on a spur overlooking the plain. Most of the *ghorfas* have collapsed, but outside the main gate is a fitfully used **underground mosque**. Follow a path around the spur and you come to two abandoned **oil presses**, still in good repair.

Back on the main track, continue south over the plateau and, crawling along an appalling surface, you eventually sight the white minaret of **KSAR HADADA** (sometimes called Ghoumrassen Hadada) and regain the tarmac. The old **ksar** here is no longer used for grain storage and half of it has been abandoned, but the other half is now occupied by the *Hôtel Ksar Hadada* (☎05/869605; ②). Run by the same management as the *Gazelle* in Tataouine, it's a bit of a tourist trap, but the only place to spend the night between Tataouine and Medenine. If you specifically want to spend a night in a converted *ksar*, this is probably not the one to choose – those at Metameur and Ksar Hallouf are better. Still, the rooms have showers and toilets, and meals in the reasonably priced **restaurant** are not at all bad.

When it's time to move on, the only **public transport** is the bus service to Ghoumrassen (4 daily; 10min), where you need to change for points beyond (although the same vehicle may actually continue to Tataouine and Medenine). If you're planning to head north of Ksar Hadada, you really need your own car. You could try hitching the 22km to Beni Kheddache but there isn't much traffic, although this may change when the road is surfaced in late 1995. From Beni Kheddache, there is tarmac and transport to Medenine (see p.337).

Ghoumrassen and around

GHOUMRASSEN, squeezed into a sharp-sided valley, 5km further south, is an ancient settlement. French officers found traces of a Roman fort nearby, with inscriptions now lost in a museum somewhere. In the fourteenth century, the historian El Tijani, accompanying the Hafsid ruler of Tunis on the *haj*, stopped at Ghoumrassen for three months. He describes a community at war with its Arab neighbours, living in caverns within the rock in the shelter of a fortress, the **Kala'a Hamdoun**.

The *kala'a* has now gone, its site marked only by a few pieces of wall at the top of the spur overlooking the main part of the town, next to the white **tomb** of the marabout Sidi Moussa Ben Abdallah (the near-legendary figure who united the Ouerghamma), the texture of its walls reminiscent of melted candlewax. A path cut into the side of the spur leads up to them. Below, the **cave dwellings**, or *ghar*, remain, cut into the softer strata at the base of the spur. Most consist of a single room, a cooking area near the front and a raised living quarter behind, but some of the larger *ghar* have several rooms separated by massive pillars of stone. A walled courtyard called a

---

MOVING ON FROM GHOUMRASSEN

If you're driving, the most direct road to Medenine commences at the eastern end of the main street. Roads to Tataouine, Guermessa and Medenine via Ksar Hadada branch off at the other end of town. The **bus station** has services to Guermessa (2 on schooldays; 20min), Houmt Souk on Jerba (1 daily; 3hr), Ksar Hadada (4 daily; 10min), Medenine (5 daily; 1hr) and Tataouine (3 daily; 45min). **Louages** serve Medenine, Tataouine and Tunis. **Hitching** to Guermessa shouldn't be too much of a problem: the tarmac road branches off the main Tataouine road just out of town.

---

houch at the front provides a private living area; the outer wall is usually a raised *ghorfa* used for storage.

Each of the five spurs on the northern side of the mountain shelters a separate part of the community, another group living at Ksar Hadada. These have long been at odds and, during the French occupation, when they were brought under the command of a single *sheikh*, there was frequent fighting. With the construction of the new town in the valley in the 1890s, however, the community was brought together and peace finally achieved. Few families now live in the *ghar*, as they are considered dangerous due to rocks frequently falling from the cliff faces onto the courtyards below. As you wander round you can see the devastation these rockfalls have caused, so do take care.

Ghoumrassen is now a market town and very lively during the Friday **souk**, which attracts tribespeople from Nefzaoua in search of the region's esteemed olive oil. Most of the town's shops are located on the long main street. There are lots of **cafés** and **patisseries** selling the Ghoumrassen speciality, *ftair* (doughnuts), but no hotel, so you'll have to go on, or back to Ksar Hadada or Tataouine. If you need a **bank**, however, you'll find two, plus a *Grand Magasin* **supermarket** and a PTT (country hours) where you can make international phone calls. The **bus station** is a block from the main street towards the eastern end of town, and **louages** leave from the middle of the main street.

A few kilometres east of Ghoumrassen is the large but unimpressive **Ksar el Ferich**, whose two storeys of *ghorfas*, still in use, lie flat on the plain. The guard posted there is happy to show people around. About halfway between the Chenini turnoff and Ksar el Feric, the new three-star *Hôtel Dakyanus* (☎05/862932; ②) caters especially for Japanese tour groups, and can be expected to meet their exacting standards. This is a cheap but rather less stylish alternative to the *Sangho*, 7km down the road (see p.347).

Guermessa

The traditional Berber village of **GUERMESSA**, 8km southwest of Ghoumrassen, is less troubled by tourists than its sister villages of Douiret and Chenini to the south (see p.347), perhaps because it was rather difficult to reach until recently. Even now, despite surfaced roads from Tataouine and Ghoumrassen, and the two daily school **buses** to Ghoumrassen, it's not exactly well connected and has few facilities.

Guermessa is built around a spur with a ruined **kala'a** on its peak, up to which leads a distinctive paved **pathway** from the valley below, no mean engineering achievement, considering the size of the slabs. Although it's still inhabited, the construction of a new village in the plains is gradually drawing families away, and within a decade or so it too will likely face abandonment.

Tataouine (Foum Tataouine) and around

FOUM TATAOUINE – meaning "the mouth of the springs" – evokes an image of the desert outpost, a palm oasis surrounded by drifting sand. This, at any rate, is the tourist blurb's pitch. Reality is rather different, for the town is new, busy and drab, built by the French administrators on an empty site some 50km south of Medenine. And though it has nothing of historic interest in itself, within a radius of 25km are some of the most impressive sites in Tunisia. With Tunisia's southernmost hotels and banks, Tataouine is a better base for exploration than Medenine, with enough accessible goals to its north and west – like Ghoumrassen, Guermessa, Ksar Hadada, Chenini and Douiret – to fill a week or more, while to the southeast of the town there are interesting *ksour* within walking distance, and further south the well-preserved *ksar* of **Ouled Soltane**. Tataouine itself, despite its lack of any historic depth, has a certain inexplicable charm – don't be surprised if you find yourself making excuses to delay leaving. In April the **Festival of the Ksour** enlivens the town in pale imitation of Douz's Saharan Festival, with pseudo-traditional marriages and a rather tame pop concert.

Tataouine's main street, **avenue Bourguiba**, is a continuation of the main road from Medenine. About halfway down it stood a statue of Habib Bourguiba, but this has now been replaced by a clock – it remains to be seen how many other Tunisian towns will follow Tataouine's example and start pulling down statues of the supreme combatant, like those of Lenin in Russia. In the meantime, don't expect to see any signs indicating the street's name.

Tataouine was built as the far south's administrative centre and **garrison town** and the military presence is still strong – be careful not to incur the wrath of army personnel by climbing the rocks behind the military camps along the Remada road for the view, which also gives you a vantage point over the camps. As late as 1950 the soldiers outnumbered the 300-odd civilians by three to one. Most of these troops were members of a penal battalion of the French army and the French Foreign Legion, and for the most part they were German. Indeed, in the 1930s, German was the town's third language.

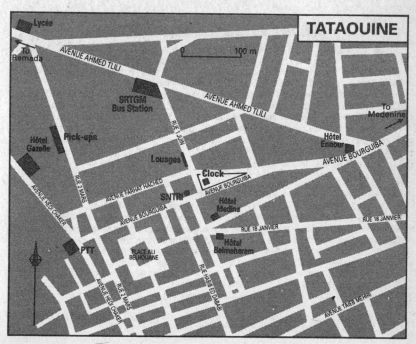

The town's other function was that of a **market centre**. At the turn of the century the French had great expectations of this market as the focus of Saharan trade. It was not to be, as trade had already dwindled and what was left passed through Tripoli, where ivory and gold could be sold openly. In 1896, commerce dried up completely after a French nobleman, the Marquis de Morès, was killed by Tuaregs while gun-running for the Mahdi's forces holding out against the British in Sudan.

Tataouine's modern **marketplace**, off avenue Bourguiba in place Ali Belhouane, is lively, and it's worth trying to coincide with the souk held on Mondays and Thursdays. The square fills with merchants from all over the south buying sheep in the early summer, olives in the autumn, and locally made blankets at any time. Other merchants, mainly from Jerba, sell groceries and dubious plastic knicknacks. It's always very colourful, with tribespeople coming in from distant villages and nomadic encampments, and peddlers stocking up with the goods they then sell from their camels' backs to people in the remotest communities.

Practicalities

The main **bus station** is on avenue Ahmed Tlili, while the *SNTRI* office is at 67 avenue Bourguiba and runs Tunis services from across the road by the clock. **Louages** park in rue 1 Juin, off avenue Bourguiba by the clock. There are also **pick-ups** and Peugeots around the region to be found in rue 2 Mars, just north of avenue Farhat Hached. Taxis can usually be found in place 18 Janvier.

You can make **international phone calls** at the PTT at the western end of avenue Bourguiba (city hours), or from **taxiphone offices** nearby at 5 avenue Bourguiba (daily 8am–9pm), and at the other end of the avenue, opposite the *Hôtel Ennour* (daily

---

MOVING ON FROM TATAOUINE

Buses operated by *SRTG Medenine* run from the bus station 200m down the Remada road and only a couple of blocks away from the clock in avenue Bourguiba. From here, there are four departures daily to Medenine (1hr), two of these continuing to Houmt Souk, Jerba (2 daily; 3hr), one via Jorf (2hr) and the other via Zarzis (2hr).

Buses from here also serve Ghoumrassen three times daily (45min) and Remada once (2hr). The *SNTRI* office is at 67 avenue Bourguiba, with two buses daily – one morning, one evening – for Tunis (8hr 30min) via Gabes (2hr 15min), Sfax (4hr 30min) and Sousse (7hr) from across the road by the clock. **Local bus services** run twice daily to Chenini (40min), and three times to Maztouria (20min) and Ksar Ouled Debbab (30min), and are best picked up at the *lycée*, 100m west and across the street, as the driver usually turns the bus there without taking it into the terminal; however, check there first.

Louages park between the two bus companies in rue 1 Juin, off avenue Bourguiba by the clock. Medenine and Ghoumrassen are the obvious destinations, but you'll also find vehicles to Remada and Dehibat, and direct to Gabes and Tunis.

There are also **pick-ups** and Peugeots around the region to be found in rue 2 Mars, just north of avenue Farhat Hached. These serve places like Chenini, Douiret and Maztouria, work on the same principle as *louages* (but with eight passengers instead of five) and cost very little (less than a dinar a place). They are most plentiful before midday, so set out early. And, as in Medenine, if there are three or four of you, you may want to negotiate a deal with a **taxi** to one or more of the local *ksour* and Berber villages (try a *louage* if there are five in your group). Taxis can usually be found in place 18 Janvier or near the *louages*. Expect to pay around 5–8TD each way to places like Chenini, Douiret and Guermessa, plus around 5TD an hour for the driver to wait while you look around.

Alternatively, you could hitch out to the villages from the Remada road, or walk or take a bus to the appropriate turnoff and hitch from there.

7am–10pm). There are several **banks** in town, mostly on avenue Farhat Hached and avenue Bourguiba. The most convenient **hammam** is down a side street by the *Mobil* garage, opposite the bus station – bear left after twenty metres and it's at the end of the street (daily 4am–8pm for both sexes; separate entrances). For supplies, the *Grand Magasin* **supermarket** is by the market in place Ali Belhouane, and there's also a **night pharmacy** at 2 avenue Bourguiba, opposite the PTT. For more serious problems, the **hospital** is 9km north of town at the Ghoumrassen turnoff from the Medenine road (☎05/860114), and there's an **emergency medical service** (☎05/860902) behind the *Garde National* office, opposite the *Hôtel Gazelle*.

There isn't a huge choice of **accommodation** in Tataouine, but what's on offer is reasonable enough.

Hotels

Belmeharem, pl 18 Janvier (☎05/860104). Charming staff make up for the slightly rudimentary rooms and sporadic hot water. ①.

Ennour, 107 av Bourguiba (☎05/860131). More than adequate for the price, but ask for an outside window. ①.

Gazelle ★★, av Hedi Chaker (☎05/860009). This is not only Tataouine's top address, but also the base for the hotel at Ksar Hadada and the *Relai* at Chenini, so you can enquire about them here. Phone ahead or arrive early as it is often fully occupied by tour groups. ③.

Medina, pl 18 Janvier (☎05/860999). A gem of a place, with staff as bright and pleasant as the rooms. Hot water only in the morning (shower early or shower cold) is a small sacrifice. Recommended. ①.

Sangho ★★★, rte de Chenini (☎05/860102). Just up the Chenini/Ghoumrassen turnoff, 3km south of town – look for the sign on the hillside (lit up at night). A very classy joint with tasteful rooms, antique decor and full facilities. A cut above the usual three-star traps. ⑥.

Eating and drinking

When it comes to **food** in Tataouine, you are not exactly spoiled for choice. One of the cheapest places is the *Restaurant Medina*, in a little square behind the *louage* station, off avenue Farhat Hached and rue 1 Juin, where you can eat outside if you like. Similarly priced is the *Essendabad*, just across rue 1 Juin from the bus station. If you want something more sophisticated, try the *Hôtel Gazelle*'s reasonably priced set menu. The *Gazelle* is the only place in town where you can get a beer. For anything posher than that, you'll have to trek down to the *Sangho*, 3km south of town, where you have the choice of reasonably priced wood-oven pizzas, a pricier buffet or an à la carte restaurant.

A Tataouine speciality, now common all over the country, is the **kab el ghezal**, *corne de gazelle*, a sweet pastry horn filled with honey and nuts, available at any patisserie in town.

The Jebel Abiadh

To the east and south of Tataouine stretches the mountain range of **Jebel Abiadh**, home of the **Ouderna** tribe – the most powerful in the south and part of the Ouerghamma confederation – and of several smaller Berber communities. Though *ksour* and villages litter the mountains, the sites aren't as dramatic as Douiret and Chenini, to the west of Tataouine (see p.347); even so, they're still pretty impressive, and have the great advantage of being free of tourist parties.

The Berbers living in these mountains lacked the independence enjoyed by the larger communities at Douiret, Chenini and Guermessa, and most shared their village with semi-nomadic groups who claimed Arab origins, or else the village was closely linked to a neighbouring nomadic tribe's *ksar*. French anthropologists used to maintain that the Ouderna, the dominant tribe, had Berber serfs who paid them olives, figs and wool in return for "protection". It was, they claimed, "a veritable slavery such that the Ouderna can spill the blood of his Berber client without fear of the law". In reality there were bonds between the Arab nomads and the sedentary Berber villagers, but these represented an exchange of services: in return for agricultural produce the nomad guarded a sedentary neighbour's herd, gaining access to widely dispersed pastures without the trouble of a lifestyle on the move.

Ksar Megalba is the easiest to reach of these *ksour*. Just head down the Remada road from Tataouine for about a kilometre and then turn right, cross the *oued* and head up towards the mosque straight ahead. It's well preserved, with three-storey *ghorfas* and the remains of storage racks and broken pottery. From the look of the place, however, most visitors have left their mark.

There's another *ksar* on a hill to the left of the Remada road, opposite the turnoff – one of a number called **Ksar Deghaghora** – but it overlooks a military camp of some sort and they don't like you to go up there, especially not with a camera.

Just south of Ksar Deghaghora, a paved road to the east, signposted "Beni Barka", takes you up into the Jebel Abiadh – "White Mountains" – proper. This road passes a large number of *ksour* in varying states of repair, though you'd need to be a serious enthusiast to want to visit all of them. The first is the deserted **Ksar Gurga**, on your right after 1km and still within walking distance of Tataouine.

After another 4km, you'll be able to see the village of **BENI BARKA**, also on your right, pitched atop the escarpment as you approach along the valley floor. You'll have to ask the bus to stop and walk up the steep track to the top. Formerly an important market, the centre of a thriving Berber community linked to the Arab community of Ksar Ouled Debbab, most of it is now in ruins. Even so, the **entrance gate**, dating from the fourteenth century or earlier, is still spectacular, standing on the very edge of the cliff and offering good views across the plain. The village has been deserted in favour of the many new cave-dwellings in the surrounding slopes, some of them excavated eight metres into the rock. As you walk up to the old village, look out for ripple marks in the rocks and fossils of ammonites and sea molluscs, proof that this area has not always been desert.

Maztouria and around

South of Beni Barka, the road passes a number of desolate *ksour*. **Ksar Zoltane** is up on the right, about 1km past Beni Barka. A couple of kilometres further, a road branching off left brings you after 5km to **Ksar Tounket**. And 7km beyond Beni Barka is the new village of **MAZTOURIA**, around 20km southeast of Tataouine, where many of the surrounding people have settled near a spring.

As you enter Maztouria town, you pass more abandoned *ksour* up on your right – a rough but passable track leads up to them from just after the Ksar Tounket turnoff. The first, round and compact, is **Ksar Ouled Aoun**. It is followed by three rectangular *ksour* starting with **Ksar Aouadad**, now restored but locked up, whose massive stone walls are highly impressive, making it look like a fortress. Next is **Ksar Kedim** (or Ksar Zenetes), also on the right overlooking Maztouria. Rather more ruined than Ksar Aouadad, it too is the object of some restoration work, particularly on its huge gateway. Inside, part of the decoration is still intact on some of the *ghorfas'* doorways and there is an underground well reached by a tunnel. According to an inscription, it was built in 1091 AD, shortly after the Hilalian invasion, and is usually ascribed to the Zenetes, the Berber ancestors of the region's tribes. Beyond it, the next *ksar* is called **Ksar Dahar** (known also as Ksar Deghaghora), entered through a strange tunnel-like gateway.

From Maztouria, the route continues 6km to the village of **TAMELEST**, also built to settle the region's nomads. Overlooking the village is the *ksar* of the same name, the thirteenth-century granary of the **Ouled Chehida**, the Ouderna's most powerful group. In 1915 their *sheikh* led the only full-scale tribal revolt against the French.

Although the Ouderna managed to overwhelm the telegraph stations in the south, the French garrisons held out, and within a month the tribespeople were defeated by a column from the north and forced into Libya as refugees. Much of the damage done to this *ksar*, and others in the Jebel Abiadh, dates from this period.

The road splits 2km beyond Tamelest. **Ksar Sedra**, with a number of cave dwellings in the rock beneath it, overlooks the right fork; the left leads to **Ksar Ouled Soltane**, 3km away and the best-preserved *ksar* in the south, its outer wall still intact. Ksar Ouled Soltane was built by the Ouled Chehida (the Ouled Soltane are descendants of that group) on low land where it can be seen for miles around, a tribute to their confidence in those troubled times. To get to the entrance, walk around the top of the hill, past the mosque and next to the shops and **café**. The two courtyards inside date from the fifteenth and the nineteenth centuries respectively and are connected by a passage made from palm wood. *Ghorfas* rise four storeys high and are still used to store grain and olives. On Friday afternoons the courtyards function as meeting places for the community, the majority of whom spend most of the year out in the pastures with their herds of sheep, goats and camels. Thus, not only is the *ksar* intact but so is the way of life that goes with it. The explanation for this situation, unique in the south, lies in the Ouled Chehida's reluctance to migrate to the cities, along with the *ksar*'s continued isolation from mass tourism. It's a community with a strong identity and a traditional lifestyle, one of the few left in Tunisia.

Three **buses** a day run from Tataouine to Maztouria, Tamelest and Ksar Ouled Soltane. If you're coming from Tataouine, you pick up the bus outside the *lycée*. After midday, Maztouria is the furthest any pick-up will go, but there's enough traffic on the road to make **hitching** easy.

Chenini

Most people approach the ruggedly scenic **CHENINI** along the paved road directly from Tataouine, 20km east. You can squeeze into a pick-up from rue· 2 Mars in Tataouine, take a taxi (around 15TD for the return trip including waiting time, but you may have to haggle) or hitch, which is easiest on market days (Monday and Thursday) when trucks return to Chenini at noon.

Chenini is best seen from a distance. This Berber village is built around a peak surmounted by a ruined **kala'a**, with a white **mosque** resting on a crook of the spur, the whole ensemble intensely dramatic in its size and desolation. From the distance each row of dwellings fronted by their *ghorfa* seems to cling to the steep mountainside. Reginald Rankin, travelling in the 1890s, was mightily impressed: "I have seen nearly all the so-called wonders of·the world and unhesitatingly say that the cave dwellings of the Saharan troglodytes seem to me the most wonderful thing of all." An inscription in one of the *ghorfas* gives the date 1143 AD, but the village is certainly older than that.

As at Ghoumrassen, the mostly inhabited **ghar** are dug into soft strata on the slopes below the fortress, and several levels of cave dwellings form bands around the spur that are joined by steep walkways. You can visit a working camel-drawn **oil press**, an underground communal bakery, and even enter some of the houses, but you'll usually be charged, so fix a price before you enter. This is increasingly a problem, as Chenini has suffered from overexposure to parties of tourists, most of whom arrive in the morning. If you want the place more to yourself, go later.

While Chenini itself is something special, the **views** from here are also quite outstanding. For a leisurely **walk** with brilliant vistas, follow the path up from the mosque in the village, along the hillside above the underground mosque (see below), down to a spring where the villagers collect their water.

Even older than the village around the *kala'a* is an abandoned village a kilometre along the escarpment. Here only the **Jemaa Kedima** (the "old mosque"), an underground mosque, survives. Below the leaning minaret are two interconnected rooms, one housing the **tomb** of a marabout, the other those of the **Seven Sleepers**. According to folk legend – quite a common one in the region – seven Christians were imprisoned in this underground hiding place during the Roman occupation. Four centuries later, when their cell was opened, they awoke as if they had been asleep. All that time, however, their bodies had continued to grow, so that they were now just under four metres tall. Only when they had been converted to Islam did they die, their bodies buried here in these long tombs.

Chenini has a *Relai* **restaurant** with a good inexpensive set menu, and even beer. You may be able to **stay** here in a *ghar* called the *Relai de Chenini* (☎05/860009; ②), but they only have room for half a dozen, so it's best to call ahead. The *Relai* is run by the *Hôtel Gazelle* in Tataouine, who may have further information. The only **public transport** from Chenini is in pick-ups, but it shouldn't be too difficult to hitch out. The very rough back route to Guermessa and Douiret is just about passable in a car if you go slowly, though a four-wheel drive vehicle is preferable. For the intrepid, there's an 8km footpath to Douiret over the mountain, although it's not easy to follow and enlisting the help of a guide might be a wise idea.

Douiret and around

The paved road turns off the Remada road 8km south of Tataouine at **Ksar Ouled Debbab**. Now abandoned, though used for a time as a hotel, Ouled Debbab is the largest *ksar* of the tribe of the same name, who claim an exotic Arab Hilalian line of descent but probably share the indigenous Berber origins of neighbouring **DOUIRET**, 11km down the paved road, utterly Berber and immediately impressive.

The town is dominated by a ruined **kala'a**, perched on peak some 700m high, with a white **mosque** on the slope setting off the soft colour of the bare stone. If you climb to the top and onto the precarious rubble of the *kala'a*, the panoramic views over the surrounding desert are stunning. The village is much like Chenini, though the **ghar**, inhabited in the nineteenth century by five thousand people, are mostly unoccupied. A new village was built on the plain in the 1960s, and many Douiri have set up home there or gone to Tunis.

Wandering around Douiret, you can find **oil presses** (three of them in use), **bakeries** and **inscriptions** in remarkably good condition. On the plain below is an old **graveyard** with the whitewashed tombs of revered marabouts, and a small building that was the office of the French officer sent to administer the community in 1888; it was abandoned after two years, when the French base was moved to Tataouine. The only part of the old village still in use is on the other side of the spur. If you stray into this quarter, women quickly disappear into their houses, so be especially tactful if you have a camera. There's an interesting **mosque** here as well, with an inscription in archaic Berber script (the only example of it known), but non-Muslims are rarely allowed in to see it.

Pick-ups back to Tataouine are most easily located in the new shopping area. Other vehicles will usually give people lifts, too.

Ksar Ghilane

If you have a four-wheel drive car, there are routes out to **KSAR GHILANE**, 75km west of Tataouine, from the track between Chenini and Douiret, from Beni Kheddache, from Douz and from Matmata. The safest and easiest of these to follow is the pipeline route from the Douz–Matmata *piste*.

On the edge of the sandy desert, Ksar Ghilane is a frighteningly desolate place; there's a well here, and such was its importance that the Romans built a **fort** to defend it. One of a chain, the *limes* extended the full length of the Imperial frontier. The main attraction of the area today is, however, the journey across the **Dahar**, a desolate and arid plateau that used to be the haunt of *fellaga*, or bandits, and the opportunity to see the desert gazelles and antelopes that used to be found all over the south. Ksar Ghilane is linked traditionally

THE BERBER VILLAGES: A LIFESTYLE UNDER THREAT

Life in the Berber villages of Ghoumrassen, Guermessa, Chenini and Douiret has traditionally revolved around **agriculture**. Considerable effort has been put into the construction of *jessour* (agricultural terraces) and cisterns so that trees can be planted in the arid landscape. Although sheep and goats were once raised here, too, they were a small part of the economy and the villagers never participated in the transhumance of their nomad neighbours. Each village had a specialist profession: the Douiri and Guermessi worked as vegetable market porters, the Ghoumrassini sold their doughnuts, and the Chenini newspapers. Young men would work in the city for a few years and then return to their village, spending the money they had saved on bride price to give to a bride's family, or a new *jessour*. Today, however, the young men go to France and Libya, stay away longer and marry outside the community. Many do not return. As you look round the villages, you'll notice that women vastly outnumber men, most of whom are old, evidence that migration is killing the community. This is doubly sad, since with these villages will die the last of Tunisia's Berber culture.

Berber was the predominant language in Tunisia under the Romans but after the Arab conquest was quickly overtaken by Arabic – the language of the new religion, of law and government. Only in the communities of the south did Berber survive, and here too it was in a gradual decline. By the end of the nineteenth century Berber was only spoken as a first language in Douiret, Chenini and Guermessa and, with the French occupation, the extension of government to the south and the imposition of Islamic law, Arabic finally made inroads here, too. However, migration and the consequent dispersal of the Berber population was the death blow. Now, only women speak the language and cling determinedly to the old traditions; the men, forced by education and work in the cities to adopt Arabic as the *lingua franca*, will soon become fully assimilated, swamped in the dominant Arabic culture.

Ironically, the French made every effort to separate the Berbers from their Arab neighbours. French **anthropologists** claimed that they were in fact Europeans who had migrated to North Africa at an early date. While the Arabs were caricatured as lazy, sly and tyrannical, the Berbers were supposedly industrious, honest and democratic (all considered evidence of their purported European origins), and for these reasons worthy of a privileged place in Tunisian society. In reality the French were trying to divide and rule, and the Berbers, on the whole, refused to play the game. While accepting many of the privileges offered by the government, including an independent administration and large tracts of Arab land, they remained just as hostile to the French as their Arab neighbours.

with the Nefzaoua area south of the Chott el Jerid, and in particular with the village of Zaafrane, whose Adhara people still spend part of the year at Ksar Ghilane with their flocks. Apart from the odd Roman remain and a spring, the only specific item of interest here is a **monument** to the Francophone African and French troops under General Leclerc who, in 1943, made an epic march of well over 2000km from Lake Chad to join Montgomery's Commonwealth forces in an assault on the Mareth Line (see p.310).

There are three places to **stay** in Ksar Ghilane, all *campements* – put up for the benefit of jeep tours from Gabes and Douz – where you sleep in traditional-style Berber tents, or you can pitch your own. The two **campsites** by the spring (①) are pretty rustic; a third, 4km away (②), has a pool and a higher degree of comfort, which some would say detracts from the true out-in-the-wilderness experience. Just how authentically Berber all this is can be gauged from the fact that the Ministry of Tourism have been asking the police to move on real Berbers in case their untidy presence upsets the chic clientele from the coastal resorts.

If you are going to Ksar Ghilane under your own steam, don't forget to bring enough food and water for your stay, and fuel for your journey, as there are no supplies in Ksar Ghilane and the water from the spring is sulphurous and unpleasant to drink. You should also inform the National Guard before setting out, and take appropriate precautions (see box below). The only way to get here without your own transport is with an organized group from Douz, Jerba or Gabes – the best is probably *Evatour* in Houmt Souk, Jerba (☎05/653172). A two-day trip should set you back about 100–150TD.

Remada and the extreme south

REMADA, 70km south of Tataouine, is yet another garrison town imposed on the south by the French and has nothing of great interest. When the French arrived, there was a small oasis and the remains of a **Roman fort** nearby, part of the *limes* (see p.350), now incorporated into the army base. The army continues to dominate the region, with Remada declared a "military zone" and first line in the defence against Libya. The border is now open and tensions have decreased in the last few years, but you may still get some strange looks and will still have to show your documents time and time again; seven "terrorists" were caught crossing the border in 1986, and everybody is on the lookout for more.

There's nowhere to stay in Remada, and your best bet is to return to Tataouine by bus or *louage* before they dry up around 3pm. If you get stuck, you'll just have to throw yourself on the mercy of the local police, who may have a spare cell for the night. The only **restaurant** in town is very basic, and you're just as well off buying food from one of the shops. Bring enough dinars with you as there's no bank either. **Market day** is Sunday. If you were hoping to get to **Ksar Segdel**, on a track to the east of town, it's only possible with a four-wheel drive vehicle.

The most feasible trips out from Remada are to the villages in the **Jebel Segdel** mountain range, 8km west along the road to Borj Bourguiba. It's an eight-hour walk over a flat

---

DRIVING IN THE DESERT

Driving in the desert is a potentially hazardous business and claims victims every year. You should not drive in desert regions – let alone think of leaving the main surfaced roads – without taking all the necessary precautions. Don't assume everything will be fine; consider what may happen if you break down in the middle of nowhere with little chance of anyone passing for hours, or even days.

First, make sure your vehicle is up to the terrain. Do all the usual fuel, oil and water checks and make sure you're carrying tools and a jack and spare tyre, preferably two. Take spare fuel if possible, and carry at least **five litres of water** per person at all times. Don't forget, either, to take high-factor suntan lotion, a sunhat and sunglasses, and appropriate clothing, including warm clothes for night-time, when the desert can get bitterly cold, especially in winter. A shovel is invaluable as even a tarmac road can get covered in drifts, and steel sand ladders or mats will help you get unstuck too. A compass is a very good idea.

Always inform the National Guard of your arrival and departure at every post on your journey. Tell them where you're going and when you expect to arrive (occasionally you may be refused permission). If you can't find the Guard, tell the police or gendarmes instead. Keep to well-defined *pistes* as much as possible and in open desert always travel in convoy, never alone.

If you get stuck in a sandstorm, stop. Point your vehicle downwind and wait until the storm abates. This will avoid damage to your engine. And if you break down or get lost, there's one fundamental rule that's more likely to save your life than any other: **stay with your vehicle**. Don't go wandering off into the desert alone, as dehydration, sunstroke and heat exhaustion can strike amazingly quickly, and a car is a lot easier to find than a person wandering around.

The *Sahara Handbook*, by Simon and Jan Glen (Lascelles), contains much timeless good advice on preparing and driving a vehicle in the desert.

DESERT WILDLIFE

Predictably, the **stony desert** or *hammada* that covers much of the southeast of Tunisia has a sparse wildlife population, but the sand desert in the southwest has even less. Neither habitat owes very much to Mediterranean influence, with the huge Sahara to the south dominating the ecosystem. **Plants** are thin on the ground, but the wonder is that they can survive at all. They do this by special adaptation, their leaves often reduced to thin strips to reduce water loss to a minimum. Another strategy evolved by some plants is to have swollen leaves which can store water; cacti are best known for this, but many other plants do it too.

The small **desert mammals** are almost entirely nocturnal, feeding on plants and seeds in the cool of the night. The big ears of the **jerboas** are not just for acute hearing – they may also serve a temperature control function in the same way as an elephant's ears do. On the other hand, **lizards** are mostly active by day – though hard to see easily since they have a surprising turn of speed.

Birds fall into two groups – those that concentrate around the oases, and the true desert dwellers that live out in the inhospitable wastes. In the oases themselves **palm doves** have their "home" habitat, and they've spread to the rest of Tunisia's towns in much the same way as the collared dove has done in northern Europe. If you're truly devoted, rubbish tips are worth exploring for scavenging ravens. Out in the desert and away from the villages and oases, you'll come across many of the steppe birds – larks, wheatears, cream-coloured coursers, shrikes and so on. Lurk around any area of oasis water in the early morning and the reward may be a flock of fast-flying **sandgrouse** coming in to drink. Tataouine is a good base for seeing desert wildlife, with the full range of species. This was the last region in Tunisia where ostriches were found, though any sighting today of a large long-legged bird with a black and white neck is likely to be the **Houbara bustard** – a little-studied rarity.

plain followed by a scramble up a steep escarpment, but you may be able to find a guide at the *Maison du Peuple*, beyond the marketplace on the Borj Bourguiba road. The area is completely deserted, with only the collapsed ruins of the villages and the eroded landscape of their terraced *jessour* remaining of what was once a flourishing economy. Between the sixteenth and eighteenth centuries, the tribes abandoned a total of 25 villages between Douiret and Dehibat. Why they left is still a mystery: the French blamed the expansion of the Ouderna people, though climatic change and plague epidemics may also have played a part. Today the only residents of these ruins are, so the locals claim, jackals.

BORJ BOURGUIBA, 40km southwest of Remada, is accessible only by Land Rover and with a permit from the *Gouvernorat* in Tataouine – which you're most unlikely to be granted. This military prison and settlement takes its name from the ex-president, who was interned here under the Protectorate (when it was called Borj Le Bœuf). Ironically enough, the prison held many of Bourguiba's own political enemies in the 1970s and 80s.

Dehibat and the Libyan frontier

There are two buses a day from Remada to **DEHIBAT**, on the Libyan border, and it's a fairly regular run by *louage*. The village has again been taken over by the army but the old **ksar**, now a barracks, is still there. From the 1880s until 1911, sovereignty over this town was in dispute between the French and the Turkish administration of Libya. The Dehibi had deserted the village to live in Matmata and Douiret a century earlier, but the French paid them to return in order to substantiate their claim. Eventually, when the Italians invaded Libya, the French forced them to concede the village and its lands. Today's military presence indicates Tunisia's continued insecurity over the district, although smuggling is another possible reason for it. There's nowhere at all to stay in Dehibat, though you're only likely to be here if you're self-sufficient and equipped for desert travel – or you intend to cross the border.

Dehibat is the southernmost point of **entry into Libya**, the only other authorized crossing being at Ras Ajdir on the coast (see p.334). Border formalities are taken much more seriously down here, and you can expect more thorough customs searches on both sides. From Dehibat, there is transport over the 18km to the Libyan border post at Wazin, and beyond that to Nalut, 47km away, where there are connections to the rest of Libya.

Southwest of Dehibat

Travelling south from Dehibat requires a pass from the *Gouvernorat* in Tataouine, which they are unlikely to grant. If you go, this is **gazelle** country, so keep your eyes peeled. South of Dehibat are the border posts of **JENEIN** (120km from Remada) and **M'CHIGUIG** (225km). **BORJ EL KHADRA** (also called Borj el Hattaba, and formerly Fort Saint) is at the southernmost tip of Tunisia, where the borders of Libya and Algeria meet. Even if you were allowed to cross, there's nothing very exciting on the Algerian side (the nearest important town being the oil terminal at Hassi Messaoud, 500km northwest) to Borj Omar Driss, over *pistes* to Tamanrasset and into West Africa. On the Libyan side, the ancient and fascinating former caravan terminus of Ghadames beckons. At present, however, the only way to get there is via Nalut.

travel details

Buses

Ghoumrassen to: Guermessa, Houmt Souk (Jerba), Ksar Hadada, Medenine and Tataouine.

Medenine to: Ben Gardane, Beni Kheddache, Bizerte, Gabes, Ghoumrassen, Houmt Souk (Jerba), Kairouan, Ras Ajdir, Sfax, Sousse, Tataouine, Tunis and Zarzis.

Tataouine to: Chenini, Debbab, Gabes, Ghoumrassen, Houmt Souk (Jerba), Jorf, Ksar Ouled Maztouria, Medenine, Remada, Sfax, Sousse, Tunis and Zarzis.

Louages

Ghoumrassen to: Medenine, Tataouine and Tunis.

Medenine to: Ben Gardane, Beni Kheddache, Gabes, Ghoumrassen, Houmt Souk (Jerba), Sfax, Tataouine, Tunis and Zarzis.

Tataouine to: Dehibat, Gabes, Ghoumrassen, Medenine, Remada and Tunis.

MARKET DAYS

Monday – Tataouine	Friday – Ghoumrassen, Ksar Jedid
Thursday – Beni Kheddache, Tataouine	Sunday – Medenine, Remada

PART THREE

THE

CONTEXTS

THE HISTORICAL FRAMEWORK

Tunisia has a long, dense and complicated history. The region was host to some of the earliest tool-making human cultures and was the centre of the still dimly understood Carthaginian Empire. The Romans left a clear mark and Islam arrived early in the faith's history at the end of the seventh century. Modern Tunisia is a comparatively recent creation, but the roots of the country in its present shape go back to the eighth century. What follows is the briefest of outline introductions to Tunisian history from the year dot to the end of 1991.

PREHISTORY

Around a million years ago, **early hominids** were living in North Africa's tropical climate, hunting with the primitive tools known as "pebble culture". These gradually gave way to heavy hand-axes, until, about 50,000 years ago, the discovery of fire encouraged what was by now almost *Homo sapiens* to live in fixed settlements. A culture known as **Aterian** began to make smaller, more specialized tools, and the next step forward was the arrival about 10,000 years ago of Caucasoid Proto-Hamites from western Asia. These people were probably fair-skinned, buried some of their dead, spoke a language related to ancient Egyptian,

and made the most sophisticated tools yet: barbed arrows and long, thin blades, which have been found near Gafsa and have given their name to the influential culture (Capsian Man) found as far away as Kenya.

The blades found at Gafsa have been dated to around 6000 BC, and for the next 4000 years **Capsian people**, perhaps with some infiltration from further east, continued to live in caves and survive by hunting and gathering. About 2000 BC the introduction of metals from Sicily brought Tunisia into the Bronze Age, but it was still a relatively small-scale society of nomadic hunters that the Phoenicians encountered when they arrived at the beginning of the first millennium BC. Contemporary Greek accounts consistently distinguish "Libyans" from "Ethiopians" in North Africa, and the so-called Libyans were descended from the Proto-Hamites, fair-skinned in contrast to the Ethiopians, and still speaking their remote Libyc language. The Greeks called them *barbaroi*, a name originally attached to any people who did not speak Greek and which found its final form as **Berbers**. Today's pure Berbers, of whom there are very few in Tunisia (most live in remote areas of Algeria and Morocco) are the descendants of these Proto-Hamites.

THE CARTHAGINIAN EMPIRE, 814–146 BC

The **Phoenicians** were originally drawn to North Africa from their home in the region of modern Lebanon because they needed staging posts for the long haul across the Mediterranean. Traders supreme of the ancient world, they were already heavily involved in exploiting the resources of Spain and beyond (principally metals), and the towns they founded (such as Sousse, Utica and Bizerte) were important transit points.

Traditionally, the earliest of these ports were founded around 1100 BC, **Carthage** itself in 814. Part of this ancient tradition was the myth of the foundation of Carthage (Qart Hadasht: New City) by Queen Dido (or Elissa) and a band of exiled nobles from the Phoenician homeland. The myth may reflect a genuine influx of the Phoenician ruling class, caused by Assyrian pressure at home in the ninth century BC; but it may just be a later rationalization of Carthage's supremacy among the cities in North Africa. There is little archeological evidence to support the gap between the foundations, and ninth-century dates all round may be more accurate.

At first, the Phoenician trading posts were more or less isolated enclaves on the coast. Links with the homeland were strong, and there was no reason to use the hinterland for more than immediate needs. Towards the end of the seventh century BC, however, a rival for Punic (Phoenician) trade domination appeared as **Greeks**, based in southern Italy and Sicily, began to extend their reach through southern France and eastern Spain. Conflict was inevitable, and the Phoenician cities amalgamated for security under Carthage – though the relationship was never to be easy. Fighting through the sixth century went Carthage's way, but in 480 BC the Battle of Himera in Sicily resulted in a decisive Greek victory. Forced from now on to fight its own battle for survival in the western Mediterranean, Carthage became increasingly independent of the homeland and simultaneously extended its control over the Tunisian hinterland: the Carthagian Empire was born. The year 396 BC saw another bad defeat in Sicily followed by domestic upheavals; then in 310 BC the Greek king of Syracuse, Agathocles, boldly eluding a Carthaginian army which had landed in Sicily, descended on Cap Bon and for three years devastated North Africa.

This episode was the last to involve Greeks against Carthage. The young and vigorous Italian city of **Rome** had been gradually superseding the Greeks in Italy and Sicily, and henceforth Carthage's struggle for domination of the Mediterranean basin and Europe was with this formidable opponent. The first of three famous **Punic Wars** (263–241) consisted mainly of naval skirmishes around Sicily, but also included one episode of war on land which became enshrined in Roman national legend. The Roman general **Regulus** landed with an army in Africa and had some success before being defeated and captured along with his force. He was allowed to return on parole to Rome to plead before the Senate for acceptance of Carthaginian terms, but when this was refused he kept his word as a man of honour and returned to certain death and a place in the pantheon of Roman national heroes. Roman versions of the story dwell with loving detail on the grief of his family and the brutality of his death at the Carthaginians' hands.

Carthage finally lost the war and had to accept Roman terms, surrendering its fleet and agreeing on spheres of influence in Spain. It was to Spain, however, that the Carthaginians soon turned their attention. After preliminary manoeuvring by both sides, the Carthaginian general **Hannibal** deliberately moved over the agreed border in 218 and proceeded to make his legendary march (with elephants) through France and over the Alps. Although he won initial victories at Trasimene and Cannae, he remained isolated in Italy for several years with no support, either locally or from home, which would enable him to take Rome. This was in part because the Roman Scipio had been tying down Carthaginian forces at home, and in 202 Hannibal was finally compelled to return. Scipio defeated him at the **Battle of Zama** in central Tunisia, winning the official title "Africanus". Hannibal fled to Asia Minor – and to his own place in Roman legend as a dreaded but respected opponent.

Carthage had to surrender its fleet again, and to refrain from training elephants. Although Carthaginian power had now been effectively nullified, for many Romans a threat remained as long as the city physically existed. The arch-conservative Cato used to end every speech in the Senate, on whatever subject, with the phrase "Carthage must be destroyed". A story goes that one day he came into the Senate and deliberately spilled some ripe figs on to the floor. Questioned, he replied that these were Carthaginian figs – the implication being that a Carthage this healthy was one Carthage too many.

The hawks won the day, and in 150 BC a third war was provoked, culminating in the final, apocalyptic **sack of Carthage** in 146 BC. Descriptions of this are predictably lurid, and the ruins were ploughed over with the proverbial salt to ensure that they remained barren. The Carthaginian Empire was well and truly obliterated, and the Romans set up the province of Africa in northern Tunisia.

CARTHAGINIAN CIVILIZATION

The Carthaginians always aroused hostility; by the seventh century BC Homer was describing a typical Phoenician as "grasping and well versed in deceit". Unfortunately, so little has survived of their civilization that we are forced to rely almost entirely on Greek and Roman accounts, which deserve the same caution as modern western descriptions of, say, Libya. "Phoenician faith" was a proverbial Roman term for dishonesty, and Roman mothers used to tell their children "Hannibal's coming" to make them be quiet.

But the Carthaginians do seem to have succeeded in antagonizing many of the people they came across. Hannibal crucially failed to secure any local support during his long stay in Italy, and the Romans later claimed to have had little difficulty in persuading North Africa's Berbers to transfer their allegiance. A simplistic explanation for this might be found in the Carthaginian **commercial vocation**. Their exploits in pursuit of profit were legendary. Two of these – fifth-century BC voyages west round the coast of Africa and north as far as Brittany – may be so legendary as not actually to have taken place, but at the very least they reflect Carthaginian interest in distant markets.

The competitiveness which made them such successful traders left them ill-equipped to get on with others, or even among themselves. The **Truceless War** (241–237 BC), which inspired Flaubert's novel *Salammbô*, is a graphic example. Carthage had always relied on its naval strength, recruiting mercenaries whenever a land army became necessary. When peace was made at the end of the First Punic War, there were no funds to pay the mercenaries. The authorities tried to get rid of the problem by sending the mercenaries off to Sicca (Le Kef), but with the support of the oppressed Berbers they turned on their erstwhile masters and a four-year struggle of unrelieved brutality ensued. After hiring yet more mercenaries, the Carthaginians finally won – but the episode indicates a reliance on wealth rather than loyalty, manifestly an unsuitable policy for a country aspiring to Great Power status.

From what can be gathered of **Carthaginian society**, it was oligarchical and conservative and permanently divided into jealous factions, which prevented any unified policy from being carried out. Power was concentrated in the hands of the ruling aristocratic families (or whichever one had the support of the army), and although many of the native Berbers were technically free, in practice the tribute demanded made them resentful of their effective subjection.

Characteristically for such a society, **religion** and **art** remained essentially anti-humanistic.

The most important gods were **Baal** and his consort **Tanit**, and their worship included child-sacrifice – a practice which, somewhat hypocritically, made the Romans throw up their hands in horror. But details of the less lurid aspects of their religion are barely known. At first the gods were worshipped at *tophets* (holy places), just a sacred area with perhaps a small shrine to hold a divine effigy, but gradually, under Greek influence, these became more substantial, with a monumental porch and a courtyard attached. By the fourth century BC some Greek cults were even introduced, though in modified form.

Carthaginian art was almost all derived from foreign sources – Egyptian, then Greek – and much of what little there is consists of incompetent attempts to reproduce what had been seen elsewhere. There are few original characteristics, and the most distinctive Carthaginian image – the symbol of the goddess Tanit, a bare circle balanced on stick legs – only proves the **anti-humanist trend**.

So few archeological remains have been found that it is impossible to say what Carthaginian **towns** looked like. Only domestic housing has so far been uncovered, at Kerkouane and Carthage, with none of the great public buildings which characterized Greco-Roman civilization. Under Greek influence, though, more regular civic planning may have come in. Outside their cities the Carthaginians eventually adapted very successfully after their early disinterest. Their expansion into the Sahel and the Medjerda Valley after the fifth century BC was successful enough to be mentioned by Agathocles' expedition of 310 BC, and the theoretician Mago wrote a treatise on farming that was so well considered that the Roman Senate ordered it to be translated in 146 BC.

ROMAN AFRICA, 112 BC–439 AD

The immediate attitude of the **Romans** to their acquisition in Africa was less than positive. The destruction of Carthage had been a preventive measure designed to protect the Straits of Sicily and ensure the safety of Italy: there were no plans for colonization, and the province of Africa consisted of no more than the Carthaginians had controlled, roughly everything east of a line from Thabraca (Tabarca) to Thaenae (Sfax).

Even so, Romans seem to have moved to Africa on their own initiative. In 112 BC, it was the native king **Jugurtha**'s misguided slaughter of Romans living at Cirta (Constantine in Algeria) which forced the Senate to intervene in Africa against his rampaging; presumably these were traders who had moved in to exploit the new territory. Jugurtha was king of Numidia, the native kingdom that stretched west from the Roman border through Algeria. He was the grandson of Massinissa, a Numidian king who had provided invaluable support for the Romans against Carthage in the second century BC; now that the Carthaginian threat had gone, however, there was no more incentive to support the Romans than there had been to support Carthage previously. The Romans had created a power vacuum in their province which they were eventually going to have to fill.

Jugurtha was finally defeated in 105 BC, and a few veterans were settled in the north of the province. It was only in 46 BC, however, when Julius Caesar finally won the Roman Civil War against Pompeii at the battle of Thapsus (near Mahdia), that **colonization** really took off. The existing province was extended to the west by a line running south from Hippo Regius (Annaba in Algeria), and to the east by the addition of Tripolitania (western Libya), and renamed Africa Proconsularis. As a symbol of the Roman presence, **Carthage** was refounded in 44 BC.

Under the Empire (from 30 BC), growth in Africa was phenomenal, made possible by a combination of political and economic factors. Politically, Africa was for two centuries one of the most stable provinces of the Empire. Where a small part of France needed four Roman legions (of 6000 men each) to maintain its defences, the whole of Africa needed only one. Its base moved steadily further west during the first century AD, from Haidra on the Tunisian border to Tebessa in Algeria, and Lambaesis near Batna; and a line of frontier forts was established, running westwards from the Chott el Jerid, and east from Ghadames at the southern tip of Tunisia. Within the province, the characteristic network of Roman roads grew, but they were designed to facilitate trade instead of the usual defence.

The **agricultural trade** in question was the basis of Africa's economy. In the first century AD, Africa is said to have provided two-thirds of Rome's grain requirements, to Egypt's one-third. As Rome's population swelled, the supply of grain grew to be of supreme importance: this is the era when Juvenal coined the phrase "bread and circuses", and when bad weather one year kept the grain ships from sailing there was panic in Rome. Accordingly, the Romans invested a great deal of time and expertise in developing the province's infrastructure, maximizing the potential which the Carthaginians had only touched on – they had had only themselves to feed, after all. In the second century AD olive oil production began to be encouraged in the Sahel, and other products included a gaudy yellow marble (from Chemtou); purple dye; wild animals for amphitheatre displays; coral; wood; and plain domestic pottery, which by the second century was being exported all over the Empire.

Throughout the first two centuries AD there was hardly an interruption in Africa's steady increase in prosperity and importance. By about 200 AD as many as one-sixth of Roman senators were of African origin, and in the Severans from Tripolitania, Africa provided a dynasty of emperors. In 180, however, there was a portent of things to come. The proconsul of Africa tried twelve Christians and executed them when they refused to recant their faith. The rise of **Christianity** in Africa, signalled also by the polemical writings of Tertullian, was a symptom of the problems threatening the Empire throughout its unwieldy expanse.

In 238 Thysdrus (El Jem) was the scene of a revolt which spread over the Empire and ushered in half a century of great unrest. The golden age was over, and while commitment to the Imperial way of life steadily dropped, Christianity became more widespread. In 312 Emperor Constantine was converted and the Empire officially became Christian. Constantine was trying in effect to restore the Empire to the hearts of its people, but in Africa he was foiled by the **Donatist** schism in the local Church. This was caused by Christians unwilling to accept priests who had renounced their faith in the face of persecution; to avoid being "tainted" by such priests, they formed their own communion. One famous supporter of the official Church, who spent his life trying to heal the rift, was Saint Augustine of Hippo (Hippo Regius, in Algeria).

Throughout the fourth and fifth centuries the Empire gradually crumbled in the face of internal tyranny and external aggression. One such tyranny in Africa, under Gildo (386–98), put Rome in a quandary: whether to put the upstart down, risking disruption of the all-important grain supply, or just to cut their losses. In the end, Gildo and his 70,000 men were suppressed. The external problem, raiding by local tribes, was equally serious. One pleasant theory holds that the tribes had discovered a secret weapon which decisively increased their combat strength – the camel; more likely, internal dissension was too great for organized resistance on any scale. Donatist supporters probably aided the **Vandals**, a Germanic tribe which invaded North Africa from Spain in the 420s. Their capture of Carthage in 439 put an end to the Roman era, and effectively cut the area off from western Europe. From now on, the region's loyalties would lie in a different direction.

IMPERIAL ROME

African society under the **Roman Empire** settled to two levels: a wealthy, urban, Romanized middle class, and a poorer, rural native culture. A good deal is known about the rich, because they left behind material remains that can be seen everywhere in Tunisia today. The life of the rural Berber population will always remain obscure, because their poverty produced only a meagre material culture. Although limited opportunities did exist for social advancement, the essential gap between the social classes was never eradicated, and the alienation of the less privileged Berbers was to be an important factor in the eventual disintegration of Imperial culture.

To be fair to the Romans, most of the better-off were of local origin: when one speaks of "Romans", this is usually a reference to Romanized Africans. The opportunity was there for Imperial citizens to make good – as never under Carthage – and many of them made the most of it, as the number of African senators and emperors shows. It's certainly difficult to imagine the equivalent happening in the British Empire. Other things sound more familiar, though: Septimius Severus, the first "African" emperor, had a wife who wasn't quite acceptable in smart Roman circles because of her strong accent.

The most striking fact about the **towns** where the middle class lived is that there were so many of them: literally hundreds. These smallish settlements of 5000 to 15,000 inhabitants provided homes for farming landlords, markets for their produce – and a perfect environment for one-upmanship. In the absence of any external pressures, wealth was diverted into civic and private rivalry: local plutocrats put their money into buildings and facilities on which their names would be prominently displayed. The ensuing prestige translated itself without too much difficulty into political office.

The basic aim was **Romanization**, and this meant building institutions which fostered Roman values. The spiritual heart of any self-respecting town was the **Forum**, a regular paved space enclosed by colonnades and surrounded by administrative and religious buildings. The most important of the town's religious buildings, the **Capitol**, was almost always in the Forum: it was dedicated to the Capitoline trio of Jupiter, Juno and Minerva, patrons of the Empire. Other temples and shrines served cults which were a curious mixture of Roman and local influences; the Carthaginian goddess Tanit, for instance, was given a Roman name, Caelestis (Heavenly One), and worshipped all over Africa Proconsularis. Priesthood was a temporal matter, open only to those of a certain social status and thus closely tied to political authority.

Baths may not seem like an obvious Imperial building type, but in fact they became almost synonymous with Roman civilization. They were magnificent buildings, their soaring vaulted ceilings impressive products of Roman engineering expertise, but it was the activity they housed which made them so central to Imperial life. Surrounded by mosaics and statuary, citizens of all ranks could pay a small fee and spend hours there. Actual bathing was only a small part of the full ritual, which also included exercising in gymnasia, reading in libraries or just sitting around. Other public facilities such as theatres and amphitheatres were usually set on the outskirts of the town, not far from the vast cemeteries of ostentatious mausoleums which lined approach roads. By 250 AD, the countryside was crisscrossed by 20,000km of roads, aqueducts and bridges.

In material terms Roman Africa was a great success, though historians have tended to exaggerate Rome's achievement, not least the French who, in their eagerness to put down the

Arabs, mistakenly attributed many of their engineering works to Rome. Culturally Roman Africa, best known for its lawyers, was less spectacular. Nevertheless the **mosaics**, used to decorate private homes and public buildings, reached heights in Africa almost without equal – perhaps partly because there was so little other artistic activity. The greatest name in **literature** was Apuleius, author of *The Golden Ass*, who was born in modern Algeria; others were Tertullian and Saint Augustine, the Christian writers. But these Christian names are a reminder of how briefly the Empire flourished. Once its citizens lost their faith in the Imperial dream, from the third century onwards, the physical fabric also began to crumble. No great Roman buildings were erected after the year 250, and those already standing went unrepaired. The only new constructions were churches, often built in the ruins of older temples and baths, and the **Vandals** that came later inherited a way of life that was only a shadow of its former incarnation.

THE VANDALS, 439–533

One of the northern tribes which harassed the Roman Empire to its end, the **Vandals** were a Germanic tribe of Arian Christians who worked their way through Spain into Africa. If the Donatist Berbers hoped that they would be rewarded for their support against the Romans, they were sadly mistaken. Religious persecution continued – including the destruction of religious and other images, which was the Vandals' main characteristic. If half the Roman statues in the Bardo, for example, seem to have had their noses and penises knocked off, that is down to the Vandals.

Religion apart, the conquerors found what remained of Roman luxury fatally congenial – there are reports of a great pleasure palace south of Carthage. They never got any further than northern Tunisia and, after the death of **King Genseric** in 477, a succession of weak rulers tried unsuccessfully to levy extortionate taxes from the ever-rebellious Berbers.

THE BYZANTINES, 533–646

After little more than a century, the Vandals offered a tempting target to the resurgent eastern half of the Roman Empire, now established in Byzantium (modern Istanbul). The great Emperor Justinian had grandiose plans for recovering the lost realms of the western Empire, and to this end dispatched **Belisarius**, his general, in 533. Belisarius sailed with his army to Sicily, now held by the Ostrogoths, hoping to exploit their differences with the Vandals. In the event, the landing and conquest were so easy that this was unnecessary.

The same cannot be said for the next century of **Byzantine rule**. As virtual absentee landlords, hoping to exploit the territory, the Byzantines found themselves no more able than the Vandals to control the insurgent Berbers of the west and south. They made a more concerted effort, building massive fortresses whose ruins are almost the only reminder of their presence, but the Berbers were gradually proving that they could not be ruled by force alone, and Tunisia was too remote from Byzantium to be a prime concern. In 646 the Prefect Gregory declared the province independent of Byzantium, but this new state lasted only a year before falling to the **Arabs**.

THE FIRST ARAB RULERS, 647–800

When the first wave of **Arab invaders** hit North Africa from the east and defeated and killed the Byzantine Prefect Gregory at Sbeitla in 647, their new religion of Islam was less than fifty years old. After victory at Sbeitla, the first invaders stayed long enough only to collect their share of the rich booty distributed. It was the third Islamic wave, led by **Oqba Ibn Nafi**, which finally put down roots, making Tunisia part of a vast Arab empire ruled by the **Ummayad Caliphs** from Damascus. Ibn Nafi founded Kairouan as regional capital in 670. The rest of the seventh century was taken up with quelling the last of the Berber resistance, led most famously by a legendary Jewish queen, Kahina; but in the eighth century it was with Berber converts in their army that the Arabs advanced to Spain (and ultimately as far as Poitiers in central France).

However, as with Donatism 400 years earlier, the Berbers turned to heresy as a way of asserting their independence. It took the form of **Kharijism**, a movement hostile to central government, which denied any need for the Caliph to be an Arab, and advocated his election from among all true believers (see p.386). This idea became very popular among the Berbers, who rose in rebellion under its banner. First defeated outside Kairouan in 742, they went on to conquer the city in 757 but were driven out four years later and their movement pushed into the south of the country, which remained part of a Kharijite state until 909. The Ibadites of Jerba are all that remains of it today but, paradoxically, it was Kharijism which brought Islam to almost all Berbers, making Islamicization of North Africa far more lasting than Romanization had ever been. Disaffection continued but the Berbers now broadly shared a faith with their rulers.

THE AGHLABIDS, 800–909

By the end of the eighth century, the **Abassid Caliphs** – who had usurped the Ummayads in 749 and moved their capital to Baghdad – were finding it ever harder to hold onto Spain and North Africa. When Ibrahim Ibn Aghlab put down a military rebellion and declared himself governor in 800, Tunisia became independent in all but name. The Caliph who accepted this situation, incidentally, was Haroun al-Rashid of Arabian Nights fame. For a century, Ibn Aghlab's descendants, the **Aghlabids**, controlled the whole country bar the Kharijite south. Unpopular in religious circles because of their dissolute lifestyle, the Aghlabids tried to make up for it by constructing and embellishing religious buildings throughout their domain. They also built a series of walled cities and *ribats*, most importantly Sousse, from where, in 827, they launched a successful invasion of Sicily. The island remained in Islamic hands until the eleventh century, and in 846 an Arab raiding party even managed to attack Rome and sack St Peter's.

The Aghlabids' building programme, their conquest of Sicily and raids on Italy, and their concern for irrigation and agriculture made their reign something of a **golden age** for Tunisia. Their effect on culture was also strong: by the time their emirate fell, more people in Tunisia spoke Arabic than Berber.

FATIMIDS AND ZIRIDS, 909–1148

Meanwhile, yet another heresy was finding fertile ground in North Africa. The **Ismailis**, a Shiite faction, sent one **Abu Abdullah** to Algeria as a missionary for their cause. He soon converted a number of formerly Kharijite Berbers, who joined him to invade the Aghlabid state in 903. When they took Kairouan six years later, the Syrian Ismaili leader **Obaidallah Said** decided to come to Tunisia and take over, but was imprisoned en route by Kharijites in Sijilmasa (Morocco). Abu Abdullah struck west and attacked the Kharijites, destroying their Tahirt-based state, which controlled Jerba and the south of Tunisia. On his liberation, Obaidallah declared himself *Mahdi* (see p.427) and took political power. Claiming descent from the Prophet's daughter Fatima, he began the **Fatimid dynasty** and built a new capital at Mahdia. He showed his gratitude to Abu Abdullah by having him assassinated.

Obaidallah and his successors made themselves highly unpopular through their attacks on the orthodox **Sunni** faith of most of their subjects – they had a distinguished lawyer flogged in the Great Mosque at Kairouan and various prominent Sunni theologians assassinated – and the extortionate taxes they levied to finance overseas military exploits. It was the Kharijites, however, who rose up against them. Led by **Abu Yazid** ("the Man on the Donkey") from Tozeur, they besieged Mahdia in 944 and Kairouan the following year. The revolt was not crushed until 947.

In fact, the Fatimids were never primarily interested in Tunisia: they had their eyes on Egypt, and then the Caliphate itself. Obaidallah launched an abortive **campaign against Egypt** in 914–15 but, driven out by an army from Baghdad, had to be content with consolidating his power base and establishing control of Morocco and Sicily. In 961, however, his great-grandson El Muizz seized an opportune moment and finally achieved the long-desired conquest of Egypt, founding the forerunner of modern Cairo. The Fatimids ruled Egypt until overthrown by Saladin in 1171. They left Tunisia in the charge of their nominees, the **Zirids**.

The arrangement lasted until 984, when the Zirids, under pressure from their subjects, withdrew their allegiance to the heretical Fatimids, later transferring it to the Sunni Caliphs in Baghdad. The Fatimids responded by unleashing against their former representatives the **Banu Hilal**, a hostile nomadic tribe who had been causing them trouble in Egypt. The

Hilalians descended on Tunisia in an orgy of destruction – Ibn Khaldoun compared them to a swarm of locusts – which may in reality have been merely the culmination of an already advanced process of disintegration. At any rate, they were more than a match for the Zirids, who abandoned Kairouan and holed up in Mahdia, leaving cities such as Tunis, Sfax, Gabes and Gafsa virtually independent, and the countryside under the control of **nomads** who had little use for the **infrastructure** of a settled society. This infrastructure, which had since Roman times helped to keep the region unified, fell into disuse. The country reverted to the fragmented, dark-ages conditions of early Phoenician times – a few isolated coastal centres, and an unproductive stateless interior.

ALMOHADS AND ALMORAVIDS, 1159–1229

This disarray was exploited by maritime Europeans: the **Normans** recaptured Sicily in 1072, then took Jerba and ports on the east coast, and finally Mahdia in 1148, thus ending the last remnants of the Zirid state.

They were evicted by the **Almohads**, a religious movement from Morocco which followed the teachings of a revolutionary preacher named Ibn Tumart, whom they had declared _Mahdi_. After driving the ruling **Almoravids** out of Morocco and Spain into final refuge on the Balearic Islands, the Almohads turned their attention eastwards to Tunisia. They took Tunis in 1159 and Mahdia the following year, and came to control an area stretching from Spain to Libya, uniting the Maghreb under a regime based in Marrakesh.

The Almohads' rule saw a massive growth in **Sufism** and an atmosphere of religious turmoil, but their biggest threat in Tunisia came in 1184 when they tried to subjugate the Balearic Islands. Pre-empting attack, the Almoravids under **Ibn Ghaniya** launched an invasion of Tunisia and set up a base in the Jerid. From there, they went on to conquer most of the country; but just as Tunis fell to them in 1203, an Almohad force captured their home base of Majorca and cut off their armies.

THE HAFSIDS, 1207–1574

Having regained Tunisia, the Almohads left it in the hands of a governor whose family, the **Hafsids**, ruled it from then on, declaring independence in 1229 when the Marrakesh regime repudiated Ibn Tumart's teachings. Many saw the Hafsids as the Almohads' legitimate heirs.

The Hafsids made **Tunis** their capital and gave the country the new orientation it needed. Contact with Europe was re-established after a gap of several centuries, and the trading state created by the Hafsids is recognizably the direct ancestor of modern Tunisia.

Mediterranean relations were both friendly and hostile, mutually threatening and beneficial. The Hafsids sent ships to Valencia in 1238 to help the Muslim citizens defend themselves against the Christian kingdom of Aragon; but with Valencia's fall, they opened trading relations with Aragon. These grew to such an extent that eventually a large number of Christians were able to live in Tunisia under Aragonese protection, and were even allowed to preach their religion.

This did not prevent a **crusade** (the eighth crusade) being led against Tunisia by Louis IX of France. Louis's expedition was prompted by a desire to convert the Hafsid Sultan el Mustansir and by debts owed to French traders in Tunis; but after taking Carthage, the French king died suddenly of plague (he was later canonized).

Trade was now booming in the Mediterranean, and Tunis was exploiting it more successfully than anyone. Complex agreements were signed with European states such as Venice, Pisa and Genoa. There was also trade across the desert with West Africa, and in 1262 an embassy even arrived from Norway.

Hand in hand with trade went piracy – the two were often indistinguishable – and the **corsairs of Barbary** (as North Africa was now known in Europe) became the legendary scourge of Christian merchants, plundering their goods on the high seas and selling their crews into slavery. Christian corsairs were just as efficient as their Muslim counterparts, and Genoa and Pisa had their own **slave markets**. Credit arrangements between Barbary and Europe included provisions for ransoming captured merchants and sailors.

With the proceeds of these activities, **El Mustansir** (1249–77) created a kingdom in Tunis that was recognized as the leading monarchy in the Islamic world. Cultural life flourished and building programmes established what became Tunisia's classic style of architecture, influenced by the Andalusian artisans who were encouraged to immigrate from Spain.

After El Mustansir's death, however, the Hafsid state was riven with internal strife and became so weak that Tunisia began to disinte-

Although **Islam** reached virtually all the Berbers, largely through the medium of rural marabouts, society was little more homogeneous than it had been under the Romans. The rulers – whether Aghlabid, Fatimid or Zirid – had little in common with most of their subjects. The resentment of the ever-oppressed Berbers was felt even in the most apparently stable periods – hence, for example, the secluded palaces built by the Aghlabids outside Kairouan. Occasionally this found focus in a leader such as Abu Yazid, "The Man on a Donkey" from Tozeur, and the rulers were forced to defend themselves.

Urban society, however, flourished. Scholarship, law and education centred on mosques and the religious tradition (see p.386), and in the first centuries Arab culture here, as elsewhere, was able to absorb and disperse the knowledge it acquired during its rapid expansion. A specific example in Tunisia was the introduction around Gabes of silk culture, which had first been encountered in China. **Ibn Khaldoun**, a truly original thinker, was born in Tunis in 1332 and lived through an eventful 74 years, which took in scholarship, exile and high political office. His best-known work, *Al Muqaddimah* (see p.419), set out historical principles several centuries ahead of its time. He saw history as a cycle reflecting the relative power of desert tribes and an urban state. The tribes were strong because life in the desert was harsh, they were constantly at war with their neighbours, and shared *assabiya*, solidarity that derived from their common descent and interests. The cities (and the states they supported) were, by contrast, weak, because the luxury of urban life corrupted people's bodies and their society. Tribes, such as the Hafsids in the thirteenth century, that were greedy for the wealth that control of a city offered, could defeat and take over a state that was internally weak. But as the new rulers settled into the same mould, they also succumbed ultimately to another tribe. And so history unfolded in a cycle of dynastic rise and fall, but not progress.

The physical breadth of Arab culture played a large part in spreading knowledge. The geographer **Ibn Battuta** was born in Tangier in 1304, and is estimated subsequently to have travelled 120,000km. Even in early centuries, before the advent of the Ottoman Turks, it was a surprisingly cosmopolitan society – much more so than the bloodthirsty and intolerant image cherished by its Christian opponents might suggest. The Fatimid general Jawhar ("Pearl"), who captured Egypt in 970, had been a Christian eunuch slave in Sicily, which was itself a remarkable example of its period: when the Normans recaptured Sicily for Christendom in the eleventh century, they found the Arab culture so congenial that they happily made the most of it while at the same time raiding the Tunisian coast. In 1270 Louis IX's expeditionary force at Carthage found itself fighting against the army of Frederick of Castile, who had been engaged by the sultan.

Islamic art, however, took a very different form from that of Europe. The ban on human and animal images removed at a stroke the narrative core of representative art, leaving an emphasis on disembodied form that came to be seen in **architecture** as well as in the **decorative arts**. For all their surface brilliance, Islamic buildings are distinguished most by their manipulation of space, whether in a courtyard or a dome. In a Christian cathedral, large spaces are intended to be filled; but while spaces in mosques – courtyards or prayer halls – are sometimes filled, it is when they are empty that they have most significance, symbolizing the all-embracing nature of Islam as a religion. Early architecture in Tunisia – the Great Mosques at Kairouan, Sousse, Tunis and Sfax – illustrates this aspect particularly well, and is outstanding in any company.

Later buildings from the Hafsid period onwards became locked into a more conservative and provincial style, with an emphasis on decoration rather than space. The classic elements of Tunisian architecture are the horseshoe arch (a more restrained version than elsewhere in the Maghreb) and internal stucco decoration, a skill first brought by Andalusian artisans. Along with other features – tiles, doorways, relief patterns on minarets – these make for a tradition that is at its best extremely elegant, at its worst trivially pretty – a sort of classical Rococo. Certainly the majesty of the early buildings was lost when the Fatimids took their skills to Cairo in the tenth century.

grate into small **city states** once again – Gabes, Gafsa and Tozeur being the main ones. Christians from Sicily occupied Jerba in 1284 and the Kerkennah Islands in 1286, and the region was twice split with rival sultans in Tunis and Bougie (Algeria). But in 1370, the Bougie sultan, **Abul-Abbas**, captured Tunis, took control of all the city states and islands, and reunited the country, beginning a Hafsid revival that lasted another century. In 1390, he even saw off a joint European expedition against Mahdia.

The Hafsids continued to rule until 1574 although their state was in decline, losing any real power after 1534. Even so, they had presided over a settled and prosperous era lasting more than three hundred years, one to which Tunisians still look back with some pride.

SPANISH–TURKISH RIVALRY, 1534–1574

The sixteenth century in the western Mediterranean was glamorous but violent. Moorish civilization in Spain was being toppled by the resurgent Christians and, encouraged by the capture of Granada in 1492, the Spanish launched naval raids on the ports of the Maghreb with some success. Opposition to these Christian corsairs arose in the form of the **Barbarossa** brothers Aruj and Khair ed Din, who based themselves on Jerba and set about winning back the Maghreb for Islam. After Aruj died in 1518, Khair ed Din petitioned the **Ottoman Turks** for support: still exhilarated by the capture of Constantinople in 1453, they needed no second invitation to contest such a vital region with the infidels, and Tunisia became the front line of an east–west confrontation, a sort of medieval Vietnam.

In 1529 Barbarossa took Algiers, then in 1534 he expelled the now abject Hafsids from Tunis, at the same time taking control of the east coast and Kairouan. This was too much for the Spanish, who sent a massive army in 1535 and restored the Hafsid **Moulay Hassan** as a puppet ruler. Events continued at this sort of pace for the next half-century, with Spain, France, Turkey, Naples and other powers all disputing the North African coast. In 1536 Francis I of France allied himself secretly with the Ottoman sultan against their common enemy, Charles V of Spain. Fully supporting the pope's denunciation of this unholy pact,

Charles tried to make his own arrangement with the real regional power, Barbarossa, under which Barbarossa would become Spanish viceroy of the North African coast in return for helping to crush France and Turkey. This eventually fell through, however, and in 1544 Charles and Francis managed to resolve their differences in another treaty which nullified at a stroke the previous two.

Fighting in the field was fierce – the pyramid of skulls which stood on Jerba until 1849 was the result of one clash between Turks and Spanish – but the Turks were gradually gaining the upper hand. **Dragut**, a pirate who had been enslaved by the Spanish and ransomed by Barbarossa, had extended his control from Jerba as far as Kairouan by 1557, and a flurry of activity at Tunis brought the war to a close. Taken from the Spanish in 1569 by an Algerian Turk, it fell to Don John of Austria in 1573, and then for the last time in 1574 to the combined Ottoman forces of Algiers, Tripoli and Turkey itself.

EARLY OTTOMAN RULE, 1574–1704

Tunis (like Algiers) was made a **Regency** of the Ottoman Empire, governed by a complex system which only helped to intensify internal strife. Power was divided between the **Bey**, a civil administrator in charge of the taxes levied from every town, the **Dey**, a military commander with access to the proceeds of foreign trade and piracy, and the **Pasha**, the Ottoman sultan's representative. At first it was the Deys who controlled the country: Othman Dey (1598–1610) and Youssef Dey (1610–37) were two commanders who left their mark on the architecture of Tunis, and by building up the fleet to renew its activities in the Mediterranean. In 1604 Jerba was brought back under Tunis's control. But while the Deys were busy with foreign and military affairs, Murad Bey and his son Hammouda Pasha (who combined the offices of Bey and Pasha), were strengthening their grip on domestic power, starting the first line of hereditary Beys, known as the **Muradids**. Firearms and the professional Turkish army allowed them to hold power far more effectively than any previous government and, unlike the Hafsids before them, they faced no threat of a tribal coup.

As the century wore on **European traders** were allowed back into the country. The first

One by-product of the Muslim–Christian struggles of the sixteenth century was to have a lasting impact on all the countries of the central Maghreb: the immigration of Spain's Muslim communities following their expulsion by the triumphant Spanish Christians in 1609.

Relations between the Muslims of the Maghreb and Spain had always been close, especially after the fall of Seville in 1248 and ensuing Christian advances. The Hafsid rulers of Tunis, who had previously held high command in Spain, were particularly welcoming and perhaps 100,000 immigrants arrived during the three centuries of their rule. Beginning in 1609, though, pressure on Muslims and Jews to leave Spain unless they converted to Christianity finally became formal expulsion orders: in the provinces of Valencia, Andalusia and Murcia in 1609, Aragon in 1610, and finally in Catalonia, Castile, La Mancha and Estremadura.

The resulting refugee problem bears comparison with contemporary examples. In 1609 alone, 80,000 refugees arrived on Tunisian territory at a time when the entire population of Tunis was probably around the same figure. The wealthy urban elite were encouraged to settle in prestigious streets that were set aside for them: Rue des Andalous in the southwest of Tunis's Medina is the most obvious example. Smaller-scale artisans were directed to existing smaller towns in the north such as Jedeida and Tebourba. And the majority, rural farmers, founded small communities in three main areas: the northeast corner of the country, between Tunis and Bizerte, where Kalaat El Andaleus' name (see p.146) is still an obvious sign; the fertile base of Cap Bon, in towns like Soliman and Grombalia; and the Medjerda valley, from Medjez el Bab westwards.

Religion apart, these immigrants were more Spanish than North African. Spanish-speaking, when their writers composed satires against the Spanish Inquisition, they wrote them in Castilian verse. More than a hundred years after their arrival, in the early eighteenth century, the French traveller Peyssonel found the inhabitants of Soliman and Tebourba still speaking Spanish. Their food and clothing were different and, with their eyes always on their abandoned homeland, they were reluctant to dilute their culture by marrying outside their community.

Eventually they became assimilated, but the Andalusian immigrants have left a lasting imprint on Tunisian culture. The single most visible and concentrated remnant of Andalusian immigration is Testour (see p.230), a small farming town in the Medjerda valley with a recognizably Spanish flavour.

permanent French consulate was built in the Tunis Medina in 1659, and an agreement was signed with England in 1662. Not that trade was any more tranquil than it had been before – in 1654 the English Admiral Blake bombarded and destroyed the pirate base of Porto Farina (Ghar el Melkh). But contact with the outside world boosted the opportunities for trade and began a short period of relative prosperity.

THE HUSAYNIDS, 1704–1881

The Muradid line of Beys came to an end at the beginning of the eighteenth century when an Algerian invasion had to be repulsed. The successful commander was **Husayn Bin Ali**, a Turkish soldier of Greek origin based in Le Kef, who now took control of the country on the basis of his success. Despite his Ottoman ties, he came to identify more and more with internal Tunisian interests, and from this time on the Ottoman connection, never very strong, was little more than nominal.

Such problems as Husayn had were closer to home. Having groomed a nephew, Ali, to succeed him, Husayn produced a son who naturally replaced Ali as heir. Ali responded by rebelling against his uncle, enlisting the support of the ever-hopeful Algerian Turks. Husayn was defeated once near the border at Le Kef in 1735, then killed at a battle near Kairouan in 1740. Now Husayn's sons in turn obtained Algerian support against the usurper: they too were defeated near Le Kef (1746), but ten years later succeeded in expelling Ali Pasha from Tunis. After seeing off (with some difficulty) their over-enthusiastic Algerian supporters, **Ali Bey** (1759–77) and **Hammouda Bey** (1777–1813) made Tunis once again a secure, prosperous and independent power in the Mediterranean.

But whatever their success in international politics, the Beys failed to bring Tunisia fully under their control. Even at its apogee under Hammouda Bey, the Husaynid state only governed the cities, the Sahel and the Tell. In the steppes of central Tunisia and in the far south the tribes were virtually autonomous. They paid their taxes irregularly, when forced to by a *mahalla* (military expedition), and though they might admit the Bey's sovereignty as commander of the faithful, they would not allow him to intervene in their affairs.

The **early years of the nineteenth century** were the turning point of Tunisia's modern history. Under Hammouda Bey the economy and the state were strong, but in the following years both collapsed under an assault from the west. Cooperation between European navies after the Treaty of Aix-la-Chapelle in 1816 effectively put an end to Mediterranean piracy, an important source of revenue for the Beys. To make up the loss they increased taxes on trade and agriculture, putting a heavy burden on the economy. At the same time industrialization gave European manufacturers a competitive edge that enabled them to subvert Tunisian products, first in the Mediterranean and then in the domestic market. By the 1840s Tunisia's balance of trade surplus had become a deficit.

Tunisia was also beleaguered politically. In 1830 France had seized the Beylik of Algiers on the feeblest of excuses, and in 1836 it signalled its interest in Tunisia by sending a fleet to discourage a Turkish invasion. To secure foreign protection without falling under the control of any one power, the Beys had to offer trading concessions to each of the European governments in turn, thereby aggravating the country's economic decline.

Ahmed Bey (1837–55) attempted to strengthen the state through internal reform, extending his control of local government and founding a **European-style army**. But this failed. The government could not afford these expenses and had to increase taxes and borrow from abroad. Furthermore, by employing French military advisers and going on a state visit to France in 1846, Ahmed Bey brought Tunisia firmly into the French camp, and once they had a grip they would not let go. Ahmed's successors, Mohammed Bey (1855–59) and Mohammed es-Sadok Bey (1869–82), were less dedicated to government reform than to a life of luxury. Their reckless expenditure on palaces and neglect of the administration brought the country to the brink of collapse. Not only did they contract debts at disadvantageous rates but, in 1864, the doubling of the **poll tax** led to a widespread

revolt. At one point the European consuls, fearing that the capital would be overrun, packed their bags and were ready to leave. In the end the revolt fizzled out when the government backed down and the tribes fell out with each other. But by then the government's weakness was clear to all inside and outside Tunisia.

Unable to increase taxes, the Tunisian government was virtually bankrupt. Trying to keep itself afloat, the country borrowed at ever-increasing rates from European (mainly French) banks in a spiral enthusiastically encouraged by the European powers. By 1869 Tunisia's main creditors – France, Britain and Italy – feared the Tunisian government would be unable to service these debts and that this might serve as a pretext for one of the powers to invade. In a rare moment of international cooperation they set up an **International Financial Commission** that effectively supervised every act of the Tunisian administration. Behind the scenes, however, the powers were jockeying for position. They fought among themselves to secure the contracts awarded by the Bey – the TGM railway in Tunis, for instance – and influence at court.

The only Tunisian who came close to arresting this decline was **Kherredin**. As a minister in Mustapha Khaznader's government (1857–64) he had masterminded a form of constitutional monarchy that guaranteed the **civil rights** of Tunisian and foreign citizens (the name of which, *destour*, meaning "constitution" in Arabic, lives on in the modern **Destour Party**). But jealousy at court and his unpopular pro-Turkish policies had led to his dismissal in 1862. When he returned from retirement in 1869, to head first the International Financial Commission and then the Bey's government, he realized that Tunisia's only hope was to play off one power against another while strengthening Tunisia from within. He reformed the administration, local government and the legal system, and seemed set to restore government control over the tribes and their finances. A rapprochement with Turkey enabled him to set the British and Germans, who did not want the ailing Turkish Empire broken up, against the French and Italians, who did, and so postpone the threatened French invasion.

Sadly Kherredin's government was shortlived (1870–77). Despite his reforms, the economy was still weak, and when he tried to embroil

Tunisia in Turkey's war with Russia, as a loyal country of the Ottoman Empire, the French consul, **Theodore Roustan**, was able to galvanize opposition at court and have him overthrown. Without his directing hand the administration foundered. Worse still, the French were able to secure an agreement on the division of the Ottoman Empire with Britain and Germany at the Congress of Berlin in 1878. In return for Cyprus, Britain gave France a free hand in Tunisia. And so Tunisia's fate was sealed. France's only rival in Tunisia was now Italy – a new nation eager to join the colonial powers – and when the Italians appeared to be getting the upper hand at court the French decided to act.

In **1881** France announced that 9000 Khroumir tribesmen had raided Algeria, an action they had encouraged as a pretext, and that it was compelled to defend its territory. A force of 30,000 men was sent across the border, occupying first Le Kef and then Tunis, where in May the Bey signed the **Treaty of Ksar Said**, ceding to the French all control over foreign affairs "to ensure the re-establishment of security and order along the frontier and the coast".

The Bey had given in without a fight, ordering his garrisons to surrender; in the words of a Tunisian song, "he sold his people like vegetables". Even so, resistance continued piecemeal among the tribes, led by a former *caid* (provincial governor), **Ali ben Khalifa en-Naffati**. But when **Sfax** fell in July 1882, bombarded into submission by nine ironclads and four gunboats, and then **Kairouan** in October, many of the tribespeople submitted. The remainder (100,000 people, one-tenth of the population) fled to Libya as dissident refugees. There, disappointed by the sultan's indifference and starving in squalid camps, they gradually gave in. By 1885 there were probably fewer than 1000 dissidents left.

Having defeated all opposition, the French secured their control of Tunisia. In 1883 the **Treaty of the Bardo** recognized the Bey as the nominal ruler but forced him to comply with any "suggestions" made by the French Resident General. Thus while Tunisian administrators retained executive powers, the French alone made policy.

THE FRENCH PROTECTORATE, 1881-1956

Colonial policy in Tunisia was less aggressive than it had been fifty years before in Algeria. There the French controlled the country directly and, following repeated rebellions, soldiers evicted Algerians to make way for colonists. In Tunisia the French were more clandestine, advancing the same policies under the cover of reforms to Tunisian law, usually with spurious claims to Islamic legitimacy. But the results were very much the same.

Large colonial estates were established in the Tell and Sahel by dispossessing Tunisians who lacked titles to their land. Tens of thousands of independent farmers were reduced to landless day-labourers. Iron, lead and phosphate mining concessions were granted to French companies. Taxation increased markedly but government expenditure only met the needs of the colonists. A Tunisian-sponsored colonization fund was established in 1897 to encourage **French immigration**. Roads, wells and dams were built to facilitate colonization, not local development. Railways and ports were provided for the export of Tunisian resources to the metropole. Markets and advantageous tariffs allowed French goods to flood Tunisia, swamping local industry and draining precious local capital. In short, colonization destroyed the Tunisian economy.

Within less than twenty years European settlers made up almost five percent of the population: 25,000 were French, but they were outnumbered by some 70,000 Italians. Most of the French colonists were government officials. They monopolized the higher echelons of the administration; few Tunisians achieved higher rank than a clerk. The **Italians**, fleeing impoverishment in southern Italy, set up small farms and businesses. Competition between the two communities was rife, occasionally violent. Eventually the French, fearing that their colonists would be overwhelmed by the militant Italians, many of whom were fervent supporters of Mussolini (and his Fascist designs on the country), had to restrict their immigration to redress the imbalance.

There was little Tunisian **resistance**, at first, because Tunisia's urban elite, always cosmopolitan, was not over-resentful of the French presence. Life for them, particularly those around the Bey, was still very comfortable, and the resentment of the poorer classes had no outlet beyond sporadic outbreaks of violence. Those who sought reform, moreover, were admirers of France's material and economic power. These **young Tunisians** wanted cooperation with "mother France", not confrontation: they wanted to learn before seeking full independence.

Unfortunately, the French were by no means as conciliatory. Led by the newspaper publisher de Carnières, a strong colonial lobby opposed every reform. They saw **education** as a particular threat because it would make Tunisians unsuitable for the role they were born to fill, that of servant and labourer. Their efforts were rewarded by cuts in the education budget and restriction of primary education to fewer than ten percent of the population.

Elitist and intellectual, the Young Tunisian movement could not rally popular support. Nor, despite demands for a wide range of constitutional rights, could its successor, the **Destour Party**, formed in 1920. Dominated by members of Tunisia's small professional and entrepreneurial middle class, they too were out of touch with the grass roots of Tunisian society, those who really suffered from colonization. Their nationalism came across as a peculiarly ineffectual blend of nostalgia and legal hairsplitting rather than an active and broad-based campaign for independence.

Throughout the 1920s, however, growing resentment was fuelled by the economic depression. Violent demonstrations against French containing measures gave it some expression, but there was little organization. Ever more reactionary, Destour had nothing to offer, and a new organ was needed to channel popular nationalism. It was to meet this need that a group of rebels formed the breakaway **Neo-Destour Party** in March 1934 in Ksar Essaf. Their secretary-general was **Habib Bourguiba**, whose life history epitomized the ideals of the new party. Born in 1903 into a lower-middle-class Monastir family, Bourguiba managed to make his own way by exploiting the few opportunities allowed Tunisians. He won a scholarship to the Sadiki College in Tunis, then another to study in Paris, where he became a lawyer and married a French woman, returning to Tunis in 1927. His political activism did not fully begin until 1932, when he started up a newspaper, *L'Action Tunisienne*; two years later the new party was formed.

With his background, Bourguiba was able to identify and give voice to popular aspirations in a way that the old Destour party never had, and

– for the first time in Tunisia's history – ordinary people acquired some (albeit outlawed) political muscle. Bourguiba was a formidable populist politician, and Neo-Destour immediately drew massive support for its aims of **self-determination and a return to Islamic culture**. Ever the pragmatist, Bourguiba could be heard in these years advocating a return to the veil for women.

The French were quick to spot the threat posed by this new opponent. Six months after its foundation, they declared the party illegal and, for the first of many times over the next two decades, arrested Bourguiba. But their insecurity, and popular unrest, continued through the 1930s, fuelled by the situation in Europe and the growing ambition of **Mussolini**'s Fascist Italy. Having helped themselves to Libya in 1912 (taken from failing Turkey), and Ethiopia in 1936 – to the horror of the ineffectual League of Nations – the Italians' hopes of a new African empire were rampant, and they had always felt cheated of Tunisia. The French built the **Mareth Line** – an African Maginot Line – south of Gabes, and when Bourguiba was arrested after another violent demonstration in 1938 he was quietly interned in France to avoid any suggestions of weakness in Tunisia.

WORLD WAR II IN TUNISIA

Ironically, when France fell in **World War II**, the **Italians** took Bourguiba to Rome, hoping for his support in their claim. Since, however, he trusted neither the Italians nor the Vichy French (nor much more, perhaps, the Free French), he consistently supported the Allies, even when the **Germans** landed in Tunisia in November 1942.

The Germans had invaded in response to a double Allied advance: the British across the desert from Egypt (after El Alamein), and the Americans from Algeria following the **Operation Torch** landings of November 1942. The Allies needed Tunisia as a base to invade Italy, "the soft underbelly of Europe"; the Nazis needed it to control the Sicilian Channel and thereby cut off Allied shipping from Egypt and India. By the end of the month the Allies had the west of the country, but as winter set in, they found the going harder than anticipated and, in February, **Rommel**'s retreating forces found a weak spot in the Americans' defences at

Kasserine and inflicted a serious defeat. In spite of this setback, American forces held the line before the Algerian border as Commonwealth troops streamed into Tunisia from the east. By this time too, the Allies were able to decode Rommel's most secret messages, enabling them to obtain details of his plans and to identify and sink his supply ships.

The Germans held the **Mareth Line**, designed to prevent the Italians invading from Libya and now used against the Allies. By stealth, however, and using routes thought impassable by the Germans, **Montgomery**'s Eighth Army managed to get round the line, and had control of it by the end of March 1943, linking up with the Americans to the west. Over the next month, the Allies advanced through the country, their toughest battle being at **Takrouna**, which fell to New Zealand troops on April 19. On May 7, the Allies took Tunis and Bizerte, leaving the Germans only Cap Bon, for which a fierce battle was expected. In the event, however, German forces in Cap Bon surrendered only two days later.

The campaign fought in Tunisia is little known compared with the "glamour" of Tobruk and El Alamein, but the Allies alone left **15,000 dead**. Without Tunisia, moreover, it would have been impossible for them to invade Europe.

THE STRUGGLE FOR INDEPENDENCE, 1945-1956

After the end of the war, colonizers and colonized took up much where they had left off, and the only permanent reminder of this violent interlude are the **war cemeteries** dotted around the country. To all appearances, Bourguiba's political support for the Allies, and the military support of the many Tunisians who had fought for them, had very little effect on relations – but French intransigence would almost certainly have been hardened still further if the Tunisians had supported the Axis. Even so, **Bourguiba** had to make a hurried exit from Tunis in 1945 to avoid arrest. He went to Cairo, and spent the next few years travelling world capitals to drum up support for his country's cause, with considerable success. A born showman, he took to the stage of world politics with some panache.

Back at home, popular nationalism was growing steadily. The **UGTT**, a Tunisian-only Trade Union federation formed in 1946, became an important vehicle of resistance in Bourguiba's absence. A strike in Sfax in 1947 was put down violently. By 1950 the French were ready to talk, and even accepted Bourguiba as a negotiator. After he put forward proposals in Paris, which included safeguards to French interests in Tunisia, a government was installed in 1951, headed by **Mohammed Chenik**, who had led a nationalist administration against the Axis occupation. But in a pattern that was to be repeated later in Algeria, the first signs of concession from the French home government produced a sudden hardening in the resistance of the Tunisian French. Under pressure from them, the French government reversed its policy. Bourguiba was exiled to Tabarca, then France, and **violence** escalated. In December 1952, **Farhat Hached**, secretary-general of the UGTT and a close friend and ally of Bourguiba, was gunned down in Tunis by the **Red Hand**, a group of French settler terrorists.

This only succeeded in promoting international sympathy for the Tunisians: the Latin American countries had succeeded in October 1952 in getting their problems onto the UN agenda, and a resolution was now passed calling for the resumption of **French-Tunisian talks**. There were those in France and Tunisia who thought the issue could be squashed, including a repressive French resident general immortalized for his statement that "There can be no question of putting Monsieur Bourguiba on trial. Tunisians, who are apt to forget easily, have already almost forgotten his name." But if there was no legal outlet for nationalism, the guerrilla gangs who began to appear in the hills showed that it could not be simply ignored. In 1954 France suddenly reversed its policy, worried by recent disasters in Indo-China and fearing that, if they did not come to an agreement with Bourguiba, more radical politicians might gain the upper hand. Pierre Mendes-France came to Tunis with plans for internal self-government. After many months of talks, agreement was reached in June 1955, and Bourguiba returned to Tunis to an ecstatic welcome.

The agreement, however, only gave Tunisia limited internal autonomy – foreign policy and some aspects of the economy were still to be controlled by France – and this gave Bourguiba's traditional opponents an angle of attack. They claimed that he had compromised and betrayed the Tunisian nation – this was the time in the 1950s when pan-Arabism, inspired by Nasser in Egypt, was running strong. Bourguiba's leading opponent, **Salah Ben Youssef**, defeated politically in December 1955, took to guerrilla warfare with Egyptian and Algerian support. By 1956, though, his revolt had been suppressed; Ben Youssef escaped to Cairo, and five years later was murdered in Frankfurt.

Bourguiba had always retained the support of the people, and he was well aware that full independence was within his grasp; on **March 20, 1956**, soon after Morocco, Tunisia became an independent state.

TUNISIA UNDER HABIB BOURGUIBA, 1956–1987

In the years following **Independence** Bourguiba set up the political and legal framework for the kind of state he had envisaged. Almost immediately **elections** were held for the national assembly, the result virtually a clean sweep for Bourguiba's **Front National**. By 1959 the constitution had been passed in the assembly. It gave Bourguiba wide powers as president, including nomination of government and civil service personnel, and initiation of legislation. Since all members of the assembly were nominees of the party (re-styled the *Parti Socialiste Destourien* or **PSD**), government really was Bourguiba's personal fiefdom. The small Communist Party was dissolved in 1963, to leave what was in theory a one-party state – in practice, a benevolent dictatorship under the Supreme Combatant. With the political framework in place, Bourguiba immediately set about bringing in the sweeping **social reforms** he had long sought. While in opposition, circumstances had dictated that he should call for a return to the Muslim veil for women, but now marriage laws were framed giving women a more powerful voice, and outlawing polygamy (though this had never been very widespread). Women were given the franchise, equal pay made statutory, family planning introduced on a wide scale, and education for women strongly encouraged (see p.395).

Another area of planned reform was more narrowly **religious**, and here Bourguiba had to tread very carefully to avoid alienating the religious establishment. He downgraded the great Zitouna University in Tunis to a theologi-cal faculty of the modern university, and in a still more daring step attempted to end the tradition of the Ramadan fast (see p.387). Working from within the Islamic tradition, Bourguiba obtained official support for the following ingenious argument: those engaged in a *jihad* (holy war) are excused from Ramadan; Tunisians are engaged in a *jihad* against underdevelopment; therefore Tunisians are excused from observing Ramadan. What is remarkable about this attempt is not the ingeni-ousness of the argument or the fact that it eventually failed, but Bourguiba's audacity both in challenging such a basic thread in the fabric of Tunisian life, and in getting official support for his challenge from the Mufti of Tunis. The main centre of resistance to change was the holy city of **Kairouan**, which had previously also opposed the enforcement of monogamy; the citizens pointedly observed Ramadan a day early, simultaneously with Cairo, in a gesture of Arab solidarity.

The first decade of independence was a period of mixed success. It took several years to hive off the last remnants of the **colonial presence**, occasionally at some cost. The first of the problems was the naval arsenal at Bizerte, where the French had stayed on after independence because of NATO's decision that it was a vital link. To begin with there was no antagonism, but then in 1958 French planes from Algeria bombed the border village of **Sakiet Sidi Youssef**. This incident, at the beginning of the Algerian War of Independence, was denounced as "a new Guernica", and the newly independent colony understandably felt strongly about it. Tunisia demanded the evacuation of Bizerte, the French refused, and the Tunisian army went into action for the first time. Some 1300 Tunisian lives were lost in a symbolic and drawn-out action before the French agreed to leave by 1963. Another moment of colonial tension came in 1964 when Bourguiba, under the influence of the young left wing of his party, suddenly **nationalized** the land of remaining settlers. Given his determination to maintain close relations with France, relations were soon back to normal, helped by Bourguiba's unusually repentant tone in conceding a lack of experience.

During this decade Bourguiba set his prag-matic style in **foreign policy** – a pragmatism that could at times seem paradoxically radical. In 1965, during a visit to the Middle East, he referred to the existence of Israel as a "colonial fact", implying that the Arabs should negotiate over the Palestinian question. At a time two years before the June War, when Arab rhetoric, led by Nasser, was more concerned with driving the Israelis into the sea, this was not a move calculated to improve solidarity. Indeed, Bourguiba's relations with Nasser remained explosive, partly because Bourguiba felt that he had been upstaged by Nasser as the leading man of the Arab world. Bourguiba's western orientation – in 1966 he actually voiced approval of US bombing in Vietnam – was another stumbling block, and in 1968 Tunisia boycotted the Arab League because of what it felt were pro-Soviet tendencies.

At home Bourguiba had his own problems of orientation, caused largely by the career of **Ahmed Ben Salah**. Once a leader of the UGTT trades union organization, Ben Salah had been forced out in 1956 after daring to claim an equal role for the unions in government. However in 1961 the president switched course, appointing Ben Salah as minister of planning, and began to direct the country along an increasingly leftist course. Collectivization was introduced, particularly in agriculture, with cooperatives being formed out of the old peasant smallholdings. Bourguiba went around the country on well-publicized outings where he was shown riding through prickly-pear fences, a traditional symbol of the smallholder's pride. But in 1969, Bourguiba decided that collectivization was a failure. Ben Salah and his policies were purged, and the country was given a violent twist to the right.

The Ben Salah affair was typical of Bourguiba's avowedly autocratic **style of government**: guided by the demands of the moment rather than by any long-term overriding principles, yet somehow still carrying the vast majority of the population. By appointing a **prime minister** to deal with executive matters – from 1969 – and so putting himself somewhere above everyday politics, he made himself a figure of almost royal detachment. When mistakes were made he could sacrifice a subordinate, such as Ben Salah, and enhance his own reputation by appearing to correct misjudgements that were ultimately his own responsibility. Ever a master of political in-

fighting, as well as the wider stage, Bourguiba resisted an attempt at the beginning of the 1970s to reduce his influence within the party, and in 1974 he was elected president for life.

As the 1970s wore on, however, Tunisia's international reputation for political stability and contentment in the developing world was being threatened. Early in the decade the government began to legislate against strikes, and the country's **human rights** record brought it mentions in the reports of Amnesty International. Deteriorating relations between the government and unions eventually came to a head when a strike in the mining industry in 1977 was followed in January 1978 by the first **general strike** since Independence, called by the UGTT. The strike was violently suppressed by government forces and arrests were made; in June the Socialist Democratic Movement was (illegally) formed. On the second anniversary of the general strike the mysterious **"Gafsa incident"** (see p.262), possibly a Libyan-backed coup attempt, was clearly an attempt at destabilization, however badly calculated.

By now, though, the government was making promises of **political liberalization**. In 1981 other political parties were legalized – providing, that is, they were representative, constitutional, "preserved national gains", and rejected fanaticism, violence and foreign dependence. This, in effect, meant that the government could choose and manacle the opposition by rejecting the applications for legalization made by parties that they considered too popular. As it was, the PSD/UGTT federation won all 136 seats in the November 1981 **election**, the first free election since 1956, prompting complaints of electoral malpractice from the recently formed Socialist Democrats and Popular Unity Movement.

Even more serious was the question of **Islamic fundamentalism**. Like every moderate Arab state, Tunisia was worried by the prospect of the Iranian Revolution spreading to its own shores and, as early as 1979, the government had banned the fundamentalists. In 1981 two religious movements appeared, the *Mouvement de la Tendence Islamique* (**MTI**) and the *Rassemblement Nationale Arabe* (**RNA**), only to be banned in July, before the elections. Soon after, over 100 of their leaders were summarily arrested and sentenced to long prison terms – arrests that presaged a new era of repression.

Meanwhile, discontent was fuelled by high **unemployment** (14 percent according to government statistics, but more realistically 20 percent and up to 40 percent among the young), by **poverty** (average income was only £1.25 per day), and by **repression** administered by the police and the Destour Party's unofficial militia. There was little chance of an organized popular opposition because of the government's crackdown on dissidents. Consequently, when Tunisia's youth eventually exploded in January 1984, following the government's announcement that it would remove the **subsidy on bread** (Tunisia has one of the world's highest bread consumptions), **rioting** was spontaneous. It began in the south and west, the poorest regions, and quickly spread to Tunis. After ugly street battles with the police, in which at least eighty people were killed, Bourguiba went on television to announce that the subsidy had been restored, and the riots ended almost as suddenly as they had begun.

At a government level there was some doubt as to who would be sacrificed – there being no question that Bourguiba, though head of state, would relinquish responsibility. After a brief period of uncertainty the prime minister, **Mohammed Mzali**, survived, and **Driss Guiga**, the interior minister, was made scapegoat. Yet although the government soon settled down to its austerity programme and raised the price of bread again within a couple of months, everyone knew that the riots had shaken the leadership. This tacit understanding in turn hardened government attitudes towards the opposition – and encouraged the regime's opponents to redouble their efforts.

The UGTT under **Habib Achour** quickly dissociated itself from the electoral alliance of three years before and began to campaign rigorously on the government's economic and human rights records. Achour, a rival of Bourguiba's since the 1950s, set himself up as the unofficial leader of the opposition, in the hope that he could rally the young behind a socialist flag and overthrow the government. He had little chance. In January 1986 he was arrested and imprisoned with twenty other union leaders on trumped-up charges.

With the unions now under the government's thumb it was the **fundamentalists** who represented the greatest threat. For a short time the government appeared conciliatory and accorded the banned MTI's *emir*, **Abd el Fateh Morou**, a sort of semi-recognition. But after continued student unrest and a series of bomb attacks on ministry buildings it clamped down harder than ever. **General Zine el Abidine Ben Ali**, the officer who commanded the riot troops in 1984, was appointed minister of the interior in May 1986. In the following month police appeared on the campuses, 1500 students were arrested, a publishing house with fundamentalist sympathies was closed down, and a purge of the civil service and armed forces began.

Bourguiba, who had virtually retired in the early 1980s, feared that he was losing control and began to reassert his authority throughout the administration. Early in 1986 he divorced and expelled his wife, Wassila, a formidable woman who had political aspirations of her own, and, under the guise of an anti-corruption campaign, arrested her relatives and minions. In June he appointed the 90-strong Central Committee of the Destour Party, a body that was usually elected by party members. Then in July, as a *tour de force*, he dismissed Mzali, whom he had publicly named as his successor only a month before, and replaced him with the economist **Rachib Sfar**.

Mzali, a liberal with dreams of opening up the electoral process, was a danger to Bourguiba and his continuing control of power. It was no surprise, then, that the **elections of November 1986** were a sham, even boycotted by the recognized opposition parties. As for the fundamentalists, Bourguiba became even more determined that they should be eliminated. They were, he stated in private, a menace to the very nature of the secular state he had created and to destroy them would be the last great service he could render his country.

Early in 1987 the police began arresting suspects on the streets and by the end of April more than 2000 people had been jailed, among them **Rachid Ghannuchi**, the new leader of MTI. The Tunisian League of Human Rights complained about torture and detention without charge, only to find its offices closed and its leader under arrest. Men shaved off their beards to avoid suspicion and women took off their *chadors*. In March the government broke off relations with Iran, claiming that Iranian

THE HISTORICAL FRAMEWORK/375

diplomats were inciting political unrest and providing the fundamentalists with arms. Shortly afterwards Rachid Ghannuchi and ninety other fundamentalists were charged with promoting terrorism and conspiring with Iran to overthrow the state.

Far from frightening the fundamentalists into submission, the campaign of repression sparked off a series of retaliatory **demonstrations and bombings**. And in August the fundamentalists showed that they were willing to strike at the government's Achilles heel: the economy. Bombs planted at four hotels near Monastir injured twelve tourists and threatened to mar Tunisia's reputation as a safe holiday resort. With **tourism** the country's most important source of foreign exchange and an employer of ten percent of the population, this would be a severe blow.

Fortunately, the government backed down from further confrontation. At the end of September only nine of the fundamentalists on trial were sentenced to death and five of them were sentenced *in absentia*. Then at the beginning of November – amid rumours of Bourguiba's ill health – Rachid Sfar resigned as prime minister to be replaced by **General Ben Ali**. Within a week (on November 7, 1987, a date commemorated in the names of many streets) Ben Ali had seized power in a **palace coup**. Bourguiba was diagnosed as senile, not surprisingly given his decrepit appearance in the previous months, and forced to retire. Ben Ali's opponents and rivals were placed under house arrest and a new administration was formed.

Most Tunisians sighed with relief. Despite continuing affection for Bourguiba, particularly among older Tunisians who remembered the French occupation, he was considered too old and out of touch to govern effectively. The question of succession had, moreover, created a great deal of uncertainty over the previous decade and its settlement was seen as a sign of returning stability.

Once in power, Ben Ali pursued a policy of **national reconciliation**, releasing 5000 political prisoners over the next six months, including MTI leader Rachid Ghannuchi. He reduced government interference in the internal politics of the UGTT trade union federation and began

to introduce **political reforms**, banning imprisonment without trial, relaxing political censorship and putting the presidency up for election every five years.

In February 1988, Ben Ali announced that the ruling PSD was to change its name again, henceforth being known as the *Rassemblement Constitutionnel Démocratique* (Democratic Constitutional Assembly, or **RCD**). Limited freedom of political activity was also introduced, with opposition parties allowed to operate, and recognized by the state, so long as they were not anti-constitutional, religious, ethnic nor regional. A number of opposition parties were legalized – though not the fundamentalist MTI.

At the RCD's first conference in July 1988, Ben Ali promised free expression and free **elections**. The latter materialized in April the following year, and resulted in the RCD taking all the seats and, apparently, eighty percent of the vote. Their main challengers were Islamic fundamentalists who, banned from fighting the election as a party, fought as independents and obtained up to a quarter of the vote in some areas. The MTI, now called **Ennahdha**, dismissed the elections as fraudulent, and Rachid Ghannuchi moved to Paris where he felt freer to speak out.

Political **liberalization** continued through 1989, with more amnesties and talk of legalizing Ennahdha, but when this proved to be little more than talk, Ennahdha began to step up its activities. In December, a group of fundamentalist students began a hunger strike in protest at government attempts to close the faculty of theology at Zitouna University in Tunis. Allegations of government inaction following the **January 1990 floods**, which killed thirty people and left thousands homeless, added fuel to the movement, together with a strike by municipal workers, riots in Nefta and Sidi Bou Zid, and clashes in Sfax and Kairouan between police and students associated with Ennahdha. The alarm bells really started ringing when fundamentalists scored a massive victory in **Algerian municipal elections** in June 1990. Arrests began in September as **repression** set in. Twelve opposition publications were closed and Ennahdha's student organization banned. Meanwhile, moves were made to bring the legal opposition into the establishment fold. Legal opposition parties were given free seats in 1991 by-elections, and guaranteed **hand-**

outs from the pork barrel. The illegal opposition were portrayed as "terrorists", with allegations of bomb-making and coup attempts. Since then, the **human rights** situation has deteriorated, and **Amnesty International** has expressed its concern. In October 1991, three fundamentalists were executed for the murder of a security guard in a raid on RCD offices.

Tensions reached a climax in 1992. While the government in neighbouring Algeria cancelled general elections that were about to be won by the FIS Islamist party, the Tunisian government held mass trials of the 300 principally **Islamist dissidents** who had been arrested a year earlier. Most were sentenced to lengthy terms in prison, and **Rachid Ghannouchi**, the Ennahdha leader, tried *in absentia*, received a life sentence although he was subsequently granted political asylum in Britain.

The trials attracted widely unfavourable coverage in the West from human rights observers such as Amnesty International, which issued a critical report in 1993 containing allegations of torture and harassment of Islamists and their women relatives. Amnesty's allegations were strenuously denied by the government, as well as by several opposition parties and prominent Tunisian women activists, but they were followed in 1994 by a critical human rights assessment from the US State Department. The government's response has been to protest its innocence on the one hand while at the same time cracking down severely on what it perceives as unfair coverage. A BBC correspondent was expelled in February 1994, and other journalists – both local and foreign – have been on the receiving end of official and unofficial sanctions. Meanwhile, the regime continues to consolidate its position. In March 1994, **Ben Ali** was re-elected president for a further five-year term, winning 99.9 percent of the vote.

TUNISIA'S FOREIGN RELATIONS

Ben Ali's problems don't stop at home. **Relations between Tunisia and its neighbours**, especially Libya, have had their ups and downs. In the late 1970s Tunisia accused Libya of interfering in its internal affairs, and it was generally believed that Libya had backed the "Gafsa coup" in 1980. After Tunisia lost a border dispute settled at the International Court of Justice, tension increased. In March 1985 the Libyan Voice of Vengeance radio station called on Tunisians to massacre their Jewish community and in the same month police arrested seven suspected "terrorists" crossing the border. Then, at the beginning of August 1985, Libya expelled 31,000 Tunisian workers, most of them illegal immigrants. Libyan troops began to mobilize on the border and Habib Bourguiba said privately that he was ready to go to war. Arbitration by Kuwait managed to avert such drastic measures, but relations between the two leaders remained sour.

Since Ben Ali took power, however, there has been a dramatic improvement. The **Great Arab Maghreb**, based on a 1983 treaty between Tunisia and Algeria, has been gradually widened to include Morocco, Mauritania and, since June 1988, Libya. Libya has compensated the workers expelled in 1985 and opened its frontier with Tunisia, while the two countries have agreed freedom of movement between them, the right

ALGERIA

Since early 1992, when the government cancelled elections expected to be won by the FIS (*Front Islamique de la Salvation*) Islamic party, Algeria's internal security situation has been slowly deteriorating into what is now virtually a civil war between the forces of the establishment (in essence, the army) and of the Islamic movement. As of early 1995, as many as 30,000 people had already died in the vicious struggle between hardliners on both sides. Victims of the security forces have included ordinary citizens suspected of allegiance to their Islamist opponents, while the Islamists have targeted not just security and government officials, but anyone involved in what they perceive as a West-tainted activity: to date this has included journalists, a *rai* (pop music) star, feminists and sporting officials. Few of the victims in absolute numerical terms have been foreigners, but two extremist Islamist groups have stated publically that they are explicitly targeting foreigners and most Western governments now officially discourage their nationals from visiting Algeria.

of their citizens to live and work in both countries, and there has been amicable settlement of a dispute over Mediterranean oil fields. The February 1989 establishment of the **Arab Maghreb Union**, an EEC-like organization of the five Maghreb states, has helped to normalize relations further.

Ben Ali has also been successful in maintaining good **relations with the West**, in particular with France and the USA. America was the first country to recognize independent Tunisia and so it is not surprising that bonds between the two countries have been solid. Tunisia has **Peace Corps** workers and American military advisers, and in 1986 the Tunisian and American armies carried out a joint exercise. Many Tunisians believe that Ben Ali, who was trained in the USA, came to power with America's tacit support if not positive blessing. Certainly Tunisia makes a valuable United States ally: not only does it lie between Algeria and Libya, but the naval base at Bizerte is one of the best in the Mediterranean.

Relations with the West, however, came under great strain during the **1991 Gulf crisis**.

Following Iraq's invasion of Kuwait, the USA and its allies, including Egypt and Saudi Arabia, sent troops and attacked Iraqi forces. In Tunisia, public opinion was massively behind Iraq's leader, Saddam Hussein, who was seen as a champion of the Arab nation against Western interests, a kind of latter-day Nasser. Fortunately, the fundamentalist opposition, funded largely from Saudi Arabia, was unable to capitalize on this feeling and Ben Ali successfully outflanked them, opposing American intervention, but not strongly enough to alienate his Western friends. Tourism, accounting for over ten percent of Tunisia's GDP, suffered badly but has now returned to normal, while elsewhere, with fundamentalism so far contained, Tunisia seems to have settled back into "business as usual".

PROSPECTS FOR THE 1990s

The **economy** is still shaky after the ravages of high inflation in the 1970s, but the IMF-imposed austerity programme introduced in 1987 has stopped the growth of Tunisia's huge national debt and brought inflation down to

TUNISIAN STREET NAMES

Throughout Tunisia, you will come across **street names** commemorating key dates and personalities from the country's recent history; the following is a brief rundown, and you'll find more details of the country's history, from p.357.

Bechir Sfar (1856–1917) and **Ali Bach Hamba** (1876–1918) were two early nationalists who co-founded the young Tunisians movement in 1907. A famous speech by Sfar in 1906 is considered one of the key events in the development of Tunisian nationalism, and he was known as the "second father of the reawakening", the first being the Turkish official **Khereddin** (see p.368). Next in the sequence of nationalist movements was the Destour party, founded in 1920 by **Abdelaziz Thaalbi** (1874–1944) but soon to be overtaken by the Neo-Destour party, founded on March 2, 1934, at the Congress of Ksar Hellal by the young French-educated lawyer **Habib Bourguiba** (1903–).

Among Bourguiba's colleagues in the movement were **Hedi Nouira**, **Habib Thameur** (1909–49) and **Ali Belhouane** (1909–58), a teacher at Sadiki College. On **April 9, 1938**,

Belhouane led an anti-French demonstration in Tunis that ended in violence, with as many as a hundred people killed; the result of the demonstration was the banning by the French authorities of Neo-Destour and the arrest of Bourguiba and other leaders. Bourguiba moved from jail in France to Rome before returning to Tunisia in 1942, but he found himself as unwelcome as before by the authorities. On March 25, 1945, he made a dramatic escape by fishing boat from Kerkennah (see p.217) and spent the next few years abroad. In his absence a reconstituted Neo-Destour received valuable support from the UGTT national union movement (*Union Générale Tunisienne de Travail*), among whose leaders were **Habib Achour** and **Farhat Hached** (assassinated in 1952). Negotiations for independence proceeded with Bourguiba in exile on the island of La Galite off Tabarca (see p.149), but on **June 1, 1955**, he made a triumphant return to Tunis to supervise the final stages, and on **March 20, 1956**, the final protocol was signed in Paris. Following Independence, Bourguiba served as president until **November 7, 1987**, when he was peacefully deposed by the current incumbent Ben Ali.

manageable levels – officially, at least, less than ten percent. Inevitably, this has involved unpopular measures such as an **earnings freeze** for public employees (the state is Tunisia's biggest employer), **devaluation of the dinar**, and **abolition of food subsidies** – only this time gradually to avoid serious repercussions like those of 1984.

The future is, however, far from certain for Ben Ali and Tunisia. As Bourguiba's heir, Ben Ali has a hard act to follow in many ways. When future generations look back they will judge Bourguiba as the father of his country. Following independence, he provided Tunisia with the framework for a constitutional and secular democracy, even if the reality did not quite live up to the ideal. His self-identification with the country's destiny gave Tunisians a national cohesion lacking in many developing countries. Tunisia's standard of living is one of the highest in the developing world, with little of the extreme poverty experienced in Morocco and Egypt. All Tunisians have access to education as far as university level and to health services. Actual social progress may have lagged behind the radical legal framework introduced nearly 40 years ago, but it is a mark of just how far Tunisia has come that it tends to be judged – not least by Tunisians themselves – by Western standards rather than those of its 1950s contemporaries.

The tradition of secularism and development seems safe enough in Ben Ali's hands, and yet as the country returns to **political repression and fundamentalist unrest**, the question remains: how many of Bourguiba's vices may Ben Ali have inherited along with his virtues?

ARCHITECTURE

Seeing the ancient sites in Tunisia inevitably takes you to mosques – which, unlike those in Morocco and much of the Islamic world, are often open to non-Muslims. They follow the same basic plan, whatever their size, style and age, the most important model in Tunisia being the Great Mosque of Kairouan (for a plan, see p.192).

Besides this religious architecture Tunisia has a wealth of domestic architecture which, unadvertised and often hidden, can say more about Tunisia than any mosque or beylical palace. The best way to see domestic architecture is just to wander around the medinas and the villages. Although you can walk into many of the semi-public outer courtyards, you should be sensitive – like most people, Tunisians get upset if strangers walk uninvited into their homes.

This brief account is an attempt to introduce and explain the design, development and function of Tunisian buildings.

MOSQUES

All mosques face **Mecca**, the birthplace of Islam, the site of the *Ka'aba*, the place of pilgrimage, and, most important of all, the direction of prayer. In the mosque this direction is shown by the **mihrab**, a shallow alcove in the *qibla* (literally, the facing) wall. This is not an altar. The direction, not the niche, is sacred and representations of the *Ka'aba* are often placed there to emphasize this point. The mosque is built around the axis passing through the *mihrab*

and at right angles to the *qibla* wall, so that the whole building faces Mecca. (Incidentally, toilets and beds are usually aligned at right-angles to the axis so as not to profane.)

The mosque is a place of worship and a sanctuary, its separation from the world outside guaranteed by high, often windowless walls and strong gates. Inside, large mosques usually have a courtyard like a house does. The parallel is important, for Islam considers its adherents a family. At the *qibla* end of this courtyard, nearest Mecca, is the **prayer hall** – broad rather than long because the front row of worshippers receives greater *baraka*, or blessing from Allah, than those behind. What restricts their breadth is the ability of worshippers at either end to hear the calls to prayer and so act in unison with the rest of the congregation.

The prayer hall has to be ritually pure, so it is usually separated from the remainder of the mosque by a step or balustrade – before entering worshippers must take off their shoes so that no dirt is carried in. The worshipper must also wash before prayer – either partially or totally depending on their state of ritual impurity – and a **washing fountain**, a well leading to the cistern below, is often provided in the centre of the courtyard (as at Kairouan's Great Mosque) or in a washing room to the side (as at the Jema'a Zitouna in Tunis).

Inside the prayer hall there is very little religious furniture. The **imam** leads the prayer and preaches from a **minbar** – a pulpit, usually just a flight of steps in ornately carved wood, occasionally a permanent structure in stone. The imam sits on the second step from the top, the highest step being reserved for the Prophet. In the days before loudspeakers the imam's voice was amplified by the **muezzin** sitting on a raised wooden platform, or **dikka**, and then relayed through the congregation by strategically placed respondents, the *muballighun*. Today the only other piece of furniture is the **kursi es-sura**, the wooden lectern, usually placed next to the *minbar*. This is important because recitation, *tawliq*, considered a great art in Islamic society, is the basis of the service. Otherwise the prayer hall is bare. There are no pews (the congregation sitting instead on a floor covered with carpets in the richer establishments and alfa matting in the poorer), no elaborate screens, and no paintings.

Other rooms or buildings may be added to this basic design according to the size and function of the mosque. There is usually a **minaret**, the most distinctive feature of the mosque on the skyline, from where the *muezzin* calls the faithful to prayer. Some mosques have **tombs**, often crowded against the *qibla* wall, sometimes the centrepiece and *raison d'être* of the building. Others have **dormitories** for pilgrims or students, or a school room and library. But all these are appendices to the basic plan, for, in essence, the mosque is simply the *mihrab* and the prayer hall. Most of the **masjid** – mosques used for daily prayer – are just that. It is only the larger congregational mosques used for Friday prayer, the **jema'a**, that have all these features.

Stylistically one can trace a gradual move towards lighter construction and more ornate decoration over time. The first mosques, those of the **Aghlabids**, used heavy columns, frequently of Roman origin, massive construction, and little or no decoration. The prayer halls were, consequently, dark, and much more impressive in their size than in their style of construction. Later the Zirids introduced the first domes and so gave prayer halls extra light and a sense of space. With brighter interiors artists were able to develop finer and more sophisticated decoration. Under the **Hafsids** these trends continued, with domes becoming larger and covering more and more of the prayer hall, and decoration becoming more detailed and sumptuous. Then, during the **seventeenth century**, Turkish architects revolutionized styles. The dome was extended to cover the whole prayer hall, the superstructure was reduced to a minimum, allowing for more windows, and **Ottoman** and **Italian** decorative features – the keel arch, painted tiles and stucco plasterwork – were adopted. Prohibitive construction costs prevented the architects of less monumental mosques from adopting the massive domes seen at the Jema'a Sidi Mehrez in Tunis, but more modest Ottoman ornamental features spread throughout the country. Since then, styles of construction have changed little, except that modern mosques are built in reinforced concrete and their tiles and arches are more likely to be mass-produced than hand-crafted.

DOMESTIC ARCHITECTURE

For Tunisians the **home** should be genuinely private. Walking around the medina in any city you are immediately struck by the lack of windows looking out onto the narrow streets. Those that exist have heavy bars or ironwork grills, and doors leading into the houses are made of thick wood reinforced with iron studs. Tunisian houses look in towards the family, not out towards the wider world.

Traditionally, family life took place within a **courtyard**, the *wust al-dar*, a private place where visitors are rarely admitted. Here women could go about unveiled, protected from the prying eyes of strangers. Between the courtyards and the outside world was a **hall**, the *driba*, with benches built against the wall, or a second courtyard, the *wust el-dwiriya*, a sort of antechamber to the house where the men of the family could entertain visitors. Within the living quarters rooms were arranged around smaller covered "courtyards" so that a single building could accommodate numerous related families.

In contrast to the plain and anonymous outside walls of Tunisian houses, these courtyards and the living rooms behind them displayed extravagant **decoration**. Since the Middle Ages floors have been made of tessellated slabs termed *keddal*, with designs of black and white marble (from the Jebel Ichkeul) in the wealthiest houses. In the seventeenth century hand-painted **tiles** from Qellaline and Nabeul became popular (to be replaced by cheap Italian factory-made copies in the nineteenth century), and most houses have tiles up to shoulder height on the walls. A fashion for ornate geometric **stuccowork** also developed in the seventeenth century, and in the houses of wealthier Tunisians this delicate tracery begins above the tiles and continues over the vaults. During the nineteenth century, **paintwork**, abandoned in the fifteenth century, regained favour, particularly on the wooden ceilings and rafters of upper floors. Consequently the houses of wealthy families were full of colour and ornamentation.

Architectural features changed with fashion. During the seventeenth century, when North Africa was opened up to Mediterranean, particularly Italian, influences, a **loggia** was often added to the courtyard, usually three "moorish" arches on classical columns. More substantial houses had peristyle courtyards, a balcony supported on vaults with ornate wooden balustrades. Twin windows were yet another Italian import.

Yet whatever changes of detail fashion might impose, the basic structure of the town house remained unchanged until the early years of the twentieth century. Not only did this design suit the social context, but it was also functional. The inner courtyards made the living rooms light and encouraged a through draught that made the rooms cool in summer. Some of the houses were **foundouks** (merchants' "hotels"), those of the European merchants doubling up as consulates; the lower floors, readily accessible through the courtyard, provided *makhzen*, storage space and stabling. The courtyard itself covered a cistern, or *madjus*, containing the rainwater that fell on the marble floors and the roofs of storage cellars.

Urban houses were crammed into the limited space inside the city walls, making housing densities very high (about the same as early Manhattan in the case of the Tunis Medina). For this reason the city streets were narrow, convoluted, and seemingly chaotic. Yet chaotic they certainly were not. Within the city each ethnic group occupied its own **fariq**, or quarter. In Tunis, for instance, the Jews were segregated in the Hafsia and surrounded by a wall, the Europeans down near the Bab el Bahr. Early on in the indigenous quarters there was no segregation by class or wealth; instead, the households were clustered in loose ethnic or family groups. Many of the streets were impasses, sometimes called **darb**, hidden from major thoroughfares by sharp bends. Family groups lived around these *darb*, which still bear their names. The street provided a sort of outer courtyard used by the wider family group.

This urban structure and building style began to change when the **French** arrived. The new grid cities they built – the **Villes Nouvelles** – became the favoured quarters of wealthy Tunisians, who gradually abandoned the medinas. Their new houses or, more often, apartments, reflected their aspirations to French culture and their assimilation of a new individualistic social order. Boulevards and segregation by wealth replaced the equality of the **medina**'s narrow streets; isolated houses

replaced the intimacy of the *darb*; and the smaller house of the nuclear family replaced the huge segmented house of the extended family.

Independence accelerated rather than reversed the process of westernization. The new Tunisian middle class soon assimilated the social values and tastes of their European predecessors and with them their architecture. Expensive **suburbs**, much like those around any southern European city, gradually surrounded the larger towns. Today some of the architects are returning to the details of traditional housing, using arches, painted (though factory-produced) tiles, and even stucco plaster, but the inspiration and the design remain fundamentally European.

The departure of the wealthy inhabitants has inevitably led to the **decline of the medinas**. Houses have been divided up into one-room apartments, *oukala*, where families live in appalling conditions of overcrowding. Without an influential political lobby some of the medinas' residents go without electricity, water or mains drainage. The fabric of the buildings has also suffered from lack of repair, unsympathetic modifications and dangerous extensions on roofs and walls. Faced with deteriorating conditions and soaring rents, many of the original residents preferred to move out, if only to a *bidonville* shantytown on the outskirts of the city, leaving the medina to recent immigrants.

A UNESCO-funded project to save the Tunis Medina's architecture is in full swing but the fruits are yet to be realized. If it is to be a success it will not be enough just to refurbish the buildings: money needs to be injected to revitalize the Medina's economy and change social attitudes so that it once again becomes a desirable place to live.

Rural domestic architecture has undergone the same transformation as urban architecture in the last century. Houses, usually of reinforced concrete, that follow the same pseudo-European design are squeezing out traditional styles (see especially "The Ksour", Chaper Nine). Tunisia's architectural diversity is being replaced by a rather tacky and depressing homogeneity.

A CHRONOLOGY: MONUMENTS AND EVENTS

Tunisian buildings often bear a plaque stating the date of construction, or sometimes of restoration or additions to the building. Although the numerals and calendar are unfamiliar, if you treat this as a puzzle to solve, it's not difficult to translate.

١	٢	٣	٤	٥	٦	٧	٨	٩	٠
1	2	3	4	5	6	7	8	9	0

The 1 and the 9 are easy enough and the others don't take long to become familiar with. As for the years, the Islamic calendar began with the Hegira, Mohammed's flight to Medina in 622 AD (which was thus 1 AH). Moreover, the Muslim year is a little shorter than the western. To convert AH to AD, you add 622, then subtract the original AH year multiplied by 3/100, ignore anything after the decimal point and you have the AD year in which that AH year began. Thus, for example, 1416 AH = 1416 + 622 - [3/100 x 1416], and therefore began in 1995 AD.

10,000–6000 BC	**Capsian Man** appears throughout North Africa	Implements found near Gafsa give name to this culture
2000	Introduction of metals from Sicily begins Bronze Age	
1100	Earliest Phoenician settlements	
c.800	**Carthage** and other major Phoenician ports founded	
600–300	Increasing conflict in western Mediterranean between **Carthaginians** and **Greeks**	
310	Expedition of Agathocles from Syracuse into Carthaginian territory	**Carthaginian civilization** almost completely lost, thanks to Romans and overbuilding. Some houses at Carthage and Kerkouane; many funerary artefacts; occasional monuments (Maktar, Dougga, etc)
263–241	First Punic War between Carthage and Rome, including Regulus expedition	
218–202	Second Punic War – Hannibal crosses Alps from Spain with elephants	
150–146	Third Punic War – Carthage sacked in 146	First informal Roman settlements in new province
112–105	Jugurthine War in province of Africa	
46 BC	Caesar defeats Pompeii at Battle of Thapsus: Roman Civil War won, Carthage refounded	
1–200 AD	Almost uninterrupted growth in prosperity of Africa as rich province of **Roman Empire**; control gradually extended west to Morocco, south to Chott	**Roman** town plans and buildings imposed throughout province: theatres, baths, temples, forums, amphitheatres, bridges, aqueducts

193	**Severan** dynasty of African Emperors from Libya	
235	Uprising at Thysdrus makes Gordian briefly emperor – end of the Empire's golden era	El Jem amphitheatre possibly built now, but after 250 AD fewer and fewer Roman monuments
312	Empire becomes officially Christian, but Donatist schism in Africa is vehicle for disaffection with Imperial rule	**Churches** built in ruins of old Roman buildings
429–535	Carthage falls to **Vandal** invaders from Germany (429), who rule province for a century	Vandals leave minor monumental marks: Basilica of Hildeguns at Maktar and chapel at Haidra
535	**Byzantine** invasion, inspired by Justinian and led by Belisarius, drives out Vandals	Many **fortresses** indicate fragility of Byzantine control
647	**Arab invaders** defeat Byzantine Prefect **Gregory** at Sbeitla	
670	Third wave of invasion under **Oqba Iba Nafi** settles and founds Kairouan as capital	First **mosque** built at Kairouan on site of present Great Mosque
800–900	Prosperous **Aghlabid** dynasty rules Tunisia from Kairouan; Sicily captured 835	Aghlabids build **Great Mosques** at Kairouan, Tunis, Sousse, Sfax, and **ribats** along the coast. Simple forms
909–970	Heretical **Fatimids** rule from Mahdia, resisting **Kharijite** revolt led by Abu Yazid (940), then move to Egypt, from where they unleash destructive Banu Hilal invasion	Fatimids build Great Mosque at Mahdia, make additions to Great Mosque at Sfax
1059–1159	**Khourassanid** dynasty rules principality of Tunis during Hilalian invasions – **Normans** and other Christians raid east coast	Hilalians destroy much vital infra-structure throughout the country; Ksar Mosque built in Tunis
1236–1534	**Hafsid** dynasty establishes Tunis as capital; a century of great prosperity and prestige, followed by gradual decline	Tunis **Kasbah** and **medersas** built; influx of **Andalusian** arti-sans brings Moorish techniques such as stuccowork; Hafsid archi-tecture becomes the "classic" style of the country; first great souks in Tunis
1270	Abortive invasion (Crusade) by Louis IX (St Louis) of France	
1300–1400	Mediterranean trade and Christian attacks; domestic insecurity	
1534–81	**Hispano-Turkish** struggles for control of Tunisia and North African coast: Tunis taken by Turks (1534), Spanish (1535), Algerian Turks (1569), Don John of Austria (1573), combined Turks (1574)	Many Spanish and Turkish **forts** along the coast (La Goulette, Bizerte, Kelibia)

1580–1705	Regency of Tunis part of Turkish **Ottoman Empire**, ruled by Deys and Beys; Othman Dey (1584–1610) and Murad Bey (1612–31) secure power	**Hanefite** mosques built (octagonal minarets) in Tunis: Youssef Dey (1616) and Hammouda Pasha (1655). increasing use of Italianate elements, but also pure Turkish Sidi Mehrez mosque in Tunis (1675)
1600–1700	**Trade** and **piracy** at their height; French Consulate established in Tunis 1659, agreement with Britain 1662; Porto Farina bombarded by British Admiral Blake (1654)	
1705	**Husaynid** dynasty established; Turkish connection increasingly nominal, internal struggles aggravated by Algerian Turks	Security and prosperity bring lavish building programmes: **Mosque of the Dyers** (1716) and **Mosque of Sahib At Tabaa** (1780s); **mederssas** throughout Tunis Medina; **palaces** (Dar Ben Abdallah, Dar Husayn)
1700–1800	Tunisia's last great era before independence under Ali Pasha (1759–82) and Hammouda Bey (1782–1814)	
1741	Expeditions against coral establishments at Tabarca and Cap Negre	
1784	French and Venetian fleets bombard Tunisian ports	
1830	**French** takeover in Algeria; slave trade ends, leaving Tunisia in increasing economic straits; England, France and Italy all manoeuvring for position	Last luxurious buildings help to bankrupt the country; **palaces** at Bardo, Mohammedia; **arsenal** at Ghar el Melkh
1860–64	**Kherredin**'s constitutional reform	Kherredin's Sadiki College built in Tunis
1869	International Financial Commission takes over bankrupt country's finances	Pseudo-oriental **cathedrals** built at Carthage and Tunis
1869–77	Kherredin prime minister; administrative and judicial reform, diplomatic measures to prevent colonization	
1881	**French invasion**, on spurious excuse of Khroumiri raids, and colonization	**French quarters**, founded outside old medinas, become city centres; vast estates created and farmhouses built in the countryside; naval arsenal founded at Bizerte
1920	Nationalist Destour Party founded	
1930	Catholic Congress at Carthage helps inspire Bourguiba's nationalism	
1934	**Neo-Destour Party** founded and soon banned by French	

1942–43	Tunisian Campaign (WWII)	Mareth Line emplacements; Commonwealth, French, US and German cemeteries stand as reminders
1952	Farhat Hached murdered by Red Hand terrorists; Tunisia problem discussed at UN	
1955	Bourguiba returns to Tunis with internal autonomy	
1956	**Independence**, March 20	
1957	Declaration of **Republic**	
1976	The first major strike, and demonstrations	
1978	The first general strike since independence sparks off a wave of government repression	
1980	Gafsa "coup" attempt	
1981	First free elections; parties restricted; accusations of vote-rigging	
1984	Bread riots start in the south and spread to Tunis	
1985	Conflict with Libya comes to the brink of war	
1987	Bourguiba overthrown by Prime Minister Zine el Abidine Ben Ali	

ISLAM: THE BACKGROUND

Since many visitors to Tunisia will be new to Islam, a very basic background is given here, comprising some theory, some history, and a sense of Tunisia's place in the modern Islamic world.

A NEW FAITH

The founder of Islam was the **Prophet Mohammed**, an Arab from the rich trading city of Mecca, now in Saudi Arabia. In about 609 AD he began to hear divine messages which were transcribed directly as the Koran. God claimed to have been misunderstood by earlier religions – Judaism and Christianity – and in Islam, Jesus is only one of a number of prophets.

The main characteristic of the new religion Mohammed founded was its directness, a reaction to the increasing complexity of the established faiths, and its essential tenet was simply "There is no God but God, and Mohammed is His Prophet". There is no intermediary between people and God in the form of an institutionalized priesthood or complicated liturgy, and worship in the form of prayer is a direct and personal communication with God. As well as the central article of faith, the four other **basic requirements** in Islam are five-times-daily prayers, the pilgrimage (*hadj*) to Mecca, the Ramadan fast and a religious levy.

The five daily times for **prayer** (bearing in mind that the Islamic day begins at sunset) are sunset, after dark, dawn, noon and afternoon. Prayer can be performed literally anywhere, but preferably in a mosque. In the past and even today in some places, a **muezzin** would climb his minaret each time and call the faithful. Nowadays the **call to prayer** is likely to be less frequent, and prerecorded; even so, this most distinctive of Islamic sounds has a beauty all its own, especially when neighbouring *muezzins* are audible simultaneously. The message itself is equally moving: "God is most great. I testify that there is no god but Allah. I testify that Mohammed is His Prophet. Come to prayer, come to security. God is great." In the morning another phrase is added, "prayer is better than sleep". The most easily recognizable phrase is *Allah Akhbar*, "God is great".

Prayer is preceded by **ritual washing** and is performed with the feet bare. Facing towards Mecca (the direction indicated in a mosque by the *mihrab* – though prayer can be said anywhere), the worshipper recites the *Fatiha*, the first chapter of the Koran: "Praise be to God, Lord of the Worlds, the Compassionate, the Merciful, King of the Day of Judgement. We worship You and seek Your aid. Guide us on the straight path, the path of those on whom You have bestowed Your grace, not the path of those who incur Your anger nor of those who go astray." The same words are then repeated twice in the prostrate position, with some interjections of *Allah Akhbar*. It is a highly ritualized procedure, with the prostrate position symbolic of the worshipper's role as servant (Islam means literally "obedience"), and the sight of thousands of people going through the same motions simultaneously in a mosque (in a *jema'a*, rather than a *masjid* or "local mosque") is a powerful one. Here the whole community comes together for prayer, led by an **imam**, who may also deliver the *Khutba*, or sermon.

The **pilgrimage**, or *hadj*, to Mecca is an annual event, when millions come from all over the world to Mohammed's birthplace. Here they go through several days of rituals, the central one a sevenfold circumambulation of the *Ka'aba*, before kissing a black stone set in its wall. Islam requires that Muslims should go on *hadj* as often as is practically possible, although for the poor, it may well be a once-in-a-lifetime occasion. In Tunisia, from the earliest times to the French occupation, pilgrims assembled at towns along a well-established route, passing through Kairouan and Gabes, to join the *rakeb*, a caravan numbering thousands of people. They would then make the journey to Mecca by foot or camel. The French made it a lot easier. They didn't want just anyone going on the *hadj*, where they might pick up bad political habits like nationalism, so they restricted pilgrims to several hundred a year and laid on transport in the form of a special pilgrim boat. Now the government still helps many of the poor to make their *hadj* by air, and the month when all the pilgrims leave for Mecca is still a great time of celebration in Tunisia. The story that seven visits to Kairouan equal one *hadj* to Mecca is really more apocryphal, expressing the unusual reverence in which the city is held.

THE EVIL EYE

The superstition that envious looks bring **bad luck**, though disapproved of by strict Muslims, is ingrained in Arab culture. Even when admiring something belonging to a friend, formulae are uttered to ward off this **"evil eye"**. More unlucky than the remarks of friends, however, are the jealous glances of strangers.

For this reason, various charms are used against the evil eye. One of the most common is the so-called **"Hand of Fatima"**. The Fatima referred to is the Prophet's daughter, although what connection there is between her and the symbol of the hand remains obscure. It may be that the five fingers of the hand, like the five points of the pentagram star, represent the **five pillars of Islam** (declaration of faith, prayer, pilgrimage, charity and observation of Ramadan).

Certainly, the symbol is often combined with a Koranic quotation, or with the names of Allah and Mohammed written in Arabic script. Then again, the pentagram and the significance of the number five predate Islam and are often associated with Jewish mysticism. It is interesting to note that Jerban Jews share this belief in the evil eye, and use similar symbols to ward it off, even more than do their Muslim neighbours.

Another charm against the evil eye is the **fish**. Again, its origins are obscure, though it's believed that it was originally a phallic fertility symbol. Whatever the truth, you'll see charms against the evil eye all over the place, in the form of car-stickers, hands and fish painted on houses, and cards pinned up on the walls of shops.

Ramadan is the name of the ninth month in the Islamic calendar, the month in which the Koran was revealed to Mohammed. The custom of fasting is modelled directly on Jewish and Christian practice, and for the whole of the month believers must forgo all forms of consumption – food, drink, cigarettes, sex – between sunrise and sunset. A few categories of people are exempted: travellers, children, pregnant women and warriors engaged in a *jihad*, or holy war. Given the climates in which most Muslims live, the fast is a formidable undertaking, but in practice it becomes a time of some intense celebration as the abstinence of the day is more than compensated for by huge consumption during the night.

Based on the five "pillars of faith" and firmly underwritten by the Koran, Islam was an inspirational faith for the Arab people and gained wide acceptance in the course of the Arab advance – particularly among the Berbers. The beginning of a new era was symbolized by the adoption of a new calendar: thus 1996 sees the start of the year 1417 in the Islamic calendar.

THE OLD BELIEFS

Whatever success Islam had during its early period of rapid expansion, it did not entirely eradicate **pre-existing religion**. Animistic beliefs in the powers of stones and trees (as at Fernana) and rites of ancestor worship were incorporated into the new faith, as was a belief in *baraka*, the power to work miracles given by God to some men. These "saints", or **marabouts**, formed a pantheon of intermediaries between the people and God. Some had particular powers, to cure disease or generate rain, and prayers and sacrifices were made to them at their tombs for these services. Others acquired reverence as founder guardians of a tribe.

Baraka was not only embodied in tombs, it was also transmitted through blood, and the descendants of these holy men enjoyed a particular respect – the *sharifs*, ancestors of the Prophet, more than any other. Some of them could even perform miracles. Ascetics and preachers might also acquire the status of a marabout, at least during their lifetime. In the fifteenth and sixteenth centuries, Tunisia was flooded with these holy men, most of them coming from Morocco. During a later time of crisis, in the nineteenth century, another wave arose, warning of the approaching Armageddon.

The dualism of the older faith was also retained as a belief in **bori**, or evil spirits, and the evil eye. These led to rituals of exorcism, many of which were performed by Africans who were believed to be particularly powerful against the *bori*. You still see little bags of herbs around the necks of children to protect them against any harm, and the hand of Fatima is a widespread symbol (see box), but today these beliefs are on the way out. They persist in remote rural areas where religious life still focuses on the marabout's tomb rather than the mosque.

ISLAM'S DEVELOPMENT

By **800 AD**, the new religion was dominant over an area stretching from Afghanistan in the east to Spain in the west. Given the rapidity of this expansion, it was inevitable that Islam would acquire some of the trappings of the older religions to which it had been a reaction, in the form of hierarchical and doctrinal disputes.

Like most religions, Islam soon developed its own institutions and with them particular interest groups. In the early years there was an understanding that consensus legitimized authority, the law and religion. By the ninth century, however, the **ulema** (the learned ones) – that is, the *imam* and the *sheikhs* of the religious colleges – had come to monopolize the interpretation of the Koran and the Prophet's sayings. They became a religious establishment, wielding considerable power and controlling great wealth. Under their control the religion itself became increasingly intellectual and dogmatic. And so the scene was set for the division of the faithful.

The **first dispute** arose soon after the death of Mohammed, and has remained the biggest single split in the faith – equivalent to the Catholic–Protestant schism in Christianity. When the Prophet died, the spiritual leadership of the faith was the object of fierce contention among several Caliphs (rulers). A substantial minority felt that the new Caliph should be in direct descent from the Prophet, and their candidate was Ali, a cousin of the Prophet married to his daughter, Fatima. Eventually, Ali's supporters broke away from the **Sunni** mainstream to form the **Shi'a** sect.

Although the two groups agreed broadly in their respect for the Koran and its tradition (the *hadith*), the Shi'ites were forced into a more allegorical interpretation of the Koran in order to support their claims for a divinely inspired leader. Even the orthodox Sunnis found themselves increasingly unable to agree on points of legal detail (all law was taken from the Koran), and by the twelfth century, four **madhabs**, or schools of legal thought, had been established within the Sunni community: Hanefite, Shafite, Malekite and Hanbalite. Together with two

Shi'a *madhabs*, these still account for the great majority of Muslims.

But there were also smaller and more radical sects. The **Kharijites**, or "Secessionists", were one of the earliest of these (see p.362). Puritanical in the extreme, they held that anyone guilty of serious sin deserved death. The rigour of this sect appealed particularly to subject peoples such as the Berbers in North Africa, alienated by the excesses of their new rulers, the more so because the Kharijites denied any necessity for Arab leadership – the Caliph, they said, should be elected for his piety from among all true believers.

Sufism, which remains a force in southern Tunisia, is not so much a breakaway sect as the name for a different emphasis within Islam, focusing on the ecstatic and the mystical rather than the intellectual niceties of Koranic interpretation. It is a blanket term for the many different brotherhoods, often spread widely over the Islamic world, who evolved various practices in the attempt to attain some sort of mystic communion with God. The name *sufi* derives from the word for wool, after the simple woollen clothes worn by early ascetics. During the eighteenth and nineteenth centuries, many of these *sufi* brotherhoods spread throughout the Islamic world, with lodges as far apart as Yemen and Morocco linked by allegiance to their founder's teachings and, in some cases, a well-structured administrative hierarchy. They became institutions – and in the case of the Senoussi of Cyrenaica, a government with a state.

The secret of the *sufi* groups' success lay in their ability to meet the **religious needs** of the community ignored by orthodox Islam. Some, such as the intellectual Rahamania, placed great emphasis on learning, whereas others adopted more colourful practices in order to reach a state of **religious ecstasy**. The Aissouia, better known as the "whirling dervishes", used self-flagellation and music to induce a trance. Many of these brotherhoods are still active in Tunisia, though their secrecy, unorthodox practices, wealth and ability to mobilize a large part of the population arouse great suspicion among the religious establishment and in the government.

With these basic institutions, Islam came to exert a profound influence over every aspect of life in one of the greatest civilizations the world has seen. Unlike Christianity – at least Protestant Christianity, which has to some extent accepted the separation of Church and State – Islam sees no such distinction. The **sharia**, or religious law, *is* civil law, and in a process of gradual accretion numerous layers have been added to the original code, the *Sunna* entrusted to the Prophet. Many controversial requirements, such as *purdah* (the seclusion of women), polygamy and slavery, have been declared not to be part of the original code – but it remains very much a question of interpretation.

Perhaps Islam's most fundamental role was in **education**, which was based almost entirely on the Koran. Young children (mainly boys) whose parents could afford it were sent to the *kouttab*, or primary school, where they learned to read and write by learning the Koran (all 6200 verses of it) off by heart. If they continued their studies, it would still be under religious auspices because the great universities, such as Al Azhar in Cairo (founded by Fatimids from Tunisia in the tenth century) and the Zitouna in Tunis, were attached to mosques. Students might live and do some of their studying in *medersas*, or residential colleges, but teaching was based at the mosque, and the syllabus remained religious. Law, grammar, science, logic – all were subsidiary to the Koranic tradition as handed down from generation to generation. For several centuries Arab philosophers and scientists produced work that built on the Greco-Roman achievements they inherited, and was hundreds of years ahead of contemporary Europe – their role in transmitting this culture to the European Renaissance has gone generally unappreciated. Ibn Khaldoun, the great historian, politician and scholar born in Tunis in 1332, set out sociological principles that have only recently become current in the West.

DECLINE AND CRISIS

Despite its vigour, there was also a very static element in Islam and, as it developed, Arab culture became oppressed by the weight of a **religious tradition** increasingly hostile to free enquiry. Anything that threatened the authority of the religious establishment was gradually suppressed, and the dynamism which had taken the Arabs so far in so short a time was replaced by a society unable to make the innovations that would keep them ahead of the

fast-rising Europeans. Peter Mansfield (see p.419) notes that the Arabs learned how to make paper from the Chinese when they captured Samarkand in 704, but refused for centuries to manufacture books mechanically because it was an invention unsanctioned by God and tradition.

At first this stagnation was relatively unimportant because the Arab world was so far ahead of the European competition in every field. But as the pendulum began to swing in the other direction, there was no facility for adapting to match the Europeans. Napoleon's expedition to Egypt in 1798 was the beginning of a century in which almost every Islamic country came under the control of one or other of the European powers; a single exception – of which all the Arabs are aware today – was Saudi Arabia. Under **colonial rule**, Islam became the focus of opposition. In Algeria and Libya, *sufi* brotherhoods led the resistance movement, drawing the support of the masses with a call to the *jihad*, a war to protect their faith as much as their country. Unfortunately, by the time it came to fight the battles, the wars had already been lost to the factories of Manchester and Lille.

It would be simplistic to blame this reversal of fortune on Islam alone. The Islamic nations were not, after all, the only ones to suffer the indignities of colonization or mercantile exploitation. But because it is such an all-embracing religion, deeply rooted in every facet of the societies which hold to it, the nineteenth and twentieth centuries inevitably saw something of a **crisis** in religious confidence. Islam had once been the basis of a great civilization and was now dominated by infidel foreigners.

There were two alternatives: either Islam could try to adapt itself in some way to the essentially secular ways which had brought success to the West, or it could reject Western influence entirely; by purifying itself, it might rediscover its former strength. In practical terms, few Islamic countries under Western control were in a position at first to adopt either alternative – but these were the poles between which Islamic thought was operating.

Then, in the post-war period, self-determination suddenly came to the Middle East. First, the **decolonization** process, accelerated in many countries by the contribution Islamic consciousness made to the nationalist movements, brought political autonomy.

Second, and even more important, **oil** wealth brought economic self-sufficiency and the possibility of spiritual independence from the West. These two developments made the problem of identity suddenly immediate and real. In a situation where many of them could afford to reject Western values, how should Islamic countries now deal with the conflicts between their religion and secular materialism?

Some countries, notoriously to Western perceptions, have chosen to return to or maintain a more or less **traditional form of fundamentalist Islam**. To see this course, as many do in the West, as a deliberate return to barbarism is an egocentric failure to understand the context. A return to the totality of Islam is to choose one consistent spiritual identity, one that is deeply embedded in the consciousness of a culture unusually aware of tradition. Most people in the West would be outraged if they were suddenly told that they must give up many of the most fundamental rights and customs of their whole culture – yet this is what they blithely expect the Arabs to do.

Conflict with the West is another aspect of the return to Islam. Adoption of Islamic values signals a rejection of Western society's values – which are perceived as having been, and being, based on greed and exploitation. Traditional Islam offers a positivist brand of freedom, with substantial historical backing, which is clearly opposed to Western secularism. The most extreme Islamic fundamentalists are not passive reactionaries thinking of the past, but young radicals, often students, keen to assert new-found independence. Islam has in a sense become the anti-imperialist religion – hence the Black Muslim movement in America – and there is frequent confusion and even conflict between secular, left-wing ideals and more purely religious ones.

But the rejection of all Western values does involve missing out on what the West sees as the "benefits" of **development**. It may be begging the question in strictly Islamic terms to say that the emancipation of women, say, is a "benefit"; but in the more liberal countries, of which Tunisia is a leader, such steps are considered desirable, and simultaneously reconcilable with Islam (see "Women in Tunisia", p.395). The hope is that the supremacy of Islam, a vital part of national identities, can be maintained while shedding what are seen as its less desirable

elements. Most Islamic countries have now embarked on this formidable balancing act in their social and political lives.

ISLAM IN MODERN TUNISIA

For a country now so advanced in its liberalization, **Tunisia** has always had a strong religious **tradition**. After Mecca, Medina and Jerusalem, Kairouan is the most holy city for Muslims, still visited at the *Mouled* every year by visitors from all over the Islamic world. The university at Tunis's Great Mosque was long respected, and Tunisia's Malekite teachers still enjoy a high reputation. Yet at the same time there is a greatly revered Jewish shrine on Jerba (the Ghriba), and although the Jewish population has diminished over the last thirty years, tolerance is still unusually high.

The majority of Tunisians have always belonged to the **Malekite** school of the Sunni orthodoxy (their mosques easily recognizable by square minarets). The Turks brought with them the teaching of the **Hanefite** school (these mosques have octagonal minarets), which still survives among Turkish-descended families; but there is little if any conflict between the schools, and since both are Sunni the two groups can use each others' mosques. Between them, these groups account for the vast majority of Muslims in Tunisia; for the outpost of **Kharijites** on Jerba, and the **Sufi** stronghold at Nefta.

Despite these long traditions, though, Tunisia – or at least Tunis itself – has always had a **cosmopolitan** element and therefore remained more open to innovation. Kherredin's attempt to introduce constitutional government in 1860 was a failure, but it was a move that several Islamic states have still to make more than a century later. Since Independence, Bourguiba had to tread a narrow path between secularization and loyalty to Islamic tradition. With evidence of willingness to adopt Western values, vital Western aid and cooperation have always been abundant. At the same time the Islamic tradition has to be respected enough for the country to remain in favour with wealthier Arab countries, for both political and economic reasons.

After Independence, Bourguiba, broadly speaking, tried to **secularize** the country – as far as possible with the religious establishment's support – and with some success. During the 1950s and 60s religious observance dropped steadily, particularly in Tunis and among the younger generation. But in the 1970s and 80s the trend reversed. Local and foreign funding boosted the number of mosques from 810 in 1960 to 2450 in 1986. What is more, the mosques are now full, with predominantly youthful congregations. Islam has had a revival that most Christian churches would envy.

Today Islam gives the young a sense of identity and solidarity in a world they see as hostile. It has also given them hope. The *imams'* calls for a **return to Islamic values** are interpreted by many as an indirect criticism of a government that has done so much to Westernize Tunisia, and of the middle classes who live affluently amid poverty. Extremists, such as the *Mouvement de la Tendence Islamique*, have gone further, demanding that Islamic values and principles are applied in law and government. They would have an Islamic Republic along Iranian lines.

It is difficult to tell how many Tunisians would support such a radical constitutional change. Most have some sympathy with the fundamentalists' point of view but cling to their Westernized and materialist lifestyle. Fundamentalism's most fervent supporters are among the **very poor** or the frustrated **lower middle class**, who have gained little from Bourguibism. But to what extent their fundamentalism is a reaction to and expression of poverty and oppression or a genuine ideological commitment is unclear.

The government has tried to deflect criticism and return moderate fundamentalists to the fold of legitimate politics. It has proclaimed its Islamic credentials, stressing the pre-eminence of Islam as the official religion rather than the secular nature of the state. Ministers now make great show of their religious observance. Affronts to Islam, such as the sale of alcohol on Fridays, have been stopped, and the outward trappings of **Islamicization** have been adopted. Arabic, for instance, is more and more important as the language of instruction at all levels of education.

These gestures may have appeased the moderates, but the **extremists** remain unmoved. As their opposition became more vocal, Bourguiba, who feared fundamentalism as a threat to both the Destour Party and the secular nature of the state he had created, grew determined to root out what he saw as a danger. Confrontation escalated into violence from 1985 to 1987, and Tunisia seemed set to fall into a downward spiral of repression, dissidence and terrorism. General Ben Ali's first years in office don't suggest he has yet broken the chain, and recent executions of fundamentalists indicate his similar determination to keep state and religion apart. It would be a great achievement if, like Hussein in Jordan, he could divert the radicals into parliamentary politics and thus institutionalize a revolutionary movement. The price the middle classes would have to pay for political stability – further, inevitable Islamicization – might be worth paying.

TRADITIONAL SOCIETY

Traditionally, the family was the foundation of Tunisian society. Now, however, that society is changing and new allegiances and values are emerging that conflict with the old.

THE OLD TRADITIONS

In traditional society (which today means in rural areas and the poorer parts of the cities), the **extended family** was the fundamental social group. Tunisians spent much of their social life with close relatives and also tended to marry within the family unit (for a man, marriage to his father's brother's daughter was the ideal), and mutual obligations meant that families were tied economically. Land in rural areas, for instance, was usually co-owned with brothers or cousins. If a man wanted to build a house or clear some land he would call on his relatives to help, on the understanding that he would reciprocate later. In the same way, if he had financial difficulties, or needed money to celebrate his daughter's wedding in proper style, he could rely on support from his close relatives.

Age and experience are revered in Tunisia much more than in the West, with more senior members of the family living with their children (usually sons), caring for their grandchildren and strongly influencing family decisions. Age commands respect and is associated not so much with frailty and vulnerability as with wisdom, experience and a lifetime of input into the family and the community. Even as a foreigner, this means that you will be treated with a certain amount of deference, and shown the respect due your years. There are no state, and few private, pensions so social security is a family rather than a state matter.

Wider social groups were defined in the same family terms by means of descent from a common ancestor. In this way traditional Tunisian society was composed of a series of ever larger families: the nuclear family, the extended family, a lineage, a village or tribe. The frequency and intensity of social interaction declined as the size of the social group

increased but, even at the scale of village or tribe, there were still communal rights and reciprocal obligations that unified the group.

Individuals were identified by their **genealogy**, a name chain in the Welsh fashion: Ahmed Ben (son of) Mohammed Ben Ahmed Ben Slim etc. The name of a distant ancestor was usually used to identify the individual's lineage inside his community, but if he travelled to another village he would adopt the village name, if he went to a city, his tribe's name. There were no surnames that identified the individual definitively or transcended social context. People were always a member of such-and-such a family.

The family also created **honour** in the sense that reputation and good name derived from the achievements of ancestors and the length of an identifiable genealogy. People whose ancestors were *sheikhs*, marabouts, or even *hadjis* (those who have made the pilgrimage to Mecca) are always identified as such. The more esteemed the ancestor, the more detailed the genealogy. A *sharif*, for instance, will trace his ancestry right back to the Prophet Mohammed.

Because honour was derived from descent and was shared by an extended group, attacks on individuals could escalate into a **vendetta**. A family shamed had to take appropriate revenge (an eye for an eye, a tooth for a tooth) if honour was to be saved, and reciprocal attacks could build up into long-lasting feuds. Most of these vendettas began with verbal or sexual attacks on women, for in this patriarchal society it was here that honour was most sensitive. Murder might be resolved by the payment of *dia*, blood-money, but never an attack on a woman.

BREAKDOWN OF TRADITIONAL VALUES

Now that Tunisians are moving to the **cities**, this traditional society is breaking down. Migrants leaving the rural areas try to find accommodation near relatives or members of the same village community. The *bidonvilles* on the edge of Tunis and the *oukala* in its Medina are full of these transplanted rural communities. Many of the migrants also return to their home for the summer marriage season, the highlight of communal life, when social bonds are reaffirmed by complex webs of visiting and hospitality. But they're no longer temporary residents in the city, returning to their village when they have earned enough to get married and set up their own farm; they are now committed to an urban lifestyle and look at the village as their origin – not their goal.

After a couple of years in the city the migrant's visits home become, typically, less frequent, and social life begins to cross communal barriers, with **marriages** often taking place outside the community. Most important of all, income differentials among urban workers discourage the mutual aid that formerly united members of the same family. Gradually the **individual**, with personal identity and interests, emerges and distant family and community fade into the background.

Among these dislocated urban dwellers new allegiances and identities develop, those of **income and class**. A new ethos of personal advancement takes the place of the redundant ideals of the community and mutual aid, and with this new conflicts emerge between rich and poor. It is this struggle, expressed in the battle between the governing party and the secular middle class on the one side, and the aspiring poor, newly educated and fundamentalist on the other, that characterizes Tunisian politics today.

CUSTOMS AND CELEBRATIONS

As traditional society has been subverted by new social structures, so **customs** have been replaced by more "refined" mores. Tunisians still love celebrations, marriages in particular, but in the cities they have lost much of their social significance and zest. If you want to see Tunisian customs at their liveliest, you have to go to the small towns and villages.

Every stage of the **life cycle** is associated with its own celebration and customs: birth, circumcision (in the far south, this includes some girls), marriage and death. It is only at **marriage**, however, that strangers are welcome. Paradoxically enough in this patrilineal society, marriage – the social relationship that crosses patrilineages – is the most public of all social events. It is a matter of honour that the celebration is as splendid and well attended as possible. Most of the village turns out, and unexpected guests, even foreigners, are always welcomed.

Marriage ceremonies differ from region to region but they are always lengthy affairs taking several days, usually in the summer when migrants return home. The first days are spent in preparation. The bride has henna applied to her feet and hands and has all her body hair removed, before being taken to the groom's house where separate receptions are held, accompanied by much music, usually performed by hired singers, drummers and pipe-players, and ritual praise-singing. The ceremony and the communal celebration follow, usually a massive feast with more music and dancing. The consummation of the marriage is, however, the climax, and in rural areas sometimes a semi-public event, with the groom's mother present to confirm her daughter-in-law's virginity. More often the sheet is produced as evidence and, at this news, guns go off and the music starts all over again.

The other major celebration in village and tribal life is the **ziara**, a communal pilgrimage to the tomb of a marabout, usually the community's "patron saint" or eponymous ancestor, again a summer event. In the past everybody participated, even in nomadic communities, where it was the only occasion in the year when everyone would camp together. As a communal – as much as a religious – activity it was important in reaffirming the bonds between members of the community. With everyone gathered around the tomb, visiting would take place, deals would be clinched and marriages arranged.

Pilgrims walked barefoot to the tomb, usually accompanied by music and singing, waving flags bearing religious slogans. There they made a communal prayer and then sacrificed an animal, sometimes a sheep but more often a bull. The **meat** was divided into scrupulously equal portions (symbolic equality being important in tribal life) and distributed to each of the families. The real celebration came afterwards with feasting and dancing.

Today, sadly, these festivals are becoming less and less common. The disintegration of village and tribal life, sapped by emigration and assaulted by affluence, is partly to blame, but the real cause is the expansion of **religious orthodoxy**. Tunisia's *imams* have no place for the marabouts next to God and so they lambast the old faith. As new mosques have penetrated the remotest villages, the marabouts' hegemony has been broken and their legitimacy undermined by the attacks of the educated religious establishment. The government encourages the trend. It doesn't want the people's religious allegiance scattered among a series of local saints, but wants it centralized instead where it is easier to control and manipulate. Consequently, schools throughout the country promote orthodox Islam and dismiss its local forms. As attendance at the mosques and schools increases, that at the *ziara* declines. Perhaps this is the last generation to participate and to see this manifestation of local Islam and tribal solidarity.

WOMEN IN TUNISIA

When still a young child, I told myself that if one day I had the power to do so, I would make haste to redress the wrong done to women.

Habib Bourguiba

Thirty years ago, Tunisian women shared the oppression experienced in most Arab countries. That their position has changed as much as it has is due largely to ex-president Bourguiba's personal vision and his ability to institute far-reaching reforms. Almost the first thing he did after Independence was to introduce the Personal Status Code, an attempt to improve the social position and treatment of women. Hitherto such issues had been controlled by the *sharia*, the Holy Law revealed by Allah through Mohammed and based on the Koran and Hadith.

This assessment of the position of Tunisian women is followed by personal accounts by women travellers in the country.

WOMEN'S TRADITIONAL STATUS

In the eighth century the **Islamic code** had in fact improved women's status: the dowry (*mahr*) was paid to the bride instead of to her guardian, rights of inheritance and control of income were restored, albeit in a very limited sense. Divorce,

though solely a man's right, was to be effective only after a three-month waiting period, the '*idda*, and the husband was supposed to maintain his wife (though the responsibility fell mainly on her brothers) and offer some explanation for his conduct. These limited reforms were, however, later ignored, and Mohammed's own conciliatory attitude (and that of Aysha, one of his wives) disappeared under the stern injunctions of the Koran itself.

Women were henceforth **veiled and segregated** to protect their virginity and reputation; **polygamy** remained common, **marriages** were contracted when the girl was young, and **divorce** proceedings became quite arbitrary. A man could repudiate his wife simply by pronouncing a formulaic saying, the *talaq*, three times in three months – but the three *talaq* were often all pronounced at one time, with no recourse for the woman and no '*idda* at all. Although it was possible to guard against polygamy by inserting a prohibition in the marriage contract, and to receive a portion of the *mahr* on divorce, such measures were seldom taken. A married woman lived in a patriarchal family and was expected to produce sons at regular intervals. Likewise the institution of **habous**, a legal entail excluding women, meant that they rarely received property through inheritance as was their right; and in the courts, a woman's word was worth less than that of a man.

Women, on the whole, enjoyed greater freedom in **rural areas** than in the cities. They were able to walk about within the village without the veil, and within the home they enjoyed considerable influence over their husbands, and power over their dependents. Most women had an independent income that came from the sale of artefacts or animal produce and they spent it as they wished. Divorce was rare, partly because parents consulted their children over the choice of spouse, and partly because of the social stigma attached. Moreover, the proximity of their own family afforded wives a certain protection and shelter. Nevertheless, their status was a far cry from Mohammed's concept of equality.

REFORM

It is against this background that the radicalism of the **1956 Code** must be measured. In Turkey another great reformer, Mustafa Kemal

(Ataturk), had simply abolished the *sharia* and introduced the Swiss Civil Code. Bourguiba, helped in certain areas by the more egalitarian personal laws of Tunisia's Malekite legal school, justified his own reforms from within the original Koranic texts and thus secured the support of Tunisia's spiritual head, the *sheikh* of Zitouna. The marriage age was raised – to 19 for women, 20 for men – and informed consent made necessary. Polygamy was outlawed completely: Mohammed had stipulated that each wife should be treated equally and this was held to be impossible. *Sharia* and civil courts were merged together, divorce became a civil matter, and the formulaic *talaq* was abolished. The Koran itself states that arbitration is needed when there is marital discord: **divorce**, reasonably enough, is felt to be evidence of this. But although a woman can now sue for divorce on grounds of "mental incompatibility", alimony is not always granted. Bourguiba also encouraged people to think of the *mahr* as purely symbolic and gave his second wife a token one dinar. Custody of children has been restored to the woman at divorce, though only until the boy is 7 or the girl 9. **Abortion** rights were introduced over the next fifteen years, along with an extensive and effective family planning campaign. Legislation was passed on equal pay and, as the French left, opportunities for work were created. Women obtained **the vote** in two stages during 1956 and 1957.

Actual **social change** has been slow to follow these comparatively radical laws. A telling indication of the staying power of traditional attitudes is the assertion, frequently heard even from young and otherwise liberal men, that women now have "too much power". Despite the efforts of the *Union Nationale des Femmes Tunisiennes* (*UNFT*), formed in 1956 to introduce the reforms to the country, female **illiteracy** is higher than male, far fewer women than men have attended secondary school and university, and it is doubtful if the rural poor, especially the Berbers, are aware of their rights at all. Opinion polls among the lower classes in the ever-expanding cities, heavily affected by unemployment, show a decline in support for a woman's **right to work**; and the difficulty of finding somewhere to live (because women living alone are still considered immoral) can frustrate most of the

independence that a job might otherwise have brought. Work itself is thus no guide to emancipation. In fact, it has been argued that male authority may actually have increased inside the family as a result, because money earned is often paid directly to a husband or male relative, or used for the dowry – the goods which the bride herself brings to a marriage.

The economic recession, combined with events in Iran, may lie behind this reaction. Since 1979 increasing numbers of women, particularly in the cities, have taken to wearing the Iranian headscarf-like veil, or **chador**, instead of the traditional Tunisian *sifsari* – the white veil-cum-cloak often gripped between the teeth to hide the face. If the apparent backlash continues, the overall process of social change will be enormously complicated and women may find themselves caught between, on the one hand, the break-up of the extended family – which is already causing problems of isolation in the cities – and, on the other, new reactionary pressures.

WOMEN VISITORS TO TUNISIA

As briefly outlined on p.47, a woman traveller in Tunisia (either alone or with a female or male companion) faces certain unavoidable difficulties. With the right approach, skill and luck, some of these can be overcome, but, as the following personal and very different accounts show, the problems are enduring ones. Further feedback and comments from women travellers – or Tunisian men or women – would be much appreciated for the next edition.

■ A SURFACE LIBERALISM
Linda Cooley taught in Tunisia for six years. The following article is reprinted from *Women Travel* (Rough Guides).

Tunisian women enjoy a measure of **freedom and equality under the law** unknown in many other Arab countries. Polygamy was abolished in the mid-1950s when Tunisia became independent. Divorce laws have been altered in women's favour. Most girls attend school. A reasonably large percentage of women are in higher education. Many women work outside the home. There are women in the professions and two women ministers in the government. An established feminist group exists, which holds regular meetings in the *Club Tahar Haddad* in the capital's Medina, and there is even a feminist magazine, *Nissa*.

But the presence of so many women in public can be misleading. It may lull you into a false sense of security when you first arrive and lead to false expectations of what you can and cannot do. If you walk around the capital (and remember, this is very unrepresentative of the rest of the country), you will see women in jeans and the latest fashions, sometimes sitting in cafés, even girls walking along holding hands with their boyfriends. But what you cannot see and should know is that these same fashionably dressed girls have fathers who expect them to be home by eight o'clock at the latest, who expect them to be virgins at their wedding and who often expect them to marry a relative chosen by the parents. The clothes may have changed in recent years, the number of women at work may have changed, but, deep down, **social attitudes** remain unaltered. The Tunisian women you see in the streets are most often going to work or going home. The idea of a woman travelling abroad on her own, in this traditional Arab society, is understandably considered strange.

It is important to realize this before setting off on solo (or even two-women) travels. And to realize, too, how superficial are many of the Europeanized images – even in Tunis. **Bars** are not like those in France, but exclusively male domains, and if you wander in for a rest and a beer you will be stared at. Similarly, you can't expect to be able to chat to the man at the next table in the café about the best place to have lunch or the best time to visit the mosque, without your conversation being taken as an invitation to get more closely acquainted. **Western movies** have done an excellent job of persuading Tunisian men that all Western women spend their lives jumping in and out of bed with any willing male.

All this may sound somewhat offputting. Yet in six years living in Tunis, I often travelled alone, I travelled with my son and I travelled with another woman. Perhaps I was lucky, but apart from the unwanted attentions of a few men, nothing happened to me. There is no part of the country that it is unsafe to visit – you can see everything.

But **travelling alone**, it is incredibly hard to get to know the people, and it is hard to relax, never being sure about how your behaviour will be interpreted if you do. I learnt to cope by avoiding direct eye contact with men, and above all never smiling at strangers. I once found myself being followed home because I inadvertently smiled at a man as we reached for the same tin of tomato sauce in the supermarket. It may irk you to keep your silence; not to answer like with like; not to show occasional disdain; but in the long run it will make your life more pleasant. After a while, the ignoring game becomes a reality; you really don't notice that anyone has spoken to you! If you cannot learn to ignore the hassle from men you will probably find yourself impatient to leave Tunisia after a very short time – it is an easy country for a woman on her own to dislike.

Travelling with a man makes it all much simpler. The stereotyped images on both sides (yours of pushy Arab men; theirs of loose foreign women) can be dispensed with and everyone can act naturally. Men will talk to you both as you're sitting in a café or waiting for a bus – and generally just for the pleasure of talking with someone different, nothing more. You may well get invited home to meet their families, where you'll be able to talk to the women in the home too, as unlike in many other Arab countries, Tunisian women and men eat together.

You can also go to the **hammam** (public baths) with the women of the house. This is very worthwhile as it is the one place where women can meet traditionally as a group, away from all the pressures of a male-dominated society. Unless you speak Arabic, it is difficult to talk to the older women there, who rarely speak French, but they are more than willing to show you how to remove the hairs from your body, to henna your hair, to use *tfal* (a kind of shampoo made from mud) and to give you a thorough scrub with a sort of loofah mitten. You could, of course, go on your own to the hammam, but it's much better to go with a Tunisian woman, and introductions are almost exclusively made through men.

Another possibility is that if you express curiosity, you may well find yourself invited to a **wedding** (you don't have to know the bride or groom – hundreds of people attend Arab weddings who hardly know the couple), or some other traditional event. Total strangers can be very hospitable when it comes to sharing their customs and food with you. I once had the most beautiful couscous brought out to the field where I was eating my picnic of cheese sandwiches: but then, I was with my son and a male companion.

Alone or with another woman it is all possible. But you do miss a great deal of what is, essentially, Tunisian life. Hopefully through more contact between foreign women and Tunisians a greater understanding will ensue on both sides, and the lone woman traveller will become more easily accepted. Meanwhile, ideas are changing – but very slowly.

■ FROM BOTH SIDES OF THE FENCE
Dee Eltaïef is an English woman married to a Tunisian and lives in Sousse.

Tunisia is one of the most **progressive** Muslim countries in the world as regards its treatment of women, who have equal opportunities in education and work, are allowed to drive, to travel abroad, to have private bank accounts, wear European clothes and watch European television, go to the cinema, choose their own husband and inherit according to the law. All of this may sound very mundane to a Westerner, but by comparison to other Arab or Muslim countries it is very enlightened.

But despite these progressive laws which protect women's rights, **tradition** also plays an important role in their lives. Girls are brought up to be homemakers and mothers, and are schooled from an early age for their wedding day (considered to be the highlight of their life), the gathering of a trousseau and the very real possibility that their marriage will be arranged by their family. To be unmarried by the late twenties is definitely considered to be "on the shelf", regardless of a career. So by being a wife, and then a mother, a girl's status in society is assured and recognized.

Traditional roles originate from economic practicalities as much as anything else. The man provides for his wife and children, and a woman's day-to-day duties involve a lot of **domestic work**, with stone floors that need daily washing and extensive food preparation (cleaning fish, plucking chickens, shelling peas, grinding spices, as well as annual tasks like preparing couscous and sun-drying tomatoes). There are no frozen foods here and only limited tinned goods, and because many families do not have a refrigerator, food has to be bought and prepared on a daily basis. Few people have vacuum cleaners or washing machines, and rugs must be beaten and clothes washed by hand. If the house has no running water, this has to be collected from the well or pump. Bearing the chores in mind, it is understandable that women's work in the home can be considered full-time, especially if you add several children as well. There are few New Age Tunisian men so the bulk of these jobs are left to the women, although men still often do the shopping. Following this scenario, the children will be trained to help and invariably follow the parental roles, with girls bearing the brunt of domestic jobs, and boys encouraged in the education stakes in order to get a good job so they can support their future wives and children, as well as their parents in old age. The girls of the family are often married, do not have an income, and therefore cannot help out financially. So from an early age the roles are set.

There is tremendous **social pressure** for marriage. Even if a girl goes on to further education, this is still often seen as a secondary status to that of a married woman, and having a job and income does not give her the same level of independence as in Europe. Until she is married she lives in the family home, helps with domestic duties and pools any income for the benefit of the whole family. But there is always a background encouragement for her to find a husband and clean her own floors instead of her parents'. **Virginity** is still a desirable commodity even in so-called sophisticated circles, and single parents and unmarried mothers are a rarity, there being considerable social stigma attached to pregnancy outside marriage. Tunisian society is interdependent on a vast network of family members and friends, meaning that there are very few places that a single woman could go to seek privacy. Even cities operate as large villages and there are few secrets in a country with only eight million inhabitants. The arranging of marriages still goes on today, although it tends to be more of a tactic approval of the couple's intentions rather than the go-between couplings of strangers.

From the **male point of view**, a husband wants his home well looked after; if his new wife is pretty, as well as a good homemaker, he considers it a bonus. The average Tunisian man will continue to socialize with his male friends after marriage, and is therefore not necessarily looking for intellectual compatibility in his wife; in fact, many believe that wives should be "moulded" by their husbands and a brilliant intellect in a woman is not a desirable characteristic. A man wants a wife to be the mother of his children and provide regular sex; he would expect to marry a virgin, probably several years his junior. Her parents will vet the prospective husband to make sure he is able to support a wife and children, and has a firm financial basis in order to buy the basic essentials for a home. He would also be expected to buy gifts for his prospective bride, usually in the form of expensive gold jewellery. This can be a costly investment from a man's point of view, so he's looking for value for money apart from anything else. He does not necessarily expect to be "in love", and if they are compatible in other areas, it is assumed love will follow. The groom is not expected to be a virgin; in fact, he is expected to have sown his wild oats and be ready to settle down. As all married Tunisian girls are supposed to be virgins, and all prospective husbands expected to be men of the world, one can only presume that a certain amount of convenient temporary homosexuality can serve a purpose, as can the local prostitutes, the discreet wife of someone else or the nubile tourists who come on holiday.

With such a complex background, the stage is set for **tourists** to provide a very attractive alternative, which leads to many misunderstandings. Firstly, many female European tourists are not inhibited in consummating a relationship with an attractive Tunisian male. The Tunisian is happy to oblige, thus being provided with sex and a certain kudos among his friends in having "pulled" a European; if he plays his cards right he might get invited to Europe, be given gifts and have his beers paid for locally. It also does not spoil his chances of a good marriage later to a Tunisian girl when he's ready to settle down.

As Tunisian girls are simply not available for this type of relationship, one can perhaps understand the gravitation of Tunisian males to European tourists. The sexual licence shown in current films also creates an image of freedom

and willingness. Many female tourists encourage the myth by not considering they have had a good holiday unless they have had several boyfriends. If the liaison gets as far as a mixed marriage, there may still be ulterior motives involved. As many of the boys who chase after tourists are not in a financial position to provide the gold dowry for a Tunisian bride, it is one way round a celibate life. Also many may use the marriage as an entrée into a European country, for which they would have no hope of getting a visa without the foreign wife.

Many Tunisian males with little personal experience of European cultures may be more influenced by what they see on television or what their own fertile imaginations can provide, so it's largely a question of clearly giving out the right signals. If you bathe topless, don't expect a lot of respect from any man who has seen your breasts. If you behave circumspectly and immediately reprove any advances, double meanings or hint of familiarity, you will earn the respect of both Tunisian men and women as you travel through their country. You will also be setting a standard which other female travellers will be happy to follow, and just as all Tunisians cannot be grouped in the same category, so they will understand that not all female tourists can be the same either.

■ SURVIVAL SKILLS
Dr C.L. Higham travelled around northern Africa and lived in Tunis for eight months.

As a fair-skinned Caucasian, I turn pink when exposed to the sun, and during my travels it was obvious everywhere I went that I was not Tunisian. Repeated advances from men taught me some basic urban survival skills that most Western women already possess to some degree.

1. Dress modestly. You will see Tunisian women in miniskirts and tank tops, but you must remember that most of them, too, are harassed on a daily basis, and also that they have connections with Tunisia. When they are in their own neighbourhood, everyone knows their family, which gives them some degree of protection, an advantage that foreign women do not have. Dressing in a long skirt and modest blouse or T-shirt will give a certain amount of immunity, although you should still expect occasional unwanted advances. My neighbours and several women I knew taught me defence skills because they felt I dressed in a way that was respectful towards their society.

2. Wear sunglasses. I found this cut down on unwanted eye contact as well as allowing me to watch out for potential trouble on public transport.

3. Make contact with Tunisian women and older men. I found that Tunisians are very observant people. The men on the front desk of the hotel we booked into became protective of me within a week, and I found I could sit in the lobby without being hassled. In our second week, I had a bad allergy reaction to some food and remained in our room for several days. The maid, Hedia, took it upon herself to check on me, and in faltering French we talked. She was very helpful and just as curious about me as I was about her. In the market, I always bought from the older men as they tended to be polite and very helpful. One day, a young man walked up and kissed me; the stall owner went after him with a broom and apologized to me about his behaviour. From that time on, he called me *binte*, or daughter, as did some of the other men – older Tunisian men do not approve of most of this licence and if they consider you a friend or valued customer, they will use their influence to stave off young men.

Because I lived in a neighbourhood for eight months, I met and befriended several Tunisian women. I also found that being friendly to Tunisian women in shops sometimes led to friendships. Women who work outside the home are not only sympathetic to your problems but they also have solutions – they know where the largely hidden restaurants are that are patronized by women.

On the street, it is best to act like you're in a large, anonymous city, but when dealing with people in shops and souks, behave as if it is a small town, always asking how people and their families are and what they recommend you buy. They will initially be suspicious but will soon become equally friendly. Remember, Tunisia is still a very family-oriented society; family connections are important, and the more connections you make, the more included you feel.

4. Be open to questions and curiosity. Often when I became friendly with women, they would ask me embarrassing questions.

One woman wanted to know why I did not shave the hair on my arms and offered to remove it with hot sugar water. Several times on the TGM, *hajas* (older women) would look through my shopping basket and ask me what a non-Tunisian was going to do with various products, then give me some good cooking tips. I always figured that if they were interested enough to ask the question and felt comfortable doing it, it was up to me to answer it.

5. Establish a pattern. I tried to patronize the same stores again and again and played on my one advantage: I was distinctive. Within a month or so of arriving, I felt perfectly comfortable exploring the souks by myself even though I spoke no Arabic, as the hawkers had come to recognize me and ignored me unless I entered their store. Then I found they were happy to answer questions and very helpful. The same was true of people in the corner stores and restaurants. We often ate at a little *gargote* on Ibn Khaldoun that served wonderful *keftagi*. One day I asked the cook what was in it. From that point on, I got special service and she would always give me *keftagi* no matter what I ordered. She would also send her son to clear a spot and wipe down the table for me. My husband found this both funny and irritating because he ended up eating standing up most of the time.

6. Overtip waiters. When I did not want to wait in the hotel lobby, I sometimes went to the *Café Africa*. Here, I applied big-city techniques, spreading the newspaper all over my table and avoiding eye contact. I also overtipped the waiters, and by the second week a newspaper was unnecessary. I could read a book, while the waiters intercepted men headed for my table. I had another advantage in my own neighbourhood: as my husband not only spoke some Tunisian Arabic but also looked somewhat Tunisian, I became an accepted member of my neighbourhood community, and was able to go into local cafés alone, with the waiters always asking about him and staving off unwanted advances.

7. Don't be afraid to confront. Early in our stay, two young men began to follow me and call out comments. I initially ignored them, but when one of them grabbed my skirt I turned around and hit him with my market basket. They instantly scattered. It was then that I became aware of the café across the street, where the men were clapping at the show I had put on.

Later, I related this story to a Tunisian friend of ours who has a daughter. He felt that once young men cross the line of touching, they deserve what they get, and had taught his daughter where to kick and how to punch. I can count on one hand the times I had to get physical or even threaten to get physical with men. I found simply turning on someone who follows you and heading towards them screaming "Izzy" does wonders. If you feel threatened, create a scene. The aggressor will usually back off, or other people will intervene.

Tunisia is like anywhere else in the world, in that strangers are more open to problems. When I saw tourists wearing halter tops and tight shorts in the souks, yelling because someone had touched them, I used to wonder what would happen if they dressed like that and walked around at a street fair in New York or Chicago. As I look back on my nine months there, I realize that I spent most of the time alone, exploring the souks, markets and museums, and I really had very few problems. Once you establish relationships with people in Tunisia, you will see a whole other part of the country that is wonderful and delightful.

WILDLIFE

For a country a mere 800km long by 250km wide, Tunisia packs in an amazing variety of habitats. Although northern Tunisia will be familiar to anyone who knows the Mediterranean – a combination of limestone and sandstone hills, pine and cork oak forest, and agricultural land – as soon as you get south of the great Dorsale ridge of mountains that splits the country, you're into something totally different: steppe deserts north of the Chott el Jerid, and true rolling sand dunes to the south, with fertile oases punctuating both.

It takes some practice to learn to identify promising wildlife sites. Look for sites with a variety of different **habitats**, such as a hillside with woodland, scrub and rocky gorges. **Fresh water** is invariably a magnet and always worth checking out. **Deciduous woodland** is terrific, but give the monotonous olive groves a miss. For flowers, look for **colour**, which often indicates richness, especially on hillsides. A site with a **wide variety of plants** will tend to be richer in insects, and hence small birds and reptiles too.

The **time of day** is important, too. While flowers, insects and reptiles can be watched right through the day and are best when it's hot, birds are most active at dawn and dusk. A walk through the woods at dawn or within the two hours afterwards can yield ten times as many birds as the same walk at midday.

CLIMATE AND HABITAT CHANGES

Climate, as always, plays a major role in determining the distribution of plants and animals.

Any visitor from northern Europe has to keep the lack of water firmly in mind – it's the dominant factor. Although Tunisia includes the wettest place in North Africa (the cork oak forests around Aïn Draham on the Algerian border), large areas of the south have an annual average rainfall of less than 50 millimetres. And average rainfall totals are highly misleading; what actually happens is that there is no rain at all for years, and then a sudden deluge. This patchiness is common in the north as well.

This is confusing for the average naturalist. It means that animals and plants have adapted to become highly flexible and unpredictable in their appearances. While in Britain you can go to a wood and see the same orchids flowering year after year, you can't always do that in Tunisia. After a very wet year, parts of the desert will bloom in a blaze of colour, the *sebkhas* will flood and suddenly support huge populations of wintering birds. After a very dry winter, annual plants may simply not germinate, some perennials will retreat into their bulbs or roots and not even flower, and the desert will remain devoid of vegetation.

Along with climate, **agriculture** is the other hugely important factor. The fertile north of the country has been used as an intensive agricultural belt from the first century BC right through to the French occupation, and agricultural pressures are no less intense now, with Tunisia's population growing at 2.5 percent annually. This has meant that the original forests have long since been cleared, and many of the scrubby Mediterranean hillside regions have been converted to arable land or greatly modified by the pressure of grazing.

Grazing accounts for changes to the desert, too, with the familiar pattern of desertification being caused by a combination of overgrazing and climatic change. Many people who live in the south depend on wood for their cooking and heating; combine this with over seven million grazing animals and you can see why forests have degraded to scrubland and desert.

FIELD GUIDES AND TIMES TO VISIT

Despite the loss of habitats, Tunisia still has abundant **plant and animal life**, and much of it can easily be seen. One problem is the lack of **identification** books. Birds are fine – many of the standard field guides include North Africa –

but **plants** are a problem since the only comprehensive guides to flora in Tunisia are highly technical, out of print, unillustrated, and in French. The following accounts therefore concentrate on species that can also be found in the northern Mediterranean, or which are covered in Oleg Polunin and Anthony Huxley's standard field guide, *Flowers of the Mediterranean* (Chatto, 1990). For general coverage of the wildlife sites of Tunisia and a detailed rundown of the species, Pete Raine's *Mediterranean Wildlife* (Rough Guides Ltd, 1990) is an invaluable companion to supplement the wildlife features in the *Rough Guide to Tunisia*.

Spring is a good time to visit. Not only are the hillsides in full flower, but April and May are also the best times for migrating birds passing through Tunisia on their way to breeding grounds further north. By **high summer** much of the country is burnt out, but good flowers are still to be found in the mountains and on the coast, and breeding is in full swing for summer migrant birds from further south. **Autumn** sees the return migration of European breeding birds, as well as a late flowering of many species of bulbs. **Winter** is the best time to visit the deserts of the south, with many of the desert plants choosing this time to flower (water permitting), and the winter season also sees the build-up of birds from Europe and Russia with huge concentrations of wildfowl and waders.

BIRDS

Tunisia's **bird** population varies widely depending on the time of the year – it's more obviously affected by migration than countries further north. During spring migration, the country can seem like the avian equivalent of Piccadilly Circus in the rush hour, when summer visitors like **bee eaters** arrive to breed from their winter quarters south of the Sahara; winter visitors, mostly **waders and wildfowl**, leave to migrate the thousands of kilometres to their breeding grounds in northern Europe; spring migrants such as **honey buzzards** pass through, sometimes in huge numbers; and the resident birds just stay where they are. In autumn, the same happens but in reverse. The best book on Tunisian bird spotting, if you can get hold of it, is the Danish-published *The Birds of Tunisia* by Peter Thomsen and Peder Jacobsen (Jelling Bey Frykheri, 1979).

FARMLAND

Farmland can be rewarding, especially where the fields are small and broken up by trees or patches of scrub. Finches are much in evidence here – familiar **goldfinches**, **linnets** and **chaffinches** are joined by the yellow **serin**, a distant relative of the canary. **Nightingales** are a common summer visitor and the colourful and exotic **hoopoe** can be found wherever there are suitable old trees for nesting. Another abundant farmland species is the resident **corn bunting**, a heavy, brown bird with a monotonous song usually described as like the jangling of a bunch of keys. The song of the small resident **fantailed warbler** is no less monotonous, a repetitive "tsip" delivered in its undulating flight. Farmland attracts **migrating quails** and is often hunted over by **black kites** – long-tailed, with level wings – and **marsh harriers**, with equally long tails but wings tilted upwards. Black and white **great grey shrikes** are also found here, often perching on telegraph wires; they're joined in summer by their smaller, red-headed relative, the **woodchat shrike**.

WOODLAND AND MOUNTAINS

Deciduous **woodlands** are really only found in the Khroumerie region in the northwest of the country, and are home to many birds which, though common in Europe, are rare in Africa. Look for **woodpeckers**, **jays**, **wrens** and **tits** all year round, with **warblers**, **nightingales** and **wrynecks** in summer. Coniferous woodlands are less exciting, although **finches**, tits and some warblers are common.

The scrubby hillsides of the north are rewarding for small species. **Sardinian warblers**, with their glossy black caps, red eyes and scratchy song, are abundant. One species found only in North Africa is **Moussier's redstart**, an extremely beautiful small bird, with a striking plumage of orange, black and white. **Stonechats** are resident in this type of habitat, and the same zones are widely used as feeding stations by migrating **wheatears**, **warblers** and **wagtails**. **Barbary partridges**, another North African species, breed on these hillsides too.

Mountains, whether the forested hills around Aïn Draham, the limestone ridge of the Dorsale, or the barren massifs of the south, are the best place to see resident **birds of prey**. **Buzzards**, **eagles**, **vultures**, **kites** and falcons all use the rocks as breeding sites, gliding out over the surrounding plains in search of food. **Blue rock thrushes**, very like blackbirds but a superb powder-blue colour, are also found in mountains, as are **black wheatears** and **rock buntings**.

THE COAST

Tunisia's **coastline** varies from the rocky shore of the north, around Bizerte, to flat mudflats in the southeast. Predictably, this is the place for **seabirds**: a wide variety of gulls and terns spend the winter here, including the **slender-billed gull** and the **Caspian tern**. The latter is the largest of the terns of the region, almost gull-sized and with a very stout red bill. The islands off the north coast have colonies of two species of **shearwater**. But it's the tidal mudflats of the Gulf of Gabes that hold the most exciting birds, with huge wintering populations of **waders** (primarily **dunlin, sandpipers, stints** and **redshank**), along with large numbers of more exotic species such as **flamingos, spoonbills** and **avocets**.

DESERT BIRDS

Finally, the hills, *oueds* (dry stream beds) and oases of the **deserts** hold their own specialities. There is a truly bewildering variety of **larks** and **wheatears** around here, enough to tax the keenest ornithologist. One especially strange lark is the **hoopoe lark**, so-called because of its long, decurved bill and black and white wings. Its song starts on the ground with a series of repeated notes, slowly ascending in pitch until the bird culminates with a final flurry of notes as it takes off vertically and then spirals down to start all over again. Another desert bird with an extraordinary call is the **trumpeter finch**, locally quite common.

MAMMALS

Although the top-of-the-food-chain predators such as lion and leopard were finally shot out earlier this century, there are still exciting species such as **jackal, wild boar, porcupine, mongoose** and **genet**, a beautiful tree-climbing carnivore with a spotted coat and a long ringed tail. The cats are still represented by **wild cats** and (it is said) **lynx**. But ignore anyone who says it's easy to see mammals; they're shy and often nocturnal, with good

reason considering the long history of hunting. But the wooded mountains of the Khroumerie hold a good range of species, as do some of the limestone mountains like Djebel Ichkeul.

Further south, small desert rodents are of interest. **Desert rats, gerbils** and **jerboas** lope around the desert at night, and a species of **suslik**, *Psammomys* (a sort of short-tailed ground squirrel with a characteristic upright "begging" posture), is common on the salt-marshes and *sebkhas* of the south. Most of the larger desert antelopes have been reduced to the point of extinction by disturbance and hunting, but a programme to reintroduce **gazelle**, **oryx** and **addax** (as well as **ostrich**, which has only been exterminated this century south of Medenine) is in progress at the national park of Bou Hedma, in the steppes near Maknassy. **Fennec foxes** (a beautiful desert fox with huge ears) certainly used to occur on Chott Djerid but may have disappeared by now.

One final **mammal** that may still exist on the shores of Tunisia is the **Mediterranean monk seal**, which is down to its last few hundred, mostly in Greece and Turkey. Perhaps a few still hang on around some of the islands off the north coast.

REPTILES AND AMPHIBIANS

Throughout the country, reptiles and amphibians are much in evidence. **Lizards** and **skinks** are everywhere on the dry hillsides, small **geckos** come out in the evenings to pursue their useful insect-eating lifestyle on the walls and ceilings of older buildings, and **frogs** and **toads** croak a deafening spring chorus wherever there is fresh water. The handsome **painted frog** is widespread, blotched in brown and green. In the desert, you sometimes see **desert lizards** running like the wind on their hind legs from bush to bush. **Tortoises** and **pond terrapins** are both, locally, quite abundant. A dozen species of **snakes** also occur; although only some are poisonous, they do include several species of **viper**, and you should be cautious when out walking on rocky hillsides – shorts and sandals are perhaps not a good idea.

BUTTERFLIES AND INVERTEBRATES

Butterflies are the most obvious insects. In spring, huge numbers of the migrant **painted**

lady cross Tunisia from further south, bound for Europe. It's a pretty extraordinary phenomenon, for although they breed in northern Europe, the young insects are doomed, as they can only very rarely survive the northern winters in hibernation. **Clouded yellows**, a deep yellow with black wing edges, undertake a similar migration but in smaller numbers. A small yellow butterfly with orange wingtips is likely to be the **Moroccan orangetip**, very common in early spring. Three striking species are the **Cleopatra**, (*Gonepteryx*), like a huge **brimstone** but with orange patches on its yellow wings, and two species of **swallowtail**. Early summer is probably the time when butterflies on the wing are at their peak. Other striking animals of the lower orders include **praying mantids**, harmless but unnerving assassins of the undergrowth and, of course, **scorpions**, which you are most unlikely to come across unless you go looking under rocks and bark.

MARINE LIFE

Finally, the **marine life** of the rocky northern coast is well worth mentioning. Some of the best snorkelling and diving in the Mediterranean is here around the **coral reefs** off Tabarca, Cap Serrat and especially off the marine national park of the Zembra isles. The coral is long dead, a memory of a time when the Mediterranean was a much warmer sea, but it holds extensive seaweed beds and numerous fish. Sadly, spearfishing is much promoted as a tourist activity.

On the other hand, the Tunisian **fishing** industry is one of the best regulated in the Mediterranean, with the National Fisheries Board (the ONP) doing a superb job in ensuring that offshore fishing remains at a sustainable level. Apparently the weight of fish per area in Tunisian waters is some twenty times the weight in areas around Sicily, where trawling is notoriously exploitative. A trip round any fish market, and especially the big one in rue d'Allemagne in Tunis, gives some idea of the range and quality of what can be caught.

FLORA

The **flora of Tunisia** stands at the crossroads between the Mediterranean flora of the north and the desert plants of the south. The forests of the Khroumerie have an almost northern European feel about them, with cork oak, flowering ash and even hawthorn growing above bracken, while only a few finely tuned species can survive in the waterless desert conditions.

FARMLAND

Farmland hosts a colourful mass of plants in spring and early summer, especially around the field margins. Characteristic plants include **scarlet pimpernel** (confusingly, bright blue in much of the Mediterranean region), **poppies**, **marigolds**, **daisies** and **campions**. The borage family is well represented; most plants of this family have hairy stems and leaves, and five-petalled flowers which are often pink in bud but blue in bloom. The **common borage** has nodding star-shaped bright blue flowers (which you can eat in salads, incidentally), the **forget-me-nots** are in the same family and so are the **buglosses**. There are a number of different bugloss species (*Echium*) in Tunisia, but they all have blue or purple trumpet-shaped flowers with protruding pink stamens. One common species in this family that breaks the blue-flowered rule is **honeywort** (*Cerinthe major*), which has unusual chocolate-tipped yellow flowers hanging in a fused tube.

Various **convolvulus** species are common: there are pink varieties in early summer and, in spring, a colourful species is the aptly named *Convolvulus tricolor* – blue around the edge, yellow in the middle, and white in between.

Although the uncultivated field margins have most of the farmland species, an occasional field will have escaped the attentions of the herbicide spray, and here you can see a blaze of colour from miles off, including the bright yellow of *Chrysanthemum coronarium*, the scarlet of **poppies**, and sometimes the nodding pink of **wild gladioli**.

A plant to watch out for on grazed agricultural land is the **asphodel** (*Asphodelus microcarpus*). It grows up to a metre in height, with flowering spikes flung up from a narrow-leaved basal bulb; the flowers are pink with darker veins. It's the classic indicator species of **overgrazed land** since livestock won't touch it, and it slowly takes over as other, more nutritious species are eaten away. In some parts of Tunisia the asphodel forms a virtual monoculture over large stretches of impoverished land.

One final group consists of introduced species. **Mimosa** or wattle is widespread, with long pendant strings of yellow flowers in spring. It's an Australian species, and well adapted to a hot dry climate. So are the **eucalyptus** (gum) trees, which have been widely planted both in forests and for roadside shade; it's hot enough for them to flower here, often very strikingly in a mass of yellow or red blossom.

On farms and around villages you're bound to see the **prickly pear**, a large cactus introduced to Europe, it is said, by Christopher Columbus. The **century plant** (*Agave amencana*) is another American species, brought over from Mexico in the eighteenth century; it produces a huge flowering spike up to ten metres high when it's ten to twenty years old, and then dies, although suckers around its edge may live on. Much smaller, but equally noticeable, is the **Bermuda buttercup**. A very common wayside plant, it flowers in spring in a sheet of absolutely brilliant yellow among bright green, trefoliate leaves. Despite its name, it was introduced from South Africa, as was the **Hottentot fig** (*Carpobrotus*). This last species now dominates sandy cliffs and banks by the sea, with its mat of fleshy leaves and psychedelic pink or yellow flowers.

THE COAST

The **coastal areas** also hold many of these farmland plants, and were in fact their original habitat in many cases. Field margins are continually being disturbed, and the plough creates an ecological niche similar to the effect of the sea and shifting sand. Three common plants around the Tunisian coast are all familiar to British gardeners. **White alyssum** (*Lobularia manbma*), beloved as an edging plant by bedding plant enthusiasts, grows sprawlingly with clusters of white flowers; **Virginia stock** (*Malcolmia mantima*), has tiny pink, red or purple four-petalled flowers; and the everlasting **sea lavender** (still known as *Statice*, although botanists have renamed it *Limonium*) has papery blue and white flowers.

Salt marshes are a common feature of the east coast, and inland there are vast dry salt lakes (*sebkkas*). These are often dominated by plants of the **glasswort** family – low shrubs with fleshy cylindrical stems and minute flowers. Only real plant freaks will want to sort them out down to species level as they're a very difficult group.

HILLSIDES AND MOUNTAINS

The scrub-covered **hillsides** of the north, and the slopes of the wetter limestone mountains of the centre, form perhaps the classic Mediterranean botanical habitat, equivalent to the *garigue* of France or the *matorral* of the Iberian peninsula. Here you can find the aromatic shrubs of **rosemary**, **sage** and **thyme**, together with the **rockroses** (*Cistus*), with their profusion of flat white or pink flowers. Limestone hills tend to have a wider variety of ground flowers than the sandstone ones; peer under the bushes for many **orchid** species, as well as **irises**, including the delightful, tiny *Iris sisyrinchium*, which only flowers in the afternoon after the heat of the sun has warmed it. A noticeable spring species here, also common on farmland, is a small **valerian**, *Fedia cornucopiae* – low-growing with clusters of pink tubed flowers. It seems to be unpalatable to goats; you see it flowering profusely where everything else has been grazed out. One plant which is heavily grazed is the **dwarf fan palm** (*Chaemerops humilis*), a low-growing relation of the ubiquitous date palm; on ungrazed hillsides (if you can find any) it can sometimes be dominant.

DESERT SPECIES

The **sand and stone deserts** south of the Dorsale mountains have a quite different flora. Plants are sparse, except in the oases where many of the farmland and hillside species mentioned above can be found, and they are highly adapted to the dry conditions. They survive in two ways. Sunlight is so abundant that they don't need big leaves to gather energy, so their leaves are reduced to **narrow stems** in order to reduce water loss by transpiration. The other technique is to try to store water, and some desert plants have fleshy, swollen leaves for this purpose. Many desert plants and shrubs have ferocious **spines**, too, as protection against grazing animals, although there's not much that can protect against the camel, which will even feed on prickly pear.

LEGENDARY TUNISIA

Long before acquiring its present name, when it still belonged primarily to early Mediterranean civilization, the land of Tunisia appeared in two of the greatest poems of European literature: Homer's *Odyssey* and Virgil's *Aeneid*. More than 2000 years later, it was this same remote past which drew many travellers to the French colony, among them the French writer Gustave Flaubert, whose novel *Salammbô* aimed to recreate one spectacular episode of the Carthaginian era.

In **Homer**'s epic of wandering and survival, the hero Odysseus, on his way home from Troy with a group of faithful but often foolish companions, is forced by hostile gods and goddesses to overcome a series of tests of his initiative before finally, after ten years, being allowed to return to his home on the island of Ithaca. Many of the episodes, such as the encounter with the one-eyed Cyclops, are now an integral part of European consciousness, and the **Land of the Lotus-Eaters** (see passage quoted on p.312) is among them.

There is an obvious and enduring fascination in the idea of a lifestyle emptied of cares by some mysterious substance, and it is hardly surprising that several places claim identity with Homer's idyllic land. Jerba's claim, however, is supported by very ancient tradition. While describing the peoples of North Africa, the fifth-century BC historian Herodotus comes to the Gindanes – a tribe, incidentally, whose

women wore a leather band around the ankle for each man they had slept with. "Within their territory," he continues, "a headland runs out into the sea, and it is here that the Lotus-Eaters dwell, a tribe which lives exclusively on the fruit of the lotus. It is about the size of a mastic-berry, and as sweet as a date. The Lotus-Eaters also make wine from it." The geographical similarity with Jerba (where the causeway connecting the island with Zarzis was probably built before Herodotus's time) is unmistakeable, and anyone who has tasted Tunisian palm-wine (*laghmi*) will agree that it is a suitably primitive source of intoxication – which might well have been in use more than 500 years before Christ.

VIRGIL: *THE AENEID*

Like Odysseus, Virgil's hero Aeneas has difficulty in escaping the seductive charms of a part of Africa, but this episode from the Aeneid is much more emotionally and politically involved. On the face of it, Aeneas's tragic love affair with Dido, queen and founder of Carthage (see p.105 for the background), is no more than that – but its implications go much deeper. Aeneas is forced to make a choice between his personal commitment to Dido and his public, divinely enforced commitment to founding a new Troy for his people – that is, Rome.

In the passage quoted here, the affair is almost at its end. Venus, goddess of love and implacable opponent of Aeneas, has made Dido fall in love with Aeneas in the hope that he will abandon the great Roman destiny planned for him by Jupiter, the king of the gods. Aeneas has duly returned Dido's feelings, their affair consummated al fresco to the accompaniment of thunder, lightning and nymphs wailing from the mountaintops – but without making any formal commitment. Dido, herself committed totally, has alienated not only the neighbouring Numidian tribes (by rejecting marriage with one of their kings, Iarbas), but, through her infidelity to her dead husband Sychaeus, also her own Phoenician people. When Jupiter sends Mercury to remind Aeneas of his destiny, therefore, Aeneas knows that to abandon Dido will be to destroy her and the whole of her life. At first he plans to leave secretly, but Dido realizes his intentions and, here, confronts him. Dido's eventual suicide on a funeral pyre symbolizes the inevitable destruction of Carthage by Imperial Rome.

The end of the affair

At last Dido accosted Aeneas, speaking first, and denounced him:

"Traitor, did you actually believe that you could disguise so wicked a deed and leave my country without a word? And can nothing hold you, not our love, nor our once plighted hands, nor even the cruel death that must await your Dido? Are you so unfeeling that you labour at your fleet under a wintry sky, in haste to traverse the high seas in the teeth of the northerly gales? Why, had you not now been searching for a home which you have never seen in some alien land, and had ancient Troy itself been still standing, would you have been planning to sail even there over such tempestuous seas? Is it from me that you are trying to escape? Oh, by the tears which I shed, by your own plighted hand, for I have left myself, poor fool, no other appeal, and by our union, by the true marriage which it was to be, oh, if I was ever kind to you, or if anything about me made you happy, please, please, if it is not too late to beg you, have pity for the ruin of a home, and change your mind. It was because of you that I earned the hate of Africa's tribes and the lords of the Numidians, and the hostility of my Tyrians also; and it was because of you that I let my honour die, the fair fame which used to be mine and my only hope of immortality. In whose hands are you leaving me to face my death, my Guest? I used to call you Husband, but the word has shrunk to Guest. What does the future hold for me now? My brother Pygmalion coming to demolish my walls, or this Gaetulian Iarbas, marrying me by capture? At least, if I had a son of yours conceived before you left, some tiny Aeneas to play about my hall and bring you back to me if only in his likeness, I might not then have felt so utterly entrapped and forsaken."

She finished. He, remembering Jupiter's warning, held his eyes steady and strained to master the agony within him. At last he spoke shortly:

"Your Majesty, I shall never deny that I am in your debt for all those many acts of kindness which you may well recount to me. And for long as I have consciousness and breath of life controls my movement, I shall never tire, Elissa, of your memory. Now I shall speak briefly of the facts. I had no thought of hiding my present departure under any deceit. Do not imagine that. Nor have I ever made any marriage-rite

my pretext, for I never had such a compact with you. If my destiny had allowed me to guide my life as I myself would have chosen, and solve my problems according to my own preference, I should have made the city of Troy, with its loved remembrances of my own folk, my first care; and, with Priam's tall citadel still standing, I should have refounded Troy's fortress to be strong once more after her defeat. But in fact Apollo at Grynium, where he gives his divination in Lycia by the lots, has insistently commanded me to make my way to Italy's noble land. Italy must be my love and my homeland now. If you, a Phoenician, are faithful to your Carthaginian fortress here, content to look on no other city but this city in far-away Africa, what is the objection if Trojans settle in Italy? It is no sin, if we, like you, look for a kingdom in a foreign country. Each time the night shrouds the earth in its moist shadows, each time the fiery stars arise, the anxious wraith of my father Anchises warns me in sleep, and I am afraid. My son Ascanius also serves as a warning to me; I think of his dear self, and of the wrong which I do him in defrauding him of his Italian kingdom, where Fate has given him his lands. And now Jove himself has sent the Spokesman of the Gods — this I swear to you by my son's life and by my father — who flew swiftly through the air, and delivered the command to me. With my own eyes I saw the divine messenger in clearest light entering the city gate, and heard his voice with my own ears. Cease, therefore, to upset yourself, and me also, with these protests. It is not by my own choice that I voyage onward to Italy."

Throughout this declaration Dido had remained standing, turned away from Aeneas but glaring at him over her shoulder with eyes which roved about his whole figure in a voiceless stare. Then her fury broke:

"Traitor, no goddess was ever your mother nor was it Dardanus who founded your line. No, your parent was Mount Caucasus, rugged, rocky, and hard, and tigers of Hyrcania nursed you … For what need have I of concealment now? Why hold myself in check any longer as if there could be anything worse to come?… Has he spared a sigh or a look in response to my weeping, or has he once softened, or shed a tear of pity for one who loved him? Depth beyond depth of iniquity! Neither Supreme Juno, nor the Father who is Saturn's son, can

possibly look with the impartial eyes of justice
on what is happening now. No faith is left
sure in the wide world. I welcomed him, a
shipwrecked beggar, and like a fool I allowed
him to share my royal place. I saved his
comrades from death and gave him back his
lost fleet ... The Furies have me now, they
burn, they drive ...! So, now, it seems, he has
his orders from Apollo's own Lycian oracle, and
next even the Spokesman of the Gods is sent
by Jove himself to deliver through the air to
him the same ghastly command! So I am to
believe that the High Powers exercise their
minds about such a matter and let concern for
it disturb their calm! Oh, I am not holding you. I
do not dispute your words. Go, quest for Italy
before the winds; sail over the waves in search
of your kingdom. But I still believe that, if there
is any power for righteousness in Heaven, you
will drink to the dregs the cup of punishment
amid sea-rocks, and as you suffer cry "Dido"
again and again. Though far, yet I shall be near,
haunting you with flames of blackest pitch.
And when death's chill has parted my body
from its breath, wherever you go my spectre
will be there. You will have your punishment,
you villain. And I shall hear; the news will
reach me deep in the world of death."

She did not finish, but at these words broke
off sharply. She hurried in her misery away and
hid from sight, leaving Aeneas anxious and
hesitant, and longing to say much more to her.
Dido fainted, and fell; and her maids took her
up, carried her to her marble bedroom and laid
her on her bed.

*Taken from Book IV of the Penguin Classics
edition, translated by W F Jackson Knight*

GUSTAVE FLAUBERT: SALAMMBÔ

*In the nineteenth century, Carthage's abrupt
and tragic end made its fabulous past irresistible to the imaginations of many Europeans,
among them Gustave Flaubert. But his decision
to write a novel about ancient Carthage probably owed as much to the present as the past;
on his first trip to the East in 1851, Flaubert had
become obsessed with "the Orient", that mythical land created by feverish post-Romantic
sensibilities. The letters which he wrote from
the Middle East (you can find some of the best
– and most lascivious – in* Flaubert in Egypt,

*published by Michael Haag) are a rich source
for these Orientalist attitudes and in* Salammbô
*are obliquely enshrined in fictional form. It
seems extraordinary that anyone could ever
have taken the historical aspect of this book
seriously. Its plot, such as it is, deals with the
War of the Mercenaries (241–37 BC) – though
with significant additions from the author's
fertile mind, including the character of
Salammbô, sex symbol supreme. Take away
the plot and you in fact lose little, as the bulk
of the novel consists of Flaubert's attempt to
recreate the atmosphere of Carthage as an
ancient Orient, something of a cross between a
Cecil B De Mille epic and a video nasty. It is
also however, highly imaginative, not to say
fantastic, and a whole generation did see the
Orient in terms quite as excessive as
Flaubert's. Eating, drinking, sex, violence,
cruelty, beauty, wealth, poverty and nearly
every human quality and activity was
grotesquely exaggerated.*

*In the episode included here, Hanno, one of
the Carthaginian generals, is in Utica snatching
in typical style a brief respite from the rigours
of campaigning against the Mercenaries, or
Barbarians.*

Hanno takes a bath

Three hours later he was still plunged in the
cinnamon oil with which the bath had been
filled; and as he bathed, he ate on a stretched
out ox hide, flamingo tongues with poppy seed
seasoned with honey. Beside him, his doctor,
standing motionless in a long yellow robe, had
the bath heated up from time to time and two
boys leaning on the steps of the pool rubbed his
legs. But the care of his body did not interrupt
his concern for the welfare of the state, and he
was dictating a letter to the Grand Council and,
as some prisoners had just been taken, wondering what terrible punishment to invent.

"Stop!" he said to a slave who stood writing
in the hollow of his hand. "Have them brought
in! I want to see them."

And from the back of the room filled with
white steam where torches cast spots of red
three Barbarians were pushed in: a Samnite, a
Spartan, and a Cappadocian.

"Continue!" said Hanno.

"Rejoice light of the Baals! Your Suffete has
exterminated the greedy dogs! Blessings on the
Republic! Order prayers to be offered!" He

noticed the captives, and then roaring with laughter: "Ha ha! My brave men from Sicca! You are not shouting so loudly today! Here I am! Do you recognize me? Where are your swords then? What terrible men, really!" And he pretended to try and hide, as if he were afraid. "You demanded horses, women, land, judicial office, no doubt, and priesthood! Why not? All right, I will give you land, and land you will never leave! You will be married to brand new gallows! Your pay? It will be melted in your mouths in the form of lead ingots! And I will set you in good positions, very high, among the clouds, so that you can be near the eagles!"

The three Barbarians, hairy and covered in rags, looked at him without understanding what he was saying. Wounded in the knees, they had been seized and bound with ropes, and the ends of the heavy chains on their hands dragged along the floor. Hanno was angry at their impassivity.

"On your knees! On your knees! Jackals! Dirt! Vermin! Excrement! So they do not answer! Enough! Silence! Have them flayed alive! No! In a moment!"

He was puffing like a hippopotamus, rolling his eyes. The scented oil ran out beneath the bulk of his body, and sticking to his scaly skin made it look pink in the torchlight.

He went on:

"For four days we have greatly suffered from the sun. Crossing the Macar some mules were lost. Despite their position, the extraordinary courage ... Ah! Demonades how I am suffering! Heat up the bricks and make them red hot!"

There was a clattering of rakes and furnaces. The incense smoked more fiercely in its large burners, and the naked masseurs, sweating like sponges, squeezed over his joints a paste composed of corn, sulphur, black wine, bitches' milk, myrrh, galbanum, and styrax. He was tormented by constant thirst: the man in yellow did not give in to this craving and, holding out a golden cup in which steamed a viper's brew:

"Drink!" he said, "so that the strength of the serpents, children of the sun, may penetrate the marrow of your bones, and take courage, reflection of the Gods! Besides, you know that a priest of Eschmoûn is watching the cruel stars around the Dog from which your illness derives. They are growing paler, like the spots on your skin, and you are not to die of it."

"Oh, yes, that is right," repeated the Suffete, "I am not to die of it!" And from his purplish lips escaped a breath more noisome than the stench of a corpse. Two coals seemed to burn in place of his eyes which had no eyebrows left; a mass of wrinkled skin hung down over his forehead; his two ears, standing out from his head, were beginning to swell, and the deep creases which made semi-circles around his nostrils gave him a strange and frightening look, like that of a wild beast. His distorted voice sounded like a roar; he said:

"Perhaps you are right, Demonades? In fact a lot of the ulcers have closed up. I feel quite robust. Just look how I eat!"

Then less out of greed than for show, and to prove to himself that he was well, he attacked cheese and tarragon stuffing, filleted fish, pumpkins, oysters, with eggs, horseradish, truffles and kebabs of little birds. As he looked at the prisoners he revelled in imagining their punishment. However he remembered Sicca, and fury at all his pains burst out in insults at these three men.

"Ah! Traitors! Wretches! Infamous cursed creatures! And you exposed me to your outrages, me! Me! The Suffete! Their services, the price of their blood, as they call it! Oh yes! Their blood! Their blood!" Then talking to himself: "They will all perish! Not one will be sold! It would be better to take them to Carthage! I should be seen ... but I have probably not brought enough chains? Write: send me ... How many of them are there? Go and ask Muthumbal! Go! No mercy! Cut off all their hands, and bring them to me in baskets!"

But strange cries, at once hoarse and shrill, could be heard in the room, above Hanno's voice and the clattering of the dishes being set round him. The noise increased, and suddenly the furious trumpeting of the elephants broke out as if battle was starting again. A great tumult surrounded the town.

The Carthaginians had not tried to pursue the Barbarians. They had settled at the foot of the walls, with their baggage, their servants, their whole satrap retinue and they were making merry in their handsome pearl-edged tents, while all that remained of the Mercenary camp was a heap of ruins on the plain. Spendius had recovered his courage. He sent out Zarxas to Mâtho, went through the woods, rallied his men (losses had not been heavy) –

and furious at having been beaten in battle, they reformed their lines, when someone discovered a vat of paraffin, no doubt abandoned by the Carthaginians. Then Spendius had pigs collected from the farms, smeared them with pitch, set light to it and drove them towards Utica.

The elephants, frightened by these flames, took flight. The ground sloped upwards, they were assailed by javelins, and turned back — and with mighty blows of their tusks and hooves they ripped, smothered, flattened the Carthaginians. Behind them, the Barbarians were coming down the hill; the Punic camp, with no defences, was sacked at the first charge, and the Carthaginians were crushed against the gates, for no one would open them for fear of the Mercenaries.

Dawn was breaking; from the west appeared Mâtho's infantrymen. At the same time horsemen came in sight; it was Narr'Havas with his Numidians. Jumping over the ravines and bushes, they drove the fugi-tives like hounds hunting hares. This reversal of fortune interrupted the Suffete. He cried out to be helped out of the bath. The three captives were still before him. Then a Negro (the same one who carried his parasol in battle) leaned over to his ear.

"Well now ...?" the Suffete slowly replied. "Oh! kill them!" he added brusquely.

The Ethiopian drew a long dagger from his belt and the three heads fell. One of them, bouncing amid the debris of the feast, jumped into the pool, and floated there for a while, with open mouth and staring eyes. The morning light was filtering in through cracks in the wall; the three bodies, lying on their chests, were streaming blood like three fountains, and a sheet of blood covered the mosaics, which had been sprinkled with blue powder. The Suffete soaked his hand in this still warm slime, and rubbed his knees with it; it had remedial powers.

Taken from the Penguin Classics edition,
translated by A J Krailsheimer

TUNISIAN LITERATURE

Across the Maghreb, modern literature is tangled up in the question of national and linguistic identity. Traditional local Arabic forms and language wrestle with the forms and language of the colonizers. The best-known work internationally tends to be written in French, but Tunisia has yet to produce a writer as widely known as Morocco's Tahar Ben Jelloun or Algeria's Rachid Mimouni. Nor does it have a resident foreign sage and interpreter to play the role that Paul Bowles has done in Morocco for the last forty years. In the first half of the century, though, two precocious writers — both fated to die young — did emerge from colonial Tunisia.

ABU-L-QASIM AL-SHABBI

Abu-l-Qasim al-Shabbi (1909–34), a native of Tozeur in the south, was the son of a judge who sent him at the age of twelve to study at the Zitouna mosque in Tunis. He subsequently studied law, but already he was more interested in poetry, which he read widely. Goethe, Lamartine and the Syrian American Gibran Kahlil Gibran were particular influences.

By the age of eighteen his own poetry was being published and in 1929 he delivered a famous and influential lecture in Tunis on "The poetic imagination of the Arabs". Rejecting the stifling weight of the past represented by classical Arabic poetry, he made a plea for the poet's "freedom to imagine". His own work, while retaining the essentials of classical form and language, expresses a distinctly Romantic sensibility. The poems are full of solitary individuals yearning for self-expression, frequently in settings that consist of mountains covered with rushing streams and leafy forests. Neither Tunis nor Tozeur has many of these, but al-Shabbi spent his summers in Ain Draham and presumably drew his inspiration from the scenery around there. He died of a cardiac problem at the age of twenty-five, but not before achieving an extraordinary reputation. His poem "The Will of Life" has been taught to schoolchildren across the Arab world. Like several of his poems, it hints at the frustrations of the colonized state in which al-Shabbi found himself and his country.

THE WILL OF LIFE

If one day the people should choose life
Fate is certain to respond.
The night will surely retreat,
and fetters be broken!
He who is not embraced by the longing for life
will evaporate in vacancy and be forgotten —
Grief to anyone not aroused by the breathing
desire for life!
Let him beware the slap of oblivion!
This is what life said to me,
this is how its spirit spoke.

The wind muttered between the ravines;
"When I aspire to a goal,
I ride my wishes, forgetting caution,
face the wilderness, the rugged trails
and flaming days —
He who does not like scaling mountains
will live eternally in potholes."

So the sap of youth churned in my heart
as other winds raged within my breast.
I bent my head, listening to
the clap of thunder,
the chime of the draft,
the cadence of the rain.

When I asked the earth,
"Mother, do you hate mankind?"
She replied, "I bless those with ambition,
those who brave danger —
I curse the ones not keeping step with time,
who are content to live a fossil life.
The vibrating universe loves what moves
and despises the dead, forgetting their
greatness.
The horizon hugs no stiffened bird,
nor does the bee kiss a withered flower.
Not even graves would hold the dead,
save for the tenderness in my motherly heart!
Woe to one not longing for life!
Let him beware the curse of extinction!"

On an autumn night laden with boredom,
I was so drunk on starlight my sadness drank
too.
I asked the dark
"Does life return the spring of youth
once it is withered?"

The lips of darkness did not move,
nor did the virginal dawn.
Then the forest gently spoke
like the quiver of a chord:
"Winter comes, winter of mist,
winter of snow, winter of rain,
and magic dissolves.
What budded and ripened,
the gleaming angles of fields
and quiet magic of the sky –
gone like branches
that fall with their leaves.
Now the wind tosses dead petals,
the flood buries them haphazardly.
All perish like a lovely dream
which shimmered in some heart then
disappeared.
Only the seeds remain, kernels of memory,
still embracing, even under the fog, the snows,
the heaps of earth –
the shadow of life that never palls,
the green germ of spring
dreaming of birdcall,
the musk of flowers, the tang of fruit."

✳✳✳

The diaphanous night revealed a Beauty
that kindled the mind.
A strange magic was flung across the skies
as a giant wizard lit the glittering stars.
Incense drifted from flowers on the moon's
quiet wings ...
a holy hymn ringing out in a temple!
Across the universe it was proclaimed:
Endeavour is the flame of life,
the heart of victory.
If the spirit chooses life,
Fate is certain to respond!

From Songs of Life *translated by Lena Jayyusi
and Naomi Shihab Nyc (Beit al-Hikma,
Carthage 1987)*

ALI DU'AJI

*Another member of the same Tunis literary
circles was* **Ali Du'aji** *(1909–49). Born into a
comfortably-off Tunis family, Du'aji wrote
plays, sketches, stories and songs, as well as
editing literary journals. Like al-Shabbi, he
wrote in Arabic but read much foreign literature: Chekhov, Flaubert, Jack London and Mark
Twain. Twain's influence in particular is detect-
able in the ironic modern tone that Du'aji incor-*

*porated into his observations of contemporary
urban life. One of his most successful works is*
Bar-hopping along the Mediterranean, *a series
of sketches about a Mediterranean cruise in
1933. Like a photographic negative of most
travel writing, this provides a rare glimpse of
what the dominant European culture looked
like to an educated colonial citizen.*

*At the Beach at Hammam-Lif, the short
sketch reprinted here, is typical of Du'aji's
portraits of everyday Tunisian life. Deceptively
casual, it carries more weight than might at
first appear. Its narrator, rootless and anonymous in the crowd, could be any alienated
urban character from the West – Albert Camus'*
The Outsider, *for example, wandering aimlessly
a few years later along Algiers' beaches. At the
same time, though, this character's cultural
references – Romeo and Juliet on the one
hand, the palace of the Al-Hambra in Granada
on the other – betray a consciousness of his
dual heritage in both the West and the Arab
world. In just a few deft paragraphs, Du'aji
conveys the complex texture of Tunis's new
urban culture: simultaneously old and new,
Arab and Western.*

AT THE BEACH AT HAMMAM-LIF

The car on the train was packed with a very
heavy woman, and heavy she was! Added to
her weight, she wore a red cape, the same
colour as her lips and fingernails. Just as she
filled the car with her flesh, she filled it with
her movements, and with her son too. Wouldn't
you know, her son had a big fat head and he
too was wearing red. I imagined that wearing
red and being fat ran in the family. The kid was
screaming like he was crying, but he wasn't
crying at all. Everyone in the car was bothered
by the screaming. They just wanted to keep
him happy by giving him what he wanted. The
questions kept coming. One person asked him
what he wanted; another bounced him on his
knee; a third patted him on the nose. But the
kid got angrier and screamed all the more, as
though he were screaming just for the sake of
screaming. He didn't want a sandwich, he
didn't want a toy horn. To tell the truth, twenty
minutes was all I could take of this little brat,
and I decided to move to another car.

I didn't see anyone at first, and I went in
thinking the coast was clear. That is, until I
walked past the second compartment where I

found a young couple whom we would classically refer to as "Romeo and Juliet". Romeo was over six feet tall, gaunt and very pale, with a long nose. He looked like a poet. Juliet was Sicilian, medium height, and wearing bright yellow, the way a king would wear an ermine robe. They were speaking in whispers and moving their hands a lot to overcome the loud noise around them. Romeo would put up his hands, then pull his left hand forward as though he were saying: "I love you and I'll kill your father with a dagger if ..." Juliet was rolling her fingers around as though she were answering: "I'll embroider you a scarf that you'll be proud to wear in front of the vice-consul."

It was unbearable, sitting next to a pair of lovers, seeing and hearing only gestures ... And for this I took the train? Yes, I took it to go to Hammam-Lif. What was important was that I get there. So I decided to leave all the cars altogether, sit out the journey on one of the car steps watching the telegraph poles and counting them where I could.

From the station to the beach, I walked quickly so I could get to see the bathers. What's nice is that it's not just the "nose" beach [a pun on Arabic name Hammam al-Anf, meaning "the nose bath"], but every-other-part-of-the-body beach as well, the thigh beach and the breast beach and ... and ... and ...

The beach was full of peanut and lemonade vendors, and of bathers too, and wonderful white sheets.

The peanut and lemonade vendors are notorious for their filthiness and arrogance. As for the bathers, men and women alike, stripped of their clothes and their modesty, they feel the heat at times and throw themselves into the water. When they get cold in the water, they stretch out exposing their bodies, catching the rays of the sun. And there they were, all day long, between hot and cold.

Tradition has it that a person who bathes all day long is considered one of the "in-crowd", while the person who gives up and gets dressed after half an hour is considered an outsider.

The white sheets are something else. Those wrapped up in them are creatures who follow the tradition of their grandmothers, covering their soft bodies. Keeping up with the times, they come out to the beach mocking this one's hair-do and that one's wrinkled

trousers. There's one who forgets that she's veiled and shows you her pretty face. Then she remembers and disappears under her veil after electrically charging up four young men on the beach who had been watching her all the while.

Walking along that road I was imagining all those bodies dressed in Andalusian clothes with wide pantaloons, belly dancing in a courtyard at al-Hambra. Then, all of a sudden, a bird drilling in air manoeuvres dropped a bomb on my fez that I didn't notice. If it weren't for the passers-by laughing and pointing at my venerable head, I wouldn't have realized that there was something there that was arousing the curiosity of all these distinguished people. I took off the fez and found it decorated from that damned bird's bomb. Who was it who described the bird as an angel? If I found him, I'd show him a devil.

It was better that I not stay at Hammam-Lif nor at "the pool" after it got out that I was wearing the target for bird manoeuvres on my head. So I headed back. By the grace of God I found the train empty except for an old man who knew every single villa along the tracks that ran from Hammam-Lif to Tunis.

From Sleepless Nights, *translated by William Granara (Beit al-Hikma, Carthage 1991)*

MUSTAPHA TLILI

*Educated in Paris and the US and a resident of New York, **Mustapha Tlili** (born 1937) writes – unlike al-Shabbi and Du'aji – in French. Lion Mountain, first published in 1988, is his fourth novel. Set in an anonymous village, it is a stark exploration of national identity in post-colonial North Africa. The villagers, represented by the narrator's mother Horia, share a strong sense of local identity and history. Virtually unaffected by the French, with Independence they ironically find their community much more threatened by the new state's demand for central control, and the story's violent ending has a sense of tragic inevitability. If the novel is pessimistic about the degree of legitimacy that independent North African states can hope for, contemporary events in Algeria since it was published suggest that it is not completely out of line. One can only hope that Tunisia is more successful in working through the troubled legacy of colonial rule.*

In the extract that follows, the village receives its first representative of the new independent government.

LION MOUNTAIN

The delegate, the new authorities' very first representative in Lion Mountain, wanted to enrol all adult males in the Party. The portrait Saad draws of him is hardly flattering. A short, slightly built young man, it seems. His forehead is low and narrow. He has a thin moustache. Like one of those circumflex accents Little Brother used to pen so neatly but with too much ink when he was still at school, the moustache sits upon a dry and bony face deeply pitted by smallpox. Petty malevolence made flesh and blood.

And the man appears to be very full of himself. Always sprucely turned out, with a perpetually dashing air. He invariably wears a three-piece suit of shiny black material. It seems that from the first day, nobody was left in any doubt at all about the man's colossal self-importance, arrogance and conceit, which he shows off at the wheel of a luxurious black Citroën, driving with ostentation and contempt through the narrow, stony streets of our poor little village at breakneck speed, making an incredible racket and leaving behind great clouds of dust.

As soon as he took charge of the Delegation, which had remained unoccupied for more than a year, our little village tyrant, who thirsted for influence and authority, selected – out of all the possible candidates to fill the office of public crier – Horia's retarded farmhand. Who would ever have imagined it?

And so from dawn to dusk for three days running, the Simpleton shouted his lungs out in every corner of Lion Mountain: in the Spring, our former French quarter; in the old village, from house to house and in front of every street stall; even at the doors of the mosque, as well as for the benefit of the ruminating camels in the livestock market, the exhausted mules and donkeys brutalized by the heat and human stupidity, assorted skeletal stray dogs, and the cackling chickens roaming freely over Highway 15 as it lay dreaming in the spring sunshine.

And what tidings did this inspired messenger bring? That the Party was the Motherland. That everyone should prove his great worth by acquiring a Party card – upon payment of a

certain sum, of course. And no holdouts, or else! Recalcitrants risked losing their share of irrigation water. Close scrutiny would unmask the guilty ones.

Since what was at stake was the life or death of their crops and tiny plots of land, the source of all wellbeing for them and theirs, all male adults had felt they had no other choice but to accept their fate and trudge off, one by one, heads bowed in resignation, to the former police station now serving as headquarters for the new authorities.

Horia's property was upstream, however, and too close to the spring to risk being deprived of its fair share of water. Following the example of the other villagers, and just to be on the safe side, Saad had nevertheless thought it wise to ask Imam Sadek for his advice. The latter, after careful consideration, had confirmed the Nubian's original opinion. No, Horia and Saad weren't at risk, that was quite true. Still, it was better to be practical, after all, and cooperate with the authorities. In a word, to avoid unnecessary complications, the imam had advised against causing any trouble, because he, too, was beginning to be apprehensive about the future.

As always, however, Saad will end up doing exactly as he pleases. As always, he'll insist on seeing things only in their simplest, most essential light. And to get to the heart of a problem, he had decided there was only one way to go.

His reasoning was crystal clear. The house isn't on fire, he told himself. The village is in no danger, right? Now, he, Saad, learned all he needs to know about danger at Monte Cassino. No one, and certainly not that scarecrow of a petty tyrant at the Delegation, has to cry danger while waving a Party card under his nose. If Horia, if Imam Sadek, or the Ouled El-Gharib clan were threatened, then, yes, it would be understandable. In which case, plenty of people can vouch for the Corporal's courage. Everyone knows what he can do. Even though he has only one leg left, through the fault of the Infidels, nobody doubts that if he had to, he would not hesitate to take up a weapon. Even ... to take the machine gun from its hiding place under the ancient mulberry tree, the same gun the Simpleton discovered one day while chasing around after partridges, and which has been kept in perfect shape, unbeknownst to anyone, not even Horia, thanks to his secret but constant attention. No, really, decided the Nubian, the house is not on fire. Thank the Party anyway for having thought of him. And thanks also to Monsieur the Delegate and Madame the Motherland. It's very nice, all that, but really, no thanks.

From Lion Mountain, *translated Linda Coverdale (Little, Brown, 1990)*

BOOKS

Publishing details below first give the British and then the US publisher where both exist. Where books are published in one country only, UK or US follows the publisher's name to indicate which. Books designated o/p are currently out of print, but still worth tracking down second-hand or in libraries. Some will occasionally be reprinted or published in a new edition.

TWENTIETH-CENTURY TRAVEL WRITERS

Norman Douglas, *Fountains in the Sand* (OUP, UK, o/p). Douglas, one of the most famous early modern travellers, as well as a pederast and a bigot, nonetheless writes in a compelling style about his travels around the Jerid. He saw the Chott, like just about everything else in Tunisia, as a symbol for the "sterility of the Arab soul".

Aldous Huxley, *In a Tunisia Oasis* (in a collection called *The Olive Tree*; Chatto and Windus, o/p/Ayer). If you can disregard the snide racist tone, this is by far the best of a largely barren English tradition of travel writing about Tunisia. Some things in Nefta have changed very little.

Reginald Rankin, *Tunisia* (1930, o/p). Wholly eccentric and spiced with prejudice, arrogance and sheer stupidity, but still a good read in spite, or because of, all that.

Sacheverell Sitwell, *Mauretania* (1940, o/p). Written by the aristocratic brother of the more famous Osbert and Edith, a member of the prewar international glamour set, who played a prolific but insignificant part in the era's travel-writing boom.

Leo Africanus, *History and Description of Africa* (translated by J Pory, 1896, o/p). Written by a Spanish Moor who converted to Christianity after being captured at sea by Christian corsairs. He got his nickname from the pope, who encouraged him to write about the Arabs of Barbary. Not surprisingly, there's more than a whiff of propaganda in some of the accounts.

James Bruce, *Travels to Discover the Source of the Nile in the Years 1768–73* (Gregg International, UK). Six volumes of some of the most entertaining travel writing ever published. An eccentric British consul at Algiers, Bruce passed through Tunisia on his way to Cairo and Ethiopia (to which most of the book is devoted; the Tunisian section was actually deleted after the first edition). Bruce's egocentric and extrovert personality made other people's behaviour a source of fascination to him – a fascination brilliantly conveyed in blunt and lively style.

D Bruun, *Cave-Dwellers of Southern Tunisia* (Darf, UK, o/p). Bruun was one of the first Europeans to live with the people of Matmata and Haddej, and his sympathetic account is still interesting if you can find it in a library. Unfortunately, at the end of the book the author attempts to divest a wandering nomad of clothes for his museum back home.

Olfert Dapper, *Africa* (translated by J Ogilby, 1670, o/p). An encyclopedic compendium of reports culled from many different sources, full of fascinating nuggets.

Alexandre Dumas, *Tangier to Tunis* (Peter Owen, UK, o/p). Dumas is not at his best here, and the editing has shortened the chapters on Tunisia, but there are some amusing vignettes in this rare translation of one of the many French travellers – Dumas visited in 1846.

Sir Harry Johnston, *A Journey through the Tunisian Sahara* (Geographic Magazine, o/p). Johnston, though handicapped by a lack of basic knowledge, was one of the first Englishmen to make an effort, during his travels from Jerba to Matmata, to understand the Tunisian people and their way of life.

Lt Col Sir R Lambert Playfair, *Murray's Handbook for Travellers in Algeria and Tunis* (Murray, o/p). Written by a British consul at Algiers whose unimaginative outlook is redeemed only slightly by his erudition.

Dr Thomas Shaw, *Travels and Observations Relating to Several Parts of Barbary and the Levant* (Gregg International, UK, o/p). The author, an exceedingly dry Scot, spent most of his time in North Africa misidentifying and cataloguing every Roman site he could find.

Sir Grenville Temple, *Excursions in the Mediterranean* (1835, o/p). An early imperialist view of Tunisia. The author, something of an amateur Romantic artist, produced some unlikely versions of the monuments and scenery he encountered.

Herbert Vivian, *Tunisia and the Modern Barbary Pirates* (1899, o/p). Vivian, if anything even more unpleasant than Lt Col Playfair (they met in a Tunis hotel, an encounter mentioned in the book), seems to have been gathering a little intelligence in the new French colony.

ANCIENT HISTORY AND LITERATURE

Peter Brown, *Augustine of Hippo: a Biography* (Penguin, UK/US); **Augustine**, *Confessions* (Penguin, UK/US). Brown's classic biography contains much interesting background material on the Africa of Augustine's time. *Confessions* is the saint's most accessible work, a spiritual autobiography.

Gustave Flaubert, *Salammbô* (Penguin, UK/US). Sex, violence and more violence: it's all here in a nineteenth-century novel that anticipates Cecil B De Mille. Flaubert claimed to have written a historical account of Carthage's brutal civil war with its Mercenaries (241–37 BC), but the book owes little to history and everything to its author's obsession with the fabulous Orient. An extraordinarily bad novel, but a very enjoyable read.

Serge Lancel, *Carthage* (Blackwell, UK/US). A new and serious history of Carthage, translated from the French.

Susan Raven, *Rome in Africa* (Routledge, UK/US). A new and well-illustrated survey of Roman (and Carthaginian) North Africa.

Sallust, *The Jugurthine War* (Penguin, UK/US); **Livy**, *The War with Hannibal* (Penguin Classic, 1970); **Polybius**, *The Rise of the Roman Empire* (Penguin Classic, 1979). These are the texts Flaubert used. Sallust's book is the shortest, but by far the most entertaining, with melodramatic accounts of African war and

Roman morality. Livy and Polybius are rather too much to the historical point.

David Soren et al., *Carthage* (Norton, o/p/ Touchstone, o/p). Written by Carthage archeologists to accompany a museum exhibition that toured North America, this is a very readable introduction to the Carthaginian and Roman cultures of ancient Tunisia.

Virgil, *The Aeneid* (Penguin, UK/US). Books I and IV of the great Roman epic poem tell the tragic love story of Queen Dido (founder of Carthage) and Aeneas (founder of Rome), an inspiration to artists of every age since. The first version is still the best: read it and decide whether you can have any sympathy for the careerist Aeneas – and to get an idea of the mystique of Carthage.

TUNISIAN AND ARAB HISTORY

Lisa Anderson, *The State and Social Transformation in Tunisia and Libya, 1830–1980* (Princeton University Press, UK/US, o/p). Don't be put off by the thesis-like title; this is a good review of Tunisian and Libyan political and social history.

E W Bovill, *The Golden Trade of the Moors* (OUP, o/p/Wiener). Hard to classify, this wide-ranging book about trans-Saharan trade is full of intriguing details about a fascinating and little-studied subject.

Fernand Braudel, *A History of the Mediterranean in the Sixteenth Century* (Fontana/HarperCollins). With over 1000 densely packed pages, this is not for reading at one sitting. It is, however, a magisterial piece of work about the century that saw Tunisia on the front line of East–West confrontation. Buy it to browse for unexpected insights into Tunisia's position in the wider context.

Leon Carl Brown, *The Tunisia of Ahmed Bey, 1837–1856* (Princeton University Press, US, o/p). A fascinating insight into nineteenth-century Tunisia and the problems faced by an Arab government struggling to keep itself out of European clutches. Available in most university libraries.

André Gide, *Amyntas* (J Lane, o/p/Ecco Press). An early work by the French writer whose experiences in the North African colonies (including meeting Oscar Wilde) were a lasting influence.

Albert Hourani, *A History of the Arab Peoples* (Faber/Harvard University Press). If you have the time to read it, this expansive and panoramic view of Arab history is the best available.

Alistair Horne, *A Savage War of Peace* (Macmillan/Penguin). The standard English-language history of the Algerian War (1954–62): a readable and even-handed account, though stronger on the French perspective.

Ibn Khaldoun, *The Muqaddimah* (Routledge, UK/US). A translation, by N J Dawood, of the masterpiece by Tunisia's great fourteenth-century historian, whose fascinating mix of sociology, history and anthropology was centuries ahead of its time.

Wifrid Knapp, *Tunisia* (Thames and Hudson, UK, o/p). The most worthwhile of several introductory history-background books that came out in the 1960s and 70s.

Peter Mansfield, *The Arabs* (Penguin, UK/US). By far the best introduction to the Arab world available. A general history of the region, from Islam's beginnings to the end of the 1970s, followed by a short section on each country and two excellent final chapters: "Through European Eyes" and "Through Arab Eyes".

Arthur Marsden, *British Diplomacy and Tunis, 1875–1902* (Scottish Academic Press, UK, o/p). If you want to see how devious and calculating the foreign powers were in dividing up the Mediterranean, then this is the book to read – very scholarly but never dry.

Charles Messenger, *The Tunisian Campaign* (Ian Allan, UK, o/p). A pictorial history of World War II in Tunisia.

Magali Morsy, *North Africa 1800–1900. A Survey from the Nile Valley to the Atlantic* (Longman, UK/US, o/p). An excellent history of North Africa in a period of crisis, placing Tunisia in the context of North Africa as a whole.

Jamil M Abun-Nasr, *A History of the Maghreb* (Cambridge University Press, UK). An authoritative history of the region by a distinguished Maghrebian historian, but not exactly light reading.

W Perkins, *Tunisia: Crossroads of the Islamic and European Worlds* (Scarecrow, UK/US). The best pocket history of Tunisia available. Authoritative and a good read.

Norma Salem, *Habib Bourguiba, Islam and the Creation of Modern Tunisia* (1985, o/p).

Another political history – a bit too much of a eulogy to be credible as a balanced review, and occasionally dull, but a nonetheless competent biography of the great man.

MODERN LITERATURE

*If you read French, look out for the publications of **Editions Sindbad** and **Editions Salammbô** in Tunisia. They publish contemporary writers in the original and in translation. Tunisian literature in English is rare.*

Paul Bowles, *The Spider's House* (Sphere/Black Sparrow). Though set in Morocco, this is well worth considering. The legendary American expatriate's best book, it is also one of the best political novels ever written, its backdrop the traditional daily life of Fes, its theme the conflicts and transformation at the last stages of French occupation of the country.

Ernle Bradford, *The Sultan's Admiral* (Hodder and Stoughton, UK, o/p). A very readable biography of Kair ed Din Barbarossa, giving an excellent taste of the corsair rivalries of the sixteenth century.

Abu-l-Qasim al-Shabbi, *Songs of Life* (Beit Al-Hikma, Carthage). Poetry doesn't translate any better from Arabic than from other languages, but this does at least provide a sense of the Romantic sensibility of Tunisia's national poet (see p.412).

Ali Du'aji, *Sleepless Nights* (Beit Al-Hikma, Carthage). Short sketches by the mid-century writer, translated – unusually – into English (see p.413).

Gisèle Halimi, *Milk for the Orange Tree* (Quartet, UK). A Jewish civil rights lawyer in France, part of Halimi's autobiographical account paints a picture of her childhood in Tunisia.

Patricia Highsmith, *The Tremor of Forgery* (Penguin/Grove Atlantic). Set in 1960s Hammamet, this is a characteristically creepy piece of work by the author of the Ripley books. Although Graham Greene described it as her finest novel, it is only spasmodically available.

Amin Maalouf, *Leo the African* (Abacus/New Amsterdam). An interesting attempt by a Lebanese writer at the fictional autobiography of Leo Africanus, the Christian convert whose career mirrors the to-and-fro of the sixteenth-century Mediterranean (see p.417).

Albert Memmi, *Colonizer and the Colonized* (Earthscan/Beacon); *The Pillar of Salt* (Elek, o/p/Beacon). Tunisia's most distinguished novelist, whose main theme is the problem of identity for North African Jews such as himself. Other books of his available in English include *The Scorpion* (O'Hara, US) and *Jews and Arabs* (O'Hara, US).

Mustapha Tlili, *Lion Mountain* (Arcade, UK/ US). Excellent characterization in this short novel about the tragic effects of progress, tourism and dictatorship on a remote Tell village.

ISLAM AND SOCIETY

The Koran (Penguin, UK/US; OUP, o/p). The word of God as handed down to the Prophet is the basis of all Islam, and notoriously untranslatable. Though the full effect is still probably lost, the OUP edition is the one to go for; Penguin's is stultifyingly prosaic.

Minority Rights Group Report, *Arab Women* (MRG, UK/US, o/p). A general survey of the status of women, country by country, through the Arab world. The small section on Tunisia is dated but still a good introduction.

Jean Duvignaud, *Change at Shebika* (Allen Lane, o/p/University of Texas Press, o/p). In the 1960s, a group of French and Tunisian sociologists spent a year living in this isolated village near Tozeur. This is an interesting, honest account of their contacts with the people, sometimes open but plagued with misunderstanding and uncertainty. Duvignaud describes the position of the women, families, religion and their working lives; in part he is vague and impressionistic but the conclusion – that local customs were inadequate in a time of social change – seems fair enough.

Ernest Gellner, *Muslim Society* (CUP, UK/US, o/p). The most comprehensive and thought-provoking study available on the subject by a brilliant and well-established scholar. Certainly not easy-going, but thoroughly recommended.

N Minai, *Women in Islam* (John Murray, o/p/ Putnam, o/p). Combines a valuable historical survey with an interesting analysis of contemporary Arab society, looking at the changing status of women from the time of Mohammed, through the Caliphate, to the Ottomans, then describing the customs and traditions in vari-

ous countries, applied at each stage of a woman's life.

Edward Mortimer, *Faith and Power* (Faber, o/p/Random House). A useful introduction to the complex relationship between Islam and politics; a general historical background is followed by six case studies of countries ranging from Iran to secularized Turkey.

S H Nasr, *Ideals and Realities of Islam* (Aquarian/Thorsons). An excellent survey of Islam, and sufficiently detailed to be convincing. The chapters on the Koran, Hadith and Sharia give especially clear explanations.

Edward Said, *Orientalism: Western Concepts of the Orient* (Penguin/Random House). A book that pulls no punches, this radical analysis of Western attitudes to the Arab world was received with some hostility when it was first published. Said, a literary critic of Palestinian origin, approaches the problem through the writings of nineteenth-century travellers (such as Flaubert), and develops it into an attack on virtually every so-called modern Western "expert" on the Arab world. Some of the literary criticism, showing how the myth of "The Orient" was created and fostered by a dominant and arrogant Europe, is extremely acute, and his accusations of modern racism are hard to deny; but it's not true that these prejudices are shared by every Western specialist.

Lucette Valensi and Abraham Udovitch, *The Last Arab Jews* (Gordon and Breach, US). The definitive study of the Jerban community, its history, sociology and prospects. Good illustrations too. Lucette Valensi has also written *Tunisian Peasants in the Eighteenth and Nineteenth Centuries* (CUP, UK).

ART AND ARCHITECTURE

Michael Brett, *The Moors* (Orbis, o/p/Salem House, o/p). A glossy picture book on the western Arabs, with an unusually well-informed text by an expert in the field. A good investment.

T Burkhardt, *Art of Islam* (World of Islam Festival Publishing, UK, o/p). A highly conceptual and impressionistic account of the relationship between Islamic doctrine and its art. Some of the best illustrations around, even if the text is at times hard to grasp.

Jerrilynn Dodds, ed., *Al-Andalus – The Art of Islamic Spain* (Abrams/Metropolitan Museum of Art). Of tangential interest, with its emphasis on Spain and limited coverage of North Africa – but a useful context.

R Dunbabih, *The Mosaics of Roman North Africa* (Clarendon Press, US, o/p). Dry and academic, this is unfortunately the only work in English about Tunisia's wonderful Roman mosaics.

Derek Hill and Lucien Golvin, *Islamic Architecture of North Africa* (Faber, o/p/Shoe String Press, o/p). It's a sad comment that this is the best available introduction to Tunisian architecture. Intended originally as an artists' guide to Islamic patterns, the pictures are numerous but of variable quality; the fuller historical introduction and notes on individual buildings are useful.

Anthony Hutt, *Islamic Architecture – North Africa* (Scorpion, UK, o/p). Little more than a picture book, but almost unique in its focus on the region.

D. Mitchell, ed., *Islamic Architecture* (Thames and Hudson, UK, o/p). Along with Rogers, the best of the books on architecture, with interesting articles on domestic architecture and regional styles.

Michael Rogers, *The Spread of Islam* (Elsevier-Phaidon, UK, o/p). In a book about the whole geographical range of Islam there's relatively little on Tunisia specifically; but this is much the best general survey around of Islamic society, art and architecture. Strongly recommended if you can get hold of it.

LANGUAGE

Arabic is a notoriously difficult language for Europeans to learn, and further complicated by the fact that it varies considerably from country to country within the Arab world, not only in pronunciation but in vocabulary. Fortunately, however, Tunisia is virtually bilingual, and even in the remotest of places you will find someone who can also speak French. With even basic school-knowledge French you'll find you can get by quite well.

For all this, though, French was the language of colonialism and any attempt at Arabic – even the most stumbling – will be well received. Included here are some very basic words and phrases; if you want to learn seriously, the Bourguiba School in Tunis (see p.98) is highly recommended and exceptional value.

TUNISIAN ARABIC

The transliteration is highly approximate, and intended to function phonetically. "Kh" represents a sound like the "ch" in loch, while "gh" represents a sort of gargling sound like a French "r".

BASICS

Yes	Ayi, Aiwa	You (plural)	Intoo
No	La	They	Hoom
Please	Minfadlik*	There's, Is there?, There are, Are there?	Famma (?)
Thank you	Bark Allahufik*, Shukran	There isn't, There aren't	Famma aysh
Excuse me	Samahanee	Good	Behi
I	Ana	Not good	Mish behi, Khayeb
You	Inti, Inta*	A lot	Barsha
She	Hiya	A little	Yasser
He	Huwa		
We	Ihna		

*In theory, there are two singular forms of "you": *inti* when addressing a woman and *inta* when addressing a man. In most of Tunisia, however, *inti* is used for everyone (to the shocked surprise of non-Tunisian Arab men). A lot of words referring to "you" end in *-ik*; strictly speaking, when addressing a man this should be *-ak*.

ARABIC NUMBERS

1	Wahad	10	Ashara	90	Tissaeen
2	Zous, Etneen	20	Ashreen	100	Mia
3	Tlaata	30	Talaateen	200	Miateen
4	Arbaa	40	Arabaeen	300	Tlaata mia
5	Khamsa	50	Khamseen	400	Arba mia
6	Sitta	60	Sitteen	1000	alf
7	Sabaa	70	Sabaeen	2000	alfayn
8	Tmaania	80	Temaaneen	5000	khams alef
9	Tissa				

GREETINGS AND FAREWELLS

Hello	*Assalama*	Good night	*Tisbah ala khir*
Good morning	*Sabah el khir*	Goodbye	*Bisalama, Filaman*
(response)	*(Sabah en nour)*	My name's ...	*Ismi ...*
Good evening	*Missa el khir*	What's your name?	*Sismik?**
(response)	*(Missa en nour)*	Where are you from?	*Mineen inti?, Mineen inta?**
How are you?	*Ashnooa ahwalik**	I'm from ...	*Ana min ...*
Fine, thanks	*Labes elhamdulillah*	Bon voyage	*Treq salama*
And you?	*Winti?, Winta?* *	See you later	*N'shoofik** *minbad*

DIRECTIONS AND TRAVELLING

Is there a ... near here?	*Fee ... qareb min hina?*	Left	*Lisaar*
Where is the ...?	*Fayn el ...?*	Right	*Limin*
Hotel	*Nezel*	Near	*Qareb*
Restaurant	*Mataam*	Far	*Bayeed*
Bank	*Bunk*	Here	*Hina*
Train (station)	*(Mahata el) tran*	There	*Radi, Hinik**
Bus (station)	*(Mahata el) car*	When?	*Waqtesh?*
Museum	*Methab*	First	*El uwel*
Ruin	*Athar*	Next	*El jai*
Toilet	*Mihath*	Last	*El akher*
Straight on	*Tul*	Could you write it please?	*Yoomkin tnajim tekta-bah minfadlik?**

SHOPPING AND ACCOMMODATION

Have you got ...?	*Andik***...?*	(Too) expensive	*Ghalee (barsha)*
A room	*Bit, Ghorfa*	Still expensive	*Mazal ghalee*
A shower	*Doosh*	Have you got anything ...?	*'Andik** *haja ...?*
Hot	*Skhoon*	... better	*... khir*
Cold	*Biird*	... cheaper	*... arkhis*
Can I have a ...?	*Yoomkin wahad ...?*	... bigger	*... akbar*
Can I buy ...?	*Yoomkin ashtiri ...?*	... smaller	*... asghar*
Can I see ...?	*Yoomkin ashoofa ...?*	I haven't got any	*Ma'andish*
How much is ...?	*Kaddesh ...?*	Open	*Mahloul*
This	*Hada*	Closed	*Msaker*
That	*Hadik**		

OTHER COMMON OR USEFUL EXPRESSIONS

Slowly	*Shwaya shwaya*	In the name of God	*Bismillah (used when starting a meal or journey)*
Go away	*Imshi, Barra*		
Later	*Minbad*		
Never mind	*Maalesh*	Money	*Floos*
The same	*Kif Kif*	Let's go!	*Yalla, Nimshi!*
Praise be to God	*El Hamdulillah (used whenever mentioning any kind of good fortune, repeated in response)*	Chill out	*Wasa balek (lit: "lengthen your mind")*
		Shame on you!	*Shooma!*
God willing	*Insh'Allah (used in any reference to hopes or the future, repeated in response)*	I don't know	*Ma'arfsh/Mish 'arif*
		I don't understand	*Mefehemsh/Mish fehem*

TIME AND DAYS

What time is it?	Kaddesh loweqet?	Now	El an
One o'clock	El wahad	Later	Minbad
Five past one	El wahad wa draj	Today	El yoom
Ten past one	El wahad wa darjeen	Tomorrow	Ghudwa
Quarter past one	El wahad warbo'o	Yesterday	El barah
Twenty past one	El wahad warba'a	Sunday	El had
Twenty-five past one	El wahad wa khamsa	Monday	El tneen
Half-past one	El wahad wa nuss	Tuesday	El tlata
Twenty-five to two	El wahad wa sabaa	Wednesday	El arba
Twenty to two	El etneen ghir arba'a	Thursday	El khemis
Quarter to two	El etneen ghir arbo'o	Friday	Ej jemaa
Ten to two	El etneen ghir darjeen	Saturday	Es sebt
Five to two	El etneen ghir draj		

FRENCH ESSENTIALS

BASICS AND GREETINGS

Yes/no	Oui/non	Goodbye	Au revoir	Open	Ouvert
Good morning	Bonjour	Please	S'il vous plaît	Closed	Fermé
Good evening	Bonsoir	Thank you	Merci	Go away!	Va-t-en!
Good night	Bonne nuit	Could you?	Pourriez-vous?	Stop messing	Arrête de
Sorry, excuse me	Pardon	Why?	Pourquoi?	me about!	m'emmerder!
How are you?	Ça va?	What?	Quoi?		

DIRECTIONS

Where is the road for ...?	Quelle est la route pour ...?	Far	Loin
Where is ...?	Où est ...?	When?	Quand?
Do you have ...?	Avez vous ...?	At what time?	A quelle heure?
... a room?	... une chambre?	Write it down, please	Ecrivez-le, s'il vous plaît
Here, there	Ici, là	Now	Maintenant
Right	À droite	Later	Plus tard
Left	À gauche	Never	Jamais
Straight on	Tout droit	Today	Aujourd'hui
Near	Proche, près	Tomorrow	Demain
		Yesterday	Hier

BUYING

How much/many?	Combien?	Like this/that	Comme ceci/cela
How much does that cost?	Combien ça coute?	What is it?	Qu'est-ce que c'est?
Too expensive	Trop cher	Enough	Assez
More/less	Plus/moin	Big	Grand
Cheap	Bon marché	Little	Petit

TRAVEL ESSENTIALS

Bus	Car, autobus	Ticket (return)	Billet (de retour)	Post office	Poste, PTT
Bus station	Gare routière	Bank	Banque	Stamps	Timbres-postes
Railway	Chemin de fer	Key	Clef	Left luggage	Consigne
Airport	Aeroport	Roof	Terrasse		d'equipage
Railway station	Gare	Passport	Passeport	Visa	Visa
Ferry	Bac	Currency	Change	Money	Argent
Lorry	Camion	exchange			

GESTURES

Tunisians are great **gesticulators**. The classic motion involves joining thumb and fingertips and holding the hand upwards; thoroughly infectious, this sign can mean almost anything, depending on the circumstances. Waved fiercely it conveys impatience, held quietly it means wait, patience, and shaken deliberately in conversation it claims ultimate authority for what's being said. As elsewhere in the Middle East, and round much of the Mediterranean, the word "no" is accompanied by a click of the tongue and toss of the head – flourishes which can at first seem contemptuously dismissive, but aren't intended that way. Also apt to be confusing is "come this way": the beckoning hand pointing downward, it often looks as though you're being told to go away. Sex in general is indicated by cutting one hand against the other.

GLOSSARY

ABBASIDS Dynasty of Caliphs who ruled the Arab Empire from Baghdad 749–1258.

AGHLABIDS Arab dynasty, ruled northern and central Tunisia from Kairouan in the ninth century.

AH (After the Hegira) Islamic date, the equivalent of AD. Islamic years begin with Mohammed's flight to Medina (see p.382).

AÏN Spring.

ALMOHADS Religious movement from Morocco, which came to control the whole Maghreb, from Marrakesh to Tunisia, in the twelfth century.

ALMORAVIDS Dynasty which ruled Morocco in the eleventh century and invaded Tunisia in the twelfth.

ARIANISM Christian heresy followed by the Vandals, based on an attempt to reconcile Christianity with Germanic pagan religions.

ASM *Association de Sauvegarde de la Medina*. An organization dedicated to preserving the architectural heritage of old Arab towns.

AUTOGARE Bus and *louage* station.

BAB Door or gate.

BACKSHEESH Alms or tips.

BARBARY European term for North Africa in the sixteenth to nineteenth centuries.

BASILICA Roman building type with aisles, later used for churches.

BERBERS The non-Arab native inhabitants of North Africa since about 4000 BC, speaking their own language. Very few pure Berbers survive in Tunisia, though they form the majority in Morocco and Algeria.

BEY Ottoman official, in practice the ruler of Tunisia in the eighteenth and nineteenth centuries (the adjective is *beylical*).

BORJ Fort.

BOURNOUSE Long woollen or camel-hair men's outer garment, often with hood.

BYZANTINE The continuation of the Roman Empire in the East, ruled from Byzantium (now Istanbul), which controlled Tunisia in the sixth century AD.

CALDARIUM Hot room in a Roman bath.

CALÈCHE Horse-drawn tourist carriage.

CAPITAL Stone "cushion" at the top of a column or pillar.

CAPITOL Central temple of a Roman town equivalent to a cathedral.

CARTHAGE Phoenician city founded around the ninth century BC, which became capital of the Carthaginian Empire finally defeated by Rome.

CELLA Inner sanctuary of a temple.

CHECHIA Red felt hat, like a soft fez.

CHICHA (SHEESHA) Café water pipe.

CHOTT Flat dry area; refers to salt lakes and occasionally beaches.

CORSAIRS Muslim and Christian pirates who operated in the Mediterranean from the thirteenth to the nineteenth centuries.

DAR House or palace.

DEY Ottoman military officer of junior rank. Their control of troops meant they effectively ruled Tunisia in the early seventeenth century.

DONATISM Fourth- and fifth-century dissident Christian church set up to avoid "contamination" by insincere Orthodox priests.

DRIBA Entrance hall.

ERG Sand dunes.

EL QUDS (EL QODS, EL QUODS, EL KUDS) Jerusalem, the third holy city of Islam.

ENNAHDHA Illegal fundamentalist political party, formerly the MTI.

FATIMIDS Dynasty of Ismaili Shi'ite Muslims who ruled Tunisia, from Mahdia, in the tenth century, and Egypt in the eleventh.

FOUNDOUK Inn, storehouse and sometimes trading base, known as a *caravanserai* in the eastern part of the Arab world.

FORUM Enclosed open space at the centre of a Roman town.

FRIGIDARIUM Cold room in Roman bath.

GARGOTE Cheap restaurant or café.

GHAR Cave.

GHORFA Room – refers in particular to the cells used to store grain inside a *ksar*.

HAFSIDS Dynasty that ruled Tunisia, from Tunis, in the thirteenth, fourteenth and fifteenth centuries. Originally governors for the Almohads, they declared independence in 1229 when the Marrakesh regime ditched Ibn Tumart's teachings. Seen as the Almohads' true heirs, the Hafsids presided over Tunisia's golden age.

HADITH Islamic legal ruling.

HAJ (HADJ) Pilgrimage to Mecca, or someone who has made this journey (older people are politely assumed to have done it, and so are addressed as *haj*).

HAMMAM (Turkish) bath.

HANEFITE One of the four schools of orthodox Sunni Islam, founded in the eighth century. Widespread in Anatolia and brought by the Turks to North Africa, the school's mosques are distinguished by octagonal minarets. The school is less austere than the native Malekite school, laying some stress on commercial success.

HILALIANS (Banu Hilal) Nomadic Arabs who invaded Tunisia in the eleventh century, were outside the control of its Zirid rulers, and severely disrupted its infrastructure.

HOUCH Jerban house, which looks like a small fortress (see p.326).

HUSAYNIDS Dynasty of Beys who ruled Tunisia from 1705 until (nominally) 1957.

HYPOSTYLE Hall supported by pillars, as in many prayer halls of mosques.

IBADITE Member of the main branch of Kharijism.

IMAM Roughly the Islamic equivalent of a Protestant pastor; leads the congregation of a mosque in prayer.

IMPASSE Blind alley.

INFIRMERIE Clinic staffed by nurses for dealing with general medical complaints.

ISMAILI Shia splinter formed on the death of the sixth Shi'ite imam (equivalent to the Sunni Caliph), which claimed that only descendants of his son Ismail could be given the title of imam.

JEBEL (DJEBEL) Mountain.

JEMAA (DJEMA'A) Great Mosque, or Friday Mosque (*Grande Mosquée*), the central place of worship in any town. During the week citizens may worship at *masjids*, smaller local mosques, but on Fridays they worship together at the *jemaa*, to hear the imam's homily.

KALA'A Stone hillfort.

KASBAH Administrative centre and/or fort of an Arab town.

KEF Rock.

KHARIJITES The "Secessionists", an early heretical sect, still surviving in Jerba, which found eager adherents among the Berbers in the first years of the Arab conquest.

KHOURASSINIDS Dynasty of princes who ruled the Tunis region during the eleventh century.

KOUBBA Dome, the correct name for the tomb of a marabout.

KOUTTAB Koranic primary school.

KSAR Communal fortified granary built mainly in the south (plural *ksour*).

LALLA Female saint.

LIMES Chain of forts built along the frontier of the Roman Empire.

LOUAGE Service taxi (see p.24).

MAGHREB "West" in Arabic, used of the countries of the Maghrebian confederation (Morocco, Algeria, Tunisia, Libya and Mauritania), especially the first three.

MAHDI The last prophet, Islam's equivalent of the second coming. Various people have claimed to be the Mahdi. Three are mentioned in this book: Obaidallah, founder of Mahdia and the Fatimid dynasty; Ibn Tumart, founder of the Almohads; and Mohammed Ahmed, who liberated Sudan from the British in 1886.

MALEKITE School of orthodox Sunni Islam, founded at Medina (Arabia) in the eighth century and dominant in North Africa for many centuries, with mosques distinguished by square minarets. More rigorous than the Hanefite, many people consider it the purest school.

MALOUF Andalusian-based traditional folk music.

MAMLUK Slave trained for high administrative office under the Ottoman Turks.

MARABOUT Holy man, and by extension his place of burial. These tombs, dotted all over the North African countryside, are often centres of cult worship. Marabouts played a vital role in spreading Islam among the Berbers.

MASJID Small local mosque, for everyday (rather than Friday) prayer.

MEDERSA (MEDRESSA) Residential college of Islamic education, usually in the form of a courtyard surrounded by students' cells. These colleges spread throughout the Islamic world from the thirteenth century onwards, generally as state foundations teaching the local orthodoxy.

MENZEL Dwelling place – in Jerba refers to the family *houch* and the enclosure around it.

MIDHA Ritual washing and latrine facility attached to mosque.

MIHRAB Niche indicating the direction of Mecca (and of prayer).

MINARET Tower attached to a mosque from which the *muezzin* gives the call to prayer.

MINBAR Pulpit from which the imam delivers homily at Friday prayers in a *jemaa*.

MUEZZIN Singer who gives the call to prayer.

MURADIDS The first hereditary line of Beys who ruled during the seventeenth century, nominally under the Ottoman sultan.

NADOR Watchtower.

ONAT *Organisation National de l'Artisanat Tunisien.* The national crafts organization: their shops are expensive but useful for pre-bargaining guidelines.

ONTT *Office Nationale de Tourisme et Thermalisme* (National Office of Tourism and Spas).

OTTOMAN Empire, based in Constantinople (Istanbul) from the fifteenth century to World War I, to which Tunisia belonged as a regency.

OUED (WADI) Seasonal river – may only carry water for a few days a year.

OUERGHAMMA Tribal confederation, based at Ghoumrassen and later Medenine, which dominated the far south of Tunisia from the sixteenth to the nineteenth century (see p.339).

PALAESTRA Roman gymnasium.

PERISTYLE Court enclosed by columns.

PHOENICIANS First great trading nation of Mediterranean history. Originally from what is now Lebanon, they founded trading posts (some of which became the Carthaginian Empire) along the southern Mediterranean coast.

PROTECTORATE The period of French control (1881–1956). The Beys stayed, and French rule was largely indirect and less repressive than in neighbouring Algeria.

PTT *Postes, Télécommunications et Télédiffusion.* Post office.

PUNIC Of Carthaginians and their culture.

QIBLA Direction of prayer, physically indicated by the mihrab.

RAS Headland or cape (literally: head).

RCD *Rassemblement Constitutionnel Démocratique.* Ruling political party, formerly the PSD.

RIBAT Monastic fortress, a building type which sprang up on the North African coast in the ninth century. *Marabout* originally meant an inhabitant of a *ribat*.

RUSTAMIDS Kharijite dynasty who ruled the south of Tunisia from Tahirt (Algeria) in the ninth century (see p.189).

SABAT Room built in vault over narrow street.

SAHEL Coast (see p.169).

SCHOLA Institutional Roman building.

SEBKHA Salt-encrusted mud flat.

SHIA Schismatic Islamic sect whose split from the Sunni majority in the seventh century remains the biggest sectarian division in the faith. Shi'ites emphasized the spiritual side of Islam in reaction to the power of the Umayyad Caliphs (see p.362).

SIDI Lord, saint – title of holy men.

SIFSARI Light women's outer garment wrapped around the body, which can also be used as a veil if held between the teeth. Tunisia's answer to the sari.

SKIFA Narrow passage, entrance.

STELA Tombstone (plural *stelae*).

SOUK Originally a covered urban market, now used of any kind of market, but especially a weekly one.

SUFI Unorthodox sects in Islam which take their teachings, often with mystical associations, from one originating teacher. Some cults spread throughout the Islamic world, transmitted by *zaouias*.

SUNNI Islamic orthodoxy; the vast majority of Muslims are Sunni, though they belong to a particular school, such as the *Malekite* or *Hanefite*.

TAXIPHONE Public telephone for national and international calls.

TOPHET Phoenician burial place.

TOURBET Islamic mausoleum.

TRICLINIUM Roman dining room.

TUAREGS Nomadic Saharan Berbers.

UMAYYADS Dynasty of Caliphs who ruled the Arab Empire from Damascus 661–749. The same family ruled Spain 756–1031.

VANDALS Germanic tribe who sacked Carthage in 439 AD and ruled in Tunisia until 535 (see p.362).

WAHABISM (1) Islamic heresy following Abdallah Ibn Wahab, founded in 782 AD and one of two branches of Kharijism. (2) Eighteenth-century Islamic, anti-colonial movement founded by Ibn Abdul Wahab.

WHITE FATHERS Order of monks cloaked in white *bournouse*-style habits founded in 1870 and based originally in Carthage, later in Thibar. They left Tunisia in 1976.

ZAOUIA Religious cult based on the teachings of a particular marabout, a sanctuary around the marabout's tomb, or a seminary-type base for his followers.

ZIRIDS Dynasty that ruled Tunisia in the eleventh century. Originally governors for the Fatimids, they declared independence in 984, incurring the Fatimids' wrath. During the Hilalian invasions, they ruled not much more than Mahdia.

ZITOUNA Olive tree.

INDEX

Abbasid Caliphs 363, 426
Abbès 278
Abortion 50
Abu Yazid 198, 200
Abu Yazid 274
Accommodation 29–31
Adventure trips (from
  Australasia) 13
Adventure trips (from Britain)
  5–7
Aggar 254
Aghir 324–325
Aghlabids 363, 426
AIDS 21
Aïn Draham 154
Aïn Ghellal 148
Aïn Oktor 131
Aïn Soltane 165
Aïn Tebournok 133
Aïn Tounga 232
Airline offices in Tunisia 180,
  187, 197, 214, 279
Airlines (Australasia) 13
Airlines (Britain and Ireland) 4
Airlines (North America) 9
Airports 315 (Jerba); 172, 180,
  185, 188 (Monastir); 206, 215
  (Sfax)
Ajim 325–326
Akouda 182–184
Al-Shabbi, Abu-L-Qasim 412
Alcoholic drinks 35
Algeria 376
Almohads 364, 426
Almoravids 274, 364, 426
Antiques 42
Arab conquest 362
Arabic courses 98
Arabic language 422
Archeological sites 39
Architecture 379
Aterian culture 357
Azaiza 310

Babouch 156
Backsheesh 51
Baggage deposit (left luggage)
  51
Banks 18–19

Banu Hilal 363
Barbarossa 315, 366
Bardo Museum 89–94
Bargaining 42–43
Bargou 230
Barrage Mellegue 245
Bechateur 148
Beja 158–161
Bekalta 188
Ben Gardane (Ben Guerdane)
  333–334
Beni Aissa 308
Beni Barka 348
Beni Kheddache 342
Beni Zelten 309
Berbers 267, 306, 329, 357,
  426
"Beznez" 49
Biar el Aouani 198–199
Biban 333
Bikes 26
Bir Jedid 184
Birds 403
Birdwatching 214–215, 216,
  218, 268, 353
Bizerte 136–143
Black market (money changing)
  19
Blankets 41
Bled el Haddar 278
Bon de Passage 20
Books 417–421
Borj Bourguiba 353
Borj Cedria 113
Borj el Khadra 354
Borj Younga 217
Bou Argoub 132
Bou Grara 331
Bou Hedma National Park 268
Boulbaba (Gabes) 302
Bounouma (Kerkennah) 221
Bourguiba, Habib 370
Brickwork (Tozeur and Nefta)
  276
Bulla Regia 162–165
Bus from Britain 7
Buses (in Tunisia) 24
Byzantine rule 362, 426

Cabs 28
Calendar 43
Calèches 28
Camping 31

Cannabis 50
Cap Blanc 148
Cap Bon 114–133
Cap Negre 149
Cap Serrat 149
Capsa 262
Capsian culture 357
Car rental 26–27
Carpets 41, 196
Carthage 103–109
Carthaginian Empire 357
Catacombs 178, 203
Cemeteries (War) 171
Ceramics 41
Chabbia (Tozeur) 277
Changing money 18–20
Chaouach 158
Chebba 203
Chebika 272
Chemtou 166
Chenini (near Gabes) 303
Chenini (near Tataouine) 349–
  350, 351
Chergui (Kerkennah) 218
Chicha 36
Children 46
Chott el Garsa 272
Chott el Jerid 286–287
Chott Mariam 174
Christianity, rise of 360
Cigarettes 50
Cilium 259
Cinema 44–45
Clothes (to buy) 42
Clothes (to wear) 39, 48, 51,
  399
Coffee 36
Consulates (foreign in Tunisia)
  214, 266
Consulates (Tunisian abroad) 14
Contraceptives 51
Coral 151
Corbeille (Nefta) 284
Cork 152
Cosmetics (traditional) 40
Costs 18
Credit cards 19
Crime 49
Currency 18
Customs 14
Dahar 350
Dar Chichou, Forest of 130
Dar el Ouessef 184

Dates 277, 326
Degache 286
Dehibat 353–354
Desert driving 352
Destour Party 370
Diabetics 34
Dialling codes 38
Disabled travellers 17–18
Discount agents (Australasia) 12
Discount agents (Britain and Ireland) 4–5
Discount agents (North America) 10
Dogs 20
Donatists 360, 426
Dougga 233–238
Douiret 350, 351
Douz 289–293
Dragut 200, 206
Dragut 315, 319, 325, 366
Drinks 33, 35–36
Driving 26–28, 352
Driving from Britain 7
Drugs 50
Du'Aji 413
Duty-free allowances 14

Eating and drinking 31–36
El Abbasaia (Kerkennah) 221
El Abbasiya (near Kairouan) 198
El Aouadid 303
El Attaia (Kerkennah) 221
El Djem (El Jem) 203–205
El Faouar 294–295
El Guettar 267
El Hamma de l'Arad 295
El Hamma du Jerid 272
El Haouaria 128
El Jem 203–205
El Kantara (Jerba) 324–325
El Kantara Continent 331
El May 328
Electricity 51
Elles 250
Embassies (foreign in Tunisia) 214, 266
Embassies (Tunisian abroad) 14
Enfida (Enfidha, Enfidaville) 170–171
Er Riadh (Hara Sghira) 328

Es Souani (Hara Kebira) 328
Esparto grass 41
Evil Eye 387
Excursions 28
Ez Zahra 112

Fahs 226
Faouar 294–295
Fatimids 199, 201, 363, 426
Feija, Forest of 165
Feriana 259
Fernana 156
Ferries 215, 218, 326
Ferries from Europe 7–9
Festivals 43–44, 45
Film (camera film) 51
Film (cinema) 44–45
Flaubert, Gustave 408
Flights from Australasia 12–13
Flights from Britain 3–4
Flights from Ireland 4–5
Flights from North America 9–11
Flora 405
Foggara 288
Food 31–36
Football (soccer) 45–46
Foum Tataouine 344–347
Foundouks 381
French rule 369
Fundamentalism 373

Gabes 298–305
Gafsa 262–267
Gammarth 111
Gay travellers 48–49
Getting there from Australasia 12–13
Getting there from Britain and Ireland 3–9
Getting there from North America 9–11
Ghar el Melh 144
Gharbi (Kerkennah) 218
Ghardimaou 165
Ghorfas 341
Ghoumrassen 343–344, 351
Gighitis 330–331
Gigolos 49
Glossary 426–429
Gremdi (Kerkennah) 221
Grombalia 132

Guellala 328–330
Guengla 148
Guermessa 344, 351
Guettar 267

Hached, Farhat 371
Haddej 307–308
Haffouz 254
Hafsids 364, 426
Haggling 42–43
Haidra 247
Hallouf 342
Hammam Bourguiba 156
Hammam Lif 112
Hammam Mellegue 245
Hammamet 116–119
Hammams 40
Hand of Fatima 387
Hannibal 358
Hara Kebira 328
Hara Sghira 328
Hashish 50
Health 15, 20–21
Hergla 184
Hilalians 363, 427
History 357–378
Hitchhiking 25–26
HIV 21
Holidays 44, 45
Homosexuality 48–49
Hookah pipes (chicha) 36
Hospitals 20–21
Hostels 30–31
Hotels 29–31
Houmt Souk (Jerba) 316–322
Hussaynids 367, 427

Ibadites 363, 427
Illness 20–21
Insurance 15–16
International calls 37, 38
Islam 365, 386–391
Islamic calendar 43

Jama 230
Jara (Gabes) 301–302
Jebel Abiadh 347
Jebel Bir 154
Jebel Bou Kornine National Park 112
Jebel Chambi 258
Jebel Dyr 245
Jebel Haouia 341–343

Jebel Ichkeul 146
Jebel Segdel 352–353
Jebel Serj 254
Jem (El Jem) 203–205
Jendouba 162
Jenein 354
Jeradou 172, 226
Jerba (Djerba) 312–313
Jessour 308, 350
Jewellery 41
Jews 31, 327
Jorf (Djorf) 330
Jugurtha's Table 246

Kahina 204
Kairouan 189–197
Kalaa Kebira 182–184
Kalaa Khasbah 246
Kalaa Sghira 182–184
Kalaat el Andalous 146
Kalaat es Senam 246
Kasserine 258
Kbor Klib 230
Kebili 288–289
Kef (Le Kef) 239–244
Kelibia 125–127
Kerachfa 343
Kerkennah islands 217–221
Kerkouane 127
Kharijites 189, 315, 329, 362,
  388, 390, 427
Khourassanids 427
Khroumirie mountains 156
Kneiss island 217
Korba 125
Korbous 131
Kosher meat 34–35
Kriz 286–287
Ksar 337, 341
Ksar Aouadad 348
Ksar Dahar 348
Ksar Deghaghora 348
Ksar el Ferich 344
Ksar Ghilane 350–352
Ksar Gurga 348
Ksar Hadada 343
Ksar Hallouf 342
Ksar Hellal 188
Ksar Jedid (Ksar Djedid) 342
Ksar Jouama (Ksar Djouama)
  342
Ksar Kedim 348
Ksar Kerachfa 343

Ksar Lemsa 230
Ksar Megalba 348
Ksar Metameur 340–341
Ksar Ouled Aoun 348
Ksar Ouled Debbab 350
Ksar Ouled Soltane 349
Ksar Sedra 349
Ksar Segdel 352
Ksar Tounket 348
Ksar Zammour 342
Ksar Zenetes 348
Ksar Zoltane 348
Ksour 337, 341
Ksour Essaf 202
Ksour Toual Zouamel 230

La Chebba 203
La Galite 154
La Goulette 102
La Kesra 253
La Marsa 111
La Mohammedia 227
La Seguia 324
La Skhirra 217
Lac Ichkeul National Park 146
Lake Tunis 102
Laghmi 277
Lamta 188
Language 421–425
Laundry 51
Le Kef 239–244
Leather 42
Leclerc column 351
Left luggage 51
Leptis Minor 188
Lotus eaters 312
Louages 24–25

M'Chiguig 354
Magazines 37–38
Mahbouine 328
Mahdia 199–202
Mail 37
Mahres (Mahares) 216–217
Maisons des Jeunes 30–31
Maktar 250
Mansourah 287–288
Maps 22–23
Mareth Line 310, 371
Markets 44, 133, 168, 222,
  296, 311, 335, 354
Marsa Ben Ramdane 131
Mateur 148

Matmata 305–307
Mausoleum of the Flavii 259
May (El May) 328
Maztouria 348–349
Mazzouna 268
Medeina 250
Medenine 337–340
Medersas 39
Media 37–38
Medical care 20–21
Medjerda Valley 156
Medjez el Bab 157
Meich 267
Meknassy 268
Melita (Kerkennah) 218
Mellita 325
Meninx 315, 325
Menzel (Gabes) 302
Menzel Abderrahman 143
Menzel Bou Zelfa 132
Menzel Bourguiba 148
Menzel Jemil 143
Menzel Temime 125
Metameur 340–341
Metlaoui 268–270
Metro (Monastir–Sousse) 180,
  185, 188
Metro (Tunis) 28
Mides 271
Midoun 326
Moknine 188
Monastir 185–188
Money 18–20
Morice Line 165
Mosque architecture 379
Mosques 39
Movies 44–45
Mrazig 291
Muradids 366, 428
Museums 39
Mustis 239

Nabeul 119–124
Nebeur 245
Nefta 280–286
Nefzaoua 287–288
Neo-Destour Party 370
Newspapers 37–38
Noddy trains 28
Normans 206, 315, 364
Nouail 295
Nouvelle Dougga 233
Odysseus 218

Olives 307–308, 326–327
ONAT 40–41
ONTT 22
Orbata 267
Organized tours 28, 181, 304, 321, 352
Ottoman rule 366, 428
Ouderna 347–349
Oued Ez Zit 226
Oued Sed 184
Oued Zarga 158
Ouerghamma tribal confederation 339, 343, 349
Ouesslatia 254
Ouled el Haddef (Tozeur) 276, 277
Overland routes from Britain 7–9
Overland tours from Britain 5–7

Package holidays (from Britain and Ireland) 6
Package holidays (from North America) 11
Pensions 30
Periodicals 37–38
Pharmacies 21
Pheradi Maius 226
Phoenicians 357, 428
Phone calls 37, 38
Photography 39, 51
Pick-ups 25
Pilgrims 31
Police 49
Port el Kantaoui 181–183
Post 37
Pottery 41
Press 37–38
Prostitution 49
PTT 37
Public holidays 45
Punic civilization 358, 428
Punic Wars 358
Rabies 20
Rades 112
Radio 38
Raf Raf 143
Railways 25
Ramadan 36, 43–44, 387
Raouad Beach 112
Ras Ajdir 334
Ras Angela 148

Ras Jebel 143
Ras Kaboudia 203
Ras Sidi el Mekki 144
Ras Taguermes 323–324
Redeyef 270
Religious festivals 45
Remada 352–353
Remla (Kerkennah) 220–221
Reqqada 196–197
Restaurants 31–33
Road conditions 27, 352
Romans 205, 359
Rommel 310
Rugs 41
Rustamids 167, 189, 428

Sabra 198
Sabria 294
Saidane 295
Sakiet Sidi Youssef 245
Sakket 267
Salakta 202–203
Saltpans (Sfax) 214–215, 216
Sand roses 42
Sangho (Sangou) 331
Sbeitla 254
Sebkha Kelbia 184
Sebkhet Halk el Menzel 184
Security 49–50
Sejenane 149
Seldja 220
Sened 267
Senior travellers 47
Sexual attitudes 47
Sexual assault 50
Sexual harassment 47–48, 33
Sfax 206–215
Shebika (Chebika) 272
Shopping 40–43
Sidi Abdel Waheb 149
Sidi Aïch 268
Sidi Bou Said 110
Sidi Bou Zid 257
Sidi Daoud 130
Sidi Fankhal (Kerkennah) 220
Sidi Frej (Kerkennah) 218–220
Sidi Jedidi 226
Sidi Khalifa 226
Sidi Mahares (Jerba) 322–323
Sidi Mansour (near Le Kef) 245
Sidi Mansour (near Gafsa) 267
Sidi Mechrig 149
Sidi Meta 309

Sidi Rais 131
Sidi Salem Dam 158
Siliana 230
Skhirra 217
Soccer 45–46
Soliman 132
Souk Lahad 287
Sousse 172–181
Souvenirs 40–43
Sponges 325–326
Sport 45–46
Star Wars 305, 307
Stoves 51
Student cards 15
Sufism 281, 364
Syndicats d'Initiative 22

Tabarca 149–153
Tacape 298
Tajerouine 246
Takrouna 171–172
Tamerza 271
Tamezret 309
Tampons 51
Tap water 21, 316
Tapsus 188
Tataouine 344–347
Taxis 28
Tea 36
Teboursouk 238
Technine 309
Telephones 37, 38
Television 38
Tell 223–260
Telmine 288
Temelest 348
Testour 230
TGM railway 28
Thala 249
Theft 15, 49–50
Thelepte 259
Thibar 161
Thignica 233
Thuburbo Majus 227–230
Thuburnica 166
Thyna 216
Tijma 308
Time 51, 38
Tipping 51
Tlili, Mustapha 414
Toilet paper 51
Toujane 309
Toukabeur 158

Tounket 348
Tour operators (Britain and
    Ireland) 6
Tour operators (North America)
    11
Tourist information offices 22
Tours (inside Tunisia) 28, 181,
    304, 321, 352
Tozeur 272–280
Trains from Britain 7
Trains (in Tunisia) 25
Transport in Tunisia 3–13, 24–
    28
Transports rurals 25
Travel agents (Australasia) 12
Travel agents (Britain and
    Ireland) 4–5
Travel agents (North America)
    10
Travellers' cheques 19
TUNIS 55–101
    Abu Mohamed Mosque 85
    Accommodation 63
    Airline offices 98
    Airport 60
    April 9 Museum 88
    Arrival 60
    Avenue Bourguiba 68
    Bab el Assel 86
    Bab el Bahr 71
    Bab el Khadra 86
    Bab Jazira 89
    Bab Jedid 89
    Bab Menara 82
    Bab Saadoun 86
    Banks 98
    Bardo Museum 89–94
    Belvedere Park 69
    Borj Cedria 113
    Buses 61
    Car rental 99
    Coin Museum 68
    Colonial architecture 69
    Dar Bayram Turki 79
    Dar Ben Abdallah 80
    Dar Hedri 80
    Dar Husayn 82
    Dar Othman 80
    Divan 83
    Eating and drinking 94–96

    Entertainment 97
    Ferries 60
    Foundouks 79
    Gammarth 111
    La Goulette 102
    Great Mosque (Zitouna) 74
    Hafsia 84
    Halfaouine 85
    Hammam Lif 112
    Hammams 99
    Jebel Bou Kornine National Park
        112
    Jellaz Cemetery 89
    Kasbah site and mosque 88
    La Marsa 111
    Lake Tunis 102
    Listings 98
    Louages 61
    Medina 70–84
    Midhat es Soltane 75
    Montfleury 86
    Mosque des Teinturiers 80
    Mosque of Sidi Mehrez 83
    Mosque of Youssef Bey 77
    Moving on 100
    Museum of Modern Art and
        Cinema 70
    Museum of Traditional Heritage
        of Tunis 81
    National Library 74
    New Town 68–70
    Nightlife 96
    Nouvelle Ville 68–70
    Place de la Victoire 71
    Place du Gouvernement 77
    Place du Marché du Blé 89
    Place Halfaouine 85
    Porte de France (Bab el Bahr)
        71
    Postal Museum 68
    Rades 112
    Raouad Beach 111
    Sahib et Tabaa Mosque 85
    Shopping 97
    Sidi Bou Khrissane Museum 82
    Sidi Bou Said 110
    Slave trade 76
    Souks 75–77, 78, 81, 85
    TGM 62
    Tourbet el Bey 81
    Tourist office 60
    Transport 61
    Travel agencies 100
    Western Districts 86

    Youssef Dey Mosque
    Zaouia of Sidi Braham 83
    Zaouia of Sidi el Halfaoui 86
    Zaouia of Sidi Kassem Jelizi 88
    Zaraia Mosque 68
    Zitouna Mosque 74

Umayyad Caliphs 362
Utica 144

Vandals 361
Vegetarians 34
Virgil 407
Visas 13
Voluntary work 52

War cemeteries 109, 111, 113,
    140, 149, 154, 157, 158, 161,
    171, 254, 371
Water 21, 316
Weddings 44
White Fathers 429
Wildlife 214–216, 218, 268,
    353, 402–406
Wine 35
Wiring money 19–20
Women 30, 33, 47–8, 395–401
Work 51–52
World War II 370

Youth hostels 30–31

Zafrane 294
Zaghouan 224
Zammour 342
Zannfour 250
Zaouias 39
Zaouiet el Arab 286
Zarat 310–311
Zarziha Rock 131
Zarzis 331–333
Zebda (Tozeur) 277
Zembra 130
Zembretta 130
Zeraoua 309
Zirids 363, 429
Zouiraa 149
Zriba 172, 226

HELP US UPDATE

We've endeavoured to make this guide as up-to-date as possible, but it's inevitable that some of the information will become inaccurate between now and the preparation of the next edition. Readers' updates and suggestions are very welcome. We'll credit all letters and send a copy of the next edition (or any other Rough Guide) for the best. Please mark letters "Tunisia Update" and send them to:

Rough Guides, 1 Mercer Street, London WC2H 9QJ,
or Rough guides, 375 Hudson Street, 3rd Floor, New York, NY 10014

THANKS TO ALL OUR READERS

A big thank-you to the many readers who took the trouble to write in with their comments and suggestions: Chris and Lynne Andrews, David Bagshaw, Hugh Bayley, Rev. William B. Beer, Kristel Bert and Bart Morel, Jenny Boff, Henry Botha, Hillary Box, Pauline Bremner, G.W. Bröcker, Kate Bruyland, R. Chahil, Christine and Malcolm Clark, Andy Connor, John Cowler, D. Damassino, Carol Anne Davis, Peter Deurloo, Tony Dunn and Katherine Dewar, Marie-Thérèse F. DuBois, J.T. Evans, Vanessa L. Fleming, Chris Frean, Mrs Robert Gosling, Jo Lynn M. Hardwick, Chris Haslett, Flook Heslenfeld, R.W. Hewitt, Robin Higham, Nick Hinchliffe and Glynis Ridley, Tim Huckler, Mike Hughes and Cathy Mutch, Mike Ivy, Iain Jackson, Anna Jauncey, Johannes Jepsen, William Johnson, Kirstin Kabasci, Joanne Knott, Rev. Mark Langham, Peter de Leeuw and Monique Bosman, Neil Lewis, Peter Lilley, Father Paul Lock, David Martin, Justin McGuinness, Oscar J. Merne, Mrs P. Mhadhebi, Ian Millard, Ella Milroy, Peter Milne, Anne and Chris Norman, E.A.A. Oomes, James O'Geran, Riitta Oittinen and Jukka-Pekka Piimies, Claire Pankhurst, David Phillips, Roberto Reveilleau, Eric Rideal, Jan and Linda Rodants, Damon Rosamond, Jens Roth, Brian and Shirley Sandford, Frank A. Sharman, Dr Elisabeth Sidebotham, Kevin Sinclair, Ian Stephenson, Maria Thomas, Thomas Tolk, Dave Tootell, James Trollope, Monique Vanstone, Florence Vuillet, Roland Webster, John Withington, Ian Wood, George Xuereb and Jim Pearce.

DIRECT ORDERS IN THE UK

Title	ISBN	Price
Amsterdam	1858280869	£7.99
Andalucia	185828094X	£8.99
Australia	1858280354	£12.99
Barcelona & Catalunya	1858281067	£8.99
Berlin	1858280338	£8.99
Brazil	1858281024	£9.99
Brittany & Normandy	1858281261	£8.99
Bulgaria	1858280478	£8.99
California	1858280907	£9.99
Canada	185828130X	£10.99
Classical Music on CD	185828113X	£12.99
Corsica	1858280893	£8.99
Crete	1858281326	£8.99
Cyprus	185828032X	£8.99
Czech & Slovak Republics	185828029X	£8.99
Egypt	1858280753	£10.99
England	1858280788	£9.99
Europe	185828077X	£14.99
Florida	1858280109	£8.99
France	1858280508	£9.99
Germany	1858281288	£11.99
Greece	1858281318	£9.99
Greek Islands	1858281636	£8.99
Guatemala & Belize	1858280451	£9.99
Holland, Belgium & Luxembourg	1858280877	£9.99
Hong Kong & Macau	1858280664	£8.99
Hungary	1858281237	£8.99
India	1858281040	£13.99
Ireland	1858280958	£9.99
Italy	1858280311	£12.99
Kenya	1858280435	£9.99
London	1858291172	£8.99
Mediterranean Wildlife	0747100993	£7.95
Malaysia, Singapore & Brunei	1858281032	£9.99
Morocco	1858280400	£9.99
Nepal	185828046X	£8.99
New York	1858280583	£8.99
Nothing Ventured	0747102082	£7.99
Pacific Northwest	1858280923	£9.99
Paris	1858281253	£7.99
Poland	1858280346	£9.99
Portugal	1858280842	£9.99
Prague	185828015X	£7.99
Provence & the Côte d'Azur	1858280230	£8.99
Pyrenees	1858280931	£8.99
St Petersburg	1858281334	£8.99
San Francisco	1858280826	£8.99
Scandinavia	1858280397	£10.99
Scotland	1858280834	£8.99
Sicily	1858280370	£8.99
Spain	1858280818	£9.99
Thailand	1858280168	£8.99
Tunisia	1858280656	£8.99
Turkey	1858280885	£9.99
Tuscany & Umbria	1858280915	£8.99
USA	185828080X	£12.99
Venice	1858280362	£8.99
Wales	1858280966	£8.99
West Africa	1858280141	£12.99
More Women Travel	1858280982	£9.99
World Music	1858280176	£14.99
Zimbabwe & Botswana	1858280419	£10.99

Rough Guide Phrasebooks

Title	ISBN	Price
Czech	1858281482	£3.50
French	185828144X	£3.50
German	1858281466	£3.50
Greek	1858281458	£3.50
Italian	1858281431	£3.50
Spanish	1858281474	£3.50

Rough Guides are available from all good bookstores, but can be obtained directly in the UK* from Penguin by contacting:

Penguin Direct, Penguin Books Ltd, Bath Road, Harmondsworth, West Drayton, Middlesex UB7 0DA; or telephone our credit line on 0181-899 4036 (9am–5pm) and ask for Penguin Direct. Visa, Access and Amex accepted. Delivery will normally be within 14 working days. Penguin Direct ordering facilities are only available in the UK.

The availability and published prices quoted are correct at the time of going to press but are subject to alteration without prior notice.

* For USA and international orders, see separate price list

DIRECT ORDERS IN THE USA

Title	ISBN	Price
Amsterdam	1858280869	$13.59
Andalucia	185828094X	$14.95
Australia	1858280354	$18.95
Barcelona & Catalunya	1858281067	$17.99
Berlin	1858280338	$13.99
Brazil	1858281024	$15.95
Brittany & Normandy	1858281261	$14.95
Bulgaria	1858280478	$14.99
California	1858280907	$14.95
Canada	185828130X	$14.95
Classical Music on CD	185828113X	$19.95
Corsica	1858280893	$14.95
Crete	1858281326	$14.95
Cyprus	185828032X	$13.99
Czech & Slovak Republics	185828029X	$14.95
Egypt	1858280753	$17.95
England	1858280788	$16.95
Europe	185828077X	$18.95
Florida	1858280109	$14.95
France	1858281245	$16.95
Germany	1858281288	$17.95
Greece	1858281318	$16.95
Greek Islands	1858281636	$14.95
Guatemala & Belize	1858280451	$14.95
Holland, Belgium & Luxembourg	1858280877	$15.95
Hong Kong & Macau	1858280664	$13.95
Hungary	1858281237	$14.95
India	1858281040	$22.95
Ireland	1858280958	$16.95
Italy	1858280311	$17.95
Kenya	1858280435	$15.95
London	1858291172	$12.95
Mediterranean Wildlife	0747100993	$15.95
Malaysia, Singapore & Brunei	1858281032	$16.95
Morocco	1858280400	$16.95
Nepal	185828046X	$13.95
New York	1858280583	$13.95
Nothing Ventured	0747102082	$19.95
Pacific Northwest	1858280923	$14.95
Paris	1858281253	$12.95
Poland	1858280346	$16.95
Portugal	1858280842	$15.95
Prague	1858281229	$14.95
Provence & the Côte d'Azur	1858280230	$14.95
Pyrenees	1858280931	$15.95
St Petersburg	1858281334	$14.95
San Francisco	1858280826	$13.95
Scandinavia	1858280397	$16.99
Scotland	1858280834	$14.95
Sicily	1858280370	$14.99
Spain	1858280818	$16.95
Thailand	1858280168	$15.95
Tunisia	1858280656	$15.95
Turkey	1858280885	$16.95
Tuscany & Umbria	1858280915	$15.95
USA	185828080X	$18.95
Venice	1858280362	$13.99
Wales	1858280966	$14.95
West Africa	1858280141	$24.95
More Women Travel	1858280982	$14.95
World Music	1858280176	$19.95
Zimbabwe & Botswana	1858280419	$16.95

Rough Guide Phrasebooks

Title	ISBN	Price
Czech	1858281482	$5.00
French	185828144X	$5.00
German	1858281466	$5.00
Greek	1858281458	$5.00
Italian	1858281431	$5.00
Spanish	1858281474	$5.00

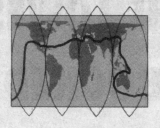

You are
A STUDENT

You **travel**
THE WORLD

You **want**
TO SAVE MONEY

Here's how

The International
Student Identity Card

Available at Student Travel Offices Worldwide.

Entitles you to discounts and special services worldwide.